Comparative, International,

and

Global Justice

⊘SAGE | **50** YEARS

SAGE was founded in 1965 by Sara Miller McCune to support the dissemination of usable knowledge by publishing innovative and high-quality research and teaching content. Today, we publish more than 850 journals, including those of more than 300 learned societies, more than 800 new books per year, and a growing range of library products including archives, data, case studies, reports, and video. SAGE remains majority-owned by our founder, and after Sara's lifetime will become owned by a charitable trust that secures our continued independence.

Los Angeles | London | New Delhi | Singapore | Washington DC

Comparative, International,

and

Global Justice

PERSPECTIVES FROM CRIMINOLOGY AND CRIMINAL JUSTICE

Cyndi Banks

James Baker

Los Angeles | London | New Delhi
Singapore | Washington DC

Los Angeles | London | New Delhi
Singapore | Washington DC

FOR INFORMATION:

SAGE Publications, Inc.
2455 Teller Road
Thousand Oaks, California 91320
E-mail: order@sagepub.com

SAGE Publications Ltd.
1 Oliver's Yard
55 City Road
London EC1Y 1SP
United Kingdom

SAGE Publications India Pvt. Ltd.
B 1/I 1 Mohan Cooperative Industrial Area
Mathura Road, New Delhi 110 044
India

SAGE Publications Asia-Pacific Pte. Ltd.
3 Church Street
#10-04 Samsung Hub
Singapore 049483

Acquisitions Editor: Jerry Westby
Associate Editor: Jessica Miller
Editorial Assistant: Laura Kirkhuff
eLearning Editor: Robert Higgins
Typesetter: C&M Digitals (P) Ltd.
Proofreader: Penelope Sippel
Indexer: Judy Hunt
Cover Designer: Michael Dubowe
Marketing Manager: Terra Schultz

Printed in the United States of America

Library of Congress Cataloging-in-Publication Data

Banks, Cynthia, author. Comparative, international and global justice : perspectives from criminology and criminal justice / Cynthia L. Banks, James Baker.

pages cm
Includes bibliographical references and index.

ISBN 978-1-4833-3238-3 (pbk. : alk. paper)

1. Criminal justice, Administration of. 2. Comparative law. 3. International criminal law. 4. International law and human rights. 5. Criminology. I. Baker, James (Denis William James) II. Title.

K5001.B36 2015
364—dc23   2015020344

This book is printed on acid-free paper.

15 16 17 18 19 10 9 8 7 6 5 4 3 2 1

BRIEF CONTENTS

DETAILED CONTENTS

ACKNOWLEDGMENTS

PUBLISHER'S ACKNOWLEDGMENTS

Dick T. Andzenge, St. Cloud State University

Joseph Appiahene-Gyamfi, University of Texas–Pan American

Mikaila Mariel Lemonik Arthur, Rhode Island College

Timothy J. Brazill, Bridgewater College

Bianca Buliga, Thunderbird School of Global Management

Ryan M. Getty, Tarleton State University

Ralph Grunewald, University of Wisconsin

Timothy C. Hayes, University of North Georgia

Patrick Ibe, Albany State University

Seokjin Jeong, University of Texas at Arlington

Peter Johnstone, University of North Texas

Mitchell B. Mackinem, Claflin University

Abu Mboka, California State University–Stanislaus

Phillip D. Schertzing, Michigan State University

Robert M. Worley, Texas A&M University–Central Texas

Glenn Zuern, Albany State University

ABOUT THE AUTHORS

Cyndi Banks is a professor of criminology and criminal justice and Dean of University College at Northern Arizona University. She has more than 24 years experience of research and project implementation in developing countries in the fields of juvenile justice, probation, justice policy, and child rights. She has worked as a criminologist in Papua New Guinea, Bangladesh, Iraq, Kurdistan, Timor Leste, Sudan, and Myanmar. She is the author of numerous articles and books, including *Criminal Justice Ethics; Youth, Crime and Justice; Developing Cultural Criminology: Theory and Practice in Papua New Guinea;* and *Alaska Native Juveniles in Detention.*

James Baker is a British lawyer now residing in the United States. He holds an LL.M. from London University with a specialization in law and development and has 30 years of experience working as a lawyer and researching rule of law and access to justice issues in Papua New Guinea, Bangladesh, Afghanistan, Iraq, Malawi, Sierra Leone, Fiji, and Timor Leste.

PART I

COMPARATIVE CRIMINOLOGY AND CRIMINAL JUSTICE

1

INTRODUCTION

This text addresses a wide range of topics relevant to criminology, criminal justice, and global justice. We use the term *global justice* to signify the totality of the fields of criminology included in the text, namely, comparative, international, and transnational and global criminologies. Although wide-ranging, the text does not sacrifice breadth for depth: discussion of each topic is characterized by a comprehensive contextualized account of a contemporary global justice issue and a critical approach. Specificity is a fundamental quality of topic discussions, and the analysis of topics and issues is scholarly but accessible, often taking the form of case studies and country profiles.

Criminology, it has often been said, is a parochial and ethnocentric discipline (Hardie-Bick, Sheptycki, and Wardak 2005, 1). As Paul Friday (1996, 231) puts it, "Criminal justice education in general has taken a narrow, pedantic view stressing knowledge of our own system and the dominant American theories of crime. If any comparative material is introduced into the curriculum, it is generally offered as a single special-topics course." As he correctly notes, this "reinforces the notion that the way things are done in the United States is the only way to do things."

This text aims to enhance criminology and criminal justice education by its focus on some of the issues engaging criminology worldwide and to prepare students for a future in which fields of study such as transnational crime are unexceptional. Not only is this important because society is now global but the topics discussed here challenge us to confront important moral, social, cultural, and political issues. The approach taken in this text recognizes the changes that have occurred in the study of criminal justice internationally, many of which can be ascribed to the process of globalization.

We agree with David Nelken (2013, 9) that the increased interest in global criminological issues has "so far gone largely hand in hand with a continuation of the older type of comparative enquiries" and "trying to keep comparative and globalization issues strictly apart has little to recommend it." René Van Swaaningen (2011, 133) gives three reasons for the emergence of a global criminology: the need to look beyond Western models in order to understand worldwide changes; the challenges to the sovereignty of the nation-state brought about by globalization; and the emergence of criminological challenges with a global scope and effect necessitating a shift from traditional levels of analysis. David Friedrichs (2011, 170) agrees that the traditional criminological framework is limited and that to be relevant in this century criminology "must increasingly become comparative international and global." Piers Beirne (2008, vii) declares that a comparative approach is limited because it cannot capture "the full complexity of globalization" but that "comparative criminology will remain a crucial avenue of inquiry for global criminology" (p. ix). We agree with these perspectives, and this text therefore incorporates issues of global, transnational, international, and comparative interest and concern.

It used to be that criminology and criminal justice studies included only comparative criminal justice or comparative criminology in a typical undergraduate degree course. This topic commonly involved a discussion of how various countries (predominantly Western) organized their justice systems. Sometimes, additional topics, such as terrorism or international police cooperation, were added. With the advent of globalization, international cooperation in criminal justice in areas such as policing, the increasing internationalization of law (especially criminal law), and the growth of transnational crime, it became apparent to many scholars that the traditional presentation of comparative criminal justice did not equip students with the knowledge they needed to understand how justice issues are organized globally.

Scholars active in the international, global, and comparative fields of study have commented on how the traditional approach has been changing. For example, Nelken (2011a, 1) has asked how the field of traditional comparative criminology has been affected by globalization. He and others have noted that traditional comparative studies accept national state boundaries and focus on explaining differences in national laws and practices. However, what of the fact that there are now multiple global links relating to crime threats and criminal justice responses? Arguably, students now need to understand how the nation-state or other locally based justice practices shape or resist global trends. The overall issue is to what extent globalization should be integrated into comparative textbooks and what comparative work might have to say to students about globalization.

It is argued that the cross-cultural study of crime and justice has evolved from a comparative or international approach to what is now being called a transnational or global approach to crime and justice (Larsen and Smandych 2008, xi). Thus, comparative approaches are inadequate to capture the complexity of these global issues, including topics such as global trends in policing, security, convergences in criminal justice and penal policy and international criminal justice, war crimes, and human rights protection. Generally, many international criminology scholars agree that trying to keep comparative and globalization issues apart has little to recommend it.

Francis Pakes argues that comparative criminal justice is "losing its relevance" (Pakes 2010, 17). For one reason, it typically compares and contrasts phenomena in different cultures, and the diffuse interrelations and complications caused by globalization are simply ignored or understated. However, Francis Pakes believes comparative study will remain a useful tool in inquiries into globalization and transnationalization. The comparative approach, he points out, is a matter of methodology, whereas globalization is an object of study. Another scholar, author of a recent text that does not follow the traditional form, seeks to show the complex processes through which the global and the local are intertwined and does not spend time comparing individual countries. Her text looks at convergences in criminal justice policy, trafficking of persons internationally, migration, transnational crime, cyberspace, and other global criminal topics. Katja Aas suggests the comparative approach to criminology should be distinguished from global and transnational perspectives. Her objective is to look at the global and transnational as an increasingly salient explanatory factor and frame of criminological reference (Aas 2007, 86).

European scholars of comparative study point to differing conceptions in legal systems and ask whether the comparative approach in fact compares like with like or whether it simply assumes system and conceptual universality (Brants 2011, 57). In attempting to understand the culturally determined meaning of concepts of and in law, they call for data on the social context in which systems of justice function and about their effects on society or about social change and its effects on the law. This, they say, points to the desirability of an interdisciplinary approach (Brants 2011, 55; Rothe and Freidrichs 2015, 3). It is also contended that most comparative studies remain too much on the surface and do not put the phenomena at study in their specific structural and cultural context: a more interpretative, cultural paradigm for comparative criminology is needed (Van Swaaningen 2011, 125). Certainly comparative textbooks have long been criticized for failing to explain the social context in which law and crime exist and operate. Nelken has noted that most work in comparative criminology does not really engage in questions of explanation or interpretation. The pivotal question of why things are different is not answered, and comparison by juxtaposition often leads to a dead end (Nelken 2011c, 185).

Others argue that global and national penal law and practice interact, leading to the conclusion that both studies of globalization and cross-national comparative research are needed and must be closely linked. Given that globalization is a powerful process that affects criminal justice and penal policies in many countries, comparative penal studies that treat countries as independent units of analysis can no longer be justified. Instead, broader comparative analyses are needed (Savelsberg 2011, 82). Consequently, Richard Vogler argues that "criminal justice can no longer be seen as a purely local phenomenon" (Vogler 2005, 3).

Looking at the effects of globalization, John Muncie (2011, 87) explains that because of globalization, a more complex and transnational level of analysis is thought necessary. State sovereignty in criminal justice seems to be challenged by international courts, human rights conventions, multinational private security enterprises, cross border policing, policy networks, and flows and technologies of global surveillance. As well, global governance and transnational justice have tended to proceed from a Western perspective, and globalization has been applied predominantly to transformations in Western and Anglophone countries. An important issue is how to adequately address the impact of the global on the local, or vice versa, when most criminal justice research continues to be parochially based in national or local contexts.

Arguing for comparative and transnational studies to be combined, James Sheptycki (2011, 145) suggests that criminology should foster both transnational and comparative studies because "patterns of governing through crime are becoming more general and more transnational." Criminology ought to be both comparative and transnational. An attempt to move toward a globalizing criminological perspective has the merit of bringing crimes that have been neglected, such as state crimes (including genocide), into better focus (Nelken 2011c, 201).

We maintain that debates concerning the recognition of the process of globalization as a field of study for criminology and the compatibility of comparative and global studies in criminology are now concluded in favor of the relevance and importance of global justice studies, and this text reflects that idea. We have therefore opted for an approach in this text that provides students with a set of topics in comparative, international, and transnational and global criminology. Whereas the comparative studies are of topics commonly contained in textbooks, the range and depth of the transnational and global topics are not found in other similar texts.

TERMINOLOGY

The most comprehensive explanation of the terminology now being used in the various fields of comparative, international, and transnational and global criminology is that of David Friedrichs (2011, 167), who has put forward the following classification and explanation of the fields of study that collectively comprise what we have termed *global justice*:

- *Comparative criminology* addresses the nature of the crime problem and the form and character of criminal justice systems in countries; a comparative criminology provides crucial data and information necessary for refining an understanding of an evolving globalized context for crime and criminal justice, the core project of a global criminology.

- *Transnational criminology* is focused principally on transnational or cross border forms of crime and endeavors on various levels to control and respond effectively to such crime.

- *International criminology* focuses on international crime or crime that is widely recognized as crimes against humanity, and international law and the institutions of international law.

- *Global criminology* is best applied to the study of the evolving context within which crime and criminal justice now exist. A global criminology increasingly provides a crucial context within which the concerns of comparative criminology and also transnational and international criminology must be understood. In recent years, we have seen more texts that adopt a transnational, international, or global focus. The traditional criminological framework and focus is increasingly limited and inadequate for a rapidly changing twenty-first century world. To be relevant now, criminology must be increasingly comparative, international, and global.

Other commentators have proposed explanations that are broadly in accord with Friedrich's analysis and have also identified where particular fields of study overlap or might link with others, revealing the impossibility of precisely fixing the boundaries between the fields of international, transnational, and global. For example, Pakes (2004, 141) points out that *transnational crimes* are offenses that involve more than one country in both their inception and effects (e.g., money laundering, drug trafficking, Internet crimes). Richard Bennett (2004, 6) explains that this field of study explores the way in which cultures and states deal with criminality that transcends borders rather than simply comparing the countries involved. Ben Bowling (2011, 363) sees transnational criminology as going beyond the boundaries of comparative analysis "to explore problems that do not belong exclusively in one place or another and can therefore only be understood by analyzing *linkages between places*" (italics in original). Michael Kearney (1995, 548) distinguishes transnationalism from globalization in terms of the former overlapping the latter but with a "more limited purview." As he puts it, "Whereas global processes are largely decentered from specific national territories and take place in a global space, transnational processes are anchored in and transcend one or more nation states."

Nelken (2011c, 198–99) suggests that *international criminal justice* encompasses a range of questions regarding international relations, human rights, truth commissions, restitutive justice, and transnational justice, but studies under one branch are linked to other branches; for example, internal human rights conventions have implications for issues such as corruption, terrorism, and immigration and also for the duration of ordinary criminal trials. Freda Adler (1996, 223) refers to international crime as being constituted by approximately twenty crimes recognized by international law, including genocide, violations of human rights, war crimes, and forms of terrorism. Ruth Jamieson and Kieran McEvoy (2005, 505) refer to "violations of human rights,

humanitarian law, crimes against humanity and the related developments in international criminal and transitional justice in the last 20 years."

Bowling (2011, 363) perceives *global criminology* as aspiring "to bring together transnational and comparative research from all regions of the world to build a globally inclusive and cosmopolitan discipline." In addition, Bowling (2011, 365) suggests that the distinction between transnational and global criminology is one of scope. Thus, the global "speaks to the idea of processes that involve, or at least aspire to involve, the whole world *considered in a planetary context*" (italics in original).

This text adopts a classification of comparative, international, and transnational and global criminology. Attempting to differentiate the transnational from the global is problematic. For example, the topic of human trafficking across borders falls within both categories because it possesses both a bilateral and a multinational or global scope and is the subject of global action intended to counter it. There are numerous links between the topics in this text; for example, violence against women in armed conflicts links international criminology in the form of international humanitarian law with the globalism of women's human rights. Terrorism involves elements of international criminal law through the various treaties that expressly sanction forms of terrorism but is also global in scope because it occurs in numerous states. One question is whether international processes on a topic, such as setting norms or standards or imposing duties on states in treaties, assign that topic to "the whole world" global criminology described by Bowling.

The categorization we have adopted should be seen as providing an organizational framework for a set of topics that link and overlap. We have indicated in each topic where there are links and connections to other topics that will enhance the knowledge and understanding of a particular topic.

WHY STUDY GLOBAL JUSTICE ISSUES?

It has been suggested that reasons for studying criminal justice comparatively include academic curiosity; preventing ethnocentrism; studying systems in neighboring countries to produce the practical benefit of enhancing levels of cooperation between those countries, such as in relation to cross border activities and fighting transnational crime; gaining benefit from simply learning from others' experience, such as in the case of criminal justice policy initiatives that might be suited to other countries; studying the ways of other countries to illuminate the way we do things in our own country (Pakes 2010, 2–7).

Other scholars argue that comparing is essentially part of the process of critical thinking. In broad terms, comparing is a way of gaining understanding of our world. We compare to learn from the experience of others. Comparing confers benefits in the fight against transnational crime (Dammer and Fairchild 2006, 8).

Philip Reichel (2013, 3–5) points out that undertaking comparative studies extends a person's knowledge beyond his or her own group because viewing the commonalities and divergences suggest how one's own society can be improved. Studying the justice systems of other countries is important because the international perspective is newly discovered in the U.S. criminal justice curriculum and the utility of that study must be demonstrated. A comparative approach offers insights into the U.S. system and challenges assumptions and the status quo, for example, that the United States has the world's best criminal justice system. In addition, comparing can generate new ideas for improvement of existing systems and substitute a global perspective for a local parochial one. Where criminal justice practitioners and professionals of one country are aware of policies and systems of practice elsewhere and internationally (e.g., the many treaties and conventions formulated under United Nations auspices that set norms and standards in the field of criminal justice), they are more easily able to interact with others and understand the elements and scope of the global justice environment. Bilateral and international cooperation in the field of criminal justice therefore benefits from adopting a global perspective.

Chrisje Brants (2011, 53), similar to Pakes, suggests that "pure intellectual curiosity" is one reason for the comparative approach and that another is to borrow ideas from other systems that seem more effective in policy terms or are more cost effective. Also, the need for harmonization of systems in the European Union makes comparison a necessity. However, Brants points out the most important reason is that comparison enables a greater understanding of one's own system, both in terms of virtues and defects. The notion of borrowing ideas from other systems can extend to determining what amounts to "best practice" in a particular field (Bennett 2004, 9).

A benefit in theoretical terms may arise from comparative studies where particular criminological theories can be tested for their generalizability in varying environments and adjusted as necessary for a particular society or can be revealed as being of limited applicability because of variances in cultures (Bennett 2004, 9; Birkbeck 1993, 307). The fundamental aim here has been described as testing whether the claims of criminology constitute more than merely local truths (Nelken 2010, 14). It is through such studies that non-Anglo-American criminologists may become more reflexive and put aside assumptions and beliefs about how non-Anglo-American systems of justice are conceived and work in practice (Nelken 2002, 176).

Although these authors explain the rationale specifically for comparative studies, the same or similar arguments can be made for global justice studies of the kind included in this text. Now that the local and the global are so thoroughly interconnected, ignoring the international dimensions of criminal justice and criminology is difficult to justify. Thus, it is not so much that international studies that focus only on the comparative approach are dated but rather that such studies in some form ought now to be mandatory in any criminal justice or criminology undergraduate course of study. This text reflects the latest academic perspective on global justice studies.

Globalization

What is globalization, how is it explained, and what is the articulation between globalization and criminology? We should be clear that terms such as *international criminology* and *transnational and global criminology* signify categories of criminology that are nondomestic. In other words, in a general sense, they are intended to describe a criminology that extends beyond the nation-state and engages with topics that in a broad sense are connected to the project of criminology. This may mean they are associated with the criminal law, or with justice, or with systems of justice, and so on. An example of this criminology is the work of Joachim Savelsberg (2010) on how to apply criminological knowledge to international crimes of genocide and violations of international humanitarian law.

For criminologists, globalization is not in itself an especially meaningful term unless it is connected to criminology in some fashion. The reason is that globalization is a process: it is not a structure or framework or a theoretical construct that necessarily implicates criminology. In broad terms then, globalization as a theoretical construct is usually explored through its links to topics where it clearly has an effect and impact. Obvious areas of connection are the environment, communications, and economic affairs generally.

Globalization as a process is discussed in terms of its impact on many of the topics in this book, for example, in policing, in human trafficking, and in juvenile justice. Globalization is a relevant part of those and other topics because it is a force that affects how they work. For example, globalization has been a prominent feature in analyses of how justice policies, both adult and juvenile, are arguably converging and imposing a common model worldwide. Similarly, globalization has impacted crime so that crime is now transnational, and globalization has required states to cooperate on issues that are no longer purely domestic in scope, for example, on policing.

There is an enormous literature on globalization, and it is possible here to give only a broad sense of how it has been explained, why some analysts contest its existence, and how theorists see globalization developing as a force in the future. We therefore sketch out the concept of globalization and then look at its application to criminology, taking account of how criminologists have addressed globalization as a topic of concern.

Explaining Globalization

Globalization has been a subject of intensive scholarship since the 1990s. There are many scholarly formulations of its meaning and one most often cited is that by Anthony Giddens (1990, 64): "the intensification of worldwide social relations which link distant localities in such a way that local happenings are shaped by events occurring many miles away and vice versa." Steger (2009, 15) offers a compressed definition of the term: "Globalization refers to the expansion and intensification of social relations and consciousness across world-time and world-space." In other words, it describes the condition of a contracting world where local developments can be traced to distant conditions and actions. For example, terrorism and crime

no longer follow territorial boundaries: they operate both globally and locally. In the developing world, as Sally Engle Merry (2006b, 42) observes, local activists disseminating the discourse of human rights become "human rights translators" and "reframe local grievances up by portraying them as human rights violations. . . . They remake transnational ideas in local terms." These distant actions include the exercise of power at a distance, for example, decisions of the International Monetary Fund (IMF) that impact a state's economy. However, the local should not be regarded as a *tabula rasa* on which to imprint the effects of globalizing processes. "Rather, the local is always already the social and historical product of movement, interaction and exchange" (Inda and Rosaldo 2008, 38).

For John Tomlinson (1999, 2) the key element in globalization is "complex connectivity," which refers to the "network of interconnections and interdependencies that characterize modern social life." Connectivity therefore operates as a framework within which criminal actors can create and seize opportunities across spaces using rapid and covert forms of communication, international modes of transport, and international markets. It also refers to a capacity to access global flows from a fixed locality, for example, the placement of illicit funds to be laundered through the international banking system.

Globalization should be distinguished from *internationalization,* which relates to independencies between bounded national states (Held and McGrew 2007, 3). Examples of internationalization are state arrangements for the extradition of offenders or policing cooperation in border control between contiguous states or in surveillance activities (see Chapter 4).

Scholars disagree about whether globalization is a new phenomenon. Many argue that it has its roots in the past. For example, Manfred Steger (2009, 19–37) provides a timeline of five historical periods from the prehistoric (10,000–3500 BCE) until the present day and is able to identify elements of globalization in each period with the modern period from 1970 exhibiting a striking expansion of "worldwide interdependencies and global exchanges."

In the debate about where the core or essence of globalization is located, many argue that it lies in the field of economics and international finance. Certainly, the processes and impact of globalization are most easily seen in how national economies have become intertwined and how capital and international trade flow worldwide. Scholars point to the rise and increased power of multinational corporations as well as the creation of international financial institutions such as the IMF and the World Bank and to the promotion of the free market and of capitalism worldwide by democratic states and by these multinational and global institutions.

Globalization also has a political dimension where a dominant argument is that the power of the nation-state has been weakened in the face of globalization—the so-called hollowing out of the state—and that since the 1960s, governance has been "deterritorialized" as national political power has been reconfigured and captured by global social formations (Steger 2009, 63). The demise of the nation-state is visible, it is claimed, in the growth and empowerment of supranational institutions and in the expansion of global civil society.

In its cultural dimension it is argued that globalization, chiefly through the Western cultural matrix of Hollywood and consumerism, is driving the homogenization of popular culture so that in time a universalization of culture will overwhelm all other forms of diversity (Steger 2009, 71). Most commentators agree that although homogenizing cultural tendencies exist, this is a far cry from contending that local cultures will be obliterated. Annette Robertson (2012), rejecting the homogenization theory, has coined the term *glocalization* to describe a contrary process in which the global meets the local in a complex interaction that produces cultural hybridity.

Ecological globalization is readily accepted as a dimension of globalization because action to counter climate change, cross border pollution, population growth, biodiversity, and a host of other ecological issues necessarily requires international cooperation and a global approach toward safeguarding the planet (Steger 2009, 84).

As explained by David Held and Anthony McGrew (2007, 5), globalization's hegemony and overall effect are contested along with its value as a worldwide project. That is, questions are asked about whether it is a process that is ethical or should be supported, rejected, resisted, or transformed. Skeptics question whether globalization is a cause or effect and believe its significance has been exaggerated because nation-states continue to act autonomously in the conduct of world affairs. The international order is therefore a product of actions by the most powerful states, not the outcome of globalization (2007, 7, 19). For reasons of space we cannot explore further the detailed contentions about globalization.[1] Arguably, however, globalization's master narrative is economic and financial, whereas other dimensions, such as the political and cultural, are received with more skepticism or with outright rejection.

Globalization, Criminal Justice, and Criminology

As we have noted, criminology has traditionally concerned itself with domestic crime and has been mindful of keeping within state boundaries. As Russell Hogg (2002, 194) expresses it, "Criminology has largely taken the form of a technical-rational project in the diagnosis and management of crime and marginal disorders *within* the state." It is only relatively recently that criminology has begun to respond to the globalization of crime and to issues of global justice by expanding its reach to better comprehend these harms. Criminology has been urged to draw on and interact with other disciplines such as international relations, economics, and environmental studies in advancing understanding of the consequences of globalization for global justice and crime (Mehigan, Walters, and Westmarland 2010, 247).

In criminology, the global is increasingly a frame of reference, and its relevance to the discipline is now generally acknowledged. Arguably, the field of criminal justice and criminology in the United States continues, however, to give much less attention to influences and knowledge from beyond even while European studies and those emanating from international organizations, UN agencies, and international civil society increasingly weave together the global and the local in their analyses of criminological issues.

Globalization does not "challenge" criminology's previous focus on comparative studies because as Nelken, Pakes, Savelsberg, and others have argued, there is clearly room for both global and comparative approaches. An example is a comparative study of the nature and causes of public disorders in British and French cities over the past thirty years in which Sophie Body-Gendrot (2012, 142) explores incidents of public disorder through several levels of analysis, including the structural, and draws attention to the economic dislocations of the 1980s, which "translated into violent outbursts in localities experiencing the transition from a Fordist to a service economy" and to inequalities created by globalization as well as austerity policies adopted by conservative governments in both countries.[2] This study demonstrates the compatibility between comparative and global inquiry concerning an issue that contains elements of both economic globalization and the local control of public order.

Globalization, Ethnocentricity, and Global Policy Flows

As Pakes (2010, 27) puts it, "The big narrative is one of globalization" and global phenomena such as international migration impact local justice systems just as U.S. mass imprisonment policies and practices enter the global discourse about punishment. Exactly how states are affected by global flows varies from state to state and inquiring into global effects will reveal the complexities of interactions between the local and the global. As Nelken (2013, 16) states, "The outcomes of globalization processes are not predetermined." This means, as Hogg (2002, 200) points out, "that the domestic populations and ways of life of western nations in the 'zones of prosperity' are no longer effectively sealed off from contemporary global disorders as they once believed themselves to be."

In criminology, the effects of globalization have been most apparent in the field of transnational crime, which has benefitted from open borders and increases in cross border trade, but globalization processes also seek to regulate criminal justice practice and procedures. For example, it is now common for international agencies to formulate and urge states to adopt codes of conduct and best international practices in areas such as policing (Chapter 4: Policing) with the ultimate aim that these codes and rules be embodied in national laws, for example, the internationally agreed rules concerning the detention of children (Chapter 7: Juvenile Justice). It is in this manner that criminal justice practices become internationalized.

The flow of neoliberal economic policies worldwide promoted by Western states and UN and international agencies has resulted in increased poverty causing illicit drug cultivation to flourish as poor farmers seek an income from growing more lucrative crops. Efficient and rapid forms of communication and transport as well as international banking facilitate criminal activity globally and enable the laundering of the proceeds of crime. The collapse of the Soviet Union and the disintegration of fragile states have opened up opportunities for cross border crime and provided safe havens for criminals. These causes and effects are discussed throughout this text.

The global flow of criminal justice policy, especially that concerning penal and crime control discourses and policies, has been widely debated by criminologists with some analysts arguing that there exists a convergence of such policies and practices and others rejecting this perspective (Chapter 6: Punishment). How states resist global criminal justice trends is one of the questions raised by the globalization debate (Nelken 2013, 9). Criminologists have not engaged significantly with other kinds of policy flows, such as the possible convergence of anti-terrorist policies worldwide post 9/11. Kelly Gates (2012, 296), for example, argues that although the concept of "homeland security" is an American signifier of national identity, sovereignty, and governmental rationality, it has also been exported beyond the United States as part of a U.S. security strategy that would necessarily constitute a global endeavor and require "international cooperation." In Chapter 12 we present case studies of three countries' responses to domestic and international terrorism: the United States, Germany, and India.

Policy flows are also a major component of UN agencies such as the United Nations Office of Drug Control and European agencies such as EUROPOL, where reports and policy recommendations circulate to governments and international civil society, constituting components of the global justice policy discourse. The United States seems largely unaware or uninterested in these discourses. The extent to which globalization might narrow criminal justice policy choices remains unclear, but agencies generating justice policy discourses have the capacity to construct dominant narratives that can marginalize alternative discourses.

Katja Aas (2012, 8) suggests that globalization affords the opportunity to transcend "established ethnocentric frameworks," and Raewyn Connell (2007, 368) notes that "with few exceptions, social theory speaks from the global North." Mitigating or even discarding globalization's Western bias and decentering the world map of criminology (Fraser 2013, 258), in favor of approaches that are more inclusive presents numerous challenges.

The think tanks, policy institutes, and government policy units are overwhelmingly located in the West, and thus far the flow has been generally one way. Nevertheless, we suggest that in addition to the academy, international civil society and UN agencies offer opportunities for non-Western perspectives on global justice issues to enter the global policy discourse, as, for example, in the field of restorative justice where many developing states possess functional traditional justice systems that apply restorative principles and practices that can inform Western restorative justice approaches. We discuss indigenous and plural legal systems in Chapter 3.

We see further opportunities to escape ethnocentric frameworks in the field of transitional justice (Chapter 8) where non-Western post-conflict states have crafted and implemented creative solutions to ending and resolving conflicts that do not rely only on the mechanisms typically found in formal justice systems. Criminologists could work with lawyers and political scientists in a flow back to the West on formulating truth-telling structures and procedures, designing justice frameworks for transitioning post-conflict states, contributing to analyses of the interaction between transitional justice and international criminal justice, and interrogating issues such as the use of traditional forms of justice in post-conflict states as occurred with the gacaca courts in Rwanda.

Connell (2007, 380) argues that colonialism, a form of metropolitan subjection, is a shared experience for the "majority world" but "does not surface as a central issue in any of the theories of globalization." We have suggested in Chapter 6: Punishment, that a "criminology of the colonial project" might include studies of colonial penality and proposed some research questions, and in Chapter 4: Policing, we have addressed the nature and persistent impact of colonial policing in postcolonial states. The push by the West to bring the principles of "democratic policing" to postcolonial states raises important issues of how the legacy of the colonial project connects with modern forms of policing.

In discussing what he terms *ideologies of globalization,* meaning the discourses associated with globalization processes, Steger (2009, 98–99) identifies social justice as a global discourse that "constructs an alternative vision of globalization based on egalitarian ideals of global solidarity and distributive justice." Steger's focus is on anticapitalist protest movements and pro-global social justice such as groups that oppose the activities of the World Trade Organization and the World Bank. These movements remain on the margins as compared with the mainstream global justice and human rights discourse promoted, managed, and operationalized by international and national nongovernmental organizations, UN agencies, and international organizations, collectively known as "international civil society."

The success of this grouping of actors in achieving forms of global justice, such as women's rights, children's rights, and the extension of international criminal law, has been recognized in the negotiation of international agreements between states such as the Convention on the Rights of the Child, the Statute of the International Criminal Court, and the Convention of the Elimination of All Forms of Discrimination Against Women (CEDAW) where international civil society mobilized resources and pressured states to reach agreement on rights protection and international criminal jurisdiction. As will be seen from discussion of these instruments in this book, international civil society's monitoring and scrutiny of state responses to these rights and justice instruments are crucial in ensuring compliance with these universalizing discourses. Criminologists have studied the association between cause lawyering and social movements.[3] Criminologists—especially those from developing states, which suffer most from crimes of globalization—could apply criminological knowledge and techniques to better understand the dynamics of the international social justice movement in terms of its capacity to mobilize international opinion and influence states.[4]

Global cities and the problem people who inhabit them is a topic of discussion in Chapter 7: Juvenile Justice, where we give an account of the development of juvenile justice in France. Notable events include the so-called social exclusion policies that have resulted in the creation of marginalized populations of young, largely North African immigrants. Manuel Castells (1998, 164–65) describes social exclusion as a "new geography" and contends that "it is formed of American inner-city ghettos, Spanish enclaves of mass youth unemployment, French banlieues warehousing North Africans, Japanese Yoseba quarters and Asian mega-cities' shantytowns. And it is populated by millions of homeless, incarcerated, prostituted, criminalized, brutalized, stigmatized, sick, and illiterate persons." Contemporary urban life for many is therefore represented by the global phenomenon of slum living and its attendant poverty and disempowerment. Analyzing global phenomena brought about by local policies of exclusion would involve an inquiry into the complex interactions between local and global, taking account of the social, economic, political, and criminological dimensions.

New International Crimes

State sovereignty over the criminological enterprise is increasingly under challenge by international discourses, practices, agreements, and institutions. States have been pressured by other states, UN agencies, and civil society to enact laws and criminally sanction practices such as child soldiering and female genital circumcision even where those crimes have never been perpetrated in their jurisdictions (Chapter 14).

Thus, international movements and other actors collectively define "new" international crimes in an international order that identifies violations of rights, criminalizes them globally, and monitors state prosecution of those crimes. States that fail to enact laws are named as defaulters in reports with worldwide circulation such as those issued by UNICEF and the CEDAW Committee on child soldiering and violence against women, respectively, or are publicly named and shamed when called to account for deficient laws or policies.

Dawn Rothe and David Friedrichs (2015, 26) identify the crimes of globalization as new crimes created by the forces of globalization and which are constituted by the "harmful policies and practices of institutions and entities." They acknowledge that these practices and policies may involve violations of the criminal law of states "or international level" and may also result in harms that are "not specifically addressed by statutory law." The authors therefore bracket crimes from other harms. There are links between this conception of harms as crimes and the claims of worldwide movements for social justice (see, e.g., Ezeonu 2008, 113). Designating international institutions' acts (which may be judged as morally or ethically questionable or objectionable, or as problematic in policy terms or in terms of social justice) as crimes, when they have not been enacted as crimes, domestic or international, is the perspective generally adopted by social justice

and environmental movements.[5] Generally speaking, few international crimes exist and largely comprise those described as violations of international humanitarian law, such as are included within the jurisdiction of the International Criminal Court (ICC) or other specially created international tribunals (see Chapter 9).

There are no international economic crimes as such, and where global harms such as cross border pollution violate international conventions and bilateral agreements between states, claims for reparations are made by states against other states under international law. Although UN agencies and institutions such as the IMF can be held accountable for violations of duties under their statutes, there is presently no applicable international criminal law. Achieving an international state consensus on what constitutes a "harm" and which "harms" committed by international agencies and multinational corporations ought to be the subject of international criminalization presents an almost insurmountable political and legal challenge when, for example, states were even unable to agree on the definition of an international crime of terrorism for inclusion within the jurisdiction of the ICC.[6]

The concept of social "harms" as crimes or of social "harms" as a separate category of wrongs outside the crime discourse but that can be sanctioned internationally has not to date been considered in any depth by criminologists. As Muncie (2000, 223) notes, "how far the recoding of crime as harm is capable of challenging and over-throwing legal definitions" is not clear, but the possibility of shaping "replacement discourses" to crime in order to capture and sanction the crimes of the powerful at the international level would be a stimulating challenge to criminologists.

Rothe and Friedrichs (2015, 83) concede that "the idea of holding international financial institutions formally accountable at this time may be unrealistic and potentially counterproductive."[7] The authors see "civil society social activism" as the only force capable of bringing about this objective (2015, 85). As noted earlier, global social movements have been very effective in shaping international conventions affecting women, children, and, most recently, the ICC. Savelsberg (2010, 32) expresses their role as "[contributing] to the creation of global cognitive scripts (or models) and norms, which, once produced, unfold considerable force." Criminology could also participate in initiatives to advance the development of the concept of "harms" as international crimes or "harms" as an alternative discourse of wrongs for which international redress would be available. Relevant studies could provide a foundation for the development of a new discourse centered on social harm and a global strategy on financial (and environmental and other) harms that took account of all the legal, political, and economic implications and could advance the cause of achieving accountability for the "crimes of globalization."

According to Held and McGrew (2007, 43), "The present age is marked by globalized insecurity." As discussed in Chapter 12: Terrorism, conflicts that were formerly interstate wars are now largely intrastate and characterized by low-intensity guerrilla type warfare, civil wars, and horrifying violence. They are fueled and financed by transnational crimes such as the illicit international purchases of arms and by the sale of national resources on international markets. In other words, protagonists in conflicts that spill over state boundaries, such as the terrorist group Boko Haram, pursue their aims by mobilizing global flows of goods and services. Moreover, actors in localized conflicts sharing similar ideologies with organized groups of terrorists may now, through global communications and linkages, extend their impact into other states distant from the conflict through acts of terrorism. Responding to the globalized nature of these conflicts and to global terrorism generally, the United States has reasserted its unilateral power and has sought to place limits on globalization by mobilizing against modes of transnational crime as described in Chapter 10 as well as through precautionary combat operations in states far from the United States.

Globalized insecurity has therefore created the conditions for the emergence of crimes that were invisible to criminology until recently. These include international crimes within the jurisdiction of the ICC, such as war crimes, crimes against humanity and rape perpetrated in violent internal conflicts (Chapter 13), human trafficking across borders (Chapter 11), and processes and procedures for not only punishing such crimes but also repairing the harms to the state and society caused by the depredations of criminal actors in the form of transitional justice (Chapter 8).

There is now general agreement among scholars that globalization will broaden the boundaries of criminology and is likely to promote more interdisciplinary studies and thereby reduce the segmentation of knowledge. As Richard Ericson and Kevin Carriere express it (1996, 515), "It is connections with myriad cultures of knowledge that are crucial to the vitality of criminology." We agree with Mark Findlay, Louise Boon Kuo, and Lim Si Wei (2013, 10) that "globalization has presented new opportunities for crime, new priorities for globalized security, new fears of new risks, and new imperatives for control." The challenge for criminology is to participate fully in the study and analysis of these and other opportunities to better understand the conditions of modern social life.

OVERVIEW OF THE TEXT

The text is divided into three parts, each concerned with a separate field of study. Within each field are located specific topics that the authors regard as contemporary and highly relevant knowledge that will assist students in gaining a fuller appreciation of global justice issues. Topics within the three fields of study overlap and often link to each other, and the three fields should not be seen as having clearly defined boundaries. Overall, the three fields of study represent a set of global justice issues.

Part I: Comparative Criminology and Criminal Justice

Part I comprises seven chapters covering the major topics commonly addressed in comparative criminology texts.

Chapter 2: "Comparative Criminal Justice: Comparing Crime across Countries" follows the traditional approach in comparative criminology and discusses issues such as the problems of comparing countries, using international crime data, what can be learned from comparing international data, international victim surveys, low crime countries, and how the United States compares internationally. We include case studies of the low crime states of Japan and Saudi Arabia.

Chapter 3: "Systems of Law: Common Law, Civil Law, Socialist Law, Islamic Law, Indigenous Law," provides descriptions of these systems and links the discussion of the different systems of law to the social, cultural, and economic context and to the historical record. So, for example, simply describing Islamic systems without any context fails to adequately convey the centrality of law in the Muslim experience. A discussion of the Islamic conception of justice provides an understanding of Sharia punishments, how Islam instructs Muslims to comprehend the idea of criminality, and the key role of Sharia law in many Islamic legal systems. Saudi Arabia and the management of modernity are discussed in the context of its legal system, revealing tensions between Sharia and modern forms of law and between the rulers and the Sharia judges. Indigenous or "traditional" law is living law in many developing countries as well as in the United States through Native American legal systems. The unique history and dynamic development of the legal system of the People's Republic of China is summarized and provides a foundation for further discussions of Chinese law and the Chinese legal system in Chapters 4, 5, and 6.

Chapter 4: "Policing" is a wide-ranging discussion of the features of policing that appear important or interesting in contemporary times both comparatively and as facets of policing itself. The discussion is linked to the historical, social, and cultural factors that relate to the emergence of these features. Thus, examining how the colonies were policed adds to our understanding of challenges to the modern notion of democratic policing because colonial policing practices remain prevalent in postcolonial states. Case studies of current and past policing styles and strategies in Russia and China explain how contemporary police attitudes and perspectives reflect policing arrangements and models of the past and how and why change and reform in police practice have been partial and imperfect. The term *democratic policing* describes Western policing practices that constitute key elements in the movement to universalize or internationalize policing practice. We explain the elements of democratic policing, how it is disseminated to postcolonial developing countries, and how, in Russia and China, its principles come into conflict with local policing practices. International police cooperation and transnational policing are explored as elements in the internationalization or globalization of policing. Transnational and national policing agencies are increasingly linked with states in intrusive forms of global policing and surveillance in the name of risk avoidance, raising questions about accountability, the policing of specific populations and minorities, and legitimate aims of this form of policing. This discussion links to Chapter 10.

Chapter 5: "Courts and Criminal Procedure" aims at understanding differences in criminal procedures, so that, for example, the importance of the judge's role is civil law inquisitorial systems can be contrasted with the importance of the defense lawyer in common law systems. Issues such as conceptions of 'truth' in criminal trials, the cultural and social conditions that brought about adversarial and inquisitorial procedures and contemporary moves toward hybrid criminal procedures are discussed. The distinctive features of the differing procedures are explored and critiqued and the strategy of reforming the inquisitorial model in Central and South America and Russia toward hybrid or even fully accusatorial systems and away from the inquisitorial is explained and assessed. The role and function of prosecutors is explored in detail, focusing on the extensive powers that prosecutors enjoy in both systems. A case study of Japanese prosecutors reveals how culture shapes prosecutorial practice there. The distinctiveness of legal developments in China is acknowledged in an analysis of Chinese criminal procedure that can be compared with a comprehensive account of the French inquisitorial system.

Chapter 6: "Punishment" discusses the rationale of punishment and compares the different custodial and noncustodial punishments applied in various states and how punishment policies in some states are said to have become more punitive through globalization. The death penalty and its worldwide decline are considered in the context of case studies of the death penalty in the United States, Japan, and China. International standards and norms relating to punishment are explained in the context of a discussion of moves to standardize punishments, or principles of punishment worldwide, based on international minimum standards or internationally recognized best practices. Although the chapter focuses primarily on the role of punishment as an instrument in crime control, the history and sociology of punishment are also explored because even though punishment has an instrumental objective, it is also formed and influenced by dynamic social, cultural, and historical forces. Case studies of penal development in China, Japan, the United States, and England describe the main contours of change in penality over time in those countries. Postcolonial countries have inherited Western forms of colonial penality that should be understood as importations from metropolitan powers at a particular time that displaced local penalities and were intended to protect the colonial social order. We look at colonial punishment regimes and suggest a set of questions within a criminology of the colonial project that would include punishment as a field of study.

Chapter 7: "Juvenile Justice" provides comprehensive studies of the development of three contrasting systems of juvenile justice: those in France, Japan, and China. In line with the aim of this text to fully contextualize topics, issues such as how juvenile delinquency is constructed and defined in those countries and what cultural and social practices, values, and beliefs over time have influenced constructions of delinquency and systems of juvenile justice are evaluated. The supposed trend toward punitiveness is explored and critically assessed in relation to each country. The detailed case studies interrogate the politics of juvenile justice and examine how justice plays itself out in the three systems. The additional focus of the chapter is the globalization of juvenile justice through the Convention on the Rights of the Child (CRC) and associated international standard-setting instruments. Analyzing international norms and the CRC (which only the United States and Somalia have failed to ratify) draws attention to the juvenile justice deficit in the United States in the context of international developments. We discuss the issue of state adherence to international standards and assess the effectiveness of the CRC in protecting juveniles in conflict with the law.

Part II: International Criminology

Part II comprises two chapters covering the topics of transitional justice and the ICC. The focus of the chapters is on the development and application of international criminal law.

Chapter 8: "Transitional Justice: Justice, Forgiveness, and Impunity" explores the development of the field of transitional justice as a response to the issue of large-scale state crimes such as apartheid, torture, and genocide as some states have transitioned from authoritarian regimes to liberal democracies. We explain the origins of this form of justice, its international legal and political dimensions, its modes of operation in post-conflict and transitional states, and its overall objectives. Post-transition justice through the normal criminal processes is rare; therefore, understanding why forms of transitional justice (such as peace and reconciliation and truth commissions) are created rather than allowing the criminal justice system to proceed and impose punishments means analyzing social, cultural, historical, and political factors. The chapter offers two wide-ranging case studies of transitional processes and their outcomes in East Timor and Rwanda. Major issues discussed include truth commissions, the granting of amnesty, lack of follow-up of recommendations made to government, and the practice of deeming reconciliation to be more important than discovering the truth. In addition, some post-conflict states adopt a culture of impunity and refuse to address issues of truth seeking or reconciliation through any formal process. This chapter explores the rationale for impunity and looks at the international pressures applied to reject impunity and institute a transitional justice process.

Chapter 9: "The International Criminal Court," only recently created, marks a significant step in the possible evolution of a worldwide justice system and in the continued international protection of human rights. Following a discussion of international criminal law to set the context for the work of the ICC, we explain the evolution of the court and describe its powers and functions under the Statute of the ICC. The United States and some other major world powers have refused to become parties to the statute, and this chapter discusses the arguments deployed by the United States and others against the ICC, how the United States has attempted to counter the role of the court, and what more recent steps the United States has taken to give it a greater degree of recognition and acceptance. We examine how the ICC has functioned and the political and legal challenges it has faced. Two studies of the ICC in action discuss its role in events in Sudan and in the Democratic Republic of Congo. The ICC prosecutor has a key role in the operations of the ICC and the functions and powers of the Office of the Prosecutor (OTP) are explored. For the first time, an international criminal tribunal has been tasked with safeguarding the rights of victims. We examine how victims participate in the proceedings of the court, what the future of the ICC is, and how it might be improved. These and associated issues are addressed in a critical review of the effectiveness of the ICC.

Part III: Transnational and Global Criminology

Part III contains five chapters and incorporates topics recognized generally as falling within the category of transnational crime, namely, transnational crime itself and human trafficking across borders. The other topics in this part fall within the general framework of global criminology.

Chapter 10: "Transnational Crime" is a general discussion of transnational crime that reveals its nature and extent and traces the development of the concept. Of the recognized types of transnational crime, studies are presented of drug trafficking, arms trafficking, smuggling of nuclear materials, money laundering, trading in endangered species, terrorism financing, and cybercrime. In each case, a critical approach seeks to interrogate the reality of such crimes in light of the absence of significant empirical evidence of many of these forms of criminality. Responses to modes of transnational crime from the United States and internationally are explored and assessed for effectiveness. The contested nature of the concept of transnational crime is explained, and critiques are presented and discussed.

Chapter 11: "Human Trafficking across Borders" shows that this is not a new crime as the discussion of "white slavery" and ancient forms of trafficking reveals. Human trafficking for the purposes of commercial sexual exploitation and forced labor (and bonded labor) is distinguished from the smuggling of persons across borders of their own free will, usually for purposes of economic advancement. Whereas the former is a crime against the victim, who is often coerced or deceived, the latter is a victimless crime against the immigration laws of a state. Trafficking has been perceived as a humanitarian issue, an issue of national security, and a crime. The different frameworks are explained and explored, especially in relation to the U.S.-Mexico border. International norms and standards protecting victims are discussed, and estimates of the extent of trafficking worldwide are critiqued in view of the problems associated with empirical investigations of trafficking. Actual instances of sex trafficking and the processes encountered by a trafficking victim are identified and assessed to uncover the human dimension. Strategies to counter trafficking show that domestic and international interventions have failed to significantly impede trafficking, and the socioeconomic conditions that cause trafficking

remain unaddressed. International efforts to control trafficking are addressed in the context of the U.S. Trafficking Victims Protection Act of 2000.

Chapter 12: "Terrorism" discusses how terrorism has become a central worldwide concern since the events of 9/11 even though it is not a new phenomenon, as the account of its evolution reveals. Nevertheless, the events of 9/11 prompted states to review antiterrorist policies and laws. This process, along with accounts of domestic terrorism, is described in three case studies of United States, Germany, and India, enabling comparisons to be drawn of national responses. The current international framework for countering terrorism is explained, and the complexities of defining and explaining what constitutes terrorism and what differentiates it from other forms of violence are discussed. We explore the concept of state terrorism and the so-called new terrorism. Terrorism can be better understood if it is situated within its particular political, social, and economic contexts. To add depth and context to this discussion of terrorism, we present comprehensive case studies of two designated (by the United States) terrorist groups—Boko Haram of Nigeria and Hamas in the Middle East—and explore the history, politics, and economic, social, and cultural context associated with each group. The chapter examines studies in the field of terrorism and religion and features a wide-ranging account of the Islamic understanding of the concept of *jihad* as it has evolved over time in the context of interactions between Islam and the West.

Chapter 13: "Violence Against Women" engages with three forms of violence against women (VAW): domestic violence (DV), honor crimes, and violence against women occurring in armed conflicts, specifically rape. VAW in its various forms has been recognized internationally as a form of discrimination and therefore as a violation of women's human rights. This chapter maps the progress of the international movement to eliminate VAW that culminated in the 1979 Convention on the Elimination of All Forms of Discrimination Against Women (CEDAW) and subsequent developments in VAW through a committee tasked with implementing the CEDAW. Focusing first on DV, we survey theories of DV and notions of gender and then present three in-depth studies of DV in Russia, Nicaragua, and Ghana. We examine gender and DV in those three countries and the national strategies employed to counter and even to eliminate DV as well as strategies recommended under international agreements. The conditions of DV in the three countries are compared with international strategies to eliminate VAW. The latter strategies are explained and assessed for effectiveness. Honor crimes, also known as honor killings, take place in countries where women are expected to conform to a set of behavioral norms designed to protect the honor of the family. We explain the nature of these crimes, reasons they persist, and the judicial reluctance to properly punish those implicated in such crimes. There has been a marked increase in the study of violence against women in armed conflict. Generated in large part by new jurisprudence from international tribunals, this area of study examines the association between rape, torture, and crimes against humanity and how the law has developed in response to the widespread rape of women in situations of armed conflict (e.g., the conflict in the former Yugoslavia). We analyze rape as an international crime and explain how new definitions and jurisprudence have rendered rape in armed conflict among the gravest international crimes.

Chapter 14: "Human Rights and Cultural Relativism: Female Circumcision and Child Soldiers" discusses two topics where global protection policies and strategies are heavily impacted by local cultural beliefs and practices. Cultural relativism is the notion that every society possesses its own moral code explaining what acts are permitted or prohibited; this notion is rejected by the discourse and practice of human rights, which applies a universalist approach to rights and practices in all societies. These universalist norms tend to be Eurocentric in nature because human rights treaties and conventions are largely the product of developed Western societies. This chapter looks at female circumcision and child soldiers as instances of practices condemned in the West because human rights discourses render them violations of women's and children's rights, regardless of the cultural and social context and of agency. We contextualize these practices and events focusing on explaining and understanding why and how they occur and how cultural and social phenomena are implicated in their practice. We offer a case study of child soldiering in Sierra Leone, show how the notion of childhood itself is socially constructed and how, in the case of child soldiers, notions of what constitutes childhood differ

between societies. Female circumcision is shown to be a complex social practice linked to marriage, gender identity, tradition, culture, and religion and to rituals concerning the passage to womanhood. The chapter explores female circumcision and child soldiers in the context of the Western critique of such practices, draws a contrast between Western perspectives and the empirical and lived realities of women and children, charts the international discourse and its outcomes, describes the international legal frameworks that have been created around these subjects, and assesses the implications for subjects of female circumcision and child soldiering.

Notes

1. Held and McGrew (2007) and other numerous globalization texts develop these arguments fully.

2. Held and McGrew (2007, 131, 133) note that one account of economic globalization identifies it as the "principal cause of growing international and world inequality as mobile capital relocates jobs and production in the world economy, trade intensifies international competitive pressures, and global finance constrains the welfare and redistributive capacities of states." The resulting dynamics include "the erosion of social solidarity as welfare regimes are unable, or politicians unwilling, to bear the costs of protecting the most vulnerable."

3. See, for example, A. Sarat and S. Scheingold, eds., 2006, *Cause Lawyers and Social Movements,* Stanford, CA: Stanford University Press.

4. Such a study ought to include an analysis of how forms of social action interact with social media and other new forms of communication, and what new dimensions these developments add to the capacity of social movements to bring about change. See, for example, M. Castells, 2012, *Networks of Outrage and Hope: Social Movements in the Internet Age,* Cambridge UK: Polity Press.

5. Social justice advocates commonly describe the formulation of international criminal offenses to address the "crimes of the powerful" as a legalistic process and adopt a sociolegal analysis of international harmful conduct that incorporates notions of both harm and criminal conduct (Cochrane and Walters 2008, 153; Gibbs et al. 2010, 129).

6. As Findlay et al. (2013, 16) put it, "International crimes are defined and incorporated into international law through negotiations between states in highly politicized forums." The process of defining such crimes includes multiple factors not least of which is protecting the interests of transnational corporations domiciled in a state participating in such negotiations.

7. Rothe and Friedrichs limit the scope of "crimes of globalization" in their study. However, there has been a "green criminology" since the 1990s (Lynch 1990, 1), and new categories of harm, including biopiracy (theft of indigenous flora and fauna; Cochrane and Walters 2008, 145), the "exploitation of hunger" (Walters 2006, 26), and "conservation criminology" (Gibbs et al. 2010, 124), have been identified by criminologists. In addition, the study of victims' rights has provided a lens through which to view international harms (Hall 2011, 371). As to a focus on harms, regardless of whether or not they constitute a crime, see P. Hillyard, C. Pantazis, S. Tombs, and D. Gordon, eds., 2004, *Beyond Criminology: Taking Harm Seriously,* London: Pluto Press.

2

COMPARATIVE CRIMINAL JUSTICE

Comparing Crime across Countries

Comparing crime and criminal justice between different countries is a methodology that serves a number of useful purposes, as noted in Chapter 1. However, there are many challenges that impact the process of comparing associated with issues such as appropriate methodology, scope of studies, and research aims. As David Nelken (2010, 15), writing of comparative research strategies puts it, "Classifications can be controversial, descriptions deceptive, explanations erroneous, interpretations interminable, translations twisted and evaluations ethnocentric." The principal issues, challenges, and approaches in comparative research are discussed in this chapter.

COMPARING CRIMINAL JUSTICE: METHODOLOGICAL ISSUES

In this section, we examine issues that affect questions of choice of methodology in conducting comparative studies. We have identified these issues as cultural difference, searching for the local, law in action, research methods, and research approaches.

Cultural Difference

Clearly, local culture will always impact meaning; therefore, theories and policies developed in the Anglo-American legal tradition and within that legal culture will not necessarily resonate with other legal cultures and countries (Nelken 2002, 175). For example, in the field of crime control, British writing assumes a close and trusting relationship between police and citizens through programs such as community policing, which exemplify the notion of "policing by consent." However, in Italy, two of the principal police forces retain an element of the militarization that effectively removes them from local pressures. The result is that this construction of policing inspires a higher level of public confidence in the police (Nelken 2002, 177).

Typically, comparative criminal justice and criminology studies juxtapose a description of one system within a society with another and then compare or contrast them. Usually, there is no explanation of any underlying cultural or social aspects of the society in question that might influence the systems chosen, and such comparisons are often ahistorical and lacking in context of any kind. Thus, as Nelken (2002, 180) points out, we must ask how we can be sure we are comparing like with like. The same point is made by Jianhong Liu (2007, 4), who, although acknowledging that criminology seeks to establish general principles and construct theories that apply to all societies, cautions that "criminology must investigate how variations in societal contexts alter theoretical statements and policy considerations."

Searching for the Local

There is often an assumption in comparative research that legal systems are the same and that they rely on the same fundamental principles, differing only in form. We tend to regard one country from the perspective of the other. This "universalizing imperative" may arise from a desire to search for what is reassuringly familiar in other legal systems or may derive from the notion that our own system is necessarily superior to others (Zedner 1995, 519). Overcoming this perspective may mean that researchers need to focus less on trying to understand how natives of the other country see things and instead look at the nature of the legal discourse there and how it "serves as an interpretative and structuring device—a means by which people seek to make legal 'sense' of conflict, confusion and disorder" (p. 519).

Lucia Zedner follows this approach in examining the discourse of law and order in Britain and Germany, showing how in Britain there is a constant media focus on reporting traditional crime, a focus that simply does not exist in Germany. In the latter, international and organized crime threaten the German concept of inner security (*Innere Sicherheit*), the counterpart to the British notion of law and order (p. 521). A major contrast between the two countries is that whereas in Britain governments have sought to diminish the role of the State in crime prevention and control by advocating and promoting community responsibility for security, Germans continue to regard the maintenance of local order as the responsibility of the State alone. There, the approach is to leave it to the professionals rather than involve the community in crime prevention or punishment. Juxtaposing these very divergent discourses about law and order reveals how an understanding of the local can illuminate deeply embedded uncritical assumptions in Britain about the content of crime control discourse.

Law in Action

Comparative studies often give little or no attention to the difference between "book law" and "law in action." Merely reciting the contents of a procedural criminal law tells us little about how it operates in practice and how the various actors charged with implementing it perceive their roles and responsibilities and their connections and interactions with other actors in the justice system of that country. A good example can be found in the empirical research of Jacqueline Hodgson which has revealed how in practice, very little supervision is exercised by French prosecutors over police despite a legal framework that suggests otherwise (Hodgson 2005). Similarly, In Italy, the law requires that prosecutors prosecute all cases unlike in the United States, where prosecutors have a significant discretion whether or not to prosecute. Of course in practice, it would be impossible to prosecute all cases at the same time, so priorities must be determined. What are these priorities, and who decides which cases are to have precedence? Only empirical research can answer these questions (Nelken 2010, 17). Researchers have also noted the gap between book law and law in action in China where "even when written rules are available, they tend to be ignored in practice" (Liang and Lu 2006, 159).

Research Methods

How can a researcher who is comparing different justice systems or undertaking other comparative studies best achieve her research goals? Nelken (2002, 179–84) suggests three possible strategies: "virtually there," "researching there," and "living there." The first comprises forms of collaboration between a researcher in the home country and a researcher in the other country. The second involves spending some time in the country under study, immersing oneself in the research site, and thereby gaining direct experience of, and exposure to, the culture and society. This strategy is likely to involve contact with local experts, but care must be exercised in determining the extent of their knowledge and assessing their possible biases in policy and practice. The third strategy envisages a lengthy period of immersion in the other culture, adopting the role of observant participator, and gaining direct experience, a methodology most associated with the discipline of anthropology. Although this seems the most valuable approach, Nelken correctly points out that the researcher will still retain cultural biases and assumptions that will affect the research issues and questions.

Engaging with these strategies then is not a seamless process. The presentational issue: the difference between what an actor in a criminal justice system does in his daily work, as compared with what that person informs a researcher he does, requires that researchers select multiple sources of information, observe actual operations within the system (e.g., court trials), and probe as deeply as possible into an actor's functions and responsibilities and interactions with others in that system. Researchers also need to be wary of relying on simplistic idealized accounts of foreign law and practice as the basis for comparison with U.S. practice. Accounts should be tested and assessed for quality and accuracy so that a deep understanding of the foreign process is gained. It is only through such careful attention to detail that potential constraints in applying foreign policies and practices in the home country can be identified.

Research Approaches

Here, we consider two approaches: the descriptive (or explanatory) and the interpretive.

Descriptive or Explanatory Approach

Studies of this kind identify differences in criminal justice systems, for example, in codes of criminal procedure. However, simply comparing laws without more data sources neglects issues such as explaining why there are differences and why a particular country has different provisions than another concerning, for example, pretrial detention. A good example of this approach is a study by Johannes Feest and Masayuki Murayama (2000, 49), who undertook a virtual comparison of how an actual criminal case that occurred in Spain would be processed (or, in the case of Spain, actually was processed) by different criminal justice systems in Spain, Germany, and Japan. In addition to identifying a number of similarities between the different criminal justice systems, the authors found significant differences, including that pretrial detention would have been ordered only in Japan; that the total period spent in jail would be much longer in Japan; that the case would have been brought to trial in Spain and Germany but not in Japan; and that the duration of the criminal proceedings would be much longer in Germany and Spain than in Japan. As Nelken (2000, 30) points out, the particular methodology employed in this study does not result in any understanding of legal culture from the inside, for example, in terms of the decision-making process of prosecutors and others working within the various systems. The study is therefore limited to one dimension and lacks explanatory power.

Interpretive Approach

An interpretive approach in qualitative research is most closely associated with disciplines such as social anthropology, where ethnographic data are interrogated to establish meaning and provide explanations of a particular social practice, society, or culture. Nelken (2002, 187) argues for an interpretivist approach to be taken in comparative studies, suggesting, for example, that such an approach would uncover how crimes are culturally constructed and would reveal why street crime is regarded differently in Germany and Italy, where the media give it little coverage, as compared with the United States and the United Kingdom, where there is a strong media focus on such criminality. Clearly, quantitative data that only rely on crime statistics cannot provide explanations of how and why particular forms of criminality occur in a particular country or how they are constructed as such by a particular culture. Denis Szabo (1975, 367), for example, questions comparing statistics between different societies without context: "What is the heuristic value of comparing statistical information concerning divorce, alcoholism, drug addiction or public disturbances, originating in countries at different levels of socio-economic development and which have cultures that are quite different?"

Fundamentally, therefore, the value of an interpretive approach lies in linking data to explanations so that the social and cultural landscape underpinning the law or form of criminality is made more explicit. As Nelken (2010, 43) explains, "The aim is to show congruence between meanings and values in criminal justice and the larger culture." However, this approach also has its drawbacks. For example, a researcher must decide who can speak for a particular culture, and given that the interpretive approach is necessarily labor intensive, it is usually not possible to employ multiple sources of information. Often the approach taken will be to study the discourse on a criminal justice topic, as Adam Crawford (2000a, 205) has done in examining the differing conceptions and meanings of mediation and appeals to the community in France and England.

In all cases, as in any form of research, access to material, places, and subjects can often be problematic. As Bin Liang and Hong Lu (2006, 163) have noted in conducting research in China, it is often critical to be able to access social networks, friends and family and former classmates and colleagues. As they put it, "One's guanxi[1] . . . plays a key role; knowing someone in the agency, particularly powerful people, helps with one's access."

INTERNATIONAL CRIME DATA

International agencies such as the United Nations collect crime data to reveal trends in crime and differences between the nature and incidence of crime in different countries. There are many problems associated with international crime data, and the principal constraints are discussed in this section. First, what sources exist for data on international crimes?

Some international bodies such as the United Nations Office on Drugs and Crime (UNODC) collect quantitative crime data as a means to measure and compare crime across countries. Analyzing that data enables us to answer questions such as the following:

- What crime risks exist in country A?

- How prevalent are crimes of violence in country B?

- How do the risks of crime compare between countries C and D?

- How does the incidence of specific crimes in countries compare with the incidence in the United States?

International data collection can present a picture of the kinds and incidence of crime reported for a country and, when examined over a period of time, can assist in revealing any crime trends. The United Nations has been collecting crime data from member countries since 1977. This effort is organized through UNODC. The data collection is known as the United Nations Surveys of Crime and Trends and the Operations of Criminal Justice Systems (CTS). Eleven surveys have been completed thus far, and the 2015 survey is currently under way.[2]

Victimization surveys, generally conducted only in countries with highly developed criminal justice systems, have become an established part of a country's efforts to understand its level of criminality. In 1989, the first international comparative victimization survey was conducted in eleven European countries, the United States, Canada, and Australia (Aebi, Killias, and Tavares 2002, 25). The International Crime Victim Survey (ICVS) is now regularly conducted by the United Nations Interregional Criminal Justice Research Institute (UNICRI) and the Dutch Justice Ministry. The ICVS conducted in the year 2000 collated information on crime experienced in 1999 in seventeen countries.[3] For example, in relation to the United States, the 2000 survey found that burglary and theft account for a greater proportion of crimes than in the other countries but that the United States comes out as average for all other crime types.

Many institutions analyze and assess international crime data. Some of the most prominent are listed here.

- The European Institute for Crime Prevention and Control (HEUNI), based in Finland and affiliated with the United Nations, is prominent in analyzing international crime statistics collected through the UN surveys.[4]

- The International Centre for the Prevention of Crime (ICPC), founded in 1994, is tasked to constitute an international forum through which governments, agencies, and international organizations can exchange experiences and policy information on crime prevention and community safety. This organization publishes material on crime issues, including international crime data collected through the UN surveys.

- The International Criminal Police Organization (INTERPOL) no longer collects or publishes crime statistics from member countries, but it does maintain a database on international intellectual property crime comprising data on trafficking in illicit goods. The organization analyzes these data for a number of purposes, including identifying "links between transnational and organized cross-sector criminal activity involving trafficking in illicit goods."[5] In addition, INTERPOL stores data in criminal databases compiled from information submitted by member countries. The principal databases include records on known international criminals, on missing persons, and on dead bodies; notices issued by the organization on fugitives and terrorists; child sexual exploitation images; DNA profiles, fingerprints, and firearms information; and stolen motor vehicles and stolen works of art.[6] INTERPOL has been described as "a dubious legal object" because although it carries out functions across and between countries, it lacks any founding document or international agreement providing for its establishment and functions. It operates entirely on the basis of voluntary cooperation among its 188 members (Savino, 2010). Given its highly informal structure, its lack of accountability to its members is problematic (Sheptycki 2004, 107).

- UNICRI was established in 1967 with the following functions: to promote greater understanding of crime-related problems, to assist in the maintenance of just and efficient justice systems, to uphold respect for international standards, and to facilitate international cooperation on justice issues. The organization's main programs address issues such as corruption, security, organized crime, violence, and cybercrime. UNICRI gathers data and facilitates information exchange on issues of criminal justice policy options, strategies, and practices.[7]

- The UNODC was established in 1997 through a merger of two other UN bodies concerned with drug control and crime prevention. The organization's functions are to assist states in the fight against illicit drugs, crime, and terrorism; conduct research concerning drugs and crime; and to help states become parties to relevant international treaties through measures such as updating their domestic laws on drugs, crime, and terrorism. UNODC now provides extensive technical assistance to countries on a wide range of crime issues.[8]

Constraints in Analyzing International Crime Data

According to UNODC, the main constraints associated with international crime data collection are the following:

- Countries define crimes differently, making it difficult to make comparisons of crime types between countries. For example, one country may define a common assault and a serious assault quite differently than another country, or conduct that would not be considered criminal in the United States (e.g., adultery) will be sanctioned severely in some Islamic countries. Obviously, this makes for differences in the number of such offenses recorded in different countries.

- Crime reporting differs between countries and is often related to the level of development. For example, whereas most crime data are based on crimes reported to police, some countries have more police posts where crimes can be reported and others have few telephones with which to report crimes to police. Also, in countries where police have an authoritarian attitude to the community as opposed to a focus on securing community safety, citizens may be fearful of police, may be reluctant to report crimes, or may believe that crimes reported will not be properly investigated and so do not bother to report them.

- The cultural and social context differs between countries, and this means that social and cultural attitudes, values, and practices can impact the level of crime reporting. For example, in some countries, women may be reluctant to report domestic violence or cases of sexual violence; this may suggest that those crimes are of a low incidence in a particular society when in fact they may be very prevalent. [9]

In addition, the unreliability and scarcity of crime data from most countries mean that no dependable worldwide crime trends can be identified (Findlay 1999, 20). Generally, only the most developed countries maintain adequate crime records from which broader trends can be extrapolated. Therefore, any conclusions about crime worldwide will be skewed by the bias in favor of developed countries (p. 35).

An associated issue is that only a limited number of countries report international crime data. Among the reasons for this are a lack of administrative capacity or technical capacity within that country to produce the required data, the belief that crime data collection is not a priority issue, the concern that reporting high crime rates will adversely affect overseas investment or industries such as tourism, and the belief that reporting will tarnish the international reputation of that country.

Countries With Low Crime Rates: Japan and Saudi Arabia

International data reveal that Japan and Saudi Arabia have consistently maintained a lower crime rate compared with other countries. What factors explain this?

Freda Adler (1983) looked at arrest rates reported to the United Nations for 1975/76 for five pairs of countries representing different regions of the world that exhibited low rates of crime. One common feature among these countries was that they seemed to have effectively maintained informal social controls such as the family, which ensured the continuance of shared values. Adler concluded that social solidarity was a factor in ensuring low crime rates in contrast to anomie[10] and lack of social cohesion that existed in countries with higher crime. Saudi Arabia and Japan were included among the low crime countries in this study (Adler 1983).

In relation to Japan, Aki Roberts and Gary Lafree (2004) agree with Adler that strong informal social controls are an important contributor to the low crime rates that Japan has enjoyed since the postwar period. Other contributing factors proposed include a low level of economic stress, a small proportion of young males within the population, and a criminal justice system that delivers a high certainty of guilt and punishment measured by high clearance rates. The strength of the postwar Japanese economy was found in one study to be an especially important element (Roberts and Lafree 2004, 179). The much-admired and copied Japanese model of small fixed neighborhood police posts called *koban* has also been noted as significant in terms of crime prevention and control. The Japanese style of policing is discussed in more detail in Chapter 4 and the Japanese criminal prosecution function in Chapter 5, but here it is noteworthy that the *koban*, at least in theory, exemplify community policing in that officers posted to them patrol on foot and on bicycle. The *koban* represent a permanent police presence close to blocks of urban residences and therefore engender a close relationship and a trusting environment for police and community relations (Bayley 1991). There is general agreement among criminologists that the social and cultural context of a country has a huge impact on its crime rate.

In Japan, recorded crime fell by about half between 1945 and 1973 (Hamai and Ellis 2006, 157). Although it has a population more than twice that of England and Wales, for the year 2004/5 Japan reported 2.56 million crimes compared with 5.6 million for England and Wales. It is likely, however, that Japan, similar to other countries, has a substantial "dark figure" of crime, given the evidence of underrecording of crime to enhance clear-up rates (p. 161). Among the twelve countries in the 2000 ICVS, Japan showed victimization rates lower than most comparable countries. Japan had the lowest reported victimization rate for violent crimes of all the countries surveyed at just 0.4 percent per 100, compared with Australia, for example, which showed the highest rate of 4.1 percent. The ICVS for 2004 shows a drop in the victimization rates in Japan from 2000 to 2004 except for thefts from cars and attempted burglary (p. 168).

The value and operation of the complex Japanese forms of social control have been documented by Nobuo Komiya (1999, 369), who explains how Japanese traditional duty (*giri*) and the notion of human relations constituted by an inner circle *(uchi)* prescribe a set of norms or behavioral rules. Neglecting one's *giri* means the likelihood of being labeled a social misfit and gradually being excluded from the group. Japanese are therefore required to fulfill their *giri* in order to benefit from the *uchi*. They feel most secure within the *uchi* world and therefore strive at all times to maintain that position (p. 373). Disputes within *uchi* relationships are settled without litigation usually through go-betweens. This not only applies to disputes between superiors and inferiors but extends to those equal in social status. The opposite of *uchi* is the *yoso* world of the outer circle composed of strangers to the group to which one belongs (p. 374). Toward strangers and outsiders there is no *giri* duty, and so the Japanese behave with indifference, arrogance, and coldness to such persons. In the *yoso* world, the law is used to redress claims against others. Here, individual autonomy is permitted in contrast to the *uchi* world where it is not.

What does this complex cultural framework mean in terms of low crime rates? The *yoso* world matters little to the average Japanese: it contains almost no sociality, and any deviance within the world of the outer circle cannot easily pollute the *uchi* world. The *uchi* group usually operates under detailed rules of conduct that constitute compelling social controls. Seniority is the paramount rule and requires that, in all interactions, members of the group practice containment and constraint behaviors and act in a manner that complies with a great number of social rules. Thus, the Japanese tend to have a strong appreciation of the norms of correct behaviors, and "accepting strong informal social control is not a sign of weakness in Japan; rather it is the proud product of self-control" (Komiya 1999, 380, 382).

There are grave social risks associated with committing crime, which include being expelled from the *uchi* group and ruining one's entire life. Thus, the Japanese cultivate the virtues of patience and caution and do not engage is risk-taking behaviors because they have too much to lose. This account of Japanese cultural values and practices reveals how social control contributes greatly to low crime rates in Japan.

In the same vein as Komiya, in his discussion of law and order in contemporary Japan, Mark Fenwick (1996, 97) identifies a "cultural framework" that includes themes of hierarchy, group orientation, and conflict avoidance that, together with other values, collectively produce a set of unique social processes.

As for Japanese organized crime in the form of the *yakuza,* researchers (see, e.g., Maguire 1997, 131) have suggested that this operates as a kind of alternative police force that polices unorganized crime with the approval of the official police force. This, it is said, explains the absence of much street crime in Japan. Aspiring local criminals are quickly brought under control by *yakusa* interventions.

Saudi Arabia

Saudi Arabia is an Islamic state and a theocratic monarchy.[11] The Islamic Wahhabi movement and its principles constitute key elements of theocratic belief in Saudi Arabia. Wahhabism interprets the Qur' an literally and rejects any modernist reinterpretations.[12] It requires strict obedience to the norms of conduct stipulated by the Qur' an, such as abstinence from alcohol consumption and smoking tobacco, and, unlike other forms of Islam that merely require Muslims to dress modestly, prescribes dress codes. The heavy emphasis on conformity means that behavior in public is regarded as a lens through which one's inner religiosity can be assessed. Thus, public opinion about personal conduct includes admonitions to those who fail to maintain prescribed standards of conduct.[13] In its insistence on strict compliance with the precepts of Islam, Saudi Arabia is perceived by many, less conservative Islamic states as maintaining a form of Islam that is socially and culturally extremely traditionalist.

Based on an analysis of INTERPOL data for the year 2000, the Saudi crime rates for various crimes per 100,000 of population as compared with rates for Japan and the United States are shown in Table 2.1.

Sam Souryal (1988, 9) has compared crime rates for seven Muslim countries (Saudi Arabia, Syria, Sudan, Egypt, Iraq, Lebanon, and Kuwait). The data show a murder rate for Saudi Arabia over the ten years from 1970 to 1979 of 0.4818 per 100,000 with the next highest rate being Syria with 3.5536 and the highest rate among the seven countries being Lebanon with 12.5429. For property crimes, the Saudi average is 2.4364 per 100,000, the next highest rate is Syria with 59.9909, and the highest rate is Sudan with 255.6455. For sexual offenses, the Saudi rate is

Table 2.1	Crime Rates per 100,000 of Population for Saudi Arabia, Japan, and the United States		
Offense	*Saudi Arabia*	*Japan*	*United States*
Murder	0.71	1.10	5.51
Rape	0.14	1.78	32.05
Robbery	0.14	4.08	144.92
Aggravated assault	0.12	23.78	323.62
Burglary	0.05	233.60	728.42
Larceny	79.71	1401.26	2475.27
Motor vehicle theft	76.25	44.28	414.17
All index offenses combined	157.12	1709.88	4123.97

SOURCE: Winslow, R. (n.d.). "Saudi Arabia." In *Crime and Society: A Comparative Criminology Tour of the World,* http://www-rohan.sdsu.edu/faculty/rwinslow/asia_pacific/saudi_arabia.html.

3.20 per 100,000; the next highest is Syria with 5.0273, and the highest is Kuwait with 28.050 per 100,000.

Souryal (1988, 11) doubts the accuracy of the data, pointing to the fact that no victimization surveys are carried out in Saudi Arabia and to the likelihood that there is a significant "dark figure" for unreported crime. His research included focus group discussions. Although he suggests that official crime rates in the country are "reasonably reliable," he believes that official rates ought to be adjusted upward by about 15 percent to account for unreported crime, police negligence in recording crimes, and possible data misrepresentation by government officials.

Generally, it is argued that Islamic belief and practices provide a social structure that keep crime rates low in Islamic states (Serajzadeh 2001, 111). The teachings of the Qur'an promote self-control, and because Islam is not simply a religion but rather a way of life encompassing the private and social lives of Muslims, it develops a strong sense of morality that contributes to a low crime rate. Seyed Serajzadeh (2001, 114) points out other specific factors that he believes contribute to a low crime rate.

- Although Islamic countries do not have homogeneous populations, the majority share the Muslim faith; thus, ethnic differences are subsumed by the unity inspired by faith in Islam.

- Family structures have endured in Islamic countries to an extent not enjoyed in the West, and therefore socialization processes and social support remain strong.

- Public opinion is highly condemnatory of criminal conduct, and severe punishments are supported generally.

Islam requires submission to the will of God and holds persons responsible for all aspects of their behavior before God on the Day of Judgment (Serajzadeh 2001, 116). This degree of accountability for conduct, including observance of the Five Pillars of Islam, strongly suggests that internal and external controls operate to enforce overall social control (p. 119). Conduct is regulated by Sharia, which "covers in meticulous detail practically every aspect of human behavior known to the scholar-jurists, from dietary rules to criminal procedures and from the rituals of worship to commercial contracts" (p. 120). Thus, Sharia serves as a source of social order and consistency in behavior.[14]

Some (e.g., Ali 1985, 45) argue that the severe punishments provided by Sharia law[15] (see Chapter 3) act as a deterrent to crime, but Souryal (1988, 19) disagrees, pointing to his research in Saudi Arabia that showed that citizens consider corporal punishment to be an act of mercy compared with a lengthy prison sentence. Moreover, where severe punishments have their genesis in the notion of an "eye for an eye" in societies where murderous tribal raids were common, the notion that Sharia punishments act as a deterrent becomes much less likely.

Other commentators regard Saudi punishments as an actual deterrent to crime. For example, Badr-El-Din Ali (1985, 48) argues that because punishments are supposed to be executed publicly according to the Qur' an, this expressive effect serves as a deterrent to criminality.[16] However, Adler (1983, 88) argues that both capital and corporal punishments are rarely carried out, so the public effect claimed seems questionable.

Serajzadeh (2001, 123–24) takes the opposite view on punishments in Saudi Arabia and gives three reasons for rejecting the notion that Sharia punishments keep crime rates low in Islamic countries. First, many Islamic countries have, over time since colonization, adopted Western-style codes and laws covering criminal conduct: only in recent times has Islamic law been the subject of a revival in some states, and therefore Sharia and its punishments are not regularly applied in such countries. Second, it is incorrect to judge the operation of Islamic law as swift and certain and therefore as possessing a deterrent effect. In practice, there are significant restrictions on the imposition of the harshest punishments, and other sanctions often depend on the wishes of the victim and his or her family. The process of arriving at a penalty is no more rapid than in other states because Islamic states, too, have levels of bureaucracy within their justice systems. Third, most criminological studies have failed to show a relationship between the severity of the punishment and the crime rate.

Serajzadeh does, however, contend that Sharia is an effective element in a low crime rate because, for Muslims, the more severe the suggested penalty is for a wrongdoing, the more sinful is the act judged to be. This argument relates to the strength of Islam in the minds of Muslims and therefore to overall public opinion about the seriousness of criminality rather than to the actual operation of Sharia (Serajzadeh 2001, 125). Ali (1985, 54) agrees that the "internalization of Islamic values among Saudi people through an integral process of socialization" influences the low crime rate but identifies strong political leadership and the resolute implementation of Sharia law as additional factors.

Other influences that contribute to strong social control in the country include the extended family,[17] schools,[18] the mosque, *ulama* (legal scholars and theologians instrumental in setting public opinion and determining policy in government), and the religious police *(motawwa'in)*. Through surveillance of the population, *motawwa'in* enforce proper conduct to ensure norms of conduct, such as attending mosque and dressing appropriately in public, are complied with.[19] Enforcement of the expectations and rules concerning proper conduct and the persistence of institutions and practices of social control suggest that "it is the complex interplay between the main social control agencies that maintains the 'low crime rate' in Saudi society" (Wardak 2005, 93).

WHAT CAN BE LEARNED FROM COMPARING INTERNATIONAL DATA?

Comparing countries can be helpful in testing criminological theories and in assessing policy interventions and initiatives to see if what works in one country can be applied in others. Understanding how crime varies across countries can give policymakers perspective on crime in their own countries. An example of theory testing is provided by Radjen Van Wilsem (2004, 92), who examined cross-national data on criminal victimization in twenty-seven countries in terms of theft, violence, and vandalism to assess whether country victimization rates supported the theory of routine activity propounded by Lawrence Cohen and Marcus Felson (1979). However, studies that compare crime in different countries will still suffer from the drawback that the social and cultural context and the relevant conceptual basis will often not be taken into account fully or at all. Thus, simply counting crime does not necessarily lead to an understanding of it.

In light of the problems associated with comparing countries or groups of countries as noted earlier, it is generally agreed that comparing is most useful for identifying trends in crime rather than any more specific factors. For example, data collected in the *European Sourcebook of Crime and Criminal Justice Statistics* include crime levels based on police data, but because of divergences in how crime is reported in the participating countries, it is argued that police data should only be used to show trends and should not be employed for comparative purposes (Aebi et al. 2002, 25). As noted earlier, the

United Nations Surveys of Crime and Trends and the Operations of Criminal Justice Systems are the most prominent data on worldwide crime trends, and some important trends have been identified from the data collected that may assist policymakers, for example, in determining best practice on a criminal justice issue (Shaw, van Dijk, and Rhomberg 2003). These reported trends include the following:

- For all reporting countries, total recorded crime data show a steady increase in crime from 2,300 incidents per 100,000 persons in 1980 to just over 3,000 in the year 2000.

- In North America there has been a significant decline in recorded crime. Since the early 1990s, the number of crimes per 100,000 persons has declined steadily in both Canada and the United States but more so in the United States.

- Surprisingly, the overall level of crime is no longer higher in the United States than in the European Union countries. One possible explanation for this is simply that greater resources, both public and private, have been devoted to crime prevention and control in North America.

- Despite decreases in North American crime volume, overall levels of crime in all regions of the world remain significantly lower than those prevailing in North America and the European Union.

- Data on the performance of the justice systems in the reporting countries show wide divergence in the proportion of cases where a conviction is obtained as compared with the number of recorded cases. For the crimes of homicide and robbery over the period 1990–2000, the data show the conviction rate in sub-Saharan Africa to be only 1 in every 18 recorded cases; in Southeast Asia and the Pacific, the rate is about 1 in every 9 cases; in North America the rate is about 1 in every 8 cases for murder and 1 in every 9 for robbery—thus below the global average for murder and just above it for robbery.

- Data on the number of persons per police officer worldwide show the average to be just over 400 persons for every police officer. Variations on this average include that in Eastern Africa the figure is almost 1,000 persons and in North America about 280 persons.

- Data on the number of judges and magistrates show that on average there are 15,000 persons for every judge or magistrate worldwide.

- In terms of the allocation of resources to parts of the justice system, the survey shows that on average, among reporting countries, 56 percent is allocated to police, 29 percent to courts, and 15 percent to prosecution services. Developing countries spend comparatively more on policing and less on courts and the prosecution function. (Shaw et al. 2003)

Unlike almost all other offenses, in the case of the offense of murder it has proved possible to make meaningful comparisons of homicide rates. This is because, unlike other crimes where definitions and reporting rates differ, the crime of homicide is generally defined in essentially the same terms in all countries and is usually reported to police (Van Wilsem 2004, 90). Using data from the World Health Organization's *World Health Statistics,* reporting on twenty-seven countries (nineteen Western [including the United States], one Asian, and seven European), Van Wilsem (2004, 98) shows that homicide is a rare crime event with about 3 victims per 100,000 persons on average among the reporting countries.

Whereas most countries have rates below that measure of 3 persons per 100,000, three countries—Estonia, Lithuania, and the United States—have high homicide rates (23.14, 10.87, and 9.64, respectively). For homicide and some other crimes, victimization rates were higher among countries with high levels of income inequality, thus giving some support to strain theory as a causative factor. Although we may learn something from data about homicide rates in different countries that seem to support at least one relevant theoretical causal explanation, the knowledge gained from such quantitative analyses is quite limited. Nevertheless, because homicide is generally regarded as a good proxy for levels of violent crime, it can be a useful indicator (Shaw et al. 2003, 40).

How Does the United States Compare Internationally?

As a major Western nation with a highly developed and well-resourced justice system, the United States is regularly included in studies comparing crime rates or aspects of criminality between countries. Such studies may be on crime rates between a range of countries, or only between the United States and another country, or between countries based on some topic associated with criminality. For example, one study by the Canadian Centre for Justice Statistics in 2001 compared the crime rates in the United States and Canada, noting that there were parallels between the two countries, economically, socially, and culturally, therefore creating the expectation that crime rates would show resemblances.

In fact, the data showed that in the year 2000, the Canadian homicide rate was about one-third that of the U.S. rate: the Canadian rate per 100,000 persons was 1.8 compared with a rate of 5.5 per 100,000 for the United States. Interestingly, one in three Canadian murders involved the use of firearms compared with two in three in the United States. The homicide rate was echoed by the aggravated assault rate (representing the most serious forms of assault), which in the year 2000 showed a U.S. rate of 324 per 100,000 persons compared with Canada with 143 per 100,000 (Gannon 2001).

Explanations for these differences would necessarily involve weighing and assessing many complex social, cultural, and economic factors. As Susanne Karstedt (2001, 285) reminds us, "crime and social control are social and cultural phenomena," and the cultural context will always shape crime prevention and control initiatives. Thus, there is no guarantee that crime prevention and control interventions that prove effective in Canada will work in the United States, and vice versa.

In another comparative study, on the topic of firearm-related deaths, deaths due to firearms in the United States in 1996 were compared with such deaths in thirty-five other high- and upper-middle-income countries (Krug, Powell, and Dahlberg 1998, 214). The one-year study of firearms covered homicides, suicides, unintentional deaths, and deaths of undetermined intent. Results showed that overall firearm mortality rates were five to six times higher in high-income and upper-middle-income countries in the Americas (a rate of 12.72 per 100,000 persons) compared with Europe (2.17 per 100,000) or Oceania (2.57 per 100,000) and ninety-five times higher than in Asia (0.13 per 100,000). The rate of firearm deaths in the United States was 14.24 per 100,000. As the study notes, the United States was "unique" among the thirty-six countries surveyed as having the highest overall firearm mortality rate, as having a high proportion of homicides resulting from injury by a firearm, and as having the highest proportion of suicides as a result of a firearm injury. Other high firearm mortality rates apart from the United States were identified in Mexico, Brazil, and Argentina (Krug et al. 1998, 219).

In considering the causal factors that might explain these divergences, the authors suggest that "social norms" might influence the low rate of firearm mortality in Asia and that a positive association between firearm ownership and rates of firearm homicide and suicide had been reported. The proportion of households possessing a firearm ranged from 48 percent in the United States to less than 1 percent in Japan.

These studies about homicide and firearms-related deaths in the United States are complemented by research that concludes that lethal violence rather than general crime is the major U.S. crime issue (Zimring and Hawkins 1997). Concluding that rates of nonviolent crime are comparable or lower in the United States as compared with other industrialized countries, the analysis of Zimring and Hawkins shows that the United States has significantly higher rates of serious violence, especially homicide. Guns are seen to be a major factor in homicides and the policy prescriptions proposed include addressing the availability of handguns.

SUMMARY

This chapter has shown that researching criminality in other countries is likely to be a complex process given the historical, social, and cultural differences that differentiate countries. Case studies of Japan and Saudi Arabia reveal how the specificity of cultural and social values and practices contribute to low crime rates in those countries. Both cultural difference and the necessity to set aside all assumptions about other countries' systems of justice, definitions of crime, and perspectives on criminality make trans-country comparative studies in criminology a challenge for all researchers. Even when researchers are able to spend considerable time in a particular country and immerse themselves in all aspects of the local legal and justice culture, they must be aware that the perspectives of their informants as well as of themselves are not objective but probably shaded by their own beliefs and values. In studying topics in criminology in other countries, researchers need to understand how others see things in that country, how criminological discourses there are shaped and structured, and how law works in action rather than how it is simply expressed in statutes.

In spite of the constraints that affect comparative work, some useful studies are being produced internationally that can show best practices in policy making, possibly resulting in helpful policy transfers to other countries. However, data flows to international agencies about crime and crime control come predominantly out of developed states, and more data are needed from developing countries to avoid skewed conclusions about how well or badly crime is being prevented and controlled worldwide. In addition, broad trends are being identified in terms of general crime rates, and more specifically in relation to crimes such as homicide and to issues such as the use of firearms. The challenge continues to be linking data to explanations.

NOTES

1. *Guanxi* is the Chinese term for social networks and influential relationships that facilitate business and dealings generally.

2. See http://www.unodc.org/unodc/en/data-and-analysis/United-Nations-Surveys-on-Crime-Trends-and-the-Operations-of-Criminal-Justice-Systems.html.

3. See J. N. van Kesteren, P. Mayhew, and P. Nieuwbeerta, *Criminal Victimisation in Seventeen Industrialised Countries: Key Findings from the 2000 International Crime Victims Survey* (Onderzoek en beleid, nr. 187, The Hague: Ministry of Justice, WODC, 2000). There are no developing countries among the seventeen countries surveyed.

4. See http://www.heuni.fi/en.

5. See http://www.interpol.int/Crime-areas/Trafficking-in-illicit-goods/Databases.

6. See http://www.interpol.int/INTERPOL-expertise/Databases.

7. See http://www.unicri.it/.

8. See http://www.unodc.org/.

9. See http://www.unodc.org/unodc/en/data-and-analysis/Compiling-and-comparing-International-Crime-Statistics.html.

10. Anomie was a concept developed by Robert Merton (1957), who proposed a functionalist theory of deviance that differentiates between culturally constructed goals and the legitimate means of achieving them. According to this view, individuals in society who have little or no legitimate access to the means of achieving the defined goals may choose illegitimate means of achieving them. Merton formulated his theory in the United States during the 1930s, when the harsh economic inequalities were difficult to reconcile with the American Dream (Downes and Rock 1988, 120). The disjunction between the dream and the means to achieve the dream was viewed as contributing greatly to high rates of crime, especially in the lower classes, thus proposing an inverse relationship between deviance and social status (p. 129). Merton attempts to show how social structures impinge on individuals by arguing that society places greater emphasis on the goals, especially economic goals, than on the means of achieving those goals. For this reason, frustration and strain are created within certain sectors of society and thus act as catalysts for deviant behavior.

11. Saudi Arabia is an absolute monarchy, whose foundational and operational legal constitutional documents are Islamic Sharia and the Basic Law of Government of March 1992. The king is the custodian of the Muslim holy sites of Mecca and Medina (Wardak 2005, 92).

12. See http://countrystudies.us/saudi-arabia/27.htm.

13. See http://countrystudies.us/saudi-arabia/27.htm.

14. Of the 6,236 verses of the Qur' an, only about 500 prescribe legal and moral rules of conduct (Duncan 1998, 3).

15. For example, the punishment for murder is a beheading in public, as a lesson to the community, but the family of a murdered victim has the right to decide on the actual punishment if an alleged murderer is convicted (Duncan 1998, 3).

16. Executions are performed in the very center of a large plaza in full view of the public. Beheading is carried out using a four-foot crescent-shaped sword while loudspeaker broadcasting from a mosque bordering the square briefly describes the crime for which the person is being executed (Duncan 1998, 12).

17. Deference and obedience to elders is expected, and rejecting parental wishes is regarded as sinful conduct punishable on the Day of Judgment. Continuous disobedience to parents can result in forfeiture of future property inheritance and social stigmatization. The fact that marriages are arranged by parents who also finance a son's or daughter's education overseas are also significant factors in parental control (Wardak 2005, 99).

18. Although both secular and religious education is provided, a large part of the curriculum is devoted to Islamic studies. This has the effect of inculcating and reinforcing, through schooling, the same values that children are socialized to accept by their parents (Wardak 2005, 101).

19. Approximately twenty thousand men perform this role; they receive a salary but are not part of the police. They are entitled to detain persons for twenty-four hours before turning them over to the police. They seem to function as the policing arm of the Saudi *ulama* in their role as enforcers of public morality (Wardak 2005, 104).

3

Systems of Law

Common Law, Civil Law, Socialist Law, Islamic Law, Indigenous Law

All countries make laws that include prohibitions and sanctions against forms of conduct, for example, against deliberately inflicting violence on another person. Violations of such laws constitute criminal offenses, which are prosecuted by the state. These laws are applied and interpreted through systems of criminal law and justice. A criminal justice system in a country commonly comprises police, prosecutors, courts, and modes of punishment (including incarceration) intended to process and punish violations of the criminal law when a person is found to have committed a criminal act. Accordingly, a legal system is constituted by a set of legal institutions and the rules and procedures they formulate and apply in their everyday work.

A legal tradition is a less concrete concept. Nor is a legal tradition a collection of institutions or rules for doing justice but rather "a set of historically conditioned attitudes to the role of law in a particular society, its characteristic mode of legal thought, and its legal sources and basic ideology" (de Cruz 2007, 27). Thus the legal tradition of a country will largely determine the nature of its institutions and legal rules and procedures and will absorb social and cultural elements of that society. The terms *legal system* and *legal tradition* are used interchangeably in this chapter, as is the norm when discussing comparative legal systems and traditions.

The differences between legal systems and legal traditions, how these divergences came about, and what makes each system and tradition unique are also explored. Generally, most legal systems today are identified in the two major legal traditions of civil law and common law. It used to be the case that a third category was identified—that of socialist law—but that category has become problematic over time. In Islamic countries and in African, Asian, and Pacific countries, elements of Islamic law and of indigenous (or customary) law remain important to varying degrees.

Examples of civil law systems are Germany and France, most of Europe and South America, and parts of Africa that were colonized by France, Portugal, and Belgium. Common law countries include the United States, England, Australia, Canada, and African countries that were colonized by the British. Hybrid or mixed jurisdictions, which are neither common law nor civil law exclusively, include Seychelles, South Africa, the Philippines, and Greece (de Cruz 2007, 36).

In civil law systems, Roman law heavily influenced the French and German models and hence civil law systems are evident in other countries. In common law systems, development occurred through the adoption of substantive principles of law on a case-by-case basis as disputes were brought before the courts for resolution. Thus the common law was developed by the courts, especially in the early period, rather than by the legislature. This contrasts with civil law systems, in which scholars and universities built on the foundation of Roman and local customary law to formulate codes of law enacted by the legislature.

A striking difference between these systems, therefore, is the role and power of the judiciary in terms of legal development. Whereas the common law system can be characterized as based on improvisation, and as pragmatic and concrete, civil law systems tend to be abstract, conceptual frameworks, heavily rule based, and reliant on comprehensive regulation for resolving disputes (de Cruz 2007, 39). Chapters 4, 5, and 6 contain detailed discussions of policing, criminal procedure, and prosecutions in the various justice systems.

The examination of other kinds of legal systems allows us to better appreciate how certain aspects of the U.S. legal system operate but also to gain an understanding of how some aspects of other legal systems might be of value to the U.S. system. Accordingly, it is important not to idealize one system at the expense of others, because, although different to the one we know best, other systems may well possess features of worth and benefit.

All legal systems are rooted in a country's history and culture and evolved as part of societal growth. Consequently, the historical record is significant in helping us to understand all legal systems and often explains many of the differences between them. This is especially true when comparing the common law and civil law systems.

Indigenous law and informal systems of adjudication have existed from time immemorial and are usually found in states that have plural legal systems where they exist alongside common law or civil law systems. There are often tensions between formal and informal systems that relate to questions of due process and gender bias in the latter systems.

Some states have incorporated Islamic law as the entirety or as a part of their legal systems, for example, Saudi Arabia where the former applies. Unlike non–theocratic legal systems, Islam not only provides a set of norms constituting proper conduct for Muslims but also incorporates those norms into a theocratic legal system that emphasizes the place of Islam in society as a way of life.

COMMON LAW SYSTEMS

By virtue of its position as a former British colony, the United States, like many countries colonized by Great Britain, possesses a common law legal system, with one exception: the state of Louisiana, once a French possession, has elements of civil law in its state legal system.

Along with its language and culture, Great Britain imported the British common law into its colonial possessions as an integral element of the colonial project. Ordinarily, former British colonies have tended to retain common law systems post independence. In some cases, for example, India, many African states, and South Pacific states such as Papua New Guinea and Solomon Islands kept the imported English common law and continued to supplement it with their own indigenous systems of law, creating plural legal systems. The historical record shows, therefore, that countries have adapted common law to suit their own needs and circumstances.

This leads us to ask how common law came into being. Given that the history of the growth of the common law is complex, it is helpful to identify events that occurred in specific historical periods to reveal the trajectory of common law development.

Roman Occupation of Britain

Despite Britain having been invaded by the Romans in 55 BCE (except for Scotland, where Roman law did not take hold), there was no significant reception of Roman law into England and Wales (Freeman 1987, 48). Therefore, England and Wales avoided a civil law system with Roman law as its foundation; however, Roman law in the form of canon law did indirectly affect the development of English common law (Glendon, Carozza, and Picker 1982, 303).

Anglo-Saxon Period

During this period, Britain was invaded by Vikings and Danes while ruled by a series of local kings, the most famous being Alfred the Great (871–99), who produced a code of laws that was basically a collection of the customs and edicts of his predecessors (Head 2011, 335). Tribal groups developed customs that achieved the status of "customary law," but England was fragmented with seven kingdoms, each having its own customs that differed significantly from those of the others (p. 335). Victims responded directly to injuries (crimes) by taking action themselves or with their tribe to punish through violence or by payment of forms of compensation. The principal courts in this period were the "hundreds," which were local in nature, but other courts included manorial courts, shire courts, county courts, and honorial courts. There was little or no central control over these courts (p. 337).

Norman Conquest

The year 1066 is commonly seen as the inauguration of the common law tradition. This is the year when William the Conqueror, a Norman from France, defeated the English at the Battle of Hastings (Merryman and Perez-Perdomo 2007, 3). It is not clear to what extent the Norman Conquest and Norman practices, or existing Anglo-Saxon customs and practices before the conquest, contributed to the development of the common law. It seems that the Normans were happy to accept elements of custom while also imposing their own ideas and merging these different elements (Hudson 1996, 17). Scholars debate whether the growth of the common law has its foundation in the later period of Henry II or earlier during the Anglo-Saxon period, or whether the Anglo-Saxon period provided the foundation from which Henry II was enabled to further formulate the common law (thus tending to minimize the perceived "genius" of Henry II; p. 20). It is clear, however, that William established centralized administration at Westminster and effectively ended tribal rule, laying the foundation for the royal courts to create a common law for the whole of England (Head 2011, 343).

At this time, citizens expected a medieval ruler to fulfill the role of a king who provided and implemented "justice." Thus citizens with claims to make would follow the king and his court to gain an audience to seek justice. According to the nature of the plea or the identity of the person making it, access to the king himself might be given (Hudson 1996, 27, 29). William exemplified this notion of the king as the dispenser of justice by proclaiming himself the fountainhead of justice (Head 2011, 338).

In spite of this focus on the king, courts could still be held without his personal presence, and royal officials who presided at courts functioned as justices, either at the king's court or as itinerant justices (Hudson 1996, 30, 33). The Normans were able to make the law uniform throughout England by having the king's officials conduct cases in the shires through the introduction of the general eyres (from Old French *erre*, meaning journey). These were regular countrywide visitations from royal judges with special powers and duties who would sit in the local courts and hear cases (Head 2011, 344). Over time, however, the royal courts broadened their jurisdiction at the expense of local courts (p. 347).

The common law grew from the bottom up in the form of decisions of the king's judges on the facts of cases brought privately or brought by the king's agents to enforce the king's peace. This contrasts with the development of civil law systems in which it was professors in universities and not judges practicing law who created forms of laws and procedures.[1] Not only was the common law developed systematically from case to case based on precedent cases, it was a truly national law applying throughout the country. This radical change in what constituted "the law" meant that the new common law replaced regional law based on custom that had applied before the Norman Conquest (Hudson 1996, 17; Van Caenegem 1973, 88). By the mid-thirteenth century, the term *de communi iure* (common law) had superseded custom as an expression of the prevailing law (Hudson 1996, 18).

Henry II

During the reign of Henry II (1133–89), common law forms of action and procedures were finally selected and systemized so that it became clear who had access to the king's courts (Head 2011, 339; Van Caenegem 1973, 100). According to Maitland (writing in 1895 at the zenith of the British Empire), it was Henry's "genius" that centralized and unified the common law (in Hudson 1996, 19).

During the twelfth century, the notion of serious crimes in the form of felonies against the king's peace replaced more ancient forms of redress that necessitated individual rather than state action and allowed for forms of compensation from offender to victim (Hudson 1996, 19). Henry's justices traveled the country trying criminal cases and enforcing public order (Van Caenegem 1973, 41). Homicide and theft were the predominant crimes, but with no police forces, medieval societies found it difficult to catch offenders unless they were able to do so red-handed (Hudson 1996, 61). It seems that only a small proportion of crimes were tried, largely because offenders who escaped would most likely never be caught (p. 68). If the offender were caught red-handed, the trial would be swift and, typically, a thief would be sentenced to death (by hanging or beheading) or to mutilation. Where guilt was not obvious, a mode of proof would be chosen from the options of ordeal, trial by cold water, and trial by iron (pp. 72–73). Later, trial by battle between the accuser and the accused became the preferred method of proof in serious crimes (p. 75).

In 1187–89, the substance of the common law was explained in *Glanvill—The Treatise on the Laws and Customs of the Realm of England Commonly Called Glanvill,* written anonymously, possibly by a clerk to justiciar Ranulf de Granvill (Hudson 1996, 154). It focused largely on describing the forms of procedure that had developed under common law. The production of a working manual of law of this nature would have assisted in standardizing practice and procedure and in understanding the scope of the common law throughout the country (p. 154). It was only in the late twelfth century that the distinction between civil and criminal causes became clear-cut. In the Norman period, the word *crimen* was used flexibly, describing not only crimes but also sins (p. 56).

Magna Carta

Although known mainly for its protection of civil rights, the Magna Carta, representing the negotiated outcome of disputes between the king and his barons, also reflected tensions between the king's courts and the baron's local courts, which had progressively lost jurisdiction to the royal courts (Glendon et al. 1982, 159). In a response to the barons' concerns, Clause 17 of the Magna Carta, for example, provided that "common pleas shall not follow our court, but shall be held in some specified place" (Hudson 1996, 224). As a future model statute and norm-creating document, the Magna Carta sustained the process of systemizing and consolidating the common law.

Common Law and Equity

The common law was shaped by causes of action and procedures that were inflexible, and if a petitioner could not bring himself or herself within the forms of action, he or she had no remedy. Equity developed alongside the common law to mitigate its severity and strictness. This sometimes led to conflicts between common law and equity. For example, the Chancery Court, formally established to apply equitable remedies, could issue an injunction ordering a person to refrain from doing an act that had been mandated by a common law court (Glendon et al. 1982, 305). In 1873, the Judicature Acts merged common law and equity and replaced the separate common law and equity courts with a Supreme Court of Judicature that exercised both common law and equitable powers (p. 305). The rule became that where common law and equity conflicted, equity would prevail.

There are a number of features of the common law, built up over time, that render it unique and special and differentiate it from other legal traditions and systems. These features include the notion of precedent and the concept of common law offenses.

The Force of Precedent

The defining feature of common law systems is the notion of *stare decisis:* the power and obligation of the courts to base their decisions on prior decisions. This doctrine that courts follow precedent is said to be a feature distinguishing common law from civil systems. However, whereas in theory at least, civil courts do not follow precedent, in practice this does occur (as described later in the discussion of civil law systems). Thus "judge-made law" that governs the outcome of future similar cases characterizes common law systems. Common law systems, therefore, not only produce positive law in the form of statutes, regulations, and the like, but also generate judge-made law through court decisions and rulings. In fact, for many centuries common law was the primary source of law in England, only giving way partially to statute law after the Civil War and then being overtaken by legislation in the mid-nineteenth century (Glendon et al. 1982, 277).

Common Law Offenses

Only in common law systems is it possible to punish persons for "common law offenses" and for contempt. For example, whereas most U.S. states have codified criminal offenses by enacting criminal codes or other statutes providing for offenses, in the United Kingdom the offense of murder, among others, is still defined by the common law rather than by statute. As for contempt, no contempt power in civil law jurisdictions exists because it is considered that giving a judge the power to punish criminally in civil actions would be inconsistent with the civil law view of the role of the judge (Merryman and Perez-Perdomo 2007, 55).

BOX 3.1   Common Law in the United States: How Did the English Common Law Come to U.S. Legal Systems?

Legal development within the original thirteen colonies was uneven because each colony was created at a different time and each had its own royal charter. The charters did not require that the local courts be patterned after those in England or that the common law should be applied: they simply stated that laws should not conflict with the laws of England.

English settlers into the colonies brought with them their knowledge of the law. Because they were ordinary citizens, this meant they transplanted their local community custom rather than the more complex common law created by the Royal Courts at Westminster. Juries were used from the very beginning, and the Bible was an early influence. As the colonies grew socially and economically, access to the common law became more frequent so that by the time independence came in 1776, English common law was the foundation of the legal system in each of the colonies. By that time there were numerous lawyers in each colony. Of the fifty-six signatories to the Declaration of Independence, twenty-five were lawyers.

By the end of the eighteenth century, law reports began to be published but the law was often ascertained from publications like Blackstone's Commentaries of the Laws of England, which first appeared in America in 1803. The American legal tradition developed further through law schools and scholarly writing with the establishment of Harvard Law School in 1829.

Despite the common law legacy, there are distinct differences between the English and U.S. legal systems. Primarily, the United States has a federal system of government with a constitution for the entire country and each state having its own separate constitution, laws, and legal system. Laws can be struck down for being in violation of the constitution, and this form of "judicial review" does not exist in England where review is much more limited.

Codification has been adopted in many states as a means of stating the law in a comprehensive manner along the lines of the practice in civil law systems, but this has not occurred in England. The background of judges and their method of appointment, the weight given to scholarly opinion on the law, and differences in trial practice are widely divergent from those in England, but in spite of this, the basic judicial approach in the United States closely resembles that of England.

SOURCES: de Cruz 2007, 108; Stoebuck 1968, 393–426.

CIVIL LAW SYSTEMS

Countries with civil law systems vastly outnumber those with common law systems. The civil law tradition is much older and has always been more influential across national boundaries. However, there are major differences between the various civil law systems in terms of procedures, rules, and institutions (Merryman and Perdomo 2007, 1). It is generally accepted that the civil law tradition dates back to 450 BCE, supposedly the date of publication of *The Twelve Tables* in Rome (p. 2).[2]

As explained by Glendon and colleagues (1982, 17) and Merryman and Perdomo (2007, 6), the civil law tradition comprises a number of elements that over time have merged and shaped the nature and content of civil law systems. The historical record is therefore very important for understanding the civil law tradition. These authors broadly agree that the constituent elements are the following:

- Roman law

- Germanic and local customs

- Canon law

- Commercial law

- The rise of the nation-state

- Legal science

Roman Law

The period covered by Roman law is immense, starting from *The Twelve Tables* in 450 BCE up to the Justinian compilations of about 534 CE. However, two distinct phases in the life of Roman law are generally identified:

- the first begins in the classical period of Roman law formulation and publication and ends in the writing and publication of the *Corpus Juris Civilis* by the Emperor Justinian; and

- the second begins around five hundred years after the publication of the *Corpus Juris Civilis* and became known in Europe as the "revival of Roman law."

Ancient Roman law reached its greatest development in the classical period from around 117 CE to 235 CE when legal professionals known as jurisconsults rendered legal opinions and advice. Foremost among them were Ulpian, Papinian, and Gaius (Glendon et al. 1982, 19). *The Twelve Tables* was a written text of customary law applicable in Rome that emerged from a political confrontation between plebeians and patricians (Head 2011, 51). *The Twelve Tables* details both procedural and substantive rules of law.

During the sixth century CE, Emperor Justinian directed the preparation of a compilation and codification of the then extant Roman law relating to persons, the family, inheritance, property, contracts, and remedies (Merryman and Perdomo 2007, 7). This publication, known as the *Corpus Juris Civilis,* represents Justinian's organization of the opinions, treaties, and commentaries written by the jurisconsults. His objective was to render any further commentaries unnecessary and capture the best work of the classical period (p. 7). To civil lawyers, the group of subjects covered by this material represents the essence of a civil law system: it is what a civil lawyer means by "civil law."

To Justinian, the *Corpus Juris Civilis* was intended to supersede all previous commentaries and make any further reference to them unnecessary. The *Corpus* was now to be the sole authoritative source and to this end Justinian prohibited the writing of commentaries on the *Corpus,* an instruction that was generally disregarded even in his own lifetime (Merryman and Perdomo 2007, 7). The *Corpus* comprised four parts: the *Institutes,* the *Digest,* the *Code,* and the *Novels,* with the *Digest* having the greatest value as the essence of the best Roman legal thinking of the classical period. It was about the same size as the Bible (Glendon et al. 1982, 20). The *Institutes* was a short introductory text for first-year law students along the lines of a hornbook, the *Code* was a collection of Roman legislation, and the *Novels* contained imperial laws enacted after the completion of the *Code* and the *Digest* by Justinian himself (Head 2011, 64).

Following the reign of Justinian, the *Corpus* fell into disuse for many centuries in Europe when the Roman Empire and its constituent parts became the subject of numerous invasions and ensuing chaos over a period of five hundred years during the period commonly known as the Dark Ages (from the fall of the Roman Empire in 476 until about the year 1000 CE). It survived, however, in the Eastern Roman Empire in the area around Constantinople for almost fourteen centuries (Head 2011, 67).

Late in the eleventh century, interest in the *Corpus* reemerged. This revival of Roman law had its origins in Bologna, Italy, where the first modern European university was established. The law studied here was the *Corpus,* which had attained an iconic status ranking alongside the Bible and the writings of Aristotle. Scholars in

Bologna called the work "written reason," recognizing its high intellectual quality. Soon, other universities in northern Italy began to study the *Corpus,* drawing to them scholars from all over Europe. The first generation of scholars, known as glossators and commentators, produced literature on the work itself (which in turn became a separate source of study; Merryman and Perdomo 2007, 9) by writing notations in the text margins of the *Digest* to explain its meaning and to resolve apparent inconsistencies (Head 2011, 77). The commentators aimed to shape the *Corpus* to the needs of the time and, in this process of modernization, used external sources such as statutes and local and commercial customs (p. 81).

When scholars returned from Italy to their own countries and began to teach, a common body of law began to develop, a common teaching style was adopted, and a common legal language was devised (Merryman and Perdomo 2007, 10). Thus a common law of Europe developed while the glossators and commentators gradually began to adapt the laws of Roman society to contemporary times (Glendon et al. 1982, 25).

Germanic and Local Customs

In governing territories they captured between the fifth and tenth centuries, the Romanized Germanic peoples applied versions of Roman law blended with their own customs. Blending Germanic customary law with elements of Roman law and then disseminating it helped to ease the legal uncertainty and confusion of the Middle Ages. Over time, the German contribution began to be written down and, through gradual refinements, evolved to produce a form of limited legal literature that, although usable, was ultimately unable to develop any further to meet the needs of the time (Glendon et al. 1982, 23). The Germanic law produced through this process was called by Europeans "vulgarized" or "barbarized" Roman law (Merryman and Perdomo 2007, 8).

Canon Law

Canon law developed through the interaction between Christian notions of law and Roman law following the Christianization of the Roman Empire beginning with Emperor Constantine. After the fall of the Roman Empire in 476 and until the eleventh-century revival of Roman law,

canon law was the only universalizing element in civil law systems (Glendon et al. 1982, 24). Canon law was designed to meet the needs of the Church, but in the universities church scholars learned both canon law and Roman law, resulting in an overlap between Roman law and canon law. A scholar of both laws would receive a degree of Doctor of Both Laws: Juris Utriusque Doctor or JUD (Merryman and Perdomo 2007, 11). The primary influence of canon law was in relation to family and succession, criminal law, and the law of procedure (p. 12).

Commercial Law

As Europe emerged from the economic stagnation of the Middle Ages, the rapid development of trade and commerce meant there was a need for commercial laws to govern business transactions. Roman law was not easily adapted to this objective and guilds and merchants were left to work out their own rules, practices, and procedures, including setting up commercial courts. In time, these procedures came to be seen as customary law, and so the "law merchant" became a recognized field of law (Glendon et al. 2007, 27). As maritime cities became international in character, so commercial law itself became internationalized. Eventually, commercial law became incorporated into commercial codes adopted throughout civil law countries in the eighteenth and nineteenth centuries (Merryman and Perdomo 2007, 13–14).

Rise of Nation-States

As nation-states began to emerge from the chaos of the Middle Ages, an opportunity arose for jurists educated at the universities to secure positions and influence in the new royal bureaucracies. In some countries, for example, Germany, Roman law was formally received and adopted into national legal systems and became foundational law. Other countries adopted more informal methods of utilizing Roman law, but its appeal was apparent and it became the *jus commune* (common law) of Western Europe (Merryman and Perdomo 2007, 10). The notion of "state positivism" developed, meaning that only the state had the power to make legal rules binding on the citizens living in that state. Thus the state was sovereign for the purposes of law making. In addition, the concept of secularism put an end to the belief that the law was of divine origin, and the power to legislate was recognized as being vested in the state (Head 2011, 158). Thus all the Western states became, over time, both secular and positivistic in relation to the sources of the law.

Legal Science

The concept of legal science was primarily the creation of the German legal scholars of the mid and late nineteenth century, especially Friedrich Carl von Savigny (1779–1861), a member of the historical school of jurists, who argued for a historically based codification of German law instead of following the French model of secular natural law (Merryman and Perez-Perdomo 2007, 61). The German scholars focused on Roman law received into Germany, as modified by German customary law, and produced highly detailed treatises culminating in the publication of the German Civil Code of 1896. The methods used by the German historical school came to dominate legal scholarship. Scholars regarded the materials of the law as data from which principles and relationships could be extracted in the same way as a scientist discovers natural laws from studying data (p. 62). The significance of the German approach lies in its systematic and orderly methodology.

Public Law and Private Law

All civil law systems categorize law as either public or private. Nowadays, ordinary courts adjudicate disputes governed by private law with the exception of criminal law, which is classified as public law along with administrative and constitutional law. Generally, public law is concerned with relations between state institutions and between citizens and the state. In contrast, private law deals with interpersonal disputes and issues, including civil law and commercial law, both of which topics are generally codified and supplemented by separate individual laws when needed.

The subject division between public and private law varies according to country. For example, some classify civil procedure as private and others public, and the same applies to labor law, agricultural law, and social security (Glendon et al. 1982, 110).

Codification of Laws

One of the principal features of civil law systems is the codification of laws; that is, these states generally have codes of law covering specific topics that contain all the legal rules relating to that topic, for example, civil law, criminal law, criminal procedure, and commercial law. Thus finding the law on a topic means reading the relevant code of that law. Unlike common law systems, there is no requirement in civil law systems to read court decisions to ascertain the law on a subject.

By the nineteenth century, Western European states had adopted civil codes containing all the rules of civil law as their civil law codes. These codes were often modeled on the French Code Napoleon of 1804. Civil codes were largely duplicates of the first three books of the *Institutes* and the Roman civil law, but in addition states sought to give effect to nationalistic pride concerning their own customary laws, and over time each state developed its own characteristic institutions and system of laws based on the coalescing of the two sets of laws (Merryman and Perdomo 2007, 13).

Codification represented a rational systematized legal system that was comprehensive in scope and an improvement on the *jus commune*. Once codified law was in place, it was the authoritative source of law replacing the *jus commune*. The French Code Napoleon 1804 and the German Civil Code 1896 have been models for most other modern civil codes (Glendon et al. 1982, 33).

Recognizing that a civil code could not cover all instances where laws might be needed and applied, the drafters of the Code Napoleon opted for a code that could be read and understood by all, and they set out general rules of law rather than try to detail rules of law for all possible cases that might arise. As one of the draftsman put it, "The function of law is to fix in broad outline the general maxims of justice, to establish principles rich in implications, and not to descend into the details of the questions that can arise in each subject" (Glendon et al. 1982, 37–38).

In contrast to the Code Napoleon, the German Civil Code was shaped not by abstract principles but by historical research. German scholars disregarded the ahistorical Enlightenment approach to code making and instead followed what they called a science of law, drawing rules and principles from historical data, whether Roman law or customary Germanic laws (Glendon et al. 1982,

40–41). The German Civil Code took more than twenty years to complete and was "constructed and worked out with a degree of precision that had never been seen before in any legislation" (p. 44). Unlike the radical Code Napoleon, the German Code was not intended to stamp out the old legal system but simply to codify principles that had emerged from careful historical research (Merryman and Perez-Perdomo 2007, 32).

Despite their conceptual and stylistic differences, both codes drew on the *jus communes* and their respective national laws, and both have their foundation in nineteenth-century liberalism as well as in concepts of personal autonomy, freedom of contract, and private property. Nevertheless, they are separated considerably in time, and because of this the German Code is more "modern" in the sense that, for example, in family law, the authority of husbands and fathers in the German Code is less absolute than in the Code Napoleon (Glendon et al. 2007, 43).

In the era of codes, French and German models have proved the most influential in other civil law countries. The Code Napoleon was brought by Napoleon himself and his armies to Belgium, the Netherlands, Poland, and Italy. In the course of the French colonial project, the Code Napoleon came to parts of the Near East, northern and sub-Sahara Africa, Southeast Asia, Oceania, and the French Caribbean. When the Spanish and Portuguese empires ended, the newly emergent states took the code for their law. The German Civil Code was influential in the Italian Code of 1942 and the Greek Civil Code of 1940 and the legal science behind the German code was influential in a number of Eastern European countries (Glendon et al. 2007, 46, 47). The Japanese and Koreans also looked to the German code as a source of law.

Codes of law are not confined to civil law countries but have also been enacted in common law countries such as the United States and Australia. For example, in Australia it has been common practice for many years for the Australian states to enact criminal codes that, in effect, codify the common law. In the United States most states have adopted the Uniform Commercial Code. Codes in common law countries do not aim to be exhaustive of the subject matter in the same way as codes in civil law systems. Conversely, civil law countries do not always have codes of law. An example is Hungary, which, until it became a socialist state, had not codified its civil law. Consequently, the existence of a code or codes is not distinctive of only civil law systems (Merryman and Perez-Perdomo 2007, 27).

Why are civil law systems so invested in codes of law? The principal reason may be the certainty that a code adds to ascertaining the law. Advance notice of the rules has a high value (Head 2011, 173). The advantage enjoyed by common law systems is their capacity to make law through judicial activism that provides those systems with a level of flexibility and equity lacking in civil law systems. The law is able to respond rapidly to changes in ideas, practice, and societal norms and values. Although common law systems also value certainty, this attribute is not generally elevated to the level of ideology or dogma in the same way as happens in the civil law tradition.

THE ROLE OF REVOLUTION AND GOVERNANCE IN SHAPING LAW

Revolutionary ideas in France, especially about the role of the state, and of law and government contributed to the fashioning of the Code Napoleon as well as to the scope of public law. Public law, especially in the form of administrative and constitutional law, emerged from the revolutionary events beginning in 1776 that included the American and French Revolutions, the Italian Risorgimento, the independence movements in Latin America, the German unification under Bismarck, and the liberation of Greece (Merryman and Perez-Perdomo 2007, 15).

This intellectual revolution brought about new ways of thinking about governance. Revolutionary developments changed the form and mode of application of the basic codes of law. Equality and the rights of man as distinct from the role of government and the proper function of government in relation to those rights were important driving forces of the new ways of thinking.

Foremost among the new concepts was the notion of the *separation of powers*: separating the legislature, the executive, and the judicial functions, and having as one of its principal purposes preventing incursions by the judiciary into the law-making functions of government (Merryman and Perez-Perdomo 2007, 16). The new theory of separation meant that the judiciary must be carefully regulated so that they limited themselves to applying the law made by the legislature and did not attempt to interpret laws written by the legislature. In contrast, in the United States and England, judges had protected citizens against abuse by rulers, and judge-made law was welcomed and understood to be a proper function within the common law legal tradition.

In Europe, and later in other civil law systems, the French Revolution and the notion of the separation of powers brought about a separate system of administrative law and courts; constraints on the judicial review of laws; and the confinement of the judges to "a relatively minor role in the legal process," at least compared to the role of judges in common law systems (Merryman and Perez-Perdomo 2007, 19).

Rejecting the common law notion of *stare decisis* as inconsistent with the separation of powers and adopting a concept of legal positivism, the civil law tradition declared that judicial decisions were not law and that only laws enacted by the legislature could enjoy that status. Gradually, therefore, the authority of Roman law diminished, to be replaced by statutes and by delegated legislation authorized only by the legislature itself until finally the sources of law in the civil law tradition came to be identified as comprising only statutes, regulations, and customs[3] (Merryman and Perez-Perdomo 2007, 24). According to some scholars, this list of sources, although constituting an orthodox statement of the status of legal sources, does not represent a modern view of the civil law tradition. The modern view contends that additional sources of law are constitutions, initiatives and referenda constituting direct law making by citizens, international law, case law, and legal scholarship (Head 2011, 161).

In reality, the courts and the judges in their daily practice in civil law countries are influenced by prior decisions even if they do not consider them binding on them. Thus "the fact is that courts do not act very differently toward reported decisions in civil law jurisdictions than do courts in the United States" (Merryman and Perez-Perdomo 2007, 47). In civil law countries, judicial decisions are widely reported so that case law (in French *jurisprudence constante* and in German *Rechtsprechung*) plays a similar role to that played in England and the United States (Head 2011, 163). For example, under French law, *arrêt de principe* holds that a series of decisions, all in agreement, will generate an established rule of law, and the *jurisprudence constante* doctrine holds that judges should consider themselves bound to follow a consolidated trend of decisions that can then constitute a source of law. Interestingly, the same rule applies in Louisiana (Fon and Parisi 2006, 520–23).

The United States, although a common law country, stands in a special position because of the way it combines elements of the civil and the common law tradition. The U.S. Constitution embodies both individual rights and judicial power—the power to strike down statutes that violate the Constitution, a feature of civil law systems. Also, by marginalizing and ignoring indigenous law, early settlers and their lawyers were able to construct laws and legal systems on what was effectively a *tabula rasa* (blank slate) without any necessity to factor in immemorial custom and usage. Consequently, the United States has claimed a certain freedom of action, for example, in enacting codes of civil procedure and criminal law and in adopting management and inquisitorial style practices such as judicial case management that emanate from civil law systems (Glenn 2010, 266–67).

SOCIALIST LEGAL SYSTEMS

Socialist legal systems are in essence civil law systems that have been impacted by Marxist-Leninist ideology and therefore view the law somewhat differently than other civil law systems. Before the communist revolution, Russia was a civil law country. China, too, had incorporated elements of civil law in the form of a civil code, a civil procedure code, and a land code prior to 1949 when the People's Republic of China was proclaimed and all existing laws, decrees, and courts were abolished (de Cruz 2007, 211). Civil law therefore supplemented its base of Confucianism (Quigley 1989, 781),[4] and as de Cruz suggests, at one level China could have been regarded as a civil law society.

The exemplar for a socialist legal system was the USSR (Union of Soviet Socialist Republics), but in contemporary Europe, legal systems previously described as socialist legal systems no longer exist. In China, the framework of Marxist-Leninist thought introduced by Maoism in 1949 sees law as simply an instrument of state policy and as a mechanism for implementing state plans (de Cruz 2007, 40). As discussed in

Chapter 5, this instrumentalist approach to law has not changed, however, and although China's situation is problematic, it is strongly arguable that it no longer possesses a socialist legal system.

Socialist scholars insist that socialist legal systems differed from civil law systems and therefore stood apart from them even though they shared many, if not all, of the features of such systems, including codification of laws, inquisitorial court systems, no doctrine of precedent, and a reliance on scholars and scholarly studies (de Cruz 2007). The fundamental assertion made by the proponents of socialist systems was that "common law and civil law traditions reflect a capitalist, bourgeois, imperialistic, exploitive society, economy and government" (p. 185).

In socialist systems, the state owns all the means of production and controls the entire economy; therefore, private law relationships are diminished and are seen as disturbing the civil law balance between public and private law because public law will predominate (Quigley 1989, 786). Socialist theorists point to the transitory nature of law in socialist societies, arguing that historical materialism means that law will eventually die out in such societies. It is acknowledged that this will not happen in a hurry but rather in stages: first there must be a sufficiency of material goods, and second, communism must be realized worldwide (p. 784).[5] The effect of this perspective is to negate the importance of law in society in general, resulting in, for example, the use of alternatives to formal justice processes such as alternative dispute resolution (Quigley 1989, 785). It would seem, however, that during the approximately seventy years of the Soviet socialist project, there was no clean break from a civil law system and no radical changes were made to the justice system that would demonstrate new principles and a new legal system.

Therefore, concurrent with the collapse of communism in Eastern Europe, socialist legal systems have become one episode in the history of socialism, except in those few countries such as Cuba, North Korea, and Vietnam, where forms or elements of Marxist-Leninist thought remain as state ideology (Glenn 2010, 347, 348). China followed the Soviet model of communism for about ten years from 1949 but broke with formal communism in 1957 at the time of the Cultural Revolution and the Sino-Soviet separation (p. 349). Almost no laws were passed during the time of Mao from 1949 to 1976 (de Cruz 2007, 212).

Legal System of the People's Republic of China

A brief discussion of the nature of the Chinese legal system is warranted because of its unique history and dynamic development, especially over the past twenty years. Here we briefly explore the nature of the contemporary Chinese legal system and ask questions such as is it a civil law system or a socialist system, or is it a mixed socialist and civil law system, and how is Marxist-Leninist ideology compatible with the now well-established privatization of state assets and the promotion of capitalism in China, exemplified in the Chinese slogan "Getting rich is glorious"? (Liu, Zhang, and Messner 2001, 26).

The latest Constitution of the People's Republic of China is that of 1982, since amended four times. In terms of socialist ideology, the 1982 Constitution praises Marxism-Leninism as providing guidance to what it calls China's "socialist legal system" (Head 2011, 615). Amendments made in 1999 and 2004 have developed this ideological statement by stating that "China is currently in the primary stage of socialism" and that "the basic task of the nation is to concentrate its effort on socialist modernization in accordance with the theory of building socialism with Chinese characteristics" (p. 616). Later, there is praise for the guidance of Marxism-Leninism and a reference to the goal of "building socialism with Chinese characteristics . . . under the leadership of the Communist Party of China and the guidance of Marxism-Leninism" (p. 616). In the latest amendment, the concept of "Chinese-style socialism" replaces the notion of "socialism with Chinese characteristics" (p. 616). The notion of Chinese-style socialism might suggest a socialist legal system, but this is problematic. China has enacted a great deal of legislation since the reforms of 1980, principally to foster the privatization of the public sector, but it is difficult to identify any overall legal framework. Rather, nowadays, legislation is being enacted piecemeal on a case-by-case basis.

According to Head (2011, 619), Chinese-style socialism is inadequate to establish what he calls a "legal ethic" for China such as could replace old-style Confucianism with a new form that would reflect the Confucian values of education and hard work, now seen as desirable in the interests of economic growth and stability (p. 612). Broadly, Head (2011) sees a need for China to establish an organizing principle or foundation (a "legal ethic") that sets the direction of progress in law and defines and explains Chinese legality. Socialism, he contends, is disqualified because it is primarily an economic ideology and in any event it has been tainted in the new China by capitalist practices. If Head is correct, China is still searching for a legal tradition that can be adequately aligned to its political rhetoric. Given its dynamic situation and the fluidity that characterizes its legal development, China cannot presently be classified as being wholly within any of the recognized systems of law.

Chinese law and the Chinese legal system are further explored in Chapters 4, 5, and 6.

ISLAMIC LAW SYSTEMS

The history of Muslim civilization dates back fourteen centuries, but by the early 1970s most Islamic law, or Sharia,[6] had been displaced by Western-style laws, especially in the form of codified law (Mallat 2006, 610). However, the 1979 revolution in Iran changed everything.[7] The installation of an Islamic government in Iran was followed by an Islamic renaissance so that by the start of the twenty-first century, Sharia was a living force again in most countries with a Muslim majority (p. 611).

The Arabic word *Islam* is usually taken to refer to submission (of oneself to God). Muslims believe that God's will is revealed in the Qur'an as dictated to the Prophet Mohammed. Therefore, "God's *word* and God's *will* are the central elements in Islamic belief and constitute the principal fixation of a person brought up in accordance with the dictates of Islamic culture" (Serajzadeh 2001, 115).

It is helpful to have a glossary of terms to refer to when discussing Islamic law. Box 3.2 lists some terms that are used throughout this discussion.

BOX 3.2   Common Terms in Islamic Law

Sharia

This is a generic term for the totality of Islamic law. Sharia means the way or path to follow. The term *Sharia* is sometimes used to mean only the Qur'an itself and the *Sunna*. Sharia is divine law intended to govern all aspects of human life as revealed to the Prophet Muhammad between 610 and 632 CE.

Qur'an (*or* Koran)

This is the key text of the religion of Islam believed by Muslims to be the actual word of God. The legal content of the Qur'an comprises only some five hundred verses.

Sunna

The Qur'an commands persons to obey the Prophet, and accordingly his words and actions constitute a secondary revelation. The *Sunna* comprises the sayings of the prophet Mohammed, as noted by those who recorded them, explaining the Qur'an. *Sunna* means literally the path taken by the Prophet himself.

Hadith

These sayings make up the *Sunna* and are statements of traditions that have been passed on in a chain of communications from the Prophet himself. Each statement is a *hadith*. There are two parts to a *hadith:* a normative statement and the chain or detail of the tradition that it has followed. Choosing among different *hadith* is part of *fiqh*.

Fiqh

This is Islamic religious jurisprudence, generally in the form of the opinions of scholars who, because of their piety and learning, are seen as fit persons to interpret the revealed texts so as to derive law.

Law Schools

There are four doctrinal schools of law: *Maliki* (an old school, prevalent in northern and western Africa), *Hanafi* (the oldest and has the greatest number of adherents), *Hanbali* (the most conservative, dominant in Saudi Arabia), and *Shafi* (most influential in Southeast Asia).

Ijma

Ijma is the consensus reached on a particular issue of doctrine after lengthy debate and discussion among qualified legal scholars. A ruling after such a consensus has the same status as an unequivocal rule in the Qur'an or the *Sunna*.

Qadi

This is an Islamic judge tasked to resolve disputes in accordance with Islamic law. In decision making, *qadis* are not required to give reasons and therefore no system of case reporting exists.

Mufti

A *mufti* is an expert in Islamic law who is asked for legal advice or opinion and provides it in the form of a *fatwa*.

Fatwa

The opinion and advice of a *mufti* on a question of Islamic law, often filed in court to assist in deliberations or provided to a family to resolve an issue to avoid having to litigate it.

Ijtihad

This means individual endeavor or effort, and refers to the process of analogical reasoning followed by Islamic judges and legal scholars to resolve a legal issue arising under Sharia. It is therefore the process by which scholars find law by the interpretation of the revealed texts—the Qur'an and the *Sunna*—when those texts provide no clear answer.

Ulama

This refers to a group of Islamic legal scholars whose views are very influential on legal issues.

Jihad

The word does not, as is commonly supposed, refer only to war but means "effort" or "striving."

Nizam

This is a decree, law, or regulation issued by the King of Saudi Arabia.

Siyasa

Meaning "policy" or "the conduct of affairs," this term denotes the right of the King or the executive power in a Muslim state to augment Sharia by making decrees and regulations for the public good. This power is recognized by the *ulama* as part of *fiqh*, meaning that *siyasa* is authorized by Sharia.

Hudud

These are mandated punishments for specified crimes under Sharia and are considered the most serious category of crimes.

(Continued)

(Continued)

Tazir

This refers to correction or chastisement and covers sinful acts (crimes) that are not specified as requiring *hudud* punishments.

Qisas or Diya

This is the punishment for murder and the infliction of bodily harm, which Sharia treats as intentional torts giving rise to civil claims that may be prosecuted by, or on behalf of, the victim. These include claims for compensation (blood money), known as *diya*. In exchange for compensation, the victim may forgive the crime and no action will be taken by the state as for a criminal offense.

Gender and Islam

How did the Qur'an affect the status of women at the time of its making? Although the Qur'an advanced the status of women, it did not replace the patriarchal Arabian society of the time. Typically, Arabian women were treated like chattels with no property rights in a tribal male-dominated society and derived their status from the nature of their relationship with a man, for example, as wife, mother, or daughter. The reforms brought about by the Prophet through the Qur'an included outlawing female infanticide, emphasizing a woman's right to contract a marriage, granting women inheritance rights (albeit inferior to those granted to men), giving women the right to control dower and property, and providing support for widows and orphans.

Although polygyny continued to be permitted, the right to have unlimited wives was replaced with a limit of four wives, and although only males could pronounce a divorce, the Qur'an stipulated a wife's right to support and maintenance after divorce (Esposito 1998, xii). Despite these changes, women continued to possess fewer rights than men in many areas of life. Effectively, the division of labor continued, with women being responsible for the home and perceived as the maintainers of tradition and men providing for the family (p. xvi).

Ahmed (1992, 37), in exploring the articulation between gender and Islam, argues that a historical construct has been developed that the pre-Islamic period was an age of ignorance, including concerning gender relations, and that the coming of Islam was the sole source of a civilized society. However, her research argues that "in some cultures of the Middle East women had been considerably better off before the rise of Islam than afterward." She points out that the politically dominant "establishment" interpretation of Islam reads women as obviously subordinate to men and subject to onerous and discrete rules of conduct allegedly articulated in the Qur'an. This contrasts with the alternative liberal view and interpretation of the Qur'an that conceives of gender "inhering in the ethical vision of Islam" (Ahmed 1992, 64). The latter reading argues that the Qur'an expresses the "absolute moral and spiritual equality of men and women,"[8] but it has been marginalized by "the androcentric[9] voice of Islam" (p. 67) and condemned as "heretical" (p. 239).

How do Islamic states treat gender under the law? Although some Islamic states have adopted liberal laws on the family, apparently giving more rights to women, in practice, the courts have not necessarily followed the legislative mandates, and conservative attitudes have weakened the intended effect of such laws.[10] For example, in 2004, Morocco amended its family laws to give greater rights to women on divorce and polygyny and raised the minimum age of marriage for women from 15 to 18 years (Alami 2013). Nevertheless, conservative judges have avoided the law by giving special dispensation to minors to marry, especially when the minor girl is pregnant, in the belief that this will save the girl's honor. In one case, a 16-year-old girl committed suicide when her family and a judge required that she marry a man alleged to have raped her.[11]

Sometimes judges are prepared, however, to apply constitutional guarantees and interpret Sharia so as to protect women, as the ruling described in Box 3.3 reveals.

BOX 3.3 Sharia in the Egyptian Courts: Is Female Genital Mutilation Authorized by Sharia?

In July 1996 the Egyptian Health Minister issued a decree forbidding the carrying out of the operation of female circumcision, whether in hospitals or elsewhere. The decree was immediately challenged by proceedings in the Cairo Administrative Court by Islamists who claimed the decree was void because it violated the principles of Islamic law, described as the major source of law in the Egyptian Constitution.

When the Administrative Court ruled in favor of the challenge, the Minister appealed to the Supreme Administrative Court. This court reviewed the ruling of the Egyptian Supreme Constitutional Court on challenges to laws founded on the supremacy of Sharia. It noted that the Supreme Court had ruled that Sharia principles are the main source of law and therefore operate to limit legislative power. The Sharia principles are not open to interpretation. However, this does not mean that a specific interpretation under *fiqh* binds the legislature because those rules are within *ijtihad* and are flexible and subject to change from time to time to cope with new developments.

When there is no definite provision of Sharia governing a topic, the legislature may exercise *ijtihad* and reason independently. The Supreme Court noted that female circumcision is not mentioned in the Qur'an and that it is a pre-Islamic custom usually sanctioned by reference to various *hadith,* the meanings of which are disputed by modern scholars. There is no consensus, the Court said, in *fiqh,* and no clear legal principle or rule can be invoked. Therefore, the issue of female circumcision can be regulated by the legislature or executive rule and the Minister had not violated Sharia by prohibiting it.

SOURCE: Balz 2000, 36–40.

The Centrality of Islamic Law

Islamic law regulates every aspect of Muslim life and is unique because it represents a personal rather than a territorial system of law: in other words, the law applies to a person because he or she is a Muslim wherever he or she goes or resides in an Islamic state. Sharia is the common law of the Muslim world (Mallat 2006, 613). There is no central doctrinal authority in Islam and, as a result, the various Muslim countries have made different choices about how Islam will be situated within their legal system, demonstrating "spheres of flexibility" (Dwyer 1990, 2). Nevertheless, Islam gives a central position to law as aptly described by Islamic law scholar Joseph Schacht: "Islamic law is the epitome of Islamic thought, the most typical manifestation of the Islamic way of life, the core and kernel of Islam itself" (quoted in Dwyer 1990, 1).

Legal systems in Muslim countries have historically been marked by codification of laws and the amalgamation of law from diverse sources (Dwyer 1990, 3).[12] With the spreading of the Code Napoleon as a model, the Ottoman Empire adopted the first Sharia-based code for the law of obligations producing the *Majalla* (the Mecelle) between 1869 and 1876, which spread to other Muslim countries—to Tunisia in 1906, and to Morocco in 1912 (Vogel 2000, 213). It remained in force in Kuwait until 1980 and in Jordan until 1976 (p. 213). In Iran, a civil code was enacted in the mid-1930s. In 1949, Egypt produced a civil code that became a model for those of Syria, Kuwait, and Libya (Mallat 2006, 629).

As early as 1880, the role of Sharia law in many Muslim states had been circumscribed to family law and issues of inheritance. For example, in Egypt where the criminal law remained Islamic from 640 through to the mid-nineteenth century until legislation in 1882 produced the first modern Egyptian criminal code having its origin in French law (Mohsen 1990, 16). After World War I, Turkey, in a radical move toward modernism, disestablished Islam and became a secular state, something no other Muslim state has done (Vogel 2000, 214).

Sharia and Local Custom

Sharia may tolerate local customs and traditions where there is no inconsistency with Islamic teaching. Islam accepts the distinction between Sharia and *urf* (law derived from local custom) (Fischer 1990, 117). Customs are important in *adat* in Indonesia and Malaysia, as well as in India, in many parts of Africa, and in central Asia, especially Afghanistan (Glenn 2010, 212, 213). In Jordan, which remains a tribal society, the state actively cultivates the tribes and this has reinforced tribal values, including forms of *urf*. The average Jordanian does not differentiate Sharia from *urf*, believing both to be required by Islam. This includes the honor killing of women for violations of family honor, a practice that has no basis whatsoever in Islam (Brand 1998, 105; see Chapter 13). A similar argument applies to the practice of female genital mutilation, which is not sanctioned by Islam but by *urf* in a number of Muslim states.

Sharia is the officially mandated law in Saudi Arabia, Iran, Sudan, and Pakistan. In other Muslim states, two broad models exist (Glenn 2010, 227). The first gives Islam a formal legal status for the Muslim population only, but it is often limited to personal status law matters such as family law and succession (personal status law remains the mainstay of Sharia in Islamic nations).[13] This is the situation in India, with its large Muslim minority population. In Africa, Islam may be recognized in parts of one state in a federal system (e.g., in Nigeria), and in a number of Southeast Asian countries, Islam coexists with customary law and with Western law.

In the second model, applying largely to the West, Islamic law is not recognized as a source of law, but it may come into play through contractual arrangements between Muslims or under claims for religious freedom or protection, for example, through human rights provisions in constitutions (Glenn 2010, 228).

Whereas the Qur'an and the *Sunna* are regarded as divine law and mandate rules of conduct revealed to the Prophet in scripture, Sharia, like common law, is man-made and subject to change over time. Islamic jurisprudence (*fiqh*) applies Sharia to concrete situations for which no absolute rule is provided by the Qur'an or *Sunna* and is thus variable according to the circumstances of a particular historical period.

Islam and Justice

For a fuller understanding of Sharia, it is important to grasp the Islamic conception of justice. This will help explain why, for example, Sharia mandates such severe punishments for certain crimes and how Islam instructs Muslims to comprehend the idea of criminality.

In Islam, Sharia is regarded as an expression of God's will and justice, and Sharia (meaning the path) shows the route to be followed to achieve God's justice, that is, to do good and avoid evil. Sharia is directed at protecting the public interest *(maslaha)*, and the interests of individual believers are only protected to the extent that they do not conflict with the interests of the collective (Khadduri 1984, 137, 138). Principles of brotherhood and equality define one's relationship with others, and within the Muslim community, a person may act as he or she chooses unless an act is forbidden by Sharia (p. 143).

Procedural justice in Islam emphasizes the qualities expected of a judge as the central figure in that process. Both judges and witnesses are required to be "just," meaning they must possess strong religious and moral values and display truthfulness and "good behaviour" (Khadduri 1984, 145).

To a great extent, Islamic justice is historically based because the Qur'an was handed down at a time when the Arabian environment privileged tribal custom and tradition, the family, and religion. Thus offenses that were regarded as undermining these institutions were subject to severe punishment in order to enforce social cohesion. In a setting where banditry, slavery, and blood feuds and tribal vendettas were common, the Qur'an highlights the importance of retribution while also pointing to mercy and forgiveness as the means of avoiding personal revenge (Holscher and Mahmood 2000, 87).

Today, Muslims in countries such as Saudi Arabia, where *hudud* punishments are inflicted, tend to believe that crimes of violence (e.g., rape and murder) are rarely committed because of the strict and harsh penalties imposed for much lesser crimes (e.g., adultery and theft; Holscher and Mahmood 2000, 89; Souryal, Alobied, and Potts 1996, 429). In addition, in the Islamic tradition, thieves are considered to be the equivalents of murderers and rapists because the Qur'an puts a high value on community, declaring that "your lives and properties are forbidden to one another until you meet your Lord on the Day of

Resurrection," and theft violates the ties that bind together the spiritual Islamic community (the *umma;* Souryal et al. 1996, 430).

Within Islam, all human actions are classified by five distinct categories ranging from those that are obligatory to those that are forbidden *(haram)*. It is considered a sin to do a forbidden act, and it is believed that punishment for that sin will be inflicted in the hereafter. Sins that are also regarded as crimes will also be visited with punishment by the mortal authorities. It is considered the religious duty of a Muslim to prevent sin; therefore, those who commit criminal acts are pressured by the family and the community to confess and compensate the victims of their wrongdoing (Serajzadeh 2001, 122). The sinfulness of an act is judged by the penalty for that sin. Thus the greater the penalty is, the greater the degree of perceived sin is (p. 125).

According to Souryal et al. (1996), the most commonly invoked explanations of the concept of justice in Islam involve first, the notion that the community is a brotherhood that requires every person to be responsible for and accountable to all others, and second, that justice amounts to a divine expression of will and, therefore, harsh punishment is to be expected given the source of the command and the enormity of violating it. Moreover, for Muslims, justice carries a deeper meaning and message because Muslims are "expected to act as if they are always in the presence of God" (Souryal et al. 1996, 432). It is argued that Islamic justice mandates punishment severe enough to act as a deterrent and ensure social cohesion, but it is also compassionate and forgiving. These values are demonstrated through the *qisas* process and by paying *diya* (p. 435).

Punishment Under Sharia

For a few crimes, the Qur'an and *Sunna* specify severe *hudud* punishments. These crimes are adultery, theft, drinking alcohol, slander imputing adultery, highway robbery, and apostasy (rejecting your religious beliefs). In Saudi Arabia, these punishments are inflicted in front of large crowds in a public square immediately following the Friday noon prayers (Vogel 2000, 242).

Crimes that carry *hudud* punishments are extremely difficult to prove. There must be a

| Table 3.1 | *Hudud* Punishments |

Crime	Punishment
Theft	Cutting off the hand
Adultery	If unmarried, flogging with 100 strokes. If married or divorced, stoning to death
Apostasy	Death by beheading
Highway robbery	Death, sometimes followed by crucifixion or cutting off one hand and the opposite foot, or exile
Slander	80 lashes
Drinking alcohol	40 or 80 lashes

confession or conclusive proof of guilt. A confession must be voluntary, and even where there exists strong evidence of guilt through other means, a confession can be avoided if the accused simply asserts that the confession was coerced. In the case of adultery, the confession must be repeated four times (Vogel 2000, 244). A confession may be retracted right up to the moment of execution.

When there is no confession, the Qur'an states that in the case of imputing adultery, there must be four male witnesses of good character and who are eyewitnesses to an act of penetration. Other *hudud* punishments require at least two acceptable eyewitnesses who can establish all the elements of the crime. Circumstantial evidence is easily rebutted; to all intents and purposes therefore, a person accused of a *hudud* crime can only be convicted through making a voluntary confession that is never withdrawn (Vogel 2000, 245).

The principle that *hudud* can be avoided through doubt is reinforced by the narrow definitions of the specified crimes. For example, theft must take place by stealth and not by snatching or by force and must involve property above a minimum specified value, must not be property to which the accused has any kind of claim to ownership, and must be stolen from a place of safekeeping. The crime can also be avoided if the accused can show that he or she stole because of famine (Vogel 2000, 243).

Tazir punishments are less severe, and securing a conviction is easier than for a *hudud* punishment. Unlike Western systems, in which there is a common standard of proof whatever the offense, in Sharia the standard of proof varies according to the crime charged. Nevertheless, the presumption of innocence applies to all crimes under Islamic law.

The rigorous requirements of proof in *hudud* mean that most crimes are dealt with under the *tazir* category (Vogel 2000, 246). In fact *tazir* covers all crimes for which no specific penalty is fixed by Sharia. Crime in *tazir* is "defined" as either an act that constitutes a sin or an act declared by the ruler to be punishable because it is harmful to the interests of society (and which is also a sin because it represents a flouting of the ruler's commands).

All the schools of law agree that certain *tazir* crimes are subject to the death penalty; these crimes include sorcery, propagandizing for heresy, and spying for infidels by a Muslim. Some crimes, such as sodomy, are defined by various schools of law as either *hudud* or *tazir* (p. 249).

Qisa crimes are fixed by the Qur'an and the *Sunna* as murder and bodily harm. The victim or the victim's family may chose *diya* or *qisas* (the right of retaliation). Thus these crimes blur the boundary between civil and criminal. Traditional Muslim states still make use of this sanction, and it has been applied to foreigners to secure their release on payment of *diya*.[14] When the crime is murder, the murderer will only suffer the punishment of execution if all the victim's heirs demand it be carried out.

BOX 3.4   Blood Money Paid to Release Briton

The dead body of Yvonne Gilford was discovered on December 11, 1996, in her bed. It was reported that she had been stabbed four times, beaten with a hammer, and suffocated with a pillow. She was an Australian national and a nurse working in a military medical complex in Saudi Arabia. On December 19, the Saudis arrested two British nurses for the murder. The nurses had worked with Gilford. The accused were interrogated for five days with no Australian Embassy representative or lawyer present. On December 24, both signed confessions and on December 30, they were permitted to see a lawyer. The subsequent trial of both accused found one guilty and the other guilty of being an accessory. They retracted their confessions during the trial. Deborah Parry, found guilty of the murder, faced the death penalty.

The case created tensions between the U.K. and Saudi Arabian governments, and there was talk of the trade relationship being affected. British newspapers carried articles condemning the legal process in Saudi Arabia and the perceived unfairness of the Saudi system of justice. No European or American has ever been executed in Saudi Arabia.

During the trial, the judges attempted to persuade the victim's family to grant mercy to the two accused, but they resisted until after the trial was concluded (Duncan 1998, 231). Ultimately, the deceased's family accepted a payment of about 750,000 U.K. pounds and Parry was not executed. The blood money payment was raised by British businesses concerned about the effect of the trial and potential punishment on trade relations (p. 231).

According to classical Islamic law, there were no fora dedicated to hearing appeals or any right to an appeal (Vogel 2000, 65). A person who was aggrieved by a judgment could seek a review by another *qadi* or by the ruler, his agents, or some special court (p. 65). Another possibility was for the *qadi* to reverse his decision if a procedural error had occurred (Khadduri 1984, 146). Nowadays, appeal or review procedures are commonly incorporated into Muslim states laws and practices.

Sharia Law and Modernity in Saudi Arabia

As is well known, "Saudi Arabia is the most traditionalist Islamic legal system in the world today" (Vogel 2000, xiv). As the birthplace of the Prophet and home to the two holiest places in Islam (Mecca and Medina), many Muslims expect that the country will be governed according to Islamic teachings (Wardak 2005, 91).

Judges in Saudi Arabia apply Islamic law exclusively and, unlike many Arab states, Western law has made little impact on the core of the Islamic legal system largely because Arabia was never colonized. Only from about the 1970s have some "modern" laws been enacted in the Kingdom of Saudi Arabia and specialized judicial bodies and tribunals created to manage and implement them. However, the King's capacity to make laws and decrees has brought the secular into conflict with the religious because the judges resist all laws other than those they find in the Word of God as transmitted to men in the Qur'an and the *Sunna*. The Ministry of Justice, aided by the Supreme Judicial Council, is responsible for the operation of the Sharia courts, and judges are guaranteed independence by a royal decree of 1975 (Wardak 2005, 107).

Saudi Arabia publicly adheres to one school of Sunni thought, that deriving from the teaching of Abd al-Wahhab, hence Wahhabism, and is therefore religiously homogeneous. Wahhabis sought to reclaim the purity of their forbearers and tried to eliminate cultural influences that had impacted Islam over the centuries. Their adherence to Islamic law has been described as "puritanical" (Vogel 2000, xvi).

The Saudi lower level courts of trial are called Summary Courts and have jurisdiction over all criminal offenses except crimes involving sentences of death or amputation, or retaliation for physical injury. Accordingly, these courts hear the majority of criminal cases, which are conducted by a single judge. The second level of trial courts is the Sharia courts (called Great Sharia Courts in the larger cities). They hear all criminal cases outside the jurisdiction of the Summary Courts, and hearing is by way of a panel of three judges (Vogel 2000, 89, 90). Appeals go to Courts of Review sitting in panels of three judges, except where sentence of death or amputation is involved, in which case five judges sit (p. 93). Unlike Western legal systems, there is no distinction in the Saudi courts between an appeal on findings of fact and an appeal on findings of law.

Legal representation is not permitted at all in criminal cases. The judges believe that a judge's dedication to the immunities provided by Sharia is sufficient to protect an accused. However, where a case involves foreigners, lawyers are routinely allowed to appear (Vogel 2000, 161).

Law making by the King takes the form of making decrees or regulations called *nizams* (Vogel 2000, 175). From the 1920s, after the establishment of the state, laws concerned with modern legal problems such as firearms, nationality, social insurance, and motor vehicles were needed. The effect has been that now *nizams* coexist with *fiqh*, supplementing *fiqh* to reflect modernity. The *ulama* are consulted before *nizams* are made, to avoid conflict with *fiqh*. Unlike common law systems, *nizams* are considered subordinate to *fiqh*: this is the opposite of a common law system, in which statutes always prevail over the common law. *Fiqh* also operates like common law, as residual law to fill gaps, and *fiqh* governs the majority of cases and all crimes other than those created by *nizams* (p. 175).

The relationship between *nizam* and *fiqh* is far from seamless because secular and religious elements of governance are in conflict over the management of modernity and the all-inclusiveness of Sharia (Vogel 2000, 177). This is true even though Sharia and *nizams* are complementary. Thus it is common practice for Sharia courts to refuse to enforce *nizams*. If the Sharia court thinks an issue covered by the *nizam* is already regulated by *fiqh*, it will decide the issue without recourse to the *nizam* at all. Conversely, if the court thinks the law making was a proper exercise of the power granted to the King under *siyasa*, it will dismiss the case from the Sharia court and allow a special non-Sharia court or administrative tribunal to decide the issue. It is the *ulama* who set the terms of this debate by narrowly defining the theory of *siyasa*[15] and deciding what offends Sharia (p. 177). In the view of the President of the highest judicial authority in the Kingdom of Saudi Arabia, the Supreme Judicial Council, all *nizams* ought to be concerned with purely administrative matters or with *tazir* criminal penalties, neither of which, in his view, are properly the concern of the Sharia courts (p. 177).

Given the *qadi* opposition to *nizams,* the King has been obliged to create non-*qadi* tribunals to enforce their provisions, starting with a commercial court in 1931.[16] The argument from the *qadi* amounts to this: although tribunals can deal with administrative or executive matters, they are not courts and should not operate as such (e.g., as commercial courts), and if they purport to be courts, they should be abolished. The task of "true" courts is to apply Sharia; therefore, institutions such as commercial courts (assuming they should be allowed to exist at all) must apply *fiqh* because they are courts (Vogel 2000, 176). The *ulama* have taken a similar approach to codification of law, by claiming that each *qadi* must be free to judge each case according to his conscience and that codification forecloses that discretion (p. 337).

BOX 3.5   Discovering Tazir Crimes in Saudi Arabia

A Saudi judge tried an Egyptian who was caught smuggling marijuana into Saudi Arabia. This constituted a crime because the King had made a regulation creating this act as a criminal offense and fixing the punishment. During the trial, evidence emerged indicating that the drugs were smuggled into the country in a copy of the Qur'an. When he heard of this crime against the holy Qur'an, the judge announced with some passion, "That is another crime!"

SOURCE: Vogel 2000, 247.

As noted earlier, even when a prosecution for a *huhud* crime fails, the person can still be convicted of committing a sinful act by being charged with a *tazir* crime where *hudud* punishments do not apply. Box 3.6 is an example of such a case.

BOX 3.6   Adultery as Tazir Crime

In Saudi Arabia, a man was accused of sodomy, which, according to the school of law followed there, constitutes adultery and is punishable by stoning to death as a *hudud* crime. The accused confessed in a written statement in his own hand, but when the trial took place for the *hudud* crime, he retracted the confession and avoided the *hudud* penalty. The case was referred to another court to be tried as a *tazir* offense. In that court, based on the same confession that had been previously retracted, the accused was found guilty and sentenced to imprisonment for one year and sixty-five lashes to be applied after six months and again at the end of his sentence.

SOURCE: Vogel 2000, 247.

In Saudi Arabia, the regular *tazir* punishment is lashing, but other possible punishments include scolding, public humiliation, cuffing, imprisonment, and fines (Vogel 2000, 248). There are rules about lashing: it must not be so severe as to break the skin; the lasher's arm must not be extended, only cocked; and the lash may only be of moderate size (p. 248).

The historical record shows how classical Islamic legal systems have been impacted by modernism in the form of civil and criminal codes of law and Western concepts of justice. There has been ebb and flow, given that some Muslim states have pushed back against Western models of justice systems. Examples can be seen in the cases of Iran in 1979 following the 1979 Revolution and in the perpetual tensions that have been occurring in Saudi Arabian jurisprudence, as described earlier.

Other states, for example, Egypt, have relegated Sharia to the field of family law and opted for the modernist model. As Khadduri (1984, 228) notes in the debate on justice, some Muslim scholars have urged caution in absorbing Western influences, whereas others have become impatient with the slowness of change and have insisted on moving forward without taking account of the likely impact on Islamic values. The outcome has been a series of protests and contestations, not necessarily about change itself but about the methods used in carrying out modernization. No doubt the debate will continue.

INDIGENOUS LEGAL SYSTEMS

Indigenous law, also known as customary law, traditional law, and informal justice (in contradistinction to the formal justice system established by positivist law) is the body of rules, practices, and usages that, through their constant repetition, constitute a set of norms regulating many aspects of life within indigenous communities (Woodman 2011). Norms are subject to change in response to social and economic variances, and because of this, custom should not be perceived as frozen forever in some distant time in the past. As Woodman (2011, 15) aptly puts it, "A norm of customary law need not have a longer history than the length of time it takes for the community to adopt it as part of its scheme of social obligations."[17] Custom is distinctly different to other sources of law, as are the customary processes that have developed for dispute settlement within communities that apply what is called "customary law." The principal difference between custom and positivist law is that normally custom has not been systematically recorded in writing (codified).

Customary norms often include mechanisms for settling disputes (including acts defined as crimes by the formal justice system) for which remedies such as payment of forms of compensation are ordered by village chiefs, tribal elders, councils and native or village courts, and even local warlords. Customary law often operates extensively in post-conflict states where the formal system has collapsed or where the state is weak in terms of formal justice institutions and is unable for some reason, usually lack of resources, to bring the justice system to all rural parts of a country (Stromseth, Wippman, and Brooks 2006, 311).

Custom and Colonialism

Although customary norms organized many aspects of daily life in precolonial systems, they were not formalized or defined with any degree of precision. The historical record shows that during the colonial period, colonizing countries brought their laws with them as part of the colonial legal order but were increasingly forced to recognize custom (or parts of it that did not conflict with their worldview of what amounted to civilized conduct) to control territory through local leaders (Bennett 2008, 645). This strategy

was referred to as "indirect rule" by the British in their colonial projects, and it included maintaining order and peace by enabling the indigenous people to operate native courts applying customary law. This raised a set of questions: How was customary law to be ascertained? Should customary law be recorded and, if so, by what means? How far did it constitute tradition, and to what extent should it be permitted to change? (Chanock 1985, 61).

As Chanock (1985, 114) notes, the purpose of indirect rule was to maintain "relationships of authority," not to bring about the rule of law. In Central Africa, for example, the native courts operated as administrative agencies of colonialism, dispensing little customary law but devoting court time to continually enforcing rules about sanitation, tree cutting, and the like, in the village area (Ranger 1983, 250). Indirect rule meant delineating tribes where none actually existed because administrators believed that every African belonged to a tribe. Similarly, customary land law evolved as the joint creation of colonial officials and African leaders and had little to do with tradition or immemorial custom (p. 250).

In ruling through local leadership and the exercise of customary law, European constructs and assumptions about what constituted law and justice meant that, for example, in Central Africa, a hierarchical justice system was imagined (and, if necessary, created) headed by a "traditional chief" (Ranger 1983, 212). Once a chief had been identified, a native court would be established and charged with administering customary law. In this process, the colonial officials "set about inventing African traditions for Africans. Their own respect for 'tradition' disposed them to look with favour upon what they took to be traditional in Africa. They set about to codify and promulgate these traditions, thereby transforming flexible custom into hard prescription" (p. 212).

British colonial administrators assumed that customary law was constituted as an already existing body of rules that could be applied to cases just like common law rules. They found that this was not the case because custom was always vague and uncertain, far from categorical, and always subject to qualifications.[18] Rather than having a substantive content of rules as imagined by the colonial administrators, custom was better understood as "a strategy for legitimizing control which assumed a 'legal' form when it was offered a 'legal' forum in which to operate" (Chanock 1985, 58). Customary law was, and is, "fluid, relational, negotiable, and intimately tied to fluctuating social and political relations" (Ubink 2011, 89).

During the colonial period, institutions such as native courts influenced and changed custom and especially the flexible customary processes, replacing them with fixed rules and procedures. Thus the outcome of the colonial process for customary law is that customary law "must be understood as an historical product created in colonial institutions" (Chanock 1985, 145). In Central Africa, therefore, developed law actually preceded a form of elaborated customary law produced from and by Western legal forms and the colonial state (p. 238).

Plural Legal Systems

Countries with legal systems comprising multiple sources of law (e.g., positivist law in the forms of written laws and rules, common law and equity, and customary law) are referred to as having *plural legal systems*. Within such systems, custom is sometimes treated in the same way as common law or Sharia; that is, it is a source of law that can be applied. Usually there are limitations on the application of custom. For example, in some legal systems, custom may not be applied if it is contrary to the country's constitution or its written laws, or to the common law, or if it is rejected as a form of law under so-called repugnancy clauses.[19] A good example is the Constitution of Papua New Guinea, which provides the following:

- Custom is a source of law and shall be applied and enforced.

- Custom that is inconsistent with the Constitution, or a statute or "repugnant to the general principles of humanity" shall not be applied or enforced.

- The rules of common law and equity in England are a source of law.

- Common law and equity is not to be applied if it is inconsistent with custom.

SOURCE: Papua New Guinea Constitution, Schedule 2, Part 1.

Unusually, this Constitution gives custom the capacity to prevail over common law and equity, reversing the status given to custom under most constitutions. Generally, custom has not played a significant role in modern legal development although it remains an active element of normative social control in many societies, including those on the African continent (Fenrich et al. 2011, 1; Ubink 2011, 83). Customary practice is often beyond the reach of the state and is preferred by many to the formal system of justice because it is usually free of charge, prompt, and understood by those who seek a remedy.[20]

In formal legal systems, custom is regularly treated by the courts as a question of fact which means it has to be proved by evidence in every case unless legislation provides otherwise (Bennett 2008, 646; Sheleff 1999, 382; Woodman 2011, 23).[21] A major issue for a state where custom is still applied from day to day is the extent to which it will permit local customs to share in rule making. As noted above, the options for custom include the following:

- Treat custom as an integral part of the legal system.

- Exclude custom in whole or in part, for example, by limiting its application to family law and succession.

- Allow custom to apply as law but subject to certain constraints.

Where a state allows custom, it may do so through customary courts called, for example, village courts, chief's courts, or tribal courts.[22] These are effectively a continuation of the former colonial customary courts. Where customary processes are permitted and even supported by the state, the relationship between formal justice institutions and customary processes and organs needs to be identified and formalized if there are to be no conflicts between the formal and the informal. One method is to formalize customary processes, as has been done in Papua New Guinea, where "village courts" were created by law in 1975 and are required to apply custom only, but with appeal rights from the village court to the formal system to check abuses.[23]

Codifying Customary Law

Lawyers have tended to ignore custom, treating it as an adjunct to state positivist law and unworthy of attention, and have left the field of study of custom to social anthropologists.[24] Nevertheless, during the colonial period and subsequently, the notion of writing down customary "rules" in a code similar to a civil law codification project has been viewed as a way of giving customary law a degree of certainty that it lacks as compared with common law or statute (Himonga 2011, 32). This kind of custom has been referred to as "official custom" or "lawyer's custom" and is principally the legacy of colonialism with some postcolonial additions. Unwritten customary law that continues to affect the daily lives of Africans is known as "living customary law," and some argue that it will continue to regulate daily lives far into the future, particularly because it possesses the capacity to change (Himonga 2011, 34; Oba 2011, 59, 64).

An alternative to codification has been the formulation of restatements of customary law, which serve as guides to identifying particular customary law and do not constitute legal codes (Oba 2011, 63). Restatements suffer from the same problem as codification in that they do not account for changes in custom unless they are systematically revised and updated. Whereas this may be a relatively easy task, persuading judges that customary law has changed since the last restatement was issued might prove more challenging (Ubink 2011, 96). In addition, unsuccessful attempts have been made to unify the plurality of customary laws within a country (Oba 2011, 66), and this plurality creates significant complexities in deciding informal cases.

Responses to codification have generally been unfavorable (Juma 2011, 130). Scholars have pointed out that codification freezes custom at a certain point in time, rendering it inert, when in fact custom is always alive and mutable within a society that is itself unsettled. The concept of "living customary law" reinforces the undesirability of codification because there may be no congruence between official customary law and living customary law (Himonga 2011, 34). Furthermore, codification effectively generalizes custom when custom is often highly localized and specific (Bennett 2008, 648).[25] One effect of codification is that changes to the code, as custom itself changes over time, would have to be made through the legislative process, often a lengthy and contentious operation (Woodman 2011, 29).

In Africa, colonial officials in Kenya resisted codification, for one reason because they objected to the courts taking over customary dispute resolution and "even when Europeans and Africans put customary law to paper, a review of court transcripts shows that African court elders continued

to employ law situationally" (Shadle 1999, 431). Tanzania codified customary law during the 1960s but opted to codify only the custom of one major tribal group. In Lesotho, the Basotho Code of Customary Law was promulgated in 1903 and with amendments remains in constant use by the courts there, but codification has not had the effect of enhancing the standing of customary law, which remains subordinate to Western law (Juma 2011, 139, 141). In South Africa, the Natal Code of Zulu Law attempted to codify Zulu custom, and the Black Administration Act 1927 codified the customary law of succession (Rautenbach and Plessis 2011, 343). Codifications of customary law are criticized for inaccuracy, for not stating the correct principles of unwritten customary law and omitting some important principles, and for giving the impression that only one system of custom exists in a country.

Leaders of postcolonial states have tended to resist incorporating custom into law. Even when they have incorporated it, they have not encouraged its application, seeing it as primitive and as an obstacle to modernity and national unity (Bennett 2008, 662). Nowadays, custom is undergoing something of a resurgence in Africa, especially in South Africa where it has been recognized by the constitution and through decisions of the courts as a separate legal system alongside the common law (Rautenbach and Plessis 2011, 339).

In the field of criminal law, custom, or what is claimed to be custom, has had the most effect in relation to punishment, especially for juveniles, in countries such as New Zealand, Australia, and Canada with indigenous populations. They have turned to indigenous custom for alternative forms of process and punishment collectively described as "restorative justice."[26] In some countries, for example, Canada, Papua New Guinea, and Australia, custom has been relied upon as a defense to a criminal charge, but generally the courts have allowed evidence of custom only in mitigation of penalty.[27] Some customary courts are empowered to deal with criminal offenses, but this approach is problematic because of conflicts with constitutional provisions that allow legal representation (commonly lawyers are barred from customary courts) and because of a lack of attention to rights such as to a formally defined criminal charge (commonly ignored in customary courts).

In the field of conflict resolution, traditional systems of settlement and reconciliation continue to flourish in indigenous communities from North America to Africa, Asia, and the Pacific, resolving all manner of injuries and keeping cases out of the formal justice systems. It is in the field of dispute resolution that custom has shown itself to be most resilient.

Of late, rule of law and justice projects of aid and technical assistance in developing countries with indigenous justice systems have begun to recognize the importance of informal systems of justice to the general population. This is largely because of their popularity with the people in speedily processing wrongs outside the formal justice system. Thus, increasingly, informal justice systems are considered worthy of financial and other forms of support by aid donors who support improvements in local justice systems. Donors have recognized that formal legal institutions do not impact rural populations or afford access to justice to many citizens for reasons of cost, slowness of decision making, and complexity of operation.

However, there are concerns about gender and human rights when forms of customary justice exclude women from decision making or favor men in dispute settlement and do not always accord fairness in adjudication processes (Stromseth et al. 2006, 336).[28] One suggested approach to this issue is to encourage the emergence of human rights norms through the development of living customary law (Himonga 2011, 50). In this way the community itself will protect rights and freedoms.

historical record reveals that elements of custom have been incorporated in both principal legal systems, and socialist systems took on key elements of the ideology of Marxist-Leninism.

Customary or traditional systems of law remain the "law in action" in numerous societies and continue to resist attempts to codify or restate custom and tradition that failed in colonial times but still retain an appeal in some countries. They represent an effective alternative to formal legal systems, but in the modern day, issues of gender bias and fair procedures before customary tribunals present a challenge. In modern times, a great deal of interest has been shown in Islamic Sharia; for example, some states within the United States have passed legislation preventing it from being applied. Comprehending the scope, meaning, and purpose of Sharia as it operates in whole or in part in different Islamic societies presents a challenge for Westerners because Sharia as law is strikingly different to Western legal traditions. The discussion of Sharia in Saudi Arabia shows how managing modernity creates tensions between the judges of Sharia and the rulers of a modern state.

This chapter lays the foundation for the detailed discussion in Chapter 5 of courts and criminal procedure in the different legal systems and how the social and cultural context and institutional practice have shaped practice and procedure and the search for truth in criminal proceedings.

Comment

The legal traditions and the legal systems discussed in this chapter reveal the significant differences between legal thought, ideology, and practice that exist between the dominant common law and civil law systems and those based on tradition and custom and on theocratic rules and norms. The role of law in civil law systems has traditionally been to offer certainty in the content of the law: a certainty based on the legislative and executive having the exclusive, or at least the dominant, role in determining the meaning of the law. In common law systems, the legislature and the executive effectively surrender control of the discourse of law's meaning to the courts. Over time, however, clear-cut differences between civil and common law systems have eroded: the United States, in particular, has taken on some aspects of the civil law tradition while civil law has proved to be amenable to judge-made law and the doctrine of precedent. The

Notes

1. As Head points out (2011, 353), the legal profession in England developed quite differently from that in Europe because English lawyers learned the common law from practitioners while apprenticed to them in the Inns of Court and relied on their example and experience rather than on scholarship.

2. This was the earliest attempt by the Romans to create a code of laws. A commission appointed to the task was able to produce sufficient laws to fill ten bronze tablets. This work was considered unsatisfactory and another commission was appointed and added two further tablets (Steinberg 1982, 379–80).

3. Merryman and Perez-Perdomo (2007, 24) explain that although custom continues to be a subject of study and can be applied as long as it does not conflict with any statute, its importance as a source of law is "slight and decreasing."

4. Head (2011, 615) is doubtful that Confucianism plays any significant role in contemporary Chinese law, but an alternative view is presented in Chapter 5.

5. According to historical materialism since the formation of the state, four basic types of law have been advanced through the laws of the slave, feudal, capitalist, and socialist societies. Quigley (1989, 799) argues that in each of the four forms, a system of law has protected the class in power.

6. *Sharia* is used as a generic term for Islamic law (Mallat 2006, 610).

7. On April 1, 1979, an Islamic Republic was declared in Iran (Fischer 1990, 117).

8. Sufism, for example, adopts a mystical view of Islam and diverges from orthodox interpretation by stressing the ethical, spiritual, and social teachings of Islam. It views "the practices of Muhammad and the regulations that he put into effect as ephemeral aspects of Islam relevant primarily to a particular society at a certain stage in its history" (Ahmed 1992, 95).

9. Focused or centered on men.

10. According to Ahmed (1992, 242), "Family law is the cornerstone of the system of male privilege set up by establishment Islam."

11. See Alami (2013). The cultural perspective that sees the rape of a virgin daughter as damaging the victim's father economically and therefore justifying not only the payment of compensation to the father by the unmarried rapist but also the marriage of the victim and the rapist can be traced back to Assyrian law (Ahmed 1992, 14).

12. "By the 1950s, Westernization had proceeded to the point that codified laws from continental Europe had come to predominate throughout the Middle East. The Arabian Peninsula constituted the chief exception since it alone had escaped Western domination and influence" (Mayer 1990, 99).

13. Personal status law has not been treated as sacrosanct because a number of nations have either abolished polygyny or amended its effect. For example, in Morocco, a wife is entitled to stipulate as a condition of marriage that she has a right to divorce her husband if he takes a second wife (Dwyer 1990, 5, 6).

14. Sometimes the victim's family will refuse to accept blood money as occurred in the case of a Sri Lankan maid who was beheaded after being convicted of killing her employer's baby. She had been found guilty of smothering the baby following an argument with the infant's mother ("Saudi Criticises World Reaction to Maid Beheading," 2013).

15. Education in the *siyasa* legal system has become a part of the curriculum of Saudi universities (Vogel 2000, 290).

16. Other tribunals include special labor courts called "labor commissions" created under the Labor Regulation and a Commission for Commercial Paper Disputes established by the Ministry of Commerce (Vogel 2000, 288).

17. It should not be assumed that custom was unchangeable until the colonists arrived. Long before colonization, long-distance trade and migrations had been triggering social changes (Woodman 2011, 16).

18. According to one provincial commissioner in Malawi writing in the 1920s, the true meaning of native law was that it was a "living expression of native public opinion" (Chanock 1985, 76). Colonial administrators and anthropologists of the time tried to discover the "rules" of custom by conversing with traditional leaders and other experts in custom and later through the study of "trouble-cases" or disputes. Subsequently, the focus shifted to the behavior of protagonists and dispute resolvers and then to the study of situational power relations (Ubink 2011, 86, 88).

19. The British in particular, in their colonial projects, commonly recognized local custom and ruled through local leaders. However, recognition would be refused where a custom was considered "repugnant" to natural justice, public policy, equity, conscience, or such factors. As noted earlier, in the case of Papua New Guinea, this formulation is still in use in Pacific states and applies also as a legacy of colonialism in several African states (Sheleff 1999, 22).

20. For example, in East Timor a survey revealed that most Timorese were "most comfortable and familiar" with customary dispute resolution processes and regarded the formal justice system as "less fair, less accessible, more complex, and a greater financial risk" (Stromseth et al. 2006, 335).

21. In Ghana, custom is specifically made a question of law by the Courts Act 1971 (Akamba and Tufuor 2011, 209; Sheleff 1999, 382).

22. See, for example, the Village Courts Act 1989 of Papua New Guinea.

23. For a full description of the powers and functions of the Papua New Guinea Village Courts, see Banks (1993, 27–31).

24. Oba (2011, 67) reports that legal education in most African countries ignores customary law, despite the fact that it is very much in use by a significant portion of the population.

25. In the then Dutch East Indies (now Indonesia), the Dutch scholar van Vollenhoven formulated an elaborate codification of *adat* (customary) law that divided the Indies into nineteen adat law areas composed of persons deemed to be culturally homogeneous (Roff 2010, 457). Islamic law was in effect excluded, except to the extent that it had been received into one of the *adat* law areas (p. 457).

26. The literature on restorative justice is now voluminous; a comprehensive text is Johnstone (2002).

27. See, for example, how the courts approached custom as a defense in Banks (2001, 102–22) and the discussion of the issue in Sheleff (1999, 262–89).

28. In Afghanistan, customary *jirgas* decide disputes; this can include, in murder cases, transferring young girls to the family of the victim as recompense so that the girl may be forcibly married to a member of the victim's family (Stromseth et al. 2006, 337).

4

POLICING

T his chapter is concerned with policing,[1] a term that may refer to an
activity that can be performed by a variety of persons, both professional and nonprofessional. For example, state regulatory agencies
"police" corporate conduct in certain fields where crimes have been created
to penalize acts that harm the environment, and private non-state security
companies provide policing services of various kinds, including static
guards and security patrols. Policing can also refer to the prevention, control, and prosecution of crime and the maintenance of public order by
professionals employed by a state in an entity known as "the police" or the
"militia" or "the gendarmerie" or in law enforcement in the general government sense. In this chapter we discuss policing and police in the latter sense
of the term.

We have selected features of policing for discussion that appear important or interesting in contemporary times but have also adopted an
approach that seeks to identify any historical, social, or cultural factors that
relate to the emergence of these features. A key feature of policing, historically and now, is the use of force, because police are generally the principal
authority within a state with the competence and authority to use force in
performing their functions and "even when they do not use force, it shapes
every interaction they have" (Bayley 1985, 8). Taking a broad perspective,
we look at police use of force in policing the colonies and current and past
policing styles in Russia and China.

Systems and arrangements for policing differ among countries: some are
purely civil in nature, whereas others (e.g., in the United States) incorporate
elements that are located in the armed forces. Many police forces were created during periods of colonialism and continue to maintain an institutional culture that sees the law as a protector of the rights of those in power
and of local elites. Why do some police agencies follow a civilian model and
others a military model, and how are these models deployed in different
countries? In exploring contemporary policing arrangements, we look at
what countries perceive to be the proper role and functions of the police and
how they organize and structure policing to achieve national goals and
objectives.

In Western police practice and through international instruments, international norms and principles of policing that are said to constitute "best practice" in policing have been formulated and formalized. The term *democratic
policing* describes these best practices. They constitute key elements in the
movement to universalize or internationalize policing practice. We explain

s of democratic policing, how it is distributed to postcolonial developing countries, and, in Russia and China, its principles come into conflict with local policing practices.

International police cooperation and transnational policing are seen as elements in the internationalization or globalization of policing. It is claimed that transnational policing has weakened the role of the nation-state in policing and that supranational policing agencies lack accountability and now exercise powers beyond the control of the nation-state. Institutionally, the International Criminal Police Organization (INTERPOL) was the first such international mutual assistance organization. Within Europe, the European Police Office (EUROPOL) brings together European policing organizations consistent with the aims of continued European integration in numerous fields of governance. These institutions are linked with states in increasingly intrusive forms of global policing and surveillance in the name of risk avoidance and are said to have adversely impacted citizens' rights and freedoms. What challenges are presented to states in light of these developments in global policing?

How has policing developed in countries that have transitioned to market economies and forms of democratization? What challenges are faced by China and Russia in democratizing authoritarian and intensely intrusive policing arrangements? Detailed case studies of policing in China and Russia provide an understanding of how history, culture, and the process of social change impact arrangements for social control as countries strive to define and shape their contemporary and future internal security needs.

ORGANIZING POLICING

Policing, in the form of organized forces, began in the West in the nineteenth century. Historians debate whether these forces were established to control the violent underclasses and protect the elite in society or simply came about as the natural progression and growth of societies (Bayley 1992, 535).[2] Revisionist accounts perceive the police as similar to the colonial police forces, with their principal task being the protection of the rights and property of the middle and upper classes of society. The traditional account of policing stresses the policing function as service to the public (Sinclair 2006, 11). There is,

however, a consensus among historians that fear caused by increases in the crime rate and failure of parish constables and the military to control public riots acted as determinants in the 1829 police reform in England (Brodeur 2010, 176).

Writers on policing tend to draw a distinction between Anglo-American policing and "continental policing," meaning policing as it was, and is, generally organized in Europe. Of course, there is no one model of policing that applies to all European states, but certain common elements exist within the notion of continental policing. These include having origins in the Roman colonial system, being constituted as more centralized, and having a wider jurisdiction than the Anglo-American model; for example, police are commonly responsible for functions such as passport control, compliance with building and some health regulations, tax collection, and even weather data collection (Mawby 2008, 23).

Robert Mawby (2008, 22) identifies the elements of continental policing (accepting, always, that there are variations between countries[3]) as centralized, militaristic, placing greater importance on political and administrative functions in terms of their overall functions, closely tied to government, and lacking in accountability to the public or the law. In addition, there is a tendency for the traditional continental model to comprise a structure in which one military or paramilitary-type police force is counterbalanced by one, or a collection of, municipal-based civilian police forces. The French, Italian, and Spanish forces follow this model and typically locate their militaristic forces organizationally within the Defense Ministry and their other police within Interior or Justice Ministries.

A police force is constituted as a *bureaucracy* with a structure and organization designed to fulfill the policing mission and policing objectives.[4] Generally, all police forces perform the following core policing functions: general duties policing (known as "patrol" in the United States), traffic control, and criminal investigation (Bayley 1992, 523–24). Most police forces have a heavily armed unit trained in handling violent confrontations such as terrorist incidents, hostage taking, and violent demonstrations. Following U.S. terminology, these units are often denominated as SWAT units. In addition, specialist units are often to be found in the better-resourced police forces, including crime prevention, a criminal intelligence unit, and community policing units

(p. 527). Police forces are characterized by their hierarchical structures and by the chain of command with this feature being more pronounced in forces that have a high degree of militarization. This usually means there are several layers of command with the degree of authority increasing along with higher rank.

Other less bureaucratic models have been proposed for policing. Some have argued that initiatives such as community policing necessitate a non-bureaucratic organizational approach that emphasizes decentralization of manpower rather than hierarchical models. This could mean adopting a flat organizational structure that eliminates middle ranks and a matrix structure approach in which expertise is gathered together in teams to meet defined objectives similar to the task force model. As this chapter's discussion about policing in China indicates, community policing may in fact represent traditional forms of policing that have never been decentralized.

Another policing study by White (2007) has proposed a "hospital model," which would focus on the wide discretion enjoyed by individual police officers, similar to that exercised by medical practitioners. The thinking behind this notion is that there would be rigorous police recruitment standards (as for entering medical school), intensive training, and no direct supervision of individual police officers but with compliance to standards required (as in a hospital) (p. 150). In addition, the management of the organization would be separated from the organizational side so as not to interfere with officer decision making, individual officers could be sued for bad practice and would need to be insured against this risk, and questionable police decisions would be assessed by a peer review panel (as does the American Medical Association). Clearly, a model of this kind would require radical changes in current organizational structures and would raise questions about police accountability generally (pp. 150–51).

Police forces worldwide have adopted, or seek, or are encouraged to adopt the attribute of *professionalism*. This term signifies "explicit attention given to the achievement of quality in performance" (Bayley 1985, 47) and encompasses a range of features, including standards of recruitment and promotion, salary levels, internal discipline, and supervision practices that in the aggregate signify that a force has been professionalized.

Professionalism is allied to efficient management of resources and personnel and the achievement of objectives and targets such as reducing the crime rate.

Centralization and Decentralization

It is common for researchers and scholars to categorize policing organizations according to whether they are centralized, decentralized (fragmented), or integrated. What is meant by these categorizations in organizational terms?

A police force may be termed *centralized* because there is a national police force under the control of the national or central government. An example of this is the French police perceived as being the archetype of continental policing. David Bayley (1985, 54) describes centralization in operational terms as existing when "operational direction can be given routinely to subunits from a single center of control." Based on data from forty-eight countries in 1985, Bayley concluded that centralization was the dominant policing model. It likely remains so because, as noted by Bayley (p. 60), "the structures of public national police systems display remarkable permanence over time." In his research on centralized police forces, Bayley (p. 65) found that there was a strong association between authoritarian countries and centralized policing. Thus, countries with authoritarian regimes were more likely to have centralized police forces and conversely those with nonauthoritarian governments to have decentralized systems of policing.

The United States is always identified as having the most *decentralized* police force, largely due to federalism and the growth of local governments within states. Decentralized policing is signified by a highly localized organizational structure with policing agencies being accountable to local authorities. This fragmentation of law enforcement in the United States has resulted in numerous police departments with very low staffing levels.[5] The tradition of local autonomy in the United States began in the early seventeenth century, and it was only in the mid-nineteenth century that state governments took control of policing in the cities. New layers and levels of policing were added over time, but local control was never erased (Bayley 1985, 61). Again, in operational terms, Bayley (p. 54) says that decentralization exists when there is "independence of command in subunits."

An *integrated* model of policing exists where the organization and administration of policing is a responsibility shared between the center or national agency and local agencies. Thus, police authorities may be accountable to both national and local authorities. Police models that fit these characteristics are found in the United Kingdom, Germany, Australia, and Japan (Bayley 1985).

The history and development of a police force are always relevant elements in assessing how a police force is organized now (Bayley 1985, 64). As the section titled "Colonial Policing" reveals, many police forces, especially those in third world states, have not substantively changed their organization in the postcolonial period and retain the colonial model. As a consequence, tradition often exerts a constraining influence over any proposed structural changes. The police institutional culture is also of great importance in terms of the probability that it will welcome or resist organizational change. Nevertheless, police systems are subject to change.

In the case of developing countries and transition-to-democracy countries, change will often occur through interventions promoting democratic policing (see "Democratic Policing" and "Case Studies of Policing: Russia and China"), but this may be a challenging process that requires many years of sustained effort at changing not only organizational structures but also institutional policing cultures because "police systems are closely embedded in the wider structure and the culture of their societies" (Mawby 2008, 39). It should not be assumed that all policing systems are converging into one model that fits all countries. First of all, local interests and pressures will often resist change in local policing, and second, even where cross border cooperation is promoted and expected along with harmonization of policies and practices (such as occurs within the European Union), there will be instances where national interests will contest such changes. For example, there have been conflicts between the Germans and the Dutch over appropriate drug policies (p. 39).

What implications flow from having a decentralized or a centralized police force? In considering this question, the civilian/military nature of the policing body becomes relevant. "It has been shown that, while it is possible to have a highly centralized civilian police, it is not possible to have a decentralized military-style police" (Weber 2001, 40). However, if the policy is to

maintain a safe and relatively crime-free environment, then decentralization will operate to bring the police closer to the community and the people that it should be serving.

In Brazil, for example, the present-day order maintenance policing[6] force *(polícia militar)* was a development of the National Guard created in 1831 for the protection of ruling groups and the repression of socially and economically disadvantaged groups, including slaves, native peoples, mixed-race peoples, and the poor (Reames 2008a, 71). As noted, police forces tend to follow either a centralized or a decentralized model with policing in the United States being the most decentralized and fragmented worldwide.[7] States with federal systems of government tend to decentralize by delegating policing to their states. For example, Brazil has twenty-six states and one federal district, and policing is controlled by the various states with each state governor appointing a Secretary of Public Security who manages the police (Reames 2008a, 64). Mexico, with thirty-one states and one federal district, resembles the United States in having a multiplicity of police forces (approximately three thousand) operating with different jurisdictions at the state, municipal, and federal levels (Reames 2008b, 100).

India is an example of a centralized police force because the police are organized and maintained by the states of the Union of India. Police power in India varies according to rank, and much like the army, the police force is divided into an officer class (superintendents), a non-commissioned type officer class (inspectors and subinspectors), and other ranks of constable and head constable. This rank distribution is reflected in the police force of every state. The officer cadre—the Indian Police Service (IPS)—is recruited, organized, and trained according to national legislation but is operationally under the control of each state. In municipal forces, the chain of command runs up to the state Home Minister (Hakeem 2008, 175).

Another centralized police force is that of Turkey, where the Turkish National Police (TNP), the *Jandarma* (gendarmerie), and the Coastal Security Guard each have a highly centralized organization with the Minister of the Interior, empowered to control and fund the three elements (Mutlu 2000, 383). The *Jandarma* is responsible to the Defense Minister for military tasks and to the Interior Ministry for policing tasks (p. 384). Police have headquarters operations in each province of the country with the chief of police in the province appointed by the Interior Minister and being responsible to the central government through the governor of the province (Cerrah 2008, 197). Every provincial appointment within the police, regardless of rank, is made centrally, and all policies and practices affecting police are made centrally (p. 198).

In France, it is said that the French policing model first appeared in 1667, when an office of general lieutenant of police for the city of Paris was established; in 1699, this model extended to the rest of the country (Dupont 2008). These arrangements confirmed the king's power over policing, consistent with other centralized royal powers over justice administration and revenue collection. By 1720, a gendarmerie had been created to patrol the roads and protect settlements located in *brigades* in strategic locations across the country. The 1789 revolution brought about the collapse of the centralized police structure, which, for a time, became decentralized to the municipalities. Gradually, the central government worked to regain centralized control of the police, a process that was completed by 1941 while France was under German occupation (Dupont 2008, 249). The French police system is regarded as one of the most centralized in the world. The director-general of the National Police, for example, is directly responsible to the Minister of the Interior. In the case of the gendarmerie, it is headed by a director-general who must be a civilian and who is responsible to the Minister for Defense, but operationally the gendarmerie is subject to the direction of the prefect of a department.

CIVILIAN AND MILITARY POLICING MODELS

Members of a *civilian police force* are usually public servants, national or local, but in a *military policing structure*, military discipline, ranks, and rules about obedience to orders (even unlawful orders) prevail. It is easy to assign tasks in a military-style structure whatever may be the nature of the task. Trade unions are not found in military structures, but it is quite common for police to have unions. Most of all, supervision and accountability are much easier to secure in the case of a civilian force

(Weber 2001, 40–41). It is usual in continental Europe to find that states deploy one national police force in the cities and another large force, which is militarized and accountable to the Defense Ministry, to police rural areas and small towns (Brodeur 2010, 11).

In Brazil, where policing is designated a state-level responsibility, each of the twenty-seven states and the federal district maintains a civil police force for crime investigations (*polícia civil*) of 150,000 and a military police (*polícia militar*) of 450,000 for order maintenance that constitutes a reserve force of the Brazilian Armed Forces[8] (Reames 2008, 65). This dual policing system is mandated by the 1988 Constitution but has had the unfortunate effect of creating two discrete policing agencies which do not coordinate, communicate or share information. Each has its own institutional culture, pay scales and rules and regulations. Due to its connection to the armed forces, the *polícia militar* is structured like a military force with officers and regular soldiers (p. 67). In addition, there is a policing unit for the federal district—the *polícia federal*—numbering approximately 15,000 officers, responsible for the country's border security and for guarding key officials and government installations. They also investigate complex commercial crimes, and handle crimes involving native groups in the Amazon region. It maintains specialist units and is the point of contact for INTERPOL (p. 68).

A similar model to Brazil applies in Mexico where police are divided into *polícia judicial*, with the function of criminal investigation and numbering about 26,000, and *polícia preventiva*, numbering about 330,000 concerned with public order maintenance. Police units operate at federal, state, municipal, and the federal district levels (Reames 2008b, 102). In the Federal District comprising Mexico City with about 19 million residents, the *polícia preventiva* total about 34,000 to which should be added 40,000 police auxiliaries and 15,000 banking police.

In Russia, the police force was, until March 1, 2011, known as the militia *(militsiya).* It is now known as the police *(politsiya;* Zernova 2012, 474). Peter the Great brought the European concept of policing to Russia and the Office of Policemaster-General was created in St. Petersburg early in the eighteenth century. Before then, Ivan the Terrible had created the first state police in 1564 in the form of a mounted military corps (Bayley 1985, 31). Peter the Great's policing system was extended to the rest of the country with paid police in the cities and unpaid police in rural areas (p. 31).

In the early period, the force was centralized and exercised a broad range of functions. This centralization continued following the 1917 revolution when, despite assurances, the policing function was never transferred to municipalities. In 1922, the secret police functions, including guarding borders and investigating crimes against the state, were vested in the KGB. By the early 1990s, the KGB had expanded its mandate so that it investigated any crimes that political authority deemed expedient, confirming its status as a totally politicized policing authority (Roudik 2008, 140–41). The Police Law 1991 divided the police into criminal police and public security police, the former responsible for criminal investigations and the latter for local police stations, detention centers, and traffic control as well as minor crimes and public order maintenance. The public security police can be local or federal and they make up 60 percent of the total number of police (p. 146). Both elements of the police force are located within the Ministry of Internal Affairs. All regional ministry departments maintain antiterrorist and serious crime units known as "Black Berets" (OMON—Special Purpose Militia Detachments) who are essentially SWAT forces. Within the police also are military units called Internal Troops, who take part in crowd control and in emergency military operations. They are similar in nature to the U.S. National Guard and number about 300,000 (pp. 147–48).

In India, police forces are still regulated by the colonial framework of the Police Act 1861 (Hakeem 2008, 173). State forces are headed by an inspector general of police, and major cities have municipal forces headed by police commissioners. State forces are comprised of armed and unarmed police: the former are tasked with running police stations and conducting criminal investigations and with the multitude of duties that police may be called on to carry out. The armed police live in cantonments[9] and are recruited and trained separately from other police. They have no contact with the public unless they are called on to deal with public order issues. Elements of armed police are either district armed police, located in the district headquarters, or special armed police, placed in a few locations within a state and commonly used for special actions such as dealing with public disturbances where their enhanced protective equipment becomes important (p. 173). It is estimated that police in the states total 765,000 (p. 175).

The Indian federal government controls some police elements, including the Indian Police Service (IPS), paramilitary units, and police in the Union territories. In addition, the Ministry of Home Affairs controls the Central Reserve Police (CRP), established by the British in 1939 to police the Independence movement. The CRP is now used to control public disturbances when a situation is beyond the control of local policing units and to protect federal installations and buildings. The Border Security Force (BSF) was created in 1965 to patrol the border with Pakistan and possesses more advanced weaponry than other paramilitary units (Hakeem 2008, 177).

The Turkish *Jandarma* (gendarmerie) is a fully armed paramilitary force with each officer carrying a personal weapon. From the 1980s more heavily armed police units modeled along SWAT lines have been set up for public order and antiterrorist purposes (Cerrah 2008, 194). The *Jandarma* numbers between 280,000 and 300,000, whereas the civilian police (the TNP) comprises about 175,000 police with almost 13,000 civilian staff. The *Jandarma* relies on national service conscripts who make up about 80 percent of its numbers and who normally serve for fifteen months after undergoing a short training program of about six weeks. The focus of the *Jandarma* is the rural areas of the country, and it lacks the professional law enforcement competence of the TNP because of its reliance on conscription (Goldsmith 2009, 35).

The French Gendarmerie (the name was adopted in 1791) was originally set up as a rural police force, but it gained its military character in 1798 during Napoleon's reign. It is basically a military force that is also responsible for civil police duties in rural areas and thus provides a line of defense against social disorder. The civil and military combination of policing based on the Gendarmerie and regular criminal investigation police was exported by France to Europe and to the French colonies (Dupont 2008, 250). A peculiarity of the French justice system is that an investigating magistrate can choose to assign a case for police investigation to the civilian National Police or to the Gendarmerie. This has resulted in strong competition existing between the two forces to secure prestigious investigations and a reluctance by each to share information or cooperate generally (p. 252). The National Police are under the control of the Interior Ministry, and the Gendarmerie is placed under the Defense Ministry. There are also a number of municipal forces in France, about 3,000 in total, but they do not compete with the National Police being used in towns and cities only for local duties such as providing a uniformed presence on the streets and enforcing municipal laws. The total personnel in municipal forces is approximately 15,400, the Gendarmerie number approximately 98,000, and the National Police 132,000 (p. 256).

The Gendarmerie is divided into the general Departmental Gendarmerie with 63,500 personnel operating 3,600 police stations in rural areas, and the Mobile Gendarmerie of 17,000, which polices riots and public protests. The famous Republican Guard is a mounted unit of 3,000 providing honor guards for state visits and guards state facilities (Dupont 2008, 256–57).

As indicated earlier, modern police forces are products of the historical context of policing in a state. In many developing countries, police forces remain embedded in the past and the colonial model of policing continues to hold sway. In understanding contemporary policing in these countries, therefore, it is necessary to acknowledge the legacy of the past. The following discussion of colonial policing explains colonial styles of policing and their impact on the shaping of postcolonial policing.

COLONIAL POLICING

A police force has been established as an armed semi-military force and is employed for the prevention and detection of crime, the repression of internal disturbances, protection against fire, the defence of the colony against external aggression and any other duties prescribed by the Governor in Council.
(Particulars of the Office of Detective Superintendent of Police – Guiana Police 1938 – Colonial Office; cited in Sinclair 2006, 1)

The colonial policing experience has shaped postcolonial policing in numerous developing countries. In countries where a militaristic colonial policing model was installed, it often endures because the postcolonial leaders, like their former colonial rulers, fear that without it their authority and control over their citizens will be diminished or even erased altogether. In addition, there is police resistance to changing a model that makes few, if any, concessions to accountability for policing actions, which legitimates high levels of police violence, and which sees no benefit in befriending the community. Many of the academic studies on colonial and postcolonial policing relate to former British colonies. For that reason, this discussion focuses largely on policing in British colonies.

Historical accounts of colonial policing trace the tension between two models of policing: (1) the *civilian model,* exemplified by the British "bobby" originating in the 1829 law that established the civilian Metropolitan Police Force in England, and (2) the *military or paramilitary model,* adopted in numerous British colonies to ensure colonial control (Sinclair 2006). These opposing policing models were perceived as indicating a choice between *policing by consent,* represented in Britain by largely unarmed British constables working closely with the community and possessing a high degree of individual discretion, and *policing by coercion,* represented by armed policing units with military ranks, military training, and military discipline. The historical account of colonial policing shows that while colonial civil servants in Britain often wanted to export the civilian policing model to the colonies, especially as decolonization approached, those ruling the colonies almost always believed they needed to militarize local law enforcement.

Evolution of Colonial Policing

Britain's imperial possessions needed to be maintained and, if necessary, defended, but by 1850 the British Army was modest in size and lacked the capability to secure all of Britain's imperial possessions. Thus, police forces provided a resource for this purpose (Sinclair 2006, 2). What were the overall objectives served by a police force in a colony? Mawby (2001, 21) suggests the following:

The British government sought to establish a policing system that was integrated with the military and civic administration and that provided tightly controlled and efficient government, where the needs of expatriates were catered for and the demands of the indigenous population suppressed where necessary.

The police performed a critical social maintenance function, and later, a political security role, in the social and political history of British colonialism. Overall, it can be said that in the early period of colonization, colonial policing had less to do with crime control and more with maintaining the social order and protecting property and privilege. In fact, order maintenance was regarded as the prime task, with justice and even the law placed after that (Harriott 2000, 146). Later, more emphasis was given to crime prevention and control and on developing explicitly civilian forms of policing, but the process was not seamless or even, as between colonies (Anderson and Killingray 1991, 6).[10]

Policing styles varied according to the stages of colonization. During the early stages, public order was the priority. In the established and stable colonial phase, the focus turned to conventional crime control and creating the legal institutions necessary to process acts of criminality. In addition, when police acted to impose control, policing became "multifaceted," with a variety of roles being performed by a colonial force that amounted to an armed constabulary with a limited civil policing capacity (Sinclair 2006, 2). Finally, in the last pre-Independence stage, mounting disorder and violence associated with nationalism called for a police response that was commensurate with threats to public order and state security that sometimes amounted to emergencies, such as occurred in Malaya and Kenya, requiring both a military response and a punitive police reaction (Mawby 2001, 21–22).

Generally speaking, colonial police forces were centralized and militaristic although some colonial administrations did ask for information about the structure and organization of the Metropolitan Police civilian model of policing, and there was often an overlap between this model of the British "bobby" and the militaristic model (Sinclair 2006, 13). Military-style police forces tended to live apart from the community in barracks and ordinarily carried weapons. In terms of their functions, police regularly gave greater priority to public order–type missions and tasks, but they also performed numerous administrative responsibilities, such as issuing various licenses. Importantly, the absence of anything we now refer to as "community policing" endorsed the role of the police as an affiliate of the colonial administration and devalued its legitimacy among the indigenous population (Mawby 2001, 21).

The policing model that Britain developed was intended to constitute the first line of defense of a colony, as well as maintain public order. In the case of most colonies, Georgina Sinclair argues that it followed a model adapted from British experience in Ireland (2006, 4). The experience of attempting to police disturbances in Ireland led to the creation of the Royal Irish Constabulary (RIC) in 1814. The legislation authorizing the RIC provided for a force to combat disturbances in Ireland where, as the legislation put it, "the ordinary police hath been found insufficient" (cited in Sinclair 2006, 14). The RIC was basically a military unit, using military ranks and uniforms and armed.[11] It contrasted radically with the civilian model that emerged as the Metropolitan Police in the 1829 legislation promoted by British Home Secretary Sir Robert Peel. Ireland was policed by the RIC from 1822 to 1922 and on the creation of the Irish Free State, many former members of the RIC took their policing experience to the colonies (Sinclair 2006, 16), in particular to the Palestine Police, the legislation for which explicitly stated that its organization was similar to that of the Royal Irish Constabulary.

The claim that all colonial police forces followed the Irish model has been challenged because, for example, while Ireland was heavily policed, most colonies were not; some forces adopted the RIC organization structure but did not follow its training practices; and some forces claimed to be organized along the lines of the British civilian policing model and others were hybrid—for example, the first police force in Hong Kong was modeled on the Metropolitan Police and the New Zealand force changed from a military to a civilian force, very much along British lines (Hill 1991, 52). Indian policing drew on both military and civilian models (Anderson and Killingray 1991, 4; Arnold 1986, 7).[12] In Jamaica, the police force formed in 1866 was a paramilitary model, and the colonial administration's concern was principally with controlling the population in a volatile, sometimes hostile environment "in the certainty that the black subjects (including most of all the stereotypical brawny police constables) were infantile, unintelligent, irresponsible, and politically unreliable" (Harriott 2000, 37).

Thus, the origin and development of the colonial policing experience in each colony raises complex questions associated with factors such as the degree of control held over a territory, the available resources that could be assigned to policing, and the extent to which other institutional justice structures—including magistrates, native police forces, and colonial civilian personnel—contributed to the work of keeping the peace (Anderson and Killingray 1991, 5). It is important, therefore, to situate the study of colonial policing within the "broader fabric of colonial rule" and social controls enforced within the colonies (Anderson 1991, 183).

Colonial Police Forces

What sort of policing units were actually established in Britain's colonies? The numerous colonies and protectorates had forces of varying sizes and quality, some always weaponized and others with easy access to arms when needed. In a paramilitary-style police force, the armed police constable usually operates as a member of a group receiving and carrying out orders from a superior. The civilian policing model, however, empowers a police constable to exercise discretion within the limits of the law and in response to all the circumstances (Sinclair 2006, 221). The police commissioner for the Gold Coast aptly expressed the difference in 1904 as follows:

> As a rule a good Policeman makes a bad soldier, and a good soldier is not necessarily a good Policeman. A Policeman has to act and act quickly on his own responsibility, a good soldier is a machine who only acts on instructions from a superior officer. (quoted in Killingray 1991, 119)

Lacking legitimacy with the indigenous population, colonial police forces favored recruiting "trustworthy strangers" to police "other strangers" and, instead of recruiting locally, recruited from places on the periphery of the colony. Examples are Indians in Mauritius, Trinidad, and Fiji and Chinese and Indians in Malaya (Anderson and Killingray 1991, 7).

In some colonies, for example, Ceylon (now Sri Lanka), initial thinking about appropriate policing favored the British Metropolitan civilian police model, but after former RIC officers had been placed in charge of police development in Ceylon, the colonial model prevailed despite attempts between 1913 and 1937 to remodel it to an unarmed civilian force. In 1944, the then inspector general of the Ceylon Police was reporting that its characteristics were those of a military body (Sinclair 2006, 29–30). In the Caribbean colonies, the Colonial Office attempted to establish a police force on the model of the Metropolitan Police, but after 1838 and slave emancipation the model changed according to the local context, and maintaining the economic order was the major concern of the colonial elite. When British troops were withdrawn from the region, police forces in the Bahamas and in Trinidad were militarized (Johnson 1991, 87).

In Canada, a military-style constabulary was thought to be needed to control the North-West Territories and the Yukon Territory, a vast expanse deemed appropriate for policing by a mounted cavalry force of riflemen, one of whose tasks would be to pave the way for European settlement by forcing the First Nations peoples to stay on the reserves allocated to them. A force along the lines of a cavalry regiment was therefore formed under 1873 legislation with field artillery and a red tunic like that of the British Army (Sinclair 2006, 44). The Canadian government regarded the North-West Mounted Police (NWMP) as more of an armed militia than a police force and it drew on RIC training methods with the addition of equestrian skills. The thinking was that if the RIC could cope with "wild disloyal Irish" the NWMP could cope with the First Nations (p. 48). The Royal Canadian Mounted Police (the "Mounties") later absorbed the NWMP.

The Royal Irish Constabulary was the model for the Egyptian gendarmerie, formed in the 1880s during the British occupation of Egypt (Tollefson 1999, 5). A notable drawback associated with the military model was the fact that "a punitive, militaristic style of policing militates against skilful detective work, can be expressed through brutality and torture, and has difficulty coping with ordinary crime.… The British came to favor the military model of policing … to aid in political repression and to hold costs down" (p. xiii). The Egyptian police, under British control and with British officers, played a leading role in countering Egyptian nationalism (p. 181).

British rule in Palestine revealed the futility of attempting a civilian policing model in a situation where the colonial police had to hold a thin line between soldiering and policing (Sinclair 2006, 104). As the internal security situation worsened, the need for paramilitary policing increased, and the Palestine Police gained experience in counter-insurgency operations that some of them put to good use during the Malayan Emergency. In 1944, the Palestine Police Mobile Force (PPMF) was established as a fully militarized unit. Its members wore battle dress, received training along military lines, and were armed with automatic weapons and mortars. The task of the PPMF was to provide support in public disorder situations. The PPMF was a model for similar units exported throughout the colonies, for example, to the Gold Coast, Northern Rhodesia, Eritrea, Cyprus, and Malaya (pp. 111, 113).

Policing the Indigenous Peoples

Colonial policing was largely about policing people of color regardless of the size of the colony or its population (Sinclair 2006, 10). For example, in some African colonies, administrations enforced a curfew that made it illegal for Africans to be out on the streets at night unless they held a pass.[13] In colonies with large white settler populations such as Kenya and Northern Rhodesia, the European community regarded the police force as their protector against the indigenous peoples and considered they ought not to be bothered by police for traffic offenses or minor thefts (p. 142).

The British colonial project involved the economic exploitation of its colonies and meant that a close connection existed between policing and the economic interests of the expatriate populations. As a result, colonial police were employed, for example, in some African colonies to enforce labor laws against African workers and to protect the economic assets of settler and European populations (Sinclair 2006, 143).[14] In Kenya, the European settler population regarded the country as theirs, and police claimed they were pressured into prosecuting Africans for the most minor of crimes, such as stealing food because of hunger (p. 145). Police became involved in maintaining the indentured labor system in the major sugar colonies of British Guiana and Trinidad because a violation of the labor law by Indian immigrants constituted a crime (Johnson 1991, 75).[15]

In Africa, under the British indirect rule model, vast rural territories were left to be policed by tribal chiefs (Sinclair 2006, 137); the colonial police dealt with more serious breaches of public order and with crimes by and against the white expatriates.[16] In other locations, the native population was largely unpoliced, but

natives who moved into towns came under scrutiny. For example, in the Transvaal and Orange River Colony in the early 1900s, the South African Constabulary (SAC) policed the native population by enforcing municipal regulations, vagrancy laws, and pass laws that were designed to preserve the "white character" of towns and prevent indigenous Africans permanently settling there, or "loitering." The SAC did not police or patrol African locations (except to collect taxes from Africans),[17] and it was regarded as a first line of defense against fears of a native uprising (Grundlingh 1991, 176–77). Similarly, by 1911, the Kenya Police was restricted to policing the larger urban areas and the "White Highlands" (the area occupied by the expatriate settlers)—essentially the European parts of the colony after the responsibility for policing "Native Reserves" was assigned to the district administration (Anderson 1991, 185).[18] A comparison between the policing of white and native areas in Nyasaland between January 1930 and December 1933 shows that only forty-one cases of theft and housebreaking were recorded in the main towns. In the surrounding villages, more than two thousand such cases were reported over the same period to which the police responded largely with indifference (McCracken 1986, 134).

In India, the policing hierarchy comprised European superintendents and inspectors (as decolonization approached, there was pressure from the emergent Indian middle class to Indianize the inspectorate[19]) and the Indian constabulary on the lowest tier. They were seen as carrying out duties of a purely "mechanical nature" and were not expected to display initiative or exercise discretion in their dealings with Indians. Their pay was low, but they nevertheless perceived themselves as of a superior status to the class from which they came. Although the British did not approve, they could do little to prevent the constabulary associating with Indians, but the nature of that relationship was essentially predatory. The constables used their power to "extort bribes and favours from anyone too weak to resist their demands" (Arnold 1986, 64).

Policing Decolonization

In the final stage of policing the colonies, decolonization brought fresh concerns about public order and gave rise to a form of "political policing." Police use of force increased to deal with disturbances associated with nationalist movements and the like. In the countdown to Independence, political policing became the norm. It involved close surveillance of specific organizations and individuals prominent in local politics. Accordingly, "colonial police became pawns in the imperial endgame" (Sinclair 2006, 189). Political policing meant having to develop police Special Branch units charged with the collection of intelligence and its assessment and with the distribution of information likely to affect public security (p. 203). In addition, police in these units were called upon to investigate subversion and sabotage and acts that might endanger the safety of the state.[20]

After World War II, British colonies began a rapid process of decolonization. As part of this process, in 1948, the Colonial Office began an attempt to standardize the Colonial Police Service. By 1948 there were 43 separate police forces in the Colonial Police Service ranging in size from the Falkland Islands with a total of 8 of all ranks to Malaya with 15,854. The aim of the Colonial Office was to export to all of the colonies the community-friendly model of the British bobby (Sinclair 2006, 56). Yet the reforms proposed came too late and were too little for the modernization that was required. In addition, there was a tension between the notion of injecting "Britishness" into these police forces and fear that installing a civil rather than a military style of policing could put a colony's internal security at risk (pp. 62–63).[21]

The Colonial Office began belatedly to express concerns about future ex-colonies having police forces that did not serve the law but were under political control (Sinclair 2006, 67). In reality, the use of force by police increased in the colonies as public order situations developed with the upcoming decolonization. In addition, Africanizing, Indianizing, and generally localizing police forces became an issue because the policy of localizing colonial police forces came too late. For example, a number of European officers remained in the Malawi Police Force until the early 1970s although it attained Independence in 1964 (p. 71). In Kenya, the segregation created by the white settlers found a parallel in the police force as between officers and other ranks, and it was not until 1961 that it was possible for an African to achieve the rank of inspector, and only in the three years prior to Independence were European officers required to identify African officers who were promotable to higher ranks (p. 145). It

appears that several hundred European officers stayed on in Kenya after Independence and policing continued to rely on traditional colonial methods. By 2005, almost a decade after Hong Kong was brought under the sovereignty of China, there were still about three hundred European officers serving in the Royal Hong Kong Police (p. 218).

By 1932 in Jamaica, despite attempts made to civilianize a force with a strong military character, the force's organization was substantively identical to that of 1866 (Sinclair 2006, 86) and military ranks, drilling, and weapons training continued as before. Anthony Harriott (2000, 30) notes that the Jamaica Constabulary Force was formed in 1866 and "is therefore perhaps more profoundly shaped by colonialism than any other state institution." He points to its current institutional culture, organization, and style of policing as elements of this shaping. In the Caribbean generally, a military policing model had initially been justified by fear of freed slaves (Johnson 1991, 71), but over time, with the formation of trade unions, the withdrawal of British troops from some Caribbean colonies, and general public discontent as decolonization approached, there was little scope for civilianizing the police (Sinclair 2006, 91).

The potential for social turmoil present in almost every colony at the end of the empire was most marked in Malaya and Kenya. The Malayan Emergency lasted from 1948 until 1960, and by 1952, one hundred thousand regular and auxiliary police were assisting the army, often working on the front lines (Sinclair 2006, 166). In Kenya, the General Service Unit was created, modeled on the Palestine Police Mobile Force (PPMF), to counter the Mau Mau emergency.

Strategies and techniques learned in Palestine were exported throughout the colonies by former members of the Palestine Police and "Palestine became the unofficial training and recruiting ground for senior colonial policemen" (Sinclair 2006, 115). The Colonial Office objective of "transplanting Britishness to territories where the tradition of colonial policing was deeply embedded within society and the end of Empire marked by increased resistance to colonial rule" proved to be unworkable (p. 131).

The British failure to export and install the civilian policing model meant that the colonial police force model with the addition of political policing was still intact at the time of Independence in most colonies. Thus, new states simply inherited the colonial model, which they found useful and effective in countering the problems associated with Independence because it was discovered in India, for example, that police could as easily serve Indian politicians as colonial officials (Arnold 1986, 227). In India, "Congress Ministers took over the colonial police organization (and its colonial mentality) largely intact, promoting to vacant senior posts Indian officers habituated to colonial policing roles and attitudes. The greatest value of the police to the new regime—as to its predecessor—was as an agency of coercion and intelligence" (p. 58). In addition, in India, the colonial police had been involved in defending and protecting the Indian elite and this role was easily transferred to Indian police at Independence (p. 4).[22] In former French, Spanish, and Portuguese colonies, policing systems adopted on Independence were similar to those of the colonizers, and in North and West Africa, the French centralized policing system was also simply taken over (Cole 1999, 96). Consequently, in many former colonial states, contemporary postcolonial policing is still focused primarily on public order maintenance and crime control, the latter using outdated techniques and often with little regard for citizens' rights. Modern policing recognizes that police need to act democratically and become service oriented, and ironically so-called democratic policing is now being exported to many postcolonial states with an emphasis on community policing (see "Democratic Policing"). Limited resources and prioritizing other services and needs other than democratic policing continue to be issues, as is the fact that authoritarian governments are loath to surrender their control over police as a means of enforcing their political will (Cole 1999, 101).

The form and manner of colonial policing is closely linked to interventions from the West to alter patterns of policing in the postcolonial developing world where policing often remains substantially unchanged since decolonization. As noted earlier, many former colonies retain the colonial policing model even though it represents a form of policing designed for a different time and political arrangement. We have looked at some of the reasons why the colonial model has been retained by postcolonial countries. The following section on democratic policing explains how policing has been globalized or internationalized through the concept of democratic policing and how developed states currently promote democratic policing, considered to represent "best international practice policing," to postcolonial states and to states in transition.

DEMOCRATIC POLICING

The notion of democratic policing has been touched on in the preceding discussion but needs further explanation to fully understand how Western formulated norms and standards of police conduct are being promoted by developed states as a way of internationalizing policing.[23] Democratic policing is a concept that originated in the developed world, where it is regarded as encompassing a key set of principles and practices that ought to be deployed in law enforcement practice. For example, police accountability to citizens is generally regarded as a critical element of democratic policing. In addition, in many police reform interventions and projects conducted in developing states, democratic policing has been promoted as the required foundation for democratic and best practice policing.

In many parts of the world, police have been traditionally regarded as protectors of the interests of the state rather than of the rights and freedoms of citizens. In Central and South America, challenges to state power from armed guerrillas have given state military forces dominance over safety and security, and the divide that commonly exists between military power and police power has been distorted by the preoccupation of both military and police with the protection of the regime. Accordingly, basic crime prevention and control have been neglected even after the overthrow of the military and the free election of reformist governments (Hinton 2006, 6). Rising crime, an acceptance of corruption in public offices, and a lack of political commitment to police reform have impeded radical changes to policing that would render it more service oriented (p. 192). As before, the tradition of "policing only the lowest rungs of state and society" and protecting the middle class and the elite endures (p. 200).

In Africa, established colonial policing practices have continued in postcolonial policing, and "most police in most African countries are fundamentally unchanged from what they were ten years ago" (Hills 2008, 216). Thus, numerous

African policing systems remain centered on order and control rather than crime prevention and justice (Hills 1996, 278).

In post-Soviet Eastern Europe, the inherited police forces have a history of being primarily deployed as a tool of the Communist Party. As in many Latin American and African states, these Eastern European forces have faced reform challenges because, as Michael Trebilock and Ronald Daniels (2008, 109) note, "Police were alienated from citizens because of the exclusive focus of the police on securing social order and defending ruling interests." In contrast, as long ago as 1979, the earliest international set of norms for policing, the UN Code of Conduct for Law Enforcement Officials, asserted that the role of police is to "serve the community" (Office of the United Nations High Commissioner for Human Rights).

Elements of Democratic Policing

Contemporary interventions aimed at reforming police forces in developing and transitional states draw on international norms and standards of policing which are presented to developing and transitional states as "best practice" in policing worldwide. They also constitute elements of democratic policing. What is meant by democratic policing? Although explanations of this term remain somewhat of a work in progress, a general consensus exists among academics and other policing experts about its composition.

At the most fundamental level of analysis, some policing experts reason that the core principle of policing should be the notion of protecting human rights and furthering justice.[24] Respect for people's human rights and dignity is said to be central to the issue of public confidence in the police (Neyroud 2003, 578). As well, scholars have argued that democratic policing is connected to the existence of a democratic society (Alderson 1998, Palmiotto 2001, Wiatrowski 2002, all cited in Pino & Wiatrowski 2006, 71). As Rachel Neild (2001, 23) puts it, "Democratic policing ... exists in a symbiotic relationship with democratic government."

Peter Manning (2005, 23) describes democratic policing as policing that "eschews torture, terrorism and counterterrorism; is guided by law; and seeks minimal damage to civility." Nathan Pino and Michael Wiatrowski (2006, 83–86) argue that democratic policing should incorporate the following normative principles:

- *The rule of law*: laws and institutions established by law originate through a democratic process, and individual and organizational conduct and disputes are regulated and resolved by application of the rule of law.

- *Legitimacy*: people and institutions exercise authority according to the explicit purposes of the law and social institutions. The foundation of legitimacy is the consent of the governed.

- *Transparency*: government operations, including policing, are conducted with transparency, and therefore citizens are always aware of government actions.

- *Accountability*: institutions and persons having authority always remain responsible to citizens and to elected or appointed leaders for their actions.

- *Subordination to civil authority*: the police will never be a law unto themselves and will always be accountable to a civil authority.

These principles do not include responsiveness to citizens, which is commonly regarded by other scholars as a core element in democratic policing.

Charles Call (2000) and Pino and Wiatrowski (2006) argue that democratic policing requires that police are placed under civilian rather than military control. He suggests that other elements of democratic policing should include that police provide a public service while adhering to human rights standards and that police are "ethnically plural and nonpartisan" (Banks 2014, 353). Bayley (1985, 223) suggests that democratic policing is grounded in the values of "responsiveness" and "accountability" and argues that the degree to which policing can be evaluated as democratic can be determined by comparing the ratio of police responses to service calls from the public to forms of police work originating through the chain of command. In his later study of democratic policing, Bayley (2006, 19–20) identifies the minimum requirements for democratic policing reforms in the following:

- Police are accountable to the law and not to government.

- Police protect human rights, especially rights safeguarding political activity in a democracy.

- Police are accountable to lay persons who are empowered to regulate police activity.

- Police give priority to the needs of citizens and groups in conducting policing operations.

In terms of international explanations of the term, one United Nations policing institution—the United Nations International Police Task Force—operating under a UN mandate in Bosnia-Herzegovina in 1996, focused on service delivery (responsiveness to the public) and fairness or nondiscrimination in the application of the law and argued that "the police force of a democracy is concerned strictly with the preservation of safe communities and the application of criminal law equally to all people, without fear or favour" (quoted in Stone and Ward 2000, 14). Consistent with this fundamental statement of purpose, the Task Force outlined the following principles of democratic policing:

- Police must function in accordance with the law.

- Police conduct must be regulated by a professional code of conduct.

- The highest priority of policing is the protection of human life.

- Police must serve the public and are accountable to the public and must communicate their actions to the public to establish the legitimacy of police action.

- A central focus of policing is the prevention of crime.

- Police must act in such a way as to respect human rights.

- Police must act in a nondiscriminatory manner.

There is now a general consensus that the fundamental policing responsibility is the protection of human rights, which is said to translate into the following specific goals:

accountability, professionalism and legitimation, supported by specific policies which will lead to their achievement: non-partisanship and impartiality in the application of law; representativeness in the composition of police personnel; personal integrity sought through proper recruitment, training and promotion and sanctioning procedures;

transparency of all operations which are not based on specifically and legitimately protected information; sensitivity to the diversity of social identities, cultural interests and non-dominant values in society; responsiveness to societal demands and norms; an orientation to public service; and a commitment to the rule of law. (Mareinin 2007, 180)

Practitioners of police reform largely agree with academic commentary concerning the content of democratic policing. For example, in its publication "Anticorruption and Police Integrity: Security Sector Reform Program," the U.S. Agency for International Development (USAID) calls for a focus on democratic policing with "reform strategies that emphasize accountability, transparency, and professional practices" and "greater responsiveness to communities" (USAID 2007, 13). Also included are "improving standards, selection, training, and salaries" and "performance indicators and well-defined job descriptions [that] will support merit-based systems for assignment and promotion" (p. 13).

Commentators agree also on the need for knowledge about ethics in policing as part of democratic policing reforms (Pino and Wiatrowski 2006, 107). Putting this view into concrete proposals, the Patten Report (1999), detailing recommended democratic policing reforms in Northern Ireland, called for a new code of ethics that incorporated the European Convention on Human Rights and for extensive human rights training for officers (p. 172).

Global Norms and Standards in Democratic Policing

International norms concerning policing conduct are widely regarded as instances of best practice in policing and are commonly incorporated into democratic policing programs. These norms are sometimes located in international treaties and declarations and may therefore be obligatory in international law for a state that is undergoing police reform. Others are internationally approved guidelines or rules that constitute nonbinding "soft law." The first of these international prescriptions was the UN Code of Conduct for Law Enforcement Officials (1979), which recognizes the key role that police play in protecting human rights and guaranteeing equal treatment under the law. The Code requires that law enforcement officials "respect and protect human dignity and maintain and uphold the human rights of all persons." There are prohibitions against using excess force, torture, and cruel, inhuman, and degrading treatment or punishment. Guidelines for the Effective Implementation of the Code of Conduct for Law Enforcement Officials were adopted in 1989 and provide that states should establish effective mechanisms to ensure internal discipline and external control as well as the supervision of law enforcement officials. In addition, the guidelines require that provision be made for the receipt and processing of complaints against law enforcement officials made by members of the public. Thus, police accountability is at the center of this instrument.

"Basic Principles on the Use of Force and Firearms by Law Enforcement Officials" were adopted by the Eighth United Nations Congress on the Prevention of Crime and the Treatment of Offenders, August 27 to September 7, 1990. Governments and law enforcement agencies are to adopt and implement rules on the use of force and firearms against persons by law enforcement officials. Nonviolent means must be applied before force or firearms are resorted to; intentional lethal use of firearms is only permitted when strictly unavoidable in order to protect life; firearms may only be used in self-defense, or in defense of others where there is an imminent threat of death or serious injury, to prevent the commission of a serious crime involving grave threat to life, and to arrest a dangerous person or prevent his or her escape when less extreme means will not serve this stated purpose. Reporting and review procedures seek to hold accountable police who wrongfully employ force or firearms, including holding superior officers responsible, access to judicial process, and the making of detailed reports of incidents.

The Optional Protocol to the Convention against Torture and Other Cruel, Inhuman or Degrading Treatment or Punishment (2006) requires that states follow a practice of making regular visits to places of police detention and to places where police interrogate suspects. The visits should be made by independent international and national bodies to places where people are deprived of their liberty, in order to prevent torture and other cruel, inhuman, or degrading treatment or punishment. The provision is therefore directed at securing police accountability by preventing police misconduct in the treatment afforded to detainees.

The Standard Minimum Rules for the Treatment of Prisoners, United Nations Rules for the Treatment of Women Prisoners and Non-custodial Measures for Women Offenders (the Bangkok Rules), and Body of Principles for the Protection of All Persons under Any Form of Detention or Imprisonment establish principles associated with ensuring that detainees are treated with dignity. They require states to make known places of detention and the identities of custody and interrogation officers so as to facilitate accountability. The 1988 Body of Principles requires that places of detention comply with a system of external visits and grants detainees the right to make a complaint to the detention authority and bring a complaint before a judicial or other authority when a complaint is rejected or inordinately delayed. Whenever the death or disappearance of a detained person occurs during that person's detention, an inquiry into the cause of death or disappearance shall be held. These instruments seek to ensure that human rights are protected when persons are detained.

The Global Standards to Combat Corruption in Police Forces/Services, adopted by INTERPOL, aim to ensure that police possess high standards of integrity and to promote and strengthen the development of anticorruption measures in police forces, including bringing corrupt police to justice. The standards include a provision authorizing the INTERPOL General Secretariat to monitor their implementation in member countries.

The European Code of Police Ethics (2001) clearly promotes democratic policing, stating that the main purposes of the police in a democratic society governed by the rule of law are

- to maintain public tranquility and law and order in society,

- to protect and respect the individual's fundamental rights and freedoms,

- to prevent and combat crime,

- to detect crime, and

- to provide assistance and service functions to the public.

The Code also provides that a state's police laws should satisfy standards required by international instruments to which the country is a party and a state must make police accountable to the state, citizens, and their representatives.

Furthermore, public authorities must ensure effective and impartial procedures for complaints against the police, and accountability mechanisms are to be promoted. Member states must also develop police codes of ethics based on the principles set out in the Code. Police training must include practical training on the use of force and limits with regard to established human rights principles. A detailed set of guidelines applies to operational policing covering the use of force, prohibition on torture and inhuman treatment, and nondiscriminatory conduct. Police conducting investigations and arresting or detaining persons are subject to specific duties and prohibitions. An explanatory memorandum to the Code states the intent of a police code of ethics is to "recommend(s) best practice for the police, and is a specialized version of habitual, everyday common-sense principled conduct."

Although there are questions about the effectiveness of programs promoting democratic policing and Western policing models, there is insufficient space here to review that issue. It can be said, however, that democratic policing has been criticized for its assumption that the deployment of Western policing discourses and practices will be effective in developing states, especially post-conflict states, and for prioritizing reform over effectiveness. As Graham Ellison (2007, 233) puts it, "Police democratization will do little to enhance citizen safety without some parallel effort to enhance police capacity and political steps to ameliorate the structural conditions of crime." Christopher Murphy (2007, 258) also takes issue with Western policing models, describing them as "often inappropriate, seldom sustainable and usually ineffective, and are sometimes harmful to the interests of local citizens and communities." It has also been pointed out that democratic policing reforms are unlikely to be effective or sustained "without fairly systemic political and cultural change, ensuring that political and civil institutions are themselves democratic in their operation" (Hinton and Newburn 2009, 23).

CASE STUDIES OF POLICING: RUSSIA AND CHINA

Apart from gaining a detailed understanding of the development and contemporary conditions of policing in these two countries, the following case studies of policing in Russia and China provide an opportunity to contrast policing in those countries with the international standard of democratic policing. It will be seen that in both countries, historical forces have substantially shaped the style and nature of policing and continue to do so today. In neither case have policing agencies significantly benefited from the impact of internationalized policing. In particular, Russian policing remains notable for its corruption, brutality, and lack of responsiveness to the public. Chinese policing is differentiated from other countries' law enforcement practices by the police power to impose various forms of administrative detention without any prior judicial process, and by policing strategies (strike hard campaigns) that involve staged public displays of state policing power and force.

POLICING IN RUSSIA

In communist countries, "the primary task of the police forces, in common with other state bodies and institutions, was to sustain the political system and safeguard its functioning" (Koszeg 2001, 1). As Louise Shelley explains, "Militia personnel were key actors in the imposition of order from above, forcing citizens to comply with the state's ideological objectives" (1996, xiii). In light of this commonly held assessment of the policing function in the Soviet Union, it might be expected that radical changes have taken place since the end of the communist regime in 1991, or even before that time as *perestroika* and *glasnost* challenged previous orthodoxies. Have such changes in fact occurred, and to what extent has the past history of policing and its place in Russian society constrained the process of police reform? Responses to such questions can provide us with explanations, however partial, about how Russian society is now policed; about how the notion of policing is understood and applied in the new democratic Russian Federation by the state and its organs; about citizens' perceptions of safety and security in this state; and about what Shelley (1996, xvi) calls "the authoritarian legacy" of Russia in relation to the former Soviet states and the formerly communist nations of Europe.

The regular police force in Russia was formerly called the militia (*militsiya*). On March 1, 2011, it was renamed the police (*politsiya;* Robertson 2012, 162; Zernova 2012, 474). It has been argued that the past success of the militia in enforcing social control in the USSR can be ascribed to its blending of "continental, colonial and communist police traditions" because each privileged the state and its interests rather than those of citizens (Shelley 1996, xviii). As a policing organization in a communist state,[25] the militia defended and protected a wider range of state interests than either the continental or colonial policing traditions (p. 4). As a Tsarist empire and then a Soviet state occupying almost the same territory, the various non-Slavic communities (later Soviet republics) were incorporated into the Soviet state with the militia operating as if it were a colonial police force, protecting Soviet property, enforcing central control, and maintaining political control. Under the Soviet policing system, Russians were appointed to key positions in all legal agencies, including the post of Deputy Minister of the Interior, the ministry responsible for the militia (pp. 12–13).

The history of the militia is one of cooperation with whatever other political policing agency operated to ensure the state's demands were enforced. Traditionally, lower ranked militia members had come from the lowest strata of society, and this practice did not change after 1917 (Shelley 1996, 20). The post-revolution functions of the militia stated in 1925 remained constant throughout the Soviet period. They included tasks that resembled colonial policing functions, for example, "fight unsanitary conditions," perform numerous regulatory functions, issue identification documents, and "ensure observance of cattle-grazing rules" (p. 26).

During the Stalin period, the various policing agencies consolidated their control over citizens and the head of the People's Commissariat for Internal Affairs (NKVD; which absorbed the militia) reported directly to Stalin. Even Communist Party officials were prohibited from interfering with NKVD operations (Shelley 1996, 31). The massive labor camp system, the size of the militia, and its extensive powers meant that crime rates remained low during this period (p. 36). The militia was dominated by Slavs from its inception, except in rural central Asia where there were few Russian speakers. In some of the Baltic states, 80 percent of republican militia staff were Slavs (p. 93).

In 1953 Khrushchev became First Secretary of the Communist Party, and although his policy of de-Stalinization involved reducing criminal penalties and extralegal procedures, there was no fundamental reform of the policing function. However, "crime control and enforcement of economic regulations became more important than political duties," and policing became much more professional (Shelley 1996, 39).

In 1973, during the Brezhnev years (1963–82), a new statute on the militia was enacted, expanding its functions on administrative and data collection, but corruption, particularly under Brezhnev's patronage system, was rampant within the militia during this period (p. 47). Anticorruption was a focus of Andropov's brief regime from 1982 to 1984, consistent with his reputation for efficiency and incorruptibility.

The Gorbachev regime lasted from 1985 to 1991 during which period he attempted to "use the law as a vital instrument of change" and establish the rule of law (Shelley 1996, 53). As part of the *glasnost* era, the militia was challenged by media revelations of brutality and abuse of citizens' rights, whereas previously there had been almost no reporting of the militia's activities. The media revealed the militia to be "not only brutal but ineffective" (p. 53), and the release of crime data in 1987 to the public for the first time reinforced this charge of ineffectiveness, showing escalating crime rates. The militia's reputation suffered accordingly (p. 53), and public fear of crime increased. Gorbachev tried to address these issues by adding new crime control units, including OMON (Special Purpose Militia Detachments added in 1987, later used in the Baltic states), and by permitting the privatization of some policing services such as guard services. The Ministry of Internal Affairs (MVD)[26] and militia response to the social change engendered by *glasnost* and *perestroika* was "chaotic and uncoordinated" because its structure was unable to support liberalization (p. 55). Overall, policing became part of the dilemma created by *perestroika*: "how to liberalize Soviet society while maintaining social order and central government control" (p. 192).

In the final years of the USSR, the troops of the MVD fought alongside the Soviet Army in suppressing local resistance to centralized rule only to find that local militias in the Soviet republics supported local interests and protected the local population (Shelley 1996, 55). Within Russia itself, continued efforts by the MVD to create a rule of law culture resulted in the dismissal of some 83,000 people from the MVD. In addition, 6,000 militia faced criminal charges and 30,000 were dismissed, often for work-related issues. At the same time, Gorbachev provided additional resources and equipment to the MVD and instituted a crackdown on ethnic movements throughout USSR, effectively reversing *perestroika*[27] (p. 57). Following resistance to Gorbachev from Russia, led by Boris Yeltsin, an abortive coup in August 1991 lasted only three days, and within months the USSR had collapsed (p. 58). In the transition from the USSR to the Russian Federation, the country faced higher crime rates, poverty, unemployment, and a general breakdown in social control (Beck and Robertson 2009, 51).

In the late 1990s, President Yeltsin favored decentralization of powers, including policing, to the regions and republics, and control of the militia passed to the governors. However, when he became president in 2000, Vladimir Putin determined to reverse this process. He persuaded the Constitutional Court of the Russian Federation that governors should not have the power to appoint regional police chiefs. Consequently, this power reverted back to the center (Solomon 2005, 232).

Legislation relating to privatization of policing services in 1992 resulted in the granting of licenses to numerous private security companies usually headed by ex-KGB or MVD staff. By 1999 there were almost 11,000 such enterprises, and almost 200,000 security agents were licensed to carry weapons. In addition, the regular militia also began to compete with security firms providing security services for standardized prices. This police "moonlighting" included working privately during official police working hours (Solomon 2005, 233). From the 1990s fear of crime increased and the shift from state-controlled media to market-driven media with heavy coverage of crime stories previously not publicized added to feelings of insecurity. In addition, press reports of militia corruption and brutality, and connections to organized crime proliferated (Zernova 2012, 477).

In 1996 a group of academics and practitioners summarized the proposed development plans of the MVD for the period 1996 to 2005. The overall goal as stated in their "Concept (Paper) for the Development of the Internal Affairs Agencies and Internal Troops of Russia" (1996) was to "make the MVD capable of guaranteeing the unfailing protection of individuals,

society and the state from criminal encroachment" (MVD 1996, quoted in Beck and Robertson 2009, 52). Included among the many programs envisaged to meet this goal were improving police accountability; a new legal, technical, organizational, and financial framework; new systems of selection and training of personnel; and reequipment and improved working conditions (p. 52). Adrian Beck and Annette Robertson (p. 55), after assessing the planned and implemented measures, note the absence of any real impact on the militia. Measures such as the transfer of the prison system out of MVD to the Justice Ministry and the fire department to the Civil Defense Ministry were supposed to make MVD a leaner and more focused organization. Departments within MVD were streamlined and downsized and decentralization plans announced, but they did not materialize (p. 56).

Summarizing the development of police reform in 2009, Beck and Robertson (2009, 50) commented that although the Russian criminal justice system had experienced change since 1991, with the aim of bringing about democratic reforms, "much of the police reform has in fact been superficial or involved the continuation—and even the reinforcement—of Soviet trends and traditions, rather than a break from past practices and principles." They assessed the prospects for the future democratization of the police as "not encouraging."

In 2011 a process of police reform instituted under the presidency of Dimitri Medvedev resulted in a new Law on the Police that included a change of name from militia to police, reduction in number of police, salary increases (a threefold increase), and changes to police and detainee rights as well as a new statement of the functions of the police that rid police of functions like organizing "drunk tanks" and investigating debtors (Robertson 2012, 164, 170).[28] The initiative seemed to be a response to adverse media reports about the militia that gradually built into a crisis of confidence as the police were shown to be not only ineffective but also dangerous to the population. For example, the chief ombudsman stated on television that "it is necessary to transform our militia from a semi-criminal, semi-feudal structure into a modern serious militia" (Taylor 2014, 9).

Initially the reforms included decentralization proposals, but these were defeated by concerns about loss of power at the center and also by fears that local authorities would be incapable of shouldering the burden. As a result, rather than substantive structural and operational reforms, the path chosen was to simply legislate a new law drafted largely by the militia itself (Taylor 2013, 14). Under the new law, militia officers had to be recertified to serve in the new police force. The recertification commission opted to follow an aggressive approach by not reappointing 143 out of 340 MVD generals, or 42 percent of the total. The reform was "judged by most observers to have failed to seriously transform the police" (p. 21).

According to Solomon (2005, 233–34), "Underfunded and underequipped, public policing in Russia is less professional now then it was in the late Soviet period," and the educational background of staff and regular militia has declined due to the availability of more attractive opportunities in the private sector for the better educated. Furthermore, the number of officers convicted of crimes, including abuse of police powers and taking bribes, increased from 504 in 1991 to 3,700 in 2000.[29] According to the Internal Affairs Ministry, in 2009, militia officers committed more than 5,000 criminal offenses, 3,000 of which involved corruption and abuse of power (Zernova 2012, 475). It is interesting to note that Russia is not under-policed according to Robertson (2012, 168–69). The current police-to-public ratio in Russia is approximately 979 per 100,000 persons. This compares with England and Wales (263 per 100,000 persons) and the United States (227 per 100,000 persons).

Citizens' views about the police surveyed in 2004 suggest low levels of trust, doubts about their capacity, and a widespread belief that police are corrupt (Solomon 2005, 234). A study conducted in 2007 and 2009 in Moscow and a provincial town in central Russia interviewed fifty-four citizens concerning their views of the militia. They saw the militia "as ineffective, corrupt, brutal, disrespectful towards the law, concerned primarily with personal enrichment, and regularly consorting with criminal groups" (Zernova 2012, 476).

Moreover, there exists a lack of support within policing agencies for implementing the kinds of radical change that are needed to bring genuine democratic policing to the Russian Federation (Solomon 2005, 238). Bribing militia is common practice ranging from a small bribe to the traffic police for a minor violation to larger bribes that, for example, avoid investigations into a driver causing the death of a pedestrian. Bribes are used to acquire fake documents such as driving licenses (Zernova 2012, 479). Based on the results of focus group discussions, Gerber and Mendelson (2008, 18) conducted in three regions in 2002, "Russians experience about twice as much police violence and corruption in the course of two to three years than Americans experience in the course of their lifetimes."

This narrative of the militia reveals that during the seventy years of Soviet rule,[30] the militia began as a militarized force, then began to fulfill the functions of an authentic law enforcement agency, and then became, in effect, a militarized force again, acting like a colonial police force in the final period of empire. Shelley (1996, 59) points out that the most radical shift in the nature of the militia occurred in the period between Stalin and Khrushchev, when at least a semblance of systematic law enforcement replaced the authoritarian and arbitrary dictates of Stalin. Shelley (p. 59) argues that Gorbachev "never intended to make the Soviet militia resemble its western counterparts" because he anticipated that governance through state socialism would continue, and therefore the militia would need to possess police powers beyond those enjoyed by Western law enforcers.[31] As noted earlier, generally analysts of Russian policing agree that contemporary policing arrangements in Russia fall far below the standards set for democratic policing and there is little expectation of change. As well as a lack of political will for changes in policing, an institutional police culture exists that has successfully resisted even moderate pressures for improvement to international standards.

POLICING IN THE PEOPLE'S REPUBLIC OF CHINA

Historically, the principal mode of policing in China was the *baojia* system: a form of localized self-government and protection centered on the family and the household. During the eleventh century, Song dynasty collections of families formed units for the purpose of carrying out militia-style functions as a mode of defense against bandits and the like. The same organization could be used for tax collection purposes and to deploy forced labor (Dutton 1992, 66). During the following Yuan dynasty, *baojia* practices evolved to make village heads responsible for ensuring order in the village, checking on the spread of superstition and conspiracy against the government and instituting a dread of the law in the villagers (p. 68). By the seventeenth century, the *baojia* system was being employed for village self-defense, for conducting police investigations, and to organize teams to protect against fire and theft (p. 72). Modern policing did not come to China until the late nineteenth century (Yue 2008, 13).

Milestones in the history of policing in China (Sun and Wu 2010, 21–24; Yue 2008, 13–17) are listed below:

- In 1901 the Capital Police Bureau, the first modern policing agency in the country, was established in Beijing to enforce the law and keep public order. In 1902 police forces were created in some provinces and towns.

- In 1905 the Ministry of Police was formed as the first stage in unifying the police system in the country.

- The era of Imperial dynasties ended in 1911. By 1911 the Capital Police Bureau comprised some four thousand police as well as patrol, detective, training, and disciplinary divisions. From 1912 to 1928, the country was controlled by various warlords and although some policing development occurred, police were also manipulated by warlords to control the people.

- From 1928 until 1949, the country was ruled by the Kuomintang, and the Division of Police Administration under the Ministry of Domestic Affairs took responsibility for unifying the police system with police departments operating at various levels of government.

- In 1937 the Central Police College was established in Nanjing and up to 1949 graduated more than forty thousand police. From 1937 to 1945, the police acted in support of the war against Japan and in repressing the rise of the Communist Party.

- The Chinese Communist Party (CCP) was formed in 1921 but controlled only a small part of the country until the late 1940s. A State Political Security Bureau responsible for investigating some crimes was set up in 1931 by the CCP.

- In 1949 the Ministry of Public Security was established. From 1945 to 1965, "mass line" policing was practiced with the police; it was used to support the new communist government, suppress opposition, and fight class enemies. The Police Regulation of 1957 contained only eleven provisions.

- During the ten years of the Cultural Revolution (1966–76), the justice system collapsed, and some police were sent to work in the countryside to perform forced labor. Police assisted the Red Guards and harshly punished political dissidents.

- From 1976 to date, the police have undertaken reforms with the objective of becoming a professionalized and specialized force that acted in compliance with the law. Western democratic policing notions migrated to China, including the strategy of community policing introduced in 2001.

Chinese conceptions of policing have their foundation in self-help, informal community-type organizations and, more generally, in reliance on the masses (Dai 2001, 153). (See Chapter 5 for a discussion of the Confucian moral order for the ideals and values in which the conception of policing is embedded, especially the notion that police were expected to enforce the moral order rather than the law.) The concept of the "mass line" representing both traditional policing and Marxist-Leninist thinking informed policing by advocating a close relationship between police and the masses (Jiao 2001a, 161). Although the mass line requires that police seek input from the public, it is said that modern professionalism and managerial techniques have shifted the focus away from the community and toward building a professionalized police force (Fu 2001, 274; Jiao 2001b, 166).

Some commentators argue that traditional community-type policing[32] has been replaced by the Western conception of police practice referred to as "community policing."[33] This claim is closely associated with the migration to China of Western-style professional policing. However, some argue that the Western conception of community policing is simply "old wine in new bottles" because policing in China has always enjoyed the characteristics of community policing in the sense that "social control has always been provided for by the local communities and intimate associates" (Wong 2001, 188; Zhong 2009, 157).

Mass line policing characterizes the police-citizen relationship as the police are fish and the masses are water (Zhong 2009, 158). Accordingly, the "mass" refers to the people, and the concept of the mass line means that public security is not seen as something to be provided only by state agencies but by the whole population (Wong 2001, 197). When the mass line conception is applied to the justice system, the effect is that informal justice, popular justice, and peoples' justice are preferred over formal and legal modes of justice (p. 201). In terms of the police, the mass line meant that "police needed to be on a first-name basis with the people and work alongside the people as one of them. Police needed to do good deeds *(ban hoshi)* for the people and stand ready to sacrifice for them, so that the police would be appreciated and remembered" (Wong 2001, 201).

Mass community organizations in urban areas are mandated by the Chinese Constitution 1982, which requires that *neighborhood committees* set up subcommittees "for peoples' mediation, public security ... in order to manage public affairs and social services ... help maintain public order" (Zhong 2009, 158). In the Chinese model of mass line policing, *work units* (places of employment) are also involved in public order and security.[34] Every medium-sized or larger work unit has a *public security unit* with direct contact to the regular police. Districts and work units may join together in *social order joint protection teams;* in 1997 there were more than two million such teams (p. 159). Gradually, the joint protection teams took on the status of auxiliary police, but abuse of powers by some members led to calls for their abolition (p. 162).

Police Professionalism, Legality, and Policing Structure

With the advent of a socialist market economy starting in 1978, the Chinese police[35] faced a number of critical challenges. How would a traditionally based police system operate in the new relatively open market economy? What changes needed to be made in the roles and functions of the police in the new economic conditions? How would police combat the challenge of economic crime, organized crime, drug trafficking, and other modes of criminality in conditions that would be radically changed from those applying before 1978? Above all, how would the police manage the transition from a once intimate relationship with the public to a less intimate connection? (Wong 2004, 200). Building police professionalism has been seen as one response to these challenges.[36] Other responses have been identified as specialization and adherence to the law (Dutton 2000, 62).

The ideology associated with the notion of police professionalism has superseded traditional forms of community policing in which the police were a "forceful part of the community more than they were law enforcement agents" (Bakken 2005, 2; Fu 2001, 274). This move has included instituting police vehicle patrols to supplement foot patrols and neighborhood policing in the cities (Fu 2001, 273; Jiao 2001b, 167). The old style of policing that relied heavily on the community is now considered to be "static" and inconsistent with a society in which there is constant migration from the rural areas to the cities and which requires a visible, mobile police presence, rendering policing "dynamic" (Fu 2001, 273). According to Allan Jiao (2001b, 169–70), "the traditional emotional cohesion and support between police and the community are barely maintained in some neighborhoods" and "Chinese officers have lost some of the moral authority they used to possess which would allow them to play the role of teachers and leaders in the community." Hualing Fu (2001, 267) agrees that professionalism is a new source of legitimacy for the police congruent with, as he sees it, the declining influence of the CCP. As the political role of the police has declined in importance, priority in policing has shifted toward conventional crime control and modernization (p. 276).

Associated with the new professionalism is the relevance of the law.[37] There is now an emphasis on "socialist legality" signified by new laws such as on criminal procedure and the People's Police Law 1995 (Fu 2001, 268; Trevaskes 2002, 673).[38] Consequently, laws have replaced the CCP directives that formerly legitimized policing (Fu 2001, 276). Police work is now conceptualized as being governed by law, meaning processes and decisions must be made in accordance with laws, that laws must be implemented, and that those who violate laws must be held accountable (Wong 2004, 209). This conception is called *yifa zhijing* (govern police by law) (p. 210).

The People's Police Law 1995 for the first time mandated the policing functions as "(1) safeguarding state security, (2) maintaining public order,[39] (3) protecting the legal rights of citizens, (4) building the police force, (5) improving the quality of the police, and (6) ensuring the legal power of the police for the socialist modernization" (quoted in Dai 2001, 152).

BOX 4.1   Chinese Policing Units

Public security police—the regular patrol/general duties police under the Ministry of Public Security which makes regulations on legal procedures, recruitment, and training standards and directs and coordinates investigations into major or complex criminal cases. There are four special public security police forces, in the areas of railways, transport, civil aviation, and forests (Yue 1997, 116). The public security police investigate crime, direct traffic, administer the household registration system, and participate in mass line policing campaigns (Yue 2008, 17).

State security police—established in 1983 and responsible for protecting state security, including investigating espionage, sabotage, and conspiracies against the state and located under the Ministry of State Security. The National Security Law 1993 sets out their duties and functions (Yue 1997, 121). A state security bureau is established in each province, autonomous region, and municipality (Yue 2008, 21).

Prison police—responsible for those in custody serving sentences of imprisonment under the Ministry of Justice, Bureau of Prison Management; the Prison Law 1995 applies (Yue 1997, 117).

Judicial police in People's Courts—affiliated with the courts and provide security, execute court orders; the Organic Law on the People's Courts 1979 applies (Yue 1997, 121).

Judicial police in people's Procuratorates—affiliated with the prosecutors and conduct searches, serve subpoenas, and provide physical and building security; the Organic Law on the People's Procuratorates applies (Yue 1997, 118, 121).

People's armed police—although not named in the law as a police unit, it was set up in 1983 by converting one million soldiers into police. The armed police conduct border patrols, guard high-ranking officials and foreigners, and guard buildings (Yue 1997, 117). The armed police are under the joint control of the Ministry of Public Security and the Central Military Committee (Yue 2008, 20).

Under the People's Police Law 1995, police are supervised by the Procuratorate and by higher level police organs that can "revoke or correct mistakes found in the punishment and decisions" (Brown 1997, 113). A Chinese characteristic of the law is that police are required to have "education and training in political affairs and ideology" as well as in police work (p. 114).

Organizationally, the Chinese police fit between the centralized and the integrated models of policing because although, in practice, they are under central control, they are accountable to both the center and to local authorities (Yue 1997, 114). The central authority for all policing units is the Ministry of Public Security, under which are four levels of public security bureaus (the patrol or general duties police), namely, provincial, regional, prefectural, and police substations. Police units established at provincial, regional, and prefectural levels are considered to be a component of the local government for that level. Each public security bureau is accountable to the immediately higher level bureau and to the local government. Thus, a provincial public security bureau is responsible to both the Ministry of Public Security and the provincial government (p. 115). A local authority is primarily responsible for the police unit within its area of operations and determines the size of the police unit, funds and equips it, and determines policing priorities.

Policing Strategies

Since the early 1980s, concurrent with the new economic freedoms, China has experienced a significant rise in crime. Despite several "severe strikes against crime" campaigns, crime has not decreased, and police effectiveness measured by the overall clearance rate showed a decline from 71.1 percent in 1980 to 57.1 percent in 1990 (Yue 1997, 113).

The overall approach to crime prevention and control initiated in the early 1980s is termed *comprehensive management of social order* (CMSO). Under this strategy it is believed that efforts to prevent crime must be comprehensive and involve government, the economy, business enterprises, the community, and society in general (Jiao 2001, 168). The aim is to combine punishment with prevention and the "strike hard" campaigns (discussed in "'Strike Hard' Campaigns") constitute the punishment element of CMSO (Zhong 2009, 160). According to Michael Dutton (2000, 63), CMSO represents a revisit to the socialist past because it follows the traditional pre-reform approach of a broad constellation of social forces led by the CCP that stresses crime prevention and social reintegration.[40] For Susan Trevaskes (2010, 4) CMSO represents the state strategy only in relation to minor crime, whereas serious crime has tended to attract the "strike hard" approach.

One significant aspect of crime control strategy has been the emergence of private security following pressure from foreign enterprises and joint ventures, who were concerned that regular policing would not meet their security needs (Zhong 2009, 161). The first such company was set up in 1985. In China, private security does not carry the same meaning as in United States or Europe because the security companies are "wholly owned subsidiaries of the local branches of the Public Security Ministry" (Dutton 2000, 86). By December 2005, there were four million security guards across the country (Zhong 2009, 162). Police have total control over the staffing of private security companies, and all senior positions are filled by senior staff from the local Ministry of Public Security. They now encompass about one third of all urban police work. As a result, security has become commodified (Dutton 2000, 86).

Yue (1997, 130) points out that before the commencement of economic modernization,[41] police had developed very successful policing strategies in the form of the *hukou* system of household registration (see discussion on "Surveillance in China") and through mass line organizations that enabled surveillance of the population. These strategies gave police the capacity "to keep a tight control over the subject population," a capacity that has now diminished greatly as thousands move from rural areas to cities in search of work; the size of this transient population is estimated at fifty to eighty million persons. Today, police are policing a dynamic and mobile society that demands professionalization and alternative methods of policing (p. 131). A sharp contrast to earlier times can be found in the multitude of laws and regulations that have been promulgated so that police conduct their actions according to law and with adequate legislative guidance (p. 133).

"Strike Hard" Campaigns

The *yanda* campaign, known in English as the "stern blows" or "strike hard" campaign was a state-sponsored, nationwide generic campaign against crime that initially ran from 1983 to 1986, and again in 1996 and 2001 to 2003. In addition, in every year since the 1980s, one or more specialized campaigns were also conducted focused on a particular category of crime, such as organized crime[42] (Trevaskes 2010, 2). The objective of the campaign was to reduce the crime rate and reinforce social order through investigating, arresting, trying, and punishing convicted criminals in public fora and through the united efforts of police, prosecutors, and the courts. According to Børge Bakken (2000, 392), "The traditional belief in China is that parading evil—or, rather, bringing evil to justice for all to see—will lead to a decrease in crime." Thus, *yanda* campaigns are motivated by a belief in deterrence that is widely accepted in China and exemplified by officials repeating traditional metaphors such as "Kill one to warn a hundred" (Tanner 2005, 173). The populist nature of the "strike hard" campaigns stands in sharp contrast to the objectives and practice of professionalism, specialization, and adherence to the law as well as the strategy of CMSO (Dutton 2000, 63; Tanner 2005, 184).

According to Trevaskes (2002, 675; 2010, 7), the significance of *yanda* is not so much in terms of crime control but as a demonstration that the Communist Party remains in control notwithstanding the post-Mao reforms. Furthermore, these campaigns express the notion of punitive justice, believed by state officials to be the correct approach to serious crimes to preserve social stability and facilitate continued economic success. Murray Tanner (2005, 172), however, sees the motivation for such campaigns as more pragmatic, that is, as a police response to the low police-to-citizen ratio in China that necessitates the police relying on activism among the masses to maintain public order. As he puts it, in view of increases in crime, police need to convince the masses that police, and not criminals, control "the balance of awe" in society (p. 173).

The model established by the first *yanda* was copied in subsequent campaigns. As a result, the 2001 *yanda* began with a national conference on the state of social order with representatives of police, prosecutors, and courts in attendance. Experts and political figures addressed the conference on the escalating crime rate: it was reported that crimes recorded by police showed an increase of 50 percent over 1999 crime figures, and that over the previous twenty years, Mafia-style gang crime[43] had increased sevenfold (Trevaskes 2002, 677).

The campaign of 2001, as previously, took the form of public arrest and sentencing rallies across the country in a shaming process in venues such as marketplaces, stadiums, community halls, and even at the site of the crime. Attendance by the public varied from only a few to more than one hundred thousand. Sometimes only a few criminals would be displayed and at other times groups would be paraded, usually having been convicted of serious crimes. After a number of speeches, the handcuffed offenders, sometimes wearing placards detailing their names and offenses, would be publicly sentenced and then driven off to be executed or imprisoned (Trevaskes 2002, 679).

The police role dominated the public arrest rally, which became popular in the 1996 *yanda*. It took the form of a line-up of suspects who were put on a stage and shown being publicly arrested by police. The 2001 *yanda* introduced joint arrest and sentencing rallies showing a symbolic link between arrest and punishment (Trevaskes 2002, 680).

The campaign approach achieved only limited success, often producing only a short-term reduction in crime and encouraging the use of extralegal measures such as torture, extensive use of the death penalty, and, within the police, the production of false statistical data in order to meet stipulated targets (Yue 2008, 32). Tensions over policy between the favored police approach of crime prevention and the high-level officials' "strike hard" strategy became apparent during the 2001 campaign (Trevaskes 2010, 102). Attacking crime came at the expense of regular police work, and funds were taken away from routine policing, forensics, and appropriate policing technology to fund the hard strikes (p. 110). By 2003 it seemed that police objections were having an effect, because in that year it was announced by the Central Party Committee's Politico-Legal Committee that "strike hard" campaigns would be "regularized" by being incorporated into ordinary crime activity (p. 118). L. Craig Parker (2013, 132) notes that Chinese government officials claim to have abandoned strike hard campaigns since about 2010.

Police and Administrative Punishments

Police in China have been authorized (sometimes problematically) to impose certain administrative punishments that in most legal systems could only be ordered by courts. Chinese police have always believed they need to possess a degree of flexibility in law enforcement, but some would argue that such flexibility enables arbitrary and even illegal practices to occur (Jiao 2001a, 177). These measures are found in the Box 4.2.

BOX 4.2   Administrative Punishments

Administrative detention—police may impose a warning or a fine, or detain a person for up to 15 days for a violation of the law that does not amount to a crime because the circumstances were minor and the harm not great (Yue 1997, 123). The legal basis for this detention is found in the Security Administration Punishment Regulation 1986, which also provides for punishment for stipulated offenses, including disturbing the public order of public places and spreading disruptive rumors (Brown 1997, 12). There are no guidelines concerning which acts warrant which punishment; consequently, police have complete discretion in both finding that an "offense" was committed and in deciding the appropriate punishment for that act.

Shelter and investigation (Shourong shencha)—created by the police to control the movement of persons in the country and to impose punishments without any court sanction. This measure had no clear legal basis but was commonly used by police against those who failed to register with police under *hukou* requirements. It was said to be authorized by various circulars and notices issued by the Ministry of Public Security. In 1985 the Ministry stated the time limit for detention to be from one to three months. Yue Ma (1997, 123) notes that police used the provision to circumvent the Criminal Procedure Law and the Administration Punishment Regulation and imposed periods of detention far in excess of three months, sometimes for years (p. 124). Foreign criticism, on human rights grounds, of the practice of shelter and investigation in the 1990s added to pressure from Chinese academics and lawyers to abolish the practice (Dutton 2000, 75).

According to Joshua Rosenzweig (2013, 76), at the time of formulating a set of amendments to the Criminal Procedure Law in 2012, an end was announced to this provision. However, many of its elements were absorbed into the draft amendments so that the final draft contained the practice which the police found very useful and were reluctant to give up. Sarah Biddulph (2005, 212) agrees that the shelter and investigation provisions were subsumed into the Code but states it was "ostensibly abolished by amendments to the Criminal Procedure Law in 1996."

Reeducation through labor (Laojiao)—administrative incarceration by police without any judicial process is effected under the *laojiao* system, which began in the early 1950s. Police may send a person to *laojiao* on their own discretion for up to three years. According to the U.S. State Department, in 1997 about 230,000 persons were so held, but in the 1980s the figure was about 400,000 (Belkin 2000, 68; Seymour and Anderson 1998, 21). *Laojiao* should not be confused with *laogai*—the latter is a criminal punishment imposed by a court. Reeducation through labor is intended for those whose conduct falls "between crime and error" (Seymour and Anderson 1998, 19). Police have the power to recommend to a *laojiao* committee that a person undergo *laojiao*. The committee makes the final decision. The person sent to undergo *laojiao* may challenge the committee decision in a court after its imposition, but the process to secure a hearing is so lengthy that the *laojiao* may be completed before the review is heard (Belkin 2000, 69). Reeducation through labor can also be ordered by the courts and by the security departments (Seymour and Anderson 1998, 20).

Laojiao camps are operated by the Ministry of Justice and constructed with bars on windows and gates around the perimeter. According to Ira Belkin (2000, 70),who visited a camp in 2000 that housed about two hundred males, fourteen "students" (as they are called) occupied one room, and there was a library and recreation room and a facility for visiting families where students may stay if they have shown good conduct. Students may write letters and receive telephone calls and may be given a period of release for significant family events. On completion of the period of *laojiao,* an employer must rehire a released student. The labor component of the reeducation is educational and no forced labor is required. Belkin was informed that 60 percent of the students were undergoing *laojiao* for petty theft, fighting, shoplifting, and vandalism. Drug abusers are also sent on the program if they fail to complete a drug abuse program. *Laojiao* as a form of administrative punishment is commonly justified as giving a person one chance to reform after he or she has committed what amounts to a minor offense. *Laojiao* does not generate a criminal record (pp. 71–72).

According to a December 2012 press report,[44] the *People's Daily* in the previous month attacked the *laojiao* system asserting it had become "a tool of retaliation" for local officials. The argument stated that the power to direct this sanction is open to abuse for lack of restraints on its exercise and is often used for corrupt purposes; for example, bribes are paid to officials to reduce sentences, or it is used to satisfy personal grudges against a person. Examples noted in the report

(Continued)

(Continued)

include a migrant worker from Inner Mongolia being ordered to undergo *laojiao* for quarreling with an official in a restaurant, and a mother from Hunan Province who publicly protested the lenient sentence given to men who raped and forced her eleven-year-old daughter into prostitution ordered to undergo eighteen months *laojiao*. Chinese human rights advocates have documented inmates sometimes working twenty-hour days to produce goods such as handbags and cardboard boxes. In addition, in November 2013, state media in China reported that China would reform its system of reeducation through labor as part of an effort to protect human rights. This decision was approved by the CCP Central Committee.[45]

Perspectives on Policing in China

According to Mao Zedong, "The state apparatus, including the army, the police and the courts, is the instrument for the oppression of antagonistic classes, it is violence and not 'benevolence'" (quoted in Dai 2001, 151). Thus, the Marxist-Leninist approach to policing sees police as an instrumentality for serving the ends of the state and the ruling class that governs it. Accordingly, during the early years of the People's Republic of China, the police were engaged in political tasks, and crime control and public order were not priorities (Dai 2001, 152). After 1979 and the advent of Deng Xiaoping, the nature of the task, according to the Chinese Communist Party (CCP), changed to one of building "socialist modernization," and consequent policing reforms were instituted.

According to Yisheng Dai (2001, 155), the commencement of the reform of policing in China can be traced back to the enactment of the 1979 Criminal Law and Criminal Procedure Law, which for the first time established the principle of the rule of law. Before that time, police operated according to the dictates of the CCP. (Chapter 3 discusses the Chinese legal system and legal reforms.)

Fu (2001, 259) takes a different view, seeing the military suppression of the Tiananmen Square student protests in 1989 as having compelled the CCP and the police to examine and assess the role of the police in post-revolutionary China. The CCP perceived the police to have failed to control the students and this uncovered deep-seated fears that their civil disobedience might spread to other cities. As a consequence, the CCP ordered in the military. Fu (p. 260) reports that two "national soul-searching conferences" of police chiefs were called after the military suppression to formulate plans for any such future incidents. Fu sees the

police as initially having the primary task of combating class enemies and investigating counter-revolutionary offenses. Early on, the enemy was constituted by spies, saboteurs, bandits, career criminals, and capitalists hostile to the new regime. Once they had been eliminated, fresh class enemies arose, namely, landlords, wealthy peasants, and rightists (p. 261). The police were tasked to safeguard the new political order and take on these dangerous class enemies utilizing the criminal law. Consequently, a crime was not simply a violation of the criminal law but a challenge to the political order newly established, and a guilty verdict validated the criminal as an enemy of the state (p. 261).

Whereas criminal justice was reserved for class enemies in this new order, the approach to the people was different: conflicts between persons were to be resolved through informal processes by education and persuasion (Fu 2001, 262). In other words, where the people were concerned, as opposed to class enemies, the mass line was the appropriate strategy. Accordingly, the neighborhood police station was responsible for most policing and was pivotal in maintaining social order. Residents' committees mediated disputes in the community under police supervision, and police educated the masses, mobilized the community to support the approved ideology, and reformed deviants. At all times the people remained subordinate to the police. Even during the Cultural Revolution, while the courts and prosecutors were reviled and attacked, the police retained their position of power (Fu 2001, 263). Police powers included rehabilitation through a procedure of preventive detention they designed and administered—the so-called shelter for examination (now abolished in name if not entirely in practice) and the process of reeducation through labor (now under challenge but still in operation).

Fu (2001, 264) points out that organizationally, police do not operate within a tightly controlled hierarchy from the center downward because police in regions, provinces, cities, prefectures, or counties are "semi-independent from each other and Party leadership is exercised through the Party Committee at the regional level." Consequently, local control dominates centralized national command (p. 264). Local chiefs of police are appointed by the local CCP committee and, apart from police salaries, a regional police force is funded entirely out of the local budget, helping to ensure local influence and accountability (p. 265). However, local funding is inadequate, and in the 1990s the police approached the public directly for funding through corporate sponsorships, the imposition of fees and levies, and the collection of fines. Having established the extent of the revenue shortfall, each police officer is given a target to reach through fine collection. Furthermore, police will only investigate commercial and economic crimes when the victim can afford to finance an investigation. Clearly these techniques designed to address revenue shortfalls can involve selective policing and corrupt practices (Fu 2005, 247).

TRANSNATIONAL POLICING AND INTERNATIONAL COOPERATION ON POLICING

International cooperation on policing can be described as police cooperation and as common action between officials and bureaucracies who derive their authority and owe allegiance first and foremost to the state in which they conduct policing (Walker 2008, 119). Hence, the state remains the main reference point in this form of policing. Into this category of cooperation fall issues on which different police forces join forces. Examples of this are bilateral projects of police assistance, usually between developed and developing states; the transfer of new technologies such as new forensic processes; sharing information about wanted criminals; and joint operations (Goldsmith and Sheptycki 2007, 11).

Transnational policing has been explained as "any sort of system or process that involves agents of state control cooperating across national borders" (Westmarland 2010, 188). Bowling and Sheptycki (2012, 3) define it very broadly as "any form of order maintenance, law enforcement,

peacekeeping, crime investigation, intelligence sharing or other form of police work that transcends or traverses national boundaries."[46] INTERPOL is a good example but is fundamentally a forum for the exchange of police messages.[47] Unlike international cooperation in policing, which is just that—police forces cooperating because it serves their national interests to do so—some argue that the notion of transnational policing could include a style of policing that transcends national boundaries and that can develop a worldwide *constabulary ethic*, that is, a set of characteristics describing desirable policing initiatives in transnational contexts (Sheptycki 2007, 31). However, others regard this as extremely problematic in light of the divergences between international policing standards and local standards, especially in developing states, and particularly in the range of approaches to police use of force (Hills 2009, 301). In any event, there may be little difference between the notion of a constabulary ethic and the idea of democratic policing. Some argue that police worldwide share the same norms and values and hence a police subculture operating transnationally exists, or alternatively, that at least specialist transnational police have their own subculture that disseminates "the discourse and practices of security, sometimes using fear to do so, further amplifying insecurity" (Bowling and Sheptycki 2012, 99).

The concept of transnational policing also implies the existence of networks autonomous of the state of origin, or which derive authority or owe allegiance to non-state entities or political communities. The European Union is the foremost example of this mode of policing (Walker 2008, 119). Transnational also suggests an activity that involves more than one country, such as the international response to the events of 9/11, which spread across many jurisdictions as countries joined together to fight terrorism (Westmarland 2010, 195). As a result, it is possible to say that *transnational policing* is likely to be multilateral in scope, whereas *international policing* may be focused more on bilateral cooperation, for example, between the United States and Mexico in the war on drugs.[48]

Policing the border regions in Europe has been identified as a transnational police operation. Often, a rapid understanding of the intentions of police colleagues on the other side of the border is essential, for example, in cases of hot pursuit after a bank robbery in one country where escape involves a border crossing. Hartmut Aden has shown that in the Dutch-German-Belgian border area for example, major practical constraints to everyday cooperation include different laws, different administrations and policing techniques, and different languages in use (2001, 102–3).

The distinction between international cooperation on policing and transnational policing is not well theorized, and different commentators offer examples of one that others believe to be examples of the other. Scholars seem to agree, however, that a key difference is that transnational policing, unlike simple cooperation at the international level, can (and does already) take the form of autonomous policing networks basically floating free of any meaningful state control and that such networks commonly incorporate elements of "high policing" (see "'High' and 'Low' Policing").

The array of policing agencies said to be transcending the nation-state includes EUROPOL, UN Security Police (comprises seconded police who protect UN installations), UN Civil Police Units (CivPol) deployed in UN peacekeeping operations,[49] and INTERPOL (Bowling and Foster 2002, 1006). To this list could be added the U.S. Drug Enforcement Administration (DEA), which operates in a number of states, apparently with few constraints (Brodeur 2010, 27) and the countless liaison officers from various national agencies such as the U.S. Federal Bureau of Investigation (FBI) and the British Serious Organized Crime Agency posted overseas.[50] Some argue broadly that every U.S. law enforcement agency with the capability to operate extraterritorially in a sustained manner "should be regarded as only loosely coupled to the state *qua* state" and that such agencies are in fact independent of the state and act transnationally (Bowling and Sheptycki 2012, 48).

To a great extent, transnational policing is an outcome of efforts to counter transnational criminals. Crimes such as drug trafficking, human trafficking, immigration crime, money laundering, and Internet-related crimes are considered to be transnational and demanding of a transnational policing response. The free movement of capital facilitates many of these crimes, but some argue there is a need to be wary because policing beyond a country's borders may also involve increased surveillance of the population (Weber and Bowling 2004, 195).

Issues in Transnational Policing

Questions such as how policing beyond the state is to be controlled and regulated and by whom, and what actions or preventive activities are legitimate to pursue in support of proper transnational policing objectives have become issues in trying to understand transnational policing (Westmarland 2010, 178). Such questions include the extent to which, in the context of globalization, the entities involved may be acting or may claim authority to act equivalent to that of a state. For example, according to Neil Walker (2008, 123), in the case of the European Union, "the political logic of police co-operation is increasingly that of a distinct political community with autonomous capacity, authority and allegiance." In addition, ethical issues in transnational policing associated with the deployment of intrusive techniques with the potential to undermine rights and freedoms, or to marginalize groups such as asylum seekers, refugees, and other immigrants considered undesirable, have also been highlighted (Bowling and Foster 2002, 1008).

Walker (2008, 122) identifies a set of political factors and a set of professional factors that contribute to the growth of transnational policing in the following:

Political features:

- International crime demands that states cooperate with each other through their police agencies and other justice institutions in order to respond to threats to their internal order and security posed by the planning and conduct of such crime.

- When states act as above, the reasons are largely pragmatic in the case of "normal" crime where states have similar criminal laws but even where the crime is not normal. For example, in the case of terrorism striking at the state itself, the state will be likely to cooperate and override distrust of a transnational approach for reasons of urgency and risk avoidance.

- Police cooperation internationally may provide domestic leverage to secure additional resources and even increased powers.

Professional features:

- Police may find trust and empathy working with colleagues in other states, colleagues who share and confront similar problems in their policing duties.

- Police, given their relative isolation from domestic politics, can more easily respond and adapt to the needs of international policing cooperation on a professional level without having to pay attention to ideological, policy, or political concerns about the acceptability of such cooperation.

In an analysis of the justification or rationale adopted by states for transnational policing, Hartmut Aden (2001, 104–5) contends that from the 1980s, new forms of danger were identified, including opportunities for cross border crime when border controls in Europe were removed, illegal immigration, and organized crime. This list would now be augmented by the various forms of terrorism that have challenged police forces everywhere since the events of 9/11. In regard to organized crime, despite the contested definition of this form of crime internationally, Aden (p. 105) asserts that it "has stayed a favourite argument justifying international police cooperation." He notes that one element in the process of legitimizing transnational policing has been the establishment of various legal frameworks to facilitate its operation, including the Schengen Convention, the Amsterdam Treaty, and the EUROPOL Convention as well as many bilateral treaties (p. 106).

In Europe, the control of, and the accountability for, decision making in transnational policing is largely dominated by police leaders. The European Commission and European Parliament play only a marginal role despite demands for greater democratization by the Parliament. The European Commission, for example, may attend meetings of the EUROPOL board of directors but may not vote (Mattelart 2010, 165). Similarly, most civil society groups concerned with citizen or consumer protection do not formally participate in policing decision making. Economic groups, however, have an interest in transnational policing because of their concern for stable conditions for investment in countries and free international trade. This explains the dominant role of anticorruption and combating organized crime in international police policy making (Aden 2001, 111). The growth of transnational policing in its various forms has drawn attention to issues of accountability and transparency, the human rights implications of this democratic deficit, and the growth of invasive laws and surveillance (Andreas and Nadelmann 2006, 250).

Some claim that the globalization of crime is driving the growth of transnational policing and international cooperation on policing. Globalization has become the "master narrative," but some argue for a more nuanced approach and claim that "political forces" have combined—through state cooperation, interventions by hegemonic states setting the international crime control agenda,[51] and social constructionist acts that have defined new deviances—to become the true drivers of this process (Andreas and Nadelmann 2006, 7). More specifically, it is claimed that transnational policing is being driven by the supposed threat of global crime, by the issue of drugs, and by terrorism (Weber and Bowling 2004, 199). Other scholars also question the "straightforward functional logic" of this claimed nexus between the globalization of crime and international and transnational policing (Bowling and Sheptycki 2012, 1).

History of International and Transnational Policing

We may think of transnational policing as a modern development but in fact contemporary "wars" on drugs and terror are fresh materializations of historical processes and events dating back to the nineteenth century when Britain tried to halt the trade in slaves, when intelligence agencies in Europe used "high policing" methods to locate and catch political activists, and when U.S. military forces attacked pirates and bandits operating off the coast of Africa (Andreas and Nadelmann 2006, vi). These unilateral and bilateral interventions, as well as treaty arrangements for extradition (and nowadays extralegal rendition), are clear examples of states acting internationally and cooperating with each other. They signify that crime control has always had an international dimension (p. 4).

Transnational policing is an outcome of crime control, and crime control is a product of the criminalization of acts such as drug production, once considered licit practices. Crimes are social constructions, and it is argued that the United States, "the world's most ambitious and aggressive policing power" (Andreas and Nadelmann 2006, viii), more than any other state, has constructed crimes, internationalized them, and promoted international policing cooperation to pursue the criminalized. Political, economic,[52] and moralizing[53] influences within the United States have played a role in crime construction, exemplified in the criminalization of drugs,[54] which, it is argued, has played a key role in creating and driving international policing practices (p. viii).

Peter Andreas and Ethan Nadelmann (2006, 105) summarize their argument this way: "The internationalization of crime control is substantially a function of domestic politics producing new criminal statutes, rather than simply a response to proliferating transnational criminal activities." Another view is that transnational policing is being justified by reference to a set of "folk devils" or imaginary fears that operate to ensure funding is maintained for policing beyond the state. This includes international legal frameworks calling for transnational police cooperation such as the UN Convention Against Organized Crime of 2000 (Weber and Bowling 2004, 199).

In the modern period, the earliest attempts at international police cooperation in Europe can be traced to the second half of the nineteenth century when some European states cooperated on issues involving what were regarded as political threats to states by the actions of anarchists, émigrés, and political dissidents[55] (Andreas and Nadelmann 2006, 66). Extradition treaties were also negotiated that strengthened the internationalization of law enforcement (p. 80). The development of criminal investigation units within police forces meant more professionalism in policing; more effective law enforcement, including across borders (p. 61); and sometimes the involvement of the "high police" (see "'High' and 'Low' Policing").

The first nonuniformed unit to investigate crime was the *Brigade de la Sûreté*, established in France in 1812. In England, the process began with the Bow Street Runners, followed by the Detective Department of the Metropolitan Police in 1842 (Andreas and Nadelmann 2006, 78). As a community of criminal investigators gradually developed, they began to share information (e.g., on counterfeiting) on criminals who had crossed borders, and multinational gatherings of police officials began to take place, the first in 1819 and others in 1909, 1912, and 1913 (pp. 81–82, 85).

By 1923, the International Criminal Police Commission (ICPC) had been established in Vienna and supplied a means for police forces to communicate on policing matters beyond individual state boundaries and for police chiefs to foster personal relationships (Andreas and Nadelmann 2006, 91). The successor to the ICPC

was the International Criminal Police Office (ICPO), later to be known as INTERPOL. Again, this provided a mechanism for police cooperation notwithstanding its dubious organizational status under international law. In the case of all these organizations, government involvement was minimal, and to some extent they functioned as "policemen's clubs" where professional and social contacts with colleagues in other states could be fostered (Walker 2008, 124). Although INTERPOL has expanded its membership over the years and taken on more functions, it has never sought to move beyond its status as an international adjunct to police forces worldwide. Indeed "it is no longer the dominant actor on the scene" (p. 125). As INTERPOL membership grew, so did "a powerful transnational police subculture within Europe" (Andreas and Nadelmann 2006, 98).

European Union and EUROPOL

In 1976, after a period of terrorist attacks in Europe (Germany, Ireland, and Spain), the European Community agreed to establish working groups at the Interior Ministry level on internal security issues, naming these arrangements TREVI. In 1985 and 1986, additional working groups were formed for better coordination in fighting organized crime and immigration (Andreas and Nadelmann 2006, 1002). In 1985, police cooperation gained further impetus in Europe with the conclusion of the Schengen Agreement (implemented in 1995 and given treaty force in the 1997 Treaty of Amsterdam) to eliminate border controls within the European Economic Community. During the 1990s, Europe's internationalization of crime control focused on continued police cooperation and particularly on cross border operations but also on extending EU policing priorities and practices especially to states wanting to join the European Union who were required to adopt European policing standards (pp. 175, 179). The integration of European states and the dismantling of border controls provided significant justification for European police forces to begin to focus more closely on collaboration and cooperation, including the notion of "pooling sovereignty" (p. 179).

The EUROPOL Convention was signed in 1995, and EUROPOL commenced operations in 1999 (Walker 2008, 128). The initial broad remit of EUROPOL covering all crimes with an "organized criminal structure" was later broadened to include operational cooperation between agencies such as police and customs and to include the capacity to undertake new functions such as establishing joint operational teams to support national investigations; assuming the power to ask national agencies to conduct and coordinate specific investigations; developing expertise that can be put at disposal of states for investigating organized crime; and promoting liaison between prosecutors and investigators working on organized crime issues (Walker 2008, 128–29). EUROPOL's mandate now includes illegal migration, cross border vehicle theft, human trafficking, nuclear smuggling, counterfeiting, and terrorism.

EUROPOL is administered by a directorate comprising a director and three deputies appointed by the EU Council of Ministers for Justice and Home Affairs. The budget of EUROPOL is approved by the EU Council, which also submits an annual report of EUROPOL's activities to the European Parliament. Each EU nation designates a police agency to function as its EUROPOL National Unit and as the contact point with EUROPOL. Directly coordinating the activities of the various National Units gives EUROPOL a significant degree of autonomy as a bureaucratic structure (Deflem and McDonough 2010, 142–43).

The EUROPOL Computer System maintains a huge database for information on criminal suspects and stolen goods. Although EUROPOL is a supranational organization, there remain impediments to, for example, giving EUROPOL arrest powers as a supranational police agency in light of the differing legal regimes and laws with the European Union (Andeas and Nadelmann 2006, 187). As a result, EUROPOL remains in some way short of becoming the FBI of the European Union.

"High" and "Low" Policing

"High policing" refers to the gathering and sharing of information by and among police forces. High policing is also conducted by the so-called intelligence community, which includes the FBI, the Central Intelligence Agency (CIA), the British MI5 and MI6, and the French Directorate of Territorial Security (DST; Brodeur 2010, 224).[56] There are three major characteristics associated with high policing:

- High policing is not concerned with actual criminal prosecutions but with the collection of political intelligence (Andreas and Nadelmann 2006, 62; Brodeur 2010, 226). This is not a new development; intelligence exchange began in the nineteenth century in Europe when undercover police tracked anarchists and political figures considered to pose a danger to a state (Andreas and Nadelmann 2006, 67).

- High police are more likely to act extralegally, for example, to conduct illegal surveillance using electronic means, conduct illegal break-ins, intercept mail, and employ torture to get information. These methods are typically employed in a number of South American states and were used in South Africa under the apartheid regime (Andreas and Nadelmann 2006, 63).[57]

- High policing methods are likely to be less straightforward, for example, using undercover agents and trickery and manipulation.[58] Human sources and undercover agents are the hallmark of high policing (Brodeur 2010, 229).

"Low policing" refers to the regular process of criminal investigation and prosecution and the overall task of protecting society. This contrasts with high policing's mission of protecting political institutions and the constitutional structure of society (Brodeur 2010, 226). High policing functions and activities are commonly separated from low policing functions by being located within different branches or units within a police force. Sometimes high policing operations are conducted by an entirely separate force, such as an internal security service. Tensions can develop between high and low policing units because in practice the extraterritorial aspects can come within the jurisdiction of both high and low units (Andreas and Nadelmann 2006, 64). The gap between high and low policing in terms of operational procedures was noted by the U.S. 9/11 Commission (Brodeur 2010, 235). Sharing information with low policing agencies is not operationally favored by high policing agencies, who fear their sources and methods will be revealed in a criminal case (p. 236). Some scholars believe transnational policing will tend to favor the intrusive and coercive side of high policing (Weber and Bowling 2004, 199).

The aftermath of the events of 9/11 included an enhanced focus on terrorism within both the United States and Europe and to a much broader use of surveillance technologies such as biometrics to track cross border movement. The Schengen Information System II has the capacity to store both image and digital and biometric data and responds almost instantly to law enforcement information requests (Andreas and Nadelmann 2006, 213). U.S. and EU cooperation in law enforcement after 9/11 included an agreement allowing U.S. agencies access to EUROPOL's computer database, the exchange of liaison officers between the FBI and EUROPOL, and a treaty between the United States and the European Union on extradition and mutual legal assistance (p. 218). Most notorious was U.S. insistence on screening passengers to the United States before departure—part of a process of shifting immigration controls into gateways away from the United States and passing responsibility to airlines for compliance (p. 219).

This brief analysis of international cooperation on policing and transnational policing has highlighted the concerns associated with the latter. Scholars of policing agree that forms of global policing that have already detached or may become detached from national state control should not be regarded as unproblematic but as in need of critical scrutiny so that appropriate checks and balances and levels of accountability are exercised over their plans and operations. Associated with these forms of global policing is the issue of police surveillance and the growth of the so-called surveillance society discussed in the following section.

POLICING THROUGH GLOBAL SURVEILLANCE AND THE MANAGEMENT OF RISK

We have seen how high policing operations can include both licit and illicit methods of intelligence collection, and we have discussed briefly the problematic nature of the association between transnational policing and surveillance activities by policing agencies. The topic of police surveillance has attracted a considerable scholarship over the past ten years or so as researchers attempt to understand and explain how such surveillance impacts a society. Police surveillance has been linked to the events of 9/11 and its aftermath as well as the fight against international crime generally. Surveillance has now become globalized through flows of surveillance data; for example, purchasing an airline ticket creates a data flow of personal details across spaces (Lyon 2001, 9).

The degree of surveillance exercised by a state over its population and beyond depends on the available resources of that state and its political will (Zureik and Salter 2005, 5). Surveillance "contributes to the very ordering of society" and "is the means whereby knowledge is produced for administering populations in relation to risk" (Lyon 2001, 6). Surveillance is a mode of practice that, when applied to a society, has the capacity to divide, classify, and enable choices and ultimately to exercise a form of control or act as a constraint (p. 4). Questions about the nature and purpose of surveillance lead to more questions about what flows from the act or acts of surveillance.

BOX 4.3   Surveillance of Muslims Post 9/11

Post 9/11, apparent police profiling or targeting of Muslims where there existed no evidence of any suspected criminal conduct was challenged through court proceedings in New Jersey. There, police officers working undercover were sent into cafes, bars, and bookstores in neighborhoods with a large number of Muslim residents. In addition, the New York City Police Department (NYPD) closely monitored the Muslim Students Association at Rutgers University and sent "mosque crawlers" into every mosque within a 250-mile radius of New York City to secure informants and monitor conversations and religious addresses to those attending the mosques.[59]

In another instance, in the United Kingdom in the city of Birmingham, the media exposed the existence of a network of surveillance cameras that were being utilized by police to indiscriminately monitor local Muslims. The project was designed to monitor any individuals entering and leaving a predominantly Muslim suburb. The data collected were then uploaded to regional and national law enforcement databases (Rushin 2011, 230).

According to David Lyon (2001, 5; 2004, 137), the concept of "risk" has contributed to an expansion of surveillance in that surveillance is increasingly tied to the mediation of risk in what has been called the "risk society." Risk[60] and its management has become a major preoccupation of governance, especially in the sense of containing behavior perceived to be threatening. In terms of policing, Richard Ericson and Kevin Haggerty (1997, 18) argue that "in risk society the traditional police focus on deviance, control and order is displaced in favour of a focus on risk, surveillance and security." In more general terms, since the 1970s, "a discourse of risk has come to permeate global concerns for security and safety" (Drake and Muncie 2010, 107).

BOX 4.4   Global Surveillance and Its Consequences

Returning from a family vacation in September 2002, Maher Arar, a Canadian citizen born in Syria who worked in Ottawa as a communications engineer, was detained by U.S. officials on a stopover in New York. It was alleged that he had links to Al Qaeda. Mr. Arar was deported to Syria (he had dual Syrian and Canadian citizenship). In an interview, the director of Homeland Security stated, "There was sufficient information within the international intelligence community about this individual that we felt warranted his deportation. . . . The decision was made, based on that information available through the global international intelligence community." In Syria Mr. Arar was imprisoned for one year and tortured. Apparently information collected in Canada by Canadian law enforcement about Mr. Arar—who was never charged with any criminal conduct—was entered into a database referred to as the security criminal intelligence system (SCIS) to which the FBI was given access.

SOURCE: Lewis 2005, 97–98.

In the modern day, in seeking security, all institutions attempt to minimize risk by collecting and assessing all factors relevant to the perceived risk, including through surveillance and examination of resulting data flows (Lyon 2001, 7). Consequently, for example, the war on terror has demonstrated "an insatiable quest for knowledge: profiling populations, surveillance, intelligence" (Aradau and Van Munster 2007, 91). Claudia Aradau and Rens Van Munster argue that post 9/11 there has emerged a "precautionary element" ("better to be safe than sorry") that has redefined risk to require that potential catastrophes be avoided at all costs (p. 91). As a driver of activities such as antiterrorist surveillance then, the precautionary approach to risk management is described this way:

> Any level of risk is now considered unacceptable; risk must be avoided at all costs. Risk minimization and other forms of risk management (such as "contingency planning") derive from the joint realization that the catastrophe will happen. The worst case scenario and its irreversible damages logically lead to a politics of zero risk. (Aradau and Van Munster 2007, 103)

Where previously a risk was deemed acceptable if it was reparable or repaired, this is no longer true. As a consequence, actions such as drone strikes, the continued existence of Guantanamo Bay prison, and the practice of extraordinary rendition are regarded as appropriate methods of governance. Surveillance seeks to incorporate the entire population because precautionary risk requires that there be no underestimation of potential threats. This means deploying multiple technologies of surveillance targeted at everyone because, aside from religious and ethnic affiliations, how otherwise can a terrorist become known to be such? (Aradau and Van Munster 2007, 104). While increasingly precautionary risk renders surveillance quite arbitrary in its scope, technologies of surveillance multiply in the face of uncertainty.[61] When the limits of surveillance are reached, naming a person as a suspected terrorist (and therefore perhaps subject to a drone strike) becomes an administrative rather than a judicial decision, and the "managers of unease" (p. 104) must act with alacrity based on their assessment of "dangerous." There is no place for due process or similar legal protections ordinarily required when surveillance was conducted to collect evidence for a criminal prosecution (p. 107).

Contemporary police transnational computer networks, especially those in Europe, have been dubbed the "police archipelago" (Lyon 2001, 97). Data not only track what happens within and between states but are shared by a broad range of justice-related agencies, such as police, customs, immigration, consulates, and private surveillance organizations, enabling them to track persons who have interacted with these agencies and with others that require knowledge of risks. As a result, there has emerged an increasingly routine and systematic focus on the lives of individuals with the aim of managing or influencing those lives. Surveillance includes not only the products of direct gazing on persons[62] but also the acquisition of personal data, including "biographical, biometric or transactional data on individuals harvested from personal communications, electronic transactions, identifiers, records or other documents" (Bloss 2007, 209). Collectively, this growth in surveillance has been referred to as the "surveillant assemblage" (Haggerty and Ericson 2000, 606) and is noted as being so broad in its scope as to lack "discernible boundaries" (p. 609).[63]

Lyon (2004, 144–46) has argued that increasingly, surveillance has become globalized as an outcome of events such as crime campaigns (e.g., the war on drugs), the increased flow of persons across boundaries, and the extraordinary events of 9/11.[64] Certain trends in surveillance have emerged in response to 9/11, namely, the privatization of policing and the militarization of police. It is now common for private policing corporations to supplement public policing. Militarized police now operate like "soft" armed forces units in places where new forms of surveillance are perceived to be necessary, namely, borders, airports, and significant urban areas. Generally, as Lyon (2003, 18) notes, 9/11 had the effect of more fully exploiting existing surveillance capacities and it "brought surveillance to the surface." According to Mattelart (2010, 198), surveillance is now so pervasive that "a new mode of governing society by tracking is now emerging, in which everyone who circulates is liable to be under surveillance. … Control societies are now coupled with suspicion societies."

A survey of forty-seven countries conducted in 2007 by the U.K. nongovernmental organization Privacy International found that surveillance had increased and privacy safeguards had declined compared with the previous year. Eight countries were rated as "endemic surveillance societies"; among these, China and Russia scored lowest. The United Kingdom and the United States were also included in the eight (Coleman 2010, 147). The following descriptions of domestic surveillance systems in Russia and China remind us that comprehensive surveillance programs have operated in some states over many years without sophisticated technology.

BOX 4.5   Surveillance in Soviet Russia and the Russian Federation

Shelley (1996, xv) states that "the heart of police power in the USSR lay in the passport and registration system administered by the militia—making the regular police a more tangible presence in the lives of most Soviet citizens than the KGB. Police controls affected every aspect of Soviet citizens' daily lives: individuals could not move, take a vacation, travel abroad, register their cars or obtain a driver's license without authorization from the police."

In the Soviet Union the issue of internal passports to citizens began in 1932 (Beck and Robertson 2009, 58). A citizen could not be issued an internal passport until age 16 years, and the permanent residence stated in the passport was the only permitted place of residence. Information about time spent in a labor camp or failure to pay child support could be included. Citizens were required to carry their passport at all times and to produce it on the request of a militia officer (Shelley 1996, 131). Other information included in the internal passport included place of birth, nationality, marital status, names of children, record of military service, place of work, and the residence stamp (propiska; Dutton 1992, 211). Any change in a person's permanent residence required the approval of the militia passport division and the issue of a residence permit, but it was not possible to relocate to cities that were designated as closed to new residents. Thus, through this mechanism, the growth of major cities was managed (e.g., Moscow or Kiev; Shelley 1996, 132).

It was not until the Gorbachev regime that a citizen had any recourse if denied a residence permit. The creation of a right of appeal against a refusal was heralded as a genuine act of *perestroika* (Shelley 1996, 133). The passport system was sometimes reconfigured to meet the needs of *perestroika:* when some price controls were lifted, a requirement that passports be shown on entering a food store, proving Moscow residence, prevented a run on food stores (p. 135). Although generally agreed as being in violation of the constitution, the *propiska* system continues to be used in the larger cities and is still administered by the militia, who regularly demand bribes from those who do not have one (Beck and Robertson 2009, 58).

BOX 4.6   Surveillance in China

The Chinese *hukou* system of household registration is a response to the challenge presented by the potential movement of the rural population to the cities. Generally, in line with the requirements of socialist planning, the potential of the masses was to be regulated and controlled according to the needs of the state. The Chinese system of household registration, unlike the Soviet model of individual passports, is based on households and not on the individual (Dutton 1992, 203). Originally the *hukou* was to cover only those living in the cities, but by 1958 the National People's Congress had resolved that it cover both urban and rural households (p. 207). The task of household registration is implemented by the police department through the household registration police (p. 209). According to the regulations, items to be listed in the household registration form include the household head, marriage, divorce, internal immigration and emigration, births and deaths, occupation, and work unit (p. 211). Registration is crucial because without it one cannot enter school, obtain employment, vote in elections, marry, or serve in the armed forces. The registration officer uses this information to make risk determinations in respect of those residing in the household (Zhong 2009, 159).

Before the recent economic reforms, a person's status was basically determined to be agricultural or nonagricultural. The latter gave an entitlement to state-provided housing, employment, a grain ration, education, access to medical care, and other welfare benefits. In contrast, the agricultural population was expected to be self-sufficient and received few state benefits. A transfer from agricultural to nonagricultural status was highly regulated. In addition, all persons were required to register in only one place of permanent residence (Chan and Buckingham 2008, 588).

Nowadays there are broadly two kinds of migration: one that involves a formal transfer of residency and one with no formal *hukou* change and therefore no right of permanent residency in the destination (Chan and Buckingham 2008, 590). The non-*hukou* residents are considered to be transients. Over the past twenty-five years, the majority of the floating, transient population are persons holding agricultural *hukou* who move into the cities (p. 590). The latest initiative concerning this complex system involves cities and towns issuing local *hukou* based on entry conditions. This is normally granted only to the wealthy or the highly educated or to those persons whose immediate family are already city residents (p. 595).

Dutton suggests that the underlying rationale that guided internal migration was based on four principles: (1) rural to urban movement must be strictly controlled; (2) movement from towns to cities, from small cities to bigger cities, and from rural areas to suburbs must be properly regulated and limited; (3) movement between places having a similar size need not be regulated or controlled; (4) movement from large to medium, or from medium to small urban places, or from urban to rural locations was to be encouraged (Dutton 1992, 213).

(Continued)

(Continued)

The challenge to *hukou* has come from the market economy model, which encourages workers to move freely and reside anywhere there are work opportunities. Nowadays, a personal identification system supplements the *hukou,* and rural dwellers are permitted to move into the cities if they have a temporary residence permit (Dai 2001, 154). According to Kam Wing Chan and Will Buckingham (2008, 583), "China's long-standing policy of 'incomplete urbanization,' as practised in the reform era, allows peasants to move to the city but denies them permanent residency rights and many of the associated social benefits." The *hukou* system now determines entitlement to forms of public welfare and to urban services (2008, 587). In 2005 the migrant or floating population was estimated at 150 million persons (Zhong 2009, 163).

In addition to the *hukou* system, a resident identification card system was established in 1986, intended to supplement the *hukou.* All residents over the age of 16 are required to carry an identification card, and police are empowered to demand it be produced for inspection (Yue 2008, 33–34).

According to Elia Zureik and Mark Salter (2005, 5), "The new dynamics of global policing and surveillance should be a central concern of modern policy makers and policy studies." In 1990, the French philosopher Gilles Deleuze wrote, "We're moving toward control societies that no longer operate by confining people but through continuous control and instant communication" (quoted in Mattelart 2010, 183). Questions such as who is monitored and surveilled, for what reasons, and with what effects and through what means are linked to issues of privacy and to the overall efficacy of surveillance and its claims to improve public safety and security. At the highest level of analysis, as Didier Bigo (2012, 280) notes, "the study of surveillance techniques and their impact on privacy and other key issues sheds light on the way citizens in general and specific population groups are governed."

Notes

1. In its original meaning, *policing* referred to general governance through the executive branch of government. Samuel Johnson's 1756 *Dictionary of the English Language* defined *police* as "the regulation and government of a city or country so far as regards the inhabitants." He adds that the word was borrowed from the French.

2. Bayley (1985, 95), citing Radzinowicz (1957), points out that the police force created in England in 1829 was a uniformed force that would stand out in a crowd and would therefore be more likely to deter violence in such situations. This fact supports the revisionist analysis that controlling the mob and preventing collective violence was the purpose of establishing the Metropolitan Police Force rather than simply dealing with increases in the number of committals for property crime—the justification offered by Sir Robert Peel for the new force (p. 94). Jean-Paul Brodeur (2010, 57) points out that the monarchs of Europe did not fear individual acts of crime but rather collective action such as riots, protests, and violence in general.

3. For example, Switzerland has decentralized canton-based police forces, and Iceland is district based; in Germany, police operate in each *Lander,* but Sweden and Ireland have centralized forces (Mawby 2008, 22).

4. In the United States, police bureaucracy was initially politicized through patronage, but by the beginning of the twentieth century, reforms had established a truly professionalized bureaucracy that was politically neutral and constituted an authentic police service (Reiss 1992, 70). Nevertheless, today, a police chief who is elected may be subjected to external pressure from the local administration (p. 71).

5. Albert Reiss (1992, 63) reports, for example, that of the 281 city police departments in North Carolina, 56 percent have fewer than ten sworn police officers. According to Reiss, any pressure to consolidate small police forces into larger units would be resisted because "any conception of a national system of law enforcement is anathema to the American citizenry" (p. 64). Reiss argues that police forces themselves resist consolidation, that local control of police is a firmly entrenched tradition, and new law enforcement bodies are continually created as populations grow beyond existing law enforcement boundaries (pp. 66–67).

6. In South America, order maintenance and public security policing is called "ostensive policing" (Reames 2008b, 101).

7. In 2007, the U.S. Bureau of Justice Statistics reported there were 12,766 local police agencies, 3,067

sheriff's departments, and 1,481 special jurisdiction agencies (Mastrofski and Willis 2010, 58).

8. Under the Brazilian Constitution, the army is also charged with order maintenance and guaranteeing internal security resulting in confusion over functions between it and the *policía militar*. To complicate matters further, the police are constitutionally ultimately responsible to the army, but on a day-to-day basis they are responsible to the state governors (Reames 2008a, 70).

9. A cantonment refers to a permanent military camp within a town or city established during the British colonial period in India.

10. David Arnold (1986, 131) suggests that in India, crime and rebellion were virtually synonymous in the eyes of the colonial administration and formed part of a "continuum of violence and dissent, appropriation and defiance." Thus, criminality carried an almost political connotation.

11. Richard Hawkins (1991, 24, 28) sees the RIC as an example of a gendarmerie along the lines of the continental model and notes that the "semi-military" nature of the RIC clearly distinguished it from the police of Great Britain.

12. The first attempt to introduce a police force in India along RIC lines occurred in 1843 in Sind. The model there separated the constabulary from the military. In Sind, even the constabulary carried weapons, and Sind was considered a worthy example of how to Indianize the RIC model (Arnold 1986, 27).

13. In Nyasaland, Blantyre (the main town) was organized from the beginning as a European enclave, and Africans who were not domestic servants or railway workers were not allowed to reside within town boundaries. In addition, local bylaws prohibited African workers from using township roads without a pass from an employer between 9 p.m. and 5 a.m. (McCracken 1986, 133).

14. Arnold (1986, 153) states that labor legislation "was a common feature of control over non-white workers in many British-ruled territories in the nineteenth and early twentieth centuries."

15. In Madras, India, it was a criminal offense for a worker to leave his place of work before the end of his contract. Insubordination and creating a disturbance on the property of the employer were also crimes. All crimes were punishable by imprisonment (Arnold 1986, 154).

16. The French preferred direct rule where Frenchmen filled all important government positions and, according to Whittlesey (1937, 367, 369), "African life is given no official recognition" and "jobs requiring only moderate technical proficiency are still performed by Europeans, including selling stamps at the post office." He notes that in relation to law enforcement, the French colonial police may have had about the same numbers as the British in their colonies, but "a large army cantonment is a feature of every important town in A.O.F." (Afrique Occidentale Française;

p. 370). The French regarded their colonies as part of France, and it was possible for the indigenous peoples to acquire French citizenship.

17. Collecting taxes from Africans was a major part of police work in Nyasaland (now Malawi). John McCracken (1986, 132) reports that in the 1920s, police collecting hut tax often kept women hostage at the district headquarters until their husbands had paid the tax. Some tax defaulters had their houses burned down, but the most common sanction was arrest and forcible public works labor.

18. D. Anderson (1991, 194) reports that in 1937, in Kenya, "more than 6000 Africans were prosecuted for being resident in townships without permission and for failing to produce a pass; 4772 for failing to pay their hut and poll tax; nearly 4000 for offenses against the Native Registration Ordinance; … [and] 1245 for vagrancy." After 1945, numerous bylaws and regulations regulated almost every aspect of African life (p. 198).

19. In 1917, the British secretary of state for India, attempting to head off Indian nationalist agitation, promised that Indians would become involved in all branches of the administration as part of the realization of responsible government for India. It was recognized that this commitment had to be honored (Arnold 1986, 83).

20. According to Arnold (1986, 190), the Special Branch in Madras, India, reported on political leaders, intercepted correspondence, kept dossiers on labor organizers (in 1933, fifty-nine labor leaders were being watched), monitored arrivals into the city, and contacted students returning from study overseas.

21. Justin Willis (1991, 222) notes that in Kenya in 1926, the police commissioner reported that policemen were being taught "bayonet fighting on lines adapted from the latest methods employed by the British army."

22. It was not until thirty years after Independence that a commission was appointed to review the operations of the Indian police. The commission's report was never implemented (Arnold 1986, 227).

23. Some commentators criticize police reform projects for being entirely directed at benefiting the interests of the donor state rather than the recipient state's policing agencies. This view is taken by Martha Huggins in her discussion of police reform projects promoted by the United States in South America. According to Martha Huggins, U.S. police training "has been used almost exclusively to promote specific U.S. national security political interests and objectives" (Huggins 1998, 7). Other criticisms relate to the uncritical importation of overseas policing models such as community policing schemes like neighborhood watch, a scheme rejected by the public in Serbia as being too resonant with schemes of the communist past when they were spied on by police and faced the fear of being spied on by their neighbors (Stojanovic and Downes 2009, 89).

24. A regional conference on policing in Southeast Asia, organized by Amnesty International and held

in Jakarta November 19–20, 2013, called for effective measures of accountability for police abuse in Indonesia, Malaysia, Philippines, Thailand, and Timor-Leste. The conference agreed that human rights should be at the center of police reform. (See Amnesty International, "Indonesia: Regional Conference on Policing in Southeast Asia Calls for Human Rights-Based Policing," November 20, 2013, https://www.amnesty.org/en/documents/ASA21/037/2013/en/.)

25. Recruitment into the militia was decided by the central bureaucracy in Moscow, and no republic controlled hiring decisions. In addition, whereas the head of the Ministry of Internal Affairs (MVD) in each republic was a member of the dominant ethnic group in that republic, his or her deputy was always a Russian. Through such means, Moscow controlled and commanded the militia in the republics as well as in Russia itself (Shelley 1996, 87).

26. The MVD was the principal organ of state control during the Soviet period and housed the militia, but the militia always remained responsible to the Communist Party (Shelley 1996, 82).

27. Shelley (1996, 85) states that by 1988 the MVD employed 3.5 million persons, including about 700,000 militia who policed a population of 280 million. Militia personnel were not distributed evenly; thus, for example, in 1987 Moscow had 56,000 police compared with 28,000 for New York with Moscow being only a slightly larger city. With only 3 percent of the population, Moscow had 8 percent of the nation's police.

28. The law contains restrictions on police use of force, including prohibitions on using force with women who appear to be pregnant, hitting persons in specified places (such as the genitals or heart), and using force to stop unlawful assemblies that are of a nonviolent nature and pose no threat to public order. Given that police misconduct is a "serious problem" in Russia, it remains to be seen whether legislative rules will be transformed into actual police practice (Robertson 2012, 166). Police salaries were also doubled in 2003, again as an anti-bribery measure, but without any obvious subsequent impact on police corruption (2012, 171).

29. In April 2009, a drunken police chief fired shots in a Moscow supermarket, killing two people and wounding seven. This incident symbolized, for many, the lawlessness of the militia (Taylor 2013, 8; Zernova 2012, 474).

30. Shelley (1996, 63) emphasizes that during the entire Soviet period from 1917 to 1999, the militia retained a quasi-military, centralized structure (a legacy of Tsarist times), the continental police tradition, and the chaos of the early years of communism.

31. As an instance of the degree of control the militia exercised over citizens' daily life, Shelley notes that every year the militia issued administrative sanctions to about one-quarter of the adult population (Shelley 1996, 128).

32. Kam Wong (2001, 198) states that consistent with Confucian ideals and values, in Chinese traditional social regulation, "indigenous groups are made primarily responsible for day-to-day social control and crime prevention."

33. There are countless definitions and explanations of community policing; see, for example, Peter Manning (1986, 486–89), where he suggests that it can be explained as "ordering or regulating an interacting group of persons within a governmentally defined territory and thus is not a unique function, objective, characteristic, or defining feature of policing. In a sense, all policing is community policing."

34. Dutton (2000, 84) disagrees with Lena Zhong, asserting that whereas once the work units had been central elements in community policing, they now focus on production, industrial espionage, and internal work unit affairs and have little to do with the formal police force. Previously they had "fed directly into police work" by such actions as compiling dossiers on dangerous persons, doing surveillance, investigating suspects and interrogating them, and opening cases for the police. Enterprises now establish their own security forces, who often wear police uniforms but are not part of the police force. Thus, mass line–based enterprise policing through work units has been rendered problematic (p. 85).

35. In China, the police are termed *gongan* (public security) and, more recently, *jingcha* (police; Wong 2004, 211). According to Jiao (2001, 163), in 1999 there were 1.57 million police in China.

36. In January 2015, it was reported that the CCP had ordered an end to "secretive performance goals that set minimum arrest and conviction rates for the police, prosecutors and the courts" and which had exacerbated pressures to render guilty verdicts. According to the state-run news agency, "There has been a stress on confessions, giving less weight to evidence, and even the use of torture to secure confessions" (Chris Buckley, "China Aims to Abolish Goals for Arrests and Convictions," January 21, 2015, http://www.nytimes.com/2015/01/22/world/asia/china-said-to-be-doing-away-with-goals-for-arrests-and-convictions.html).

37. Dutton (2000, 66), points out that under Mao, China was ruled by general published regulations, specific CCP edicts and directives, and *People's Daily* editorials and commentaries.

38. Between 1979 and 1991 alone, over 50 percent of China's laws governing public security were enacted (Dutton 2000, 67).

39. Wong (2001, 207) states that all types of social disorder, including civil uprisings, and crime are described by one word in Chinese: *luan* (chaos). Disorder is condemned in China because a disorderly person reflects poor family discipline and therefore poor morality; a disorderly community reflects poor administration and governance; and, historically, a

disorderly state presented a challenge to the legitimacy of the emperor.

40. Dutton (2000, 64), in his analysis of the return to mass line policing, states that police employed financial incentives to bring back the mass line, rather than turning to a strategy of political mobilization. Thus, wages paid to mass line activists were increased substantially (p. 80). Monetary incentives began to be employed throughout the policing system through the issue of contracts, for example, to police informants who began to replace activists as sources of information about crime. Dutton therefore sees a convergence between the economic reforms and the monetization of policing. By June 1981, all police stations in the five main cities were ordered to implement a system that linked police performance to financial rewards (p. 75).

41. In December 1978, the third plenary session of the Eleventh Central Committee of the Communist Party of China under the leadership of Deng Xiaoping endorsed modernization by way of economic reform and the opening of markets (Wong 2004, 199).

42. For example, a "People's War on Drugs" specialized campaign ran from 2005 to 2007 and a specialized war on organized crime from 2006 to 2007. Other targets have been prostitution, human trafficking, gambling, robbery on highways, and itinerant criminals (Trevaskes 2010, 18). It was thought that specialized campaigns would overcome the issue of adequate funding for general police work and that combining criminal justice system resources would control the rise in crime (p. 30).

43. Six principal categories of Mafia-style gang activities have been identified within organized crime in China: violent acts of terrorism, including murder and robbery; kidnapping; protection rackets; criminal acts, such as obtaining stolen goods; hiring "hitmen"; and smuggling rackets associated with gangs outside the country (Trevaskes 2002, 688).

44. See Andrew Jacobs, "Opposition to Labor Camps Widens in China," *New York Times,* December 14, 2012, http://www.nytimes.com/2012/12/15/world/asia/opposition-to-labor-camps-widens-in-china.html.

45. See "China to Abolish Reeducation through Labor," Xinhua News Agency, November 15, 2013, http://news.xinhuanet.com/english/china/2013-11/15/c_132891921.htm.

46. *Global Policing,* the title of Ben Bowling and J. W. E. Sheptycki's text, refers to "the capacity to use coercive and surveillant powers around the world in ways that pass right through national boundaries unaffected by them" (2012, 8). It is not clear how this differs from international and transnational policing, which also denotes these powers.

47. Interpol is not an association of states because its membership is constituted by police forces and it is a supranational association (Bowling and Sheptycki 2012, 54).

48. In an instance of police cooperation between the United States and Italy, it was reported in the media in February 2014 that after a two-year investigation conducted by police in both countries, a series of arrests had been made in connection with the trafficking of drugs and weapons involving the Gambino crime family of New York and the Italian Mafia. It was reported that FBI agents and Italian police had worked undercover on the joint operation. (See Lizzy Davies and Ed Pilkington, "Police Break Atlantic Network of US and Italian Crime Families," *Guardian*, February 11, 2014, http://www.theguardian.com/world/2014/feb/11/police-arrest-crime-network-gambino-ndragheta.)

49. In 2010 the UN policing capacity had grown to more than 17,500 officers from 98 states deployed in peacekeeping operations (Bowling and Sheptycki 2012, 4).

50. In 2010 the UK Serious Organized Crime Agency had 140 liaison officers posted overseas. The Royal Canadian Mounted Police posted 35 Mounties in 25 locations outside Canada, and the Australian Federal Police had 80 liaison officers in 27 states in 2009 (Bowling and Sheptycki 2012, 6).

51. Recent successful U.S. efforts in gaining access to offshore financial havens and bank accounts in countries such as Switzerland attest to the power of U.S. pressure in pursuing alleged money laundering operations. As Michael Levi (2002, 181) puts it, in social constructionist terms, "what was formerly a genteel sovereign right of any nation to ensure 'customer confidentiality' has become redefined pejoratively as unacceptable 'bank secrecy' that facilitates the drug trade."

52. Britain's decision to abolish the slave trade was influenced by economic arguments that slavery was a highly inefficient system (Andreas and Nadelmann 2006, 28).

53. Moralizing influences can include "religious beliefs, humanitarian sentiments, faith in universalism, paternalism, fear, prejudice, and the compulsion to proselytize" (Andreas and Nadelmann 2006, 13). See also Chapter 11 for an instance of moralizing that produced global norms and international cooperation as well as U.S. unilateralism in the form of domestic legislation on this topic.

54. It is worth noting that morphine and heroin were initially greeted as huge advances in the medical treatment of pain and that both drugs, along with cocaine, were commonly added to restorative and curative tonics to improve health. The association of these drugs with fear of new immigrants and of marijuana with Mexican immigration played a significant role in their prohibition (Andreas and Nadelmann 2006, 39–41).

55. A good example of a police agency charged with surveillance and intelligence collection about its country's émigrés is the Tsarist political police agency, the Okhrana, created in 1881 after the assassination of Tsar Alexander II (Andreas and Nadelmann 2006, 68).

56. There is insufficient space here for discussion of the now widely appreciated significance of private

policing as an element of the entire policing network, but as Brodeur (2010, 288) points out, private high policing is a major activity of private security agencies.

57. In intelligence work, a distinction is made between intelligence from human sources, called HUMINT, and that obtained from electronic means, including from data mining by computer programs (SIGINT; Brodeur 2010, 247).

58. Aden (2001, 101) points out that convergences in policing policies and practices among developed states, including the promotion of undercover policing by the United States, have led to the development of standards for the conduct of undercover operations. This process is also another form of transnational policing.

59. These activities were challenged in the Federal District Court in New Jersey in a lawsuit brought by eight Muslims who alleged violation of constitutional rights because the mass surveillance was based solely on religious affiliation. On February 21, it was reported that the federal district judge had dismissed the lawsuit. (See Ed Pilkington, "Federal Judge Tosses Out Legal Challenge over NYPD Surveillance of Muslims," *Guardian* February 21, 2014, http://www .theguardian.com/world/2014/feb/21/nypd-muslim-surveillance-legal-challenge-judge last seen February 23, 2014.)

60. The notion of the "risk society" is most closely associated with the work of Ulrich Beck, beginning with *Risk Society: Towards a New Modernity* (London: Sage, 1992). On the terrorist threat, see Beck, "The Terrorist Threat World Risk Society Revisited," *Theory, Culture and Society* 19, no. 4 (2002): 39–55.

61. In the United States, legal impediments to police surveillance have been greatly reduced by federal counterterrorism laws. The Patriot Act enhanced police wiretapping powers, introduced "roving wiretap warrants" that allowed surveillance against unspecified persons, expanded the power to use "pen register" and "trap and trace devices" for recording telephone numbers to include the recording of computer IP addresses, and reduced the standard of proof to obtain a wiretap from probable cause or reasonable suspicion to "certification," a mere statement by police that the warrant sought related to a law enforcement purpose (Bloss 2007, 216).

62. In Britain it has been estimated there are some five hundred thousand closed circuit television (CCTV) cameras operating in public and private spaces (Haggerty and Ericson 2000, 614). It is argued they provide a symbol of safety in a fear-dominated society perceived to be ridden with risks (Wood and Webster 2009, 263). By 2008 the United Kingdom had one CCTV camera for every fourteen people, the highest rate of penetration worldwide (Drake, Muncie, and Westmarland 2010, 13).

63. In budgetary terms, it is significant that the George W. Bush administration allocated US$38 billion in spending for homeland security in the fiscal year 2003 (Lyon 2003, 67).

64. But Lyon (2003, 139) also notes, "The result of globalized surveillance is not global surveillance." Lewis (2005, 102–3) points out that there is no central authority or power that directs, controls, or stores information or intelligence and that information systems are "loosely connected and unstable."

5

COURTS AND
CRIMINAL PROCEDURE

Exploring the differences in criminal procedures between countries reveals how the dynamics of justice vary within legal systems. These differences include the dominant role of the judge in civil law inquisitorial systems, the prominence of the defense lawyer in common law systems, and the role of the prosecutor as compared to the functions of an investigating magistrate. Through such comparisons, the distinctive features of the U.S. system can be better appreciated, and the value and efficacy of elements of civil law systems that do not exist in common law systems can be recognized and assessed. This assessment might in turn lead us to question whether some civil law elements could improve justice systems in the United States. Increasing our knowledge of differences in justice systems expands our thinking about how best to achieve an effective and efficient justice system that also protects the rights of individuals.

This chapter examines issues such as the search for truth in a criminal prosecution and how this is achieved through criminal process; the cultural and social context which has produced sometimes radically dissimilar procedures; and contemporary repositioning in some states toward a system that is hybrid, containing both common law and civil law elements. We provide an account of U.S. interventions to realign countries in South America and Eastern Europe away from inquisitorial procedures and toward hybrid or even fully accusatorial systems. We ask why this policy of procedural reform has been pursued by the United States and how successful it has proved to be in practice.

We examine variances in the role of the prosecutor within civil law countries and in its scope between civil and common law countries. Questions about the power possessed by prosecutors, and its limits, are examined in the context of the social and cultural context within which prosecutors function.

Indigenous or informal systems of justice are enjoying a resurgence in many parts of the world as policymakers have come to realize they offer citizens rapid and affordable justice, especially in the resolution of disputes, that formal justice systems have failed to deliver. This leads to questions concerning the potential for the further development of informal systems, how they should interact with formal systems, and whether such systems constrict or hamper human rights and gender equality.

Islamic justice systems are generally poorly understood, and misconceptions about process and punishments continue to be fostered by Westerners suspicious of Sharia law. We contextualize Islamic systems within Islamic culture and history and examine Islamic conceptions of justice. Are all Islamic systems resistant to change, or is it the case that there is no single Islamic model applicable to all Muslim states and therefore that some systems will readily change and others will not?

ADVERSARIAL, INQUISITORIAL, AND HYBRID SYSTEMS OF CRIMINAL JUSTICE

Justice systems are commonly categorized as adversarial, inquisitorial, or hybrid, the latter referring to a system that incorporates features of both of the other systems. Regardless of the categorization, justice systems increasingly appropriate elements from one another so that it has become difficult to identify a justice system that could be described as "pure" adversarial or "pure" inquisitorial.

A common claim about the inquisitorial system is that it focuses on a search for the truth, whereas the accusatorial process is said to be a contest between the parties in which the truth may sometimes be obscured for tactical reasons but may sometimes emerge. A more insightful explanation of the difference is that "the inquisitorial process places a higher value on the discovery of truth, whereas the adversarial process is only prepared to discover truth within strict evidential and procedural boundaries" (Nagorcka, Stanton, and Wilson 2005, 462). In its search for truth, the inquisitorial system privileges this truth over the protection of the rights of an accused. For example, there is restricted access to legal advice in most civil law systems because lawyers are considered to be hindrances to truth seeking. Moreover, the inquisitorial process has no place for technical rules of evidence that exclude relevant facts based on rules about hearsay or evidence improperly obtained. This is congruent with the need to find out the truth and, in any event, criminal civil law systems rely on professional judges to assess the probative value of all evidence admitted during a trial. With no system of jury trial, there is no need to filter evidence for prejudicial effect.

At a more general level of analysis, the divergence between the systems is associated with the distrust that the adversarial system holds for the exercise of the power of the state compared with the inquisitorial system's confidence that the state will protect the innocent.

Adversarial and Inquisitorial Models

Over time, researchers and scholars have identified a set of characteristics possessed by each of these justice systems and these features are described in the following discussion to illustrate the differences. The various elements considered normative or decisive in each system are also examined.

Under the *adversarial* model, trials are seen as contests between rivals on an equal footing who are primarily responsible for defining the issues and investigating and processing the case. Usually, in serious cases there is judgment by one's peers (the jury) and a heavy emphasis on the oral presentation of evidence. The reliance on lay decision makers in the form of the jury means there is a necessity for rules of evidence intended to ensure that the jury receives only reliable evidence. (Unlike judges, juries are believed to lack the capacity to assess the probative value of all and any evidence given in the trial and so cannot filter out unreliable facts.) Judges in adversarial trials play the role of umpire (e.g., deciding what evidence can be admitted) but otherwise leave the presentation of all evidence and issues of law relevant to those issues to the parties. Judges have the capacity to call witnesses themselves or to question witnesses but generally do not do so. Accusations are processed in stages with a pretrial process and a trial process (when there is no plea bargain negotiated, which happens in 95 percent of cases). The latter continues day by day until a verdict is reached. Sentencing after a verdict of guilty may take place sometime after the trial in a separate hearing. If the accused pleads guilty, usually following a plea bargain, there is no trial and the process is quite speedy. In the adversarial system, there is a good deal of discretion in decision making.

In the *inquisitorial* model, the trial process is enacted as an inquiry aimed at establishing the truth of the events that resulted in the commission of a crime. The court controls the process through rules and procedures that tend to be rigid and that the parties may not limit it in any way. Plea bargaining is considered inconsistent with the ideal of finding the truth (although in practice forms of plea bargaining do actually occur. This model favors documentary evidence, and trials always take place whether or not the accused admits guilt because a trial is required to establish the truth. Rules of evidence are basically nonexistent because there are no juries in the form adopted for the adversarial system and verdicts are decided on by professionally trained career judges.

The variances between the two models give rise to many differences in practice from police investigation to sentencing. For example, in the Netherlands, which uses a civil law model, there is an emphasis on written documents which heightens the significance of recording statements of witnesses and the accused. Given that there are written statements of the witnesses, Dutch courts are reluctant to hear oral evidence at trial. Where additional witnesses are found necessary at trial, the trial court will usually adjourn in order for written statements to be recorded from the additional witnesses and submitted to the trial court (Van Koppen and Penrod 2003, 4). This usually means that the trial is interrupted, and this may occur several times. The outcome is a long trial process for an accused (p. 4). Other differences at various stages in proceedings are identified here.

Commonalities are found within almost all justice systems and include

- the need to satisfy a standard of proof to establish a guilty act;

- a presumption of innocence in some form;

- a right to legal representation, although the details of when this can be accessed will differ; and

- a right, in some form, to question the evidence brought against an accused.

In spite of these commonalities, adversarial and inquisitorial procedures are not alternative ways to serve the same purpose. Rather, they represent radically different views of the purpose of the law and of the state in administering the law (Damaska 1986). In a liberal state based on the principle of *laissez-faire*,[1] it is entirely consistent in an adversarial system for the trial to be fashioned as

a contest between parties and therefore for the decision to make no claim to be a truth statement. Mirjan Damaska (1986, 73) argues that the role of the "reactive" state is to provide a framework for persons to pursue their goals through self-management. On the other hand, the "activist" state, as in an inquisitorial system, far from merely designing forms within which citizens may pursue their goals "tells citizens what to do and how to behave" (p. 82). Thus the inquisitorial process constitutes principally a managerial approach to justice administration that is sustained by a highly developed bureaucracy capable of methodically assembling a written record of information on which to base decisions.

What is the nature of the process that has produced these two quite different models of justice? In his analysis of the foundations of the two systems, Damaska (1986, 38) suggests that the Anglo-American model of justice reveals a strong affinity for lay decision makers (justices of the peace and jurors). Although the historical account of the development of adversarial justice supports this assessment, in contemporary England, 97 percent of criminal cases fall into the less serious category and are disposed of without jury trial in the magistrates court (Glendon et al. 2008, 197, 253). In the United States, 95 percent of serious cases are plea bargained and never come before a jury at all (Luna and Wade 2012, 84).

There are a number of studies concerning which system is considered the "best" (better expressed in terms of the "most efficient" or "the fairest"; see, e.g., Thibaut and Walker 1975). These studies have generally shown a strong preference for the adversarial system, but the surveys on which those results were based involved only U.S. participants (Anderson and Otto 2003). A study of fairness, involving 120 participants, half from Chicago and half from the Netherlands, found that each showed a clear preference for their own system. This outcome is unsurprising because it is likely that each group opted for the system with which it was most familiar; an alternative explanation, however, is that a system also reflects one's beliefs and values (Anderson and Otto 2003, 557). In addition, conclusions about the merits of one system may be based on ignorance of the other. For example, persons engaged with the adversarial system find that having control over the presentation of the facts and therefore ensuring that a court has all relevant facts before it is its most valued feature. However, in the case of inquisitorial systems, although it is true that the court controls the evidence, the facts of a case may be considered anew on appeal, providing a chance to secure a second opinion of the merits (Crombag 2003, 21).

Adversarial systems have come under scrutiny because of the number of wrongful convictions that have been discovered over the past twenty years (National Registry of Exonerations 2013).[2] Among the reasons for these defects is the quality of legal representation of the defense—a significant factor in light of the prominence of the lawyers in any criminal trial under an adversarial system (Roach 2010, 387). Despite its imperfections, adversarialism is deeply rooted in the competitive culture of the United States and in popular culture generally, which teaches through media representations of policing, prosecutions, and trials that the adversarial process "uncovers the truth about past events" and that "lawyers working within an adversary system are champions of justice and liberty" (Asimow 2007, 655–56).

Development of the Adversarial Model

The adversarial mode of trial, fashioned in the mid-eighteenth century in England, infers a lawyer-dominated process founded on a set of due process rights, including the presumption of innocence, the right of silence, the right to call witnesses, and the right to cross-examine (Vogler 2005, 129).

Pre-adversarial Procedures

How were trials conducted before the coming of the adversarial mode? During this period, an accused essentially stood trial as a passive actor in the judge-dominated proceedings (Vogler 2005). The judge directed the course of the trial, sometimes with the aid of depositions, and was the only legal authority in court. From at least the twelfth century, a person accused of a felony (other than treason) had no right to counsel, except that counsel could address the court only on matters of law. This was because it was believed that no person should be able to have assistance in challenging the king (Vogler 2005). Determining guilt or innocence was seen to be a simple matter for the jury to decide on the facts presented in evidence. The

trial process was crude, relying almost entirely on oral evidence, and was accusatorial in nature. The victim, supported by a constable, would apprehend the alleged offender and bring him or her to a justice of the peace, who would take depositions from the victim and any witnesses. The accused had few rights, and was not told of the case presented or allowed to be present when depositions were taken. In this process the judge, in effect, acted as prosecutor, consistent with the then strong prosecutorial bias in the justice system; once satisfied there was a case to answer, the judge would bind over any witnesses and commit the accused for trial (p. 132).

After being committed for trial, the accused was kept in custody in a jail, usually in appalling conditions, often for extended periods, because the Assize Court sat only twice a year in the provinces (Vogler 2005, 132). The defense was not shown the indictment or the prosecution evidence and had no process to compel its witnesses to attend the trial. Until at least 1703, defense witnesses and the accused, unlike the victim and his or her witnesses, were not heard at trial on oath (p. 133). The trial process itself was rapid and, because of the constraints imposed on the accused, tended to force an accused to speak in his or her own defense. Records show that in 1751, an Assize trial could last as little as half an hour, thus pressuring an accused with no skills at speaking in public and who was hardly in a physical state to be able to conduct a cross-examination (p. 133). The aim was to force an accused into submission and passivity.

The actual procedure at trial involved the presentation of the indictment and then a confrontation between the victim and the accused. The accused was obliged to comment on the evidence as it was presented (Vogler 2005, 134). The absence of a properly structured procedure meant that the judge could act as an interrogator and greatly influence the jury. The accused had the right to a trial but little more because there was no right to bail, no burden of proof placed on the prosecution, and no rules of evidence excluding, for example, hearsay evidence, and most importantly, no right to counsel (p. 135).

The Lawyers

How did trial practice and procedure change so radically in the common law courts so that accused persons came to possess rights and protections?

Evidence of the changes lies chiefly in the Sessions Papers of the Old Bailey Criminal Court in central London from 1674 to 1834 (Vogler 2005, 136) showing that whereas counsel appeared only occasionally in late 1710, by 1735 appearance was becoming much more common until by 1795 records show counsel appearing in well over one third of cases (p. 137).

Changes in practice and procedure were brought about by the lawyers with the concurrence of the judges through the imposition of a structure for the trial process that involved a clear distinction between prosecution and defense cases, between examination-in-chief and cross-examination, and between evidence and submissions or argument, with counsel acting as zealous advocates for their clients (Vogler 2005, 139). Lawyers began, in their arguments, to suggest that the prosecution had not discharged the burden of proving guilt, thus establishing the presumption of innocence. At the same time, the pre-trial proceeding before the justice of the peace also became a structured process with the accused entitled to be present with counsel. Clearly, advocacy and the rights of the accused figured greatly in these new procedures (p. 139).

By 1836, the Prisoners' Counsel Act had authorized representation by counsel in an accused's defense and legal representation at the committal for trial proceedings, and had given the defense the right to access prosecution statements of the case against the accused (Vogler 2005, 145). It thus constituted an endorsement of the concept of adversariality. In 1848, legislation mandated the right to silence and a caution, and in 1865, the Criminal Procedure Act gave the defense the right to speak last in the criminal trial, consolidating and affirming the adversarial concept (Vogler 2005, 147). The final stage in completing the formulation of the adversarial model came in 1898 when the Prisoners' Evidence Act made the accused and the accused's spouse competent but not compellable to give evidence in the trial (p. 149).

Although the lawyers played a crucial role in this radical refashioning of the trial, other factors were also important, including the development of the rules of evidence by the judges, the professionalization of the prosecution function, and the increased engagement of lawyers in criminal work when their commercial business collapsed (Vogler 2005, 140–44). Changes in criminal procedure and practice paralleled,

meshed with, and were part of the broad sweep of social, political, and economic changes that occurred during this period in ways too complex to discuss here.

Adversarial Procedures—Comparing the United States and England

The development of the adversarial process brought about an emphasis on rights and the protection of the accused during the trial process. The role of the judge was diminished with a corresponding enhancement in the functions of the prosecution and defense lawyers. Today, adversarial systems of law share many common features, but it is instructive to consider how the United States and England differ in certain respects in elements of the trial process.

The most significant difference lies in the way in which major changes in criminal procedure have been achieved. In the United States, this has generally come about through litigation, chiefly at the Supreme Court level, which has resulted in the creation of a pre-trial set of rights and the regulation of criminal procedure. In England, broadly the same outcome has been achieved through systematic legislation enacted by Parliament mandating changes to pre-trial and trial procedure, and most recently, institutional change in the establishment of the Crown Prosecution Service (CPS), centralizing prosecutions (Kagan 2009, 61). While this difference in approach is, to a large extent, the outcome of the United States having a system of judicial review based on a written constitution, as Robert Kagan (p. 61) has noted, "Procedurally, American criminal justice is structured and pervaded by adversarial legalism—lawyer driven legal contestation in a relatively nonhierarchical, organizationally decentralized system."

Table 5.1 outlines divergences in the criminal procedures of England compared with those of the United States, which have been observed by Mary Ann Glendon et al. (2008) and Richard Vogler (2005).

INQUISITORIAL PROCEDURE IN FRANCE

A greater understanding of how inquisitorial systems process the various stages of a criminal prosecution helps highlight differences and

Table 5.1   Criminal Procedures: Comparing England and the United States

England	United States
The prosecution function has the capacity to be much more widely exercised in England because there is scope for citizens to bring private prosecutions, although this is rare and is discouraged by the CPS.	In the United States, "the opportunities afforded by the criminal justice systems for private prosecutions are sparse and rarely utilized" (Krug 2002, 643).
In England, since 2003, in serious cases, the decision to charge an accused is exercised by the CPS and not by the police.	In the United States, the decision to charge rests with the police.
The Grand Jury was abolished in England in 1933.	In the United States, grand juries operate in about half the states and at the federal level. The grand jury passes a true bill declaring there is sufficient evidence for an accused to stand trial: the true bill is the indictment.
In England, legal aid for an accused is linked to the legal profession and there are no public defenders. Nevertheless, the growth of legal aid services in England has resulted in lawyers increasingly appearing at the pre-trial process.	There are public defenders in the United States. The U.S. "lawyerization" of the pre-trial process through public funding is more comprehensive than in England.
The English system has a structure of judges and barristers who have common roots (senior judges are appointed from the ranks of barristers who have usually specialized in trial advocacy for many years).	The English structure of judges seems to U.S. eyes to be suggestive of a closer bond between counsel and judges than is appropriate and to be susceptible to inhibiting the presentation of a strong defense. This kind of close association does not exist in the United States.
Police interrogation techniques in England are based on the concept of "investigative interviewing," which involves hearing the suspect's full story repeated twice before questions can be put to him or her. In addition, interviews are recorded in England.	Although investigative interviewing occurs in some U.S. states, it is not widespread, nor is the recording of interviews.
In England, the judge has discretion to admit evidence obtained illegally by police, if it is relevant, but with some exceptions.	When a court in the United States finds that evidence was illegally obtained by police, regardless of its relevance, that evidence will be excluded.
The right to silence is not regarded as absolute in England in the same way as in the United States. For example, in England, if an accused fails to mention a fact on which she relies at trial after having been cautioned ("given her rights" in U.S. terms), an adverse inference can be drawn from her silence on that fact. In England, taking the stand is irrelevant in considering whether to admit a record into evidence.	The right to silence is regarded as an absolute. The United States allows past records of an accused only when the accused takes the stand.
In England, the trial judge is allowed not only to rule on legal issues and submissions but also to comment on facts, recall witnesses, or question witnesses where she believes issues and facts were not fully debated.	In the United States, the judge must limit herself to matters of law.

England	United States
A voir dire procedure does not exist in England and although in theory a challenge for cause can be made, this is rarely done. The rule in England is basically to accept those called together to form a jury. England does not assess likely jurors to the extent done in the United States.	In the United States, a voir dire is conducted that allows counsel to challenge the fitness of potential jurors. There is an elaborate assessment of the likely jurors in the United States if the defense has the resources (including so-called jury experts, who psychologically profile jurors).
There is no wide publicity through media reporting of trials in England where contempt of court rules limit this kind of publicity.	There is wide publicity through media reporting that will generally occur when trials involving prominent persons or dramatic events occur.
In appellate reviews of trials, English appeal judges are far more reluctant to interfere with the discretion of the trial judge than is the case in the United States. In addition, there is much more emphasis on the oral presentation of argument in an appeal in England. In England, at the conclusion of oral arguments on appeal, the view of each appeal judge is given orally (except in the highest appeal court [the House of Lords], where appeal decisions are reserved and are written).	This contrasts with the U.S. practice where lengthy and printed briefs are prepared for the appeal court. This compares to U.S. practice where judges regularly reserve judgment sometimes for lengthy periods.
As a result of 1996 legislation in England, the accused is required to supply the prosecution with a defense statement outlining the general lines of the defense and identifying issues where the prosecution evidence will be challenged.	There is no such obligation in the United States.

CPS, Crown Prosecution Service.

SOURCES: Glendon et al. 2008, 251–74; Vogler 2005, 151–55.

commonalities between adversarial and inquisitorial systems. In addition, exploring inquisitorial procedure in some depth provides us with an understanding of how the legal culture of a particular civil law country may influence the criminal prosecution function in relation to issues such as protection of rights. It also leads us to ask questions such as the following: Does the inquisitorial process protect the rights of an accused sufficiently in police interrogation or during the pretrial process? Is the investigating judge (an institution often praised by proponents of the adversarial) a model that should be adopted in the United States? What value is gained by court officials compiling a dossier of all the facts and evidence and relying on this dossier rather than on oral evidence at trial to determine guilt? What is the underlying philosophy at work in the process of an inquisitorial prosecution? In attempting to answer these and other questions, this section examines the inquisitorial criminal procedure in France, considered to be one of the "purest" inquisitorial systems in Europe.

As an introduction to the striking differences between common law and civil law criminal procedures, the following description of how witnesses are examined in a continental inquisitorial process provides us with an immediate sense of the inquisitorial system.

1. There is no distinction between witnesses for the prosecution and for the defense: all witnesses are sources of information and facts for the judge and not for the parties. This is consistent with the inquisitorial objective of searching for the "truth."

2. The parties may not affect or prepare the evidence of witnesses.

3. At trial, a witness will be asked by the judge to narrate the facts of the case within his or her knowledge. The witness will only be interrupted with questions by the judge when he or she has not expressed himself or herself well, when clarification of a fact is considered necessary, or when the witness needs to be guided back to the facts at issue.

4. Only at the conclusion of this period of informal communication will the interrogation proper commence by the judge: again, this will seem informal and not in the style of a cross-examination conducted in an adversarial trial.

5. At the conclusion of the judge's interrogation, the parties will be permitted to ask the witness questions. (Damaska 1975, 1083)

Turning now to the French system of criminal prosecution, the following table describes the steps taken in French criminal procedure in the case of a serious offense from the police investigation onward.

As can be seen from Table 5.2, the French criminal procedure has three distinct phases:

1. the preliminary investigation phase, including the *garde à vue;*

2. the judicial investigation phase conducted by the *juge d'instruction;* and

3. the trial phase.

The system envisages early involvement of the prosecutor or the *juge d'instruction* concurrent

Table 5.2	French Criminal Procedure
Police investigation	• Judicial police carry out the investigation supervised by public prosecutor. • Police can detain and interrogate a suspect after arrest on the *garde à vue.* Under this procedure, police may, for the purpose of interrogation, detain in custody a person caught at the time or soon after an offense and suspected of having committed it.
Investigating judge **(Juge d'instruction)** *Pre-trial judge* **(Juge de la mise en état)** *Committal court* **(Chambre d'accusation)**	• For offenses called *délits and contraventions,* punishable with imprisonment from two months to five years, a prosecutor may decide to refer to an investigating judge for investigation but is not required to do so. • For all crimes punishable by five years imprisonment or more (known as flagrant offenses or *flagrants délits* or *les crimes*), a prosecutor must refer to an investigating judge. • The investigating judge is independent and is tasked to search for the material truth by discovering facts both for and against the accused. • An accused is entitled to have a lawyer present at any time he or she is interrogated by the judge. • The investigating judge can order searches, interrogate persons, obtain reports of experts, and prevent a person in pre-trial detention from communicating with others for a period of ten days. • A judge may order detention on remand, grant bail, or dismiss the case where there is insufficient evidence. • The judge may delegate the investigation to the judicial police or give the police instructions to gather evidence. • The judge may order the setting up of interception devices or order medical examinations. • Counsel for the accused may inspect the *dossier* (the collection of documents resulting from the investigation), but the accused may not unless representing himself or herself. • The judge must decide if there are grounds to commit the accused to stand trial, in which case the judge will refer to a tribunal according to the nature of the charge. For example, where the accused is charged with a *délit flagrant,* the case will be referred to the *chambre d'accusation,* which will decide if the accused will stand trial in the *cour d'assises.* • After the accused is committed for trial, the case goes to a pre-trial judge who determines the trial date and may ask questions of counsel, supervise discovery, hear arguments on points of law, and hear any facts she considers necessary for resolution of the case.

| Trial court—serious cases (Cour d'assises) | • Court of trial for *délit flagrant* comprises the presiding judge, two assessors, and nine lay persons known as *jurés*.
• The trial process begins with procedural objections.
• The indictment is read.
• The presiding judge summarizes the dossier and asks the accused questions to elaborate on the dossier.
• The accused does not plead to the indictment.
• The accused is examined on her background, including previous convictions, and any differences from facts stated in the dossier will be closely followed up.
• Prosecutor and defense counsel may suggest questions to be put to the accused by the presiding judge or may ask to put questions themselves.
• Lay jurors and assessors may only ask questions if given permission by the presiding judge.
• The accused does not take any oath before being examined.
• At the conclusion of the examination of the accused, the judge calls any witnesses and asks questions about their background and then asks the accused to make a statement with no interruptions, after which the judge may ask questions. There is no cross-examination as such, but counsel may suggest questions to be put to the witnesses.
• At the conclusion of presentation of evidence, the prosecutor addresses the court and usually asks for a specific punishment to be imposed.
• Defense counsel then addresses the court.
• At conclusion of trial, judges will retire to consider verdict; all members of the court, including the *jurés*, will consider together. A two-thirds majority is required for a guilty finding, and in most cases the *jurés* are greatly influenced by the professional judges.
• The decision must be given in writing and state what evidence has been accepted and the probative value of each piece of that evidence—this facilitates any appeal. |
| **Trial court—less serious cases (Tribunal correctionnel)** | • Court of trial for *délits* normally comprises three judges but can be a single judge in less serious cases. |

SOURCES: McKillop 1997, 527; Nagorcka et al. 2005, 448.

with the police investigation. The decision to charge and the offense to be charged is not made by police but by the prosecutor (Hodgson 2001, 345). Each of these phases will now be further explored to provide a greater understanding of the social and cultural aspects of the French system.

The police investigation in France is conducted by the *police judiciaire* who conduct investigations into crimes subject to the direction of investigating judges and prosecutors (McKillop 1997, 530). They must inform the prosecutor immediately of a *crime flagrant* (a crime committed within the previous eight days; p. 531).

The *garde à vue* (GAV) has been a contested procedure within the French system for many years because of claims that it gives excessive powers to police and fails to properly protect suspects (McKillop 1997). While the GAV was already well established in practice in police procedure, it was recognized through legislation in the French Criminal Procedure Code only in 1958. Similar to interrogation practices in Anglo-American systems, it affords the police an opportunity to hold a suspect in custody to secure a confession or at least damaging admissions that can be used in evidence against her.

Over the years there has been an increased focus on the need to regulate the GAV to avoid contravening the terms of the European Convention on Human Rights, which assures persons arrested or detained of certain rights.[3] Traditionally, it has been the responsibility of the prosecutor to supervise the GAV (although some research suggests that this duty has been interpreted so as not to interfere with police action) and not to make physical inspections of the conduct of an actual GAV. Since 2000, the supervision role has been shared with a new figure within the system: *le juge des libertés et de la détention* (Dorange and Field 2012, 156–57). Arguments in favor of limiting access to legal advice during the GAV have centered on claims that a suspect is protected by a judge and a prosecutor.

Legislation in 1994 permitted the accused to have an interview with a defense lawyer after twenty hours of detention. In 2000, the law was changed so that the right applied from the commencement of time in custody and again if custody was extended beyond twenty-four hours (Dorange and Field 2012, 157). However, lawyers were given no right to access the contents of the dossier and could not be present when the suspect was interrogated. Also, police were not required to advise a suspect of his or her right to silence (p. 157).

In July 2010, the constitutionality of the limits on rights to legal representation in police custody was challenged in the French Constitutional Court, and on July 30, 2010, the court declared the legal framework of the police custody phase unconstitutional, in part because of violations of the European Human Rights Convention, which is superior to domestic law under the French Constitution (Dorange and Field 2012, 159). The decision reasoned that the presence of a lawyer in police custody was essential, that only limited exceptions could be made to that rule, and that no conviction could be based solely on confessions made while in custody if a lawyer was not present (p. 159). On April 14, 2011, a new law came into force regulating the GAV (Law 2011–392).[4] The elements of the new legislation are shown in Box 5.1.

BOX 5.1   Elements of French Law 2011–392 on Police Custody

- For the first time the legislation defines the nature of the GAV.

- It requires that there be one or more plausible reasons for suspecting that the detained person has committed or attempted to commit offenses *punishable by imprisonment* (therefore, offenses punishable by fines no longer justify GAV).

- It requires that GAV may only be applied if it is the sole means of achieving at least one of six specified objectives.

- Persons who are not suspects must not be interrogated for more than four hours.

- The maximum period of detention remains twenty-four hours and may be extended for a further twenty-four hours, but an extension must be approved by the prosecutor.

- The prosecutor remains primarily responsible for supervision of the GAV and must be informed at the start of the period of detention.

- Where the period of detention is extended, the suspect must be brought before *le juge des libertés et de la détention* within twenty hours, and from that time, only that judge may further extend the detention.

- A suspect is entitled to have a thirty-minute consultation with a lawyer from the start of detention and on each extension and is entitled to have a lawyer present during interviews and *confrontations*[5] with witnesses.

- Where a suspect has asked for a lawyer, no police interrogation may commence for two hours. Where the lawyer arrives later than this time, the lawyer may consult privately with the suspect by interrupting an interrogation that has already commenced. Even where the lawyer arrives late, she is entitled to immediately attend the interrogation.

- Police have a right to postpone access to a lawyer in defined circumstances for up to twelve hours if approved by the prosecutor or *le juge des libertés* or for longer periods where "organized criminality" is found to exist.

- Lawyers may now consult specified documents in the *dossier* and may take notes of statements but are not entitled to copies.

SOURCE: Dorange and Field 2012, 159–66.

Despite the new legislation, there remain several issues of concern for defense lawyers. For example, lawyers are still not able to consult the full dossier or obtain copies of all documents; lawyers are only allowed a thirty-minute consultation period; limits are still imposed on the timing of lawyer involvement; and the prosecutor remains in control of the GAV while many believe it should be supervised by a judicial officer.

In civil law systems, the *dossier* is crucial in advancing the trial process—it shapes the form the trial will take and will be read in any appellate review of the trial court proceedings. It is not a police file but the outcome of a judicially supervised inquiry, and therefore it is said that statements contained in it may be accepted without the need for oral evidence and cross-examination (Hodgson 2001, 345). The components of a French dossier are outlined in Box 5.2.

BOX 5.2   French Dossier

- Record of the investigation, including original police report, depositions taken, experts' reports, and results of searches and of any modes of surveillance

- Record of the accused's pre-trial detention, if applicable

- History and background of the accused, including details of prior convictions

- Record of warrants, requisition orders, and directives

SOURCE: McKillop 1997.

Given its importance in the process,[6] the written dossier makes the French system a written one. It is significant that no transcript is made of the trial proceedings, including the oral evidence of witnesses (who are expected to confirm their depositions contained in the dossier), and therefore, on any appeal, the appellate tribunal sees only the dossier. The value of the dossier lies not only in its completeness but also because it contains statements from witnesses and the accused that were made soon after the alleged crime was committed and when memories were fresh (McKillop 1997, 582). This compares to an adversarial trial, which may take place many months after committal for trial when memories have dimmed. Furthermore, the dossier is compiled by professionals (police, investigating judge, prosecutor, experts), and this accumulated bureaucratic input gives legitimacy and validity to the account presented in the dossier, placing corresponding pressure on an accused (p. 582).

In France, there are no *rules of evidence* such as found in Anglo-American law, and any means of proving a fact is accepted although it can be challenged (Dorange and Field 2012, 164). So, for example, hearsay evidence is admissible. This approach reflects the concept that the duty of the court is to collect facts and search for the truth—a duty entrusted to a professional judge. In trials throughout Europe, *evidence of prior convictions* can be given during the trial. This is explained in terms of the accused being judged and not only his or her crime.

Unlike the U.S. practice, *expert evidence* is given by experts appointed by the court from lists of experts kept by the court and not by the parties. Expert evidence can be challenged; if a challenge succeeds, the court will appoint additional experts. Thus, unlike Anglo-American systems, experts are not expected to be partisan and do not burden juries with assessing the weight of what may be highly technical expert evidence from both sides without professional assistance (Dorange and Field 2012, 164).

A *confession of guilt* by the accused can be made, but it is not binding and so an accused may be acquitted even if there is a confession that has not been retracted (Dorange and Field 2012, 164). The judge evaluates the probative value of any confession based on the judge's "inner belief" (French Code of Criminal Procedure, Article 353). Similarly, in the French system, the conviction of an accused is founded on the "inner conviction" of the finder of facts. The legislation of 2011 (Law 2011–392) has restricted this rule, stating that in serious and middle-level cases, persons may not be convicted solely on the basis of declarations made by them without the advice and assistance of a lawyer (Dorange and Field 2012, 164).

In the French system, it is unlikely that the accused will be found not guilty because all the evidence has already been considered during the pre-trial process and the judges have read the dossier before the trial (McKillop 1997, 565). Consequently, when an accused is committed for trial, this will generally mean that he or she will be convicted. In this sense then, the actual trial becomes more of a public review of the dossier and a confirmation of the facts stated there. The investigation is therefore the key element in the process and the trial simply adds the public dimension by presenting the outcome of the investigation (p. 565).

It is only in serious or complex cases that the prosecutor must open an *information* and refer the case to a *juge d'instruction* (the investigating magistrate). Such cases constitute less than 7 percent of all cases, making the process quite rare in practice (Hodgson 2002a, 805).[7] As well, in practice police are delegated the task of investigation by the *juge d'instruction* once the case is referred to him or her. By that time the *garde à vue* will have already been completed by police. It is rare for an investigating judge or prosecutor to intervene in a police inquiry. Accordingly, it is the prosecutor who is central to the judicial supervision of the criminal justice process (Hodgson 2001, 346). The role of the French prosecutor is discussed later in the section "Prosecutors and the Prosecution Function."

The *right to silence*, a highly valued right and protection in adversarial systems, is subject to certain social and cultural influences in the French system. In the GAV, the new legislation (Law 2011–392) requires that persons detained must be informed immediately of their right to remain silent. While the investigating judge is required to warn the accused that he or she does not have to answer questions, this does not have to be repeated at each appearance that the accused makes during the investigation. According to Bron McKillop (1997, 577), while an accused does not have to respond to questions, it is rare for the accused to remain silent. Two possible explanations for the willingness of accused persons to reply to questions are that the traditional centuries-old inquisitorial process in France

has socialized citizens to cooperate with public officials and that the accused cooperates because of the adverse effect silence will have in the process. In the French system, the court is entitled to draw adverse inferences from the failure of an accused to cooperate in the investigation. Therefore, an accused who fails to respond to incriminating evidence runs a very real risk of being penalized in the outcome. However, according to the jurisprudence of the European Human Rights Convention, a national court must not convict solely on the basis that a suspect chose to remain silent.

There are significant differences between the perception of *defense lawyers* in France and those practicing in the United States. In France, the defense lawyer, the *avocat,* is seen as outside the criminal justice system. Prosecutors, *juges d'instruction,* and trial judges are all *magistrats*[8] that is, professional justice officials who have undergone the same training and share the same values in terms of the legal culture. The *magistrats* are regarded as engaged in the public interest in a search for the truth, whereas defense lawyers are perceived to be acting solely for money in the interests of the accused. As a case in point, Jacqueline Hodgson (2002a, 789) quotes a *juge d'instruction:* "The lawyer, he works as a liar, to see how far he can distort the law." Both criminal defense lawyers and *magistrats* perceive the purpose of their presence during the *garde à vue* and the pre-trial process as to ensure that procedures are complied with and not to engage with the substantive process on behalf of a client (p. 789). The following comment by a senior prosecutor on the role of a defense lawyer is illustrative: "In France, the lawyer is there not to advise the person, but to signal any problems in the condition of the *garde à vue;* to provide not so much legal advice as moral support" (Hodgson 2004, 178).

Comment

This exploration of French criminal procedure reveals radical divergences between the U.S. and the French systems. Those familiar with adversarial systems of justice will justifiably ask a set of questions that would include the following: While the French may be said to have made some advances in protecting the rights of an accused at the police station, do the protections now available equal those enjoyed by accused persons under the U.S. Constitution? Is the investigating judge really an important element in the French procedure when so few cases are actually referred for pre-trial investigation? If the investigating judge delegates her duty to investigate to the police and distances herself from police work, does this process in practice conform to a pre-trial judicial investigation in the sense intended by French law? Is it appropriate for the pre-trial investigation phase to be conducted by a judge, or is this task better handled by a prosecutor? In light of the importance of the investigation phase as compared to the trial, where the trial is essentially a public demonstration of a decision already made during the investigation, does this not delegitimize the trial as a public display of justice in action?

REFORMING THE INQUISITORIAL MODEL: LATIN AMERICA

The changes occurring in French criminal procedure are paralleled to an extent in Central and South America and in Eastern Europe as well as in Russia, all of which formerly maintained inquisitorial systems. However, unlike the French case, in these regions some elements of the adversarial system have been directly incorporated into their criminal procedure codes. Transforming inquisitorial criminal justice systems by importing institutions and procedures shaped in foreign adversarial system states is a challenging task. The following account of these developments provides an understanding of the constraints faced by these states in making these policy transfers as well as the rationales for such action.

Over the past twenty years, many Latin American countries have not just amended but have comprehensively revised their criminal procedure codes as well as introducing other reforms into their justice systems[9] (Santiso 2003, 114). During the Spanish colonial period, Spanish codes applied. Following their Independence, these countries adopted the civil law model and an inquisitorial system based largely on the Spanish Code of 1822 (Bischoff 2003, 34). Reforms to those codes starting in the 1990s have introduced significant elements of the adversarial system. Among the several questions arising from this development are the following:

- What was the rationale for reform, and what factors influenced these states in deciding to reform their codes so radically?

- What reforms have occurred?

- Have the reforms improved their justice systems, and if so, how?

The following discussion attempts to provide a summary response to these important questions. While there are many other issues associated with reform efforts in the region—including corruption, securing the independence of the judiciary and of prosecutors, inefficiency throughout justice systems, and severe limits on citizens' access to justice (see, e.g., Ciurlizza 2000, 218–20)—these issues will not be explored here in any depth. Instead, the focus of this discussion is on criminal procedure code reforms in the region. While there are commonalities[10] within the region in the reforms that have taken place, there are also variances because criminal procedure reflects the cultural, historical, and political values, beliefs, and expectations of a society.

Democratization and Neo-Liberalism in Latin America

The South and Central American reforms were an outcome of changes in government that have occurred in many countries marked by the cessation of military rule and the coming of *democratization*, a term that commonly includes a commitment to adhere to the rule of law. It is generally accepted policy that entrenching democracy necessitates strengthening the rule of law, and this in turn requires an efficient justice system (Dodson 2002, 201). In addition, economic theory argues that there are causal connections between the rule of law and economic development so that sustaining the former is said to promote the latter by enabling business to grow in a nurturing free market environment (Ciurlizza 2000, 211; Santiso 2003, 113–14).

The United States Agency for International Development (USAID), with its history of providing support for Central and South America in various forms,[11] was a strong advocate of democratization and, along with other international organizations, was keen to strengthen legal systems as a means of supporting both economic and democracy development (Langer 2007, 619).[12] In transitioning to democracy and gaining an enhanced

to form a view of a case, judges were prone to treat each piece of evidence discretely and thereby find insufficient evidence of guilt (p. 209).

In *Colombia,* a new adversarial model criminal procedure came into force in 1992. It transferred the functions of the investigating judge to a new office of prosecutor *(fiscalía),* an initiative followed in a number of other states (Pahl 1992, 619). The prosecutor ranks as a judge and is appointed by the Supreme Court and must possess the qualifications of a Supreme Court judge (p. 619). The prosecutor is tasked with investigating alleged offenses and laying charges as well as with directing the judicial police in executing those functions. Extensive police powers have been vested in the prosecutor, including issuing arrest orders, ordering wiretaps, and conducting searches, all without any judicially issued warrant. Those in support of granting these powers to the prosecutor argue that prosecutors are able to exercise proper restraint because of their previous experience as prosecutors and judges in the inquisitorial system and that these powers simply reflect the more extensive role of the state in an inquisitorial system, a tradition that has continued despite the new procedures (Pahl 1992, 629–30).

In *Chile,* judges, lawyers, and academic lawyers all resisted reforms. According to Alberto Binder, an expert and proponent of reform who experienced the reform process in many Latin American states, the inquisitorial system had created a culture of conservatism and ritual within the legal community (Riego 1998, 447–48). This culture rejected changes to the system and emphasized formality and procedure at the expense of substantive issues and concerns. Thus the procedure became an end in itself, and its social utility was never weighed or assessed.

Training for Reform

In training lawyers and judges in the adversarial mode of proceeding, Leonard Cavise (2007, 804) found that most resistance was expressed toward the jury trial, with judges and lawyers taking the view that a jury chosen from citizens at random would not possess the capacity to decide complex issues of fact and that only "competent people" with legal training could possibly serve on a jury.

Similarly, the notion that under the adversarial system, the defense lawyer investigates the facts of the case against the defendant independently of police and the prosecutor, sifts through the evidence, decides what evidence the defendant should present, assesses the weight of the prosecution evidence, and interviews witnesses was found difficult to accept (Cavise 2007, 807).

Even criminal defense lawyers receiving training were reluctant to believe that it was the professional duty of a defense lawyer to challenge all state evidence, where possible, as was the notion that the defense lawyer enjoyed equal status with the prosecutor and the judge (pp. 808, 812). Fundamentally, accepting that the outcome of a trial could depend on the quality of the advocacy was a notion antithetical to Latin American criminal lawyers (p. 815).

Questioning Reforms

Introducing widespread and radical changes to Latin American criminal procedure codes was seen as unproblematic by advocates, and there was minimal discussion about the policy transferability of adversarial reforms. This is because they were perceived as somehow natural, and even inevitable, due perhaps to the view that they were essential elements in building democracy or necessary precursors to increased foreign investment, or as indispensable to establishing the rule of law. Jorge Esquirol (2008, 75), who notes that the standard discourse of law reform projects in the region over the past fifty years has been "law's failure," asks salient questions about the merits of this approach. In his view, this discourse "denies much of any value to existing law anywhere in the region" (p. 75) and "keeps a range of questions off the table, depriving all of the Americas of any real engagement with the pre-reform options embodied in the law of Latin American states" (p. 75).

Esquirol points to critiques of aspects of the U.S. adversarial system debated within the United States that have not been reviewed or assessed in policy terms in the context of the Latin American reforms but have nevertheless been adopted almost unquestioningly (Esquirol 2008, 88). For example, he asks if it is appropriate, in view of the historical record of prosecutorial abuse of powers in the region, to give prosecutors expanded discretion. While prosecutor's offices are strengthened, what of public defenders who have not enjoyed the same level of additional resource allocation? Why is it considered that the investigating judge is so inferior in performance to an investigating prosecutor? Will the defendant's rights be as zealously protected by a perhaps inexperienced defense lawyer compared to judicial protection under the inquisitorial system? Has the change from written to oral proceedings accounted for the greater expenditure of time and resources now taken on trials? Additionally, will there be the same level of accountability as existed previously?[17] It might also be appropriate to question the merits of plea bargaining and the value of jury trials in light of the criticisms of plea bargaining practice and the now rare use of juries within the United States because of plea bargaining.

In the end, as William Prillaman (2000, 6) correctly points out, regardless of arguments about the desirability of policy transfers, the success or otherwise of reforms in the region will depend significantly on sustained political stability, whether political will to implement reforms endures, and whether the reforms are adequately resourced on a continuing basis—again a political issue, because "judicial reform, for better or worse, is an inherently political rather than a technical process entailing a series of political judgments at every stage."

REFORMING THE INQUISITORIAL MODEL: RUSSIA AND EASTERN EUROPE

Following the collapse of the Soviet Union in 1991, Russia and the Commonwealth of Independent States (CIS) began to introduce reforms to their justice systems as part of democratization projects. Their justice systems were based on the inquisitorial process and, like Latin America, they opted to introduce elements of the adversarial model. For some former Soviet Union states such as Poland,[18] this proved to be a relatively painless process, but in the case of Russia, actors in the justice system who suffered, or were likely to experience diminished powers, firmly resisted reform. The traditionally authoritarian nature of the state and the absence of the rule of law during the communist period adversely impacted the reform process.

During the communist period, law was regarded merely as one of many instruments that facilitated governance. Political decisions and regulations made by the executive always prevailed over law, and the court's jurisdiction to challenge executive acts was very limited (Solomon and Foglesong 2000, 4). In criminal cases, judges faced pressures to convict, and records were kept of judges' performance to assess their "stability of sentences," that is, the extent to which their cases were changed on appeal. Records of this nature influenced the career prospects of the judiciary, their potential bonuses and professional standing, and could result in disciplinary action if an excessive number of cases were reversed on appeal.

Judges depended on the largesse of local officials for personal benefits such as housing and vacation time and for infrastructure support for the courts. Local party leaders were influential in the regular "election" of judges and thus judges tended to cooperate with local officials' needs, even extending this to interventions in cases in their courts (Solomon and Foglesong 2000, 6–7). These factors contributed to the low standing of judges with citizens as well as to the low self-esteem of the judges themselves (p. 8).

The following discussion focuses on events in Russia.

The *Prokuratura*

The unusual and powerful office of *prokuratura*, first established by Peter the Great in 1722, not only was charged with the exercise of the investigation and prosecution function in criminal matters but also possessed supervisory powers along the lines of a Western-style administrative tribunal aggregated with an ombudsman function (Diehm 2001, 31). In 1917, the Bolshevik regime abolished the *prokuratura* and all other Tsarist courts and legal institutions. However, by the end of 1921, the Communist Party had restored the general supervisory powers that had been granted to the *prokuratura* by Peter the Great.

During the communist years, the *prokuratura* was the guardian of socialist legality, empowered to suspend court proceedings if it thought the court was acting contrary to socialist legality and able to detain persons without trial for months at a time (Diehm 2001, 23). It was placed above all legal institutions, cooperated with the KGB in investigating and prosecuting dissidents, and operated as a feared organ for state-sponsored coercion and oppression (Orland 2002, 133). The *prokuratura* enjoyed authority and influence within the legal system exceeding that of the judiciary, and the procurator general possessed greater status than even the highest judge (Greenberg 2009, 11).

The end of the Soviet Union in 1991 brought about the end of the *prokuratura* but only temporarily, because in January 1992 legislation reinvented the Russian *prokuratura,* possessing the same functions, organizational structure, and bureaucracy as the previous institution but without the power to supervise judicial acts (Greenberg 2009, 12). The dual prosecutorial/supervisory mandate of the *prokuratura* has been criticized because it denies the principle of "equality of arms" between the prosecution and the defense in criminal cases. Nevertheless, the institution continues to possess and exercise those supervisory functions. The new Russian criminal code (see "New Russian Criminal Procedure Code," later) reduced its powers over pre-trial detention, but lobbying by the *prokuratura* has eroded some pretrial custody rights (p. 16). Further, under the new Code, a practice has developed of prosecutors and judges interacting over a case in the absence of defense counsel, again offending against the equality of arms principle (p. 21). That the *prokuratura* continues to cause concern is evidenced by comments from journalist Edward Lucas (former *Economist* Moscow bureau chief), writing in 2008:

> The most flawed part of the justice system is not the courts themselves, which few Russians use and fewer trust, but the prosecutor's service, "the Prokuratura." This unreformed Stalinist relic is the engine of state illegality. Prosecutors can freeze your bank account, putting you out of business; they can have you imprisoned in a disease-infested hell-hole; they can concoct evidence that will keep you there for decades; they can intimidate any witnesses, defense counsel, and even judges who try to stop them. With a few heroic exceptions, the prosecutor's office is the best friend of the authoritarian bureaucrat and the well-connected gangster. (Lucas 2009, quoted in Greenberg 2009, 36–37)

Trial Process in the Former Soviet Union

Trial process in the former Soviet Union included a feature not found in Western inquisitorial systems; that is, when the court conducting a trial determined there was a need for more evidence, the trial could be terminated and the case referred back to police and prosecutor for further investigation. Subsequently, the case could be brought back for trial based on any new evidence discovered. The existence of this process naturally rendered acquittal a rare event (Diehm 2001, 25).

Given that Russia was a state accustomed to autocratic rule for over a thousand years (Diehm 2001, 16), rulers of Russia, from the Tsars to the communist regime that began in 1917, have always perceived the law as an instrument for accomplishing the aims of the regime in power. An inquisitorial system based on secret procedures, an absence of transparency, and minimal protection for an accused person served this instrumentalist approach well. A contributing factor may have been the stipulation in communist doctrine that when communism became fully established there would no longer be any need for law (p. 22). During the Soviet period, the Soviet judiciary was not respected and was expected to obtain clearance from the Communist Party before deciding a case (Boylan 1998, 1327–28).

The Jury

From 1866, under reforms instituted by Tsar Alexander II, a jury system was in force in the country until abolished by the communist revolution in 1917 (Diehm 2001, 22). It appears that juries were effective even in the time of the Tsars because they rendered verdicts against the government[19] (p. 22).

A radical feature of new criminal procedure in Russia has been the *reestablishment of the jury,* a right provided for by the new constitution.[20] Initially, in 1993, juries were authorized in only nine of Russia's eighty-nine regions and only for defendants charged with offenses punishable by death or deprivation of liberty for more than ten years (Diehm 2001, 31–32).[21] Unlike Western jury systems, Russian juries do not give a verdict of guilty or not guilty but, following the French model, render a verdict on four issues: whether the crime was committed; whether the defendant committed the acts charged; whether the defendant is guilty of the crime; and whether any lenience is merited (the jury must answer this question despite having no knowledge of the defendant's criminal record or background generally).

The twelve-member jury is permitted to give a majority verdict[22] after three hours of unsuccessful deliberation or a unanimous verdict. Jurors may submit questions for witnesses if they are deemed appropriate by the judge (Diehm 2001, 34). Relaxed rules of evidence can mean that the jury is exposed to testimony that in Western adversarial systems would be considered prejudicial to the defendant. In addition, the presence of the victim and a victim's representative with no legal training often leads to outbursts in court and improper comments that can also be considered prejudicial (p. 35).[23] One interesting power given to the jury is that during their deliberations, they have the authority to request the court to reopen the evidence and ask that additional evidence and witnesses be produced (De Muniz 2004, 94).

New Russian Criminal Procedure Code

The new Criminal Procedure Code of the Russian Federation came into effect on July 1, 2002, after a dozen years of formulation. It moved the Russian justice system in the direction of adversarialism and into a "neo-inquisitorial" system along the lines followed in Western Europe generally (Solomon 2005a, 77). Previously, the pre-trial investigation had been conducted by a court investigator and subsequently by the prosecutor, and then, in the Stalin period, exclusively by the police. Defense lawyers had few rights during the pre-trial phase with access to the accused only possible at the conclusion of this phase and no access to the court file. At the trial, the *dossier* was admitted into evidence, and the judge verified its correctness through questioning of witnesses. Judges were biased in favor of the prosecution, and usually the prosecutor did not even attend the trial. Judges were expected to convict and, in cases of difficulty, to return to the investigation process (p. 79).

Reformers wanted to lessen this accusatorial bias through radical reforms in criminal procedure. In the 1990s, bias in favor of the prosecution was clearly established by the very low rate of acquittals, averaging only 0.4 percent overall. After the new code came into force, the rate of acquittals rose, doubling the previous rate, so that by 2003 the rate was 0.8 percent (0.6 percent if only state cases are included and not private prosecutions), but a significant number of acquittals were reversed on appeal (Solomon 2005a, 90–91).

The "Concept of Judicial Reform," prepared by nine leading jurists, offered a critique of Soviet justice and advocated maximum adversarialism in all phases of criminal procedure (Solomon 2005a, 80). It also recommended that the powers of the *prokuratura* be significantly reduced (De Muniz 2004, 82), and supported life tenure for judges along with guaranteed housing and access to health services, as well as adequate resource allocation for the courts (Solomon and Foglesong 2000, 11).

The new Code declares the presumption of innocence and places the burden of proof on the prosecution (Solomon 2005a). The expectation is that the accused person will be legally represented, and where there is no such representation, most evidence obtained during that time will be excluded. The court and judges are made fully independent of the prosecutor and are no longer subject to prosecutorial supervision for the conduct of trials. In the trial phase, the prosecution evidence must be actually presented by the prosecutor, and the presence of counsel for the defense is generally required also. The same evidence contained in the *dossier* must now be presented orally at trial, and new evidence rules exclude hearsay and testimony given during the pre-trial phase. The power to send a case back for further investigation as a method of ending a trial is now eliminated. However, during the preliminary hearing a judge may remit a case to the prosecutor for a five-day period but only to remedy any violations that would impede the trial.

In spite of these radical changes, the pre-trial investigation retains the inquisitorial form and continues the distinctly Soviet procedure of having the pre-trial investigation managed and controlled by the investigator who is not part of law enforcement or the prosecutor's office. The *dossier* remains key to the case as a basic source of knowledge about the crime charged and is transmitted to the court with the indictment. This seems at odds with the adversarial direction of the proceedings and can be said to have "tainted" the judges' minds even before the trial commences (Pomorski 2006, 142).

Pre-trial detention may only be ordered by a court, and searches, seizures, and wiretaps also require judicial orders. In terms of police and prosecutor relations, police and investigators have no power to open a case against a suspect and must request a prosecutor to do so, thereby providing a check on the evidence quality. An accused has a right to have counsel no later than twenty-four hours after the actual detention and before any interrogation takes place. After that time, counsel may meet with an accused at will for periods of up to eight hours, and counsel may attend all interrogations of the accused, witnesses, and experts.

The defense may see documents in the *dossier* as soon as they are compiled and will be given access to the entire *dossier* at the conclusion of the investigation. While the defense may interrogate witnesses, it is only able to have this new evidence introduced into the *dossier* if the investigator interrogates the person whose evidence is sought to be included. The defense itself is unable to compile a record of witnesses' statements and put them into evidence (Pomorski 2006, 142). One adverse change for the defense is that now the investigator no longer has to seek and give attention to exculpatory evidence because the underlying foundation of adversarialism shifts this duty to the defense (Solomon 2005a, 84–85).

Police objections to the new Code center on their inability to formally open a case, this being a power now given to the prosecutor. Police complain about the extra time needed to locate a prosecutor in remote areas, and the pressure to restore police powers continues (Solomon 2005a).

Prosecutors have found it difficult to supply sufficient officials for every trial and have objected to delays in starting trials when defense lawyers did not finish reading the *dossier* within a reasonable time. Also, prosecutors and police were very concerned by the new rule that both sides had to agree to evidence given in the preliminary inquiry being admitted at trial because generally defense counsel did not agree (Solomon 2005a, 88). By 2001 almost every region had established trial by jury and the national acquittal rate was 15 percent.[24] However, one-third of acquittals were reversed on appeal and remitted for new trials (p. 97). Many critics have described the abandonment of the inquisitorial principle of "truth finding" as the principal goal of judicial proceedings as "unpalatable" (Pomorski 2006, 135).

Comment

Tracing the history and evolution of criminal procedure reforms in these regions throws light on the bias toward conviction and the absence of rights for an accused in the postcolonial and Soviet codes of criminal procedure. In both regions, the collapse of authoritarian regimes brought about justice policies that aimed at democratization and the entrenchment of the rule of law. These policies stimulated little political interest and were regarded as technical exercises necessary to capture aspects of the adversarial system of justice and therefore ruled unproblematic. The specificity of the reforms in the regions seemed to the technicians of the justice system (i.e., the police, prosecutors, and judges) to present challenges to their domains of power and authority and met with resistance. The case studies demonstrate that justice reforms are political exercises that, when confronted with resistance, can only be mediated politically. Legal culture, long established modes of practice, and a bias toward conviction combined to delegitimize reforms that were often seen as benefitting the accused and producing more crime. While on the surface reforms have been put in place, nevertheless, powerful institutional players such as prosecutors have taken care to ensure that their established powers have not been overly diluted. Agitation for reversal of some reforms continues, justified by claims about the need to ensure public safety and security.

Based on this summary account, the transfer of U.S. justice discourses through USAID and international agencies to these regions can be seen as the Americanization of the Latin American and Russian legal systems, or as an element of the globalization associated with the establishment of new democracies thought to require entrenchment of the rule of law and human rights protection in order to create conditions for capturing capital flows and investment. Certainly, in Latin America it was the belief of many governments that reforming their justice systems to align more with adversarial justice models would benefit them economically. At the same time, this occurrence of the flow of the discourse of adversarial justice encountered local resistance, with the result that some reform elements were discarded after an initial period of uncritical acceptance while other features were circumvented. The outcome in both cases is an unfinished hybrid system in a state of flux as players within the system continue to contest elements that challenge their former capacity to control the process of criminal justice.

CRIMINAL LAW AND PROCEDURE IN CHINA

The radical course of Chinese history, especially since 1949, and China's special characteristics as a nation with a justice system that has undergone many dynamic changes over time mean that China must be included in any discussion of justice systems worldwide. Perhaps more than most states, China's social, cultural, and political context has configured Chinese forms of justice and justice systems in unique ways and for distinctive purposes. For this reason, this section includes a discussion of how Chinese authorities have perceived law, justice, and the rule of law in the past and now.

BOX 5.3   The Chinese Legal Tradition

Chinese legal development took place over many centuries. Some of the most important events are listed here.

- *Confucianism.* In about 500 BCE, Confucius wrote his philosophy of proper behavior and proper governance, stressing the need to have virtuous leaders who govern by enlightened example and follow a strict code of conduct based on compliance with rituals and subordination and respect in relationships such as father and son and ruler and governed. The inferior must respect and obey the superior, and the younger must respect and obey the older. Familial obligations based on respect and subordination to one's elders closely resembled the power structure. Thus *li* (informal law and custom) was superior to *fa* (formal law). A king should rule by virtue, setting a moral example for his people. Confucius saw law as having only a minor role in governance; proper rituals and virtue were the key principles. He considered punishment as a poor method of persuading the people to behave well, preferring benevolence and good example. While the law can convict and punish, it cannot teach the virtues of kindness, benevolence, and compassion (Ren 1997, 21). Controlling one's own conduct was regarded as one of the highest qualities of human virtue and submission to the authorities, and confession of wrongdoing and repentance were important mitigating factors in assessing punishment (p. 29). Criminality was not seen as a rational choice but rather as a lack of self-control or the outcome of insufficient moral education (p. 30). By the time of the Han Dynasty (206 BCE–220 CE), Confucianism had taken the role of the leading political ideology and remained so for successive generations of emperors (p. 22). Confucian values remain a key element in Chinese society and are especially reflected in Chinese forms of punishment where it regards human nature positively, believing that the virtuous elements of human nature can be amplified and enhanced by persuasion and good example.

- *Legalism.* The Legalists became active during the Qin Dynasty 221–207 BCE. They took issue with Confucianist views, arguing that governance should not operate on social distinctions but on law applied equally to all persons; that punishment, not moral example, was more likely to persuade people; and that rule by law was better than rule by men. Legalists believed that persons sought gratification, and therefore all were capable of criminality, and that social order could only be maintained through enforcing the law. A ruler must act swiftly and inflict serious punishment on those disobeying the law to curb the impulse toward self-gratification (Ren 1997, 21). Whether contemporary developments in law reform in China are designed to implement the rule *of law* or merely rule *by law* continues to be debated.

- *Law Codes.* Among the Chinese dynasties, issuing legal codes was something like issuing a constitution for a dynasty. The codes sought to maintain the stability of the government and contained detailed regulations about how persons were to behave and the punishments that could be inflicted for sanctioned acts. For example, the Tang Code, made around 617 and again

(Continued)

(Continued)

in 653, specified how beating with a light stick was to be organized (from ten to fifty blows) and specified its dimensions and composition. The Tang Code provided that criticism of the emperor was punishable by decapitation and forging an imperial decree by strangulation. The Qing Code provided a punishment of "slicing" for plotting rebellion and high treason, and strangulation for "fornication with force" (Ren 1997, 39). Punishments under this Code were adjusted according to social status; for example, if a slave hit a commoner and broke a limb, the punishment was strangulation. However, a master who killed a slave who had committed some offense would receive a punishment of only one hundred blows with the heavy stick. Status was judged according to four groups: intellectuals, farmers, workers, and merchants (p. 39).[25]

- **Cultural Revolution.** The Cultural Revolution was launched by Mao in 1966 to purge "counterrevolutionaries" in the Chinese Communist Party (CCP). From this time until Mao's death in 1976, the shutdown of the legal system was almost absolute. In this period, the legal system was displaced by working-class families forming revolutionary committees to arrest, interrogate, torture, try, and punish alleged counterrevolutionaries in ad hoc courts. Consequently, tens of thousands were sent to labor camps and prisons. It is estimated that during the ten years of the Cultural Revolution, forty million died as a result of riots, torture, execution, and suicide (Ren 1997, 100).

- **Legal Reform.** From 1979 until the present, the government of the People's Republic of China (PRC) has made more than two thousand laws, regulations, and decrees, many concerned with economic reform, but these also include a Law of Criminal Procedure in 1996; Laws on Judges, Lawyers, and Procurators 1995, 1996; People's Courts and People's Procurates 1979; Regulations on Arrest and Detention 1979; and on Detention Centers 1990 (Head 2011). Levels of street crime have increased dramatically since legal reform (due in large part to migrating rural dwellers moving into the cities). The crime rate has tripled, and new crimes, especially economic crime and drug-related crime, have demanded new measures of control (Liu, Zhang, and Messner 2001, xii, xiv, 67).[26]

- **Legal Scholarship.** Chinese legal scholars enjoy the same status as judges, prosecutors, and lawyers (Head 2011, 589).

BOX 5.4   Contemporary Chinese View of Law

- The influence of the Chinese legal tradition, including dynastic imperial attitudes to law, is reflected today in the Chinese view of law as "an instrument of state power, to be wielded for the purpose of maintaining order, stability and efficiency" (Head 2011, 590). Current legal reforms are a fusion of the imperial legal tradition, Western law, and socialist law, but traditional legal culture restrains the penetration of foreign legal liberalism (Potter 2001, 7; Ren 1997, 3). Although legal reform involves applying Western liberal models of law and legal institutions as policy transfers, local values and norms always affect and shape those models (Potter 2001, 6).

- In the Chinese view, a constitution is regarded as a political document and not a strictly legal one. It is regarded as a document of legal formalism and as a statement of general justice policy—it is not seen as creating substantive legal rights (Ren 1997, 78). Law is a tool for disseminating and implementing directives from policy-making organs and is itself a type of political directive (Castellucci 2007, 41, 51). It is therefore fundamentally instrumentalist (Potter 2001, 10). Accordingly, while there are constitutional guarantees of freedom of speech, assembly, and association, at the same time all citizens are required to obey the leadership of the CCP and follow the socialist road. The right to speak, therefore, means speaking in a manner consistent with CCP orthodoxy (Ren 1997, 103).

- Chinese laws are "often side-stepped by the government officials," and China's authoritarian tradition and lack of a democratic voice in social control have not been changed as a result of economic openness (Ren 1997, 2–3).

- Chinese legislators enact laws that are deliberately vague and ambiguous, thereby affording bureaucrats the utmost flexibility in their interpretation and application of laws and regulations (Potter 2001, 11).

- Over the past twenty years, the Chinese legal system has developed through a process of "selective adaptation, by which borrowed foreign norms about law and legal institutions have been mediated by local legal culture" (Potter 2001, 1–2). While foreign lawyers will recognize the structures that have been put in place for dispute resolution, "the norms and practices these institutions apply often depart quite significantly from the expectations of those familiar with liberal legal systems. . . . local legal culture . . . acts as a normative filter through which flow the influences of foreign and international legal models" (p. 37).

Contemporary Chinese Legal System

The reform of the legal system began in 1979 with an emphasis on developing the legal infrastructure and the creation of many new legal initiatives by the National People's Congress (NPC), State Council, and the ministries (Brown 1997, xxi). The NPC is the highest legislative body and has about three thousand deputies (Li 2014, 39). In explaining this initiative, some argue that the Chinese leadership's new emphasis on economic growth necessitated the creation of a legal framework to underpin and support that policy, thus linking the state-planned economy with legal reform (Potter 2001, 1). Nowadays, China's laws and courts incorporate elements of foreign systems but with "Chinese characteristics" (Brown 1997, xx). With the enactment of a Judge's Law, Police Law, Procurator's Law, and a Lawyer's Law there has been a professionalization of law enforcement. The Chinese believe that the criminal justice system is moving toward an adversarial system (p. 28).

The dominant legislative branch of government is the NPC, run by its Standing Committee which operates through three organs: the State Council, under which is located the Ministry of Public Security (police); the Supreme People's Procuratorate (prosecutors); and the Supreme People's Court (Brown 1997, xi). Major laws emanate from the NPC, and the NPC also receives guidance from Communist Party organs, which parallel the administrative organs of the government (p. 7).

In the administration of a law, there is an interaction between the CCP and the government (p. 7).

The Supreme People's Court is located in the capital and under it are located a provincial court system comprising a High People's Court, an Intermediate People's Court, and the Basic People's Court. There are also many municipal court systems and several specialized courts, such as the People's Liberation Army, the Railway, and the Maritime (Brown 1997, 4).

Prosecution Function

The Procuratorate exercises the following functions:

- Approving arrests and appearing in court to prosecute. Where the Procuratorate does not approve an arrest, the person must be immediately released (Brown 1997, 9–10). The time limit for deciding whether or not to prosecute a suspect in custody is one month. If the decision to prosecute is made, the procuracy files a bill of prosecution in a People's Court (p. 14).

- Investigating certain types of cases such as government corruption involving violations of the law by officials.

- Supervising the courts in criminal cases by a "protest" (a kind of appeal) against first and second instance decisions through a process known as adjudication supervision.

• Supervising the activities of public security organs for legality and of prison and labor. The functions of the public security bureaus (which are established at all levels of government) are to investigate crime and maintain public safety and public administration. In order to make an arrest, they must seek an arrest warrant from the procuracy. In terms of public administration, their functions include traffic, maintenance of public order, registration and compliance with health standards, and administering reeducation through labor programs (p. 11).

Courts—History and Function

According to Ronald Brown (1997, 123), from 1949 the law and courts were seen as a tool to control "undesirable elements" in society, but changes in attitude were shown in 1978 with the rule of Deng Xiaoping and the law began to be used in a different way, namely, as an inducement for foreign investment under the national drive for modernization; during the transition to a socialist market economy with laws being utilized to achieve competition; and in the move into global participation requiring adherence to international law and standards.

From 1949, the courts operated as an arm of the state and under the guidance of the CCP. During the period of the Cultural Revolution from 1966 to 1976, law and the courts "were not present in any recognizably 'legitimate' form" (Brown 1997, 128). With the arrest of the Gang of Four in 1976, the Cultural Revolution ended and Deng was installed in 1978 with the trial of the Gang of Four taking place in 1980 and 1981. During the period 1949 to 1979, the courts were subject to a large element of political direction. In 1979, the Central Committee of the CCP issued a directive that the CCP would no longer directly intervene in the day-to-day operation of the courts or in specific cases but would instead simply monitor the work of the courts and give only general policy guidance (p. 128).

Courts and Judges— Political Influence

One of the "Chinese characteristics" of the Chinese legal system is the exercise of political influence over the acts and decisions of the courts. The absence of the doctrine of separation of powers in Chinese law and politics means that the Chinese court system does not follow Western models that adhere to that principle. Instead, "Chinese courts operate as specific organs of the state, implementing the state policy at a local level, through the legal system, through judicial directives, hierarchies and internal procedures" (Castellucci 2007, 51).[27]

From 1949 to 1979, the CCP exercised absolute control over the judiciary in terms of policy and through a system of examination and approval of court judgments by CCP committees within the courts (Li 2014, 53). Today, there is general agreement among commentators that the courts are subject to the political mandate of the CCP but no agreement on influence beyond that. In the 1990s, the CCP set overall policy guidelines, for example, specific campaigns of law enforcement, like the anti-corruption directives of the mid-1990s and the "strike hard" campaigns first launched in 1983 (p. 51).[28] The courts may seek advice on issues that are politically sensitive, and the CCP is involved in the appointment process for judges and judicial personnel and in continuing education and materials included in judicial tools such as judge's handbooks (Brown 1997, 34).[29] Politically, the court is subject to CCP leadership at the local level. Hualing Fu points out that the CCP determines the priorities within the judicial workload, is involved in coordinating the courts' relations with other institutions in the legal field, and actually makes the decisions in important and contentious cases (Fu 2003, 193, 203). As with other units in the legal system, the work of the courts is subject to the supervision of the procuratorate, and if the procuratorate protests a decision, the court is required to review the case (Fu 2000, 2003).

The following methods employed to influence the courts have been identified:

• Under the somewhat euphemistic rubric of "leadership" or "supervision," the courts are required to enter verdicts as directed by the CCP or by the government in cases that are nationally or locally important, for example, major corruption cases involving senior CCP or government officials, and in cases involving the economy where the outcome could affect stability in a region such as in a labor dispute.[30]

• The most common method of interference is a written note to the court instructing it to judge a case in a certain way. Where an off-the-record approach is considered advisable, the telephone or a person-to-person approach to give instructions or gauge the court's attitude to a case will be adopted.

- Judges may resist or counter interference by delaying a trial or trying a case speedily if they expect to receive an instruction. Sometimes, they simply ignore the political direction, although generally they follow CCP instructions and may even invite CCP intervention (Fu 2003, 206).

- Judges may be hounded by persons carrying messages from local cadres seeking favors or making threats if decisions are not made in the manner they wish, or bringing bribes, reminders, or requests (Ren 1997, 59).[31]

Other commentators do not believe there is direct involvement by CCP officials in court decisions but do accept that the CCP influences the courts by setting broad judicial policy agendas and that it also has the capacity to influence the courts by maintaining internal disciplinary procedures over court members' conduct. (Brown 1997, 77). Nevertheless, in strict law, judges are granted autonomy in the performance of their duties under the law (Brown 1997, 105). The same right is given to the Procuratorate (p. 109). For example, the Organic Law of the People's Courts provides: "The people's courts shall exercise judicial power independently, in accordance with the provisions of the law, and shall not be subject to interference by any administrative organ, public organization or individual" (quoted in Brown 1997, 127).

However, Ignazio Castellucci (2007, 56) argues that judicial independence refers only to the independence of each court considered as a whole with respect to other organs of the state and is not meant to refer to individuals acting as judges within a specific court. Within the court system, judges are responsible to other, more senior judges in the judicial hierarchy, imposing significant constraints on actual judicial independence, as it is generally understood (Head 2011, 586).

Another view of judicial independence offered by a Chinese scholar asserts that interference with the court involves only conduct that is illegal, such as "replacing laws with personal orders," and that mere "guidance" from an official is not illegal conduct such that it amounts to interference (Head 2011, 602). John Head suggests that in the Chinese context, judicial independence is a working rule and not a key principle of political organization in terms of the separation of powers (p. 602).

Western concepts of judicial independence and autonomy consistent with the liberal notion of the rule of law should therefore not be assumed to apply in China as a matter of course, even where translations from Chinese legal texts refer to "the rule of law." The legal system should not be regarded as an isolated element working within the society according to its own rules, free from other influences. Rather, it should be seen as "part of an integrated political-legal system of governance" (Castellucci 2007, 63). Accordingly, as one chief justice of the Politburo Standing Committee (PSC) of the CCP expressed about the autonomy of the courts, "The courts must exercise the independent power of the judiciary under the leadership of the Party. Adherence to the party's leadership means that the people's courts independence in decision making must be monitored and approved by the Party." This perspective reflects not only the Mao style of governance but also the Chinese tradition of political centralism (Ren 1997, 56–57).

Court Structure, Decisions, Operations, and Corrupt Practices

BOX 5.5

Chinese courts are established under the Organic Law of the People's Court as

- Local People's Courts at Basic, Intermediate, and Higher levels—the BPCs handles 80 percent of first instance cases;
- Special People's Courts—military, railway transport courts, maritime, and other special courts; and

(Continued)

(Continued)

- Supreme People's Court (SPC)—does not generally deal with cases at first instance except cases that "are likely to have a major bearing on the country as a whole" (Brown 1997, 51).

The relationship of the SPC to the lower courts includes making use of various modes of interaction so that the latter can receive advice and direction from the SPC on issues of law. Unusually, as compared to Western systems, this occurs regardless of the fact that decisions of the lower courts may be reversed on law or fact on review by the SPC. The aim in seeking advice is to prevent judgments from being overturned and having a case sent back for re-trial. As well, the SPC through adjudication supervision may revisit lower court judgments—Brown likens this advice function to the common law system of precedents (Brown 1997, 70; Li 2014, 27).

The Supreme People's Procuratorate exercises "supervision over the judicial activities of the people's courts to ensure they conform to the law" (Brown 1997, 142). This follows the Soviet model and was intended to ensure that the unified application of law would be guaranteed. It extends to protests or appeals as a form of supervision of court adjudication (Li 2014, 63).

Similar to the courts, there is a hierarchy of Procuratorates with the Supreme People's Procuratorate at the top and Procuratorates at the provincial, city, and county levels. Their main function is to investigate crimes, approve arrests, conduct prosecution, and exercise supervision (Li 2014, 59). In practice, the organs of public security conduct most criminal investigations (p. 59).

SOURCES: Brown 1997, 51; Li 2014, 7, 11.

In terms of the actual process of producing court decisions, as in other civil law jurisdictions, the decision generally is relatively brief and non-analytical as compared to common law jurisdictions. There are no published dissents and no precedents are cited, but it is clear that the lower courts receive guidance on legal interpretation (Brown 1997, 78).

According to Brown (1997, 82) about whether decisions act as guidance or precedent, Chinese court decisions have elements of both civil and common law systems. It is significant that the Supreme People's Court (SPC) has mandated that "all opinions and instructions given by the SPC on the application of laws shall be followed, but it is not appropriate, however, to cite them directly" (Brown 1997, 82).

The Supreme People's Court has the power to issue "judicial explanations" that are effectively a form of legislation as far as the courts are concerned. The term refers to statements issued by the SPC clarifying legislative provisions. Explanations are regarded as binding and have the status of an addendum to laws and are therefore themselves a source of law. The SPC also issues "replies," and these replies are responses to questions raised by lower courts (Head 2011, 588).

Judges under the law do not have the power to punish for contempt of court, but penalties are provided for noncompliance with court judgments (Brown 1997, 84). Chinese judges come from three distinct backgrounds: government bureaucracies, the military, and universities and law schools (Fu 2003, 206). Judges appointed from the bureaucracy may come from departments that have been downsized and lack any practice or qualifications in the law, or they may be appointed because there is a shortage of court personnel. This group has been diminishing as more law graduates are appointed. China has a long tradition of appointing ex-military as judges, and demobilized soldiers are appointed because they fall into the category of persons treated as "instruments of the state" (p. 207). As judges, they continue to safeguard the state in a different guise. Although they may not possess legal qualifications, they are valued for possessing qualities of discipline, determination, and a propensity to obey orders (p. 207).

According to Fu (2003), Chinese criminal judges are competent and are assisted by the relative stability of the criminal law. In the Chinese approach to alleged criminality, the emphasis is on seeking the truth from a set of facts and on ensuring that the correct outcome is reached based on facts. Consequently, issues of law scarcely arise (p. 209). Most judges are members of the CCP and receive regular training from the CCP on party policies. As CCP members, they are expected to comply with the party's wishes on all issues of concern to the CCP (Li 2014, 51).

Corruption in the judiciary (as opposed to limitations on their autonomy) is associated with issues of personal relationships *(guanxi)*, favors *(renqing)*, and bribes *(jinqian)*. Corruption has become more sophisticated over time as Fu (2003, 211) illustrates: "Where once judges traded in cash, restaurant meals and cigarettes, alcohol, and other goods, today the currency of misconduct is more likely to be a trip overseas for 'study,' the 'loan' of a car, or a foreign education for a judge's child."

Third parties are commonly involved in corrupt practices. For example, a judge may refer a claimant or defendant in a case to a particular lawyer who negotiates the gift for the judge and organizes the evidence and arguments that will determine the issue before the court. Bribes can also be passed to judges through gambling. Lawyers play a prominent part in judicial corruption, and as facilitators they have assisted in institutionalizing corruption (Fu 2003, 211). In criminal cases, it is possible to buy a shorter sentence (p. 212).

BOX 5.6   Social Contact With Judges in China

Unlike judges in the West, who commonly restrict their contacts with lawyers to courtrooms, judges in China conduct themselves the same as other government officials and are active in social circles. For example, they may gamble with lawyers and procurators for large sums of money.

SOURCE: Fu 2003, 217.

Criminal Procedure in China

For the Chinese, criminality is not seen as simply breaking the law (Fu 2003, 195). Rather, it is the expression of "an insurgent act against the state authority and as a retrogradation of the normal relationship between the ruler and the ruled" (Ren 1997, 130). Accordingly, surrender and confession to the authorities become vital elements in demonstrating an offender's desire to integrate back into society and show contrition for what is regarded as anti-state activity. In addition, according to Yuwen Li (2014, 127), public opinion in China privileges the interests of the majority (the public) over those of minorities (including criminals), and this has resulted in a balance in favor of punishment rather than legal rights.[32] Whereas the law provides that a person cannot be found guilty if guilt cannot be established according to the evidence, "the common practice is that, in cases of doubt, the accused will not be released but will rather be punished with a more lenient sentence" (p. 127).

Writing after an exchange visit with Chinese prosecutors in 2000, Ira Belkin offered the following view of the operation of the Chinese criminal justice system:

The system is marked by long periods of investigatory detention, a high rate of confessions, and administrative penalties that are tantamount to incarceration without trial. Criminal suspects have no right to refuse interrogation, enjoy no presumption of innocence, and have no right to confront their accusers or compel the presence of witnesses to testify in their defense. The right to counsel is extremely limited in the investigatory phase of a case and, although there is a right to counsel at trial, that right is circumscribed by the absence of pre-trial discovery and the limited ability of the defense to conduct its own investigation. (Belkin 2000, 61)

Court cases in China are classified as criminal, civil, economic, or administrative. The courts handle only serious criminal cases because the police determine guilt and impose punishment for minor offenses. Minor offenses are regarded as *unlawful* acts as opposed to *criminal* acts. Each year the police deal with some three million minor offenses, and the criminal courts process about five hundred thousand criminal offenses (Fu 2003, 194).

There was no criminal procedure code in the first thirty years following the declaration of the

People's Republic of China in 1949 because attempts to formulate a code were frustrated by the general chaos in government caused by the political and social campaigns waged by Mao. In the absence of criminal laws, criminal conduct could be defined by resolutions and decisions of the CCP, but there were no standards defining what body had the authority to lay down rules about punishment (Lawyers Committee 1998, 12–13).

A Criminal Procedure Code was finally enacted in 1979, based on the Soviet inquisitorial model, but it proved inadequate to the task. For example, principles such as the presumption of innocence, the right to counsel and due process were not included (Head 2011, 591–92). In addition, the 1979 code contained instances of moralistic language not easily interpreted by legal professionals such as "stirring up trouble," "hooligan activities," "odious circumstances," and "the people's indignation is very great" and failed to provide procedures for the conduct of criminal cases (Lawyers Committee 1998, 16).

In 1997, a new Criminal Procedure Law was enacted, having been drafted largely by scholars and experts in criminal procedure. Revisions to it were made in 2012 (Li 2014, 88). It was revised to take account of the changes brought about by economic growth and as a response to international human rights criticism (Potter 2001, 106). The effect of the revision was to:

- Give defendants earlier access to lawyers and more opportunity to secure release on bail, but in practice lawyers may not be permitted to meet an accused in private or not permitted to meet at all without any reason being given for refusal except possibly on grounds of "state security" (Li 2014, 111).

- Give defense lawyers access to prosecution evidence prior to trial. They may have access from the time a prosecutor begins to examine a case for prosecution (Li 2014, 108). However, where lawyers collect evidence that contradicts the prosecution evidence, they run a risk of being accused of falsifying evidence or preventing the authorities from obtaining evidence and of being prosecuted (Li 2014, 113).

- Require prosecutors to offer reliable and ample evidence of guilt.

- Give prosecutors and defense lawyers the right to examine and cross-examine witnesses, but generally they are not called to give evidence so this right is essentially illusory (Li 2014, 104).

- Eliminate the practice of permitting persons to be convicted of offenses not established by law by using analogous provisions. (This meant a person could be convicted of an offense that was not prohibited by law.)

- Eliminate "counterrevolutionary" crimes, but nevertheless diminish the effect of this by creating an offense of "endangering state security" where no intent needs be proved.

- Specifically address economic crimes, including protection of intellectual property, corporate governance and securities, banking and finance, and stock market activity.

- Reduce the application of the death penalty (Potter 2001, 106–7).

- The judge no longer conducts a pre-trial examination. Instead she conducts only a procedural review, ensuring the adequate completion of the dossier file comprising the charges, index of evidence, copies of relevant documents, and list of witnesses (Liu et al. 2001, 144).

- Ensure the trial judge continues to play an active role in the trial, as in inquisitorial systems, even though the trial is adversarial in nature (Liu et al. 2002, 145). Functions previously exercised by a judge in an inquisitorial system (e.g., questioning witnesses) and reading written testimony are now performed by the prosecution and defense. In reality, the system is now a mixed adversarial/ inquisitorial model. Judges rarely interrupt prosecutors who control the course of trials (Li 2014, 104).

- Continues the problematic nature of the presumption of innocence. Article 12 notes that "no person should be determined guilty without a judgment rendered by a People's Court according to law." Chinese scholars are divided as to whether this statement amounts to a presumption of innocence, and many argue it simply says that courts determine guilt. The official explanation of Article 12 points out that the presumption of innocence found in the West was not wanted, but at the same time that the drafters were "firmly against the presumption of guilt" (Li 2014, 90). Others argue, however, that Article 12, taken together with the law as a whole, reflects elements of this principle and that it is clear that proof of guilt is the responsibility of the prosecutor—the accused does not have to prove innocence (p. 91).

- Maintain the fact that there is no right of silence. The 1997 law and the 2012 revision of the law give no right to remain silent as the corollary to the presumption of innocence. A criminal suspect is required to "answer investigators questions truthfully" and may only refuse to answer questions that are "irrelevant to the case," a fact determined by the investigator (Li 2014, 92). According to Li (p. 93), the refusal to confer a right to silence reflects the historical reliance on confessions. Without a confession, police consider an investigation incomplete and prosecutors are reluctant to prosecute and judges to make a finding of guilt. It is likely that an accused who did not confess will receive a harsher sentence than one who provided a confession.

- Ban the use of torture to obtain a confession and the use of other illegal means to secure evidence, and such evidence is to be excluded (Article 50). In addition, the 2012 revisions require that interrogations of suspects must be recorded by audio or video (Li 2014, 104).

Stages of Trial

The Criminal Procedure Code established four principal stages in criminal procedure: pre-trial stage, first instance, second instance, and execution of criminal punishments.

Pre-trial stage. The People's Procuratorates may file cases for investigation (Belkin 2000, 11), state police may also file cases, and private prosecutions are also possible. If police refuse to file, the Procuratorate may require police to explain their decision and if their response is considered unsatisfactory, the Procuratorate may require police to file (Belkin 2000, 11, citing Article 87 of the Criminal Procedure Law). Inquiries into an alleged criminal act are conducted by the public security organs, and in certain cases the courts and the procuratorates may also conduct inquiries.

Interrogations of suspects are performed by the Procuratorates, investigators, public security organs, and by a People's Court. After a case file has been opened, a suspect may undergo up to twelve hours of interrogation, and he or she may not consult with anyone during this period (Belkin 2000, 12). After the expiry of the twelve-hour period, if the police wish to continue holding the suspect, they must use the detention power regulated by Article 61 of the Criminal Procedure Code. This allows police to detain when

- a suspect is discovered immediately after committing a crime or preparing to or in the process of commission,

- the suspect is identified as the offender by a victim or eyewitness,

- the suspect has evidence of the crime on his or her person or in a residence,

- the suspect attempts suicide or to escape after committing a crime,

- the suspect is likely to destroy evidence,

- the suspect does not provide a true name and address or where identity is unknown, or

- the suspect is strongly suspected of committing a series of crimes or as a member of a gang. (Belkin 2000, 12–13)

According to Belkin (2000), an estimated 90 percent of suspects are detained using this procedure during investigation, rendering the process virtually automatic.

BOX 5.7 Confession

As in the case of Japan, a Chinese tradition of confession exists: voluntary or forced *(tanbai)* and of self-surrender *(zishou)*. Historical accounts reveal that great importance was always attached to confession and surrender and that leniency in punishment was the norm when offenders did so. Consequently, the typical justice model requires lenient treatment for those who confess and severe punishment for those who reject the accusation of criminality (Ren 1997, 116).

Voluntary confession has been employed as a strategy of crime control in China. Law enforcement and government agencies have issued warrants urging offenders to come forward and confess their crimes. It has been common for tens of thousands to take advantage of what amounts to an amnesty for confessions of guilt and repayment of stolen property and moneys obtained fraudulently or through extortion or bribery (Ren 1997, 122).

A person may arrange for a lawyer to provide representation. The investigating authority may attend meetings between the suspect and his or her lawyer. The Procuratorates determine whether or not to prosecute a case based on the existence of reliable and sufficient evidence (Head 2011, 594–95). The investigating authority has the right to decide whether a suspect should be kept in custody or released, but there appears in practice to be a presumption against release (Belkin 2000, 12).

Under Article 69 of the Criminal Procedure Code, between three and seven days after the initial detention, police must seek the Procuratorate's approval for formal arrest, but this period can be extended to thirty days and the Procurator must give a decision within seven days of that thirty days. Effectively then, police may keep a suspect in custody for up to thirty-seven days (Belkin 2000, 13). Taking into account the period allowed for the Procuratorate to decide whether or not to prosecute and the permitted extensions

of that period, Belkin suggests that a total period of up to seven and a half months could pass before the final decision to prosecute is made, during which a suspect may be held in custody (p. 14).

Investigators are permitted to conduct searches without judicial or other outside approval and need not establish the probability that a search will reveal evidence of a crime (Belkin 2000, 17).

First instance. A People's Court in the place where the alleged crime was committed has jurisdiction. A panel of either three judges or a panel of one judge and two people's assessors judge trials at first instance in the Primary and Intermediate People's Courts. However, in cases where summary trial is possible, only one judge is necessary.[33] In the higher courts, the panel comprises between three and seven judges and/or assessors. Generally cases are heard in public except where state security is involved. Trial procedure is outlined in Box 5.8.

BOX 5.8   Trial Procedure

1. The court begins the trial by questioning the defendant about identity, status, and the progress of the case. The defendant may request the recusal of the judges and the prosecutor.

2. The prosecutor reads the charges and the defendant is asked to respond to them. The defense lawyer and the victim have the right to question the defendant.

3. The prosecutor reads aloud the evidence and the court asks the defendant if he has any opinion about the evidence. Where the prosecutor calls a witness or if the victim is a party to the trial, the witness and victim may be questioned by the defense and the victim may question the defendant. (It is uncommon for witnesses to give actual evidence at the trial, and written witness statements may be given in evidence even without any opportunity to cross-examine the witness.[34]) The defense then presents its evidence.

4. The prosecutor, defense lawyer, defendant, and victim may then speak on the case with the defendant being the last to speak. The standard of proof is "the facts are clear and the evidence is reliable and sufficient" (Criminal Procedure Code, Article 162).

5. The panel of judges then retires and returns with a verdict and sentence (the death penalty is provided for in some thirty-five Articles of the Criminal Procedure Law for offenses ranging from homicide to rape to drug trafficking, bribery, and fraud.

SOURCE: Belkin (2000), 19–21.

Second instance. This term refers to an appeal or protest from a first instance decision based on an alleged error having been made by the lower court. The Procuratorate may protest a decision,

as may the victims of the crime on facts or law, and the appeal or protest need not be heard in public.

Execution of criminal punishment. The Procuratorate is entitled to supervise the execution of punishments by executing organs. The death sentence may be imposed but is subject to confirmation by the Supreme People's Court.

Comment

The Chinese legal tradition, Confucian influences, the impact of Marxist-Leninist doctrines, and the modernization of China have combined to create a distinctly Chinese model of criminal procedure. Chinese legal tradition shows that the law was used as an instrument of rule and control in the time of the emperors and that the role of law in society remained substantially unchanged under the communist system: the notion of the rule of law as opposed to rule by law was inimical to tradition and incompatible with communist doctrine. After a period of ten years with no functioning legal system, China embarked on a modernization phase during which it has appropriated models of criminal procedure from the West. However, in writing its codes of criminal procedure, China has fashioned criminal procedures with "Chinese characteristics" and located them within a system of law that is subject to outside political influence and pressure, thus maintaining the traditional view of the law as instrumentalist.

The Chinese system of criminal procedure mixes elements of the adversarial and inquisitorial but continues to rely on confessions, sometimes obtained through torture, to establish guilt. It is characterized by the power to impose lengthy periods of detention, by searches that do not need prior judicial approval, and by restrictions on access to lawyers. Indeed, defense lawyers like those in France, have no credibility among other actors in the system. It is probable that more empirical studies of the criminal justice system and its procedures will reveal a substantial variance between the law on the books and the law in action.

Prosecutors and the Prosecution Function

The prosecutor is a dominant figure within every criminal justice system—inquisitorial, adversarial, or hybrid. According to the country, the role of prosecutor may be termed *ministerio público, prokuratura, procurator,* or *procureur.* Depending on the nature of the system and national laws,

prosecutors may possess some or all of the following powers: investigatory, prosecutorial, supervisory, and sentencing. They may be elected, or they may be appointed as a public official within a hierarchical structure that is part of executive government. They may possess very broad or more limited discretion in deciding whether or not to prosecute, and they may be subject to minimal or greater levels of accountability for the proper exercise of their functions. Prosecutors may enjoy absolute independence in carrying out their functions, or they may be subject to some level of control or direction, either directly by some person or authority or through the medium of guidelines or instructions.

In this section, a number of important themes associated with the office of prosecutor will be explored, namely, prosecutorial discretion, the independence of prosecutors, guidelines for prosecutors, accountability of prosecutors, the status of the prosecutor, prosecutors sentencing powers, police and prosecutor relations, and the convergence of criminal justice systems in terms of the prosecution function. This discussion illustrates very significant differences between a U.S. prosecutor and prosecutors in other justice systems. This in turn raises many questions about the appropriateness of the U.S. model of prosecutor and the desirability of other models. We address questions such as the following: What features of the office of prosecutor are essential for its proper operation? Why are there such variations in the prosecutor model across countries, or are these variations more apparent than real? What underlying philosophy do laws mandate that should guide a prosecutor in deciding whether or not to charge? How and why does prosecutor *law in action* differ from *black letter law?* Why do prosecutors plea bargain, and is this a legitimate practice if it improves the efficiency of the criminal justice system? How can prosecutors be made more accountable without infringing their independence? These questions are addressed within a framework that examines how U.S. prosecution practice differs from that of other states.

As a starting point, the following is a useful summary of the powers generally possessed by prosecutors in the United States:

> The American prosecutor rules the criminal justice system. He determines whether to accept or decline a case, what crimes to allege,

and the number of counts to charge. He decides whether to participate in plea negotiations and sets the terms of the resulting agreements. He directs pretrial and trial strategy, and frequently sets the convicted defendant's sentence. (Luna and Wade 2012, xi)

American prosecutors have been described by Tonry as "lawless" and the American system of public prosecution as "unique in the world" (Luna and Wade 2012, 5) because prosecutors possess such a wide discretion, almost unreviewable by the courts,[35] and because harsh sentences under "three strikes" laws, mandatory minimum penalties, and laws punishing repeat offenders allow prosecutors to threaten and charge offenses carrying severe penalties. Fearing a lengthy sentence (often out of proportion to the alleged criminality), a defendant will accept an offer to plead guilty to a lesser offense with a lighter penalty, sometimes even when he or she is innocent of any guilt (Tonry 2012, 5).

Prosecutorial Discretion

The principal prosecutor (the district attorney) in a county within a state in the United States is generally an elected official.[36] She prosecutes all state crimes charged by her office. Every district attorney is able to exercise the prosecutorial power free from any direction or control by any other prosecuting authority, including the state attorney general. Accordingly, in the decentralized U.S. prosecution system, the elected district attorney (who heads up an office of prosecutors and may manage that office but not conduct prosecutions) is said to be accountable to those who voted her into office.

Federal prosecutors (the U.S. attorney for a district), who only prosecute federal crimes, are politically appointed to ninety-three judicial districts and, as political appointees, have no guarantee of being reappointed when there is a change of presidential administration (Moohr 2004, 196). Among adversarial systems, political appointments are far from the norm. For example, in Canada, the United Kingdom, and Australia, prosecutors are career public servants, selected on merit after an open hiring process has been conducted. A similar situation prevails in inquisitorial systems, where prosecutors are usually located in the judicial or executive branch of government. In some states, the structural location

differs. For example, in Norway and Denmark, prosecutors are situated within divisions of police departments but are independent from police (Tonry 2012, 14).

To get elected, potential district attorneys must take account of the fact that U.S. voters generally expect them to advocate for a tough line on law and order and, once in office, to secure convictions. If they fail in this regard, they will not be reelected to office. Accordingly, district attorneys may be said to be directly accountable to those who elect them for the performance of their functions, especially in regard to securing convictions. Nevertheless, U.S. state prosecutors have almost complete discretion in making the decision to charge and almost total immunity in making that decision (Gottfredson and Gottfredson 1988). This discretion has been described as "the single most unreviewed exercise of the power of the criminal law available to an individual in the American system of justice" (p. 14) and as conferring on a prosecutor the status of a godlike figure (Moohr 2004, 165). As a result, although they work within hierarchical organizational frameworks, individual U.S. state prosecutors have great freedom in their charging decisions.[37]

Luna and Wade point out that in both U.S. and European systems, the decision-making powers enjoyed by prosecutors make them the most powerful actors within their respective criminal justice systems (Luna and Wade 2012, 1). It is therefore important to ask questions such as the following: What constraints may operate to limit this discretion, other than the possibility of not being reelected? Are there internal constraints within prosecutor's offices, or do the courts impose limits or readily review exercises of discretion?

In *Germany,* prosecutorial discretion has "widened dramatically" in recent years (Boyne 2012, 37) despite the fact that Germany is a civil law jurisdiction, which applies the "legality" principle requiring that comparably situated persons must be treated in the same or similar way and that all cases are prosecuted to trial when sufficient evidence of guilt exists. This expansion in discretion is evidenced in part by the percentage of cases that actually go to trial. Germany is in the bottom range among European countries. Shawn Boyne (2012, 38) points out that German prosecutors submit less than 20 percent of incoming cases to trial. A comparison reveals that England and Wales, Finland, and Hungary bring more than two-thirds of cases to trial (p. 38). Thus German prosecutors, despite the legality principle, have in practice a wide discretion to divert cases away from the trial process. In practice, prosecutors apply the "expediency" principle under which prosecutors dispose of cases in good faith based on sound reasons (Tonry 2012, 10).

German prosecutors regard themselves as objective and as fact finders with a duty to discover the truth. This is reflected in the fact that German prosecutors have the right to ask a court to acquit a defendant, if, after trial, the evidence does not support the charges, and also the right to appeal what they consider to be a wrongful conviction (Boyne 2012). The position is similar, in theory, for *Italy,* where prosecutors are charged to be impartial and to disclose both exculpatory and inculpatory evidence. However, in practice, Italian prosecutors focus on discovering evidence of guilt and leave defense counsel to find any exculpatory evidence (Caianiello 2012, 251).

In *Italy,* prosecutors are members of the judiciary (both are categorized as *magistrati*) and entitled to the same independence as judges. Both judges and prosecutors can transfer from judicial to prosecutorial functions (Caianiello 2012, 250).

In *France,* the *procureur* as well as being responsible for prosecutions, also makes the decision to charge. Like the trial judge and the investigating judge, the *procureur* is a *magistrat* (judicial officer rather than a judge as such) and exercises judicial functions, receives a common judicial training along with judges and has a professional ideology directed toward representing the public interest (Hodgson 2012). In other words, the *procureur* is immersed in the same professional legal culture as other *magistrats.* Her discretion extends to the investigation of criminal offenses, and she may direct police and possesses police powers (p. 119; see also "Inquisitorial Procedure in France" for a discussion of the role of the *procureur* in the *garde à vue*). In addition, the *procureur* alone decides whether to refer a case to the investigating magistrate (p. 131).

Prosecutorial Guidelines

One way to limit the discretion of prosecutors is to set guidelines on matters such as charging and sentencing. Guidelines can be set by law or administratively. Guidelines also bring a degree of accountability because prosecutorial actions can be reviewed for compliance with guidelines.

Although U.S. state prosecutors may have some general office guidelines relating to their functions that set internal policies, this has little effect on the extent of their discretion (Podgor 2012, 9). Other than processes for assigning work and discussion of individual cases, most state prosecutors are left to make their decisions entirely without any effective accountability.[38]

The same cannot be said of federal prosecutors because the Department of Justice issues guidance or guidelines for federal prosecutors in the form of the *United States Attorneys' Manual* and the *Criminal Resource Manual.* Memoranda issued by various attorney generals must also be taken into account. Although these documents do not have the force of law, prosecutors are expected to follow them, and allegations of noncompliance with the guidelines are supposed to be reviewed by the Department of Justice, Office of Professional Responsibility (Podgor 2012, 10).[39] These texts are updated regularly and must be consulted on issues such as when specific approval is needed before proceeding with a prosecution, how to interpret statutes and rules, and what the "principles of federal prosecution" are specifically (p. 12). These principles cover a wide range of prosecutorial activity, including initiating and declining to prosecute, selecting charges, probable cause requirements, plea agreements, and sentencing issues (p. 13). Despite the guidelines, Moohr claims that the Department of Justice "does not approve or otherwise constrain the decisions of field attorneys" and that "independence and flexibility are prized in the belief that federal prosecutors should be free to respond to local circumstances" (Moohr 2004, 194).

In *Germany,* prosecutors work in hierarchically structured organizations located within the Ministry of Justice in each state. There is also a federal prosecutor's office but the state offices operate independently of the federal level. Decision making within offices is aided by office guidelines, and there are informal sentencing guidelines for common mass offenses such as traffic violations (Boyne 2012, 48). Management does not instruct how an individual case should be handled, and research has revealed that most prosecutors do not believe their discretion is affected by guidelines because each case can always be said to be unique and outside the guidelines (p. 48). Furthermore, supervision extends only to scrutiny that the law has been complied with and does not include a review of decision making or judgments of individual prosecutors on a case-by-case basis (p. 49).

In the *Netherlands,* the Board of Prosecutors General issues directives concerning the sentencing recommendations that prosecutors should make in trials. This assists in removing sentence disparities, and prosecutors are expected to apply these directives (Tak 2012, 144). Similarly, an instruction from the Board stipulates one hundred grounds on which a prosecutor may apply for nonprosecution. According to Tak (p. 147), a decision of that nature is taken in one of every ten files submitted by police to the prosecutor.

Prosecutors and Independence

In light of the position of the prosecutor as the gatekeeper of the criminal justice system, it is clearly important that prosecutors not be subject to political or other controls in determining who should be charged and prosecuted. However, reconciling independence with accountability can be problematic (Di Frederico 1998, 372). Tonry (2012, 3) reports that in the United States, Republican U.S. attorneys have been dismissed for refusing to engage in politically motivated prosecutions. Also, in the United States, elected prosecutors, although perhaps not directly controlled by those who elected them, must satisfy expectations that they will adopt a particular prosecution policy, and this has historically been of a punitive nature. As noted earlier, federal prosecutors are subject to guidelines and guidance but are otherwise free from direction and control. Tonry (p. 2) sets out the factors that may influence U.S. prosecutors: "American prosecutors sometimes openly and unashamedly take media reactions, public opinion and political considerations into account when deciding what cases to prosecute and how to handle them."

Today, in their practice, *German* prosecutors apply the legality principle only to the most serious crimes[40] despite its value in seeking to eliminate political interference and corruption by prosecutors. Prosecutors now follow the "expediency" principle and may dismiss or defer prosecutions in certain cases such as in minor crimes and in cases the public interest would not require that it be prosecuted. Prosecutors also possess the power to impose obligations on a suspected person, such as the imposition of a fine as a condition of nonprosecution (Boyne 2012, 41). These practices assist in the management and clearance of heavy caseloads experienced by German prosecutors (p. 45).

While German prosecutors discuss cases with each other and less experienced prosecutors seek advice from their senior colleagues, this workplace interaction operates more as a support system than a restriction on independence. Nevertheless, in some states, prosecutors believe that ignoring or rejecting informal instructions will harm their career prospects, but once a prosecutor has achieved seniority, he or she enjoys job tenure and this enhances the degree of independence (Boyne 2012, 50).

In *Italy,* the equality principle requires, in theory, that the prosecutor take action in all criminal cases no matter if the offense is minor in nature. Accordingly, all actions should theoretically end in a judicial decision. In practice, the mandatory prosecution principle is not applied because it is unworkable and impracticable given the large caseloads of prosecutors (Caianiello 2012, 254).[41] The constitution explicitly states the independence of prosecutors, and the Constitutional Court has noted that the legality principle implies total independence (p. 255). In addition, prosecutors are members of the Higher Council of the Judiciary, an institution created to safeguard the independence of the judiciary. This council appoints prosecutors.

The Minister for Justice in *Italy* has no power to direct or control prosecutors in exercising their functions. However, again, theory and practice do not always mesh because the Minister for Justice does have power to bring disciplinary proceedings against a prosecutor, and the Council determines such charges. As well, the minister has some appointment powers in regard to prosecutors and can give an opinion on the roles of prosecutors (Caianiello 2012, 256). Prosecutorial accountability remains a concern, especially in light of the abandonment of the legality principle; consequently, some scholars support the notion of creating a set of guidelines that can control prosecutorial discretion to some degree (p. 257). Some research also indicates that the close ties between judges and prosecutors (both of whom are members of the *magistrati,* share a common legal training, and enjoy equal status) facilitate informal discussions on cases, especially during the investigative stage, on issues such as custody, and whether a case should be taken to trial, raising questions about independence and accountability (Di Frederico 1998, 382).

In the *Netherlands,* prosecutors do not possess the degree of independence enjoyed by the judiciary even though they are members of the judiciary. The prosecution service for the country is part of the judiciary and prosecutors are civil servants, but the Board of Prosecutors General directs the service. It is formally headed by the Minister for Justice, who is politically responsible to Parliament for the proper operation of the prosecution service. This means the Minister can be asked by Parliament about policies and about specific individual prosecutions (Tak 2012, 135). Despite this chain of responsibility and potential board and ministerial direction, prosecutors are required to apply the law, meaning that prosecution decisions must be made free of political influence or bias. In fact, no Minister for Justice has ever given directions in an individual prosecution, and ministers are reluctant to become involved even in setting general prosecution policies (p. 136). Additionally, a special procedure must be followed before the Minister can issue an instruction in an individual case, which includes putting the instruction in writing and informing the court that the prosecutor has received a ministerial instruction (p. 141).

In *England and Wales,* by convention, ministers do not involve themselves in individual prosecution cases. This includes the Attorney General, except in cases where his consent to a prosecution is required. However, arguably the law does allow for direction because legislation states that the Director of Public Prosecutions (the head of the CPS) must discharge his functions under the superintendence of the Attorney General. While superintendence clearly covers prosecution policy, it appears that successive attorney generals have believed that it also requires that they be informed about difficult and high-profile cases so that, if necessary, they can issue a direction. The history of the conflict in Northern Ireland reveals that between 1972 and 1994, for example, directions were given about prosecutions as well as policy by the Attorney General (Jackson 2006, 46–47).

In *France,* the *procureur* is a *magistrat* and considered a judicial authority according to French law. This becomes problematic when the *procureur* conducts or supervises a criminal investigation and is responsible for the conduct of the *garde à vue* (Hodgson 2010, 1363). A question then arises as to the compatibility of the *procureur's* judicial status with his or her functions as a

procureur, especially when in the French judge-centered system, the defense does not possess equality of rights with the prosecution. There is a distinction within the French judiciary between the sitting judiciary and the standing judiciary. Whereas a sitting judge is free from executive control, the standing judge (which includes the prosecutors, the body collectively known as the *parquet*) is accountable to the Minister for Justice and the executive government. In fact, the minister is able to issue written instructions to the *parquet* and has the power to transfer and nominate *procureurs* (p. 1367). Some still argue that the ministerial power to direct the *parquet* is limited, because although instructions can be issued to the chief prosecutors, they are not themselves empowered to issue instructions not to prosecute a case (p. 1390).[42]

Plea Bargaining

In the United States, plea bargaining is such a huge part of a prosecutor's function (95 percent of all criminal cases are resolved using this process) that it can be said not to simply constitute a part of the system but to *be* the system (Luna and Wade 2012, 84). U.S. federal judge Gerard Lynch, for example, argues that the practice means that the prosecutor becomes the "central adjudicator of facts" and that "potential defenses are presented by the defendant and his counsel, not in a court, but to a prosecutor, who . . . decides the charge of which the defendant should be adjudged guilty" (quoted in Luna and Wade 2012, 85). In his view, this brings the U.S. prosecutor closer to the model of the prosecutor as adjudicator found in inquisitorial systems.

The U.S. practice allows unrestricted plea bargaining in relation to both the charge and the sentence, with the prosecutor recommending a sentence to the court, which it generally adopts (Bradley 2012, 95). Plea bargaining has been criticized on numerous grounds, for example, because some prosecutors deliberately overcharge[43] a defendant with offenses for which there is no probable cause in order to secure a conviction, or when the evidence of guilt is weak but the prosecutor nevertheless bargains to obtain a conviction rather than dropping the case (Banks 2009, 118–19). Others point to punitive U.S. sentencing practices, which can effectively force a defendant to accept a plea because the risk of conviction and attendant harsh sentence are too great, and to the weak controls the court may exercise over prosecutors (Pizzi 2012, 195–97). Nevertheless, judges, prosecutors, and defense lawyers all support plea bargaining because the stark reality is that without it, U.S. justice systems would quickly grind to a complete halt because every case would have to go to trial.

In *Europe,* "no-holds-barred American plea bargaining" (Tonry 2012, 23) does not exist, and the practice of plea bargaining has always been resisted. For one reason, it is inconsistent with the principle of legality. However, the reality is that it takes place in different forms, for example, in Germany, where it has been found to have been in existence since the 1970s but usually without recording a conviction and with no sanction of imprisonment (Boyne 2012). In *England and Wales,* plea bargaining has similarly been condemned until recently when it was recognized and given legislative form. It now covers 87 percent of cases. There are two forms of plea bargaining in England: the defendant can bargain with the court directly for a one-third reduction in sentence in exchange for a plea of guilty, or the defendant can bargain with the prosecutor. In England, the U.S. practice of "charging up" as part of the bargaining is strictly forbidden, and charges may not be brought at all unless there is a "realistic prospect of conviction" (Bradley 2012, 96; Pizzi 2012, 198).

European civil law states continue to debate whether the practice of plea bargaining is consistent with the tenets of the inquisitorial system, which require, in theory anyway, that every case go to trial on the merits even when the defendant confesses guilt (Bradley 2012, 93). However, the ongoing need to process cases through overloaded and inefficient justice systems seems to be forcing the issue in favor of processes that closely resemble American-style plea bargaining. Nevertheless, German prosecutors, for example, are not subject to the same pressures as U.S. prosecutors to secure convictions and obtain career advancement or reelection given that they are semi-judicial figures located in a public service career structure that rewards seniority and efficiency rather than a high conviction rate. This means they are much less likely to seek plea bargains in weak cases, instead of taking them to trial (Turner 2012, 108).

The *German* method of plea bargaining has now been recognized by statute law and involves the defense lawyer and the trial judge bargaining directly for a reduced sentence if the defendant confesses to the crime charged. A trial is conducted, but more along the lines of a U.S. guilty plea trial.

In the *Netherlands,* there is no plea bargaining in the U.S. sense of the term, but diversionary practices and procedures are available and used extensively so that, in practice, only 10 percent of crimes charged result in an actual trial. Prosecutors are able to suspend charges if the defendant accepts conditions (Tak 2012, 136).

Plea bargaining in *France* is not permitted for serious crimes but is allowed for crimes punishable by up to five years imprisonment. In 2004, France created a form of plea or sentence bargaining when a case is taken to court on a plea of guilty (the French system did not have a system for pleas before this measure). Similar to other corresponding European practices, this form of plea bargaining is limited to less serious charges—in the case of France, to imprisonment for five years or less—and the sentence proposed by the *procureur* or by the defense may not exceed imprisonment for one year or one-half of the maximum punishment for the offense charged (Hodgson 2012, 127). Ten days are allowed for the defendant to consider the offer, and legal representation is required. Bargaining between the prosecution and defense is not permitted, "but in practice the sentence is negotiated between the two" (p. 127). This represents almost a total adversarial approach where the parties decide the issue and not the judge, who may only accept or reject the agreed sentence and has no power to change it (p. 128).

In *Italy,* amendments to the Criminal Procedure Code in 1989 introduced many elements of the adversarial approach, including a form of plea bargaining. Only sentences may be bargained, and the defendant's term of incarceration may be reduced by up to one-third of the sentence that would have been imposed if the prosecution and defense had agreed (Bradley 2012, 93). The court must approve the sentence. Like France, the procedure may only be used to allow final sentences not exceeding five years (p. 94). This procedure does not involve any actual plea of guilty even though a criminal conviction is recorded against the defendant. Also, the defense may ask the court for the one-third reduction in sentence even if the prosecutor fails to agree, and in such cases, the prosecutor must state his reasons for refusing the proposed sentence (Pizzi and Marafioti 1992, 21). This reflects the intent of the law, which is to make the procedure available to all defendants, regardless of the attitude of the prosecutor (p. 22).

Turning to Asia, *Japanese* law does not permit plea bargaining, at least not explicitly. However, Japanese defendants will confess to crimes to gain sentencing discounts or have the sentence mitigated in some way (Turner 2012, 111). This is far different from the explicit U.S. practice and reflects the Japanese cultural practice of showing remorse in order to demonstrate rehabilitation and reintegration into society (p. 111).

In *Russia,* the notion that consensual arrangements could lead to a conviction without trial met with considerable opposition, it being argued that such arrangements would "demean the investigator, the prosecutor and the judge since they will have to bargain with the criminal" (Pomorski 2006, 135). Nevertheless, faced with overcrowded courts and case backlogs, the legislature has established a guilty plea procedure applying to cases when the maximum penalty for the crime charged does not exceed ten years imprisonment. With the consent of the prosecutor and the victim of the offense, the defendant may agree to the accusation presented to him or her (it is arguable that the defendant does not have to in fact confess but only agree to the accusation) and ask the court to enter a conviction foregoing a trial (p. 135). There must be consultation with defense counsel, and the agreement must be made in the presence of counsel. If the court is satisfied that the charge is "well founded," it may convict and sentence the defendant to imprisonment for a term not more than two-thirds of the maximum provided for the offense charged. Where the court is not satisfied, the case must proceed to trial.

Some argue that this process amounts to a form of plea bargaining because it implies a negotiating process in order to secure the consent of the defendant to the accusation (Pomorski 2006, 140). Clearly, it is not plea bargaining American style because the prosecutor has no charging discretion and no authority to offer a reduction in charges. Data suggest that the procedure is gaining popularity because whereas in 2002 district courts used the procedure in 7,800 cases, by 2004 this had increased to 117,700 cases representing 16.4 percent of the total (p. 141).

Prosecutorial Adjudication

Although plea bargaining can be described as a form of prosecutorial adjudication, there are more distinct and explicit forms of adjudication under legislative powers possessed by European prosecutors, all of which are designed to dispose of cases without trials. They are therefore better described as forms of diversion from prosecution or trial.

In *Germany,* a prosecutor may dismiss a case if there is insufficient evidence to show guilt. About 27 percent of cases fall into this category. A further 20 percent of cases are dismissed with no formal punishment imposed because the offense is not serious and it is not in the public interest to prosecute (Boyne 2012, 43). It is only when the crime charged carries more than the minimum penalty that the prosecutor must seek the consent of the court to dismiss the charges. Prosecutors also have the power to dismiss cases conditionally where a suspect consents and complies with specific requirements imposed by the prosecutor. In the year 2003, almost 53 percent of case dispositions involved dismissals according to these criteria (p. 43). A further 12.9 percent of cases were closed through the process known as a "penal order." Such orders can be made in the case of minor crimes. The procedure involves the prosecutor submitting a proposed verdict and sentence to the judge, who decides if the proposal is appropriate. If so, a provisional judgment is entered, which a defendant can contest or accept. If a defendant contests, the case proceeds to trial. This occurs in about 20 percent of cases. Only in 1.3 percent of cases do judges fail to approve prosecution dispositions (p. 44). Penal orders account for about two-thirds of all convictions. A confession of guilt is not usually required, but the prosecutor must be satisfied that sufficient cause exists to charge (Thaman 2012, 158, 166, 168).

In *France,* it is common for the *procureur* to charge a low-level offense (*délit*) and save the time and resources that would be involved in a trial for a more serious offense. This is not plea bargaining since the *procureur* is really conducting a process of case management (Hodgson 2012). An example would be charging drug importation as a customs offense where there is a rapid trial procedure rather than drug importation where there is not. In this decision making, the defendant is not consulted. When a defendant admits an offense, the *procureur* can propose a range of punishments as an alternative to a prosecution, including fine, community service, payment of compensation to the victim, attending drug rehabilitation, and restriction on freedom of association (p. 125). The court validates the agreement and if the defendant complies, there is no trial. Again, this is not a negotiated process and therefore not a plea bargain.

In the *Netherlands,* a number of diversionary processes are available to prosecutors that keep cases out of the trial process. These include a suspended prosecution where the prosecutor suspends a prosecution and imposes conditions (e.g., attending drug rehabilitation or not associating with certain named persons) that, if not complied with, will revive the case (Tak 2012, 149). Criminal charges can also be resolved by way of a "transaction" consisting of a financial payment to the Treasury or as specified by the prosecution. This process can be utilized for crimes punishable by imprisonment of up to six years. More than one-third of all crimes are now settled by way of this process despite it giving virtually unlimited power to the prosecution service to avoid trials.

Under statute, the prosecution service also has the power to impose sentences through the making of "penal orders." It is intended that these orders will replace transactions. The sentences possible under penal orders include performance of community work, a fine, an order to pay money to a victim, and withdrawing a driver's license for up to six months. The order becomes final unless opposed by the defendant, in which case the prosecution will bring the case to the court and a regular trial will occur.

Interestingly, the Dutch Bar Association has questioned the legitimacy of these orders on the basis that the prosecution is deciding both guilt and sentence—functions assigned to the courts under the Dutch Constitution. The counterargument was that no penal sanctions were being imposed and the penalties were administrative only, an approach well established under Dutch law (Tak 2012, 154).

As indicated earlier, in *Italy* prosecutors can manage their caseloads by allowing routine, nonserious cases to become statute barred and filing a request for dismissal with the court, a request that is normally granted (Caianiello 2012, 263). Cases can also be dismissed for insufficient evidence, or they can follow an expedited procedure. Given the legality principle, it is generally only possible for prosecutors to finalize cases through a judicial process. There is, however, a procedure not initiated by the prosecutor, which allows a defendant to request an abbreviated trial (without a jury and based on the investigation file alone), and by waiving his right to trial by jury, the defendant may receive a reduction in penalty of one-third of the regular sentence or conversion of a life sentence to thirty years (p. 263).

In *Italy,* special procedures under the 1989 Code of Criminal Procedure were intended to give the parties, and not the judge, the capacity to resolve cases in a way that would promote efficiencies in the justice system (Pizzi and Marafioti 1992, 2). The prosecutor was given power to proceed by way of a penal decree involving the prosecutor offering to resolve the case by imposing a discounted fine. This applies only to minor offenses, and when the defendant accepts the offer, there is a 50 percent fine reduction and no trial (pp. 20–21). Other special procedures do not give the prosecutor an adjudicatory role but require a trial process, sometimes abbreviated.

Police and Prosecutor Relations

Relations between police and prosecutors are crucial in progressing criminal complaints and suspected crimes, yet research shows there are sometimes organizational tensions (Harris 2012, 54). In the *United States,* prosecutors do not control the police although they may consult with police in ongoing investigations, providing legal advice and assistance on technical issues (p. 55). When police and prosecutors work in separate silos with police conducting the crime investigation and then submitting the case to the prosecutor, this means police are not accountable to the prosecutor. To whatever degree, working in this mode of isolation can mean that police misconduct and abuse of powers go unchecked (p. 55).

Although police and prosecutors ought to maintain a relationship of mutual support and assistance, tensions between them can arise in issues such as the appropriate charge to be made arising out of a criminal act (Harris 2012). Police may feel that prosecutors are not tough enough, and prosecutors may have concerns about the lawfulness of police action in obtaining evidence in a case. However, neither can afford to alienate the other, and prosecutors have to conduct themselves with caution if rendering critical judgments about police work (p. 57) and may "look the other way" rather than take issue with police malpractice or misconduct (p. 63).

In the *Netherlands,* the prosecution service takes final responsibility for all criminal investigations and must ensure that police comply with laws and regulations. In practice, however, police conduct investigations without any input from the prosecution service, and their interaction is basically limited to broad policy issues (Tak 2012, 140). As well, police have the power to divert cases out of the criminal justice system without seeking the approval of prosecutors. When prosecutors issue an instruction to police, it is binding on police, and noncompliance will be a disciplinary infraction. An example of such an instruction occurred in March 2003 when the Board of Prosecutors General issued an instruction that police must always conduct an investigation when the offender is known, except in trivial cases, and that the depth of the investigation must relate to the seriousness of the offense (p. 141).

Before 1986, when the CPS was created, no public authority responsible for prosecutions in *England and Wales* existed. Traditional arrangements that had developed over time involved the police laying all charges and employing private lawyers to conduct trials. Resistance to the creation of the CPS centered on the police who did not want to lose their power to charge and private lawyers who did not want to lose the income gained from presenting cases in court (Lewis 2012, 215). The creation of the CPS initially involved making some compromises, with CPS having no investigation function, police continuing to lay charges in less serious cases, and private lawyers continuing to present serious cases in courts.

In 2003, important changes were made to the CPS, including giving CPS the exclusive power to charge and making prosecutors the gatekeepers of cases, hence giving them more influence over police investigations (Lewis 2012, 221). Police and CPS are now working closely together at the local level, especially on the seizure of assets gained through crime. CPS influence over police does not extend to the service having investigation powers, and it relies on police to conduct inquiries into alleged crimes. Prosecutors are required to review every case submitted by police to ensure all information and evidence is present. This means that typically prosecutors will

provide guidance and advice to police about lines of inquiry and evidence issues. It is clear, however, that CPS prosecutors have no power to direct police (pp. 223–24).

In *Sweden,* either the Public Prosecution Service (PPS) or police may lead an investigation, with the police taking precedence if the matter is of a "simple nature" (Zila 2012, 240). This rule is supplemented by general instructions issued by the Procurator General and the National Police Board requiring that police and PPS reach agreement at the local level but listing the offenses that should normally be considered of a simple nature. When police investigate, the PPS normally has no involvement, and when the PPS conducts the investigation, it cannot always count on police assistance because police claim to lack the resources to aid PPS (p. 240).

It *Italy,* prosecutors do not supervise police inquiries and investigations and, with some slight exceptions, have no disciplinary power over police (Caianiello 2012, 251). However, in the course of a police investigation, a prosecutor possesses the capacity to give directions to police units called *zia giudiziaria* (judicial police) that assist and support investigation by other police units (p. 251).

In *France,* the *procureur* must be informed when a person is placed in *garde à vue* (police custody). The *procureur* has specific powers in relation to that detention, including the power to extend it, and to order release of the suspect at any time (Hodgson 2010). The *procureur* also determines what charges to bring and whether the case should be referred to an investigating magistrate. This judicial oversight function to be provided by the *procureur* may not be very effective in practice because there is no expectation that the *procureur* will actually visit the police station to conduct any such supervision (p. 1396). He or she will always tell police in advance of any intended visit, and while technically the police are accountable to the *procureur,* in practice police cooperation is essential. All this calls into question the capacity of the *procureur* to act as an effective supervisor of police activity during the *garde à vue* (p. 1396).

It is important that police and *procureur* develop mutual trust and confidence. Hodgson suggests that "a model of supervision based on challenging and verifying the investigative work of the police would create antagonism and undermine this trust" (Hodgson 2004, 182).

(Continued)

Defense lawyers can require prosecutors to disclose all the evidence against the accused, including exculpatory evidence, only if they obtain a court order to that effect, and such orders are granted under narrow circumstances. Generally, defense lawyers believe they should cooperate with prosecutors. For example, over 60 percent surveyed reported they had never actively advised a suspect or defendant to remain silent (p. 75). Lawyers who advise their clients to maintain their right to silence have been described by prosecutors as "going too far" and even of "violating the law" (p. 78).

Skilled and zealous defense lawyers in Japan are faced with the almost certain loss of a case at trial because of Japan's very low acquittal rate. In fact, the low acquittal rate has the effect of suppressing the criminal defense bar's capacity to grow and increase its expertise. This explains why criminal defense work is considered "not worth performing" (p. 81) and why many lawyers refuse criminal work.

Prosecutor Culture

According to Johnson's survey research, the most important objectives for Japanese prosecutors are

1. discovering the truth about a case,

2. making a proper charge decision,

3. invoking remorse in defendants, and

4. *rehabilitating and reintegrating defendants into the community.* (pp. 98–99)

By comparison, in a Seattle prosecutor's office in the United States, less than 9 percent of respondents believed remorse to be an objective, compared to more than 90 percent of Japanese prosecutors surveyed (p. 100). The emphasis on rehabilitation also has no parallel in the United States, except possibly in juvenile cases. Similarly, "repairing relations between offender and victim" (p. 102) was thought important by two-thirds of all Japanese prosecutors surveyed, but not a single Seattle prosecutor considered that objective important.

Johnson suggests that beliefs about the importance of remorse and rehabilitation in Japan are congruent with Confucian values about human perfectibility (p. 102). The absence of a truly adversarial system of criminal justice, light caseloads, and lack of political pressure in Japan may also be factors that displace U.S. prosecutors' primary objectives of "protecting the public" and "giving offenders their just deserts" (p. 100).

The Charging Decision

In determining whether to charge a suspect, the most important factors considered by Japanese prosecutors are the following:

- *Damage done by the offense*

- *Likelihood of reoffending*

- *Whether the suspect repents*

- *Suspect's motive*

- *Whether suspect compensates victim*

- *Victim's feelings about punishment*

- *Prior record* (Johnson 2002, 111)

This compares to the United States where generally the most important factors are the seriousness of the offense and the existence of a prior record of offenses. The list of factors taken into account by Japanese prosecutors includes seriousness and prior record, but the Japanese system is distinctive in its reliance on a set of factors that emphasize the individuality of the suspect, namely, factors relating to repentance, confession, restitution, and rehabilitation (p. 111). These factors scarcely figure in determinations by U.S. prosecutors although it must be noted that in U.S. cultures, remorse is not a norm and is less likely to be shown by alleged offenders. In Japan, remorse is expected because it is a norm associated with wrongdoing, and therefore when suspected offenders in Japan fail to show remorse to prosecutors, or are defiant or noncooperative, this can cause the prosecutor to become more punitive (p. 114).

Regard for the feelings of the victim is, according to Johnson, "a guiding principle for Japan's procuracy" (p. 115). The views of the victim about appropriate punishment are often central to the charging decision and can make the difference between a charge and a suspended prosecution. As a result, defense lawyers will urge their clients to compensate the victim in anticipation that this will cause the prosecutor to take a lenient approach.

Organization: Managing Prosecutors and the Influence of Culture

Unlike the offices of U.S. prosecutors, where office policy tends to be made and enforced informally or not at all, Japanese managers "articulate and communicate specific criteria in written manuals, guidelines and standards" (p. 128). Standards for case dispositions and recommended sentences are in regular use in prosecutors' offices and are valued as important sources of job information. Deviations from standards must be justified and explained to supervisors. Managers require some prosecutorial decisions to be cleared by supervisors through the *kessai* system of consultation and approval. *Kessai* discussions can take a few minutes or more than an hour, and they involve face-to-face interactions between managers and prosecutors. This process aids prosecutors in attaining consistency in their decision making and actions across similar cases (p. 131). Repeated poor performance at *kessai* can affect a prosecutor's career advancement.

As well as standard setting and the *kessai* process, a third control is the audit, or *kansa*. This comprises a yearly sample of case dispositions which managers examine for consistency. Cases not charged are also reviewed, and whenever a case was not prosecuted but is judged to have been appropriate for prosecution, an explanation must be provided (p. 132).

The collective nature of the management and exercise of prosecutorial discretion in Japan contrasts sharply with the individualistic U.S. style of managing prosecution in the same way that the collectivist nature of Japanese culture and values contrasts with the individualistic, autonomous U.S. culture.

"Correcting" Suspects and Offenders

Given that Japanese prosecutors conduct interrogations of suspects (principally to persuade them to confess and thereby show remorse), they are able to appeal directly both to a person's self-interest and also to social norms. It is common practice for prosecutors to "instruct" suspects during interrogation (p. 185). Much instruction is informational and provides facts that relate to the suspect's self-interest (e.g., "If you use drugs, you will harm your health" or "If you continue to behave badly, you will spend a long time in prison"). Instruction also draws on social norms, especially the cultural morality of Japan, using the language of "shame, disapproval, rebuke and exhortation" (p. 186). Prosecutors act like teachers, delivering lectures on duty and morality with the aim of invoking guilt and stimulating repentance and remorse.

A display of remorse shows that a person respects the values of the community. An absence of, or refusal to show, remorse directly challenges community values. In the collectivist Japanese society, such a challenge is unacceptable (p. 189). Remorse is perceived as manifesting a desire for reintegration into society and as a willingness to abide by the community moral order. Accordingly for prosecutors, an authentic show of remorse is essential in order to understand a suspect's character, and a knowledge of character is vital in determining whether or not to charge and what punishment to recommend.

(Continued)

(Continued)

With its stress on compliance with community moral and social norms comes a willingness to show leniency in punishment, provided the suspect shows that he or she is remorseful. Reintegration and rehabilitation are the norms relied upon as compared to the U.S. tendency to stigmatize and marginalize criminality (p. 191). There is also a confidence that the strong Japanese informal social controls can draw offenders back to the correct path.

However, leniency is only available for those considered correctable. Repeat offenders who have shown no capacity to be corrected are treated harshly. Those who offend collective values through their conduct, such as vagabonds and persons pursuing a different lifestyle that involves living on the margins, are not viewed sympathetically (p. 193). The Japanese system is therefore inclined to be punitive in its approach to the underclass. A similar approach is taken to Japanese gangsters, who are treated severely because they are considered depraved and dangerous; they stand at the far end of the spectrum of correctability. Drug cases are also dealt with in a stern manner with a very low suspension from prosecution rate compared to other offenses (p. 195).

The Japanese view the United States as being too lenient with drug offenders, who they categorize as "dangerous criminals" and "threats to the social order" (p. 196) and incapable of correction. Gun crimes are also taken extremely seriously because Japan is virtually a gun-free society and most guns are used in altercations between gangsters. Consequently, the Japanese system of criminal justice reveals both leniency and punitiveness, depending on the nature of the offense and the offender's individual circumstances.

Conviction Rate and Acquittals

Where a defendant is acquitted in a trial process, the acquittal is perceived by the prosecutor, the media, and a majority of citizens as a disgrace (*shittai;* p. 46). Police say that prosecutors are overly concerned with the possibility of an acquittal and so do not charge cases that should be tried. The expected result from the public and by other prosecutors for acquittals is harsh criticism, and even partial acquittals in minor theft or assault cases generate headlines and public complaints.

The Japanese criminal justice system is renowned for its high conviction rate (about 97 percent) or, to put it another way, its very low rate of acquittals. Johnson estimates that the acquittal rate is 3.38 percent for nonjury trials in Japan. This compares to a U.S. rate on jury trials of 27 percent (based on the rate for twenty-six U.S. jurisdictions; p. 216). Johnson attributes this difference to the practice of Japanese prosecutors making very cautious charge decisions that effectively screen out almost all cases with a chance of acquittal at trial. There are two elements at play here: the fact that the prosecutors have a detailed knowledge of each case based on having conducted the actual criminal investigation themselves, and the fact that only cases with a high probability of conviction are taken to trial. Most judges agree with this analysis and one judge has written,

> Prosecutors value their authority a great deal. To prevent harm to their authority they investigate and filter cases very carefully. I think this is the cause of our country's high conviction rate. What in Japan is called "precise justice" *(seimitsu shiho)* is in fact a reflection of the careful, strict investigations which precede indictment. (Quoted in Johnson 2002, 220)

The existence and strict implementation of charging and sentencing standards, audits of cases, and ongoing *kessai* consultations collectively contribute to the decision-making process. One prosecutor explained that the acquittal rate is low "because prosecutors act like judges at the *kessai* stage and because frontline prosecutors have internalized the *kessai* standards themselves" (quoted in Johnson 2002, 226). In addition, organizational controls in the form of transfers of prosecutors to undesirable positions in the structure and to unattractive locations sanction poor decision making that results in "negligent" acquittals and can affect status. For that reason, acquittals hurt career prospects; career advancement comes from avoiding mistakes that may mar one's reputation. A further organizational sanction in the event of an acquittal is that the trial prosecutor must produce a detailed report on the case with a focus on the issues that brought about the acquittal. The trial prosecutor and others deemed responsible for the mistake must also attend a series of "appeal deliberation meetings" chaired by elite prosecutors where the written reports are analyzed.

NOTES

1. *Laissez-faire* refers to an economic system based on individual transactions free from any interfering restrictions by government (such as tariffs, subsidies, and regulations, seen as disruptive), because the natural order of things is self-regulating and harmonious (Gaspard 2004, 5).

2. The National Registry of Exonerations was created in the United States in 2012. By December 28, 2013, the total number of exonerations (DNA and non-DNA) registered was 1,275 (see http://www.law.umich.edu/special/exoneration/Pages/Exoneration-by-Year.aspx).

3. Article 6 of the European Convention on Human Rights guarantees the right to a fair trial through a set of guarantees that apply before the actual trial. Protection includes the right to legal advice while in custody (Hodgson 2004, 174).

4. Loi no. 2011-392 du 14 avril 2011 relative à la garde à vue (referred to as Law 2011–392; see http://www.loc.gov/lawweb/servlet/lloc_news?disp3_l205402683_text).

5. It is common practice in French police stations to bring suspects before witnesses or other suspects to compare divergences in their accounts (Dorange and Field 2012, 165).

6. The criticality of the dossier is illustrated by the police talk of wanting to create a dossier that is *carré* (squared away or made straightforward), meaning all exit doors are closed, whereas defense lawyers talk of "exploding" the dossier (Dorange and Field 2012, 157).

7. In Germany and Italy, the position of investigating judge was abolished when elements of the adversarial system were adopted (Vogler 2005, 166).

8. *Magistrats* comprise the French judiciary, meaning the public prosecutor *(procureur)*, the *juge d'instruction*, and the trial judge (Hodgson 2004, 171).

9. Argentina adopted an adversarial system (at the federal level) in 1989; Peru in 1991 and 1994; Guatemala in 1992 and in effect in 1994; Colombia 1992; El Salvador and Venezuela 1998. Chile began the reform process in 1997 and completed it in 2005; Costa Rica reformed between 1996 and 1998; El Salvador 1998; Uruguay 1998; Bolivia, Venezuela, and Paraguay in 1999; Ecuador in 2000; Nicaragua 2001; Honduras and Dominican Republic 2002 (Bischoff 2003, 41; Cavise 2007).

10. Similarities between the states' codes are due to the sourcing of legislation to the Model Code of Criminal Procedure for Ibero-America of 1988, which is derived from the seminal Cordoba (Argentina) Code of 1939. Both codes provide for orality. Generally all the reformed codes strive to increase system efficiency while still protecting rights and to disperse power away from the investigating judge to the prosecutor (Bischoff 2003, 42).

11. In the 1960s and 1970s, USAID operated two programs concerned with legal reform—one related to legal education and the other providing training to law enforcement personnel (Langer 2007, 647). During the 1980s, USAID began to provide assistance to many states, including Bolivia, Colombia, Costa Rica, Dominican Republic, Guatemala, Honduras, Panama, and Peru. This assistance covered training courses for justice professionals, case management, and infrastructure support such as materials and supplies for the judiciary (p. 649).

12. According to Peter Solomon and Todd Foglesong (2000, 5), a productive market economy and democracy in a legal transition require "the development of strong and respected institutions of the law—especially courts; and the presence of powerful constituencies that need and support law."

13. Over the past twenty years, an array of international financial and donor institutions have invested in justice reform and institutional strengthening, including the World Bank, the Inter-American Development Bank, European Union, UN Development Program, and USAID (Dodson 2002, 201).

14. In Mexico it is common for the judge's secretary to take charge of the investigation while the judge seldom appears (Cavise 2007, 790).

15. Between 70 and 90 percent of inmates in Latin American prisons are being held pending trial (Hafetz 2002, 1754).

16. Prillaman (2000, 97) reports that in 1995–97, legislators in Brazil proposed a bill to introduce the doctrine of precedent into the justice system in the interests of reducing a staggering number of duplicate cases at the federal level. Immediately, judges began publicly to compare the proposal with Nazi Germany and complained that having to follow the decision of another court would suppress the independence of individual judges. Similarly, when in 1999, legislators agreed to conduct an inquiry into judicial corruption, judges stopped work, and senior magistrates declared that the inquiry would be "unconstitutional" (p. 110).

17. In Argentina, the introduction of orality initially caused trial delays to increase by a factor of eight, and courts using oral procedure at trial accumulated a backlog of cases seven times greater than the backlog of courts still using written procedure. Later, it was found that although orality expedited the trial process, it also led to more persons being convicted within the same time period as before, thereby putting increased pressure on prison capacity (Prillaman 2000, 122).

18. For example, Jeffrey Sachs (1998) argues that Poland was a law-based society, and civil society organizations and the Roman Catholic Church operated to keep government accountable.

19. One such verdict involved the acquittal of the revolutionary Vera Zasulich, member of an anti-Tsar terrorist group, on a charge of murdering the municipal governor of St. Petersburg in 1878 despite her having confessed (Deville 1999, 74; Diehm 2001, 22).

20. The 1993 Constitution of the Russian Federation, Article 123(3) declares, "Judicial proceedings shall be conducted based on the principle of adversariness and equality of the parties" (Pomorski 2006, 129).

21. A defendant may waive the right to a jury trial, and a large proportion of Russians do so in favor of trial by a court of lay assessors or by a panel of three judges (Thaman 1999, 239).

22. The jury deliberates in secret, and the presiding judge is not permitted to participate (Thaman 1999, 253).

23. Many officials are reluctant to entrust ordinary citizens with jury trials, believing they need legal training to deal with, for example, trials of persons involved in organized crime (Deville 1999, 80).

24. Prosecutors have consistently been rated as "poor to dismal" and either do not participate in the trial in any meaningful way or perform inadequately when they do (Pomorski 2006, 147). The same can be said for defense lawyers who, when appointed by the state to act, tend to act passively because either they are not paid or they receive grossly inadequate payment from the government for their legal services (p. 148).

25. This valorization of status is today seemingly reflected in possession of CCP membership. For example, when a newspaper reported that the deputy director of a foreign trade bureau in a city had accepted a bribe in the form of a television and a camera from a businessman in Hong Kong for a false contract, the Disciplinary Inspection Committee (DIC) of the Central Committee of the CCP investigated the case. The offender was removed from his position, but no criminal charges were brought. Pressured to report why the deputy director had received such favorable treatment, the DIC explained that he was an old high-ranking member of the party and that it would be "too embarrassing" for him to be put on trial like a common offender (Ren 1997, 82–83).

26. The Chinese government published few crime data until 1987, when the first Chinese Law Yearbook was published with less than perfect statistics on crime (Liu et al. 2001, 9).

27. Regarded as just another instrumentalist state organ, the courts "have relatively low political status" and command little attention from other organs (Potter 2001, 30).

28. See Chapter 4 for a discussion of these campaigns.

29. It should be noted that political and economic advancement require CCP membership, and every profession has a ceiling above which it is not possible to rise without possessing CCP membership. Writing in 1997, Xin Ren (1997, 60) reports that 95 percent of judges were party members.

30. According to Li (2014, 42), supervision of individual cases by the local-level National People's Congress has no basis in law because the constitution gives only a general power to supervise the work of courts and ensure laws are respected and enforced.

31. As Ren (1997, 59) notes, "Favoritism and nepotism have their deep roots in Chinese familism which highly values family ties and interpersonal relationships. Kinship-oriented officialdom was regarded by Confucius as the greatest human virtue."

32. In terms of public opinion about crime, Randall Peerenboom (2006, 846) states that "China's weak legal institutions have been unable to resist the combined pressure from an angry public demanding heavy punishments to deter criminals and a political regime seeking to shore up its legitimacy by pandering to the public's appetite for vengeance."

33. The summary procedure applies to cases with clear facts and sufficient evidence punishable by less than three years imprisonment; to cases handled only on complaint; and to minor cases prosecuted by victims. It is estimated that less than 50 percent of all criminal cases are dealt with through summary procedure, but in 2003 the SPC and the Ministry of Justice issued a regulation to allow summary procedure where the accused pleads guilty and does not contest the facts. Trial is by a panel of three judges. This has been criticized as a form of plea bargaining (Li 2014, 96–97).

34. It is reported that witnesses appear in only 5 percent of all criminal cases, and in some courts the rate is less than 1 percent. In most cases, judges refuse lawyers' applications to call witnesses (Li 2014, 99).

35. For example, in *Bordenkircher v. Hayes* (434 U.S. 357 [1978]) the U.S. Supreme Court ruled that most prosecutorial decisions, including charging, plea bargaining, and dismissing charges were nonjusticiable because prosecutors are elected officials in the executive branch, according to the separation of powers. The courts, it was said, have no authority to second-guess exercises of a prosecutor's discretion—that is a matter for the electorate.

36. In Alaska, Connecticut, and New Jersey, the elected state attorney general appoints district attorneys (Harris 2012, 59).

37. Johnson (2002, 153) notes that hierarchical review in U.S. prosecution offices is rarely found as compared with Japan. He notes, "What stands out is how infrequently and superficially superiors monitor their subordinates' decisions."

38. Manuals or handbooks located in prosecutor's offices "amount to elementary instruction books for junior prosecutors which describe the procedures to be followed in particular types of cases and the applicable rules of law. If they occasionally lapse into statements of policy designed to guide discretion, that policy is usually of the most general and unsophisticated sort" (Abrams 1971, quoted in Johnson 2002, 130).

39. Although the U.S. courts do not enforce compliance with Department of Justice guidelines, they will refer violations to the Office of Professional Responsibility, thereby enforcing the accountability of federal prosecutors (Podgor 2012, 18).

40. Under the German Penal Code, a serious crime is a crime punishable by a minimum period of one year's imprisonment (Boyne 2012, 41). Eighty-five percent of annual crimes comprise less serious crimes. Many crimes categorized as felonies in the United States are considered less serious crimes in Germany, including rape, child sexual abuse, and human trafficking (p. 42).

41. In practice, prosecution offices establish general priority classes of cases and allow routine cases to become statute barred from prosecution in order to manage the overall caseload. (Two years is the maximum allowed to complete an investigation of a complex or serious crime, with eighteen months being ordinarily permitted for most nonserious crimes.) Many are fearful that officially replacing the legality principle with the opportunity principle would make prosecutors liable to political direction by the minister for justice (Caianiello 2012, 261).

42. Hodgson (2002, 236) reports that not only have cases involving the misappropriation of public funds for political purposes attracted media attention, but ministers for justice, in conjunction with the prime minister, have ordered investigations to be delayed or ceased completely.

43. Johnson (2002, 148) narrates a discussion with a prosecutor (Larry) in Oakland, California, who described two styles of plea bargaining, both common in Oakland: "Some prosecutors make high offers ('overcharge') and then negotiate when the defense attorney counters. This strategy gives the prosecutor more leverage over the defense. Other prosecutors make 'rock-bottom' offers right away, leaving little room for negotiation." Larry reported he preferred the second style, because "it saves time and monkey business."

44. Johnson (2002, 42) includes the absence of jury trials as a factor here, but juries were reintroduced with effect from 2009 (after having ceased in 1943) with the objectives of securing more citizen participation within the justice system and as a check on the judiciary (Bloom 2006, 36). A jury comprises six citizens and three professional judges, and jury trials are available only for serious offenses (p. 38). In his 2009 assessment of the new jury trials, Johnson reports that prosecutors "seem to be proceeding with an extra measure of caution" (p. 3) because in the first two months after the introduction of juries, prosecutors charged only about half the expected number of cases per month. Furthermore, there was some evidence of prosecutors systematically reducing charges to less serious to avoid jury trials (p. 3).

6

PUNISHMENT

Most countries have systems of trial and punishment for acts adjudged to be criminal. Ordinarily, punishments for specified violations of the criminal law are prescribed by law or regulations and may include imprisonment, the death penalty, as well as less severe penalties such as fines, probation, and community work. This chapter focuses primarily on the role of punishment as an instrument in crime control but also explores the history and sociology of punishment because while punishment has an instrumental objective, it also possesses "a cultural style and an historical tradition" (Garland 1990, 19). A fuller understanding of punishment will therefore be gained if it is thought of as being formed and influenced by dynamic social, cultural, and historical forces.

In terms of punishment as crime control, comparative aspects of punishment systems, especially differences in the nature and severity of punishments, are examined. For example, some countries treat drug cases leniently, believing the appropriate response to drug abuse is treatment and not punishment, but as is well known, the United States, in particular, has tended to impose very severe penalties for drug abuse.[1]

As a social formation, punishment is a product of social, historical, and cultural movements and associated factors and gaining an understanding of comparative penality[2] requires some appreciation of how punishment has been shaped by these forces. Each country possesses a penal culture shaped by its general ideology and material conditions. This chapter therefore begins by locating punishment within a comparative frame that explains its history and social and cultural production. Due to space limitations, this must necessarily be only a summary of the experience of a number of countries, but it will add important context to the discussion. Case studies of penal development in China, Japan, the United States, and England describe the main contours of change in penality over time in those countries.

Gaining an understanding of punishment involves the study of society. As such we must ask, How do different countries and their cultures perceive punishment for criminal conduct? What do they regard as the purpose of punishment, and how do they understand punishment as a social practice? Do some believe punishment will reform a person, or is the overall perspective one of retribution for criminal conduct? What events in history have impacted countries' systems of punishment, and what cultural differences determine the nature of punishments?

Postcolonial countries have inherited Western forms of punishment from their colonizers. Forms of colonial penality should be understood as importations from metropolitan powers at a particular time that displaced local penalities and were intended to protect the colonial social order. What kind of regime of punishment was imposed by the colonizers, and how did race, the colonial economy, and the complexities of local cultures play a part in formulating and applying penal policies?

Has the severity of punishment increased over time, perhaps in response to increases in crime or perceptions of such increases? In the United States since the mid-1980s and in England and Wales since the mid-1990s, there has been an explicit trend toward imposing harsher punishment, especially on incapacitating prisoners for very lengthy periods of time. To some extent this trend has been followed in Europe also. This raises the question as to why some countries adopt punitive punishment policies while others do not, and the extent to which there is a justice policy convergence based on U.S. "get tough on crime" policies. Are there any moves to standardize punishments or principles of punishment worldwide based on international minimum standards or internationally recognized best practices? We consider these questions and discuss applicable international standards.

THE RATIONALE FOR PUNISHMENT

Criminologist David Garland (1990, 3), writing about the sociology of punishment, points out that "punishment today is a deeply problematic and barely understood aspect of social life. The rationale for it is by no means clear." Garland (1990), Michel Foucault (1977), Norbert Elias (1994), and other scholars have drawn attention to facets of the topic of punishment previously ignored, including the need to understand its cultural and social foundations, the currents in social thinking that have affected the nature of punishment, and attitudes of tolerance and intolerance that frame punishment. At a more functional level, numerous scholars over the past ten years or so have asked questions about criminal punishments in the United States, especially about punitive populism and criminal justice policies that have resulted in mass imprisonment.

Sociologists such as Émile Durkheim and Max Weber have provided accounts of punishment that, in the case of Durkheim, see punishment as being driven by moral and religious forces that express outrage producing social solidarity: the role of punishment was to reinforce moral commands and to express condemnation of breaches of the moral code (see Garland 1990, 44). Weber's notion of bureaucratic rationality is today seen in the managerial approach to crime control and punishment where experts manage and administer systems of social control that have little to do with morality. Marxist theorists have asked why incarceration persists as the dominant form of punishment when it has not been shown to be an effective deterrent to crime (Rusche and Kirchheimer 1939). Georg Rusche and Otto Kirchheimer (1939) argue that penal policy is situated within the class struggle and constitutes a method for controlling the poor. It is not, therefore, simply a response to crime but has broader implications for social structures and forces.

Elias (1994) demonstrates how, through the "civilizing process," human sensibilities changed from the late medieval period over a long period of time so that as personal conduct became more refined, violence came to be monopolized by the state with the effect that local levels of aggression and violence were diminished. Civilized norms and standards of behavior began to recognize human dignity and worth, and private forms of violence were minimized by the exercise of individual self-control (Garland 1990, 220). Elias explains that through a privatizing process, aspects of social life such as death, sex, and violence that were formerly public became hidden because they were considered crude and unmannerly (in Garland 1990, 222). However, violence did not disappear; rather it was (and continues to be) housed behind the scenes in places like prisons (p. 223). In terms of penality, there are clear equivalences to the social process of "civilizing" identified by Elias in that punishments like death, corporal punishment, and forms of shaming ceased to be performed in public and were removed behind the scenes to be later done away with altogether and replaced with sanctions such as imprisonment that reflected public concern about visibly inflicting pain and suffering (p. 224).

The question of punishment and discipline came in for radical reexamination in Foucault's *Discipline and Punishment* (1977). His account of punishment and discipline within society explains how inflicting bodily pain through early brutal means of punishment gave way to new forms of power that disciplined incarcerated persons in ways that were carefully regulated and secretive.

Prison should therefore be seen as an institution where techniques of control are exercised to the fullest extent (Garland 1990, 134). For Foucault, prison disciplining practices created delinquents by rendering the individual criminal a subject of study and control and by stigmatizing offenders through establishing the conditions for recidivism (see Garland 1990, 148). In following Foucault's perspective on power and penality, Garland (p. 198) advocates an approach to punishment that takes account of sociological and philosophical perspectives so that punishment is seen as a "complex cultural artefact" and not simply as a mode of crime control.

Several theories associated with the rationale or purposes of punishment have been advanced. These theories of *deterrence, retribution, just deserts, incapacitation*, and *rehabilitation* are briefly explained here.

Theories associated with *deterrence* are grounded in utilitarian philosophy. Utilitarians argue that we punish because we seek to deter crime and, in this sense, punishment will have beneficial consequences for citizens. Unfortunately, studies do not confirm this theory (B. Hudson 1996, 23; Ten 1987, 9; Walker 1991, 16), but this position continues to be advanced whenever justification for a particular punishment is debated, for example, in the case of the death penalty. Research has shown that speed and the certainty of punishment have more impact in ensuring compliance with the law than severe punishment and that those who commit offenses have a poor understanding of the penalties that would be attached to their criminality (Clear and Frost 2014, 121).

Retribution is the notion that punishment is justified because it is deserved; in other words, we should punish the guilty because it is just to do so (Duff 2001, 19). This approach reflects our intuitive feeling about criminality. It causes us to ask questions such as the following: How can punishment best reflect the censure that society attaches to this criminality? How can this offender best repay his or her debt to society? (Walker 1991, 73). Retributivists argue that an offender, through his or her wrongdoing, has taken unfair advantage of others and victimized them, and punishment will erase that unfairness (Ten 1987, 5). Opponents of retribution argue that it amounts to vengeance or revenge.

The notion of *just deserts* is an aspect of retribution theory standing in opposition to the freedom formerly given to judges or parole boards to determine an appropriate sentence for an offender. Just deserts theory is applied through sentencing guidelines that set the punishment for each offense calculated according to the nature of the offense. Social and economic factors relevant to the situation of the offender are usually disregarded in setting these tariffs.

Incapacitation is the policy of confining offenders so they no longer have the freedom of movement nor the capacity to commit further offenses. It is fundamentally a warehousing approach to criminality that sees taking offenders off the streets as the most effective form of crime control. This theory assumes that an offender will re-offend at some time in the future, an assumption that is morally problematic. It also assumes that others who offend do not immediately replace those locked away through incapacitation. The idea that offenders can be reformed is expressed through the notion of *rehabilitation*. Thus proponents of this theory argue that not only should the offense be of concern but also the offender and his or her social and economic background. In other words, the punishment should fit the offender, and individual circumstances ought to be taken into account in determining the appropriate penalty. Crime is perceived, therefore, to be a symptom of a social disease, and offenders can be reformed through appropriate programs and interventions that nowadays are largely cognitive behavioral in nature.

PUNITIVE PUNISHMENT

Over the past decade, extensive scholarly attention worldwide, both theoretical and empirical in nature, has been directed on the topic of punitive punishment, also known as "populist punitiveness"[3] (Bottoms[4] 1995). An early focus of this research was a series of criminal justice policy changes in the United States since the 1970s that have resulted in a staggering increase in the number of persons imprisoned. At year-end 2013, the U.S. prison population totaled 1,574,700 (Carson 2014, 1), and between 1978 and 2009, the number of persons held in state and federal prisons increased almost 430 percent, from 294,400 in 1978 to 1,555,600 in 2009 (Carson and Golinelli 2013, 1). When other forms of punishment such as probation and parole are taken into account, about 6,899,000 offenders were under the supervision of adult correctional systems at year-end

2013 down from 6,940,500 at year end 2012 (Glaze and Kaeble 2014, 1).[5] It is not the case, therefore, that increased incarceration has diminished probation and parole numbers; in fact, these punishments have all but ceased their original function of reintegrating offenders and instead have become control and surveillance mechanisms[6] for even minor probation and parole violations and have resulted in significant levels of reincarceration.

How do developments in incarceration in the United States compare with worldwide imprisonment rates? The tenth edition of the World Prison Population List covering rates of imprisonment between September 2011 and September 2013 reveals that the United States has the highest prison population rate worldwide, comprising 716 per 100,000 persons (Walmsley 2013, 1). This compares to Russia at 475 per 100,000, a median rate for Europe of 98, for Oceania (including Australia and New Zealand) of 151, Japan of 51, England and Wales of 148, and a world prison population rate overall of 144 per 100,000 (pp. 1–3). Clearly, U.S. justice policies have placed it well outside the ranges and rates of incarceration experienced in the rest of the world. As Clear and Frost (2014, 1) explain, "Nowhere else in the democratic world, and at no other time in Western history, has there been the kind of relentless punitive spirit as has been ascendant in the United States for more than a generation."

The U.S. mass incarceration phenomenon has taken place in spite of the fact that crime, especially violent and property crime, has been on the decline since the early 1990s (Clear and Frost 2014, 11). As crime rates have fallen, opinion polls indicate that crime has ceased to be a paramount public concern (p. 11). Curiously, it appears that changes in crime have had little effect on incarceration rates, suggesting that the relationship between crime and incarceration is complex and often contradictory (Cavadino and

Dignan 2006b, 46). For example, the last crime peak occurred in 1994, and crime rates have fallen steadily for more than a decade (Clear and Frost 2014, 34). However, during that period, incarceration rates increased by two-thirds (p. 36). Punitive justice policies continued to be shaped and implemented long after the crime rate had stabilized and into the period when crimes rates were falling (p. 59).

U.S. criminal justice policies that have resulted in this mass incarceration include mandatory minimum prison sentences for persons convicted of a third offense, sentencing guidelines mandating a fairly narrow range of punishments based on the current offense and prior criminal history, the abolition of parole, truth in sentencing laws requiring that violent offenders serve at least 85 percent of their sentence before being considered for parole, the "war on crime" dating from the 1960s, and the "war on drugs" first declared in 1972.[7]

In the United States, crime has become heavily politicized and sensationalized by the media. Crime frames the exercise of political and executive action and has created a culture of fear and risk avoidance to such an extent that Jonathan Simon (2007, 4) has asserted that "the American elite are governing through crime." Scholars have tried to assess whether the U.S. punitive punishment model has migrated to Europe and other countries.[8] In other words, they ponder whether criminal justice policies have begun to converge within globalization to create a homogenized criminal justice policy framework worldwide. An associated issue is the extent to which there is international regulation or standard setting in relation to punishment against which U.S. and other penal policy initiatives can be measured. However, there is insufficient space here to fully address the contours of this debate, but in considering the issue of policy convergence and homogenization, the two research studies presented in Box 6.1 are examples of divergent views.

BOX 6.1   Globalization and Penal Policy

Michael Cavadino and James Dignan (2006a, 435) assert that globalization has not resulted in a "global homogenization of penal policy and practices." Their work draws on data from twelve capitalist countries to which they apply a political economy analysis categorizing them as neoliberal (United States, England and Wales, South Africa, Australia, and New Zealand); conservative corporatist (Netherlands, Germany, France, and Italy); social democratic corporatist (Sweden, Finland) and oriental corporatist (Japan). A survey of rates of imprisonment for these countries reveals an association between the specific political economy and penal policies. Thus, with one exception (Netherlands), all the neoliberal countries have higher imprisonment rates than all the conservative corporatist countries, followed by the social democratic corporatist countries and then by the one orientalist corporatist, with the lowest rate of all (p. 446). Cavadino and Dignan argue that cultural attitudes toward the deviant and the marginalized—a part of the political economy—show a correlation with the differing rates of imprisonment. So, for example, the neoliberal category values an "individualistic ethos" that supposes that individuals and not the state must take responsibility for themselves and that economic failure is attributed to the actions or inactions of free-willed individuals rather than society, all of which results in a weak or minimal social safety net. As Cavadino and Dignan argue, "The social soil is fertile ground for a harsh 'law and order ideology'" (p. 448) that promotes a "culture of control" (Garland 2001). Cavadino and Dignan (2006b, 36) are careful to point out that their model does not explain all variations in penality by reference to the different political economies they identify and that other factors are also in play.

In contrast to the structural political economy analysis of Cavadino and Dignan, Setsuo Miyazawa (2008, 47) offers a more empirical level of analysis contending that in Japan there is rising penal populism and that the criminal justice system there is characterized by "increasing punitiveness." He sees the same penal populism developing in Japan (denoted by the Japanese term *genbatsuka,* meaning increasing the severity of punishment) that exists in the United States. His argument relies on data from the media showing how a discourse of *genbatsuka* has been generated by several notorious murders, some involving young children both as victims and perpetrators, and by the growth of the victims movement in Japan, which he traces from its inception in 2000. In cases involving serious crimes, in 2007, the victims movement succeeded in changing the Code of Criminal Procedure to allow victims' family members to go far beyond the victim impact statements typically found in the United States. Victims can now sit beside and give opinions to the prosecutor about the proceedings, question witnesses and the accused about mitigating circumstances, obtain civil damages, and present an opinion on the evidence, including about the appropriate sentence (p. 68).

Miyazawa links the discourse of *genbatsuka* and its outcomes with distrust of government and with experts in the justice system. He believes a similar analysis of these factors by Franklin Zimring and David Johnson (2006) in relation to the United States is applicable to the situation in Japan. As Zimring and Johnson (2006, 276) put it, "as soon the chain of expertise is discredited, the man in the street (or his state representative) is every bit the expert as the judge, the parole board, or the correctional administrator." The same view is expressed by John Pratt (2007, 4), namely, that one of the levers of penal populism is "disillusionment with existing political processes and declines in deference to elite opinion formers." This public perspective is aligned with a focus on the victims of crime to the virtual exclusion of the offender—"the sentence has to fit the offence not the offender" (Pratt 2007, 5, 48).

While this does not necessarily reveal a process of actual criminal justice policy transfer from the United States to Japan, it does suggest that notions about appropriate penality and victimization in the United States have gained traction in Japan through the global international traffic in information about punishment. (The case study on punishment in Japan in Box 6.5 [p. 156] indicates that country's readiness to import ideas and practices from the West.)

Generally, it has been argued that globalization facilitates "one size fits all" type penal policies that can travel effortlessly between jurisdictions because they have mass appeal (Baker and Roberts 2005, 132). This may explain trends across nations that share a similar language, social organization, culture, and ideology, where similar penal policies have been pursued over the past decade or more (Baker and Roberts 2005, 121; Cavadino and Dignan 2006b, 14). This process is aided by slogans such as "three strikes and you're out" and "zero tolerance," which can easily be turned into media sound bites for political purposes (Baker and Roberts

2005, 123). Accordingly, Baker and Roberts suggest that a "plausible argument can be made that globalization forces have created a homogenization of criminal justice problems and policies" (p. 131). At the very least, while the effects of a penal globalization may be uneven, there is no doubt that U.S. justice policies are influential outside the United States (Cavadino and Dignan 2006b, 11).

Some criminologists (e.g., Jones and Newburn 2007, 162–63) draw a distinction between detailed policy transfers that result in new penal laws in the receiving state (an example would be enacting "three strikes" legislation modeled on U.S. laws) as opposed to "soft" policy transfers that encompass rhetoric and labels and the discourse of punitive punishment generally. Where the latter takes place, the discourse is appropriated, but local policies may differ from those in the United States. This view therefore rejects the notion that U.S. policy exercises hegemony in this policy field.

Many commentators take the view that globalization flows are always mediated by local interests, culture, practices, and contingencies and thus responses to such flows are often jurisdiction-specific. In some cases, countries (e.g., Canada) actively seek to differentiate themselves from the United States (Baker and Roberts 2005, 122; Cavadino and Dignan 2006b, 11). Savelsburg (2011, 70) points out that the global and the local interpenetrate and that local actors often make policy changes to gain legitimacy internationally but do not actively implement those changes. Consequently, there is a need to fully understand the processes involved when the global and local appear to converge. This raises the question of how local actors such as public officials address the global domain.

David Brown (2005, 27) argues that punitive populism and increases in incarceration rates are the outcome of changes in social, cultural, political, and economic organization of a general nature, not simply to specific justice policies, and are therefore attributable to the conditions of life in what is termed *later modernity*. These changes are theorized through discourse analysis and include matters such as globalization; the rise of the risk society; the extension of ideas associated with neoliberalism; the growing distrust of government, bureaucracy, and experts, coupled with a corresponding rise in populism; and the failure of the state to control crime. This in turn leads to states retreating from claiming sole responsibility for crime control and later to reasserting its right to punish.

Punishment: Setting International Standards

International standards can play a role in fostering penal convergence, especially given that these standards may arise as an outcome of treaty obligations that nations are required to adhere to. International standards are also said to constitute best practice on an issue, for example, in relation to the conditions in which persons may be detained (Cavadino and Dignan 2006b). This continues to be an emerging field; however, decisions made under the European Convention on Human Rights have been instrumental in harmonizing the rights of prisoners in Europe (p. 12). Nevertheless, in real terms, little progress has been made on achieving a worldwide consensus on the goals of punishment and associated normative issues, especially given that the United States is notorious for resisting international and "foreign" concepts and practices (Frase 2001, 285). For example, a Council of Europe "Consistency in Sentencing" recommendation in 1993 failed to recommend any particular sentencing rationale (Kurki 2001, 360). This contrasts with the international attention paid to standards of criminal process about which there has been broad agreement (Kurki 2001, 368).

Since 1948, the international community has prohibited cruel, inhuman, or degrading treatment or punishment through the Universal Declaration of Human Rights, and subsequent regional human rights conventions have repeated and elaborated on this prohibition. These conventions include the European Convention for the Protection of Human Rights and Fundamental Freedoms, the American Convention on Human Rights, and the African Charter on Human Rights and Peoples' Rights. Likewise, the International Covenant on Civil and Political Rights (ICCPR) 1966 provides a global standard of treatment and punishment. As well as these general human rights instruments, specific elaborations of treatment and punishment exist in the Convention against Torture and Other Cruel, Inhuman or Degrading Treatment or Punishment

(1984) and its regional European and American counterparts.

International treatment standards are further detailed in the 1955 UN Minimum Standard Rules for the Treatment of Prisoners setting out "what is generally accepted as being good principle and practice in the treatment of prisoners and the management of institutions" (p. 1). Standards of a general nature are prescribed on topics that include separation by age and gender within institutions, food, hygiene, discipline, and punishment. As an example, in relation to the latter, Rule 33 provides as follows:

33. Instruments of restraint, such as handcuffs, chains, irons and strait-jackets, shall never be applied as a punishment. Furthermore, chains or irons shall not be used as restraints. Other instruments of restraint shall not be used except in the following circumstances:

(a) As a precaution against escape during a transfer, provided that they shall be removed when the prisoner appears before a judicial or administrative authority;

(b) On medical grounds by direction of the medical officer;

(c) By order of the director, if other methods of control fail, in order to prevent a prisoner from injuring himself or others or from damaging property; in such instances the director shall at once consult the medical officer and report to the higher administrative authority.

34. The patterns and manner of use of instruments of restraint shall be decided by the central prison administration. Such instruments must not be applied for any longer time than is strictly *necessary* (emphasis added).

Punishment in the form of solitary confinement is the subject of the Istanbul Statement on the Use and Effects of Solitary Confinement formulated by a working group of twenty-four international experts and adopted on December 9, 2007. It calls on states to limit the use of solitary confinement to very exceptional cases, for as short a time as possible, and only as a last resort. The statement defines *solitary confinement* as "the physical isolation of individuals who are confined to their cells for twenty-two to twenty-four hours a day. In many jurisdictions prisoners are allowed out of their cells for one hour of solitary exercise." Such conditions currently prevail in the so-called supermax prisons in the United States.[9]

A number of international instruments are concerned with the death penalty and establish punishment standards. For example, the ICCPR states that the death penalty may be imposed only for the most serious crimes,[10] it shall not be imposed on persons under the age of 18 years or on pregnant women, and a person sentenced to death has the right to seek a pardon or commutation of sentence. The Second Optional Protocol to the ICCPR of 1989 expressly aims at the abolition of the death penalty. It commits states that ratify it to prohibit the death penalty and not to execute persons. A set of Safeguards Guaranteeing Protection of the Rights of Those Facing the Death Penalty was approved in 1984. One such standard is "Where capital punishment occurs, it shall be carried out so as to inflict the minimum possible suffering" (p. 1). Although this standard is accepted in the United States, events in 2014 concerning the carrying out of the death sentence using lethal injection have shown that this method can be problematic in terms of minimum suffering in situations where commonly used drugs to ensure death have become no longer available.

BOX 6.2 Administering a Cocktail of Drugs

According to media reports in April 2014, condemned prisoner Clayton Lockett was administered a cocktail of drugs by the state of Oklahoma in a twenty-minute attempt to execute him. The drugs failed to kill him, and he was "left writhing on the gurney" until a heart attack brought about his death. The cocktail of drugs had never been used before in American executions. It was intended to replace the European supply of a lethal drug used previously after supplies had been stopped by companies there opposed to capital punishment (Fretland 2014).

CAPITAL PUNISHMENT

It is well known that the United States retains the death penalty for certain crimes; however, here we address the view of the international community regarding the death penalty. As noted earlier, international standards have circumscribed its use, and majority international opinion is firmly against the death penalty as a punishment, reflecting this approach. For example, in 1998, the newly created International Criminal Court was given no power to impose the death penalty, even for those convicted of genocide (Garland 2010, 99).

The European-led movement to abolish the death penalty worldwide is founded on the argument that the principle of respect for human rights renders the death penalty an unacceptable punishment (Hood 2001, 337). While the trend is toward abolition of the death penalty for all crimes, states are generally categorized as either retentionist or abolitionist (see Box 6.3).

BOX 6.3   Retentionist and Abolitionist States on the Death Penalty in 2013

- Abolition states, having abolished it for all crimes—98 states

- Abolitionist for ordinary crimes only states, retaining it for only exceptional crimes, such as under military law—7 states

- Abolitionist in practice, have not imposed it during the last 10 years, have made an international commitment not to impose it, or have a policy or established practice of not conducting executions—35 states

- Total abolitionist in law or practice—140 states

- Retentionist states—retain it for all crimes—58 states

SOURCE: Amnesty International, 2014, 52.

It may take a state some time to move from retaining the death penalty for exceptional crimes to abolishing it for all crimes. A good example is the Irish Republic, which abolished the death penalty for murder in 1954 but not for all crimes until 1990. Similarly, the United Kingdom did not abolish the death penalty completely for all crimes until 1998, having abolished it for all crimes except for piracy, treason, and some military offenses in 1965 (Hood 2001, 333). Generally, resistance to abolition is often associated with arguments that death penalty abolition is not a human rights' norm let alone an element of international law, and retentionist states have argued that the European abolitionist movement is "insulting and culturally imperialistic" (p. 340).

In the developed West, only the United States continues to retain the death penalty; it is permitted by thirty-two states with eighteen states considered non-death-penalty states (Hood and Hoyle 2015, 45). Historically, two-thirds of U.S. executions have been carried out in the states of Texas, Virginia, Florida, Missouri, and Louisiana (Hood 2001, 334). In 2013 Texas, Oklahoma, and Florida accounted for 74% of all executions in the United States (Hood and Hoyle 2013, 46).

Islamic nations permitting the death penalty are Afghanistan, Bahrain, Bangladesh, Egypt, Indonesia, Iran, Iraq, Jordan, Kuwait, Lebanon, Libya, Malaysia, Oman, Pakistan, Palestinian Authority, Qatar, Saudi Arabia, Somalia, Syria, United Arab Emirates, and Yemen (Death Penalty Worldwide 2012). The various methods used are hanging, shooting by firing squad, stoning, beheading, and lethal injection (Death Penalty Worldwide 2012). The use of the death penalty is congruent with the application of Sharia law in these states even though only Saudi Arabia and Yemen apply Sharia systems of law in full (Hood and Hoyle 2013, 86). Islamic states that are abolitionist in practice are Algeria, Brunei,[11] Morocco, and Tunisia (pp. 77, 88, 150, 166). The retentionist Islamic states have argued at the United Nations that "capital punishment is a divine right of some religions. It is embodied in Islam and these views must be respected" (cited in Hood 2001, 341).

In Southeast Asia, China, and the Caribbean, the death penalty is retained for its supposed deterrent value and because it is widely supported by the public (Hood and Hoyle 2008, Chap. 3; Hood and Hoyle 2013, 539; Simmons 2009, 189). Compared to China, India, although a populous nation of 1.1 billion, has a low death sentence rate, estimated at fewer than ten executions a year (Zimring and Johnson 2008, 105). Nearly half of Asian states with retentionist policies have in fact maintained periodic moratoria on the death penalty. Interestingly, within Asia, those states with the highest levels of execution do not have high concentrations of Islamic population (p. 105).

One important aspect is the correlation in some states between the suspension of judicial executions and extrajudicial killing by law enforcement and other state agents. For example, in Thailand, the police summarily killed more than three thousand suspected drug dealers in 2003, and in the Philippines, extrajudicial killings are quite common involving police and the military (Zimring and Johnson 2008, 111). Similarly, in India, the rate of capital punishment is affected by police encounters with alleged criminals where police kill the alleged offenders who might otherwise be sentenced to death (p. 111).

BOX 6.4 United States—Death Penalty

Why does the United States retain the death penalty in the face of a worldwide abolitionist trend? The U.S. position on the death penalty may be considered abnormal in light of its professed role as the principal liberal democracy and world guardian of human rights (Hood 2001, 343). Many commentators, including Zimring (2003), have pointed out that the U.S. federal system of government allows each state to make its choice concerning the retention or otherwise of the death penalty, and most executions are performed in a small number of states. Consequently, to speak of the United States as being a retentionist nation is misleading. Zimring (2003, 49) also argues that the attention given to victims of homicides in the court process and by the media generally means that the death penalty is, in effect, a policy response to murder that represents an "undertaking of government to serve the needs of individual citizens for justice and psychological healing." This focus on the victim has replaced the attention previously given to the situation of the offender.

In a recent analysis of the American death penalty, Garland (2010, 14) argues that it is necessary to engage with the death penalty in the United States in a holistic fashion and focus not on the morality or policy of the death penalty but on its situation in a "complex field of institutional arrangements, social practices and cultural forms" that he calls the "capital punishment complex." The American form of capital punishment has adapted over time: for example, harsher forms of execution such as hanging have been replaced by less violent lethal injections, and minors and mentally challenged offenders are no longer liable to be put to death (p. 18). According to Garland, it has evolved into "an assemblage of practices, discourses, rituals and representations" following the demands of society and the various forces that influence its operation (p. 19). Like other commentators on this topic, Garland (2010, 35) sees links and commonalities between the death penalty and lynching.[12] Thus,

- executions are concentrated in the South,

- the death penalty is a subject of local politics and populism expressed in the election process at various levels and for various offices,

- the death penalty disproportionately targets poor blacks who commit crimes against white victims, and

- support for the death penalty is energized by heinous crimes and racial hatreds and continues to provide drama.

He asserts that many of the social forces that prompted lynching also promote capital punishment (p. 35). Accordingly, the death penalty in the United States has some uniquely American

(Continued)

(Continued)

features. An example is the link between capital punishment and the justice system and due process. The due process protections that are available to condemned prisoners mean that the average time spent on death row in the United States is lengthy—in 2007 it was twelve years (p. 45). This compares to China where the execution process can be very rapid and to Japan where it is also lengthy but for reasons that remain unclear because of the secrecy associated with it but which do not relate to due process issues.

Most significantly, in the United States, the death penalty represents an expression of the "people's will" and hence the death penalty for Americans expresses democracy in action. As Garland (2010, 62) puts it, "The death penalty is depicted as a vital expression of local community sentiment, as moral outrage authentically expressed, as collective choice, and community justice." The community in this sense can extend down to the state and even county level control of sentencing. The requirement that judges, prosecutors, and police chiefs be elected by a popular vote in many states ensures that community sentiment about capital punishment is made explicit in law enforcement policies and operations. Not only is the death penalty the epitome of an expressive punishment, but also advocacy for it symbolizes being "tough on law and order" generally (pp. 121, 162, 246).

In policy terms, clearly the U.S. federal government lacks that centralized control of justice policy that has enabled European nations to abolish the death penalty, sometimes against the wishes of the population.[13] Instead, the death penalty is continuously litigated as a constitutional issue with the effect, as Garland (2010, 191) explains, that the rulings of the Supreme Court "enhance the perceived lawfulness and legitimacy of capital punishment and thus act as a force for its conservation." Regional differences among the states in the South[14] in terms of the incidence of executions (and the history of slavery, racism, and lynching) compared to the remainder of the country also provide explanations of U.S. divergence from the mainstream. Differences are reinforced by a commitment in the South to notions of state rights, local autonomy, and an anti–big government stance on policy issues (pp. 122, 159).

In sum, according to Garland, historical and cultural legacies, institutional structures, deeply rooted democratic forms and practices, and a shift to a victim-centric law and order politics, all working together, have created constraints and barriers to the total abolition of capital punishment throughout the United States. The "capital punishment complex" in the United States today exists independently of any association with crime control, instead serving various partisan and political interests as well as those of the media. Given that it exists in a form peculiar to the United States, it is resistant to arguments that have brought about its total abolition in other nations. Accordingly, capital punishment is an assured element of contemporary U.S. culture (Garland 2010, 286).

As noted earlier, Japanese law provides for the death penalty. The following case study of punishment in Japan reveals that throughout most of its history, Japan has administered death as the dominant punishment. During the post–World War II occupation of Japan by the United States, no initiative was taken to abolish capital punishment. This contrasts with Germany, where the death penalty was abolished in 1949.

BOX 6.5   Japan—Death Penalty

Today, hanging is the means of execution provided by the 1908 Penal Code (Johnson 2006, 258), and Japanese death penalty practice is notable for its extreme secrecy. Prosecutors and politicians alike are reluctant to describe death penalty practices. Embarrassing events, such as that which occurred in the 1980s when four death row prisoners were declared innocent and released, contributed to an apparent desire to preclude any criticism of the death penalty.[15] From November 1989 to March 1993, Japan operated a moratorium but no proposals for reform were legislated (p. 262).

If Miyazawa (see Box 6.1) is correct, then public opinion in Japan generally continues to favor retaining and implementing the death penalty in appropriate cases. In fact, in a poll conducted in 2005, 81 percent of Japanese respondents favored retaining the death penalty while only 6 percent thought it should be abolished (Johnson 2006, 269). In spite of this support, executions are still rare in Japan, with an average of four hangings a year over the past decade—about seven times lower than in the United States as a whole and thirty-four to thirty-eight times lower than high death penalty states like Texas and Oklahoma (p. 267). In 2013 there were eight executions in Japan and at year-end, 130 prisoners were being held under sentence of death (Amnesty International 2014).

Japanese death penalty practice is notable for its lack of consideration both to the condemned and to his or her relatives. Those waiting on the Japanese death row are not notified of the date or time of execution until about an hour before it takes place (Johnson 2006, 266). This contrasts with China, where 80 percent of all executions are announced several days in advance and inmates are allowed to meet with relatives and friends (p. 266). Condemned prisoners in Japan are kept in virtual total isolation with cells constantly lit, are not permitted to stand or lie without permission, and are required to sit and sleep in certain approved postures. They may exercise alone out of their cells two or three times each week for only fifteen minutes each session (p. 272). Relatives of the condemned person are advised of the execution only after it has taken place and given twenty-four hours to collect the body. The victim's relatives are told nothing, and only government officials are permitted to witness an execution. It is unclear why some persons on death row are selected for execution while others are not. The Ministry of Justice does not explain its process for selection, but the length of time on death row appears to be one factor that is taken into account (p. 255).

In Japan, unlike in the United States and to a certain extent China, the death penalty is not a social issue, nor is it a subject for scholarly attention as in the United States.

Amnesty International (2014) reports that China performed "thousands" of executions in 2013. The organization was unable to provide an exact figure due to government secrecy. According to calculations made by Roger Hood (2001, 336), China executed a total of 12,338 persons between 1994 and 1998, far ahead of the next highest nation for that period, Iran, with 505. Based on Amnesty International data, 6,145 persons were sentenced to death in 1996 with violent crime being the primary offense type, while about 3 percent constituted economic and corruption cases, and about 1.3 percent involved drug trafficking (Lu and Zhang 2005, 370). Hood and Carolyn Hoyle (2015, 170–71) note that between 8,000 and 10,000 executions took place in 2004 and 2005 while only 1,620 were carried out in 2013. According to Susan Trevaskes (2008, 394), the figure for executions may have been as high as 10,000 a year up to 2004 or even 15,000 each year.[16]

BOX 6.6   China—Death Penalty

During the Chinese imperial era, the death penalty was a common punishment. In recent history, during the early period after the defeat of the nationalists between 1950 and 1960, extensive use was made of the death penalty to target counterrevolutionaries through ad hoc revolutionary people's tribunals (Lu and Zhang 2005, 369). While nowadays Chinese public policies appear to impose strict limits on the exercise of the death penalty, human rights organizations insist there is a gap between policy and practice that results in China executing more persons than all the rest of the world combined (Jiang 2014, 120). For example, during the "strike hard" campaigns (see Chapter 4), it was reported that the death penalty rate increased substantially and that convictions were based on expediency rather than an adequate trial process (p. 121). During the time of the first strike hard campaign in 1983, the Supreme People's Court (SPC) was excluded from the death

(Continued)

(Continued)

penalty approval process when the power to review and approve death sentences was delegated to provincial courts; this was done to ensure "severe and swift punishment" against strike hard targeted offenders (Trevaskes 2008, 395). The power was subsequently returned to the SPC in 2006.

The current applicable criminal legislation in China provides that the death penalty is reserved for "extremely serious crimes." In the Chinese context, this includes acts that affect the essential interests of the state (Jiang 2014, 125). The method of execution is lethal injection (p. 172). The first Criminal Code of 1979 named twenty-eight capital offenses (fifteen of which were counter-revolutionary in nature); this increased to seventy-four before the law was revised in 1997 due to the increase in crime that followed the economic reforms; and in the 1997 reform of the code, capital offenses increased again to sixty-eight and focused on areas of national security, economic order, and corruption. In 2011, the number of economic-related crimes was reduced by thirteen (Li 2014, 115). This can be compared to the United States where the federal Death Penalty Act mandates about sixty capital offenses, including murder of federal officers, treason, espionage, and felony drug offenses (Lu and Zhang 2005, 370).

China has a unique death penalty feature: the two-year suspension of the death penalty. Under the 1979 Code, when a person is sentenced to death but immediate execution is not "essential,"[17] a two-year suspension of the sentence can be ordered and reform through labor performed instead. In effect, therefore, in appropriate cases the sentence can be suspended for two years while the offender is observed. If the offender shows remorse after two years, the sentence will be commuted to life imprisonment; if the offender shows remorse and has shown merit in work, the sentence can be reduced to between fifteen and twenty years imprisonment; but when the offender shows no indications of reform after two years, the death sentence must be carried out (Lu and Zhang 2005, 370–71). These provisions were changed in 1997 so that when no crime is committed during the two-year period of suspension, the sentence is commuted to life imprisonment. However, when a crime has been committed, the death sentence must be performed. Otherwise the provisions were unchanged.

A new provision in the 2012 revisions to the 1997 law requires that in a review of sentence, the SPC shall question the convicted person and where the person's lawyer so requests, the SPC must hear his or her opinion on the sentence (Li 2014, 117).

Kandis Scott (2010, 63) argues that the two-year suspension of the death sentence, the operation of which commonly converts death sentences into life sentences, has reduced the number of death sentences carried out, perhaps by as much as 40 percent. The recent debate about crime and how to control it has revived a dictum of the revolution—*Shaosha Shensha,* meaning "Kill Fewer, Kill Cautiously" (Trevaskes 2008, 393). This lenient approach to the ultimate penalty stands opposed by the harsh strike hard perspective (p. 393). This debate has taken place during the period when the power to approve death sentences was returned to the SPC in 2006 and when a policy of "balancing leniency and severity" was adopted by the then President (chief justice) of the SPC. This policy envisaged decriminalizing minor offenses and encouraging noncustodial sentencing as well as restricting the number of executions (pp. 399–400).

Since then, a new President has been appointed to the SPC. On March 10, 2014, the official news agency Xinhua reported that the President of the SPC, Zhou Qiang, in his report to the twelfth National People's Congress, stated that "the SPC has been cautious about reviewing death sentences and has carefully examined facts, evidence and application of law in these cases" and "we have ensured that the death penalty was imposed on a very limited number of people convicted of extremely serious crimes" ("China's Chief Justice Pledges to Fight Terrorism" 2014, 1).

While some Chinese scholars recommend limiting capital punishment, the public is generally supportive of it. One Chinese scholar (cited in Scott 2010, 67) explains this as the result of "the Chinese cultural tradition of retribution and lowly-regarded individual rights." At the same time, Scott argues that there appears to be no censorship of media stories about erroneous convictions, which may indicate that the state is not adverse to stimulating public interest, which in turn could result in a change in attitude toward the death penalty (2010, 73).

COMPARING PUNISHMENTS

Despite similarities in legal processes (police, prosecutors, independent courts, reliance on imprisonment for serious crimes) and responses to crime, there are distinct differences in punishment policies between nations (Tonry 2001, 3), notwithstanding the arguments about policy convergence and the globalization of justice policies. Reasons for these differences include

- the basically nonpolitical nature of criminal justice issues in states other than the United States;

- the lack of an intense media focus on crime, which is most developed in the United States and England;

- and the fact that justice system professionals are career public servants in most of Europe and do not face reelection challenges or the need to advocate for "getting tough on crime." (Frase 2001, 276; Tonry 1999, 48)

Here, we will briefly look at different punishments: *incarceration, day fines, community work* or *community service, suspension of prosecution subject to conditions,* and *intermediate sanction.*

In terms of punishment policies, the United States stands out compared to other Western developed states for its retention of the death penalty, for its life sentences without parole, and for its lengthy terms of imprisonment (Tonry 2001, 4). The United States also maintains the most punitive[18] penal policies: first, the incarceration rate per 100,000 persons is vastly higher than the rates of other developed states, and second, penalties in the United States are much harsher than elsewhere in the developed world. For example, only the United States has life sentences without parole and mandatory minimum sentences that run to twenty-five years.

In Europe, maximum sentences tend to be in the ten- to fifteen-year range, for example, in Germany, Norway, Finland, and Denmark (Tonry 2001, 16, 25). Moreover, the mass imprisonment policies pursued in the United States seem to have been promoted without regard for the staggering costs of constructing new prisons and hiring thousands of additional prison staff. In the United States in 2001, correctional authorities spent $38.2 billion to maintain state correctional systems, with an average annual operating cost

per inmate of $22,650. Between 1986 and 2001, state prison costs per U.S. resident doubled (Stephan 2004, 1). The Cost-Benefit Analysis Unit of the Vera Institute of Justice's Center on Sentencing and Corrections calculated the full cost of prisons (including the costs beyond prison walls of employee benefits, capital costs, in-prison education services, and hospital care for inmates) to taxpayers in forty participating states was 39 billion in 2012, 5.4 billion more than was revealed in corrections budgets (Henrichson and Delaney 2012, i, 1–2).

In other countries, resource constraints have been a major influence on penal policy. In Germany and Austria, prison sentences of less than six months are regarded as serving no useful purpose (Tonry 2001, 4). However, in Sweden and Finland, certainty but not severity in punishment is seen as important, and short sentences of days or weeks are imposed (p. 4). Although England introduced mandatory sentencing in 1997 requiring the imposition of an automatic life sentence for a second conviction for a serious violent or sex offense, it also provided that where exceptional circumstances existed, the rule would not apply (Stern 2001, 89). The overall approach in Europe is therefore less focused on harsh, lengthy punishments, whereas in the United States noncustodial sanctions are seen as insufficiently tough (Tonry 1999, 49, 58).

Within Europe, some countries' penal laws provide the punishment of a *day fine,* imposed for less serious offenses and as an alternative to a short term of imprisonment (Tonry 1999). This sanction was established early in this century in Scandinavia. According to the U.S. Department of Justice, day fines (also called *structured fines*) "are based on a simple concept: punishment by a fine should be proportionate to the seriousness of the offense and should have roughly similar impact (in terms of economic sting) on persons with differing financial resources who are convicted of the same offense" (Justice Management Institute and Vera Institute of Justice 1996, 1).

Consequently, in sentencing, a court considers the seriousness of the offense and the income of the offender. The process involves first determining the number of fine units for the crime committed based on a table that ranks offenses according to their seriousness. Then the amount of the fine is arrived at by multiplying the number of fine units by a proportion of the offender's net daily income adjusted to take account of dependents and other special factors. A pilot project using day fines was established in New York and later extended to four other states. However, day fines were not introduced primarily as an alternative to short prison terms, and in most of the pilot sites, day fines could only be imposed for misdemeanors.

At an Arizona site, the goal was to use day fines as an alternative to probation and at another site, it was introduced to raise funds from low-risk offenders and reduce the workload of probation officers (Tonry 1999, 54). In England and Wales, day fines were introduced, but adverse media publicity surrounding some anomalous outcomes ensured they did not survive (Tonry 1999, 53). In Germany, day fines have been possible since 1969 and have become the typical sanction for larceny, small fraud cases, non-aggravated battery, and drunken driving. To a great extent, Germany has followed a policy of replacing the sanction of imprisonment with economic penalties (Weigend 2001, 195).

In Europe, including England and Wales, *community work* or *community service* is generally ordered as an alternative to a short sentence of imprisonment. Not only is this a less expensive option but it has received a high degree of public support (Tonry 1999, 56). After pilot projects in the 1960s and 1970s, community service was widely used in Australia, Canada, New Zealand, Ireland, Italy, Norway, Denmark, France, Portugal, and the Netherlands. Ironically, the first program started in California in 1966 allowing traffic offenders to perform community service rather than pay fines. Hundreds of such programs were set up in the United States in the 1970s, but nowadays orders are generally made as a condition of probation and not as sanctions in their own right, and are intended to make probation more punitive (p. 58).

The discretionary power given to some prosecutors in Europe, for example, in Germany and the Netherlands, to *suspend prosecution* and instead impose a fine or other monetary sanction (see Chapter 5) also has no counterpart in the United States. In Germany, in misdemeanor cases, the prosecutor is empowered to require restitution be paid to a victim by a suspect, or to have the suspect make a payment to charity or to the state in exchange for waiving criminal charges. This power has been in operation since 1975 (Weigend 2001, 189).

The United States has experienced great challenges in formulating and implementing what it calls "intermediate sanctions"—those sanctions between imprisonment and probation, designed to reduce the prison population. One reason for this failure is the difficulty in determining sentencing guidelines for these sanctions, which can include intensive probation, community service, drug treatment, victim restitution, day fines, home confinement, forfeitures, and forms of treatment in the community (Reitz 2001, 249). In relation to fines generally, Pat O'Malley (2011, 549) points out that while in Europe the practice of substituting fines for some short terms of imprisonment appeared at the end of the nineteenth century, this practice did not occur in the United States. O'Malley (2011, 550) points out that it is frequently argued that fines are not imposed in the United States because they do not rehabilitate offenders; however, the same can be said of short terms of imprisonment.

PUNISHMENT IN THE WEST: SOCIAL, HISTORICAL, AND CULTURAL BACKGROUND

Contextualizing punishment practices and systems assists us to gain a better understanding of how punishments originated, how and why they change over time, and what social and cultural forces bring about those changes. For example, as described in the case studies below on various countries including China and Japan, modes of punishment in both China and Japan changed in response to their perception that the Western powers of the time would never permit their citizens to be tried and punished in Chinese and Japanese courts unless both the trial process and the sanctions that could be imposed met Western standards of "civilized" treatment. Until these countries met this standard, Western powers would continue to enforce extraterritorial treaties that exempted their citizens from the local legal system.

Explanations of colonial punishment regimes are provided to show how the abolition of slavery and racism in general prompted discrete penal policies designed to reinforce order and control over populations that were benefitting from new political and social freedoms, and how the economy of a colony benefitted from convict labor.

In addition to the case studies of Japan and China, a summary is presented of the development of punishment in the West, namely, in

England and the United States. The space available does not permit a fuller account of the development of punishment, especially of the prison, in the West.

In the Western world in ancient times, forms of punishment took the form of individual responses to perceived wrongs, and the state as such was not involved in administering or determining guilt or punishment. Punishment took the form of private vengeance, and tribal societies settled disputes through blood feuds (Blomberg and Lucken 2000, 12). Codes of law gradually evolved (as occurred in China). The Roman Code of Justinian of 529 CE, for example, prescribed a scale of punishment and compensation for specified wrongs (p. 18). During the Middle Ages, three basic modes of determining guilt, and therefore punishment, developed: trial by battle, the ordeal, and compurgation (Barnes 1972, 7). The thinking underlying these practices was that the innocent party would be favored by local divinities by having survived the experience. Generally, these methods of guilt-finding and punishment had ceased by the thirteenth century when recourse to the king's courts became available (p. 26). Torture was widely used in Europe to obtain evidence of guilt in the form of a confession (p. 10). In England, the introduction of trial by jury in the king's courts in the thirteenth century meant that justice was centralized and the state recognized as the authority dispensing justice.

BOX 6.7   Punishment in England

The gradual development of capitalism threatened the privileges and wealth of rulers as vagrants and beggars showed their potential to become a criminal class. Idleness was seen as equivalent to immorality, and by the second half of the sixteenth century the *workhouse* had evolved as a punishment for the poor and for vagrants. Labor and discipline were judged to be the instruments to be applied in changing and reforming those deemed to possess criminal characteristics. Scholars believe the workhouse evolved into the jail and then the prison because of the association between idleness, vagrancy, poverty, and punishment. As long ago as 1557, the City of London opened an institution to lock up vagrants at Bridewell, confining them for several years. Similar sites existed in Europe, chief among them the Dutch Rasp House, established in the 1550s (Ignatieff 1978, 12). The overall aim was to replace the perceived "habit of idleness" with a "habit of industry" (Hirsch 1992, 14).[19]

Among the forms of *corporal punishment* used until the close of the eighteenth century were *flogging, mutilation, branding, the stocks,* and *the pillory* (Barnes 1972, 56). Until about 1800, *flogging* was the principal method of punishing offenders; it was done using an instrument comprising nine knotted cords or thongs of rawhide attached to a handle (p. 58). *Mutilation* was justified by the *lex talionis* (an eye for an eye) and as a deterrent; thus thieves had their hands cut off and spies had their eyes removed. Women found to have committed adultery suffered removal of the nose or other disfigurement to render them unattractive (p. 60). In England, mutilation as punishment continued until the eighteenth century. *Branding* was used in Roman times, and as late as 1699, English law required that criminals be branded on the face with a letter that designated the crime they had committed. Branding was also employed as a punishment in colonial America; for example, the laws of New Jersey required that a first offense of burglary be punished by branding the letter T on the hand of the criminal and a second offense by branding an R on the forehead (p. 62). Branding was abolished in England in the second half of the eighteenth century, but the *pillory* was used in England until 1837, often in combination with other punishments such as branding and flogging.

Between 1780 and 1865, prisons were transformed from a condition of disorder and neglect to a state of quiet and orderliness. In the eighteenth-century prison, inmates wore their own clothes, some living in comfort and others in squalor. By the mid-nineteenth century, inmates were subject to strict discipline, wore uniforms and masks, and enjoyed a level of reasonable hygiene (McGowen 1995, 71). By the eighteenth century, a wide variety of punishments existed

(Continued)

(Continued)

in England; for minor offenses, which included fines and public shaming through the stocks and the pillory. Many condemned to death were conditionally pardoned by being transported to the Australian colonies. People were confined awaiting trial, but few were actually imprisoned as punishment. Places of confinement were the *jail* and the *house of correction (the Bridewell)*, the former holding debtors, those awaiting trial, and felons, while the latter held minor offenders serving short terms of incarceration (p. 72). The house of correction was intended to reform as well as to punish, and magistrates continued to believe it deterred vagrants and disciplined disobedient servants (p. 75).

Both transportation and the house of correction signified a move away from punishing the body in public displays of brutal punishments to instead stressing labor and confinement. From 1780 to 1865, most prisons (comprising jails and houses of correction) remained under local control. The passing of the Penitentiary Act in 1779 led eventually to the construction in 1816 of a national penitentiary at Millbank[20] with a capacity for one thousand prisoners, huge by the standards of the time (p. 85). In 1842, another, the Pentonville prison was opened in London. Based on the Pentonville separate system, it held 520 inmates in separate cells who wore hoods when they emerged from their cells and who were rendered nameless by being issued with identity numbers (p. 92).

In 1853 the introduction of a Victorian form of *parole* called "ticket of leave" created a moral panic when street robbery, alleged to have been committed by ticket of leave men, was amplified by the media into the "modern peril of the streets" and "a reign of terror." This form of robbery, termed *garroting,* prompted political action in the form of the return of flogging, which had been abolished in 1861 (Wilson 2014, 73–74). In 1863, the Garrotters Act was enacted and would remain in effect until 1948. It authorized up to fifty strokes of corporal punishment as a supplement to any other punishment imposed (p. 75).

The punishment of *transportation* was a significant component of the English justice system for a number of years.[21] Prisoners were initially transported to the American colonies and, when that was no longer possible after the end of the War of Independence, to Australia. Transportation can be equated with the punishment of exile in countries like China and Japan even though the latter was largely a domestic exile. Shipping criminals out of England was perceived to be an appropriate means of ridding the country of its criminals (Barnes 1972, 69), and the initial legislation of 1717 providing for transportation to the American colonies stipulated transportation for persons otherwise liable to be flogged or branded or sent to the workhouse (p. 70). When transportation was no longer possible to the American colonies, prisoners were housed in old rotting decommissioned warships known as "the hulks" (Wilson 2014, 68).

Between 1820 and 1861, the reform of the English criminal law was completed and the death penalty was removed as the penalty for all offenses other than murder, treason, and piracy (Barnes 1972, 103). This meant that by the mid-nineteenth century, incarceration had become the predominant punishment for most offenses. Imprisonment was perceived to be more humane than the death penalty (Hirsch 1992, 44).[22] English prison reformer John Howard visited carceral institutions in Europe that separated prisoners by placing them in cells and maintained systems of inmate classification. Adapting the existing knowledge of workhouses and monasteries, Howard designed a regime of prison discipline that required *hard labor* in the day and *solitary confinement* at night. His ideas began to be implemented in the 1780s in English jails. Solitary confinement was believed to prevent inmates from morally contaminating each other so that each could regenerate morally as an individual (Colvin 1997, 49), but some reformers focused on the terrors associated with the solitary state as appropriately augmenting the punishment of incarceration (Masur 1989, 83).

Developments in the design of the penitentiary in the United States (see Box 6.8) resulted in England adopting a variation of the Pennsylvania separate system (Barnes 1972, 143). In the end, the Pennsylvania system was adopted in England, Belgium, Sweden, Denmark, Norway, and Holland (p. 144).

The Prison Act 1865 amalgamated the jail and the house of correction and adopted the term *prison* (McConville 1995, 119). With the passing of the Prison Act 1877, the state took over control of all of the penal system in England, Scotland, and Wales, replacing prisons run under contract for local magistrates (Wilson 2014, 38, 54). The 1898 Prison Act abolished hard labor, allowed prisoners to speak within prisons, and introduced remission for good behavior (p. 86).

Between 1908 and 1939, the prison population in England and Wales declined by half from about twenty-two thousand to about eleven thousand, resulting in the closure of about twenty prisons (Wilson 2014, 89). This was due to penal policy initiatives that reflected public disquiet about the value of prison. The policy change meant that those previously sentenced to imprisonment for short terms or for nonpayment of fines were no longer incarcerated: in 1910 about two-thirds of inmates were serving sentences of two weeks or less (Wilson 2014, 91). The creation of a probation system in 1907 also aided the decarceration process so that imprisonment was no longer perceived as the only punishment option (p. 95). However, later events subverted this trend toward decarceration, and by 1970 a prison population of less than ten thousand in 1940 had increased to just under forty thousand (Wilson 2014, 110).

BOX 6.8   Punishment in the United States

During the colonial period in America from the creation of Virginia in 1607 until 1776 and the War of Independence, most punishments had their foundation in English law and practice, given that England was the country of origin of most colonists. Consequently, the so-called Bloody Code prescribing the death penalty for some 225 offenses applied. In practice it tended to be interpreted quite flexibly in the colonies (Ignatieff 1978, 17; Wilson 2014, 33). Each colony could choose its own discrete approach to punishment, and this meant that a variety of systems and practices applied with population being a major factor (Preyer 1982, 326). Crime and religion were perceived as interconnected and because crime was considered a sin, it had to be punished (Blomberg and Lucken 2000, 26). Prosecutions were dominated by morality offenses such as profanity, drunkenness, flirting, and blaspheming (Preyer 1982, 334). Puritan beliefs influenced the nature of punishment by seeing it as a process customized to individual needs with the aim of reintegrating the criminal back into the community. Thus confessing guilt and showing remorse aided in minimizing punishment (Cahn 1989, 127).

The most common punishments during this era were *fines, whipping, banishment,* and *shaming techniques,* including *the stocks, branding, mild mutilation,* and *forms of bondage* (Preyer 1982, 335). Public spectacles of punishment were common, both for the supposed deterrent effect and to display the power of the king (Rothman 1990, xxiii). Death was imposed for murder, arson, theft of horses, and for being an incorrigible criminal (Colvin 1997, 33). Jails and workhouses were established: the jails to lock up debtors and religious offenders as well as those awaiting trial, and the workhouses for housing vagrants and paupers. Workhouses were often situated as an adjunct to the local jail (p. 47).

Between 1776 and 1825, America was exposed to the ideas of the European Enlightenment, including its ideas about punishment. The population of the United States exploded during this period, and towns developed rapidly into cities with high labor mobility and the opening up of the West. The previously communal life was replaced by the individualism for which the United States is now known. With population increase came increased crime, especially property crime (Hirsch 1992, 36), and a belief that traditional sanctions were no longer effective; for example, banishment from a small community now had little meaning (Hirsch 1992, 39). Americans now believed the imported criminal laws with their severe punishments were in themselves causes of deviance

(Continued)

(Continued)

(Rothman 1990, 59). By the second decade of the nineteenth century, most states had changed their criminal codes to replace the death penalty with imprisonment (Rothman 1990, 61), and some, such as New York, replaced corporal punishment with hard labor in the workhouse (Hirsch 1992, 42). Imprisonment became the dominant form of punishment and led to the development of the penitentiary.[23]

Theorists differ about the reasons for the growth of the penitentiary in the United States. For example, David Rothman (1990) argues that reformers believed incarceration would instill self-discipline in offenders and that the penitentiary was a response to fears about social disorder, whereas David Ignatieff (1978) contends that the United States simply adopted the English model of the prison with its factory-like routine and detailed rules. French philosopher Michel Foucault (1977), on the other hand, sees the emergence of the penitentiary as an outcome of the application of power to punish and discipline those considered a danger to society. Other scholars see the birth of the penitentiary as a response to economic dislocation in which the poor came to be perceived as criminal or as a means of controlling surplus labor. All agree, however, that it represented a new mode of social control that focused on reforming the individual character of an offender, principally through the application of discipline, including forms of labor.[24] As Foucault (1977, 82) expresses it, the aim was "not to punish less, but to punish better."

John Howard's ideas about prisons influenced U.S. prison reformers, and when Massachusetts opened a new prison in 1805 with a capacity of three hundred, inmates began to serve their sentences in isolation and then moved into cells where they worked from dawn to dusk (Hirsch 1992, 11). By the turn of the nineteenth century, eight of the sixteen states had programs and facilities providing for incarceration. A key event in the development of the penitentiary in the United States was the conversion of the Walnut Street jail, built in 1773 as a county jail, into a state prison for Pennsylvania and its adoption of what came to be called the Pennsylvania system of imprisonment. This system kept those convicted of serious crimes in separate cells in solitary confinement to commune with their conscience. Communication between prisoners was prevented by the physical construction of the penitentiary itself, which also tried to ensure they could not see anything of the world outside. Only the prison chaplain was able to access inmates (McGowen 1995, 91), and inmates were not permitted to work.

In 1818 and 1821, laws provided for the construction of the Eastern and Western State Penitentiaries in Philadelphia (Barnes 1972, 129) mandating solitary confinement. The Cherry Hill Prison (Eastern State Penitentiary), built in 1823, was a massive stone construction with a thirty-foot wall with cell blocks radiating out from a central core. Inmates were isolated from each other and wore hoods when they left their cells, and labor was regarded as a privilege to be earned (Friedman 1993, 79).

In 1816, New York legislation, prompted by the reforms in Philadelphia, authorized a new prison at Auburn, but it used the congregate method of housing inmates with double cells and rooms that could accommodate ten or more inmates (Barnes 1972, 134). By 1819, New York had adopted the elements of the Pennsylvania model of solitary confinement as its penal policy, but Auburn did not use that method. Instead, Auburn prison administrators began to experiment with a new model of incarceration based on discipline and labor (Barnes 1972, 135). The Auburn system comprised congregate work during the day and separation at night, accompanied by total silence and enforced by measures such as the lockstep[25] and whipping. The goal of this system was to break an inmate's spirit and bring about a state of total submission to authority (Colvin 1997, 31). Whether or not an inmate could be reformed after this state had been reached was a matter of debate. Some thought education after total submission was possible, whereas others considered the regime to be a form of deterrence that induced terror while also providing cheap labor (Colvin 1997, 91). In 1828, Sing Sing prison opened for occupancy in New York. It operated the Auburn system and gradually increased the level of internal discipline and punishment so as to include not only whipping but beatings by warders and lacing wounds with salt (Christianson 1998, 125).

The Auburn and Pennsylvania systems were seen as competing systems, but the Pennsylvania system was soon abandoned by all states except New Jersey. Auburn was preferred because it was promoted extensively and it had economic advantages (Barnes 1972, 139). In the Pennsylvania system, the emphasis was on individual small-scale production of craft goods, but in the Auburn model, labor was aggregated and focused on high production factories (Colvin 1997, 84). Europeans who came to inspect the two systems favored the Pennsylvania model because it was perceived to be more intense in its effect on inmates and was regarded as producing honest men whereas Auburn produced obedient men. Effectively, the Auburn system had given up on reforming inmates, but the Pennsylvania model remained committed to redemption through solitary and silent contemplation supplemented by labor (p. 83).

After 1860, the competition between the systems ceased when the Irish model of imprisonment was adopted in the form of the Elmira Reformatory system, regarded as far more sophisticated (Barnes 1972, 141). In addition, overcrowding, the impossibility of maintaining the rule of total silence, and prisoner mistreatment turned opinion against the penitentiary models. They would be reinvented, however, in modern form in the so-called supermax prisons, where inmates live in lockdown conditions that also amount to solitary confinement.

In the U.S. South, the coercive nature of the penitentiary offended southern notions of freedom, and the South resisted wholesale adoption of the northern prison models. Furthermore, southern ministers of religion rejected the idea of salvation through the penitentiary experience because penitentiaries were not mentioned in scripture. They also believed that corporal punishment and the death penalty were more effective punishments (Ayers 1984, 49; Colvin 1997, 212). Southern beliefs in the efficacy of labor and the slave system meant that specific forms of punishment were developed there that meshed with these values and beliefs. Consequently, convict leasing and chain gangs[26] became a peculiarly southern response to the need to punish criminals. Chain gangs mirrored slavery, and convict leasing enabled freed slaves to be forced into labor for the benefit of southern plantation owners who had lost their slave labor and needed a substitute labor force (Colvin 1997, 199). Within fifteen years of the end of the Civil War, all former confederate states were allowing private contractors to bid for convict labor (Ayers 1984, 189). Nine out of ten leased convicts were black, and blacks were commonly arrested for trivial offenses and awarded heavy sentences to resupply the labor pool (Fierce, in Gorman 1997, 450). Conditions in the chain gangs were brutal: prisoners slept in iron cages shackled together and were regularly placed in sweatboxes for lengthy periods for infractions (Colvin 1997, 246). In the 1890s and early 1900s, convict leasing began to decline as the comparative advantages of convict over free labor reversed, but in Mississippi the system continued until 1916 and in Florida and Alabama into the 1920s (p. 252).

In the Progressive period from the 1880s to the 1930s, new forms of punishment included the reformatory, indeterminate sentencing, and probation and parole, which, at least in theory, would permit a prisoner to be reformed even after his or her term of imprisonment had ended. As Garland puts it, the prison became "decentered," becoming only one of a set of penal options (Garland 1985, 23). Individualized care and the scientific treatment of criminals became the new penal approach to reform, and this was to be accomplished through adult reformatories linked to indeterminate sentencing, systems of inmate classification, academic and vocational training, labor, systems of parole, and humane discipline (Blomberg and Lucken 2000, 71).

In this climate of reform, the Elmira Reformatory was opened in New York State in 1876, followed by others in Michigan in 1877, Massachusetts in 1884, and Pennsylvania in 1889. The reformatory system involved an indeterminate sentence ranging from a minimum of one year with a fixed maximum. At the end of the minimum sentence, a prison board would decide a release date and the inmate would be released on parole under supervision. By 1900 every state had a parole system, and by 1923 half of releases were on parole (Blomberg and Lucken 2000, 73). The reformatory movement came to an end in 1920 when Elmira was seen to have failed in its goals,

(Continued)

(Continued)

largely because it operated a cruel and brutal regime. An official investigation found it to be over-crowded, understaffed, and grossly mismanaged (Pisciotta 1994, 33).

The era of *rehabilitation,* the belief that through appropriate programming and interventions criminals could be reformed during their punishment lasted into the 1960s. It was believed that offenders could be corrected within the community and that informal solutions found within communities could succeed where the coercive force of the prison system had failed (Blomberg and Lucken 2000, 153). Community punishments also seemed attractive as cost-saving measures and provided an opportunity for intensive application of therapeutic techniques not possible in prisons. However, these punishments have never gained the acceptance and value credited them in Europe and Canada: public opinion within the United States views them as inadequate and lacking in punitiveness (Tonry 1999, 5–22). While conservative critics claimed community punishment was the same as being "soft on crime," liberals warned of "net widening." Ad hoc punitive responses to criminality were developed and included programs such as *boot camps, intensive supervision* of those on parole and probation, as well as *house arrest* and *electronic monitoring.*

A turning point came with the political elevation of crime and criminality to an issue of national security when it was announced that a war on crime was to be waged using professionalized managerial solutions. Rehabilitation through individualized treatment was now considered to have failed, and the argument in 1974 that "nothing works" (Martinson 1974) found favor, politically resulting in an approach to punishment that privileged incapacitation and retribution.

Crime control became a political issue in 1964 during the presidential campaign of Barry Goldwater and has been high on the political agenda ever since. Getting tough on crime means getting tough on offenders, which meant the mass incarceration of offenders as well as the implementation of measures such as "three strikes and you're out" that guarantee that the prisons will remain at full capacity. The notion of *just deserts* advocates that all offenders committing similar crimes must receive proportionate sentences often determined by applying legislated sentencing guidelines.

Warehousing prisoners has come to be regarded as the correct solution to dealing with habitual offenders. Measures such as mandatory minimum sentences, the war on drugs, truth in sentencing, and the abolition of parole in many states have combined to generate an explosion in the prison population and in prison construction. Consequently, by 1991 the United States had more than a million persons incarcerated and the highest rate of imprisonment of any country (Christianson 1998, 283). By 2013 the extent of criminal punishment through incarceration, parole, and probation was as follows:

- About 6,899,000 offenders were under the supervision of adult correctional systems at year-end 2013, declining from 6,940,500 offenders during the previous year.

- The decrease during 2013 was the fifth consecutive year of decline in the U.S. correctional population.

- Although the correctional population declined by 0.6 percent during 2013, this and the 0.7 percent decline the previous year (2012) are the slowest rates of decline observed since 2009, when the population first decreased.

- In 2013, about 1 in every 35 adults in the United States, or 2.9 percent of adult residents (unchanged from 2012; see Glaze and Herberman 2013), was on probation or parole or incarcerated in prison or jail, the same rate observed in 1997.

- An estimated 1 in every 51 adult residents was supervised in the community on probation or parole at year-end 2013, compared to 1 in every 110 adults incarcerated in prison or jail. (Glaze and Kaeble 2014)

COLONIAL PUNISHMENT REGIMES

Examining how colonial powers punished subject peoples reveals how the colonial project deployed punishment, and especially prisons, in ways that reflected colonial ideas about social and racial categories and how the colonizers institutionalized those notions (Arnold 1994, 170). As such, colonial punishment regimes become a key site for gaining a greater understanding of the colonial project and its ordering processes.

Colonial powers in Africa, India, and South America imported their laws and practices, including notions about punishment, as part of the colonial civilizing project with the principal aims of controlling subject populations and providing a source of free labor to settlers arriving from the metropolis. In contrast to the mission of reforming criminals they undertook in their own countries, for the most part colonial powers did not think their subject populations were worthy of such interventions.[27] In this sense, punishment, especially imprisonment and the prison itself, should be understood as having been brought to the colonies in culturally specific ways and as having been impacted by local practices, contexts, and cultural and social dimensions (Dikötter 2007, 1, 6). These local contexts included the issue of caste, social hierarchies existing outside the prison, the status of the political prisoner, and racism (p. 7). Prior to the European colonization, penal incarceration was generally unknown or rarely found in sub-Saharan Africa societies (Bernault 2003, 2; Killingray 2003, 100) or in India or South America.

Africa

At the end of the nineteenth century, colonial powers created prisons in Africa on a significant scale. Racial differences between the colonizers and the colonized were demonstrated through the management and architecture of their prisons, and Africans were constructed as "objects of power" (Bernault 2007, 55).

In Africa generally, precolonial punishments had relied on the payment of compensation and for more serious wrongs, death, banishment from the community, and sale into slavery (Bernault 2007, 56). From the sixteenth century on, colonial powers began to construct jails within coastal forts and garrisons (e.g., in 1816 a prison opened in Freetown, Sierra Leone), and in the main, these jails housed military personnel or traders who were incarcerated there prior to trial (p. 58). The prison was "an early instrument for the subjugation of Africans" and English law "was largely about racial dominance and economic hegemony" (Killingray 2003, 98). However, unlike reforms in Europe, it did not replace flogging and public sentences, nor was it an instrument for reforming criminality or erasing racial distinctions (Bernault 2003, 3). In the Belgian Congo in 1898, for example, the law permitted capital punishment and public executions some thirty years after these penalties had been repealed in Belgium (p. 15).

Operating within plural legal systems comprising imported foreign laws and traditional custom, the British model of indirect rule gave punishment powers to native tribunals over indigenous persons while colonials were subject to courts that applied imported criminal laws. In the French colonies, the local French administrator presided over native tribunals applying customs to wrongs committed by Africans, whereas French and European settlers were tried by *tribunaux de second degré* run by French judges following criminal codes applying in metropolitan France (Bernault 2007, 61). Punishments considered "repugnant to natural justice and humanity," such as mutilation, enslavement, and torture, could not be applied in native courts and tribunals in British-ruled Africa, and with only a few exceptions, they could not sentence anyone to death (Killingray 2003, 99). Similarly, in French colonies, native tribunals from 1910 onward were forbidden to use criminal penalties that were "contrary to the principles of French civilization" (Bernault 2007, 61–62).

In British Africa, during the establishment of colonial rule, punitive expeditions into "unsettled" areas punished through coercion and force, including destroying houses and crops and taking away cattle. As colonial rule became better established, courts were set up and penal policies were created and applied. Generally, it was argued that flogging was the most appropriate penalty because fines required a developed cash economy and incarceration was expensive and only resulted in locking up a potential labor force. The scant evidence about punishment suggests that its nature and extent varied from place to place and that individual discretion was a key factor (Killingray 2003, 98).

In French colonies, from 1881 in Algeria, later extended to Senegal, French West Africa, and

Jamaica

When Britain abolished slavery in its colonies in 1833, it instructed colonial governors to plan for changes in systems of justice. In the early post-abolition period, a program of prison reform and construction broadly following the metropolitan policy model was adopted (Paton 2001, 275). This model focused on rehabilitation and reformation, but by the 1850s this initiative was regarded as a failure. The outcome was that while imprisonment remained the dominant punishment, flogging was reintroduced and convict labor was exploited for the benefit of private enterprises (p. 276).

The failure of the prison reforms was attributed to two principal causes. The first was that prisons were thought to be too comfortable so that inmates suffered no real hardship. The prisoners were, according to the local media, "well housed, well clothed, and well fed," given their nature as "debased and brutal minded wretches" (quoted in Paton 2001, 291). The second cause of failure was the contention that Jamaicans consistently failed to condemn those convicted of criminality because they lacked the understanding that "civilized people" should always stigmatize criminals (Paton 2001, 293). The claim that criminals were seen as "martyrs" was made frequently in the media, with the obvious conclusion that imprisonment could not work but whipping would (p. 293).

In 1865 a law known as the "Whipping Bill" made second and subsequent convictions for theft punishable by up to fifty lashes. While theft was on the increase, arguments for reintroducing whipping as a punishment did not so much turn on increases in theft as on punishing a series of sexual crimes with this particular penalty (Paton 2001, 283). Moreover, the perceived failure of prison reforms was thought to justify recourse to whipping as an alternative punishment. In the end, whipping was proposed as the penalty for almost any crime but with a strong focus on crimes involving sexuality. For example, local media emphasized the need for flogging to counter "the depraved beings who are the slaves of unruly passion" (quoted in Paton 2001, 284). A racist discourse emerged, one that compared black people to animals and the other declaring that according to the degrees of civilization headed by Europeans or the British, Jamaican society was regressing. According to these arguments, punishment needed to be directed to the body (through the application of the whip) and not to the mind (through imprisonment). It was also claimed that flogging was a more effective deterrent than incarceration (Paton 2001, 285). In the end, flogging remained a criminal punishment well into the twentieth century, given in addition to imprisonment (p. 286).[33]

During slavery, the prison had supplemented private forms of discipline exercised on slaves on the plantations. For slaves, the most common reason for punishment in prison was running away. Other reasons included incarceration according to the wish of the slave's master; detaining and holding runaway slaves who had been caught, until collected by their master; and slaves accommodated in prison to protect them from their master (Paton 2001, 277). The emancipation changed this pattern so that by 1840 all prisoners were being held under the criminal law.

In 1854 a Penal Servitude Act allowed for the release on license of prisoners who had served more than half of their sentence. The condition of their release was that they serve as agricultural laborers for three-quarters of the remaining sentence. This system of release on license anticipated the convict lease system in the United States. For Jamaican planters who had complained about the unreliable labor supply since the end of slavery, this proved to be a significant benefit as they found convict labor to be "an example of industry and civility." This probably reflects the high degree of compliance required of forced labor compared to free labor (Paton 2001, 289).

Comment

This brief study of colonial punishments suggests some of the possibilities inherent in developing a "criminology of the colonial project" which might include accounts of punishment.[34] Such a criminology would add to our knowledge of colonial "crime control," social control, ordering practices, and ways in which colonial punishments assisted in the process of subjugation. Pursuing an interdisciplinary approach through postcolonial studies and accounts of anthropology and history would add significantly to the knowledge base of this criminology.

The preceding discussion reveals that even though notions of appropriate punishment changed in the metropolitan centers as the "civilizing process" advanced, colonial officials and the colonial justice systems continued to impose punitive punishments on persons in Africa, India, and elsewhere, who were deemed uncivilized. To what extent did this colonial inertia in developing punishment policy constrain postcolonial punishment policies, and what have been its long-term consequences generally? How is punishment understood in postcolonial states after the colonial experience? In what ways were local punishment practices impacted by the colonial punishment project? Was there resistance to arbitrary punishments, and if so, what forms did it take and what was the response to it? These and other questions arise from themes that emerge from this brief study. Themes include punishment as a form of labor exploitation to support the colonial economy; the part played by the complexities of local cultures in formulating and applying penal policies, for example, the caste system in India; why some colonies did not impose discriminatory punishments; how some punishments came to be defined as "repugnant" but others that inflicted similar or greater pain were not, and how the discourse of "repugnant punishments" came to be imposed; the nature of the interaction between the jailers and the jailed; and how those jailed and flogged or otherwise punished experienced the various punishment regimes.

Criminal Punishment in Japan

Daniel Botsman's (2005) study of punishment in the Tokugawa period (1603–1867) and in the following Meiji era (1868–1912) reveals how ideas and practices about punishment in Japan played a key role in the shaping of Japanese relations with the West. Japanese scholars have argued that the harsh punishments of the Tokugawa period were gradually ameliorated over time in a linear progression. However, according to Botsman (2005, 10), rather than focusing on the harshness of those punishments and the lessening of their severity, Tokugawa punishments should be seen "as one part of a complex set of strategies for ordering society and exercising power."

Accounts of punishments in Japan claim that the most barbarous punishments were applied in the sixteenth century, when local warlords controlled the country and fought each other for power and territory. These punishments included beheading, quartering, impaling, mutilations of the body (such as severing the ears, nose, and fingers), and boiling alive. With the coming of the Tokugawa Shogunate, who exercised control over one-third of the country, and the reunification of the country, conducting intimation and fostering fear in order to maintain control of territory and populations were no longer seen to be necessary (Botsman 2005, 14). Thus modes of punishment changed and became standardized throughout the country even though two-thirds was still controlled by local warlords or *daimyo*. The Shogunate required that *daimyo* enforce its laws. Inspectors toured the country to ensure compliance. While the right of the *daimyo* to punish in their own domains was recognized, they were required to follow the practices of the capital, Edo (now called Tokyo) in doing so.

Punishments were made public during the time of the eighth shogun, Yoshimune (1684–175), when a list known as One Hundred Articles was published as a kind of penal code, itemizing a list of crimes and the punishments that could be imposed. Although the Tokugawa punishments were severe, they were not arbitrary and formed part of a logical system of order and security under the shoguns (Botsman 2005, 18). Moreover, for the leadership, punishment was perceived to possess a moral purpose because it encouraged citizens to give up evil ways and embrace the good (p. 43). Accordingly, in the eyes of the Shogunate, government was a benevolent institution and punishments should not be so harsh as to undermine that belief (p. 44).

BOX 6.10   Crucifixion, Japanese Style

The first European traders and missionaries who reached Japan in the mid-sixteenth century identified a punishment they associated with Christianity and therefore referred to as a form of crucifixion. In fact, this punishment, comprising stringing up a person on a wooden frame, dates back to the twelfth century. The changes in punishment practice that came with the shoguns did not affect the practice of this punishment, and records show that from 1862 to 1865, fifteen crucifixions were performed in Edo (now Tokyo; Botsman 2005, 16).

(Continued)

(Continued)

Crucifixion involved roping the condemned person to a wooden frame: if a man, his arms and legs were stretched wide apart; if a woman, the legs were bound so she formed the shape of a cross. The frame was lifted and dug into the ground. Spear carriers stood on either side of the condemned. One pushed his spear into the prisoner's gut, pushing across and up so that the spear emerged below the opposite armpit. The second spear carrier then did the same from the other side of the body. The two spear carriers continued to alternate spear thrusts in this manner for some twenty or thirty times. When the signal was given, one of the spear carriers took up a barbed pike and used it to hold the prisoner's hair so that the prisoner's head was steady. The other spear carrier then ran the tip of his spear through the prisoner's neck from right to left. The corpse was left on display for some days before being thrown into a shallow grave (Botsman 2005, 17). When the prisoner undergoing crucifixion died before the punishment could be carried out, the body was often pickled in salt and then crucified as if alive.

Public executions in the form of crucifixion and burning at the stake[35] were conducted in Edo at two public execution grounds. From the 1620s, however, bans were issued on public gatherings, and executions for the most part were performed within the walls of the Kodenmacho Jailhouse. This greatly diminished the chance of public disorder arising from such spectacles. Beheadings also were generally conducted at the jailhouse, but the headless corpse was often dismembered with swords by warriors in a practice of "trial cutting" (Botsman 2005, 20). The harshest form of beheading dated back to medieval times and involved taking the severed heads from the jailhouse to an execution ground and placing them on specially built stands for display over several days, thus displaying the results of the execution but keeping the actual process of punishment hidden. Using bodies as signs in a penal display was a Tokugawa practice, and the execution grounds regularly featured human heads and disfigured bodies viewed by both citizens and foreign ambassadors who passed by (p. 24). In addition, it was common practice to parade condemned criminals through Edo on their way to execution accompanied by a large contingent of armed men and a banner stating his name, crime, and punishment.[36]

Tattooing and flogging punishments were introduced in 1720 to replace the penalty of severing the nose and ears. Flogging of fifty or one hundred blows was inflicted with a cane across the back for minor crimes and was often combined with tattooing. The latter was inflicted for a second offense of theft and involved marking two lines across the forearm, signifying a recidivist. A third offense might mean death. Sometimes characters signifying the word *dog* or *evil* were tattooed on foreheads (Botsman 2005, 27). Thus tattoos came to be associated with criminality.

Imprisonment was not a common form of punishment in the Tokugawa era. The main rationale for the jailhouse was holding persons suspected of crime while investigations were conducted. Imprisonment was reserved for cases where circumstances prevented the imposition of a regular punishment and long-term incarceration was not mentioned as a penalty in the One Hundred Articles but was sometimes used as an alternative to the death penalty (Botsman 2005, 28). Short-term incarceration for up to thirty days was used as substitute for flogging in the case of women, children under the age of fifteen, and infirm men. Banishment was also a common punishment, and "exile to a distant island" was regarded as a severe penalty (p. 28).

Differential Punishments According to Rank and Relationships

Punishments were graded according to the circumstances of the criminal act and to the social rank of the protagonists. While this may in part be due to the influence of Confucianism, the social ordering of the time paralleled that of eighteenth-century England, where servants who murdered their masters were hanged, drawn, and quartered, and women who murdered their husbands were burned at the stake. In both cases, the law presumed the existence of a relationship involving "special obedience and subjection" (Botsman 2005, 31). In the case of a murder where the victim had a superior rank to the perpetrator, a simple execution was not sufficient, but when the victim's standing was inferior, execution was considered too severe (p. 30). In situations when the relationship between the victim and the perpetrator was defined through a master and servant connection, any serious injury to a master would be punished according to the One Hundred Articles by the pillorying of the servant or retainer for three days, followed by crucifixion. Similarly, when a servant killed a master's relative, he would be paraded through the streets and then beheaded with the head being placed on public display.

Under the One Hundred Articles, the punishment for parents who killed their children was banishment, but when children committed the murder, they would be paraded through the streets and crucified (Botsman 2005, 30). Crucifixion was also mandated for pupils who killed their teachers and for adulterous wives who murdered their husbands, whereas a husband's infidelity was not even recognized as a crime. When a husband caught his wife and a man in flagrante, he was entitled to kill both of them on the spot. The rape of a married woman carried a sentence of death, and that of an unmarried woman was punishable by a severe form of banishment (p. 31).

Botsman (2005, 32) explains that the practice of differential punishing linked the Shogunate to the "micro level power structures that formed the basis of everyday social relations in Tokugawa Japan." In other words, through differential punishments, a message was sent to servants and retainers about the importance of hierarchy; this also reinforced the position of those considered superior in that society.[37] Furthermore, the public display of punished bodies signified to the polity that the outcome of breaking the shogun's rules would be harsh and severe sanctioning.

Public Knowledge of Punishments

The basic punishment text (the One Hundred Articles) was not publicly available in an official form, but official notices were posted prohibiting specific conduct (Botsman 2005, 34). The bodies and signposts located in public spaces also provided information about crimes and punishments.

In practice, however, unofficial copies of the One Hundred Articles were available in private hands. However, there was no certainty about the information, and other than revealing a system of crimes and punishments, there was no guarantee that public officials would adhere to it. This meant that officials with power to determine such issues were regarded with respect and generally feared (p. 35).

Confessions and Torture

The Shogunate placed great importance on securing *confessions* in criminal investigations, and for this purpose, where the crime was serious and the evidence clearly showed guilt, *judicial torture* was permitted. From the mid-eighteenth century, there were four standard techniques of judicial torture (Botsman 2005, 37). The first and most common was beating with a short whip. The second, called "hugging the stones," involved the prisoner kneeling on a platform with sharp triangular grooves cut into its top. Two heavy stones would then be placed on the thighs, and if this failed to produce a confession, guards would add their own weight to the stones by pushing down on them. As many as ten additional stones might be applied. The next technique was the "lobster," in which the suspect was tied up uncomfortably with ropes. In the final method, called the "suspension," the person's arms were tied behind his back with a rope that was then used to suspend him a few feet off the ground. He would be kept in this position for several hours with the likelihood that his shoulders would be dislocated (p. 38).

Mitigating Punishments by Acts of Benevolence

Harsh punishments might be mitigated to show that governance could also be benevolent. Thus threats of harsh punishments were balanced by flexibility and a willingness to mitigate or even circumvent punishment altogether (Botsman 2005, 45). One way of granting mitigation was to award punishment concessions to social groups who commonly enjoyed public sympathy. Accordingly, children younger than fourteen who committed murder or arson were not executed but placed in the custody of relatives until they attained their majority and then exiled to a distant island (p. 45). Women were not flogged but instead punished with short terms of imprisonment and torture, and execution of pregnant women was prohibited. A person judged to be too infirm or sick to endure a flogging might instead suffer a short term of imprisonment; however, generally it was the practice simply to apply the blows less rigorously than usual (p. 45).

The punishment for evading official checkpoints along major highways was crucifixion, but in practice, officials often overlooked the large numbers of people who circumvented these checkpoints. The public regarded this latitude as a form of benevolence (Botsman 2005, 46). Again, leniency was commonly exercised in the case of accidental fires where the prescribed punishment was burning alive. In practice, the penalty would not be imposed if the head of household took refuge in his family's Buddhist temple for a short period because this would be accepted as a display of contrition (p. 47).

As well as officials turning a blind eye to transgressions or imposing lesser punishments, the shoguns were able to maintain their benevolent image by giving responsibility for assisting with or executing severe penalties to groups of outcasts[38] (Botsman 2005, 49). Sometimes, outcasts acted simply as assistants to officials in managing death-related pollution, for example, in beheadings, where they would hold the prisoner in the correct position for a clean cut and then after decapitation, position the torso so the blood flowed into a hole dug for that purpose (p. 53). Groups of outcasts would accompany prisoners paraded through the streets to their execution and take down and dispose of mutilated bodies that had been crucified (p. 54). This practice permitted the shogun's officials to distance themselves from the unpleasantness associated with severe penalty and projected an image of the outcasts as the true executioners and torturers (p. 55).

Incarceration in the Stockade

From about 1789, influenced by the traditional Chinese punishment of penal servitude, the idea of a *long-term jail* was put forward, and in 1890 construction began of what came to be known as the *Inspector's Stockade for Laborers,* located on an island at the mouth of a river in Edo (Tokyo) Bay. This soon came to function as a kind of halfway house where persons punished for petty crimes were sent after punishment so that they did not go back to the streets to cause more trouble (Botsman 2005, 103).

Crop failures, a famine, and natural disasters in the late 1780s led peasants to abandon their land and migrate to the cities, where they were forced to commit crimes to survive, including breaking into the stores and property of merchants believed to be hoarding rice. The Stockade seemed to provide a solution to the problem of vagrancy in the city and to this kind of urban unrest. After 1820, criminals who had been formally sentenced to banishment were sent there, and in 1837, after many displaced peasants had migrated to the capital following a series of major crop failures, it was decreed that after being housed in relief shelters, those not repatriated would be sent to the Stockade. This caused the Stockade population to increase from an average of 130 to 140 to almost 500. This indicates that the Stockade was seen primarily as a means of controlling the "dangerous class" of potential troublemakers in and around the capital (p. 109).

Outsider Influences— *Gaijin*[39] and the Meiji Restoration

In 1853, the arrival of Commodore Perry and his gunboats was the precursor to competing visions and struggles for reform that culminated in the overthrow of the Tokugawa regime and the restoration of direct rule by the emperor, Meiji, in 1868 (Botsman 2005, 115). The Meiji Restoration promised the abolition of evil practices and seeking new knowledge from all over the world (p. 115). Gathering information from and about the West included making Japanese translations of Dutch texts, including the Dutch Criminal Code and Code of Criminal Procedure (the Dutch had a trading post in Nagasaki). English-speaking missionaries explained to Chinese officials about punishment and prison reform in the United States, and this information was passed on to Japanese officials.

In this way, Japanese reformers came to learn about the decline in public punishments and the shift to a penal system based on incarceration and reform of the individual criminal in the West. One outcome of the Enlightenment in Europe was that punishment had come to be perceived as a marker of a society's level of civilization, and Western travelers had noted in their reports home that punishments in Japan in 1623, for example, included "rosting, burning, crucifying both waies, drawing with four Bulls, and boyling in Oyl and Water" (from a *True Description of the Mighty Kingdoms of Japan and Siam* by Francis Caron and Joost Shorten, quoted in Botsman 2005, 130). This and other accounts placed Japan firmly behind Western nations in contemporary conceptions of human progress and meant that the "civilized" nations had an obligation to protect their citizens in Japan from such barbarity (p. 131).

The primary method that European powers and the United States used to protect their citizens involved signing treaties (the so-called unequal treaties) under which the Japanese agreed that their legal system would not exercise any jurisdiction over European and U.S. citizens residing in Japan. Instead, foreigners would be judged in consular courts and by members of the foreign community living in Japan (Botsman 2005, 132).[40] Until the Japanese were able to show that their legal system and its punishments reached the standard of "civilized," the unequal treaties would remain in place (p. 140).

The new Meiji leaders were quick to reform Japanese penal laws, first by limiting crucifixion to cases of regicide[41] and parricide[42] and abolishing the penalty of burning alive. Banishment was replaced with penal servitude, and capital sentences required the explicit approval of the imperial court. The Meiji replaced older forms of execution with the Chinese punishment of "strangulation" in 1871 (Botsman 2005, 169). This penalty proved difficult to administer because the special garroting device, consisting of a single wooden post with a hole at neck level through which a rope could be passed to form a noose, was ineffective in some cases (i.e., some prisoners returned to life after being "executed" with it).

In early 1873, the British punishment of hanging was included in the Japanese collection of modes of imposing death for criminality. By mid-1869 the practice of parading condemned criminals through the city and pillorying were abolished, and tattooing was prohibited in 1870. In early 1871, the first national criminal code was promulgated (Botsman 2005, p. 144) on an interim basis, and in 1880 the first Western-based penal code was issued. It provided for only one form of death penalty (hanging) and for various forms of incarceration (p. 170). By mid-1872, flogging had been replaced with short periods of hard labor and life imprisonment with hard labor. Now, penal servitude could be

imposed from ten days to life. In 1879, judicial torture and the public display of severed heads were abolished (p. 169). These measures were not sufficient in themselves to overcome extraterritoriality because law in action (how it was in fact applied), rather than written law, was the paramount consideration. Revising punishments and codifying the criminal law did not ensure that attitudes and practices had changed (p. 145).

Prisons, Flogging, and Colonization

Japan's *first modern prison,* designed along the lines of a Western jail, forming a cross shape with two stories and eighty cells, was completed at the end of 1874.[43] In 1908 a law on prisons was promulgated. By 1895 key elements of a functioning justice system were in place, including "a Western style penal code, a system of independent law-courts, a national network of prisons. . . . and finally, a group of academic and bureaucratic experts who would monitor, study and scrutinize the system and keep Japan abreast of the latest international trends and developments" (Botsman 2005, 165). Extraterritoriality and the unequal treaties finally ended in July 1899 (p. 198).

A network of prisons was established based on European and British models of strict discipline, and prison labor became an important element in Japanese economic development and in its colonization of Hokkaido (Botsman 2005, 202–3). Botsman (p. 204) argues that a link can be made between the use of prison labor and the extensive use of Korean forced labor in Hokkaido and elsewhere in the 1930s and 1940s, and that possibly this practice of exploiting prison labor was reflected in the Japanese Army's use of prisoners of war to build railways, roads, and bridges during World War II in the Pacific.

In 1895/96, Japan gained control of *Taiwan* in the first Sino-Japanese War and extended the provisions of the Japanese penal code to the new colony. Makeshift prisons were constructed and when the decision was made to keep Taiwanese prisoners in Taiwan, plans were made for the construction of three new prisons, which were completed in 1904 (Botsman 2005, 207). This same year, *flogging* for Chinese and Taiwanese men found guilty of minor crimes was also introduced (p. 211). Flogging was abolished by the Japanese when they took over the island but had been used by the Chinese previously and in its reinvented form was used by police as a form of

(Continued)

Mrs. Li (née Chang), after having been widowed for many years happened to hear of someone getting married in her neighborhood which so aroused licentious thoughts in her that she enticed Li Ming-tse, a son of her deceased husband, through a former marriage, to have sex relations with her. Li had been reared by Mrs. Li during his childhood and in allowing himself to be enticed by her showed complete disregard for her status as a stepmother. Both persons are thus equally guilty of licentious behavior destructive of the primary human relationships. The code, however, contains no article dealing with sexual relations between a son and his stepmother. Therefore Mrs. Li and Li Ming-tse, subject to final approval from the throne, are both now sentenced to immediate decapitation by analogy to the statute providing this penalty for fornication between a man and the wife of his paternal uncle.

SOURCE: Bodde and Morris 1967, 433.

During the *Republican period* (1911–27), a new prison system was introduced that included recognition of the reformative potential of the prison, the construction of model prisons in provincial capitals: the promulgation of prison regulations based on global standards, the adoption of single and shared cell imprisonment regimes based on Western designs, and the collection and compilation of criminal statistics (Dikötter 2002, 60–61). By 1918, a prison building program had constructed thirty-nine model prisons with a capacity for more than fourteen thousand inmates (p. 66). Prison rules were issued that stated the three principles of reformation (*ganhua*) as forced labor of seven to ten hours a day with an inmate receiving some payment, moral instruction, and basic education (p. 67).

In March 1912, a Provisional Criminal Code was promulgated in which the principal punishments were the death penalty, imprisonment for life, and imprisonment for a fixed term according to five categories: from ten to fifteen years, from five to ten years, from one to three years, and from two months to a year. Other punishments included fines of not less than one dollar and deprivation of civil rights. These punishments remained in force during the Republican period (Dikötter 2002, 62).

In the *Guomindang (GMD) period* (1928–49), the notion of prisoner reformation remained penal policy even while doubts about its efficacy influenced penal policies globally (Dikötter 2002, 143). By 1923, a juvenile reform school had been established, the Beijing Reform School, which promoted learning productive skills and habits, and in 1933 and 1934 provincial juvenile prisons opened in some provinces providing vocational training, basic education, and a focus on diligence and discipline (p. 177). In this period the method of execution was hanging, but beheading and shooting were also employed until 1949 (p. 178). Stern discipline and military-type regimentation characterized prison life, but family visits promoted reform efforts (p. 245). Prisoners performed various kinds of labor, but the contribution of prison labor to financing the justice system was negligible (p. 250).

In this period, prisoners were sent to perform agricultural work in remote frontier provinces, and schemes to reclaim wasteland were approved, inspired in part by reports of labor camps in Siberia (Dikötter 2002, 250–51). As the prison population grew, congestion became a major challenge. Drug users filled the prisons in the mid-1930s (p. 265), and conditional releases on parole and granting bail to those detained or kept in custody helped alleviate overcrowding (p. 266). Wealthy prisoners were able to buy their way out through commutation of prison sentences or through paying a fine, leaving the inmate population dominated by the poor and the marginalized (p. 268). Educated persons, including political prisoners, were given preferential treatment, but most inmates were illiterate (p. 290).

In the late 1930s and 1940s, the GMD created a variety of institutions for confinement outside of the formal justice system, including police detention centers, military prisons, and internment camps, as well as secret prisons run by the secret service in response to pressures from the communists. Detention was effected without any judicial warrant under emergency laws and could not be challenged (Muhlhahn 2009, 129). In this period, a parallel system of military justice with its own codes, courts, and prisons sought to induce terror and discipline and made significant encroachments into the civil justice system. Military punishments included executions by firing squad and torture (p. 130).

Both the GMD and the communists focused on the penalty phase of the criminal justice process. The trial was a brief formality, and sentences were determined within hours by administrative decree. Accusations without supporting evidence came to form the basis of a finding of guilt (Muhlhahn 2009, 172). For the communists, instilling fear and terror through show trials and rallies served to educate the masses and discipline them for the future struggle.

Japan conquered Manchuria in 1931 and occupied Beijing and Tianjin in 1937. In November 1937, Shanghai fell to the Japanese invaders, and the massacre in Nanjing took place soon after. The civil war between the nationalists and the communists finally forced Jiang Jieshi to flee to Taiwan with his followers in 1949. In areas where the Japanese invaded after 1937, the prison system suffered severe damage (Dikötter 2002, 324). Prisoners were released to serve in the army, and minor offenders were released on bail (p. 329). In moving to the hinterland, the GMD abandoned many prisons and suspended building new ones (p. 330). As the nationalists retreated in the face of the communist advance, many prisoners were released, and by the time the communists entered Beijing on January 31, 1949, the prisons there were almost empty (p. 364).

In the period *post 1949*, the penal system was continually shaped and reshaped as it responded to political change and internal party disputes. Merged into other forms of bureaucracy, the boundary between the criminal justice system and institutions of governance began to blur, and at the same time informal agencies took control over functions previously allocated to established institutions such as the investigation of crime and its prosecution. From 1951 onward, most punishments took the form of labor reeducation, because from the start, the communist program regarded *laogai* as playing a key role not only in criminal justice but in the overall project of building socialism (Muhlhahn 2009, 175).

Between 1949 and 1953, the judicial system was dismantled. Despite discussions among communist leaders about new laws, instead of formulating new legal codes, numerous decrees and regulations were issued on specific topics. For example, in February 1951, a law was made on counterrevolutionary activity, defined as activity aimed at overthrowing or undermining the socialist system (Muhlhahn 2009, 179). Ninety-five percent of the offenses specified in this law carried the death penalty, life imprisonment, or determinate imprisonment (p. 179). People's courts, a procuracy,[49] and public security organizations were created, but trained judges were in short supply, leading to backlogs. The Communist Party wanted harsh sentences imposed against enemies of the state, and when the judges refused to do this, 80 percent of judicial personnel were purged (p. 179).

People's tribunals and military courts began to assume jurisdiction and impose the death sentence and imprisonment alongside the people's courts for specific periods and purposes in their efforts to punish "local despots, bandits, special agents, counter-revolutionaries, and criminals who violate the laws and orders pertaining to agrarian reform" (Muhlhahn 2009, p. 181). They conducted mass trials and accusation meetings to mobilize the masses, educate them, and deter criminals through public punishment (p. 181). Purges were conducted of corrupt bureaucrats, counterrevolutionaries, capitalists, and intellectuals using these methods. During this time, an estimated four million arrests were made without the involvement of the official courts, and perhaps one-fourth of those received the death sentence in a public execution. The main purpose was to engage the masses and bring about active participation so that the regime would gain popular legitimacy (p. 184).

From 1954 until 1957, efforts were made to create a socialist justice system closely following the Soviet model.[50] Work on a new draft criminal code was started in 1954 but was continually interrupted by internal political disputes. Administrative decrees took the place of comprehensive laws such as the Security Administration Punishment Act established in 1957, which specified minor delinquencies but was not enforced through the regular court system but instead through administrative powers. This act was directed at punishing disturbances to public order and security and allowed for detention for fifteen days by administrative order (Muhlhahn 2009, 188).

During the period 1958 to 1978, all the previous developments were abandoned and the judicial system effectively ceased to operate. This was because Mao had come to believe that complex systems for justice administration and governance perpetuated the bourgeois values that the socialist system had rejected and that these systems inhibited the ability to make rapid changes to facilitate the revolutionary project (Muhlhahn 2009, 190). Consequently, he decided a national rectification campaign was needed in the form of the Great Proletarian Cultural Revolution. The Red Guards were instructed to smash the police, the procuracy, and the courts as part of the bourgeois legal order. Instead, military tribunals and mass trials disposed of serious criminal cases, and the party line guided the sentencing process with party supervision (p. 192). This emphasis on the political meant the abandonment of the Soviet-style justice system.

The Punishment of Reform Through Labor *(Laogai)*

The principle of prisoner transformation through education and labor is reflected in the idea of punishment through labor, *laogai* (labor reform), which is itself a reflection of the 1982 Constitution, which stipulates that work is the right and "glorious duty of every able-bodied citizen" (Jiang 2014, 222). Forced labor had become common in China by the seventeenth century for both economic and reformative purposes (Seymour and Anderson 1998, 12). The *laogai* system, developed from 1951 in the form of labor camps, reflected this tradition as well as the socialist belief in redemption through labor. Consequently, prisoners serving sentences of five years or more would be organized into detachments and administered at the provincial level through *laogai* units. Major construction projects would be assigned to these units, which would also be given political and ideological education (Muhlhahn 2009, 224). This form of convict labor rapidly became an economic asset because by 1954 there were 4,671 *laogai* units (p. 227).

During the period 1955 to 1958, the system of labor camps became integrated into the national economy, but from 1959 to 1966 the system was constrained by the Great Leap Forward policy and then by the Cultural Revolution occurring from 1966 to 1976 (Muhlhahn 2009, 228). Before 1978, few prisoners were able to return to their homes after being held in labor camps because they had lost their residential registration when sentenced. They were consequently retained in the camps as "free convicts" indefinitely (p. 228).

Reform through labor was brought into the prison system as a scheme for the deployment of productive prison labor and was centrally planned on a large scale in the form of Regulations on Reform through Labor of the People's Republic of China (Dutton 1992, 295; Jiang 2014, 225). Previously, *laogai* units had focused on making handicrafts (Dutton 1992, 299). 1994 a prison law was finally enacted, Article 3 of which provides: "Prisons practice the principle of combining prisoner punishment and remolding and combining prisoner education and labor to transform prisoners into law-abiding citizens" (Seymour and Anderson 1998, 252). Local prison work units perform labor in agriculture (e.g., grain and cotton), public works, or manufacturing (Seymour and Anderson 1998, 103) under strict discipline and often in remote areas. Following military practice, labor is organized into platoons, companies, battalions, regiments, and corps within a provincial or municipal region, and a camp may be platoon size or corps size (Shaw 1998, 187). Although manual labor is considered the paramount activity, education officially constitutes the primary reform goal, comprising mass meetings, studies, and interactions between inmates and prison staff. Prisoners are required to participate and to achieve specific goals. A system of rewards and penalties involves production contests, reporting runaways and performance violations, and punishment for infractions (p. 189).

According to a former prisoner detained in the northwest province of Xinjiang, if a prisoner failed to perform a sufficient amount of labor by the end of a working day, it was common for him to be required to jog for many hours or to pull a cart loaded with stones (Seymour and Anderson 1998, 177). Another punishment was to place prisoners in small cages in solitary confinement. Beatings carried out by corrections officers, or more commonly by a cell boss, were regularly administered (p. 177). Other forms of ill treatment included applying electric stun guns to parts of the body, requiring prisoners to stand for hours, and forcing prisoners to drink urine or eat garbage (p. 178).

"Strike Hard" Campaigns

These public arrest and sentencing rallies are described in Chapter 4. Although they are intended as a means of reducing the crime rate, Trevaskes (2002, 688) argues that their practical effect has been to exacerbate violent crime and increase criminality because of their brutalizing effect. In this sense, they are perceived by citizens to be an act of state violence (p. 688). Describing the *Yanda,* or strike hard anticrime campaigns of 1983 to 1986, Børge Bakken (2000, 392) explains that the Yanda targeted the emerging criminal gangs and their leaders, aiming to prevent the further recruitment of juveniles. However, the gangs multiplied, and there was a reduction in the ages of gang members. By the late 1980s, gang crime accounted for 60 to 70 percent of all criminal offenses in the country. In terms of punishment then, there are significant risks in conducting harsh punishments in public that can make it counterproductive in terms of crime control generally.

Comment

This summary account of punishment in China reveals how social control was maintained through the family and how imperial rulers saw the family as linked to modes of punishment, sometimes in the form of clan punishments but otherwise as a means of reinforcing efforts to reform criminality. The horrendous punishments applied in the feudal and imperial eras can be compared with similar punishments found in the West during the early modern period. The Meiji restoration radically modernized the framework of punishment, but contemporary strike hard campaigns revived the public element of punishment and demonstrated the state's belief that, in China, social control is sometimes most effectively enforced through strategies that explicitly express the power of the state to punish criminals through shame, humiliation, and capital punishment. However, in a sign of modernization, it appears that the Chinese leadership has now largely abandoned strike hard campaigns as a crime control and punishment strategy.

The philosophical underpinnings of punishment established traditionally and in the time of Confucius, and reinforced by the Marxist focus on productive labor, remain in place today and continue to influence modern forms of punishment, especially imprisonment, in forms such as *laogai.* The Chinese belief in moral education, their dominating cultural values, and the discipline of the group continue to shape the nature of social control and punishment choices so that the maintenance of social order does not depend on the deterrent value of penal law but primarily on moral socialization (Chen 2008, 382). At the same time, punishment fulfills several broad political objectives, including demonstrating the power of the state; sustaining a form of social order based on socialist principles with "Chinese characteristics"; ensuring the continuation of modernist policies; where necessary, bringing a focus to crime control, including punishment, that satisfies the public demand for social order; mobilizing the masses so the state is seen to be the people's guardian; and demonstrating that the state can control crime through an emphasis on punishment (p. 383).

Although punishments were severe during the imperial era and executions were held in public, as was the case in England and Europe in the eighteenth century, Chinese events did not match the "spectacles of suffering" held in the West that drew huge crowds and were celebrated like carnivals (Muhlhahn 2009, 40). An order from the Qing dynasty is witness to the restrained nature of the Chinese public execution: it required that guards be dispatched in advance to maintain order and that crowds of noisy spectators would not be permitted. No platform or stage was employed to display the spectacle, and the execution itself was a rapid operation (p. 41).

NOTES

1. The number of persons incarcerated for drug offenses in the United States grew from less than fifty thousand in 1980 to more than five hundred thousand in 2007 (Clear and Frost 2014, 43). By 2010, drug offenders represented almost 20 percent of the total inmate population, and at the federal level more than half of all inmates are incarcerated for drug offenses (p. 43).

2. *Penality* refers to not only the practices of punishment but also the laws, processes, discourses, and institutions of punishment that collectively constitute what is penal in nature (Garland 1990, 17).

3. Justice policies that are more punitive advocate primarily retribution and incapacitation and give less attention to rehabilitation (Drake, Muncie and Westmarland 2010, 40). Bottoms coined the phrase "populist punitiveness" to describe one of the influences he saw working on justice policy making. It was "intended to convey the notion of politicians tapping into and using for their own purposes, what they believe to be the public's general punitive stance" (Bottoms 1995, 40).

4. Numerous texts have been produced on this topic; see, for example, Clear and Frost, 2014; Garland 2001; Pratt 2007; Pratt et al. 2005; Simon 2007.

5. Clear and Frost (2014, 5) contend that the political salience of crime control has weakened and point to the fact that some states are closing prisons, having now fully appreciated the budgetary impact of the correctional expansion. They believe a turning point has been reached in mass imprisonment and that it will begin to be ameliorated. They cite the example of the state of Georgia, whose prison population doubled between 1990 and 2010 when the state was spending a billion dollars a year on corrections; they add that 60 percent of the state prison population constituted nonviolent offenders. In May 2012, a law was passed in Georgia to avert the growth in prison population and costs over the next five years (p. 5).

6. These include taking regular urine samples for drug testing and submitting offenders to lie detector tests (Clear and Frost 2014, 122).

7. Clear and Frost (2014, 39) make the point that declaring that a war is needed to counter a social problem legitimizes strategies that might otherwise fail adequate policy assessments or lack rational justification. The War on Drugs began under President Nixon but gained its full dimensions under President Reagan (p. 42).

8. In relation to Australia, for example, Williams has noted that the location of large U.S. correctional corporations in Australia has led to American-style correctional facilities becoming the new standard and correctional policies from the United States being adopted in Australia through truth-in-sentencing, three strikes, and other practices (cited in Cavadino and Dignan 2006a, 438). In Finland, however, the opposite has taken place with a dramatic reduction in the prison population between 1976 and 1999 through policy action partly responding to a perception that the imprisonment rate was excessive for a Western European nation (p. 440). In contrast, despite constitutional guarantees and court decisions about limiting imprisonment, Spain has one of the highest rates of imprisonment in the European Union (Cid 2005, 148).

9. For example, the U.S. Federal Penitentiary at Marion, Illinois, is a supermax facility holding four hundred high-risk inmates. Prisoners are subject to a lockdown, meaning that they are confined to their cells twenty-three hours each day and are allowed outside the cell for exercise only one hour a day (Welch 1999, 200). For a comparative study of supermax prisons, see J. I. Ross (2013).

10. The concept of "most serious crimes" has been refined by the Economic and Social Council of the United Nations as "it being understood that their scope should not go beyond intentional crimes with lethal or other extremely grave consequences" (cited in Hood 2001, 345).

11. In April 2014, media reports indicated that Brunei would impose strict Sharia punishments in stages that would include "death by stoning for offenses including sodomy and adultery" ("Sultan of Brunei Unveils Strict Sharia Code," 2014).

12. There is some evidence that state officials in the United States associated lynching with hanging and "frontier justice," and as a result, alternative methods of execution were explored (Garland 2010, 119).

13. Opinion polls have revealed majority support for capital punishment in almost all nations in which it has been abolished, both at the time of abolition and subsequently (Garland 2010, 184).

14. Public hanging continued in Kentucky and Missouri up to the 1930s, and southern states allowed the death sentence for rape, robbery, burglary, and arson up to the 1960s, even when the rest of the country had restricted it to first-degree murder (Garland 2010, 124).

15. The *New York Times* reported on April 6, 2014 ("Japan's Death Row" 2014) that the world's longest-serving death row inmate, Iwao Hakamada, was released after 48 years in prison, when a judge found that "the possibility of his innocence has become clear to a respectable degree."

16. The figure of 10,000 came inadvertently from a National People's Congress delegate; the figure of 15,000 comes from a leaked Communist Party document that reported 60,000 executions from 1997 to 2001 (Trevaskes 2008, 394).

17. The meaning of "essential" in the suspension provisions relates in practice to certain offense characteristics, namely, an offender surrendered voluntarily to police, assisted law enforcement in arresting others, or provided important information to law enforcement; an offender was involved in gang crimes, but the ringleaders for those crimes have already been executed; the victims shared some responsibility for the crime; to retain live evidence; and the offender has overseas connections (Lu and Zhang 2005, 371).

18. Jan Van Dijk (2008, 260) points out that it is difficult to determine the "punitiveness" of justice systems globally, but a detailed study made of eight Western states (Farrington, Langan, and Tonry 2004) showed that the United States has higher conviction rates than the other seven states for arrested burglars and robbers even though it does not experience higher rates of burglaries and robberies, and it more often imposes custodial sentences for such crimes. Mean actual months served in custody by these groups of offenders are also highest in the United States. As David Nelken (2011b, 14) puts it, "The debate on which factors are key to explaining punitiveness is far from settled."

19. By the eighteenth century, English law allowed a maximum period of two years hard labor in a workhouse (Hirsch 1992, 31).

20. Millbank suffered from problems associated with finance, administration, and health and was demolished in 1893 (McConville 1995, 120).

21. It is estimated that between 1718 and 1775, some 50,000 criminals were transported to the American colonies and about 165,000 to Australia starting from 1787 (Wilson 2014, 45–46, 69). A sentence of transportation was usually for seven or fourteen years but could be for life (p. 67).

22. Despite the fact that imprisonment with hard labor was not a public spectacle like executions or corporal punishments, proponents of incarceration argued that the very structure of the prison would be a deterrent because of the looming thick walls and the starkness of the architecture generally (Hirsch 1992, 44). Removing the prisoner from the eyes of the public also mitigated any risk of public empathy for the prisoner's suffering (Ignatieff 1978, 90).

23. The term *penitentiary* was first used in 1779 in the English Penitentiary Act (Colvin 1997, 47), which provided for the construction of two penitentiaries in London. Prisoners would be housed in solitary confinement at night and in the day would perform labor. Both clothing and diet were to be "coarse" (Ignatieff 1978, 93–94).

24. Alexis de Tocqueville, writing in 1832, stressed the importance of work, regardless of its impact on reforming the character of the prisoner: "Perhaps, leaving the prison he is not an honest man but he has contracted honest habits. He was an idler, now he knows how to work" (quoted in Duguid 2000, 71). Those advocating hard labor also contended that their labor would cover the costs of their incarceration (Hirsch 1992, 17).

25. The lockstep was a discrete method of movement that required prisoners to march in a human chain in strict formation. It was likened to a military funeral or to culprits marching to the gallows (Christianson 1998, 117).

26. The first chain gangs appeared in Georgia in 1866 when local counties were authorized to use convict labor to build roads or to lease them to private enterprises (Colvin 1997, 220).

27. For example, in India, proposals for penal reform between 1830 and 1920 were commonly rejected by officials as impractical or inexpedient and policy changes in penology in Britain were not automatically imported into the colonies (Dikötter 2007, 7).

28. Most colonial prisons graded food by race and social status. For example, in Northern Rhodesia (now Zimbabwe) the prison distinguished between "Europeans, Cape Boys, Asiatics and colonial kaffirs, and uncivilized natives" (Killingray 2003, 104).

29. Corporal punishment under judicial order was not abolished in England and Wales until 1948 (Killingray 2003, 109).

30. The Mau Mau emergency refers a 1950s uprising in Kenya when the Mau Mau attacked whites to resist British rule and force the expulsion of white settlers. The British implemented a state of emergency and rounded up Mau Mau members, subjecting them to torture and hard labor in prison.

31. For example, in 1858 a convict colony was established in the Andaman Islands, where the convicts remained completely separate from the often hostile indigenous population that lived adjacent to the penal colony (Anderson 2007, 207). There were numerous convict escapes that were punished by flogging or, in one case, by the mass hanging of eighty-one convicts who had attempted escape. Other overseas penal colonies were located in Burma, Mauritius, and the Straits (p. 208).

32. Contemporary concern over amenities provided to prisoners in the United States is associated with "tough on crime" attitudes that, for example, regard the provision of television, radios, and weight-lifting equipment as giving prisoners a higher standard of amenity than is enjoyed by the ordinary person on the street. This perspective is exemplified in a statement from a U.S. senator who complained, "We've got to stop building prisons like Holiday Inns" (Lenz 2002, 500). As Lenz points out, for correctional officers, simply keeping inmates busy is of value because it helps maintain order. Rewards for good behavior in the form of amenities can be taken away as punishments, and this also helps maintain order (p. 506).

33. On November 16, 2012, the *Guardian* reported that Jamaica was preparing to abolish flogging and whipping. The last person to suffer this punishment in 1994 received four years imprisonment and six lashes for stabbing his mother-in-law. He complained to the UN Human Rights Committee, which ruled in 2004 that the form of corporal punishment applied violated his rights. After that decision, Jamaican courts ceased to order the punishment. The Justice Minister said, "The time has come to regularize this situation by getting these colonial-era laws off our books once and for all" ("Jamaica to Abolish Flogging Punishment" 2012).

34. See, for example, the ordering process, including punishments, imposed on Native Alaskan cultures by the U.S. military, missionaries, and traders in the nineteenth century and into modern times in the "internal colonization" of Alaskan Native cultures described by C. Banks, "Ordering the Other: Reading Alaskan Native Culture Past and Present" in M. Bosworth and J. Flavin, eds., *Race, Gender, and Punishment: From Colonialism to the War on Terror* (New Brunswick, NJ: Rutgers University Press, 2007).

35. After completion of the burning and the death of the prisoner, the flames were extinguished and flaming torches applied to the genitals of males and the breasts of females, and on the nose, with the aim of producing a grotesque sight for public display.

36. Parading the offender with name, crime, and sentence through the streets to the stadium where the execution was public was also practiced by the Chinese in the 1980s.

37. In the Tokugawa period, the word for official punishments, *oshioki,* survives in modern Japanese as

a term that describes punishments that parents inflict on small children (Botsman 2005, 39).

38. Botsman (2005, 50) explains that from early times, Japanese rulers were concerned about pollution arising from deaths, sickness, and births and therefore required forms of ritual purification and cleaning to be conducted. Over time, outcast, marginalized groups began to develop survival strategies such as forms of craft production and engaging in the removal or cleaning of waste from temples, handling corpses, and disposing of large animal carcasses. Under the Tokagawa rulers, outcasts who had only a limited role in punishment broadened that participation "to play a key role in almost every act of punishment ordered by the warrior state" (p. 53).

39. *Gaijin* now means foreigner or outsider but originally was the exclusionary term used for foreigners perceived as "barbarians."

40. Sometimes the sentences imposed by consular courts on foreigners frustrated the Japanese authorities because, as compared with Japanese punishments, they were perceived to be too lenient. Botsman (2005, 133) cites an 1868 case in which a U.S. sailor was put on trial after stabbing a samurai in the back while drunk, resulting in his death. The sailor was convicted of assault with a deadly weapon but not of murder because there was no evidence of premeditation. His sentence was deportation from Japan and imprisonment for one year. According to Japanese practice, a mortal injury would have resulted in the penalty of death by beheading.

41. *Regicide* is the act of killing a king.

42. *Parricide* is the act of killing one's father (patricide), mother (matricide), or close relative.

43. In the first half of the 1880s, samurai rebellions and other forms of resistance led to a significant increase in the prison population from 33,000 in 1882 to 63,000 in 1885. Also in 1885, the number of new admissions to prison was 167,000. In comparison, the prison population in 1999 was 46,000 from a population four times larger than in the 1880s (Botsman 2005, 179).

44. Flogging in Korea and Taiwan was abolished in the aftermath of the March First Movement in Korea in 1919, when the repression that accompanied Japanese military rule in Korea was challenged and the police, unable to control the demonstrations, reacted with extreme violence and brutality toward the local protesters (Botsman 2005, 225).

45. The Chinese penal codes are collections of rules, the content of which varied from dynasty to dynasty but all of which stated the elements of every offense and the circumstances that would affect the punishment to be inflicted. In this sense they resemble modern penal codes, even having commentaries on the articles (MacCormack 1990, 49). There was no Chinese equivalent to the common law doctrine of precedent, but judicial decisions were regularly followed by tribunals in similar cases (p. 54).

46. According to Muhlhahn (2009, 37), no more than 20 percent of capital sentences were eventually confirmed by the emperor.

47. The prisoner was tied to a cross and, through a series of cuts, his body was sliced beyond recognition with the coup de grâce being given usually on the third cut but with as many as 120 cuts being inflicted (Bodde and Morris 1967, 93).

48. Special courses on prison administration were offered at Peking Law School after 1906, taught by a leading Japanese scholar of penality and Japanese prisons, Ogawa Jijiruo (Dutton 1992, 159).

49. A procuracy is considered the highest national-level agency responsible for prosecution.

50. The major elements of the state-administered punishment system in the Soviet Union were the correction and reeducation of all offenders and, drawing on the perspective that crime was an outcome of parasitism and laziness, the belief that labor should be the chief instrument of correction. In the labor camps, labor was associated with lengthy working days, production targets, collectivism, competition between labor groups, and food and privileges contingent on the scope of work completed. Labor camps were organized on a huge scale with prisoners deployed on large-scale projects such as reclaiming wasteland and extracting resources, generally in inhospitable locations. Little attention was paid to rehabilitation (Muhlhahn 2009, 158).

7

Juvenile Justice

Worldwide, juvenile justice systems differ significantly in several aspects. As always, in investigating justice systems, it is important to understand systems as law in action and not simply as law in books. This can be a challenging task where there is an absence of empirical studies and scholarly research is scant or superficial. For example, the focus on rights and due process found in U.S. juvenile systems is not followed in Japan, where complex cultural and social values influence the social construction of delinquency and the control and protection of youth generally,[1] or in China, where bottom-up approaches to juvenile justice through the ideology of the "mass line" and the perceived value of reform through labor offer a very different view to that of the West in how to counter delinquency.

In this chapter, we examine three contrasting systems of juvenile justice in France, Japan, and China situating those systems within the historical, cultural, and social practices of those countries associated with youth deviance and punishment. This is necessary because "the manner in which each country has resolved the 'youth justice' problem is almost certainly best understood within the broad context of that country's history and justice institutions" (Doob and Tonry 2004, 1). These detailed case studies (in contrast to the usual brief descriptions of juvenile systems found in other comparative texts) make up the bulk of this chapter. In these explorations, the central issues will be the following: How is juvenile delinquency constructed and defined in those countries, and what cultural and social practices, values, and beliefs have influenced constructions of delinquency and systems of juvenile justice over time? How do those countries deal with juveniles who come into conflict with the law? How does justice play itself out in those systems?

Mandatory international norms of juvenile justice created by the 1989 Convention on the Rights of the Child (CRC) and associated instruments should impact almost all countries' juvenile justice systems because all countries except the United States and Somalia are parties to the Convention. In terms of punishment for juveniles, the CRC promotes the notion of rehabilitation and favors restorative justice measures in contrast to other strategies, especially those prevailing in the United States and England and Wales that are generally regarded as punitive.[2] Why do countries follow the U.S. punitive model when the CRC mandates the welfare and protection approach, and just how effective is the internationalization of juvenile justice? Where the CRC and associated norms that do not apply to the United

States are discussed, this draws attention to the international deficit in the United States concerning juvenile justice.

It is helpful to read this chapter together with

- sections of Chapter 5 that discuss the French criminal justice system, the Japanese prosecutor, the Chinese legal system and their respective legal cultures;

- Chapter 6 on criminal punishment in Japan and China; and

- Chapter 4 on policing in China.

A reading of these sections will provide a deeper historical, social, and cultural context for the material in this chapter focused on juvenile justice in France, Japan, and China.

CHILDHOOD, CRIMINAL RESPONSIBILITY, AND JUVENILE JUSTICE SYSTEMS

Conceptions of youth, juvenile, and child are cultural and social constructions specific to each country. They may be defined in laws and through social practices. Internationally, the CRC stipulates that a child is a person under the age of eighteen, and United Nations declares that a youth is a person between the ages of fifteen and twenty-four.[3] Regionally, however, the African Youth Charter,[4] for example, defines a youth as a person between the ages of fifteen and thirty-five. In some cultures and societies there is little or no concept of a *juvenile* as this term is known and recognized in Western societies and Western justice systems. In fact, internationally, the term *youth* is more often used in discussions about non-adults who come into conflict with the law.

The distinction between a youth and an adult blurs when in some juvenile justice systems such as those in most U.S. states, a juvenile can be tried as an adult when he or she commits an especially serious offense or where other criteria are satisfied. Accordingly, the notion that there is a special system of justice for juveniles that will apply to them until they attain the age of majority breaks down when a juvenile can be dealt with in the adult justice system and even be sent to an adult prison.

Minimum Age of Criminal Responsibility

The fact that someone is a certain age affects notions of his or her responsibility for criminal conduct and liability to punishment because most legal systems have rules on the minimum age of criminal responsibility (MACR). These rules vary greatly worldwide and are always subject to change. If a child is below the MACR, he or she lacks the capacity to commit a crime under the law and cannot be prosecuted for a criminal offense, whatever the nature of the act. Thus the MACR recognizes that a child is different than an adult in that he or she has not attained the necessary degree of maturity to be held responsible for his or her actions. Compared to adults then, children make poorer decisions due to differences in cognitive capacity, maturity of judgment, perceptions of risk, and a greater susceptibility to peer influence (Grisso et al. 2003, 333).

According to the CRC, states must establish "a minimum age below which children shall be presumed not to have the capacity to infringe the penal law" (Article 40.3[a]). In 2007 in General Comment 10,[5] the CRC Committee expressed the view that twelve years should be the MACR and that an age below twelve years "is considered by the Committee not be internationally acceptable." The Committee stresses that states should not reduce their MACR to twelve where it has already been set higher and strongly encourages states to introduce a higher MACR, for example, fourteen or sixteen years of age. In addition, Rule 4 of the Beijing Rules recommends that any MACR "shall not be fixed at too low an age level, bearing in mind the facts of emotional, mental and intellectual maturity."[6]

In Europe, Cyprus raised its MACR in 1999 from seven to ten years and again in 2006 from ten to fourteen years; Spain raised it from twelve to fourteen years in 2000; Ireland in 2001 from seven to twelve years; and Switzerland from seven to ten years in 2007. In contrast, only thirteen states in the United States have set an MACR, and most rely on the common law which says from ages seven to fourteen children cannot be presumed to be responsible, but this presumption is rebuttable. In Africa, the average minimum is nine years and in Asia/Australia/Oceania, ten years. In Europe the average is thirteen years, but in Greece and Scotland the MACR is eight years (Rap and Weijers 2014, 88). It is common for states to adjust the MACR when public pressure forces changes in the law that express a more punitive approach to juvenile delinquency. In many developing countries, age determination is an issue because rates of birth registration are low and there is no definitive recording of the date of birth. There is evidence from some countries that this lack of clarity about age is exploited by police to prosecute children who are in fact below the MACR.

The maximum ages for the jurisdiction of juvenile courts also vary from country to country. This is the age at which offenders become liable to receive the same treatment as adults in the criminal justice system. In New York, for example, it is fifteen, but most U.S. states apply eighteen (Office of Juvenile Justice and Delinquency Program 2013). Thus, in New York, a person aged sixteen or older is dealt with by the adult court. Elsewhere, Japan applies the age of 20 years.

When persons under age eighteen are transferred to adult courts for trial, this has the effect of reducing the age of criminal majority.[7] In the United States it is estimated that as many as 250,000 juveniles are tried each year in the adult court system.[8] Barry Feld (2006, 432) points out that extending the maximum age of jurisdiction of the juvenile court would reduce pressures to transfer youth to adult court and argues for an age limit of nineteen or twenty-one for the juvenile court.

JUVENILE JUSTICE SYSTEMS: COMMONALITIES AND TRENDS

The international standard, declared by the Committee on the Rights of the Child established by the CRC, is that a special juvenile justice system ought to be in operation in a state for young persons until they attain the age of eighteen years. The Committee advises states that have a lower upper age limit to extend the application of juvenile justice provisions to young person up to the age of eighteen and abolish any provisions that allow for youth under the age of eighteen to be prosecuted in adult criminal courts (CRC Committee 2007, paras. 34, 36, 37). Scandinavian countries have no juvenile systems as such, and deal with young offenders exclusively within their child welfare systems. They try youth aged fifteen and older in their regular criminal justice systems using special procedures, sentencing options, and welfare-oriented dispositions instead of criminal sanctions (Tonry and Doob 2004).

Prosecuting youth under age eighteen in adult courts is possible in a number of European states and in the United States but under a strict model which employs a fixed upper age limit (linked to longer maximum periods of detention in the juvenile system). Within Europe, Germany, Greece, Italy, Spain, and Switzerland do not prosecute youth under eighteen in adult courts (Rap and Weijers 2014, 88). Applying adult laws to juveniles through waivers or transfers from one system to the other challenges the foundational principle that juveniles ought to receive special treatment based on their degree of maturity and "reflects a cultural and legal reconfiguration of youth from innocent and dependent children to responsible and autonomous adult-like offenders" (Feld 2006, 421).[9]

While each country may have developed its own discrete juvenile justice system, influences from the United States and from various states within Europe may well have shaped aspects of those systems in the West. In non-Western systems, concepts developed in the West have also been influential, as has colonization or occupation. For example, as the case study on Japan in this chapter demonstrates, the Japanese juvenile justice system was heavily influenced by U.S. ideas about juvenile justice during the U.S. occupation of Japan after World War II. Many former colonies upon Independence inherited juvenile laws and models of juvenile justice mandated by their colonizers which may since have been revised as countries became parties to the CRC. For example, India did not adopt a unified system of juvenile justice until the enactment of the Juvenile Justice Act 1986; previously, Indian states operated under colonial laws enacted in most cases in the 1920s and earlier (Kumari 2004, 86).

Some countries, like Japan, have always recognized a distinction between juveniles and adults in terms of punishment, but others did not come to that view until much later. Reform movements concerned with child protection became active in the West during the nineteenth century. One example is the "child savers" of the United States (Platt 1977), who were instrumental in one of the most significant developments in juvenile justice, that is, the creation of a separate system of justice to deal with children coming into conflict with the law. Associated with this concept but considerably predating it (it can be traced back to medieval times in England) was the notion of *parens patriae*—the idea that the state, through the courts, should intervene to protect children's welfare as the ultimate guardian of a child (Banks 2013b, 5). The notion of the separate juvenile court and its role as *parens patriae* took root in most common law countries. While common law countries' juvenile systems may share the same key features—for example, a close resemblance to the adult system of criminal justice in their organization and a focus on punishment—other systems, like those in Scandinavian countries, deal with juveniles in conflict with the law under age 15 through social welfare processes (Janson 2004, 391).

Norway enacted a law on neglected children in 1896, and in 1899 the first Juvenile Court was established in Chicago. England and Canada established juvenile courts in 1908. France, Belgium, and Switzerland passed juvenile laws in 1912. In 1945, France enacted a juvenile law that prioritized protection and education of delinquent juveniles. Japan enacted juvenile legislation in 1948 under postwar occupation by the United States. As juvenile systems of justice spread across the West, some distinct commonalities emerged:

- Juvenile judges were given a wide discretion to act in the interests of a juvenile based on the notion that the juvenile court was exercising the *parens patriae* power; the focus was placed therefore on the needs and concerns of the individual child and not on the offense that had brought him or her before the court.

- Juvenile courts adopted a welfare and protection approach and were often able to call upon an array of ancillary services provided by social workers, probation officers, and the like (sometimes attached to the court or part of government agencies, sometimes private agencies) to inform them about the circumstances of the child and assist them in making a disposition that would reflect the child's best interests.

- Courts often operated informally, in what is now referred to as a "child-friendly" environment as distinct from the formality usually associated with displays of the justice system in action.

- Proceedings involving children were not public, and courts were aware of the need to protect the privacy of juveniles.

- Except in the United States (after the decision in 1967 in *Re Gault*),[10] it was not considered necessary to follow rules of due process in the juvenile system of justice because an inquiry mode of procedure was better able to understand how best to cater for the interests of the child in fashioning a rehabilitative or educative disposition. (Junger-Tas 2008, 508)

Welfare/Protection and Crime Control/Justice Models of Juvenile Justice

In discussing countries' juvenile justice systems, a common approach is to categorize a country as having a welfare/protection model or a crime control/justice model. The former connotes a protective approach to juvenile offending that focuses on the circumstances and needs of the offender while the latter generally means focusing on the offense and not the offender, paying greater attention to issues of due process, and focusing on punishment rather than rehabilitation or reeducation (Doob and Tonry 2004, 12). In terms of procedure in the court, the welfare approach is associated with an inquiry mode and with informality while the latter is regarded as adversarial and therefore more formal.

Researchers have identified at least six models of juvenile justice worldwide which are differentiated by the emphasis placed on the welfare/protection of juveniles as opposed to their punishment; by the nature of the procedures used, that is, whether they are formal or informal; and by the extent to which the proceedings are cooperative and collaborative, as between the court and the parties and youth specialists in court, or purely adversarial in nature. At the extremes of this spectrum of approaches, at one end are systems that are informal (often referred to as "child friendly") that approach delinquency as the task of reeducating and rehabilitating a juvenile who has gone astray and apply the principle of the best interests of the child, and at the other end are those who regard a juvenile as an independent actor, to be held accountable and punished for actions taken, and to be dealt with through formal due process (Hartjen 2008, 86). While it is still possible to identify the essential or "classical" orientations of the welfare and crime control models, finding ideal types of welfare or crime control models is now very problematic. Rather, there are mixed systems that borrow elements from each of the classical models.

The Shift Toward a Crime Control/Justice Model

Debate continues about changes in systems of juvenile justice and especially about trends away from the commonalities noted earlier and toward a more punitive juvenile "justice" model.[11] Questions include the following: Have juvenile justice systems become more or less punitive? How have globalization and the supposed convergence of more punitive justice policies associated with globalization influenced justice systems, or have local practices resisted trends of this nature? These are complex questions, especially when applied to numerous different jurisdictions. They have been explored largely in the context of Europe. In this chapter, we consider the situation in France in a detailed case study of that system and the social, political, and cultural context in which it functions. Generally, however, Doob and Tonry (2004, 15) argue that the importance of the welfare approach to juvenile justice "as an organizing principle in many (but not all) systems appears to be on the decline." As John Muncie (2009, 369) puts it, "The emphasis has become one of fighting juvenile crime rather than securing juvenile justice."

Causal explanations of "penal populism" or increased punitiveness are associated with fear of crime, a desire for retribution, the desire to hold juveniles accountable (termed *responsibilization*), sensationalist media depictions of crime, and social and economic justifications. For example, in France, issues with ethnic minorities and their marginalization in segregated city areas as well as aggressive policing strategies seem to have been influential in the introduction of more repressive juvenile policies. In Japan, fear of crime has been enhanced by a recent media focus on sensational crimes, the media scrutiny of policing effectiveness, changes in crime reporting practices, and the entry of crime as a topic into political debate. Just as in parts of Europe, in Japan the public now defers less to crime experts on accountability and punishment issues, and crime prevention and control have become populist topics. In China, the rapid modernization of the country since the 1970s has resulted in increased crime and a breakdown of the strong informal controls that previously controlled the level of delinquency.

In determining juvenile justice policies, including punishment levels, countries are required to give effect to the CRC. In the CRC a paramount principle in dealing with juveniles in conflict with the law is the best interests of the child (Article 3.1). In other words, it repeats the foundational guiding principle of juvenile justice. What then has been the effect of the CRC on countries' juvenile justice policies and systems in light of its binding nature? Do the mandates of the CRC restrain states from shifting to a crime control/justice model? These questions are considered in the following section.

The welfare protection approach to juveniles in conflict with the law did not substantially change until the 1970s. After that time, there was a gradual incorporation of new elements into North American and European laws, matched by similar developments in Australia and New Zealand. Among the Anglo-Saxon legal systems then, there was a definite punitive turn. The new approach to juvenile justice seems to have acquired the following characteristics:

- A youthful offender has now come to be regarded as responsible for his or her action for which he or she must always be held accountable.

- The focus has shifted away from the offender to the offense that has been committed.

- The victim movement has drawn attention, including especially media attention in the case of sensational crimes, away from the offender so that victims are now central figures in juvenile justice systems.

- There has been a convergence between the adult criminal justice system and the juvenile justice system in favor of the former, as more juveniles (especially in the United States) are waived for trial as adults. (Junger-Tas 2008, 509)

JUVENILE JUSTICE SYSTEMS: FRANCE, JAPAN, AND CHINA

This section will explain juvenile justice systems in France, Japan, and China, taking account not only of how each system works today but in each case, its history and development and the cultural, social, and legal context in which it functions.

(Wyvekens 2008, 179). Juvenile judges were now to consider the concerns of victims and apply a risk management strategy.[19]

Debates about a welfare approach or a repressive approach to juvenile delinquency continued between experts and scholars, supplemented by alarmist media accounts that generated public support for punitive approaches (Ossman and Terrio 2006, 10). Conservative strategies identified Maghreb immigrants as a risk population and attempted to link their Muslim heritage to transnational crime and terrorism.[20] Liberal strategies defended the welfare approach which had guided the juvenile system for many years. Rather than identifying race as a factor in the punitive ideology, pro-welfare experts framed the issue as one of class bias in the courts. They also pointed to the underrepresentation of immigrants in law enforcement, political offices, and the magistracy. These debates set the stage for the riots that occurred in 2005 (Ossman and Terrio 2006, 11, 13).

In November 2005 urban riots began in an impoverished suburb in Paris where half of the residents were under the age of twenty-five years and 25 percent were unemployed.[21] The unrest was sparked by the accidental deaths of two boys of North African ethnicity who were running away from police. The rioting spread across the nation over three weeks and focused attention on France's immigrant problem in suburban ghettos. Nine thousand vehicles were set on fire, hundreds of buildings destroyed, four thousand rioters arrested, and a state of emergency declared (Schneider 2008, 136). On November 9, 2005, the then Interior Minister, Nicholas Sarkozy, issued an executive order for the deportation of all foreigners found guilty of rioting. In the legislature, calls were made for laws against polygamy and family reunification because of an alleged overrepresentation of North African teenagers in those arrested while others blamed radical Islam (Ossman and Terrio 2006, 6). Only one elected leader suggested that police abuse was an issue: she was the only North African senator elected in 2004 from a district that included several *banlieues* (Schneider 2008, 138).

Juvenile Crime Data

Accurate data on juvenile crime are difficult to locate but according to Ministry of the Interior data covering the period 1988 to 2001, delinquents were becoming younger and more violent (Ossman

and Terrio 2006, 57). Data indicate that there was an increase of 137 percent in juvenile arrests from 1974 to 2000, and it is estimated that juveniles are responsible for 21 percent of all crimes, with the highest juvenile involvement in street crime and property crime (p. 56).[22]

With respect to crimes of violence committed by juveniles, the rate per 100,000 recorded for such crimes increased by 143 percent between 1974 and 1992 (the increase for adults was only 31.6 percent). Between 1992 and 1994, police-recorded violent crime for youth aged ten to seventeen increased by 23.5 percent, and the total increase in violent juvenile crime between 1984 and 1994 was 86.7 percent (Pfeiffer 1998, 284–85). Possible explanations for this increase include there was a real rise in the incidence of such crimes; the change resulted from an increase in the reporting of such crimes; or the ~~change resulted~~ from law enforcement practices, for example, by increased policing in some locations and a correspondingly greater number of arrests (p. 298). Of significance may be the unemployment rates for males and females under twenty-five years of age which indicated a rate for males of 15.8 percent in 1990, increasing to 23.7 percent in 1995. For females the corresponding rates for those years were 3 percent and 31.1 percent (p. 307).

From 1994 to 1996, the number of juveniles brought before the juvenile court increased from 18,100 to 26,500, an increase of 46 percent. Net-widening through prosecuting behaviors not previously sanctioned through the juvenile justice system, such as petty violence in schools and using public transport without paying, and the punishment of "incivilities" may account for part of the increase (Bonelli 2007, 110). Between 1990 and 1999, a time associated with a perceived rise in juvenile crime, there was actually little change in the number of minors convicted of offenses: 30,507 in 1990 and 38,580 in 1999. However, while in 1990 13 percent of suspects were minors, 21.32 percent were minors in 1999 (Terrio 2009, 295).

Young immigrant males are disproportionately unemployed and some argue they resort to theft.[23] A self-reported delinquency survey conducted in 2000 indicated that 22 percent of male offenders of North African ethnicity said they had at least three friends who had been arrested for theft as compared to 7 percent of nonimmigrant youth, and of those under justice supervision, 43 percent had parents born out of France. It has been estimated that in the age range eighteen to twenty-four, those with a North African father are 9.27 times more likely to be prosecuted than those with fathers born in France (Ossman and Terrio 2006, 60).[24] The ban on disaggregating data according to ethnicity means no mechanisms exist to address the treatment accorded to French juveniles who have an ancestry as immigrants. As French nationals they become invisible, but observation has shown, for example in the Paris Juvenile Court, that they constitute by far the majority of juvenile court prosecutions (Terrio 2009, 27).

In spite of a more punitive trend since the 1990s, it is argued that French juvenile justice retains a commitment to a welfare and protection approach, and the chief administrative court (*Conseil d'État*) has rejected measures that would allow mayors to declare curfews and control begging (the latter would only be permitted with safeguards included (Ossman and Terrio 2006, 55). From 1993 to 2000, the number of juveniles sent to prison increased from 2,247 to 3,790, and in the Paris region alone, juvenile incarcerations increased by 72 percent (Sobanet and Terrio 2005, 22–23).

Juvenile Court System

The French system comprises three tiers or levels:

- the juvenile judge (*juge des enfants*),
- the juvenile court (*tribunal pour enfants*), and
- the juvenile assize court (*cour d'assises des mineurs*).

In practice, unless a serious offense is involved, or a second offense, most juvenile dispositions are arranged informally by the juvenile judge. The juvenile judge is therefore the "central person in the youth justice system" (Ministère de la Justice 2005, 5). While it has been said that the welfare and child protection philosophy and orientation of French juvenile justice has not changed since the present system was adapted in 1912 (Hartjen 2008, 132), the more recent legislative developments suggest that a more punitive approach has developed over time. As well as having jurisdiction in criminal cases, the juvenile judge has jurisdiction in civil protection cases that are not criminal. In Anglo-Saxon systems these cases are known as status offenses and include running away from home, failing to attend school (truancy), and consuming alcohol. Status offenses are acts that would not constitute a crime if committed by an adult (Rap and Weijers 2014, 98).

Informal Hearing

Generally, the French juvenile justice system gives priority to educative care, and this is arranged without any hearing before a court by a juvenile judge in an informal proceeding.[25] For many years it has been the practice of the juvenile court judge to deal with juvenile delinquency by way of educational assistance and not through criminal proceedings. Educative measures can include restorative justice type compensation orders. These involve the juvenile undertaking reparation, perhaps writing a letter of apology, or working to reimburse the victim for loss suffered. Reparations are supervised by a youth worker who reports to the juvenile judge. This measure is commonly imposed for minor offenses such as bicycle theft (Blatier 1999, 249). Restorative measures are regularly ordered before prosecution but may also be imposed during proceedings and at sentencing.

Educational services are provided by the court's social service and probation service, *Service Éducatif Auprès du Tribunal pour enfants* (SEAT), part of the PJJ, which consults with minors and families, supervises minors placed in pre-trial detention, undertakes probation supervision (*liberté surveillée*), oversees community service and reparations and educational measures, and provides the judge with updates on the progress of a juvenile. In 1956, juvenile caseworkers adopted the description *éducateurs* and established a profession around youth advocacy, social justice, and protection rather than repression. They are recruited through state examinations and must have two years of university education but generally have no training in diversity or culture and no specialized knowledge of the ethnic groups they are most involved with (Terrio 2009, 145). Nowadays, they are largely middle class and female, and state inspectors have noted the wide social distance that separates them from juveniles who come under their supervision and control (p. 139). According to Terrio (2009, 145), they are too often guilty of "ethnocentric stereotyping" or tend to read culture as something that prevents immigrants from adapting to French values and society.[26]

Educational sanctions are a new penalty introduced in 2002, falling between educational measures and criminal sanctions. For a child between the ages of ten and thirteen, the judge may order the following educational sanctions:

- confiscation of the object used in the commission of an offense,

- a ban on associating with the victim or any accomplices to the offense,

- a ban on traveling to the place where the offense occurred,

- compensation to the victim, and/or

- mandatory education.

If the juvenile fails to comply with these sanctions, the judge may order placement in an institution and the sanctions will constitute a criminal record.

Residential centers are managed by the PJJ. These may be secure educational centers (centres éducatifs renforcés [CER]), where sessions run from three to six months with groups of five to seven youth; emergency placement centers (centres de placement immédiat [CPI]); or closed educational centers (centres éducatifs fermés [CEF]) for minors aged thirteen to eighteen years for a period of six months (Wyvekens 2008, 184–85).

Minors aged thirteen to eighteen can be placed on probation conditionally if they agree to comply with measures of protection, assistance, supervision, and education arranged by the PJJ or by a private approved facility or comply with the conditions for placement in an educational center, especially a closed educational center (centre éducatif fermé [CEF]), for a period of six months, extendable for a maximum additional six months. The center is said to be "closed" not because it is secure but because noncompliance with placement conditions can result in pre-trial detention in jail (Wyvekens 2008, 185).

Unlike probation in other jurisdictions where sanctions can be imposed if a probationer decides to run away from a residential treatment center, in France attendance is voluntary and there is no arrest sanction. Jim Hackler suggests that this approach means that probation officers in France must make more use of persuasion and negotiation in dealing with juveniles than is the practice in other jurisdictions (Hackler 1988, 479).

Comment

The French juvenile justice system has many problems, including heavy caseloads, insufficient staff, lack of specialized facilities, and lack of licensed emergency and long-term residential facilities (Terrio 2009, 15). As noted earlier, some commentators believe that the welfare and protection approach is firmly embedded in the French juvenile justice system. Others argue that the "territorialized" approach to urban crime that targets marginalized immigrant populations has forced changes on the system that have caused it to become more punitive. Clearly there are deeply troubling issues associated with immigrant populations and their living conditions that have not been addressed in a systematic manner. Similarly, police use of force and the interactions between police and the immigrant population have not been substantively analyzed as areas in need of policy change. Research has shown that immigrants comprise almost all juveniles appearing before the Paris juvenile courts. The French police could learn from the experience of other European states about policing immigrant populations. The U.S. experience in policing its inner cities, as well as the numerous studies that detail issues in police and African American interactions involving youth, provides relevant comparative material (see, e.g., Banks 2013b, 103–33).

Commentators point to more aggressive policing, net-widening and increased penalties, and to the change in the MACR from thirteen to ten years as indicators of repression (Terrio 2009, 15). According to Terrio (2009, 253), "The shift away from classic penal welfarism can be heard in the discourses of judges, prosecutors, and éducateurs who focus on civility, respect for mainstream values and individual responsibility."

The juvenile judge was for many years the key actor in the system, invested with the power to ensure all rehabilitative and educative opportunities were employed in the interests of a juvenile and subject to very little interference by the public prosecutor. A dense web of ancillary services has been developed over time using both public and private resources to support the educative goal in juvenile justice. As occurred in Japan, revisions of the law have strengthened the position of the prosecutor vis-à-vis the juvenile judge. In addition, a number of specific changes to the law, such as the educative sanctions and changes in pre-trial detention rules, have argu-ably reduced the protection that juveniles have been afforded since 1945. Nevertheless, on bal-ance, the consensus of expert opinion is that the fundamental orientation of the French system has not been substantially impacted by new, more punitive justice policies.

Japan

The Japanese justice system is highly centralized with no division of powers between the center and the forty-seven prefectures. Thus the juvenile jus-tice system in each prefecture is identical, unlike in the United States where wide variations exist between states (Elrod and Yokoyama 2006, 213). While in many ways similar to Western systems of juvenile justice, the specificity of the Japanese sys-tem lies in its participatory or communal approach so that "responding to delinquency is not simply the responsibility of various formal juvenile justice agencies" but rather "the responsibility of a wide array of social institutions and individual volun-teers in the community" (p. 226). The following discussion draws substantially on the insightful account by David Ambaras of Japanese construc-tions of delinquency over time and the develop-ment of a juvenile justice system from 1895 to 1945 (the only such account in English).

Development of Juvenile Justice System in Japan

For juvenile justice purposes the most rele-vant periods of Japanese history are the Edo period from 1603 to 1867, when Japan was ruled by the Tokugawa Shogunate, and the period after the Meiji Restoration in 1868, from which time Japan began to introduce a legal system based on Western concepts and models. The change from one period to another marked the change from feudalism to capitalism and the beginnings of formal social control (Jiang et al. 2014, 38). In 1889, Japan enacted a Constitution but the emperor and the government remained above the law until the making of the 1947 Constitu-tion. The defeat of Japan in 1945 and its occupa-tion by the United States brought about further changes to the law, with the United States operat-ing as a model in a range of juvenile policy areas.

The history of juvenile delinquency and juve-nile justice in Japan is characterized by recurring public panics caused by public and police con-structions of juvenile delinquency "discovered" in youth social practices and subcultures, by an intense police and citizen surveillance of youth to ensure conformity with Japanese values and cus-toms, and "by a regime of socialization premised on the notion that every aspect of a young per-son's life should be rendered visible and subject to intensive guidance" (Ambaras 2006, 192).

The pace of social change in Japan over the Tokugawa and Meiji periods and beyond was so rapid that juvenile delinquency became associ-ated with the perceived dangers and perils of the cities and industries that grew as Westernization and modernity radically changed Japan (Ambaras 2006, 7). These social practices and values con-tinue to impact Japanese conceptions of delin-quency and youth subcultures today.

While juvenile reformers (the Japanese ver-sion of the U.S. "child savers") ascribed delin-quency to progress and modernization, the kinds of youthful cultural practices they identified, whether distinct subcultures or simply juveniles at play, actually had their roots in Tokugawa Japan (Ambaras 2006, 9).

Tokugawa Period (1603–1867)

Preceded by bloody civil wars, the Tokugawa period was regarded as one of peace and stability when one's status was an organizing principle of governance. Occupation and residence defined the dominant status groups, and regulations pre-scribed the correct mode of dress, hairstyle, and body markings for each status group. Enforcing a system based on this level of correctness meant resisting challenges from youth (mainly servants or samurai without masters [ronin]) who had decided to flout the rules in their dress and physical appearance. This style of resistance took a violent form when gangs of youth (yakko) who adopted the attitudes they associated with the samurai roamed the streets of Edo (later Tokyo) fighting and robbing and killing townspeople (Ambaras 2006, 13).

Who was considered a youth? In 1742 the Rules for Determining Legal Matters defined those under the age of fifteen years as children and allowed for more lenient punishments for that category of persons. Adulthood was more difficult to determine however. Under customary rules, for example, peasant communities often regarded men who were not householders as still having the status of youth, and this could continue until the age of forty in some parts of the country (Ambaras 2006, 10). Thus "youth" was a flexible social construction.

Responding to the *yakko*, the Shogunate set up city guardhouses, prohibited breaches of the status rules, forbid citizens to shelter these delinquents, and prohibited the formation of groups and private fighting. Police began to conduct sweeps through the city and conducted roundups of deviants. In 1787, riots broke out after massive famines and rumors that food was being hoarded. It was claimed that youth aged fourteen to eighteen had been riot leaders and an edict was issued that these youth were to be brought to the guardhouses by neighborhood chiefs, homeowners, and landlords and then dealt with and punished (Ambaras 2006, 18).

Vagrants also presented a public order problem and many minors were members of the *hinin* (a status group of licensed beggars), who carried out public health functions in exchange for a monopoly on begging. In 1790, the Edo stockade was established to remove vagrants from the streets and hold and transform them into productive and law abiding citizens but not to punish them. Youth formed a significant element of the stockade population, and in its purpose can be seen a concern for youth education and rehabilitation and a precedent for socializing juveniles that was to be continued in later projects (Ambaras 2006, 28).

Meiji Period (1868–1912)

The Meiji restoration abolished the status system of the Tokugawa era and established a centralized state, a new police force, and compulsory elementary schooling, but the image of the "outlaw hero" from the Tokugawa era would continue to figure in the Meiji period and beyond, as would the fighting and brawls of the working-class youth in the city tenements (Ambaras 2006, 29). Arriving with the development of Tokyo and plans for industrialization was a group of middle-class experts on society who aimed to rescue working-class youth from their environments and bring them into the nascent industrial economy. They worked within and outside government, studied working-class life, and mobilized public opinion to support their reform goals. Their initiatives resulted in the 1900 Reformatory Law that permitted delinquent or dependent children to be placed in reformatories "conceived as utopian models of diligence and domesticity" and in elementary schools (p. 31).

The pace of change in Japan at the opening of the twentieth century caused great alarm. Wars with China and Russia in the late 1800s and early 1900s spurred industrialization and the city populations exploded, with Tokyo rising from 1.8 million people in 1893 to 2.9 million in 1915. New immigrants to the cities filled the industrial jobs or the lower class of casual laborers. This social change was accompanied by reports of crime, poverty, and labor unrest (Ambaras 2006, 33). Social problems included juvenile crime. The number of juveniles sentenced to imprisonment tripled from about nine thousand in 1882 to more than twenty-seven thousand in 1894. Experts concluded the cause was poverty, which caused children to run away from their homes or workplaces or be abandoned by their families.

Children who became beggars were taught to pick pockets (Ambaras 2006, 36), and street children set fires and burned buildings "for the pleasure of seeing the flames" (p. 37). These children came to be seen by the middle class as the visible manifestation of the dangers posed by the urban lower class. Girls, too, posed a danger to the social order because while they were less involved in scavenging and begging, they easily found work as unlicensed prostitutes. As slum dwellers, they were regarded as sexually precocious and represented a public health danger to the city (p. 41). As a source of cheap labor, children were exploited and abused by local merchants and in apprenticeships, and this caused them to steal food. Mothers who took factory work could not assume the full-time domestic roles of the middle class, but to many middle-class reformers, it appeared that the lower classes had not internalized the norms of family life. Accordingly, state agencies and private persons determined their role was to act in *loco parentis* and protect lower-class children and shape them into the future respectable working class (p. 44).

Having studied Western prisons and aiming to create a new penal system, state officials began to target delinquent children for incarceration in special institutions. The 1872 Prison Regulations provided for the establishment of houses of correction that would provide education and vocational training for inmates under the age of twenty, who, having completed a term of imprisonment, were still thought to have criminal tendencies, or who, because of poverty were likely to drift back into criminality. These institutions could also detain children committed at their parents' request (Ambaras 2006, 44).

By 1879, police had studied classification and treatment systems used in juvenile facilities in France and Belgium, and houses of correction were replaced with correctional centers for the rehabilitation of minors below the age of criminal responsibility, set at twelve years by the Penal Code 1880. At this time there were no alternatives to imprisonment, and judges routinely ordered incarceration for most convicted children regardless of the seriousness of the crime. The outcome was that by the early 1890s minors in prison numbered between 20,000 and 28,000 (Ambaras 2006, 46).

This overreliance on prisons resulted in adoption of the Western model of juvenile reformatories separated from the prison system. Religious groups of Protestants and Buddhists started to open small reformatories in the cities and asked for government funding, and in 1885 the Tokyo Reformatory opened. The Reformatory Law 1900 required that each prefecture establish a reformatory to hold children between ages eight and fifteen (later raised to seventeen) who were not provided with proper parental control, engaged in begging, associated with delinquents, or were sentenced to terms under the Penal Code (Ambaras 2006, 47). Inmates could be detained under the age of twenty or discharged earlier if they had reformed. Parents could also commit their children for six months in special "houses of discipline" even beyond the age of majority.

The lack of specificity about the criteria for commitment meant that there was wide discretion in sending youth to these reformatories. This was later revised to include youth who presented a "threat of delinquency." This broad formulation attracted criticism in the legislature but was justified in terms of the "protection" of children and the priority for social order over due process. In the new Penal Code 1907, the age of criminal responsibility was raised to fourteen from twelve and in 1908 the Prisons Law established juvenile prisons or segregated sections of prisons for juveniles aged fourteen to eighteen and new laws allowed for suspended sentences of imprisonment (Ambaras 2006, 49).

By 1910 fifty-three reformatories accommodated 1,021 predominantly male youth across the country. There was no support for similar facilities dedicated to girls who were detained most often for petty theft and vagrancy: police did not class underage unlicensed prostitutes as delinquents (p. 50). Girls were considered hard to reform but received instruction in household duties and morality despite the fact that, as one reformatory director put it in 1914, "Once a girl has known a man, there is no way to reform or improve her" (p. 57).

Private reformatories, using the cottage system, were also established, mostly away from the cities where it was claimed by reformers that "health, spirit and vitality reside" to provide delinquents with the "proper homes" they lacked (Ambaras 2006, 51). The notion of a good home *(katei)* especially inspired reformers who regarded this as the cornerstone of a proper social structure along with domestic chores, family life, and the maternal love of a woman. Religious or moral instruction was also central, as were physical disciplines like cold baths, military drill, and scheduled labor so that youth could participate as disciplined, industrious workers in the new imperial Japan (p. 52). Unfortunately, reformatories lacked resources and so could not hire qualified or enough personnel with the result that there were numerous escapes, some because street life was preferred and others to escape abuse by older youth (p. 54).

During the early 1900s, social studies of lower-class delinquency and slum housing reinforced the view that middle-class norms ought to be communicated to delinquents. The lower classes were treated as objects of ethnographic inquiry, and journalists explored the world of the underclass in sensationalist publications. Home, school, and work were the key elements in the vision of civilizing the underclass, along with laws that were intended to control not just delinquents but all young people in a broader project to counter feared social strife (Ambaras 2006, 64).

During this time a new discourse of *student degeneracy* emerged that expressed a moral panic about the dangers faced by the middle class from student boys and girls who organized themselves into gangs and committed public acts of violence using short swords and knives (Ambaras 2006, 69). Some students became aggressive political agitators and were labeled as delinquent (p. 74). Female students became objects of moral outrage and erotic fantasy and were blamed for drawing male students to popular amusement centers (p. 77). The extent of student delinquency was minor, however, when measured against a student population of fifteen thousand in 1912 and a police roundup of 347 students as delinquents with an additional six hundred justifying continued scrutiny. Delinquent girls were even fewer, perhaps only about forty (p. 83). Reformers' concerns again focused on deviations from the prescribed sex roles, class, and status that might impact the national project of "reproducing Japan's respectable classes" (p. 94).

One way of countering student degeneracy was to establish school surveillance programs. To this end, "student oversight departments" within schools were established. They operated like police agencies, sending inspectors to students' lodgings and interrogating their landlords and providing confidential reports to school authorities. Teachers patrolled public spaces where students congregated, and girls were forbidden to go out without a chaperone (Ambaras 2006, 91).

Modern Period (From 1913)

Juvenile protection began to expand from 1918 to the mid-1930s when the rise and collapse of the "Taisho Democracy" occurred as the country moved toward broader representational government through extensions of the franchise and the growth of political parties as well as extending international engagements. During the 1920s moral panics again erupted over fears of juvenile depravity as youth of different classes sought out sites of play and amusement such as cinemas and cafes. These fears of national collapse were exacerbated by the Great Depression and the collapse of Taisho Democracy that by 1932 gave way to authoritarianism and aggressive imperialism in Asia (Ambaras 2006, 98).

In 1922 the Juvenile Law was enacted, and by 1923 juvenile courts established in Tokyo and Osaka were using new methods of casework in responding to juvenile cases (Ambaras 2006, 98). The law applied to persons under age eighteen, and the prosecutor determined if a juvenile case should be referred to the adult court or the juvenile court. A high proportion of cases were sent to the adult court because prosecutors believed that all juveniles aged fourteen and older should be punished where no special circumstances existed. Even so, punishments were much less severe than

for adults (Tanioka and Goto 1996, 192). The policy approach emphasized protection as a form of social work that ought to be performed in a "spirit of social solidarity" (Ambaras 2006, 105).

From 1923 to 1937, juvenile courts in Tokyo, Osaka, and Nagoya handled about 240,000 cases with about two-thirds of cases in the Tokyo court not moving forward because they were considered too minor to warrant protection. This suggests the rapid increase in cases was due to increased reporting and not social unrest (Ambaras 2006, 106). Most cases involved working or unemployed males and offenses of theft, fraud, gambling, or assault. The courts utilized a network of ancillary agencies to police protective measures, and the Justice Ministry conducted outreach to secure public cooperation, including in 1928, "Juvenile Protection Days" featuring public lectures, media articles, and films (p. 109). The new juvenile courts effectively encouraged police to bring cases where previously they had given informal warnings and reprimands.

Generally, the public became more interested in delinquency as concerns and fears were fed by sensational media accounts. Notions that there was an obligation on all members of society to contribute to the growth of the whole polity and to offer protection where needed informed the attitude of the public and government. The Justice Ministry embraced this notion of collective social responsibility as it formulated juvenile policies for the juvenile system (Ambaras 2006, 100).

In this period, social policy initiatives included the promotion of forms of social work and casework, the establishment of children's shelters for vagrants, child counseling, and prefectures hiring child protection commissioners to conduct social work in the poor parts of the city. Volunteer, unpaid welfare commissioners, often local business owners, assisted in implementing campaigns focusing on thrift, morality, and reverence of the emperor (Ambaras 2006, 102). Monitoring children's conduct outside school meant that teachers gained a detailed knowledge of families and home conditions and reinforced notions about collective social responsibility. Overall, a range of actors, both public and private, were mobilized for surveillance, supervision, and socialization (p. 128).

In the 1920s and 1930s, reformers "often argued that young people's presence in the workforce rendered them particularly susceptible to delinquency" (Ambaras 2006, 130). This concern extended to forms of play, when for one or two days a month, youth could frequent the cheap and plentiful pleasures of the city (Ambaras 2006, 132). Work and play for males connected with the emergence of the new working woman, or "modern girl," in clerical and other service occupations. Girls began to work in restaurants and coffee shops, jobs seen by reformers as "morally dangerous" (p. 140). Modern girls wore Western clothing, enjoyed consumerism,[29] and were regarded by reformers as in need of surveillance and discipline. The police, for example, prohibited waitresses in bars and cafes from leaving work in the company of customers (p. 159). This challenge to established gender roles, together with perceptions of depravity associated with forms of play and pleasure, caused police "to apply raw coercive power against youthful behavior that contravened dominant notions of work, morality and gender" (p. 131).

Working-class youth culture in the 1920s repeated past patterns as youth, often armed with swords and knuckle-dusters, harassed people on the streets, mugged others, and created uproar in eating and drinking places. These youth, referred to as "locals" or "no-goods," congregated in cafes, coffee shops, and empty houses in the city; formed gangs; and fought with students in the streets (Ambaras 2006, 145). The continued policing of morals led Tokyo police to conduct roundups of students and others: in 1938 police conducted a three-day sweep and arrested about 7,300 youth in cafes, restaurants, billiard halls, and places of pleasure who were guilty only of spending their free time off campus (p. 162).

Police challenges to youth culture had been a feature of urban life since the turn of the century, but their response by the late 1930s intensified because of perceptions that modernization had "radically destabilized orthodox constructions of class, status, family, gender and sexuality" (Ambaras 2006, 164). By this time youth cultures had been repressed by police and citizen groups who jointly policed the streets and places of play and pleasure to "protect" students and workers (p.164).

In the period 1937 to 1945, Japan was involved in wars that required the mobilization of youthful industrial workers from the schools to support the war machine. It was estimated that by 1943, from 50 to 80 percent of industrial workers were aged between fifteen and twenty years (Ambaras 2006, 166). Fears of delinquency fueled an expansion of agencies considered essential to

ensuring that youth understood the significance of their labor, practiced self-improvement, and did not conceal any part of their lives from scrutiny. The policing techniques used in this period would continue for decades afterward to reinforce the Japanese social order (p. 167).

The high salaries earned by young factory workers caused authorities to be concerned they were wasting their salaries in movie theaters, cafes, and unlicensed brothels and that they would become delinquent when they had spent all their earnings. Rising salaries seemed to be associated with more assertiveness by youth when teenage workers resisted police attempts to arrest them for being "spendthrifts." Later, when wages dropped, the fear was that low wages would result in delinquency. In response, police followed their time-honored strategy of rounding up thousands of so-called delinquents (Ambaras 2006, 170). Wartime protection and socialization measures created "a dense net of surveillance agencies over Japanese working youth and their families" (p. 190).

Following the end of World War II, in 1947 the Prison Branch specialist in the U.S. occupation force in Japan ordered a total revision of the Juvenile Law and subsequently submitted a draft Juvenile Court Code based on a draft prepared by the U.S. National Probation Association (Morita 2002, 367). It included provisions for a *parens patriae* role for the court and that it would not be a criminal court. In 1948 a new Juvenile Law was enacted establishing the Family Court and defining juveniles as those under the age of twenty and generally giving effect to the U.S. proposals. The law made protective measures the focus of the Family Court, prohibited screening of cases by the public prosecutor, but did permit criminal trials of juveniles aged over sixteen (p. 367).

After the end of the U.S. occupation in 1952, there were attempts to revise the law because of criticism of the reduced role of the prosecutor and a perceived imbalance in favor of the welfare and protection approach as against accountability. In 1966 the Ministry of Justice produced an amendment proposal which provided for the prosecutor to participate in hearings, and later a more specific proposal after the U.S. Supreme Court decision in the *Re Gault* case which decided that in the United States, juveniles possessed the same due process rights as adults. However, the 1973 Japanese Supreme Court decision disagreed with the Ministry, noting that "the juvenile law adopts a nonadversary, inquiry approach to hearings because this mode is necessary to the application of the educational ideal in juvenile cases" (Morita 2002, 369). Finally, in 1977, the Justice Ministry abandoned its approach and compromised on participation by the prosecutor but subject to the discretion of the court, but even this never eventuated after opposition by the Japanese Bar Association (Morita 2002, 369).

In the 1960s, youth culture was characterized by student protests against the political establishment. From the end of the 1970s to the first half of the 1980s, an affluent society emerged in Japan (Kawasaki 1994, 189). During the late 1970s, a policy of preventing juvenile delinquency included measures that increased the size of the police force, establishing more police and community delinquency prevention programs and the enactment of the Business Affecting Public Morals Law, which further restricted youth behavior in public places (Yoder 2011, 21). In the 1980s, journalists began to pay close attention to youth culture, explaining a new type of youth, seen as individualistic, consumerist, and expressive (Kawasaki 1994, 191).

Following amendments to the Juvenile Law in 2000, the general approach to juvenile delinquency in Japan continues to favor the welfare approach that promotes rehabilitation and community participation in the treatment of young offenders. Nevertheless, the victims' rights movement and a conservative push for more punitive juvenile laws since the 1990s have impacted this overall welfare model (Elrod and Yokoyama 2006, 218). The revisions in 2000 were due to be reviewed after five years, based on research conducted into the effect of the revisions. While the experts and academics who compiled and reviewed these data supported a return to a more complete welfare model, this view was resisted by the public. Accordingly, the Juvenile Law was further revised in 2007 and 2008 to increase police powers to investigate and report on serious offenses, strengthen sanctions for probation violations, permit children over the age of twelve to be sent to juvenile training schools, and expand the rights of victims (Yokoyama 2015, 186).

It is important to note the changed nature of Japanese society in relation to youth issues. As an aging society, Japan had the oldest population worldwide in 2005, and the average life expectancy is expected to increase to eighty-eight years. In 1989 the fertility rate dropped to 1.57 when only 1.25 million births were recorded, due largely to women not marrying and giving birth. The average age women marry is now about thirty years, and illegitimate births outside marriage are rare. It is estimated that by 2025, almost 30 percent of the population will be aged sixty-five or older with barely two persons of working age supporting every retiree of sixty-five years and older. The population reached its peak of about 128 million in 2006. Conservative estimates suggest it will reduce by about 40 percent by the end of the century, but others suggest a reduction of 50 percent or even 70 percent, giving a population of about 40 million. There continues to be strong resistance to immigration from any source (Goodman 2012, 163).

Japan has few natural resources other than its youth, and as the population grows older and smaller, the burden placed on them, and consequently on their well-being, will increase. Therefore, the manner in which youth are socialized to meet the needs of the future is of crucial importance. These facts may account for many of the concerns that are expressed about nonconforming behaviors in Japanese youth (Goodman 2012, 164). As a result, Japan's aging population and low birth rate mean that parents have become more protective of their children and more susceptible to increased fear of crimes committed against juveniles, whether by adults or other juveniles (Yokoyama 2015, 190). At the same time, as the historical record reveals, authorities in Japan and the Japanese media are ready to label conduct delinquent "when subcultural values and traits are seen to be a threat to the status quo as an alternative lifestyle or just by their very difference clash with what the dominant subculture group propagates and upholds as culturally appropriate and normative lifestyles and behavior" (Yoder 2011, 10). According to Yoder (p. 10), this labeling occurs most often in relation to working-class youth and foreign migrants.[30]

Data suggest that youth have been the principal target of police and government action since 1945. From 1976 to 2008, offenses under the Penal Code committed by youth exceeded those committed by adults by between three and five times. In 2008, of all Penal Code offenses (excluding traffic cases) cleared by police, the percentage of youth offenders was 8.9 per 1,000 youth as compared to 2.4 per 1,000 adults for adult offenders. Predelinquency offenses (status offenses) more than doubled from 1972 to 1983, and in

2008 some 1.3 million youth were sanctioned for predelinquency, amounting to some 9 percent of the youth population with most citations for predelinquency being for curfew violations, smoking, drinking alcohol, unsound companionship, and gang activity (Yoder 2011, 37).

Japan: Youth Violence and Punitive Populism

For the first time since World War II, crime was a key issue in the 2003 elections in Japan. A survey in 2004 revealed that public concerns about crime had doubled since 1998: from 19 percent in 1998 to 40 percent in 2004. In the 1990s, a series of police scandals changed the way the media reported on law enforcement, prompted policy changes that ensured more minor offenses were reported,[31] and consequently boosted crime data. These events in turn resulted in the growth of punitive populism in Japan (Hamai and Ellis 2006, 157). Confidence in the police was shaken by crimes that included the stabbing to death of a business consultant and his wife in Tokyo, together with their eight-year-old daughter and the strangling of their six-year-old son, and the stabbing of twenty-one children and two teachers (eight of the children died) by a psychiatric patient who ran amok in an elementary school (p. 158).

Some have argued that several recent incidents of youth violence have been sensationalized in the media, causing a public fear of juvenile crime. Such incidents include a fourteen-year-old boy killing two children and injuring three others in Kobe in 1997. One of the victims was eleven years old, and the killer severed his head and placed it on a school gate. In 2003, a twelve-year-old boy pushed a four-year-old boy from the roof of an eight-story parking garage after he had molested him (Elrod and Yokoyama 2006, 215). In 2003, in Nagasaki, a twelve-year-old student admitted murdering a four-year-old boy who was abducted and killed in a parking lot, and in 2004, in Sasebo an eleven-year-old girl stabbed and killed her classmate because she had posted messages on an Internet bulletin board that criticized her appearance and weight (Hamai and Ellis 2006, 158).

A striking fact about juvenile violence in its various forms, some of which are discussed here, is that youth participate only marginally in discussions about causes and effects. Youth issues are seen as the province of "experts," and their claims are seldom challenged, resulting in adult-dominated categories and beliefs about youth problems in general (Toivonen and Imoto 2012, 16). Since most Japanese regard themselves as members of the middle class, it is their perspective that sets the boundaries for "proper" youth behavior and it is this group that decides which social issues concerning youth need to be brought to public attention (p. 23).

School violence and bullying has been perceived as a serious social problem since 1964 but began to attract media attention starting in 1985 when several victims of bullying *(ijime)* took their own lives. One was a thirteen-year-old student at a public high school who was found in a restroom at a train station (Sugimori 1998, 175). In 1994, another student committed suicide, stating in his suicide letter that he had been threatened by his classmates who had demanded that he pay them amounts between US$500 and US$1,200 (p. 176). It is arguable that the public grew less tolerant of any form of violence and therefore focused on violence and bullying in schools as serious violent crime declined (Yokoyama 2002, 331).

Bullying takes the form of physical assaults, verbal abuse, hiding belongings, making threats, and ostracism, and it may be prolonged. Victims are usually bullied by others in the same age group (Feldman 1998, 20). It is said that bullying may be the outcome of a school system that stresses homogeneity and that students sought, through bullying, to differentiate themselves from others (Sugimori 1998, 185). According to Yoder (2011, 45), students bully other students they regard as nonconformists, such as those who learn more slowly or more rapidly than others, students who are loners, and students who have resided overseas for some time.

There have been a number of "peaks" in reporting this phenomenon previously regarded as natural but defined as a social problem from the 1980s. The number of cases of bullying peaked in 1985, then again in the mid-1990s, and again in 2006, triggered by the suicide of a twelve-year-old girl in Hokkaido, with a dramatic increase from 20,143 cases in 2005 to 124,898 cases in 2006. Explanations for the increase include a requirement that both private and public schools report instances of bullying and an expansion of the definition of *ijime.* There has been a leveling off since 2006, but attention is now being focused on cyberbullying (Toivonen and Imoto 2012, 11–12).

After the suicides attributed to bullying, the government set up hot lines to report bullying and encouraged a public response, resulting in a high level of reporting (Feldman 1998, 21). It has been noted that *ijime* was first perceived to be a problem at a time of anxiety about the Japanese education system, including especially its focus on intensely competitive examinations. As a discourse about schooling, *ijime* has resulted not only in the creation of telephone hotlines but also in a "new profession of school counselling" and much medical and psychiatric research and "the new field of clinical educational studies" (Toivonen and Imoto 2012, 10).

We have seen how in the past, juvenile activities and youthful subcultures that were considered to violate Japanese cultural conventions and values were judged "delinquent," for example, youth engaging in consumerist play and pleasure activities. Modern-day Japanese constructions of delinquency have extended to categories of persons who, in the West, might be considered to have simply temporarily "dropped out" of society, but who, in Japan, evoke alarm and even fear because they refuse to conform to cultural and social expectations of close association and social interdependence. In Japan, youth "dropouts" may be labeled[32] as *Hikikomori,* a term used to describe a group of youth who have withdrawn from social life and have had no relationships outside of the family for more than six months.

Hikikomori do not work or receive education and sometimes simply remain at home for several years (Elrod and Yokoyama 2006, 215; Furlong 2008, 309). The condition has been diagnosed as a cognitive malfunction and therefore is treated generally as a health issue (in practice and in the scholarly literature), but in 2002 publicity was given to a *Hikikomori* who was said to have turned "into a violent tyrant in his own home" and whose mother felt she could only sleep safely in a car with the doors locked, thus linking the condition with delinquency (Watts 2002). In addition, the condition became associated with violence when the domestic media reported on a seventeen-year-old *Hikikomori* who left his isolation to hijack a bus and killed a passenger in the process. Linking *Hikikomori* to violence was fostered by psychiatrists and parental associations who speculated that up to 80 percent of such cases were associated with violence in the home. This perspective increased the likelihood that *Hikikomori* would be seen as an unstable group in need of control (Horiguchi 2012, 128).

Andy Furlong (2008, 313) notes that two other crimes associated with *Hikikomori* involved the murder of a primary school student in Kyoto and the abduction of a young woman in Niegata and suggests that as a social act, dropping out in Japan "is often viewed with suspicion," in part because Japan lacks the Western tolerance for "drifting" and "false starts" because of the need to "get it right" the first time in the Japanese labor market. The medicalization of the condition has been criticized, and generally its basis is contested. Some see the condition not as pathological but as a necessary process in some persons' lives and as a temporary retreat from the pressures of the world (Horiguchi 2012, 130).

Informal Social Controls in Japan

Japanese informal social controls can be traced back to the fourth century, when the Japanese adopted Confucianism and Buddhism and integrated them into the local religion of Shintoism, which stressed the importance of duty and obedience within the relationship of parents and children. Japanese still prefer to settle disputes informally and regard the law as the last resort. During the Tokugawa era, five-family associations were developed to control conduct in a community and to mediate local disputes. Today, thousands of volunteer probation officers continue to exemplify traditional social controls (Jiang et al. 2014, 37). The collectivist nature of Japanese society stresses the importance of group goals, and individuals will withhold personal opinions, preferences, and emotions when they differ from those of the group. Collectivists are sensitive and attentive to the expectations of the group, fulfill group demands, and conform to group opinions (Yamamiya 2003, 31).

Japanese cultural values and social practices and the nature of Japanese society have always fostered informal social control as a means of contending with nonconforming or delinquent youth. These values are to be found in the schools, family, and the workplace. Accordingly, juvenile crime is regarded as a public concern, and citizens have consistently involved themselves in responding to it through a variety of interventions. For example, town associations sponsor community activities for youth, and there are numerous nongovernmental organizations that undertake forms of youth work and that are commonly sponsored by police and government agencies (Elrod and Yokoyama 2006, 218–19).

Juvenile Guidance Centers, first established privately in 1952, are government-funded institutions since 1964 that engage in crime prevention programs, including street patrols in areas where youth are known to congregate, counseling parents and youth, and improving the role of the community as socializer of children (Elrod and Yokoyama 2006, 219). In 1997, Juvenile Guidance officers cautioned about 366,000 juveniles while making street patrols and provided individual counseling to 156,000 youth (Yokoyama 2002, 337).

Police provide formal controls through law enforcement but also, to an extent not found in most countries, engage in delinquency prevention[33] programs, including providing police counselors for drug abuse education and conducting conferences with schools. Schools and police work together on juvenile crime prevention, for example, through joint street patrols, and police may notify schools of students who have committed crimes (Yoder 2011, 22). Police departments in all prefectures have established Juvenile Support Centers for offenders and victims of juvenile crime (Elrod and Yokoyama 2006, 219).

In spite of police efforts, police inaction has shaken confidence in conflict resolution *(kaiketsu)*. For example, in 1999, when a young woman complained to police that she was being stalked by a former boyfriend, police requested that she not pursue a formal complaint. She was subsequently stabbed to death, and three police officers were later found guilty of falsifying evidence in connection with the original complaint (Hamai and Ellis 2006, 162).

As noted in the historical account of the development of juvenile justice, schools have been, and continue to be, key institutional support mechanisms for social control. When a youth commits a delinquent act such as shoplifting, the shopkeeper may report the act to police and to the minor's school, which will usually impose a sanction against the youth. Teachers often patrol the neighborhood along with parents, and schools may have a set of rules about student conduct outside the school itself. Some schools even go so far as to prohibit students from obtaining a motorcycle or driver's license during their school years even though the law allows this after the age of sixteen or eighteen (Tanioka and Goto 1996, 203). At school, students must wear uniforms specific to their school, making it easy for police and others to make reports to the school when students violate school rules

outside of the school (Yoder 2011, 29).[34] In 2013, after a man had stabbed three boys in front of the gate of their elementary school, schools began to increase patrols around the schools, and teachers and parents brought children to and from school in groups (Yokoyama 2015, 190).

Ensuring conformity means that adolescence is a time when strict controls are exercised over youth by social control agents. Violating norms of conduct and creating youth subcultures with alternative lifestyles are not regarded as a natural outcome of adolescence as they are in the West. Consequently, youth are questioned about how they are dressed and their behavior by teachers, crime prevention patrols, and police, and "threats and punishments are used against them should they deviate from the myriad of controls imposed on them by adults" (Yoder 2011, 55). These threats and sanctions include being cited for predelinquency offenses or for violations of school rules and regulations.

As Mark Fenwick (2007, 125) points out, Japan's supposed "unique" culture and society has often been cited as an explanation for its low crime rates in criminology studies of Japan. Japan has succeeded in modernizing its society without long-term increases in crime, a rare event for countries that have modernized so rapidly. However, ascribing the Japanese success in crime control to its "unique" culture is problematic in that it often ignores aspects of Japanese society that are not "racially pure" and does not bring into the analysis other East Asian countries such as South Korea. As well, Japan experienced significant increases in crime in the immediate postwar period, subsequently throwing doubt on the explanation of cultural uniqueness. This suggests there needs to be a more detailed exploration of the association between Japanese cultural specificity and crime control in Japan.

Victims' Rights in Japan

Until quite recently, little attention was given to victims in Japan, but concern about juvenile crime has spurred a victims' rights movement which has in turn complained about perceived lenient treatment to serious juvenile offenders and called for stricter punishment for violent crimes (Elrod and Yokoyama 2006, 215). Victims now have the right to give an opinion to the Family Court or the Court probation officer concerning a juvenile in conflict with the law. There is also a right to information about decisions or dispositions of the Family Court. In response to victims' requests, the Court will provide the name and address of a juvenile offender, the disposition of the Court, and the reasons for the disposition. A victim may see the original record of adjudication, but information on the record that can be supplied is limited to facts concerning the delinquency and the reasons for it. The personal circumstances and background of the juvenile remain confidential (Yokoyama 2015, 185).

In revisions to the Juvenile Law made in 2007 and 2008, victims are granted the right to attend disposition hearings in the Family Court when a serious offense has been committed, but the Court must hear argument from the juvenile's lawyer before granting this permission. In addition, where a victim so requests, the Family Court must explain the reasons for a juvenile disposition in a closed session, and the right of victims to inspect the original record of the disposition has been expanded (Yokoyama 2015, 186–87).

Juvenile Law: Welfare or Control Model?

Current and past juvenile law in Japan is to be found in several laws: the Juvenile Law and the Correctional School Law, both passed in 1922; the Juvenile Training and Education Act 1933; and the Juvenile Law 1948. The age of criminal responsibility has changed over time: the 1880 Penal Code fixed it at twelve years, the 1907 Penal Code raised it to fourteen years, and the Juvenile Law 1948 raised it to sixteen years. It remained at sixteen until reduced in 2000 to fourteen years (Elrod and Yokoyama 2006, 217).

Japanese law recognizes three kinds of behavior as constituting delinquency depending on age and conduct:

1. crimes committed by youth aged fourteen and above but under twenty years of age,

2. acts committed by juveniles under the age of fourteen which would constitute a crime under the Penal Code if committed by a person fourteen or older, and

3. predelinquent juveniles "aged 20 and younger who had not yet committed a crime or delinquent act but who were considered likely to do so and were therefore in need of treatment." (Tanioka and Goto 1996, 193)[35]

Juveniles in categories 1 and 3 who are at least fourteen must be referred to the Family Court.

The 2000 revisions to the Juvenile Law introduced a more punitive approach to juveniles in conflict with the law. In the debate that preceded the revisions, aspects of the Juvenile Law were challenged. First, it was claimed that the Law was aimed only at protecting offenders and not victims or society in general. Second, some argued that the assumptions of innocence associated with childhood were outdated and that it was time for offenders to take responsibility for their actions. Third, the fact that juvenile records were erased when an offender reached the age of twenty suggested to some that the law lacked deterrent force and that minimal consequences were attached to criminality. Fourth, the Law lacked a punitive element; for example, the prosecutor was excluded from the Court, custodial sanctions were limited, and judges were reluctant to refer cases to the prosecutor for trial in the adult courts. The fact that the revisions might conflict with Japan's obligations under the CRC was not considered. The dominant public rhetoric expressed dissatisfaction with the protection principle and was one of penal populism (Fenwick 2006, 151).

In the revisions, the purpose of court proceedings was declared to be that all participants cause a juvenile to reflect on his or her offense ("soul searching") and that the Family Court causes a parent or guardian to realize their responsibility for the offense (Fenwick 2006, 153). As well, the Court was empowered to give instructions and a warning to parents, reflecting public concerns about poor parenting as a cause of delinquency (p. 154). These revisions reflect a conservative desire to focus on responsibility for illegal acts rather than on the protection of the juvenile (Yokoyama 2002, 327–28). They may also express the belief of the policymakers that protection begins after expressions of remorse and acceptance of accountability (Fenwick 2006, 153).

As well, the revisions reduced the age of criminal responsibility from sixteen to fourteen years, empowered Courts to incarcerate juveniles in Juvenile Classification Homes for longer periods, gave prosecutors more extensive involvement in the Family Court where serious offenses were being dealt with, gave victims greater access to Family Court records, gave victims the right to be heard in hearings in court, and created means to inform victims of court decisions (Elrod and Yokoyama 2006, 215–16).

Data on Juvenile Crime in Japan

Data suggest there was a steady increase in recorded juvenile crime from 1946 until it reached a peak in the 1980s. Since then, there has been an overall decline in recorded juvenile crime except for a period of three years in the mid-1990s. Despite the overall decline, slight increases have been indicated for homicide and robbery, with larger increases in school and domestic violence (Elrod and Yokoyama 2006, 216).

Apart from traffic violations, the most prevalent juvenile offense is theft, accounting for almost 61 percent of juvenile offenses handled by police in 2000. Embezzlement, which in Japan refers to the taking of bicycles, is the second most common offense, accounting for about 19 percent of offenses handled by police in 2000 (Elrod and Yokoyama 2006, 216). In 2011, 54.3 percent of convicted thefts by juveniles were for shoplifting and 18.8 percent for bicycle thefts (Yokoyama 2015, 190). There is a low incidence of both motor vehicle theft (1.1 percent) and breaking and entering and stealing (4.3 percent; p. 190).

According to Yokoyama (2002, 329), the peak of juvenile offending was in 1951 when the rate of juvenile offending was 9.5 per 1,000 youth between ten and twenty years of age. The second peak was 1964 when the rate rose to 11.9 per 1,000, and the third was in 1983 when the rate increased significantly to 17.1 per 1,000. However, this increase may reflect net-widening because of more active policing of juveniles for minor offenses. The rate for 1995 was 12.1, rose to 15.5 in 2003, and declined to 9.7 in 2011. The percentage of juveniles committing offenses under the Penal Code declined from 19.7 percent in 2004 to 11.8 percent in 2011. According to Minoru Yokoyama (2015, 189), "Japan no longer regards juvenile delinquency as a serious social problem." Net-widening may be the cause of a rise in the number of juveniles convicted of an offense under the Minor Offenses Law. An example is juveniles riding on a train but not paying the proper fare. Where previously the railway company would have taken no action if the youth had paid the deficit in the fare, now more youth are being reported to police for this offense. Police charge them with "entering without any due reason into a prohibited place" (p. 193).

During the third peak, female delinquency increased dramatically with the number of non-traffic female offenders rising from 11,866 in 1966 to 54,459 in 1983 (Yokoyama 2002, 332). The increase is arguably attributable to reduced police tolerance for female delinquency. After the third peak, the rate female delinquency declined to 12.1 in 1995 and then increased to 15.0 in 1998. After 1997, in response to sensational reports of juvenile crime, police began to "charge up," that is, to charge juveniles with more serious crimes than was the previous practice. Consequently, theft involving injury might be charged as robbery involving injury (p. 330).

Among all female offenders in 1998, the most prevalent offenses were theft (largely minor shoplifting) and embezzlement of bicycles (Yokoyama 2002, 333). There has also been an increase in females using illicit drugs, notably sniffing substances like thinner or toluene. Most juvenile offenses in Japan are committed by youth aged fourteen and fifteen years (Yokoyama 2002, 334).

Japanese Juvenile Justice System

The Family Court has jurisdiction over certain juveniles in conflict with the law. Police investigate allegations of juvenile delinquency and refer cases to the public prosecutor or directly to the Family Court when the offense or illegality is minor and punishable by a fine only. The prosecutor is nevertheless required to send the juvenile's file to the Family Court because only the Court has authority to decide the outcome of a juvenile case. In revisions to the law in 2007, police were given the right, in the case of serious offenses, to investigate and report directly to the Child Guidance Center when the child involved is below the age of criminal responsibility. The Child Guidance Center may refer the case to the Family Court for the possible imposition of educative measures.

In the case of youth under the age of fourteen, the Child Welfare Act applies. Child offenders or predelinquent children under fourteen must be referred to a Child Guidance Center, and the head of that Center may decide to refer the case to the Family Court (Tanioka and Goto 1996, 197). If not, the case is dealt with in accordance with the Child Welfare Act and is not taken to court. In a situation where the predelinquent is aged fourteen or more, the juvenile must be referred directly to the Family Court.

Family Courts are located in judicial districts within prefectures and staffed by professional judges. After a case has been referred, the Court will commence an inquiry and a probation officer will be assigned to conduct social inquiries into the case to assess the background and circumstances of the youth and his or her family. Victims are now entitled to give their views to probation officers and to the Family Court.

Pending the final disposition of a case, a judge may order protective detention in a Juvenile Classification Home operated by the Ministry of Justice and established under the Reformatory Law. Protective detention ordinarily lasts for no more than four weeks, but it can be extended for up to eight weeks following amendments to the law in 2000. In this period, further information can be obtained about the psychological state of the individual juvenile. This testing is known as an order for "measures for case and custody" (Tanioka and Goto 1996, 197).

At the conclusion of the background and circumstances inquiry, a judge reviews the file on the juvenile to decide whether the case should go to the Family Court or to a Child Guidance Center. When the judge decides there is no need for a hearing, he or she may dismiss the case as "dismissal without hearing" (Tanioka and Goto 1996, 197). In 1965, dismissals without a hearing comprised 55.7 percent of all juvenile cases, and by 1998 increased to 75.4 percent of all cases but fell to 68.7 percent in 2011 (Yokoyama 2015, 201; Yokoyama 2002, 343). Cases can be dismissed when the offender has confessed to the crime and shows remorse and an intention not to re-offend and when the parent or employer of the juvenile gives a commitment to work for the juvenile's rehabilitation (Morita 2002, 375).

Hearings are usually conducted by a single judge, are closed to the public, and are to be conducted in an informal "child-friendly"[36] manner. In the past, few juveniles contested charges brought against them, but as lawyers began to participate in cases from about the 1980s, the pattern changed and juveniles sometimes contest cases using adversarial techniques previously unknown in the Family Court. This shift prompted proposals by the Supreme Court, Ministry of Justice, and the Japanese Bar Association for amendments to the hearing procedure in 1999 that would have allowed adversarial hearings in serious crimes while maintaining the inquisitorial procedure for most cases. These proposals were seen as an attempt to introduce

due process to an unacceptable degree, and the proposals failed to secure government approval (Morita 2002, 377).

The public prosecutor does not appear in cases in the Family Court except in serious cases involving intentional killing or where a crime punishable by death, life imprisonment, or a term of imprisonment exceeding two years is charged (Elrod and Yokoyama 2006, 221–22). The scope of cases in which the prosecutor is permitted to appear was expanded in 2014 by revisions to the law passed by the parliament (Yokoyama 2015, 187).

Sanctions that can be imposed by the Family Court include probation, commitment to a home for training and education, commitment to a home for dependent children or to a Juvenile Training School, and an order that parents take measures to support the juvenile and his or her well-being (Elrod and Yokoyama 2006, 222).

Probation

Juveniles can be placed on probation up to the age of twenty. Probation is commonly used in traffic cases but also for robbery and status offenses. In 2000, about 20 percent of all Family Court dispositions were probation. Probationers are supervised by volunteer probation and parole officers (*hogoshi*) and in 1999 these numbered 48,815 (Yokoyama 2002, 346). The average age of volunteers rose from about fifty-three years to about sixty-three years in 1999, thus appreciably widening the generation gap. The percentage of female volunteers increased from 7 percent in 1953 to 23 percent in 1999 (p. 346). Probation orders may include conditions such as community work (Elrod and Yokoyama 2006, 223). When a probationer violates probation conditions, he or she receives a warning. Now, under revisions made to the law in 2007, when the warning is disregarded and the violation continues, the probationer may be referred back to the Family Court (Yokoyama 2015, 186).

Juvenile Training School (JTS)

JTS' are categorized according to the age, criminal background, and characteristics of a juvenile. *Primary schools* are for youth aged fourteen or fifteen, *middle schools* for those aged sixteen but younger than twenty, and *advanced schools* for those at least sixteen but younger than twenty-three with more serious criminal backgrounds. There are also *medical schools* for those between fourteen and twenty-six with serious mental or physical disorders. Schools are single sex. Treatment programs are conducted in these schools, including education, life skills, and vocational training, and they make use of volunteers in their programming (Elrod and Yokoyama 2006, 224). Under the 2007 revisions to the law, a child over the age of twelve years may now be sent to a JTS (Yokoyama 2015, 186).

Commitment to a JTS may be for a short period (less than one year) or until the youth reaches the age of twenty years. A more punitive approach since 2000 has resulted in an increase in the number of commitments (Elrod and Yokoyama 2006, 223). Once a treatment program in a JTS is completed, a juvenile is eligible for discharge and juveniles are commonly released from a JTS on parole. A more punitive approach since 2000 resulted in an increase in the number of commitments (Elrod and Yokoyama 2006, 224), but this has now been reduced. Consequently, from 4,758 commitments in 1983, there was an increase to 6,052 in 2000 with more than 60 percent receiving long-term commitments. By 2011 there was a decrease in commitments to 3,486 (Yokoyama 2015, 203).

Residents of a JTS must satisfy a detailed catalogue of regulations that regiment activity throughout the day, from early "morning music" to "lights out." The disciplinary regime complements the objective of training residents to follow a law-abiding lifestyle. Every rule must be observed and never questioned, and marks are deducted for rule violations. Earning demerits for violating rules means a longer period of detention in the JTS (Metzler 2003, 229). Rigorous physical training is a key element in the training and often pushes residents to their physical limits, but toughening the body is seen to be building resistance to falling back into delinquency.

The educational program commonly absorbs nearly fifty hours each week, including evenings and weekends, and there is little provision for leisure, which residents are urged to use for self-reflection or for cleaning their rooms (Metzler 2003, 230). Social skills training features role plays to internalize the correct rules of social conduct displayed by an "orderly member of society," including how to behave correctly when using the telephone and when dealing with friends, superiors, colleagues, and family members. Thus Metzler contends that the inculcation of such norms and values goes far beyond the need to learn to be a law-abiding citizen and extends to leading a "conforming life" (p. 243). In this sense, time spent in a JTS can be seen as "a rigorous continuation of scholastic education" (p. 243). Former residents have described the experience of the regime in a JTS not as education and assistance but as severe punishment (p. 248).

Juvenile Prisons

There are eight such prisons in the country to accommodate juveniles tried as adults and sentenced to a term of imprisonment by the District Court. Youth between the ages of sixteen and twenty may be sent to these prisons: if younger than sixteen they must be sent to a JTC until they are sixteen and are then transferred to a Juvenile Prison. In 2000 there were only fifty commitments to all eight Juvenile Prisons which provide individualized treatment for youth. A more punitive approach since 2000 has resulted in an increase in the number of commitments (Elrod and Yokoyama 2006, 225).

Child Education Training Homes, Homes for Dependent Children

These institutions are established under the Child Welfare Law. Child Education Training Homes are operated by the national or prefectural governments but may also be privately operated and are intended to care for delinquent or pre-delinquent youth. Homes for Dependent Children house dependent, abused, or neglected children and may be government or private operations (Elrod and Yokoyama 2006, 224). In 2011 only 270 children were sent to these homes (Yokoyama 2015, 202).

Juvenile Classification Homes

In 2011 there were fifty-two such homes. With police arresting more juveniles in the late 1990s, the number of admissions to these homes rose from about 23,000 in 2003, but admissions in 2011 totaled only about 13,000 (Yokoyama 2015, 200). These homes are for the temporary detention of juveniles under inquiry before referral to the Family Court.

Transfer for Trial as Adult

The judge may refer a case to the prosecutor where a youth aged fourteen or older (recently lowered from sixteen) is charged with a serious offense punishable by death or imprisonment. In such a case, he or she will be dealt with as an adult, analogous to the U.S. practice of trying juveniles as adults. Where a youth over the age of sixteen is alleged to have committed homicide or has intentionally caused another's death, the Family Court must transfer the case to the prosecutor subject to certain exceptions. The transfer is made to the District Court for trial as an adult. Under the Juvenile Law, the death sentence may not be imposed on a youth who is convicted of a serious offense and is under the age of eighteen years at the time of the offense (Elrod and Yokoyama 2006, 222). In 2014 the parliament passed a revision to the law that increases from fifteen to twenty years the maximum sentence that can be imposed on a youth under the age of eighteen where an offense is punishable with a life sentence for an adult.

Comment

The historical record of juvenile delinquency and juvenile justice in Japan reveals recurring moral panics brought about by public and police constructions of juvenile delinquency thought to be present in youth social practices and subcultures, and an intense police and citizen surveillance of youth to ensure conformity with Japanese values and customs. The iterative themes emerging from the Edo period until modern times show that juveniles have been subjected to "a regime of socialization premised on the notion that every aspect of a young person's life should be rendered visible and subject to intensive guidance" (Ambaras 2006, 192). Whenever youth displayed individualistic behavior or flouted social mores, they rapidly became the subject of police attention and arrests and roundups.

There are parallels between the U.S. "child savers" and the middle-class reformers of Japan: both saw their task as the inculcation of middle-class values in troubled juveniles, and both regarded a proper home environment, strict discipline, and work as the principal reform instruments. Industrialization, the growth of the cities, and social change generally arising out of World War II all played major roles in exacerbating the fears of citizens that youth might escape social control. Each moral panic that challenged middle-class values was met with a policing response and net-widening. In Japan, the outcome has been peaks of what appeared to be increases in juvenile criminality, followed by periods of low delinquency. Nowadays, there is little to fear in terms of juvenile crime other than aberrant individual acts of violence or behaviors that cause public alarm because of media sensationalism and which are often simply attempts to display individualism.

Recent policy changes, apparently in response to punitive populism as well as some weakening of aspects of the system of informal social control, have led one commentator to express the view that the outcome of the 2000 revisions was that while the rehabilitative ideal was not entirely displaced, it had "lost its preeminent status" and that Family Court proceedings now more closely resembled proceedings before an adult criminal court (Fenwick 2006, 153). As well, the reforms introduced a new moral perspective of accountability, remorse, and culpability (p. 155). The expansion of victim rights follows a Western trend that favors victims' interests and concerns in responding to criminality, adult or juvenile. Overall, Japanese policymakers have resisted any radical changes to the original juvenile justice model, which in any event already allowed for delinquents to be taught the benefits of a "conforming life" within Japanese society.

PEOPLE'S REPUBLIC OF CHINA

China has around 340 million juveniles under the age of eighteen years, accounting for about 26 percent of its population (Zhao et al. 2015, 138). During the period commencing with communist rule in 1949 until 1966, China had no juvenile justice system, and delinquency was dealt with either by the adult court system or through neighborhood committees. In that time, delinquency was not seen as separate from overall crime and was regarded as a remnant of the capitalist system (Wong 2001, 495). In 1966 the Cultural Revolution encouraged youth to undertake ideological struggles with their parents, schools were closed, and traditional values and practices challenged. As society became chaotic, youth became involved in antisocial conduct in the absence of adequate parental controls.

In the late 1970s and early 1980s, an increase in juvenile crime was attributed to the Cultural Revolution, probably as a means of diminishing the influence of the so-called Gang of Four (Wong 2001, 496). In 1982 the first national conference on juvenile delinquency was convened during which the causes of delinquency were discussed. The conference attendees agreed that crime could be the result of defects in social systems, including schools and the family. A need was recognized there to reverse the Maoist policies of deemphasizing education by strengthening reeducation and improving discipline within the family unit (Wong 2001, 497). In 1985, Shanghai passed a Juvenile Protection Law (Wong 2004, 56).

The juvenile justice system began to develop from the 1980s, with significant events being the enactment of the Juvenile Protection Law in 1991 and the Juvenile Delinquency Prevention Law in 1999 (Zhang 2008, 149). The first juvenile court opened in Shanghai in 1984 in the form of a panel to hear juvenile cases. There are now more than 3,300 juvenile courts in the country (p. 154).

In China, the term *juvenile delinquent* is not found in the law. Under law, those persons under the age of eighteen who commit crimes are termed *minors* (Ren 1996, 61). The term *youth* as used in China includes those in the age group fourteen to twenty-five. As a result, minors and youth are different but overlapping categories (Chen 2000, 334). The concept of *parens patriae,* meaning the state as protector of minors, is not reflected in Chinese law, which continues to hold families responsible for the delinquency of their children (Ren 1996, 63).

The minimum age of criminal responsibility in China is fourteen years. Youth aged between fourteen and eighteen are within the jurisdiction of the juvenile court. A juvenile court hearing is informal and is closed to the public. According to the law, education is the principal measure for dealing with delinquency and punishment is considered a subsidiary measure. Since 1996, the death penalty has not applied to juveniles who were aged under eighteen at the time the offense was committed, but before that time, juveniles aged from sixteen to eighteen were subject to the suspended death penalty of two years[37] if the crime was especially grave (Bakken 1993, 52; Zhang 2008, 154).

The Chinese model of delinquency control differs from Western models in that it blends formal and informal controls (see "Informal Social Controls in China"). Another variance is that there are no special procedural laws for dealing with juvenile offenders such as would guarantee due process or differentiate juvenile from adult criminal procedures. Instead, a model of procedure has been endorsed by the Supreme People's Court and is applied in many courts (Dai and Pi 2006, 191).

Given the informal tradition and the Maoist conception of the "mass line" police, schoolteachers, parents, and neighborhood associations can be involved in designing solutions to youth behavioral issues at an early stage and without recourse to the juvenile justice system. Police involvement includes the power to place children in detention as an administration measure for violations of rules and for acts that would be regarded as status offenses in common law Western jurisdictions.

Juvenile Laws in China

Significant increases in juvenile crime in the 1980s prompted the government to devise a comprehensive strategy that required various government institutions to combine together in a kind of "whole of government" approach to deal with delinquency (Zhang and Liu 2007, 543). Efforts were made to standardize juvenile justice practice and procedure among the different juvenile courts, and the 1996 revised Criminal Procedure Law and 1997 revised Criminal Law mandated the legal procedures to be applied in juvenile cases. The 1991 Juvenile Protection Law (JPL) provides a comprehensive legal regime for the protection of minors and their interests, and sees juvenile protection as a delinquency prevention measure. The JPL

- defines juveniles as youth below the age of eighteen years;

- provides that education is the principal measure for dealing with delinquency and punishment is a subsidiary measure;

- requires that juveniles be separated from adults when kept in custody or for punishment;

- states that juvenile trials are not open to the public and that information about juvenile cases may not be disclosed; and

- states that families, schools, government agencies and other social organizations are to assume responsibility for protecting juvenile rights. (Zhang and Liu 2007, 545)

The 1999 Juvenile Delinquency Prevention Law, first formulated in 1994, represents the government reaction to rising delinquency rates (Zhang 2008, 154). In terms of prevention, it focuses on the delivery of moral and legal education as both a pre-delinquency measure and as a means of preventing minor delinquency escalating into serious offenses, and it targets recidivism prevention. The law states a principle of "education first, and punishment second" (Zhang and Liu 2007, 545) and for this purpose stipulates a series of educational agencies as well as neighborhood committees that should implement education so as to "nip crime in the bud" (Zhang and Liu 2007, 546). The law specifies acts (status offenses in Western systems) that should be prevented; these acts include truancy, running away from home, carrying weapons, fighting, begging with force, gambling, possessing pornography, entering non-juvenile places of entertainment, and damaging public order and morality. Parents are allotted the primary responsibility in preventing status offenses and minor acts of delinquency and must educate their children not to smoke or drink and must not allow them to live alone.

The JPL describes a set of serious offenses that do not warrant criminal punishment (basically aggravated or repeated status offenses) and provides for informal and formal rehabilitation measures, including the collaboration of schools and parents to enforce discipline and supervision. The formal measure is committal to a work-study school which is referred to as an administrative and not a judicial measure for juveniles (Zhang and Liu 2007, 547).

The responsibilities of juveniles are also stated in the JPL. They include obeying laws; establishing self-respect, self-discipline, and self-development; and "strengthening tendencies toward law abiding behavior and self-protection, and enhancing awareness of resisting instigation and inducement to crime" (Zhang and Liu 2007, 548).

Preventing recidivism is also an objective of the JPL and is to be accomplished through education, with punishment being a supplementary measure. Parents, schools, and communities are to adopt effective measures to rehabilitate those

younger than fourteen, parolees, and those serving noninstitutional punishments. The law gives police the right to warn and discipline parents who fail to properly supervise and monitor their children's behavior (Zhang and Liu 2007, 549).

Essentially, the JPL continues the policy of the *mass line*[38] for social control developed under Mao in that it represents a total society strategy for promoting delinquency prevention. This means there should be a concerted effort and mobilization by all stakeholders to prevent and control delinquency (Zhang and Liu 2007, 551).

Juvenile Crime Data—China

Sources of data on juvenile crime and delinquency in China are the *Law Yearbook of China* and the *China Statistical Yearbook*. These publications report the number of juvenile offenders, the percentage of juvenile offenders among all offenders, and the number of incarcerated juveniles. No data on types of offenses by juveniles are published. Generally, the data are considered unreliable, and making comparisons with other countries is virtually impossible (Zhao et al. 2015, 143). It is also important to note that juvenile crime data in China report only on crimes committed by minors and not on misbehavior and serious misbehavior (similar to status offenses and minor offenses in Western systems) which are often dealt with by administrative sanctions that can include lengthy periods of detention (p. 143). It is therefore difficult to provide any accurate figure about the scale of delinquency, especially since changes in the juvenile population are not taken into account.

Data show that during the 1950s to 1970s, juvenile offenses as a percentage of total crime ranged from 0.2 percent to 3 percent while during the 1990s the percentage ranged from 15 to 30 percent (Zhang 2008, 149). According to Børge Bakken (1993, 38), youth offenses among those aged fourteen to twenty-five years accounted for about 20 percent of total crime in 1952, increasing to 74.1 percent in 1989. Among those aged fourteen to eighteen, during the 1950s to 1960s juvenile offenses accounted for 0.2 to 0.3 percent of total crime, increasing to 19.9 percent in 1989 (p. 39). Bakken could not explain this increase by reference to a change in the youth population. In 1956, youth aged fourteen to twenty-five comprised 24.4 percent of population over fourteen but committed only 18 percent of total crime. By 1988, this group made up 34.3 percent of the population but committed 75.7 percent of total crime. In 1990, for youth aged fourteen to twenty-five, delinquency comprised 69 percent of total crime, falling to 60 percent in 1993, and rising again to 65 percent in 1996 (Wong 2001, 493).

In 1990, of all persons tried in criminal courts those aged fourteen to eighteen made up 7.2 percent of the total and numbered about 42,000. In 2001, the rate was 6.7 percent and numbered approximately 49,000. The range from 1990 to 2001 was between 6 and 7 percent, dropping to 5.9 percent in 1997 (Dai and Pi 2006, 206). By 2011, the number of juveniles tried in criminal courts had increased to 67,000, representing a 60 percent increase over twenty years and a rate of 6.49 percent. During the same period, China's population increased by about 18 percent. Zhao and colleagues (2015, 142) cite comparative figures for Hong Kong (for youth aged between ten and 20) where juveniles accounted for 16.9 percent of all crime in 2012; Macao in 2013 (for youth aged between thirteen and 20), 4.5 percent; Korea in 2010 (youth aged under eighteen), less than 3.6 percent; and Japan in 2013, where juvenile arrestees comprised 25.6 percent of all arrestees.

Informal delinquency controls are much less effective than in the past because in modern China since the 1970s large groups of youth have lived apart from the influence of their families, thus providing a basis for fears about disorder and delinquency (Bakken 1993, 47). Now, "young people have come to be seen as potential delinquents in need of closer adult supervision" and "may also break petty rules in an attempt to delineate a sphere of independence for themselves" (p. 48). Young independent women are said to be responsible for 90 percent of all crimes defined as "sexual transgressions," but this category of crime includes "promiscuous behavior" because the concept of prostitution is very widely defined (pp. 34, 49).

Patterns and types of juvenile crime and crime trends since 2000 in China were extracted from various area studies by Zhao and colleagues (2015, 141), who reported the following:

- Most juvenile crimes are property crimes, primarily robbery and theft, with violent crimes making up a small percentage of total juvenile crime but with an increase in the most serious violent crimes, including rape and homicide, which were formerly rarely committed by juveniles.

- Drug offenses have been increasing, and numerous crimes are committed to obtain money for drug purchases.

- Sexual assaults and juvenile organized crime have increased.

- Juvenile crime tends to be opportunistic rather than planned, and juveniles commit most crimes in groups, especially property crimes, and most crime occurs in public spaces.

- The average age of juvenile offenders is decreasing; in one city it has reduced from between sixteen and eighteen to between fourteen and sixteen and on average, from 2000 to 2007, the reduction has been two years.

- Most juvenile offenders have low levels of education, and in urban areas the majority of juvenile offenders are children of rural workers who have migrated to the cities from the country: the "migrant/floating population."

- There has been an increase in the number of female juvenile offenders.

Chinese Formal Juvenile Justice System

The approved form of procedure to be followed by juvenile courts is not fixed by law. Its elements include

- a pre-trial hearing that follows an inquisitorial form and investigates the social and family background of a youth and which relatives and teachers are invited to attend and offer views;

- an informal trial process that takes the form of a roundtable discussion;[39]

- the judge's delivery of a statement (before announcing the penalty) that aims to educate the juvenile against further criminality (Dai and Pi 2006, 192); and

- the preponderance of judges and lay assessors on most juvenile courts (Dai and Pi 2006, 205).

The 2012 Criminal Procedure Code contains a new chapter on juvenile criminal procedure addressing issues such as legal aid, presence of adults during the interrogation of juveniles, and conditional non-prosecution. In spite of these revisions and improvements, China cannot be said, in the Western sense of the term, to have a separate juvenile justice system because juveniles are regularly tried in criminal courts in the same way as adults and are subject to many of the same punishments as adults.

Prosecutions in the juvenile court are handled by prosecutors specializing in juvenile cases. They generally follow common rules and principles in dealing with juveniles, including that the prosecutor must approve a warrant of arrest of a juvenile, that as few arrests as possible should be authorized (Article 269, Criminal Procedure Code 2012), and that only dangerous juveniles should be placed in pre-trial detention. Once a case comes to the prosecutor, it will usually be prosecuted to trial. For example, data from Guangzhou City covering the period 1995 to 2000 indicate a prosecution rate of 84.45 percent of all juveniles arrested by police.

Prosecutors may also divert juvenile cases out of court by electing not to prosecute and placing juveniles liable to imprisonment for not more than one year with a Social Help and Educational Group (see section titled "Educational Supervision by a Social Help and Educational Group", p. 221) for three to twelve months conditional on showing repentance (Dai and Pi 2006, 204). This conditional non-prosecution is contingent on the prosecutor consulting the police and any victims and on the offender complying with a set of standard probation conditions (Zhao et al. 2015, 156).

Juvenile Misbehavior, Crimes, and Punishments

The Juvenile Delinquency Prevention Law creates three categories of deviance and criminality applying to juveniles (Dai and Pi 2006, 197):

- *Juvenile misbehavior.* This includes the following acts: truancy; staying away from home overnight; possessing prohibited knives and weapons; fighting, battering, and insulting others; forcefully demanding others' property; theft; vandalism; gambling; listening to, watching, or reading pornography; entering places of public entertainment where underage customers are prohibited; and other violations of social norms. Sanctions for violations of these misbehaviors are strengthening parental and school education of a juvenile and giving official warnings to parents who are failing in their parental responsibilities.

- *Serious juvenile misbehavior.* These acts constitute minor offenses that violate some laws and regulations, including gathering in groups to disturb public order, repeatedly possessing prohibited weapons despite warnings, assault, demanding property with force, disseminating pornography, engaging in prostitution or other activities in the sex trade, repeated theft and gambling, possessing drugs, and other violations of social norms. The sanctions for this kind of misbehavior are ordering parents and schools to strengthen education, surveillance, and management. In serious cases the sanctions are work-study school (*gongdu*), administrative punishment under the Administrative Punishment of Public Order Management Law, rehabilitation through labor, detention shelter for rehabilitation, mandatory detention in a rehabilitation camp, educational supervision by a Social Help and Educational Group.

- *Juvenile crimes.* The conduct that falls into this category constitutes "juvenile delinquency" but in China is referred to as "crime committed by minors." It therefore describes juveniles who commit offenses against the Criminal Law (Article 17). That law prescribes the punishment based on the age of the offender. The provisions state (Yisheng and Yujin 2006, 202, 203)

  o where an offender is fourteen but under eighteen and commits a serious crime such as homicide, rape, robbery or drug trafficking, he or she must be given a mitigated punishment;

  o where a person is under the age of sixteen, the head of his or her family shall discipline him or her and the person may be sent by the government for rehabilitation; and

  o where the circumstances show that the criminal act was minor and did not cause serious harm, no crime shall be considered to have been committed and the person may be reprimanded, or ordered to make a statement of repentance, or make an apology or pay compensation for any loss or be subjected to administrative penalty or sanction.

Work-Study Schools (Gongdu)

Juveniles aged twelve to seventeen who have committed serious juvenile misbehavior may be sent to a work-study school operated by the Ministry of State Education. These schools combine middle school education (compulsory for nine years in China) with light labor to teach moral values and self-discipline, and detention is normally for up to two years. Schools, police, neighborhood committees, and parents may request that a juvenile be placed in work-study (Zhang 2008, 155, 156), but parental approval, which was once required, is no longer necessary. The time spent in a school is not regarded as legal punishment (Dai and Pi 2006, 198). Schools are required to provide at least twenty-four hours of class instruction and twelve hours of work each week (Ren 1996, 73).

Administrative Punishment Under Public Order Law

Most of the acts specified as serious juvenile misbehavior also constitute violations of this law, and police have the power to impose punishment for a violation by a fine or administrative detention not exceeding two weeks. According to data for 1991, in that year, violations of this law by juveniles accounted for 19.60 percent of all such violations. In 2003 there were about 4.8 million violations recorded by all persons, adult and juvenile (Dai and Pi 2006, 198, 199).

Reeducation Through Labor (laodong jiaoyang)

This punishment can be ordered for juveniles between the ages of fourteen and eighteen for periods of one to three years by a committee in which the police have the principal decision-making power, or by the juvenile court for criminal offenses or serious misbehavior (Wong 2004, 60). (It is also a principal sanction for adult offenders and is discussed in Chapter 6 as reform through labor [laogai]). In 1991, 2,656 juveniles were sent to reeducation through labor and this increased to 4,019 in 1995. Questions have been raised about the legitimacy of detaining juveniles for such lengthy periods through administrative rather than judicial action (Dai and Pi 2006, 200).

Detention Shelter for Rehabilitation (shou rong jiao yang)

In practice, this form of detention by administrative order is used for homeless juveniles who have committed acts of serious misbehavior. In 1991, 1,747 juveniles were sheltered for rehabilitation and by 1994 this number had risen to 2,221 (Dai and Pi 2006, 201).

Mandatory Detention in a Rehabilitation Camp

Offenders over the age of fourteen or who are engaged in sex-related businesses may be sent to these camps for six months to two years. This sanction is considered less severe than reeducation through labor. It is also used for those addicted to drugs and if, after three attempts the addiction has not ceased, the offender may be sent to reeducation through labor. There are no separate camps for juveniles, but they are kept separate within a camp (Dai and Pi 2006, 201).

Educational Supervision by a Social Help and Educational Group

This measure is not considered to be administrative or criminal punishment and is a program that targets juveniles between thirteen and eighteen who have committed serious misbehavior or have been expelled from their work unit or from school for discipline violations. It is intended to be used as an alternative to detention (Wong 2004, 59). Juveniles released from prisons or from work-study schools and who have not displayed sufficient repentance for their acts and require supervision can be included in the program. Juveniles sent to the program are supervised and monitored by a group of between three and five persons who are tasked to rehabilitate them. Since the 1980s more than one million such groups have existed (Dai and Pi 2006, 202). This measure can be used as a form of probation for crimes committed by minors (p. 206).

Reformatories

Reformatories are correctional and rehabilitative institutions to which juveniles aged fourteen to eighteen are committed for serious offenses following adjudication by a juvenile court. They apply the principle of reeducation through labor and the period of committal ranges from one to three years (Zhang 2008, 155, 156). If they reach eighteen while still serving a sentence, they are transferred to adult prisons (Dai and Pi 2006, 208).

Generally, it is contended that the sanctions regime for juveniles places too much emphasis on labor and gives insufficient attention to education and training. In practice, youth are often required to work extra hours and labor is prioritized over study. As well, long-term detention does not address the causes of delinquency, which are often located in poverty, unemployment, and lack of opportunity (Wong 2001, 503).

The legal policy of "leniency to those who confess and severity to those who resist" is said to negate any form of due process for juveniles because youth will confess to acts they did not commit in order to receive a more lenient sanction (Wong 2001, 503). Generally, it is said that the Chinese juvenile justice system follows a crime control or justice model but with an increased emphasis on education rather than punishment (Zhao et al. 2015, 150).

Informal Social Controls in China

Like Japan, China has traditionally relied on informal social controls to maintain social cohesion and prevent crime. Confucianist thinking holds that if a ruler behaves correctly, the people will obey without orders but when the ruler does not, the people will not obey. The concept of a ruler as a figure of authority extends to parents, teachers, and government officers. Obedience and responsibility are implicated in five Confucian relationships of ruler and ruled, father and son, husband and wife, elder to younger brother, and friend to friend. Confucian beliefs privilege moral over legal control because moral controls are internalized from birth, while legal controls are imposed externally and may only be followed because of compulsion and not because of lengthy socialization (Jiang et al. 2014, 37). These beliefs, low levels of personal mobility, a strong family and clan system, and the collectivist nature of Chinese society created the traditional framework for social control (Jiang et al. 2014, 37).

Given the radical changes that have occurred in Chinese society since the 1970s, including vastly increased mobility, rising crime, corruption by leaders at all levels, and increased individualism among the young, it is arguable that, at least in the urban areas, informal controls are no longer effective alone and that a combination of formal and informal controls are now needed for social harmony. In fact, increases in crime have resulted in calls for increased formal controls and better policing and law enforcement (Jiang et al. 2014, 38). Nevertheless, as discussed in Chapter 4 on policing in China, informal controls that rely on the "mass line" are still thought to be efficacious in crime prevention and control in the cities. Similarly, grassroots organizations like village committees continue to play a role in policing communities.

Informal controls include a Residents' Committee, a security and defense committee, and a mediation committee. The function of the Residents' Committee is to implement government policies concerning youth and to coordinate the activities of all neighborhood bodies. The Security and Defense Committee is tasked with education and awareness on legal and public safety issues, helping to maintain public order, assisting police, and reporting unusual occurrences. This committee may impose sanctions on juveniles who commit minor acts of delinquency and are considered to be acting beyond parental control. The Mediation Committee is to resolve neighborhood conflicts. These committees are voluntary bodies operating at the grassroots level (Wong 2001, 498).

Bang-jiao programs, which deliver community-based rehabilitation, function as social support groups and comprise parents, relatives, friends, a representative from the Neighborhood Committee, and a police officer. The program takes minor offenders, those released from correctional institutions, and persons on parole from such institutions (Zhang 2008, 156).

Youth released from reform institutions may receive a form of aftercare in the community, usually in the form of work in the community that is supervised by work units or neighborhood committees (Wong 2001, 499, 500).

Community-based informal controls have been criticized for being more concerned with enforcing ideology than with the reform of the individual offender; for nonstandard decision making in the absence of a law or set of regulations to guide activities with damaging results in terms of public confidence; for the local nature of these organizations where many members are familiar with or are even related to offenders, giving rise to a risk that decisions may not be totally objective; and for the committee's lack of representativeness because they rely on the elderly in the community for members—there is no financial compensation to attract others (Wong 2001, 500, 501). It is also contended that these committees should act with more transparency. It has proved difficult to assess their effectiveness.

Comment

The Chinese juvenile justice system is generally depicted as following the justice/crime control model. Its harsh sanctions, especially those authorizing nonjudicial detention of juveniles, are not found in most juvenile systems. Court-ordered detention appears less concerned with ensuring that loss of liberty is a last resort (as stipulated by the CRC) and more intent on punishing acts perceived to be antisocial and that in the West would constitute only status offenses. Commentators have described the Chinese system as having "a social control orientation" and as being a blend of "informal control" or "low level institutionalization" and as expressing "formal control" and "a surveillance approach" (Wong 2004, 57). Wong points out that the 1984 Shanghai juvenile court was not modeled on Western practice. He believes that the "practices of judicial officials and judges are highly arbitrary" (p. 57), that there is currently a strong emphasis on political education and labor, and that the system offers less protection of child rights and fewer programs for rehabilitation than are commonly found in Western systems (p. 62). The informal controls exercised over juveniles, originating in cultural and political practices, remain a distinguishing factor in Chinese juvenile justice. According to Wong (p. 64), about 55 percent of juvenile offenders are dealt with informally and the remaining 45 percent are "likely to be placed in Work Study Schools or Re-education through Labor institutions." Nonjudicial placement in various programs is common practice, especially by police.

Generally, no separate juvenile justice system exists in China, thus increasing the likelihood that a crime control model will be followed, and there are doubts about the capacity or willingness of the judges dealing with juveniles to follow the admittedly loosely constructed juvenile laws. Juvenile justice in China, as compared to systems elsewhere, meets the description of juvenile justice "with Chinese characteristics."

GLOBALIZING JUVENILE JUSTICE

In this section we examine the notion that there has been a convergence of juvenile justice systems around a more punitive model, crime control/justice, and explore the role and effect of the CRC in juvenile justice policy. Both the supposed convergence and the CRC are instances of the globalization of juvenile justice through the migration of juvenile justice policies from the West and through international standard setting by the CRC and its associated instruments.

Convergence and Juvenile Justice Policy

Some argue that globalization processes have caused both adult and juvenile justice systems to converge around a more punitive model, especially in the global North. One reason given for this supposed convergence is economic: it is claimed that international capital will only move into countries that maintain similar policy and justice environments. Another is that free market, neoliberal perspectives support a reduction in welfare models of justice and a move toward privatization and accountability associated with stricter penal policies (Muncie 2007, 17). In the juvenile justice field Muncie (p. 18) contends that the view that juvenile justice has become a crime control and justice model, as opposed to a welfare model, because of globalization "can be sustained only at the highest level of generality." While it may be correct that globalization poses a challenge to countries to conform to a model of juvenile justice that is largely U.S. inspired, analysis tends to show that countries mediate global forces and adapt and change them to meet local circumstances and needs (Muncie 2007, 19). Anthony Giddens (1999, 3) for example, has argued that in fact "globalization is the reason for the revival of local cultural identities in different parts of the world. . . . Local nationalisms spring up in response to globalizing tendencies."

In Europe, the mandates of the CRC concerning the best interests of the child and the European Convention on Human Rights constrain attempts to erode the concepts of child protection and child rights. Thus, while a number of countries (including France) have added punitive elements to their juvenile justice systems, there is evidence that overall, child protection remains the prevailing ideology and that the United States and the England and Wales models of justice and crime control have not been adopted (Muncie 2007, 36). Sonja Snacken (2010, 281) has suggested that the resistance to penal populism[40] in Europe is attributable to the welfare state orientation of European constitutional democracies allied with a concern for democracy, the rule of law, and human rights such as are found most clearly in the Scandinavian countries. Accordingly, globalization becomes only one element in a complex mix of processes that include the strength of public opinion and political responses and strategies that impact juvenile justice policy (Muncie 2007, 49).

The case studies of Japan and France discussed in this chapter indicate that while changes in law and practice that have occurred in each have reinforced the crime control elements in their systems, these revisions are not so radical that they challenge the foundational principles of juvenile justice in these countries. Consequently, while an observable tension has arisen between punishment and education/rehabilitation in the adjudication of cases that did not previously exist, any globalizing trends toward punitiveness have been contested by local beliefs and values. The more extreme crime control models associated with juvenile systems in the United States and England and Wales are not found in Japan and France.

Convention on the Rights of the Child and Associated Instruments

Over the past twenty-five years, the international community has developed juvenile justice standards through the United Nations and regionally through the Council of Europe. Supplementing the international instruments that bind states are nonbinding declarations and statements that have produced codes of "soft law" concerning young offenders and their rights. At the international and regional levels, the following are relevant to juvenile justice:

- The Convention on the Rights of the Child 1989, Article 40

- United Nations Standard Minimum Rules for the Administration of Juvenile Justice (the Beijing Rules), 1985

- United Nations Standard Minimum Rules for Non-custodial Measures (the Tokyo Rules), 1990

- United Nations Guidelines for the Prevention of Juvenile Delinquency (the Riyadh Guidelines), 1990

- General Comment No. 10 (2007) of the Committee on the Rights of the Child on Children's Rights in Juvenile Justice

- Guidelines of the Committee of Ministers of the Council of Europe on Child-Friendly Justice, 2010[41]

The CRC expresses the concepts that children possess rights and have agency and elaborates these. For our purposes, the key article is Article 40, which deals with juvenile justice, and especially with due process rights. The due process rights stated in Article 40 are those that apply to adults, except that children are given the additional right to have their privacy protected at all stages of proceedings.

In 1985 the United Nations adopted the UN Minimum Standard Rules on the Administration of Juvenile Justice (the Beijing Rules) intending that they stand as a model for national juvenile justice systems as representing best international practice. They apply to "all juveniles in conflict with the law" and therefore include status offenses as well as acts constituting crimes. Similarly, the Tokyo Rules and the Riyadh Guidelines set standards that, according to the CRC Committee (2007, para. 4), should be integrated into all juvenile justice policies. The Tokyo Rules contain a set of basic principles to promote the use of noncustodial measures, as well as minimum safeguards for persons subject to alternatives to imprisonment. The Riyadh Guidelines state that youth justice policies should not criminalize children for minor criminal acts and provide a detailed strategy for preventing juvenile delinquency. Collectively, Beijing, Tokyo, and Riyadh, if enacted in legislative form, would meet international standards of best practice and policy for a country's juvenile justice system.

The Council of Europe Guidelines aim to "serve as a practical tool for member states in adapting their judicial and nonjudicial systems to the specific rights, interests and needs of children" (Preamble to Guidelines) and draw on decisions of European institutions, including the European Court of Human Rights, in formulating a comprehensive statement of children's rights in judicial proceedings and other proceedings involving children. The Guidelines endorse alternatives to judicial proceedings such as mediation, diversion, and alternative dispute resolution. Restorative justice and victim offender mediation are examples of such techniques, and both have gained currency worldwide, with restorative justice being the primary tool in the New Zealand juvenile justice system.[42]

In terms of international standards of juvenile justice then, these international and regional instruments set rules of best practice, which in the case of CRC principles bind state parties to the CRC. They constitute collectively a globalization of juvenile justice (Muncie 2009, 361). In this section we examine the principal international standards. To what extent do states adhere to them?

Status Offenses

Status offenses are behaviors that can only be committed by children, such as truancy and running away from home. Japan and China prescribe numerous status offenses as do the U.S. states.[43] In the United States, according to Thomas Bernard (2010, 16), since the time of the Puritans, reformers have tried to control children's behavior (especially girls' behavior) that they perceived to be offensive or immoral, even while it was not criminal. The effect, therefore, has been to sanction and punish children for noncriminal acts, which, if performed by adults, would not be punishable based on the argument that status offenses indicated signs of future criminality (in Japan, these behaviors are called "predelinquent" and in China "misbehavior" and "serious misbehavior"). This contradiction has led to arguments for decriminalizing status offenses or at least providing that juveniles cannot be institutionalized for committing a status offense. In China, while some juvenile behaviors that would constitute status offenses in the West are not legally punishable as crimes, administrative sanctions are applied that can include institutionalization and reform through labor.

What international standard concerns status offenses? The CRC Committee stated in 2007 that the behaviors criminalized as status offenses "are often the result of psychological or socioeconomic problems." The Committee recommended that "State parties abolish the provisions on status offenses in order to establish an equal treatment under the law for children and adults." It adds that behaviors categorized in this manner "should be dealt with through the implementation of child protective measures, including effective support for parents and/or other caregivers and measures which address the root causes of this behavior."

"Best Interests of the Child"

This constitutes a fundamental principle of the CRC and in relation to juvenile justice systems requires that the best interests of the child should be the primary consideration. According to the CRC Committee (para. 10), this means "that the traditional objectives of criminal justice, such as repression/retribution, must give way to rehabilitation and restorative justice objectives in dealing with child offenders. This can be done in concert with attention to effective public safety."

Deprivation of Liberty as a Measure of Last Resort

The CRC Committee has stated that after completion of a trial in juvenile court, the law should provide the court with a range of alternatives to institutionalization and deprivation of liberty to ensure that, as required by Article 37(b) of the CRC, deprivation of liberty is used only as a last resort and for the shortest possible period of time. The Committee stated, "A strictly punitive approach is not in accordance with the leading principles of juvenile justice contained in Article 40(1) of the CRC" (Committee on the Rights of the Child, 2007, para. 71). Attention should be given not only to the circumstances and gravity of the offense, but also to the "age, lesser culpability, circumstances and needs of the child, as well as to the various and particularly long-term needs of the society" (2007, para. 71). Specifically, the Committee stated that no child under the age of eighteen at the time the offense was committed should be sentenced to life imprisonment without the possibility of release on parole (2007, para. 77).[44]

Death Penalty

Article 37(a) of the CRC affirms the international standard that the death penalty may not be imposed for a crime committed by a person who was under the age of eighteen years when the crime was committed. As the Committee notes (2007, para. 75), this stipulation "means that a death penalty may not be imposed for a crime committed by a person under 18 regardless of his/her age at the time of trial or sentencing or of the execution of the sanction." In March 2005, the U.S. Supreme Court in a 5–4 decision prohibited the execution of offenders for crimes committed while under the age of eighteen *(Roper v. Simmons 125 S.Ct. 1183)*. As noted by Feld (2006, 422), "The dissent in *Simmons* strongly criticized the majority for relying on international law as authority for its decision and for citing Article 37 of the United Nations Convention on the Rights of the Child, which the United States has not ratified."

Committee on the Rights of the Child—Concluding Observations on States' Juvenile Justice Systems

As well as issuing General Comments on specific topics, the Committee on the Rights of the Child receives periodic reports from the state parties to the CRC on the operations of their juvenile justice systems. To an extent, the Concluding Observations issued by the Committee following review of these reports and discussions with representatives of the state parties to the CRC give an indication of the extent to which states are complying with the CRC, including its provisions on juvenile justice. The Committee therefore becomes a site of contestation between the globalization of juvenile justice and local cultural and social practices and values, including challenges to the welfarism of the CRC. For example, in 2004, in the case of France, the Committee expressed concern about the "orientation" under the 2002 law (discussed next, in the case study of France), "which tends to favor repressive over educational measures" (2004, para. 58).[45]

In its 2007 General Comment No. 10, the Committee said that states "often pay quite detailed attention to the rights of children" but also stated that "many State parties still have a long way to go in achieving full compliance with the CRC," singling out for attention the areas of procedural rights, measures to deal with children other than resorting to judicial proceedings, and using deprivation of liberty only as a last resort measure (2007, para. 1). Observations of the Committee that apply specifically to the

countries studied in this chapter (France, Japan, and China) are discussed next.

France

In its 2009 Concluding Observations, the Committee reiterated its concern about "the legislation and practice in the field, which tend to favour repressive over educational measures" and noted specifically reforms under a 2007 French law that allows the judge, in the case of offenders between sixteen and eighteen suspected of having committed a serious crime of a violent or sexual nature, to waive the principle that first offenders will receive a reduced (mitigated) punishment because of their status as youth. The reform also provides that the principle of mitigation is not applied automatically to repeat offenders aged sixteen to eighteen unless specifically invoked by the judge. In addition, the Committee was concerned about mandatory prison sentences for recidivists and a 2004 law which permits children aged sixteen to eighteen, suspected of organized crime and terrorism, to be placed in police custody for up to 96 hours.

In regard to minorities, the Committee continues to be concerned about de facto discrimination faced by "minority groups and indigenous peoples of Overseas Departments and Territories" in the exercise of their economic, social, and cultural rights, including the right to adequate housing, education, and health. As noted by Muncie (2009, 378), this brings to the forefront the issue of the "racialization of youth justice in Western Europe" described earlier in this chapter in the case study of France.

Japan

In its Concluding Observations of 2004,[46] the Committee is concerned that the reforms to the Juvenile Law (see case study on Japan) were "not in the spirit of the principles and provisions of the Convention and international standards of juvenile justice." The Committee makes specific reference to the lowering of the minimum age of criminal responsibility from sixteen to fourteen and the increase in permitted pre-trial detention from four to eight weeks. Notably, there is also criticism of the intense social control over juveniles in Japan and of net-widening where "children exhibiting problematic behavior, such as frequenting places of dubious reputation, tend to be treated as juvenile offenders." The Committee recommends abolishing the power of the Family Court to transfer a child aged sixteen or older to be tried as an adult and abolishing life imprisonment for juveniles.

In its Observations in 2010,[47] the Committee reiterated its concern that the juvenile law reforms had "adopted a rather punitive approach," and noted that a new development meant that lay judges could deal with juvenile cases, as opposed to a specialized juvenile court. This the Committee considered "an obstacle to the treatment of child offenders." The Committee was also concerned about juveniles' lack of access to legal counsel that it said had resulted in "coerced confessions and unlawful investigative practices."

China

The 2005 Observations of the Committee indicate that fundamental deficiencies exist in the design and operation of the Chinese juvenile justice system compared to required international standards. The Committee's sweeping comment is that "existing legislation, regulations and administrative procedures do not adequately set out the detailed obligations of the authorities and the judiciary for the protection of children in conflict with the law." The impenetrability of the system and the high levels of discretion enjoyed by actors in the system, including the police, are described in the case study of China. The numerous detailed recommendations from the Committee include the following:

- Implement international standards of juvenile justice.

- Abolish life sentences for those who committed offenses when aged below eighteen.

- Make legislative changes to ensure that children have the right to challenge the legality of measures that deprive them of liberty and ensure that such deprivation is a last resort.

- Seek technical assistance from named UN agencies.

In a subsequent set of Observations of 2013, the Committee engages in a wide-ranging critique of China's juvenile justice system, especially the administrative detention of children. The Observations recommend that reform through labor and work-study schools be abolished, calls for the abolition of secret detention facilities for children, advocates for children to be given access to justice and legal aid, and proposes that the best interests of the child be the key consideration in actions involving children.

Comment

In its Observations, the Committee exposes the failure of many states to adhere to the principles of the CRC and to the detailed rules concerning many aspects of the administration of juvenile justice. The CRC gives states considerable discretion in the design of their juvenile justice systems. Few states have fully implemented the CRC, and many appear to consider the CRC to be a symbolic instrument (Brown 2005, 204). Nevertheless, the Committee (with assistance from numerous international nongovernmental organizations [NGOs] who submit reports on state practices) achieves a level of continuous international monitoring of juvenile justice systems and a degree of accountability that enables it to challenge practices that do not meet international norms. Moreover, the UN treaty strategy of "naming and shaming" states who violate their treaty obligations has shown that progress can be made over time in the realization of rights (see, e.g., similar reporting under the Convention on the Elimination of All Forms of Discrimination Against Women [CEDAW], discussed in Chapter 13).

Questions remain about the efficacy of the CRC, despite its virtually universal acceptance, given the apparent unwillingness of state parties to adhere to its terms. Barry Goldson and John Muncie (2012, 61) see its "capacity to drive and sustain progressive juvenile justice reform" as "severely limited," but this seems an overly pessimistic viewpoint. The Committee's management of standards is part of an iterative process of globalizing juvenile justice for the benefit of juveniles in conflict with the law. These standards "represent an effective benchmark against which law, policy and practice can be measured in a whole range of areas and in the system as a whole" (Kilkelly 2008, 191). They signify a long-term goal that will only be realized after a lengthy period of state compromise, acceptance, and assimilation, a process that is significantly under way cases, discussing them in detail and often reaching agreement on the appropriate sanction prior to the trial. The prosecutor addresses the court on the appropriate disposition for the juvenile after the adversarial debate in a *réquisitoire*, which "symbolizes the power of the state to accuse and identify the threat posed by a delinquent youth" (Terrio 2009, 239).

29. Kawasaki (1994, 187) states that urban youth culture in the 1930s was "basically consumerist and was not supported by the middle class."

30. "Working-class family" has been explained in Japanese society as a two-parent family where both parents' education was in high school or below, where their occupations are of a low status, and where the family resides in an area occupied mainly by other working-class families. It is estimated that between 20 and 30 percent of families are working class (Yoder 2011, 34).

31. A change in police practice meant that all reported incidents were to be recorded without any police discretion. Previously, police had exercised discretion not to record incidents and instead resolve them through informal dispute resolution *(kaiketsu)*. Recording all incidents meant that crime data showed a massive increase in reported violent crimes, including crimes such as indecent assaults on young women on public transport which had not previously been recorded (Hamai and Ellis 2006, 166).

32. For a discussion of juveniles and labeling theory, see Banks (2013b, 27–32).

33. According to Yoder (2011, 22), delinquency prevention in practical terms means continual surveillance and monitoring of youth. There are no specific delinquency prevention programs as such, and police and volunteers are much more active in working-class areas, including working-class entertainment districts, than elsewhere.

34. In middle school, students "are confronted with strict school regulations prescribing wear of the school uniform, hairstyle, mannerisms, codes of conduct. . . . Middle schools resemble the military— authoritarian, disciplinarian and highly regulated" (Yoder 2011, 169).

35. Yoder (2011, 20) states that the majority of predelinquent cases are categorized as "unwholesome-activity juveniles," also called "misbehaving juveniles." While cases of "crime-prone" juveniles are commonly sent to the Family Court, those that involve misbehaving juveniles are not. The kinds of misbehavior that can be committed only by youth include carrying a weapon, behaving roughly, runaways, truancy, curfew violations, sexual enticement, drinking alcohol, smoking cigarettes, and unhealthy amusements that can include frequenting bars or pachinko parlors (or other places off-limits to youth) and reading a pornographic magazine (Yoder 2011, 20). In the case of a misbehaving youth, a reprimand will be given, a police record created, and parents and school will be notified, or where a youth is employed, his or her employers will be notified.

36. The term *child friendly* appears in the *Council of Europe Guidelines on Child-Friendly Justice*, adopted in 2010. The General Elements of Child Friendly Justice include the following: "In all proceedings, children should be treated with respect for their age, their special needs, their maturity and level of understanding, and bearing in mind any communication difficulties they may have. Cases involving children should be dealt with in non-intimidating and child-sensitive settings" (http://www.coe.int/t/dghl/standardsetting/ childjustice/default_en.asp).

37. See Chapter 6 for a discussion of the death penalty in China and the two-year suspension of the penalty.

38. The mass line is a system of democratic centralism where "correct leadership is necessarily 'from the masses, to the masses.' This means take the ideas of the masses (scattered and unsystematic ideas) and concentrate them (through study, turn them into concentrated and systematic ideas), then go to the masses and propagate and explain these ideas until the masses embrace them as their own, hold fast to them and translate them into action, and test the correctness of these ideas in such action. Then once again concentrate ideas from the masses and once again go to the masses so that the ideas are persevered in and carried through. And so on, over and over again in an endless spiral, with the ideas becoming more correct, more vital and richer each time. Such is the Marxist theory of knowledge" (Mao quoted in Starr 2015, 148).

39. Zhao et al. (2015, 156) state to the contrary that the court proceedings are formal and adversarial.

40. "Penal populism" is explained by John Pratt (2007, 12) as comprising multiple elements that include "the way in which criminals and prisoners are thought to have been favored at the expense of crime victims in particular and the law-abiding public in general." "Populism" in this context refers to an unmediated direct link between the public and their political leaders (Snacken 2010, 282).

41. See "Guidelines of the Committee of Ministers of the Council of Europe on Child-Friendly Justice," 2010, http://www.coe.int/t/dghl/standardsetting/child justice/Source/GuidelinesChildFriendlyJustice_EN.pdf.

42. A description and critical review of restorative justice and associated initiatives can be found in Banks (2013b, 227–53).

43. In 2004, more than four hundred thousand youth in the United States were arrested or detained for status offenses. The 1974 Juvenile Justice and Delinquency Prevention Act (last reauthorized in 2002) prohibited placing status offenders in secure confinement, but a 1980 amendment undermined this rule by allowing status offenders to be detained for violations of a valid court order (e.g., a court order not to run away), which, if violated, can result in detention.

Research in the United States has shown that placing minors in detention for a status offense fails to provide the help and support they require and in fact is likely to exacerbate their problems (Arthur and Waugh 2008, 555, 557).

44. According to the Sentencing Project, the only country that imposes a life sentence without parole on persons who were juveniles at the time of the offense is the United States. In the United States there are more than 2,500 persons serving such sentences for crimes committed when juveniles. The U.S. Supreme Court has banned mandatory life sentences without parole for juveniles and has determined in the 2012 decision in *Miller v. Alabama* that the federal government and states are required to consider the unique circumstances of each juvenile defendant in determining his or her sentence. See http:// http://www .sentencingproject.org/doc/publications/jj_Juvenile_ Life_Without_Parole.pdf.

45. See CRC/C/15/Add.240, p. 13.

46. See CRC/C/15/Add.231, pp. 12–13.

47. See CRC/C/JPN/CO/3, pp. 15–16.

the name of reconciliation by the liberation organization SWAPO which rejected prosecutions and a truth commission and instead promoted the necessity to forgive and forget, maintaining that only this strategy would end the circle of violence. In fact, the SWAPO approach was not endorsed by Namibian society and the churches commenced a reconciliation-type initiative in the mid-1990s which was heavily contested by SWAPO (Renner 2012, 54).

In South Africa, a new development in regard to amnesty occurred when the South African Truth and Reconciliation Commission (TRC), through its Committee on Amnesty, agreed to grant amnesty to individual persons who had made a full and public disclosure of a politically motivated crime.[8] The political settlement reached in 1993 committed a future government in the interests of "national unity and reconciliation" to an amnesty that applied to "all acts, omissions and offences associated with political objectives and committed in the course of the conflicts of the past" (Constitution of Republic of South Africa Act).[9]

It is now argued that developments in international law and the creation of the International Criminal Court have so impacted state sovereignty that "amnesty outcomes are no longer within any individual state's or institution's control" (Freeman 2009, 3). The nexus between amnesty and TJ remains highly controversial largely because an amnesty constitutes an absolute bar to prosecuting persons for past criminal conduct and failure to punish at all is itself seen as an injustice (Freeman 2009, 19–20). As Teitel puts it (2000, 54), "Transitional amnesties amount to a 'selling out' of justice to transient political interests, to the detriment of democratic prospects. Many now agree that international law prohibits the granting of amnesty[10] because states' treaty obligations require they prosecute for serious offenses and because other binding requirements exist that mandate human rights abuses to be investigated and remedied.[11] As Louise Mallinder (2008, 7) describes this position, "Anti-impunity campaigners argue that any form of amnesty for serious violations of international law would violate states obligations to ensure victims' rights to truth, justice and reparations."

Those who disagree with this position argue that since international law does not *expressly* prohibit amnesty in any human rights, humanitarian, or criminal law treaty, there is nothing to prevent the grant of amnesties for whatever may be the crime alleged (Freeman 2009, 32).[12] Some scholars take a middle position, agreeing that while international law does prohibit the granting of broad amnesties, granting limited amnesties is lawful and, as a practical matter, is a power that amounts to an "important tool in the conflict resolution process" (Mendez 2012, xxv).

Amnesty granting as part of TJ was first treated by the United Nations Secretariat as a political issue but is now regarded as an issue of international law impacting the sovereignty of a state. As a result, the United Nations would not now see South Africa's limited amnesty model as legitimate (Freeman 2009, 92). In 2004 the UN Secretary-General issued a report titled "The Rule of Law and Transitional Justice in Conflict and Post Conflict Societies" by which the UN Secretariat undertook to ensure that peace agreements "reject any endorsement of amnesty for genocide, war crimes, or crimes against humanity, including those relating to ethnic, gender and sexually based international crimes [and] ensure that no such amnesty previously granted is a bar to prosecution before any United Nations–created or assisted court" (Freeman 2009, 45). Shortly after the issue of this report, the United Nations opted out of the Commission on Truth and Friendship jointly established by Indonesia and Timor-Leste because the Commission had been empowered to recommend amnesty for those who provided confessions of violations of human rights in its proceedings (Freeman 2009, 90).

Michael Freeman argues that amnesties are justified in circumstances "where public security and the human rights related thereto are jeopardized on a mass scale by the threat of prosecution" (2009, 8). In adopting this approach, the Sierra Leone Truth and Reconciliation Commission described the amnesty provisions of the Lome Peace Accord as "necessary in the circumstances that prevailed at the time" and noted that "disallowing amnesty in all cases would be to deny the reality of violent conflict and the urgent need to bring such strife and suffering to an end" (Mallinder 2008, 44). Critics of those who favor amnesties for these reasons accept that prosecutions should not be promoted where there exists "a genuine and serious threat to national life" but believe "states should assume 'reasonable risks' associated with prosecution, including military discontent" (Aukerman 2002, 39).

How then can it be determined whether or not an exception to prosecution should be pursued? Summarizing the views of commentators, Darryl Robinson (2003, 497–98) suggests that the test is to balance less than comprehensive prosecution against the most complete advancement of accountability and that the following questions would decide where the balance falls in a particular case:

- Was the alternative to full and complete prosecution adopted by an exercise of democratic will?

- Is the departure from full and complete prosecution based on necessity in terms of social, economic, or political realities that cannot be resisted or ignored?

- Will there be a full and effective investigation into the facts and events?

- Will the fact-finding institution identify perpetrators of abuses?

- Will the relevant fact-finding body be independent and adequately resourced?

- Will some form of punishment be imposed on named perpetrators, such as being named, being required to come forward, being required to perform community work, or being subject to lustration?

- Will reparations be made to victims?

- Will the chosen approach be likely to provide closure in the sense of victims believing they have received justice?

- Will there be a commitment to adhere to other human rights obligations?

It can be argued that the purpose of retribution in the form of prosecution and punishment is to fulfill a moral duty and not to secure future benefits for a society. Therefore, where the principal objective is peace for the future, amnesty is an appropriate measure (Teitel 2000, 55).

Moreover, in Latin American as well as Anglo-American legal systems, the power to pardon is vested in the executive, not the judiciary. This conveys the notion that a pardon involves political and policy considerations and is an act of mercy and not simply a refusal to punish. It is argued then that a decision to grant an amnesty is therefore specifically justified in TJ when it serves the objective of securing peace and reconciliation because it is a decision that involves a political and policy assessment of the circumstances (Teitel 2000, 56–57).

When amnesty procedures follow a participatory democratic procedure, such as being debated in parliament and incorporated into law as occurred in South Africa, or are the subject of a referendum of the people, as happened in Uruguay, they gain the greatest legitimacy (Teitel 2000, 58–59). In the end, "both punishment and amnesty help define the regime shift, as by establishing past wrongs they help construct the political legacy" (p. 59).

Seeking and Telling the Truth: Truth Commissions

TJ advocates claim that it is essential to establish the "truth" about a state's past wrongdoing[13] in order to properly lay the foundation for a new democratic order in a state in transition. Truth telling is said to be a response to victims' demands for justice and to be a facilitator of national reconciliation. Some scholars have attempted to define *reconciliation* as it is employed in TJ discourse. For example, Philip Clark (2008, 194) says that, broadly defined, reconciliation "involves the rebuilding of fractured individual and communal relationships after conflict, with a view to encouraging meaningful interaction and cooperation between former antagonists."

In TJ discourse, reconciliation is always opposed to retribution and punishment, but in many cases there appears to be little analysis of how reconciliation is actually performed in transitional states and societies (Renner 2012, 51), and simply confronting the past is deemed a prerequisite for attaining democracy and reconciliation. Judith Renner argues that once the truth is made public, events in the future will be different. Thus, it can be argued that the notion of reconciliation lacks specificity as to the expected outcome even though it constitutes an important discursive statement in the TJ process (p. 55).[14]

Teitel points out that the discourse of truth telling is "progressive and romantic" and exemplifies contemporary liberalism (Teitel 2000, 111, 116). As the decree creating the Chilean National Commission on Truth and Reconciliation expresses it, "The truth had to be brought to light, for only on such a foundation . . . would it be possible to . . . create the necessary conditions for achieving true national reconciliation" (cited in Teitel 2000, 110).

The elements of TJ truth seeking and truth telling include the following:

- The truth should be ascertained and made part of a state's history.

- There must be both knowledge and acknowledgment.

- The historical account of events must be officially recognized, recorded, and made public; by these means, "history is marshaled in the service of political change." (Teitel 2000, 69, 117)

Truth telling is commonly accomplished through commissions of inquiry called "truth commissions" or similar names. Knowledge concerning the past is generated by those who give testimony to these bodies which are non-adversarial in nature. The normative role and purpose of these commissions is well described by Renner (2012, 57) as follows:

Truth commissions are considered to create a space where victims and perpetrators can tell the public about their past experiences, receive empathy, compassion and healing, associate their private fates with the narrative of the whole community, and contribute to a process of national catharsis in which the moral base of the society is recreated and a new foundation for communal life is discovered.[15]

Thus, truth commissions rely heavily on the testimony of victims of the regime, which, when aggregated and narrated by the commission, takes on the character of a national story (Teitel 2000, 82). For the victims, giving testimony is thought to be cathartic as they express openly their experiences under the outgoing regime (p. 82). It is not entirely clear why truth telling should actually lead to reconciliation, but this tends to be treated as self-evident and not as something that might necessitate empirical validation (Hayner 2002, 6; Renner 2012, 58).

In South Africa, according to Moon (2007, 163), reconciliation was associated with "therapeutic discourses on 'healing'" and the South African Truth and Reconciliation Commission established both the testimonial[16] and the confessional as key

practices of reconciliation. Importantly, religious beliefs about confession and forgiveness intended to produce a "lost harmony" between victims and perpetrators emerged as crucial elements in the conception of reconciliation. As well, reconciliation was strongly contrasted with the notion of revenge and the Xhosa conception of *ubuntu* stood opposed to Western notions of both revenge and retribution (Renner 2012, 68). As Moon puts it (2007, 163), the therapeutic nature of the discourse about reconciliation "shaped the assumptions central to reconciliation, namely that the TRC was mandated to heal the individual and social body and to repair the national psyche."

While some commissions have the power to issue subpoenas, none have the full powers of a judicial body. Commissions tend to be managed by elite citizens of known integrity, and commissioners are expected to be neutral (Teitel 2000, 81). They have a staff and a budget and sometimes both are substantial, as in the case of the South African Truth and Reconciliation Commission. The documentation of commissions tend to be voluminous, yet detailed accounts are valued because "the greater the detail, the stronger the counterweight to prior state silence" (p. 83). Moreover, the greater the level of detail is, the less likely the narrative can be refuted, the more credibility it enjoys, and the less room there is for competing accounts.

As Teitel points out, truth telling for foundational purposes in TJ represents an idealized conception of history because truth telling does not occur in a vacuum but builds on previous accounts and narratives. The truth that emerges in TJ is socially constructed and represents a collective narrative of those who participate in the truth telling. Thus, the process is "less foundational than transitional" (Teitel 2000, 70). Moreover, truth is not the same as justice—it is better understood "as a virtue of justice" (p. 89).

While criminal trials of those accused of past abuses may constitute a form of truth telling, clearly the procedures, rules, and rigidities associated with the criminal trial cannot fully accommodate the needs of truth telling in a TJ process, nor can a trial be guided along a certain path that will reveal the truth that is sought. In addition, questions arise when successor trials are conducted merely to establish a historical record of events rather than to fulfill the proper purposes of prosecution and punishment (Teitel 2000, 75).

Geography of Truth Commissions

Where have truth commissions been appointed? South America and Central America were the first regions to create truth commissions in various forms and under various names, followed by Africa and Asia.

In *Argentina,* the discovery that the military rulers of Argentina had "disappeared," their political opponents—during military rule from 1976 to 1983, between ten thousand and thirty thousand persons were abducted, detained, tortured, and made to disappear without trace—made the *desaparecidos* symbols of that authoritarian rule (Robben 2010, 179). The new regime had to explain the fate of these victims or allow the military to enjoy impunity. In Argentina the solution was seen to be a commission of inquiry. The National Commission on the Disappeared (CONADEP) was tasked to discover the truth about the disappeared, and only after that was national reconciliation to be attempted (Robbens 2010, 180; Teitel 2000, 78). CONADEP visited military bases, police stations, former secret detention centers, and hospitals; inspected the records of cemeteries and morgues; and conducted forensic exhumations (Robbens 2010, 182). After nine months of investigation, CONADEP issued a report, *Never Again (Nunca Más),* naming nine thousand victims and identifying perpetrators by name (Robbens 2010, 192; Teitel 2000, 79).[17]

In *Chile,* under military rule from 1973 to 1990, the successor regime established a National Commission on Truth and Reconciliation (the Rettig Commission) in 1991 to inquire as to the *desaparecidos* with the task of not only seeking the truth but also securing national reconciliation. However, the presidential decree establishing the commission prohibited it from naming suspected perpetrators (Robbens 2010, 180, 192). Subsequently, a National Commission on Political Imprisonment and Torture (Valech Commission) published a list of about thirty-eight thousand victims (Collins 2012, 403).

In *El Salvador,* following the end of a ten-year civil war with 75,000 dead and thousands displaced, the 1992 peace accords mandated the creation of an international truth commission to investigate serious abuses. Comprised entirely of foreigners, the commission delivered its report, titled *From Madness to Hope,* in 1993. It implicated most of the army high command in the killing of six Jesuit priests in 1989 and "named names" but

did not recommend prosecutions. However, only five days after publication, a broad amnesty law was passed protecting the perpetrators of serious crimes named in the report (Hayner 2002, 40). An attempt to have the amnesty law declared unconstitutional was rebuffed by the Supreme Court, which appeared to regard the issue as wholly political. It has been suggested that the military and political elites in the country made a conscious decision to impose a "forgetting" on past abuses (Popkin and Bhuta 1999, 108).

In *Guatemala,* where about two hundred thousand persons had been killed or were "disappeared" in a civil war lasting thirty-four years, the truce required that the truth be established. The Commission on Historical Clarification, established in 1994 and reporting in 1999, found ethnic cleansing and genocide. The armed forces were found responsible for most of the documented violations, which were stated to have been directed by the state against "the excluded, the poor, and above all the Mayan people" (in Hayner 2002, 48). The Commission was restricted from naming those actually responsible but specifically stated that state agents committed acts of genocide between 1981 and 1983 against the Mayan people (Hayner 2002, 48; Popkin and Bhuta 1999, 117).

In *Honduras,* after a decade of disappearances, a Commission for the Protection of Human Rights was created. Its 1994 report identified almost two hundred cases of disappearances and named members of the military as perpetrators. Previously, in 1987, 1990, and 1991, Honduras had passed broad amnesty laws (Popkin and Bhuta 1999, 114).

In *Haiti,* a National Commission on Truth and Justice was set up in 1995 to investigate alleged abuses of human rights between 1991 and 1994 and assist in reconciliation efforts (Teitel 2000, 79).

In *Brazil,* under military rule from 1964 to 1985, it proved impossible to create a commission immediately, and the tasks commonly undertaken by a commission were performed by priests, who produced an unofficial report based on files they obtained clandestinely from the military (Teitel 2000, 80). In 2007, however, a Commission on Politically Motivated Deaths and Disappearances was created and a Truth Commission was pending in 2011 (Collins 2012, 403).

The same approach on truth seeking was followed in Africa, where truth commissions were created in Uganda, Chad, and South Africa. In Asia, a novel form of truth commission was

staffed and complex processes implemented with little or no consultation or outreach with or to the Timorese. Consequently, TJ concepts were introduced in a social context in which there existed multiple localized meanings of justice, and these concepts were "vernacularized" within local value and belief systems.

In terms of the overall TJ process in East Timor, it is argued that "stability" concerns, which revealed Indonesia's economic and strategic influence in the region, came to overshadow retributive justice goals and that East Timor's TJ process was "short-term, apolitical and externally driven" (Kent 2012, 46).

BOX 8.2   Rwanda

(Except where otherwise indicated, this account of events concerning Rwanda is taken from Gerald Gahima, *Transitional Justice in Rwanda: Accountability for Atrocity,* Abingdon, UK: Routledge, 2013. Gahima was Deputy Minister in the Ministry of Justice, Rwanda, from 1996 to 1999 and the Attorney General from 1999 to 2003.)

Timeline

Mid-eighteenth century: Rwanda is inhabited by the Twa, Tutsi, and Hutu communities. It is an absolute monarchy ruled by a king through a group of chiefs, the majority of who were Tutsi. In precolonial times the terms *Tutsi* and *Hutu* were fluid, but the Hutu constituted the majority of the population.

Colonial period 1890s on: At a conference in Brussels, Germany was given Rwanda as a colony, and missionaries and settlers arrived in 1897. The Germans remained in control until 1919. They believed the Tutsi to be a superior race which originated in northern and eastern Africa and adopted policies that favored them and discriminated against the Hutu, who they believed belonged to the Bantu people and were indigenous to the country. Allegedly, the Tutsi resembled Europeans while the Hutu were perceived to be common farmers.

1919: Belgium accepted a mandate from the League of Nations to govern Rwanda along with its existing Congo territory. In the 1920s and 1930s, the few remaining Hutu in government positions were removed and only sons of the Tutsi elite had access to education and formal employment. Colonial policies reinforced societal stratification and each person was issued with a racial identification card. These racial policies were justified in a written history, but no traces have been found to confirm them.

1945–1961: Rwanda became a Belgian Trust Territory. A movement to free the Hutu from colonial and Tutsi domination began after 1945. Instead of seeking to settle the issue between them, the Tutsi promoted a plan for decolonization to preserve their control. The colonial government and the Catholic Church pushed ahead with a transfer of power from Tutsi to Hutu, the 1959 revolution, and this led to ethnic violence directed against the Tutsi chiefs with hundreds killed on both sides. On July 1, 1962, Rwanda became an independent republic in a Belgian-assisted coup that toppled the monarchy and created a republic, and in 1965 it became a one-party state. By the time of Independence, some two hundred thousand Tutsi had been forced into exile in the neighboring states of Burundi, Uganda, and the then Zaire (Lemarchand 2009, 485).

1973, July 5: Defense Minister Habyarimana staged a coup and took power establishing another authoritarian regime dominated by elites from his home area in the north. He remained in power for twenty-one years and refused to acknowledge that Tutsi refugees who had fled the country in the face of persecution and discrimination had any right to return to Rwanda; in fact he encouraged them to integrate into the countries from which they received asylum. The refugees decided they had no option but to fight to return. They acquired military skills in Uganda, serving in the National Resistance Movement rebellion there.

1987: The Tutsi in exile formed the Rwandan Patriotic Front (RPF) with the intention of waging an armed struggle against Habyarimana.

1990, October 1: The RPF began its invasion of Rwanda. Thanks to French paratroopers, Habyarimana was able to repel the initial invasion and commenced a new wave of persecution of the Tutsi within Rwanda. This included forming Hutu militia comprising young men. Ethnic violence increased. The RPF invasion weakened the regime, and in 1991 it agreed to share power with the RPF. The attacks on the Tutsi continued, and the militia members were provided with training by the Hutu military.

1993, August: Habyarimana finally signed a peace treaty with the RPF, the Arusha Accords, that provided for a broad-based transitional government. Habyarimana was forced to accept the right of return of Tutsi refugees and the presence of the RPF in the transitional government. However, the peace agreement did not end the war. The Habyarimana regime had given substantial concessions to the RPF only because of pressure from the international community; it had no political will or desire to implement the Accords. By the beginning of April 1994, pressure to implement the Accords had increased.

1994, April 6: President Habyarimana and the President of Burundi were killed in a plane crash near Kigali airport, and this set in motion the violence that led to the genocide of the Tutsi and the killing of Hutu opponents of the regime in Rwanda. Between April and July 1994, about eight hundred thousand to one million Tutsi were murdered.

1994, April 21: The United Nations reduced its force in the country to only 250 after the murder of 10 Belgian soldiers protecting the moderate Hutu Prime Minister who was killed while the Belgians were tortured, shot, and hacked to death.

1994, June 22: The UN Security Council authorized sending a mainly African UN force to Rwanda, but there were delays in organizing and deploying it. The Council authorized the deployment of French forces in southwest Rwanda who created a "safe area" in territory controlled by the government.

1994, mid-July: The RPF gained control of Kigali, and the Hutu government fled to the Congo. The RPF installed a national unity government. Discussions began on a response to the genocide.

1994, August: the Rwanda government agreed to trials for genocide before an international tribunal.

1994, November: the International Criminal Tribunal for Rwanda (ICTR) was established in Arusha, Tanzania.

1995, December: The Rwandan government organized a conference with the international community on accountability for the genocide and decided to conduct domestic trials based on accountability by all persons participating in the genocide. Persons were assigned to categories according to the seriousness of the crime alleged against them. A proposal to create a hybrid court within Rwanda comprising local and international personnel was rejected. A truth and reconciliation commission was never seriously considered because it was regarded as a grossly inadequate response to the genocide and to the country's entrenched culture of impunity. There was no extensive public consultation on the accountability proposal.

1997, January 10: In the first genocide trial before the ICTR, Jean-Paul Akayesu, a local government official, was accused of ordering mass killings in his area.

1997, February 26: Citing mismanagement and inefficiency, the UN Secretary-General dismissed the registrar and the deputy prosecutor of the ICTR and made fresh appointments. By this date, the court had indicted twenty-one persons.

1998, June: A total of 135,000 genocide suspects were held in custody awaiting trial in Rwanda, and most had been held for several years. The justice system was unable to cope with the workload due to lack of personnel, lack of resources, cumbersome legal procedures, and poor working conditions of staff. As well, some were critical of the criminal justice process because it did not provide any means for public participation in securing accountability.

Rwanda: Planning and Execution of the Genocide

The organizers and planners of the genocide remain unknown, but extremists opposed to the peace process hunted down and killed both government and opposition leaders, including the Prime Minister, who could have frustrated their plans. Most commentators agree that the genocide was planned and was not a spontaneous outbreak in response to the shooting down of the President's plane. For example, a U.S. Defense Intelligence Agency (DIA) report of May 9, 1994, stated clearly that the violence was not spontaneous but directed by the government with lists of victims prepared well in advance. The DIA reported that an organized effort of genocide was being implemented by the army (Power 2007, 355).[26]

According to René Lemarchand (2009, 488–89), by 1992 "the institutional apparatus of genocide was already in place." He identifies this as a core group comprising the wife of the deceased President, the President's three brothers-in-law, and some trusted advisers who planned and orchestrated the genocide; the rurally recruited organizers numbering from three hundred to five hundred; the militia, who often operated with the police and the gendarmerie in charge of the actual killing; and the presidential guard of about six thousand who were directly involved in killing government and opposition politicians immediately after the crash of the President's plane.

The genocide organizers took control of the bureaucracy. A group of military officers allied to the late President established a military crisis committee and took over control from the civilian authorities. They appointed Hutu from the south to important government positions. The organizers, having gained control of the government, military, and security services, supervised and supported local government from province level down to village level to ensure that all Tutsi in their area were killed. Army, police, and local leaders organized the killing and relied on the militia to carry out massacres. Other strategies adopted were designed to ensure that the killing was not interrupted or impeded. These strategies included

- killing Belgian peacekeepers to intimidate the international community;

- using the media, especially the radio, to incite and control atrocities: the militia (Interahamwe) were urged on by the privately owned Radio Mille Collines which broadcast messages like "The enemy is out there—go get him!" and "The graves are only half full!" (Lemarchand 2009, 492);

- imposing a curfew to prevent escapes or organizing resistance;

- restricting movement through travel permits and roadblocks;

- using national identity cards to identify Tutsi;

- creating a so-called self-defense system comprising night patrols to ensure that Tutsi did not escape at night;

- encouraging victims to gather at hospitals, churches, and similar public places on false promises of security or protection to facilitate their massacre;

- intimidating communities opposed to the killing or ready to protect victims;

- deploying militia to areas where there was less enthusiasm for killing and offering money, alcohol, and food and assurances of rape and looting to encourage support for killing; and

- searching forests, swamps, fields, and the homes of Hutu sympathizers when all Tutsi in homes or public places had already been killed.

The killing of the Tutsi was accompanied by great brutality, including torture and extensive use of the machete to cut off victims' limbs. Wooden clubs with nails embedded were used to crush skulls. Victims were not always killed immediately and were sometimes tortured over a number of days. Others were buried alive or drowned with their legs and arms tied, and some were forced to kill their children, spouses, or relatives before they were themselves killed. Tens of thousands of women were raped, often in public places, and often with great brutality such as piercing their genital areas with sharp objects or having parts of their body cut off. Some rape victims were kept as sex slaves, and many were infected with HIV/AIDS.

According to a 1994 report by the Physicians for Human Rights, "The *interahamwe* used the following methods of killing: machetes, *massues* (clubs studded with nails), small axes, knives, grenades, guns, fragmentation grenades, beatings to death, amputations and exsanguination, live burials, drowning or rape. Many victims had both Achilles tendons cut with machetes as they ran away, to immobilize them so that they could be finished off later" (quoted in Lemarchand 2009, 493).

It is believed that three quarters of the Tutsi population were killed and that another one hundred thousand to two hundred thousand Hutu sympathizers were also killed during the genocide. More than two million persons fled the country. Both the war and the genocide left the country and its economy in ruins. Every segment of Rwanda society, from political and military leaders to police and members of political parties, participated in the genocide. However, the militias were the backbone of the civilian participation operating as mobile groups under the direction of mayors or governors or local military commanders. Much of local government organized and directed killings. Civil society also participated, and not even the Church spoke out against the killing. State-owned and private media were instrumental in stirring up and inciting hatred and violence. The hundreds of thousands of ordinary citizens who responded to incitements and persuasion to participate constitute one of the distinctive features of the Rwandan genocide.

Rwanda Gacaca Courts

In precolonial and postcolonial times, Rwanda traditional dispute settlement took the form of public gatherings of respected male elders in a community to adjudicate disputes, often involving land or inheritance. *Gacaca* means "small grass," referring to the ground where such meetings were customarily held (Longman 2006, 210). Serious crimes were not brought before gacaca. Decision making was consensual, and sanctions typically involved compensation payments.

The government of Rwanda discovered that the domestic trial arrangements they wished to pursue to punish those involved in the genocide were unable to cope with the sheer numbers of persons involved. By mid-1998, more than 135,000 genocide suspects were in custody awaiting trial (before the genocide, the capacity of the corrections system was only between 12,000 and 15,000 prisoners); many had been held in custody for many years and conditions of detention in the country's prisons were appalling. Rwanda had never had an independent system of justice before the genocide, and the judicial system was deeply flawed with an understaffed

judiciary, unskilled personnel, and a general lack of resources. It was estimated that after the genocide, only 20 percent of staff remained to service the court system. There had never been any public confidence in the justice system. A solution was needed to the issue of prosecuting so many persons with many thousands already dying in prisons each year from poor medical care, lack of hygiene, and abysmal living conditions. The justice system was overwhelmed, and some, including the President, did not feel the criminal justice process allowed for popular participation in the process of ensuring accountability.

The government organized a series of meetings to discuss how to manage the transition from arrangements adopted in 1994, termed the Urugwiro Reflection Meetings, and justice issues were discussed during eleven meetings held between August 1998 and February 1999. The meetings concluded that the formal justice system was not the appropriate mechanism for processing crimes committed during the genocide. The President proposed to adapt traditional gacaca[27] as an appropriate processing mechanism—in effect, gacaca would be reinvented in a modern form for a specific purpose. Legislation was enacted establishing the gacaca courts, and in 2008 virtually all genocide cases in the formal justice system were transferred to gacaca courts.

A principal reason for this approach was that gacaca would be seen as a legitimate response to the killings by the general public, even though victims might have reservations about it being a form of amnesty and lawyers would be concerned about its failure to protect the rights of the accused. Nevertheless, it was considered that gacaca would bring stability, expose the truth about the genocide, stigmatize the perpetrators, and ultimately promote reconciliation by reintegrating persons accused of genocide into their communities. Gacaca would make the community the judges of genocide cases alleged against members of their own community and promote closure of the issue. Addressing the grievances of the Hutu community was also an objective because many believed that thus far only "victor's justice" had been applied.

The new gacaca courts formally established on March 15, 2001, combined restorative and retributive functions. It was mandatory to appear before the gacaca for the accused and the public. Four categories of offenses were created and all except category 1 cases would be dealt with by the gacaca courts. Public officials could not hold office as gacaca judges, and judges (originally set at nineteen but later reduced to nine) were to be elected from persons of integrity and who enjoyed that reputation within the community. Proceedings were commenced by the court taking on a dossier compiled from a prior investigation or starting its own investigation.

The first stage was gathering information about those persons who had moved away or had died and those accused of being perpetrators; the second stage involved categorizing suspects identified in the first stage; and the final stage was the gacaca trial. Proceedings were conducted informally, and normal criminal procedure was not applied. No lawyers were permitted to appear, and suspects could be tried in absentia. The courts could impose any penalty provided for by the criminal law, including life imprisonment, but sentences had to be within the range allowed for each category of offense. Across the country, the gacaca courts quickly disposed of cases, completing almost all trials within two years.

How did communities react to gacaca, and what has been its effect on reconciliation and community reintegration? The goals of retribution and restoration of relationships proved to be contradictory, and in many communities retribution meant a bitter contest between perpetrators and survivors. The focus on genocide had the effect of discouraging active Hutu participation because the approach was seen to be less than even-handed in relation to the acts of the RPF.

According to Jennie Burnet (2010, 96), "My findings indicate how well gacaca has functioned varies a great deal from community to community. The most important variable appears to be the character of the *inyangamugayo* (people of integrity) who serve as judge and jury in the gacaca system." In employing gacaca to try genocide suspects, "Gacaca deepened cleavages within the communities and sowed distrust on all sides. Perhaps any justice mechanism would have had

the same side effect" (p. 112). Gacaca was also used by some for gain—"stories of people denouncing others before Gacaca to take their land are rampant—I heard them in all the communities I visited—story may be more of a metaphor for gacaca and its injustices" (p. 112).

A female Tutsi genocide survivor quoted in Burnet (2010, 105) reported: "We can't look into the hearts of men, certainly there are those who are happy and others who are not happy. In general, we pretend to get along." One informant reported that certain *génocidaires* did not have the right to rejoin the community because even though they asked for mercy and pleaded guilty and admitted to the acts alleged against them, they did not show remorse (p. 103). In the eyes of Rwandan Tutsi genocide survivors or Hutu who did not take part in the genocide, confession was not equivalent to accepting moral responsibility and showing remorse (p. 105). The theme of lasting trauma is conveyed by a Tutsi widow (quoted in Burnet 2010, 107):

> I can't forget that I am left alone. When I don't have water in the house and night is falling, I think that I should have someone to go draw water. When there is no wood for the fire, that reminds me that there should be someone to go and collect wood. When I want this or that, I should have someone to help me. With everything that I do, I am reminded that I am alone. That's how it is, we go to Gacaca, we try to be patient but forget all that; it will never happen.

In December 2007, the executive secretary of the National Service of Gacaca Courts stated that 712,723 cases had been completed out of a total of over 1.12 million and by May 2009 the majority of prisoners had either been released or transferred to TIG camps—*travaux d'intérêts généraux*—a form of community service but similar to prison work camps (Burnet 2010, 100). In June 2012, the gacaca courts were formally closed (Gahima 2013, 158).

BOX 8.3   The International Criminal Tribunal for Rwanda (ICTR)

The ICTR was established in November 1994 following the model of the ICT for Yugoslavia. In its early period, the ICTR was heavily criticized for inaction, delay, and poor management. The ICTR was located in Tanzania because it was thought that it needed to be away from Rwanda to secure its independence. However, siting the ICTR in Tanzania rendered it virtually impossible for Rwandan citizens to attend hearings. Moreover, trials were not translated into the local Rwandan languages. Rwandan radio broadcast five- to ten-minute summaries of the trials daily. It was not until four years after its creation that the ICTR finally established a Victim and Witness Support Unit funded through separate donor contributions and not from the ICTR budget. Before then, the Tribunal believed it needed to separate itself from victims to preserve its independence. In 2002, an Information Center was set up in Kigali and commenced an internship program as an element of outreach. Still, the ICTR operations remained a mystery to most Rwandans who lived in the rural areas (Lambourne 2012, 240–41).

It was not until February 1995 that the UN Security Council designated Arusha, Tanzania, as the seat of the ICTR with the first judges being elected in May 1995. The first Registrar was not appointed until September 1995 and the Tribunal finally moved into its premises in November 1995 with its first indictment being confirmed on November 28, 1995, and the first trial commencing in January 1997. The task of the ICTR was to prosecute and try persons responsible for genocide and serious crimes under international humanitarian law. It was also envisaged that it would play a role in rebuilding Rwanda's judicial system. The Tribunal Registry and Office of the Prosecutor came in for the most criticism, but the Chambers and the President also contributed to the poor reputation of the ICTR by failing to coordinate its business and control its proceedings. As a result, the Tribunal frequently went on recess and ordered or granted adjournments of cases for lengthy periods. At the same time, it has to be conceded that the Tribunal faced considerable difficulties in tracking down suspects because virtually all persons having a significant role in the genocide had left Rwanda in 1994, many seeking refuge in the Democratic Republic of the Congo and then relocating to many different countries.

Tensions arose between the government of Rwanda and the ICTR Prosecutor over plans to investigate and prosecute crimes alleged to have been committed by the Rwanda Patriotic Front (RPF)—this mission was included in the Tribunal's mandate. The Tribunals had four prosecutors and while the first two prosecutors instigated no action against the RPF, the third prosecutor, Carla Del Ponte, openly announced that she would pursue such investigations.

Del Ponte was rebuffed when she sought assistance from the Rwandan Military Prosecutors Office and informed that the Rwandan government would not cooperate. It appeared that Del Ponte had little international support for this investigation and this reinforced the Rwandan government's refusal to assist. In September 2003, Del Ponte ceased to be Prosecutor and the fourth and final prosecutor merely announced every year that he was reviewing RPF cases and made no decision on prosecutions.

Rwandans criticized the ICTR for its acquittal of several notorious defendants,[28] its slow pace of work, and its sentences, that in the opinion of genocide survivors were too lenient relative to the crimes committed. The Tribunal had no power to impose the death penalty. There was also said to be no effective witness protection system, and witnesses were not prepared for cross-examination in an adversarial system. As well, Rwandans were not impressed by the international standards of accommodation and treatment granted to those in custody, which far exceeded conditions in the Rwandan domestic justice system and even those enjoyed by many Rwandan citizens.

Finally, the ICTR had no power to order reparations—an issue that displeased survivors. In the end the ICTR brought indictments against ninety-three persons; these were the most senior military and civilian leaders together with members of civil society who played roles in the genocide. All of those trials have been completed and the Tribunal now sits to consider only appeals and expects to complete its mission by July 2015 (ICTR Newsletter January/February 2014). Nevertheless, the failure to investigate alleged crimes of the RPF has affected its credibility so that its work is perceived to be "victor's justice," at least among the Hutu. "There is abundant evidence that the RPF may have committed very extensive human rights violations during and immediately after the genocide" (Gahima 2013, 125).

In terms of cost and staffing, the Tribunal has more than eight hundred staff and an annual budget of around US$100 million. It is claimed that these funds could have been put to better use strengthening the Rwanda justice system (Lemarchand 2009, 496).

The Tribunal's legal work has included some groundbreaking decisions. The 1998 case of Jean-Paul Akayesu was the first ever conviction by an international court for the crime of genocide, and in 1999 the Tribunal registered the first plea of guilty to the crime of genocide. As well, for the first time, a person was convicted of rape as a crime against humanity (Uvin and Mironko 2009, 466).

Assessments: Rwanda

Gahima (2013) argues that situations of mass atrocity involving large-scale popular participation require a unique TJ approach that must involve investigation and prosecution of human rights by the domestic courts. However, a maximal approach to accountability aiming to pursue all suspected perpetrators is unlikely to satisfy the goals of TJ identified in TJ scholarship. The maximal approach results in unfair trials that undermine the rule of law and human rights, fail to promote reconciliation, amplify social divisions, and produce instability rather than peace. The most appropriate response is a "blend of responses from within and beyond criminal justice that addresses the specific challenges that each of these societies faces" (Gahima 2013, p. xl). Such responses can include traditional conflict resolution processes but overall responses need to be part of a "wider process of reforms that address the fundamental causes of conflict in that society" (p. xl).

In Rwanda, justice was sought through multiple mechanisms: an ad hoc international tribunal, foreign courts, the Rwandan justice system, and the gacaca courts. Adopting a radical TJ approach, Rwanda elected to put "most of the nation on trial" (Waldorf 2006, 3). The government reinvented a traditional dispute settlement mechanism, gacaca, beginning with a pilot project in 2001 and with a nationwide rollout in 2005 that enlisted the entire population in judging an estimated 761,000 suspects accused of genocide (Burnet 2010, 95). The Rwanda government strategy of maximal prosecution meant that every person who participated in the genocide, from the planners down to the peasant farmers or looters, would be prosecuted and punished. The gacaca courts were criticized by human rights groups and commentators for "the lack of provisions for the defense of alleged perpetrators, the poor training of judges, the failure to respect the principle of 'double jeopardy' and the fact that only crimes of genocide (i.e., Hutu crimes) are allowed to be discussed" (Zorbas 2007, 26).

An enduring issue for Rwandans and for genocide survivors is knowledge of when, where, and how their loved ones died (Burnet 2010, 101) because keeping the ancestor spirits happy requires a sacred burial and regular ritual offerings of food and drink. While some have recovered relatives' remains, thanks to the gacaca court proceedings, for others the truth remains undiscovered (p. 102). The legacy of the genocide has shaped Rwandan society since 1994 to the extent that "the Rwandan government's genocide commemorations and national mourning practices generate a polarizing discourse that defines all Tutsi as genocide victims and all Hutu as genocide perpetrators" (p. 110).

OBSERVATIONS AND CRITIQUES: TRANSITIONAL JUSTICE

As the previous discussion indicates, mechanisms for TJ are now multifaceted and justice processes are increasingly drawn out with prosecutions commencing twenty years or more after the alleged offense. TJ is acknowledged as a limited or compromised form of justice because of political and also resource constraints.

Commentators have now discarded the dominant "justice" approach in favor of a mode of TJ that is capable of fulfilling more comprehensive goals. For example, Rama Mani (2002) argues for a holistic and integrated approach to transition justice with three dimensions: legal, rectificatory, and distributive. The first is concerned with the rule of law, the second with direct human rights abuses, and the third with systemic and structural injustices resulting from economic and political discrimination and inequalities. Similarly, Rosemary Nagy (2008, 278) argues, "There has been a tendency to underrate the gendered and socioeconomic ramifications of violent conflict, which may include HIV/AIDS, widowhood and poverty." Instead, TJ has been heavily impacted by the "international legalist paradigm" with its focus on generating compliance with international humanitarian norms (p. 278). However, "a technocratic focus 'on the law' abstracts from lived realities" (p. 279).

The emphasis in TJ thinking and practice has shifted from top-down approaches to a focus on the community and its needs and concerns. This is well expressed by Fletcher and Weinstein (2002, 637):

> To date, truth and justice have been the rallying cries for efforts to assist communities in (re)building in the aftermath of mass atrocities. These employ a paradigm that focuses on individuals who have been wronged (victims) and those who inflicted their wounds (perpetrators). Missing is an appreciation for the damage mass violence causes at the level of communities.

The importance of the local in TJ practice should, it is argued, be privileged over "a cluster of liberal normative goods, such as the rule of law, peace, reconciliation, civil society, human rights, combating impunity, and justice," and gaining an understanding of how a community defines "justice" (or its absence) is critical in planning TJ in a locality (Hinton 2010, 1).

Alexander Hinton (2010, 5) argues that expectations for truth and reconciliation commissions are disproportionate and that such commissions do not advance strategies that would achieve societal repair following conflicts involving genocide or mass violence. In other words, some believe commissions should be intimately concerned with issues of development and social justice and that local justice practices ought to be integrated into the TJ process where this is possible and appropriate, as, for example, occurred in Rwanda and East Timor (p. 5). This reasoning implies that local communities should "take part at every stage in the process including conception, design, decision making and management" (Lundy and McGovern 2008, 266).

A common critique of TJ practice has been its tendency to be perceived by its practitioners as a technocratic exercise where unpacking the "TJ toolkit" is all that is required and where "one size fits all." The basis for this technocratic perception of TJ is its underlying discourse of "transition" or "progress," signifying a shift from illiberal to liberal, from violence to peace. Thus, TJ rests on a foundation of "breaking with the past" exemplified by criminal trials and truth commissions (Moon, 2008, 19). Criminal trials are expected to promote human rights, apply retribution and accountability, and show a shift away from a culture of impunity, whereas truth commissions are invested with a discourse of reconciliation and restoration that promotes conflict resolution through truth telling and forms of justice like restorative justice. When both retribution and reconciliation narratives apply a toolkit approach, this may result in eliding complex historical, social, and cultural issues that affect a state's ability to establish stability (Kent 2012, 30–31). As such, the transition paradigm suggests that states move in a linear fashion from post-conflict situations to democracy. In this model, state building is promoted as simply a technical exercise, that is, the completion of a checklist of strengthening and rebuilding projects. The rapid process of change brought about by the liberalization approach is

liable to ignore the destabilizing effects of such rapid change which, in themselves, can result in more violence (Kent 2012, 28).[29]

The technical approach to TJ can often have the effect of displacing the political dimension of transition. Most states emerging from internal conflicts and mass violence lack resources and rely heavily on international institutions such as the United Nations, the World Bank, and the International Monetary Fund (IMF) for financial and administrative support in the transition to democracy. These organizations, it is argued, promote only the dominant liberal democratic free market model of development and thus "are directed at reconstituting post-conflict societies in the image of Western liberal democracies, establishing such models as the ideal type. . . . This has been likened to a new form of neo-colonialism" (Lundy and McGovern 2008, 276–77).

Critical scholars argue that liberal state-building projects in post-conflict societies reproduce many aspects of the colonial civilizing mission and that post-conflict states are regularly categorized as undeveloped, violent, and corrupt. While state-builders claim to install democratic elections, the rule of law, and human rights observance, the authority of the state in which it is occurring is greatly reduced and influenced by international organizations sent in to save the economy in line with the tenets of economic liberalism (Kent 2012, 27–28).

While truth commissions have demonstrated their effectiveness in creating narratives and histories of past events, commentators have criticized the overall concept of truth telling on a number of grounds. These include

- their tendency to reopen old wounds, possibly promoting polarization of groups;

- that the truth revealed is only partial and contingent;

- that their top-down approach can have the effect of marginalizing victims;

- generally, that the trade-offs between truth and justice and stability and practical politics are often hard to accept; and

- that their focus is usually narrow and often does not engage with the socioeconomic aspects of abuses. (Lundy and McGovern 2008, 270–71)

Concerning the partial nature of the truth revealed in truth commissions, the South African

TRC is a good example of the limitations imposed by the truth commission mechanism because

> both the Christian-inspired ethos of "reconciliation" and that of "rainbow national-building" precluded certain things from being said by the relatives of victims and those who had been tortured by the apartheid regime, particularly in the public hearings. Some have argued that this led to a form of "second-order traumatization" probably doing more individual harm than good. (Lundy and McGovern 2008, 271)

In terms of responses to victims, it has been contended that truth commissions tend to inhibit recognition of state crimes because they always present only a partial recognition of crimes, victims, and perpetrators; that they tend to simplify identities and needs to fit the political landscape by equating all victims as having similar issues or stressing reconciliation and forgiveness over victims' expressions of retribution; and that their main concern is to establish an official recognition of those who have been victimized and to prime transitional states for more radical change.

Likewise, commissions are always limited by a narrow mandate and tend to be established for only short periods, often less than a year. Some victims, notably the poor and the marginalized, are less likely to be given space to speak. Women may be excluded in traditional societies where men dominate in public events, such as in East Timor, so commissions often struggle to afford recognition to all who want it; they "may simplify identities and stress homogeneity in an attempt to secure political consensus" (Stanley 2005, 591). A good example of this consensus seeking is the South African TRC when Desmond Tutu announced that everyone had been wounded by apartheid and "negated diversity and proposed there were no boundaries between individual experiences" (in Stanley 2005, 592). Thus, in effect "the Commission managed victims' feelings and misrepresented their needs to make them more acceptable to transitional powers" (p. 592).

As to prosecutions in national courts, or before ad hoc international tribunals (and now before the International Criminal Court), according to Gahima (2013, 15), "The ideal forum for prosecutions of human rights violations are the national courts of the states in which the crimes were committed" because they have the capacity to

- enhance the legitimacy of a new government,

- provide a focus for rebuilding and strengthening the local justice system,

- render verdicts that are familiar to the local community,

- handle a larger number of trials than international tribunals,

- provide a sense of ownership of the accountability process,

- provide a sense of empowerment to victims,

- have an impact on human rights standards and practices in the post-conflict society, and

- be far less costly and a better use of international assistance to post-conflict states than costly internationals tribunals.

However, international tribunals have a set of attributes not found in domestic courts. For example, they are better able to convey a message that the international community will not tolerate atrocities; they are more likely to be staffed with the expertise capable of managing the complexities of human rights and humanitarian law; they can be seen as functioning as independent entities rather than as vehicles for retribution; and they will be better resourced and therefore capable of advancing international norms of human rights and are more likely to be able to bring wrongdoers to trial where national authorities cannot apprehend them or bring them into custody through extradition (Gahima 2013, 15).

Debates about TJ now occur in states that have not experienced any fundamental political transition or where widespread human rights abuses still take place. In others, for example, in Rwanda, there has been no liberalizing process associated with the transition. Therefore, TJ discourses are applied increasingly to contexts that include non-liberal transitions. This has prompted discussion of the limits of the field and claims that it is becoming too vague or is subject to manipulation (Hanson 2014, 109–11). Where TJ is applied to complex situations, it "cannot easily resolve complex legacies of conflict and there needs to be a corrective to the 'celebratory impulse'" (Scheper-Hughes 2004, 27). For example, in celebrating the UN administration of Timor, the Deputy Special Representative of the UN Secretary-General announced, "In the rather

chaotic history of UN peacekeeping operations . . . East Timor stands as an undeniable success. In two and a half years, . . . this totally
devastated country was entirely reconstructed—
rather I should say: constructed—and brought to
independence" (quoted in Kent 2012, 45).

NOTES

1. According to McEvoy (2007, 412–13), the field
of TJ is characterized by "the dominance of legalism"
and is perceived through "a narrow legalistic lens
which impedes both scholarship and praxis."

2. This instance of a timeless prosecution for
crimes against humanity is recognized internationally
in the UN Convention on the Non-Applicability of
Statutory Limitations to War Crimes and Crimes against
Humanity (Teitel 2000, 63).

3. Priscilla Hayner (2002, 14) identifies at least
twenty-one official truth commissions since 1974 under
various names.

4. For example, in Argentina, General Augusto
Pinochet remained head of the armed forces during
the TJ process (Kiss 2000, 70).

5. "Truth seeking" is a complex concept, but
Hayner (2002, 183) argues that some advocates of TJ,
especially international nongovernment organizations,
identify the concept as a necessary part of TJ, especially
where the victims of abuse claim it.

6. According to Hayner (2002, 24), the characteristics of a truth commission may include "to discover,
clarify and formally acknowledge past abuses; to respond
to specific needs of victims; to contribute to justice and
accountability; to outline institutional responsibility
and recommend reforms; and to promote reconciliation
and reduce conflict over the past." Truth commissions
should not be seen as equivalent to a judicial trial process (p. 16) but rather as complementing "a very weak
judicial system" (p. 88).

7. The South African TRC was the first truth
commission to be given the power to grant individual
amnesty (Hayner 2002, 98).

8. A total of 7,116 applications for amnesty were
received, most from lower level offenders (about 300
came from the security forces), and amnesty was
granted to 16 percent of applicants (Mallinder 2008,
136). Juan Mendez (2012, xxiii) believes that the
amnesty power granted in South Africa in 1994
would, if granted today, be "inconsistent with international law" because its terms covered war crimes,
crimes against humanity, and torture. Other examples
of limited amnesties would be restricting them to
members of specified organizations, offering them
according to rank held in the armed forces, and giving
them to persons who committed specific crimes
(Mallinder 2008, 75).

9. In 2002 then President Mbeki granted pardons
to thirty-three persons in prison for crimes he judged
to be politically motivated, despite the TRC having
tried to forestall such action in its report by recommending against future "blanket amnesties through a
pardon process" (du Bois-Pedain 2012, 475–76). Thus,
special treatment for political crimes was not confined
to the time of transition.

10. International nongovernmental organizations
(NGOs) such as Amnesty International, Human Rights
Watch, and the International Commission of Jurists
generally advocate against forms of impunity. In a 2005
statement condemning a proposed amnesty in Algeria,
these NGOs and the International Center for Transitional
Justice said, "Amnesties, pardons and similar national
measures that lead to impunity for crimes against
humanity and other serious human rights abuses, such
as torture, extrajudicial executions and 'disappearances,'
contravene fundamental principles of international law"
(Mallinder 2008, 8).

11. The Inter-American Commission on Human
Rights has held that amnesties granted by Uruguay
and Argentina for grave human rights violations violated the duties imposed on those states under the
American Convention on Human Rights—specifically,
the duty to protect and ensure those rights and the
rights of victims to seek justice (Teitel 2000, 55).

12. According to Freeman (2009, 34), the only
explicit mention of amnesty in a multilateral human
rights–related treaty is in Article 6(5) of Protocol II to
the Geneva Conventions covering non-international
armed conflicts. It provides that when hostilities cease,
the authorities shall endeavor to grant the broadest
possible amnesty to persons who have participated in
the armed conflict and to those detained or interned.

13. Modern theory denies there is any such thing as
objective "truth" in historical accounts. Understanding
history is always contingent on the political and social
context, and there is no single "truth" (Teitel 2000, 70).

14. Hayner (2002, 163–65) suggests that five elements are necessary for reconciliation: (1) an end to the
violence or threat of violence, (2) acknowledgment and
reparation, (3) forces that can bind opposing parties, (4)
addressing structural inequalities and material needs,
and (5) sufficient time allowed for reconciliation.

15. The notion that there is a process of national
catharsis is disputed by therapists, and while research has
shown that testifying in public was of value to some victims, others did not benefit from it (Roht-Arriaza 2006, 4).

16. The TRC conducted fifty public hearings all
over the country where selected victims of abuse could
give their accounts. Hearings were marked by a strong
therapeutic and religious ethos in which victims often
broke down and were consoled by the commission
members (Renner 2012, 69).

17. In 1955 a naval officer confessed his role in
throwing captives who had been disappeared out of
planes flying over the South Atlantic (Robbens 2010, 188).

18. In international law, there is a right to reparations under the 1987 Convention against Torture and Other Cruel, Inhuman or Degrading Treatment or Punishment and under the 2005 Basic Principles and Guidelines on the Right to a Remedy and Reparation for Victims of Gross Violations of International Human Rights Law and Serious Violations of International Humanitarian Law.

19. The United Nations has issued *Basic Principles on the Use of Restorative Justice Programmes in Criminal Matters* and a *Handbook on Restorative Justice* (Hoyle 2012, 189), and there is now a very substantial scholarly and practitioner literature on restorative justice.

20. It should be noted that the U.S. Alien Tort Act gives the U.S. courts jurisdiction for claims against foreigners for violations of "the law of nations." Torture and unlawful executions have been held to be compensable under the Act, for example, for tortures committed in Argentina, the Philippines, and Paraguay (Teitel 2000, 144).

21. The English word *lustration* derives from the Latin *lustratio,* meaning ritual cleansing through sacrifice in the sense of cleansing from accusations (Czarnota 2012, 427).

22. The terms *lustration* and *decommunization* are often conflated, but decommunization can refer to "all political and legal strategies, one of which is eradication of the legacies of communism in a social and political system" (Czarnota 2012, 427).

23. In Czechoslovakia, in 2003, a list identifying 75,000 spies and informers who had denounced others to the regime was posted on the Ministry of Interior website and made available in print form. In February 2005, a Polish journalist obtained a list of 240,000 alleged collaborators that was later published on the Internet (Elster 2006, 6).

24. In Indonesia, the military "represents an elevated, powerful institution in Indonesian society and enjoys a culture of impunity that permeates the entire judicial process" (Cumes 2009, 495).

25. According to Cumes (2009, 495), "The [Indonesian] A-G's office and the public prosecution service are founded and operate on the basis of a military culture which inculcates military values of loyalty and discipline to the state above technical, legal preparation, and prosecutorial work. The values and goals of state policy are given greater precedence than values of law and justice, with the result that the role of these offices is to enforce government policy rather than independently uphold the law."

26. In relation to the U.S. response to the genocide, Samantha Power (2007, 373) notes that "the Clinton administration did not actively consider U.S. military intervention, it blocked the deployment of UN peacekeepers, and it refrained from undertaking softer forms of intervention." To a considerable extent, the U.S. response was shaped by the events in Mogadishu, Somalia, in October 1993 when eighteen U.S. soldiers were killed going to the aid of UN peacekeepers. There was no appetite in the United States, therefore, for any similar undertaking in Africa (Williams, 2008, 45).

27. It is problematic to describe gacaca as traditional justice because it only adjudicated cases arising from the 1994 genocide and did not involve itself in the RPF killings (Burnet 2010, 96). "As with any local process, Gacaca is a site of friction where local, regional, national, and international processes intersect" (Tsing 2005, cited in Burnet 2010, 96).

28. An example is the case of Jean-Bosco Barayagwiza, a Rwandan media leader who incited the Hutu to take up arms against the Tutsi and who has been called the "number one" culprit in the Rwandan genocide. In November 1999, the ICTR dismissed the case against him on the grounds that Mr. Barayagwiza's fundamental rights had been violated by prolonged detention without trial (Aukerman 2002, 50–51). Subsequently, the prosecutor asked the Appeals Chamber to reconsider the case and submitted "new facts" and the Chamber granted the application, finding that while Barayagwiza's rights had been violated, the new facts rendered the dismissal of the case "disproportionate" (Danner 2003, 531).

29. Over 40 percent of post-conflict societies return to conflict within five years (Lundy and McGovern 2008, 279).

9

THE INTERNATIONAL CRIMINAL COURT

The International Criminal Court (ICC), created in 1998, marks a significant step in the possible evolution of a worldwide criminal justice system and in the continued international protection of human rights. This chapter begins with a discussion of international criminal law to provide the context within which the ICC operates. This provides the context for how international criminal law has developed and how important the jurisprudence of the international criminal tribunals for the former Yugoslavia and for Rwanda is within that development.

How did the ICC come into being, and what was the process that led to the finalization of the Statute of the ICC setting out its powers and function? This process is explored and a detailed explanation provided of how the Court operates and the complexities associated with the exercise of its jurisdiction. The limits of the Court are highlighted as well as how it functions in association with the sovereignty of states and the United Nations Security Council.

Although the United States and some other major world powers (e.g., Russia and China) have refused to become parties to the Statute establishing the ICC, more than one hundred states have become parties. Among the questions addressed in this chapter are the following: What were the arguments deployed by the United States and others against the Court, and what steps has the United States taken to ensure that its nationals are protected in relation to states that are parties to the ICC Statute? Are U.S. objections warranted, or is the U.S. stance based on American exceptionalism and the United States' desire not to weaken the role of the UN Security Council in controlling world events?

Another question asks how the ICC has functioned since its establishment and what constraints it has encountered. The Prosecutor has a key role in the operations of the ICC, and the functions and powers of the Office of the Prosecutor (OTP) are explored here. For the first time, an international criminal tribunal has been tasked with safeguarding the rights of victims. We examine how victims participate in the proceedings of the Court, what the future of the ICC is, and how it might be improved. These and associated issues are addressed in a critical review of the effectiveness of the ICC.

This chapter should be read together with Chapter 8: Transitional Justice, especially in relation to amnesties and the International Criminal

Tribunal for Rwanda, and Chapter 13: Violence Against Women, in relation to violence against women in armed conflicts, where there are discussions of international humanitarian law and of the international tribunals for the former Yugoslavia and for Rwanda.

INTERNATIONAL CRIMINAL LAW

The ICC exercises criminal jurisdiction in international law. Understanding the role of the ICC requires an awareness of the nature and content of international criminal law. Like the domestic criminal law of states, international criminal law identifies specific international crimes and requires states to prosecute and punish at least some of those crimes (Cassese 2003, 721). It also prescribes procedures to be followed in processing international crimes.

International Crimes

The list of international crimes is not lengthy. Initially, in the late nineteenth century and for some time after, only war crimes were categorized as international crimes. After World War II, however, new crimes were formulated, namely, crimes against humanity and crimes against peace. These were developed through the instrumentality of the International Military Tribunal at Nuremberg (IMT) for crimes committed by German forces in Europe, and the International Military Tribunal for the Far East (IMTFE) for crimes committed by Japanese forces in that region.

In 1948, a Convention covering the crime of genocide was agreed to, and in the 1980s torture became another specific international crime, again under a Convention (Cassese 2003, 722). More recently, international terrorism has been criminalized internationally through several treaties (see Chapter 12). While international criminal law now specifies a number of international crimes, it is still in the development stage. International criminal law does not deal at all with the penalties for such crimes (p. 723).

While international law had criminalized certain acts, until the creation of the ICC, it was left to states to prosecute such crimes in their national courts. This means that states enacted offenses in their laws based on the content of an international crime and applied their own rules to prosecuting those crimes. States have also refined concepts and crimes that were defined rather broadly in international law.

When international tribunals like the IMT, IMTFE, and, more recently, the International Criminal Tribunal for the Former Yugoslavia (ICTY) and the International Criminal Tribunal for Rwanda (ICTR) were set up, these tribunals operated under statutes that specified which crimes the tribunal was to exercise jurisdiction over. The process of establishing tribunals and fixing their jurisdiction has been ad hoc in nature, and they have been created as a response to specific international events, for example, the ICTR in relation to the 1994 genocide in Rwanda. This was necessary because no international criminal code exists that specifies all international crimes, defines them comprehensively, and identifies which tribunals can automatically apply. Accordingly, deciding on the jurisdiction of each international tribunal has always been a one-off process (Cassese 2003, 723).

Sources of International Criminal Law

Where is international criminal law to be found? The chief sources are the numerous treaties and conventions concerning international human rights law and international humanitarian law. Many declarations and conventions have impacted international criminal law, for example, by setting out minimum standards for a fair trial, the rights of suspects, and the rights of victims. As well, elements of states' national laws have migrated into international criminal law in the form of concepts such as *mens rea*, categories of criminal liability (joint responsibility rules for criminal conduct, accessories, and aiding and abetting) because tribunals have canvassed domestic laws for appropriate concepts and models. (An example of this appears in that part of Chapter 13 dealing with violence against women in armed conflict where the definition of rape was considered by both the ICTY and the ICTR, and both drew on definitions found in states' domestic laws.)

This means that international criminal law draws on both international and state practice and laws, making it a hybrid branch of law. In this sense, its development resembles that of the common law where judicial precedent and statutes collectively develop legal rules and principles. Antonio Cassese (2003, 724) suggests that through the instrumentality of the ICC, it will be possible to begin to standardize and codify international criminal law.

Liability of States and Individuals for Criminal Acts

International criminal law is concerned with both states and individuals who are nationals of states. States regard most international crimes as violations of international law. Accordingly, when a war crime or genocide, for example, is committed by an individual, two forms of liability arise: that of the individual for his or her criminal conduct that falls within international criminal law, and that of the state and its responsibility. That both legal avenues arise is evidenced by the events in the former Yugoslavia when Bosnia brought proceedings in the International Court of Justice (ICJ; the forum for claims by states against other states) against Yugoslavia for genocide, while at the same time the ICTY conducted criminal trials of individuals (Cassese 2003, 725).

International Criminal Tribunals

With the end of the Cold War and the breakup of the former Soviet Union, there was a rise in nationalism and an increase in ethnic tensions in some parts of the former Soviet bloc. These ethnic tensions had previously been held in check under the old international order of the two superpowers. The fundamental changes that swept across Europe included the creation of new democracies and recognition of the importance of the rule of law and of human rights. Change took various forms in the new order in Europe, but in what was then known as Yugoslavia, it resulted in armed conflict between ethnic groups, atrocities, death, and gross violations of international humanitarian law. In response to world outrage, the UN Security Council established the ICTY. When an internal conflict in Rwanda indicated genocide and killings and rape on a mass scale, the UN Security Council established the ICTR. Each tribunal had its jurisdiction, powers, and procedures determined by its own Statute.

Considerable resources had to be applied to establish the ICTY and the ICTR, and the time and the attention they required from the UN Security Council militated against setting up further similar tribunals. However, similar situations in Sierra Leone, Timor, and Kosovo required attention.[1] The approach adopted in those cases was to establish hybrid or mixed courts made up of international and national judges and with aspects of national and international jurisdiction. Accordingly, for example, the Special Court for Sierra Leone was created with its own Statute in 2002 (Cassese 2003, 734).[2]

Within this context concerning how international criminal law is constituted and how it has been developed, especially through the various international criminal tribunals, we now turn to the establishment of the ICC. As the first permanent international criminal court with global jurisdiction, the ICC marks a departure from the practice of establishing ad hoc tribunals as instruments to ensure accountability for war crimes and atrocities committed anywhere in the world. (See also Chapters 13 and 8 on the ICTY and the ICTR.)

CREATION OF THE INTERNATIONAL CRIMINAL COURT

The concept of a single international criminal court dates back to the aftermath of World War I. The eventual realization of this notion in the form of the ICC went through the following stages:

- Early attempts that proved abortive in the period 1919–1945

- The Nuremberg and Tokyo Tribunals established after World War II

- The creation of ad hoc tribunals for the former Yugoslavia and Rwanda in 1993–1994

- The drafting of the Statute of the ICC in 1994–1998 (Cassese 2003, 726)

Drafting of the Statute of the International Criminal Court, 1994–1998

In 1989, the UN General Assembly, in a session on drugs, agreed to a proposal that an international criminal court be set up to deal with drug trafficking and asked the International Law Commission (ILC)[3] to look at the issue. The ILC submitted a report in 1990 and then a draft text of a Statute in 1993, which was further refined in 1994. The creation of the ICTY and the ICTR gave impetus to a possible ICC which, unlike the two tribunals, would exercise jurisdiction globally.

In 1996, the UN General Assembly established a Preparatory Committee on the Establishment of an International Criminal Court (PrepCom). At a diplomatic conference in Rome from June to July in 1998, the PrepCom submitted a Draft Statute and Draft Final Act for consideration leaving a number of issues still to be addressed (Cassese 2003, 730). The Rome conference also agreed on the formation of an additional Preparatory Commission that would arrange the operational details of the Court, develop rules on procedure and evidence, and specify the elements of crimes the Court could prosecute (Bosco 2014, 59). During subsequent discussions on the Statute and Final Act, three major groups of states were formed:

- First, the *Like-Minded Group* of sixty-three states was led by Canada and Australia. This global grouping wanted a strong court with automatic jurisdiction, an independent prosecutor with the power to initiate proceedings, and a broad definition of war crimes to include all crimes committed in the course of armed conflicts.

- A second group comprising the *permanent members of the UN Security Council* (except for the United Kingdom and France, which aligned themselves with the Like-Minded Group) all of whom were opposed to automatic jurisdiction and to the prosecutorial power to initiate proceedings, wanted no jurisdiction over the use of nuclear weapons, and were opposed to jurisdiction over the crime of aggression.

- A third group, comprising *members of the Non-Aligned Movement (NAM)*, wanted the ICC to have jurisdiction over aggression, while some wanted jurisdiction over drug trafficking and terrorism. They opposed any role for the Court over war crimes committed in internal armed conflicts and wanted the Court to be able to impose the death penalty. They also opposed the Security Council having any role in the operation of the Court.

In addition to the 161 states attending the conference, there were also 235 accredited nongovernmental organizations (NGOs) under one organizational umbrella: the Coalition for the International Criminal Court (CICC). The CICC constantly lobbied delegates for the most independent ICC. Included in the Coalition were the American Bar Association, Amnesty International, Human Rights Watch, and the Lawyers Committee for Human Rights. The CICC was said to have monitored all the working committees and "helped to strengthen the resolve of the 'like-minded' countries to resist the pressure applied by the United States" (quoted in Ball 2009, 499).

As a result of discussions in committee, the various positions taken by the groups of states were reconciled, and the Conference adopted the ICC Statute by 120 votes to 7, with 20 abstentions (Cassese 2003, 730). The United States and China voted against adopting the Statute. The ICC Statute entered into force on July 1, 2002, and in February 2003 the first judges of the ICC were elected.

As of September 2014, the number of countries who have ratified the Statute stands at 122 (Russia and the United States[4] have not ratified but did sign, and China did not sign or ratify; Cassese 2003, 731). The ICC comprises eighteen judges who will approve prosecutions, conduct trials, and hear appeals; a prosecutor and one or more deputy prosecutors; and administrative staff under a Court Registrar. An Assembly of States Parties, with one vote for each delegation, elects the judges and prosecutors and may remove them for misconduct (Mayerfeld 2003, 98).

The first prosecutor, Argentine Luis Moreno Ocampo, was elected unopposed on April 21, 2003, and sworn in for a nine-year term. On June 15, 2012, Fatou Bensouda, from the Gambia, took office as the Prosecutor for a term of nine years. The nine-year, nonrenewable term means that the Prosecutor need not be preoccupied with questions about being reelected (Bosco 2014, 54).

The ICC comprises an Appeals Chamber, Trial Chamber, and a Pre-Trial Chamber (Greenawalt 2007, 586). In the short time in which the ICC has been in operation, staff has grown to more than one thousand employees spread across its constituent organs. In 2011, its budget exceeded 100 million Euros and it has established six African field offices[5] and a liaison office in New York to handle contacts with the United Nations (Shany 2014, 247).

STATUTE OF THE INTERNATIONAL CRIMINAL COURT

The Statute contains the powers and functions of the Court and its associated organs.

Jurisdiction of the International Criminal Court

The Preamble to the ICC Statute (para. 4) states that the ICC is to have jurisdiction only over "the most serious crimes of concern to the international community as a whole" and that such crimes "must not go unpunished and that their effective prosecution must be ensured by taking measures at the national level and by enhancing international cooperation."

Typically, international crimes go unpunished in states' national justice systems because they are tolerated by the state or by an armed force in charge of events in a state. For that reason, the tenor of the ICC Statute is to eliminate impunity (Mayerfeld 2003, 98). According to Article 5, these "serious crimes of concern" are the following:

- *Genocide.* This crime is defined by the Genocide Convention, 1948[6] and requires an intention to destroy, wholly or partly, a national, ethnic, racial, or religious group by committing acts such as killing or causing serious bodily or mental harm to group members; inflicting conditions on the group calculated to bring about its physical destruction, wholly or partly; imposing measures to prevent births in the group; or forcibly transferring children of the group to another group.

- *Crimes against humanity.* These are defined under general international law and require a number of elements: they constitute a serious attack on human dignity or a grave humiliation or degradation, they are part of a government policy or a systematic or widespread strategy or policy of committing atrocities, they can be committed in time of war or peace, and the victims may be civilians or persons who did not participate in armed conflicts (Cassese 2003, 741).

- *War crimes.* These are serious violations of customary international law or of treaties concerning international humanitarian law. The armed conflict may be international or internal, and the crimes can be perpetrated by armed forces against other armed forces or against civilians, or by civilians against armed forces. If criminal conduct is to amount to a war crime, it must be linked to an international or internal armed conflict (Cassese 2003, 739–40).

- *The crime of aggression.* At the time of finalization of the Statute, this had yet to be defined. It is the most "political" of the enumerated crimes because it asks questions about why a conflict was waged and not about how it was conducted (Bosco 2014, 54). In May 2010, a conference was held in Kampala to review the work of the ICC to that date. At the Kampala Review Conference, agreement was reached on the meaning of this term and a regimen that will determine how jurisdiction will be exercised on claims of aggression. It will become an operative part of the ICC jurisdiction in 2017. Scholars argue that aggression is recognized in customary international law as the planning, organization, preparation, or participation in the first use of armed force by a state against another state where the acts of aggression have large-scale and serious consequences (Cassese 2003, 747). An example would be the Iraq attack on Kuwait in 1990. The Review Conference agreed that the individual crime of aggression is constituted by the planning, preparation, initiation, or execution by a person in a leadership position of an act of aggression. Importantly, the act of aggression must constitute a manifest violation of the Charter of the United Nations. An *act of aggression* is defined as the use of armed force by one state against another state without the justification of self-defense or authorization by the UN Security Council. When the Security Council refers a situation alleging aggression to the Prosecutor, the Prosecutor may investigate. In all other cases, the Prosecutor has the discretion to investigate but only in situations when a state makes a referral after first ascertaining whether the Security Council has made a determination of the existence of an act of aggression (under Article 39 of the UN Charter) and after waiting for a period of six months; and when that situation concerns an act of aggression committed between States Parties; and after the Pre-Trial Division of the Court has authorized the commencement of the investigation (Coalition for the International Criminal Court, n.d.).

Attempts to include terrorism and drug trafficking in the Court's jurisdiction failed because these crimes lacked a clear international definition (Bosco 2014, 52). Nevertheless, over time, the extent of ICC jurisdiction can be expanded with the consent of the parties. It has been suggested that while not normally regarded as "core crimes," that is, outside the category that comprises the most heinous crimes of genocide, namely, war crimes and crimes against humanity, the crimes of torture and terrorism should be entrusted to an international judicial body (Cassese 2003, 745).

Preconditions for Exercise of Jurisdiction

When can the ICC act on a criminal case?

Article 12 states that the ICC can only act where (a) an alleged crime has been committed in the territory of a state party or (b) a person accused of a crime is a national of a state party. Article 12 also allows non-state parties to give jurisdiction to the Court in relation to a crime committed within its territory, basically on an ad hoc basis.

The Court's territorial and personal jurisdiction arises because states ratifying the Statute delegate jurisdiction to the Court over their nationals and over the crimes committed within their territory. This means that states that ratify the Statute agree they will prosecute any of their citizens who commit war crimes or will surrender those citizens to the ICC if they fail to prosecute. The fact that jurisdiction is derived from state party consent ought to facilitate state cooperation in the operations of the Court; however, experience has shown this is not always the case (Dutton 2013, 1; Shany 2014, 238).

Reading together Article 12(a) and 12(b) means that when an accused is a national of a state which is not a party to the ICC Statute, the ICC can exercise jurisdiction if the act took place on the territory of a state party. For example, an American national can be brought before the Court if he or she is accused of committing a crime in Australia (the United States is not a state party, but Australia is a party).

However, this provision also means that under the "traveling dictator exception," leaders of non-ratifying states can commit crimes in their own territories with no fear of prosecution. Consequently, Jack Goldsmith (2003, 91) argues that impunity for international crimes is granted for those human rights violators who abuse their own citizens within their own borders; this is perhaps the largest category of violators over the past century. The only exception to this would be a referral by the Security Council where sovereignty can be overridden even when a non-ratifying state is involved (p. 92).

Principle of Complementarity

A key feature of the ICC jurisdiction is that it is intended to complement national criminal law jurisdictions: it is not intended to supplant national jurisdiction over international crimes. In fact, domestic courts have priority over the ICC. Accordingly, under Article 17, when a case is being investigated or prosecuted (or has been investigated) by national authorities, unless the state is "unable or unwilling" to carry out the investigation of the case, the case must be declared inadmissible before the ICC and the ICC cannot deal with it. This principle reflects that of state sovereignty (Cassese 2003, 732). Consequently, the principal responsibility for enforcement of international humanitarian law rests with national governments with the ICC exercising its jurisdiction only when states fail to act (Mayerfeld 2003, 98). In deciding "unwillingness" in a particular "case," the Court must consider three matters:

- Were or are the proceedings being taken to shield a person from criminal responsibility for crimes over which the Court has jurisdiction?

- Has there been an unjustified delay in the proceedings inconsistent with intent to bring the person to justice?

- Were or are the proceedings being conducted impartially or independently, and are they or were they being conducted in a way that is inconsistent with intent to bring the person to justice?

The ICC is the judge of the adequacy and legitimacy of the domestic proceedings, not the concerned state. When the Court determines, for example, that the proceedings are a sham, it can declare a case to be admissible and proceed with prosecution. The Court would be expected, therefore, to give close scrutiny to a state's domestic laws and proceedings before declaring a case inadmissible under this principle. Inability considerations would include "whether, due to a total or substantial collapse or unavailability of the national judicial system, the state is unable to obtain the accused or the necessary evidence and testimony or otherwise unable to carry out its proceedings" (ICC Article 17[2][d]).

Here, critics of the Court argue that there is potential for political bias by the Court (Funk 2010, 56–57) in that this judgment could be made on political rather than legal grounds. As explained by Tom Ginsburg (2008, 501), a state is able to avoid having its nationals prosecuted by the ICC by bringing a credible investigation or prosecution. It follows that the only states liable to have their nationals prosecuted are

- those who desire an ICC prosecution and wish the costs to be met by the international community through the ICC, or

- those that lack the capacity to conduct a credible investigation or prosecution.

Trigger Mechanisms

How does the ICC become involved in a situation; in other words, what triggers ICC involvement?

Referrals to, and investigations conducted by, the Prosecutor are termed *situations*, referring to conflict situations rather than to specific cases.[7] Here, there was a fundamental dispute between the United States and other states about the role of the UN Security Council. The United States wanted the Security Council, and only the Security Council, to be the trigger that referred situations to the ICC, but other states disagreed because they believed the Court should not be subject to political control by the Security Council or by states if it was to be a credible institution (Cassese 2003, 733).

The trigger mechanism in Article 13 provides that a situation can come before the ICC in three ways, where

- a situation has been referred to the Prosecutor by a state party, in which case it must be investigated if the Prosecutor believes there is a reasonable basis to proceed;

- a situation has been referred by the Security Council under Chapter VII of the UN Charter; in this case any person anywhere is subject to potential prosecution and the case must be investigated if the Prosecutor believes there is a reasonable basis to proceed; or

- the Prosecutor initiates an investigation on his own authority *(proprio motu)* and examines information received and, where she considers there is a reasonable basis to initiate an investigation, requests authorization from the Pre-Trial Chamber. Where authorization is given, the Prosecutor conducts an investigation.

In each case, the Prosecutor commences with an informal investigation, called a "preliminary investigation," to collect evidence, examine witnesses, and determine if crimes within the jurisdiction of the Court have occurred. The power of the Prosecutor to initiate an investigation proved highly contentious in the negotiations over the ICC Statute, and a number of safeguards have been included in the Statute to guard against an overzealous exercise of this power by a Prosecutor. The safeguards provide the following:

- The Prosecutor must examine "information" on alleged crimes and must ask for the authorization of the Pre-Trial Chamber of the ICC if there is to be a more thorough, formal "investigation" (ICC Article 15).

- The Security Council under Article 16 has the power to pass a resolution under Chapter VII to block the commencement or continuance of investigations for periods of up to twelve months at a time (ICC Article 16).

- The Prosecutor's decision to proceed with an investigation or prosecution is subject to judicial review by the Pre-Trial Chamber.

- When the Prosecutor wishes to obtain an arrest warrant or a summons, she must apply for it to the Pre-Trial Chamber.

- When a suspect is arrested or voluntarily appears, the Pre-Trial Chamber must hold a hearing to confirm the charges.

The role of the Prosecutor is discussed in the section "The Prosecutor and the Office of the Prosecutor," later in this chapter.

Punishment

The Court is empowered to impose a sentence of imprisonment "for a specified number of years, which may not exceed a maximum of 30 years" (ICC Article 77[1][a]) and a term of life imprisonment where this is justified by the extreme gravity of the crime and the individual circumstances of the person convicted (ICC Article 77[1][b]).

The Court can grant/order release after part of a sentence has been served, but this should not be seen as a form of conditional release or parole because, once granted, the decision cannot be reversed. Reductions in sentence can be given if a person has been convicted of more than one crime or a set of specified criteria are satisfied, namely, willingness to cooperate with the Court on a range of matters, including in the enforcement of judgments and orders, in investigations and prosecutions, and in locating assets that could form part of reparations; and where other factors are present that establish a change of circumstances justifying a reduction in sentence.

Fines may also be imposed in addition to imprisonment, and the Court can order the forfeiture of assets derived directly or indirectly from crime (Schabas 2011, 336–37).

U.S. OPPOSITION TO THE INTERNATIONAL CRIMINAL COURT

In the past, there was some support in the United States for an international court that could deal with transnational crimes such as violence against diplomats and hijacking,[8] and in 1988 the U.S. House of Representatives passed a resolution that the United States "should pursue the establishment of an International Criminal Court to assist the international community in dealing more effectively with those acts of terrorism, drug trafficking, genocide and torture" (quoted in Feinstein and Lindberg 2009, 30). Again in 1990, Congress recommended that the President explore the creation of an international criminal court to combat transnational crimes (p. 31).

While the Clinton administration opposed the Statute, it nevertheless signed it on the last possible day, but at the same time Clinton advised President Bush not to send it to the U.S. Senate for ratification, arguing that there were "significant flaws in the treaty" (quoted in Feinstein and Lindberg 2009, 39). This, despite the fact that the Clinton administration originally supported the creation of the ICC, actively participated in the drafting process, "expressed satisfaction with most elements of the resulting Statute," and was a strong supporter of the ICTY and the ICTR (Mayerfeld 2003, 95; Orentlicher 2004, 416).

The concern expressed by President Clinton at the time of signing was that the Court would "not only exercise authority over personnel of states that have ratified the treaty, but also claim jurisdiction over personnel of states that have not" (quoted in Feinstein and Lindberg 2009, 39).

When the George W. Bush administration took office in 2001, it, and the U.S. Congress, took a number of deliberate steps to try and limit the effectiveness of the ICC and to exempt the United States as far as possible from the ambit of the Court's powers (Bosco 2014, 71). Despite having signed the Statute early in 2002, the United States advised the United Nations that "the United States does not intend to become a party to the treaty" and that "accordingly, the United States has no legal obligations arising from its signature on December 31, 2000" (quoted in Goldsmith 2003, 97).

Since this act of repudiation, the United States has continued its opposition to the ICC and has taken steps to mitigate its possible impact on the United States. Significantly, this action has been taken despite U.S. support for the cause of human rights. Generally, U.S. opposition to the ICC "is widely seen as a manifestation of America's deeper . . . antipathy toward multilateral institutions" (Orentlicher 2004, 415).

It is now helpful to consider the principal objections raised by the United States to the ICC, many of which continue to hold sway within the U.S. government and Congress. These objections center on the independence of the ICC from the Security Council, the perceived lack of accountability of the Court, the perceived independence of the Prosecutor, the potential for the Court to bring U.S. citizens before it, and its potential to conduct political, anti-American cases against the United States.

Prosecutions

The United States argued generally and fundamentally that ICC prosecutions should be limited to cases referred to it by the Security Council and therefore the Prosecutor should have no independent power to commence a prosecution. Other states considered that having the Security Council as the gatekeeper of the ICC would undermine the very concept of the ICC and that the veto-holding permanent members of the Security Council would effectively render the permanent five members (United States, Russia, China, France, and the United Kingdom) immune from prosecution (Goldsmith 2003, 90).

The United States continues to maintain its opposition to the independent power of the Prosecutor despite the safeguards against the arbitrary or capricious exercise of the power. These safeguards are that

- investigations by the Prosecutor must first be approved by the Pre-Trial Chamber of three judges,

- the Prosecutor can be removed for misconduct by a simple majority of state parties,

- there are generous procedural protections for defendants, and

- the complementarity principle "virtually assures that the ICC will not hear cases against major international military actors such as the U.S." (Ginsburg 2008, 500)

Accountability

The United States continues to assert that the ICC lacks accountability and, in particular, is not placed under the supervision of national governments. The key objection continues to be the capacity to act without the approval of the Security Council and therefore evade the veto that the United States has the right to exercise as one of the five permanent members (Mayerfeld 2003, 105).

The United States claims that its objections are not peculiar to the United States but are instead matters of universal concern. While continuing to advocate the primacy of human rights, the United States believes that the ICC is not an appropriate means of enforcing those rights. Instead, the United States has asserted that human rights are best protected by promoting democracy at the national level and not through creating international enforcement instruments (Mayerfeld 2003, 106, 118).

It is argued that, given its position favoring the Security Council on the instigation of prosecutions, the United States is in effect declaring that the Security Council is a better instrument for enforcement of rights than the ICC. The problems with this position include the fact that there are checks and balances affecting the ICC that the Security Council is not subject to, and that the ICC is accountable to member states that have the right to remove judges and the Prosecutor. The same cannot be said of the five permanent members of the Security Council (Mayerfeld 2003, 125).

UN Security Council and the International Criminal Court

One scholar believes that U.S. policy in relation to the ICC is fundamentally grounded in the relationship between the ICC and the Security Council. While other technical reasons are advanced for its opposition to the Court, the independence that the ICC enjoys from the Security Council is seen as the key basis for U.S. "hostility" to the ICC; its other objections merely flow from the fact that under the Statute, the Security Council does not control the Court (Schabas 2004, 701). In concurring with this argument in terms of U.S. control of an international entity, Allison Danner (2003, 516) argues, "Some states, such as the United States, refuse to trust an entity whose jurisdiction they cannot directly control."

The original International Law Commission draft of the ICC Statute was acceptable to the United States because it provided for an international criminal court that was subordinate to the Security Council and fundamentally constituted a permanent version of the ICTY established by the Council a year before. In particular, as the head of the U.S. delegation to the negotiations stated,

> Though not identical to U.S. positions, the ILC draft recognized that the Security Council should determine whether cases that pertain to its function under Chapter VII of the UN Charter should be considered by the ICC, that the Security Council must act before any alleged crime of aggression could be prosecuted against an individual, and that the prosecutor should act only in

cases referred either by a State party to the treaty or by the Council. (Quoted in Schabas 2004, 712–13)

As William Schabas (2004, 713–14) notes, this U.S. focus on the role of the Security Council vis-à-vis the ICC appears in other subsequent major policy declarations including, the following statement: "Unlike other war crimes tribunals, such as for Rwanda and the former Yugoslavia, the ICC does not operate under the functional supervision of the UN Security Council, and is thus further removed from the will of sovereign states."

There is no doubt that the nexus between the ICC and the Security Council was a major issue in the negotiation of the Statute. The Like-Minded Group was determined that the ICC would possess judicial independence and be free from political control, including especially that of the Security Council. It is argued then, that all other U.S. objections to the ICC flow from this issue, and as Schabas (2004, 716) summarizes the issue, "If a permanent member of the Security Council can effectively block prosecutions, then the United States is in control.… It can only do it with difficulty, and without legal certainty, under the Statute as it now stands."

U.S. Nationals

The notion that U.S. military and other personnel might be deployed in states which are parties to the ICC Statute and therefore could, in theory, be targeted for war crimes trials before the Court caused the U.S. military to mount a substantial lobby against the ICC. The lobby included briefings to more than one hundred foreign military attachés in Washington about the "potential menace" posed to their troops by the Court, dissemination of a statement that the United States wanted to avoid "the wrong kind of Court" and warning other states about the threat posed by "independent prosecutors with unbridled discretion," and the dispatching of a team of senior Pentagon officers to European capitals to convey the U.S. arguments against the Court (Ball 2009, 495). These concerns were subsequently reflected in the American Servicemembers' Protection Act (ASPA) discussed in the following section.

Countering the International Criminal Court: U.S. Responses

The United States early on adopted a number of measures to counter the possible actions of the ICC in the belief that it might become "a runaway court" and because of its potential to exercise jurisdiction over nationals of non-state parties (Orentlicher 2004, 418). These measures are discussed in this section.

American Servicemembers' Protection Act (ASPA)

In August 2002, a month after the Statute of the ICC came into effect, the U.S. Congress showed its rejection of the ICC in the enactment of this law. It authorizes the President to use all means necessary and appropriate to bring about the release from captivity U.S. or Allied personnel detained or imprisoned on behalf of the ICC and prohibits any cooperation with, or financial support to, the ICC. It further prohibits military aid to nations supporting the ICC (except for NATO states and other allies) and requires the President to certify that U.S. forces that participate in peacekeeping will not be subject to ICC prosecutions. It also prohibits U.S. participation in peacekeeping forces to states that are parties to the ICC Statute (Mayerfeld 2003, 95). The President has a waiver power in the national interest of the United States.

By the mid-2000s, the Bush administration's position on the cessation of military aid had begun to soften as U.S. officials began to believe it was adversely affecting U.S. national security because aid to states seeking to combat terrorism was being denied to them. In addition, by October 2006, ASPA had been amended to remove restrictions on providing military training to all nations. By January 2008, all prohibitions on forms of military assistance had been repealed (Dutton 2013, 56).

Nethercutt Amendment

In December 2004, Congress adopted the Nethercutt Amendment as part of the U.S. Foreign Appropriations Bill. This legislation is far more wide-reaching than ASPA and authorizes the loss of Economic Support Funds (ESF) to all countries, including many key U.S. allies that have ratified the ICC treaty but have not signed a bilateral immunity agreement with the United States (ICCnow.org). The President has the authority to waive the provisions of the Amendment, and in March 2009 the Amendment was not included in the annual Omnibus Appropriation Act. On November 28, 2006, President Bush waived funding restrictions under the Nethercutt Amendment for fourteen countries whose ESF aid had previously been cut (ICCnow.org). However, three countries—Ireland, Brazil, and Venezuela—still have a total of approximately $15 million in ESF aid threatened (ICCnow.org).

Article 98 Immunity Bilateral Agreements

Formulated as part of its campaign against the ICC, these Immunity Bilateral Agreements commit states that enter into them with the United States to send a U.S. national requested by the ICC back to the United States instead of surrendering him or her to the ICC. No European Union states[9] have signed these agreements, and Canada and Australia have also refused to sign.[10] The United States approached almost all countries to enter into the agreement regardless of whether it had ratified the ICC Statute (Kelley 2007, 575).

Peacekeeping

The United States maintains that the power of states and of the Prosecutor to refer a case to the ICC renders members of the U.S. Armed Forces participating in peacemaking operations worldwide open to prosecution by the ICC and that such prosecutions could be motivated by political hostility to the United States (Cassese 2003, 733). As the only superpower and provider of the bulk of finance and military forces for peacekeeping operations, the United States considers it essential that its personnel be protected from politically inspired legal action in the ICC (Ball 2009, 501).

In mid-2000 the United States succeeded in having the Security Council give UN peacekeepers whose governments had not ratified the ICC Statute immunity from ICC investigation for twelve months with yearly renewals of this immunity permitted "for as long as may be necessary" (Goldsmith 2003, 97). The United States had threatened to veto all future peacekeeping operations if permanent immunity was not granted. However, pushback from other states resulted in the United States accepting one-year periods of immunity with the possibility of renewals (Mayerfeld 2003, 95). On June 23, 2004, the United States formally withdrew its request to the Security Council to renew the resolution that granted this immunity, and the resolution expired on June 30, 2004. It seems therefore that this element of policy toward the ICC is no longer to be employed (Stahn 2005, 699).

CHANGES IN U.S. ATTITUDE TOWARD THE INTERNATIONAL CRIMINAL COURT

Generally, the U.S. attitude toward the ICC softened with the change in the U.S. administration in the 2008 election. "In effect the great tide of Bush's anti-ICC legislation had receded by the time President Obama took office" (Feinstein and Lindberg 2009, 53). Nevertheless, the United States has not been convinced that it should delegate its sovereignty to the Court, and it remains wary of the power of the Court to punish noncompliance (Dutton 2013, 56).

A major influence on the U.S. attitude was the humanitarian crisis and conflict in Darfur, Sudan, where the United States stated that genocide had taken place (Bosco 2014, 113). In March 2005, the United States did not veto but abstained on a resolution before the Security Council to refer the Darfur situation to the ICC, thereby giving tacit approval to the ICC having jurisdiction (Feinstein and Lindberg 2009, 53–54). The United States has also enacted laws—the Genocide Accountability Act and the Child Soldiers Protection and Accountability Act—that give the United States a clear basis to prosecute war crimes, indicating that the United States has enhanced its legal regime to prosecute U.S. nationals who commit such crimes. This action avoids any potential ICC claim to jurisdiction and gives concrete effect to the complementarity principle (p. 57). Similarly, the United States agreed with the UN Security Council to refer the situation in Libya to the ICC for investigation. However, in the cases of both Darfur and Libya, the United States insisted that a special provision be inserted in the resolution exempting from ICC jurisdiction any alleged crimes committed by non-parties to the Statute arising out of the operations authorized by the Council (Dutton 2013, 57).

Other action taken by the United States suggests that in recent times, the relationship between the United States and the ICC has become much less hostile and much more cooperative (Dutton 2013, 55). For example, in 2010, the United States issued a public statement disapproving Kenya's decision to invite Omar Al-Bashir, the President of Sudan, to attend a celebration of its new constitution (see Box 9.1 on Sudan). It also supported an investigation by the Prosecutor into postelection violence in Kenya and urged leaders there to cooperate with the ICC (p. 58). Nevertheless, the negotiation of exemption provisions for nonparties and its unease about ICC jurisdiction over the crime of aggression signify that the United States "remains uncomfortable with an independent court and prosecutor with broad jurisdictional reach" (p. 59).

THE INTERNATIONAL CRIMINAL COURT IN ACTION

To date, all international criminal tribunals have conducted lengthy procedures and faced complaints about the slow pace of justice. The ICC has proved to be the slowest since the Nuremberg trials. Comparing the ICC with the ICTY reveals that the first ICTY trial began slightly more than one year after the first appearance of the accused.

At the ICTR the period was seven months, and at the Special Court for Sierra Leone the period was fifteen months.

Inquiries, Arrests, Prosecutions, and Trials Since Inception

According to the Prosecutor, as of September 2014, the OTP was investigating nine "situations": Uganda, Democratic Republic of Congo (DRC), Sudan, two situations in Central African Republic (CAR), Kenya, Libya, Côte d'Ivoire, and Mali. Of these, Uganda, DRC, CAR, and Mali were referred by the states themselves; Sudan (Darfur) and Libya were referred by the Security Council; and Kenya and Cote d'Ivoire were begun by the Prosecutor (ICC, Situations and Cases). On September 24, 2014, the Prosecutor announced that she was intending to inquire into atrocities in the CAR arising during months of fighting that left about five thousand people dead. The OTP is also conducting preliminary examinations into alleged crimes committed in Honduras, Afghanistan, Korea, CAR, Comoros, Ukraine, and Iraq and is assessing if "genuine national proceedings" were being carried out in Georgia, Colombia, and Nigeria (ICC Situations and Cases).

We consider two countries where the Prosecutor has brought cases before the ICC, namely, Sudan and the Democratic Republic of the Congo (DRC). In relation to Sudan, the decision to issue an arrest warrant for the President of that country was controversial. The prosecution record in relation to the DRC is mixed. The pace of proceedings has been described as "glacial" and a source of disappointment and anxiety to civil society and victims there (Glasius 2009, 512).

BOX 9.1   Sudan and the International Criminal Court

The Darfur conflict began in 2003 when local groups accused Khartoum of neglecting the region and favoring some ethnic groups over others. There were disputes over land and access to natural resources, and the situation became violent. Rebel groups attacked police and military units (Feinstein and Lindberg 2009, 70). Responding to the events in Darfur, the government bombed villages and supported Janjaweed militias comprising members of Arabic-speaking tribes providing them with arms and weapons. The resulting violence killed more than 200,000 civilians and displaced 1.6 million persons. Hundreds of thousands fled across the border into Chad seeking refuge (p. 70). In May 2004, Human Rights Watch accused the government of massive ethnic cleansing, and the UN Security Council declared that those responsible must be held accountable.

In July 2004, the U.S. Congress passed a resolution declaring the crisis to be genocide and on December 9, 2004, the U.S. Secretary of State testified before the U.S. Senate Committee on Foreign Relations that genocide was occurring in the western region of Darfur (Schiff 2008, 175). President Bush called for a full UN investigation, and the following month the UN Security Council authorized a commission of experts to examine reports of atrocities and identify those responsible (Bosco 2014, 105). While the commission did not find genocide because of lack of appropriate evidence, it did find that grave crimes had been committed (Schiff 2008, 175).

The issue of arrest warrants against Omar al-Bashir, the President of Sudan, by the ICC focused attention on the conflict and, it is argued, led to a period of intense diplomacy seeking a peaceful settlement (Feinstein and Lindberg 2009, 74).

On March 31, 2005, the UN Security Council, by Resolution 1593, acting under Chapter VII of the UN Charter, after considering a report from the International Commission of Inquiry on Darfur, Sudan, agreed (with the United States and three other states abstaining) to refer the situation in the Darfur region of Sudan to the ICC. This was the first time the UN Security Council had referred a situation to the ICC. While the Sudan is not a state party to the ICC Statute, the Security Council is nevertheless given power by the ICC Statute to take such action.

In June 2005, the ICC Prosecutor officially announced his office would open an investigation into the situation in Darfur, Sudan.

In April 2007, the ICC issued a warrant of arrest for Ahmad Haroun, formerly Minister of the Interior and Minister of State for Humanitarian Affairs of Sudan. He was charged with twenty counts of crimes against humanity (murder, persecution, forcible transfer of population, rape, inhumane acts, imprisonment or severe deprivation of liberty, and torture) and twenty-two counts of war crimes (murder, attacks against the civilian population, destruction of property, rape, pillaging, and outrage upon personal dignity). On one occasion Haroun flew by helicopter to Darfur and urged the Janjaweed militia to treat Darfur villagers as "booty." Following his visit, several villages were set on fire and many civilians were found dead (Bosco 2014, 128). He remains at large.

Also in April 2007, an arrest warrant was issued for Ali Muhammad Ali Abd-Al-Rahman ("Ali Kushayb"), alleged to be the leader of the Militia/Janjaweed. He was charged with twenty-two counts of crimes against humanity (murder, deportation or forcible transfer of population, imprisonment or other severe deprivation of physical liberty in violation of fundamental rules of international law, torture, persecution, and inhumane acts of inflicting serious bodily injury and suffering) and twenty-eight counts of war crimes (violence to life and person, outrage upon personal dignity [in particular humiliating and degrading treatment], intentionally directing an attack against a civilian population, pillaging, rape, and destroying or seizing property). Information against him included evidence that he had personally inspected a group of naked women before they were raped by men wearing military uniforms (Bosco 2014, 128).

In responding to the charges against these two men, President Bashir promoted them within the government and began a campaign to discredit the Court, claiming it was anti-Sudan and anti-African (Feinstein and Lindberg 2009, 55). The government declared it would not surrender the two accused or any other Sudanese to the ICC and that the charges were politically motivated.

In July 2008, the ICC Prosecutor asked the ICC to issue an arrest warrant for the Head of State of Sudan, Omar al-Bashir, on charges of war crimes, crimes against humanity, and genocide. Bashir had been President since 1993. The proposed prosecution related to events occurring in the Darfur region of Sudan. It was feared that launching a prosecution in the ICC against the President of Sudan would adversely affect peace arrangements then being negotiated, and NGOs active in the region expressed concern this would make their task much more problematic (Ralph 2011, 76). In addition, every permanent member of the UN Security Council communicated concern about this action (Bosco 2014, 144).

In March 2009, the Chamber agreed to the issue of an arrest warrant on an indictment that, while dropping the allegation of genocide, included five counts of crimes against humanity and two counts of war crimes. A second arrest warrant was issued in July 2010. The charges

(Continued)

(Continued)

assert that mobilizing the state apparatus is evidence of a plan by the President to destroy ethnic groups. The Prosecutor estimates that thirty-five thousand persons have been killed through use of the government apparatus and another one hundred thousand have died from starvation in displacement camps in the desert. Rape is alleged to have been integral to the plan (Ginsburg 2008, 503).

In reaction to the charges, the Sudan government expelled more than a dozen aid agencies working in Darfur. Diplomats agreed that they should avoid meeting with the President when he was under indictment. In July 2009, the African Union declared that its member states were not obliged to honor the arrest warrants and warned of the impact of the indictment on the peace process in Sudan (Bosco 2014, 155, 157). Al-Bashir remains at large despite having traveled outside the Sudan to numerous countries, a number of which, including Chad and Kenya, as state parties, were required to cooperate with the Court and arrest him. Some states refused to accept him (Egypt), warned that he would be arrested if he visited (Denmark), or discouraged him visiting (Turkey; Bosco 2014, 157).

The United States suggested the Prosecutor should proceed and made it clear it would veto any Security Council resolution deferring the prosecution under Article 16 (Ralph 2011, 77). The Prosecutor was also criticized for not seeking a sealed warrant that would be made public only when Bashir traveled outside the Sudan. Pressure was exerted on European governments to have the UN Security Council postpone the investigation under Article 16 of the Statute in order to give Bashir an opportunity to pursue peace. The British were heavily criticized in the media for supporting what was described as a "shocking moral abdication" (Bosco 2014, 146). France came out against this proposal, but President Bashir lobbied hard for it and persuaded the African Union and the Arab League to support him. China indicated it might support postponement. The United States did not support a deferral, arguing that it would send the wrong signal to the President and undermine efforts to ensure accountability. The UN Security Council, with the United States abstaining, voted to extend the mandate of the African Union–UN Mission in Darfur and rejected the postponement option (Bosco 2014, 146; Feinstein and Lindberg 2009, 57).

On March 1, 2012, an arrest warrant was issued for Abdel Raheem Muhammad Hussein, Minister for National Defence, former Minister of Interior, and former Special Representative of the Sudanese President in Darfur. He was charged with seven counts of crimes against humanity (persecution, murder, forcible transfer, rape, inhumane acts, imprisonment or severe deprivation of liberty, and torture) and with six counts of war crimes (murder, attacks against a civilian population, destruction of property, rape, pillaging, and outrage upon personal dignity). He remains at large.

BOX 9.2   Democratic Republic of Congo (DRC) and the International Criminal Court (ICC)

The conflict in the DRC is long-standing involving ethnic tensions and fighting between militias. Between January 2002 and December 2003, the growth of violent militias was exacerbated by fighting between DRC militias and forces from Rwanda and Uganda. Tensions between ethnic groups resulted and more than eight thousand civilians were killed and half a million people displaced. Sexual violence and use of child soldiers characterized the conflict (Feinstein and Lindberg 2009, 65). Thomas Lubanga had been the leader of a militia group since 2001 in the Ituri region of the northeast of the country, one of the most violent regions. The Lubanga group (Union of Congolese Patriots) drew on the Hema ethnic group but also had links to Uganda and Rwanda militaries. Lubanga was involved in an attack on UN peacekeepers in February 2005 that killed nine Bangladesh military. He was arrested following a UN crackdown against the main militia groups. Lubanga had been a target of the ICC Prosecutor since the start of his investigation into events in the DRC, and there was solid information on his use of child soldiers but inadequate evidence that showed him ordering violent crimes. The Prosecutor was concerned he might be released by the Congolese authorities (Bosco 2014, 124).

Human Rights Watch reported that soon after the ICC announced an investigation into events in the DRC government and insurgent leaders warned their followers against committing war crimes or attacking civilians (Feinstein and Lindberg 2009, 75).

- July 2003: One month after being sworn in as Prosecutor, the Prosecutor announced that he had selected the situation in Ituri Province in the DRC as "the most urgent situation to be followed" (Glasius 2009, 498). In April 2004 the DRC government, led by Joseph Kabila, after having been urged to do so by the Prosecutor, referred "crimes within the jurisdiction of the Court allegedly committed anywhere in the territory of the DRC" to the Prosecutor (Glasius 2009, 498; Schiff 2008, 212). Also, in 2004 the Prosecutor announced that he had been discussing cooperation with the DRC: "We would contribute by prosecuting the leaders who bear the greatest responsibility for crimes committed on or after July 1, 2002. National authorities, with the assistance of the international community, could implement appropriate mechanisms to address other responsible individuals" (quoted in Schabas 2008, 752).

- March 2005: Thomas Lubanga Dyilo, leader of the Ituri-based Union of Congolese Patriots (UCP) was arrested by the DRC authorities on charges of genocide and crimes against humanity. In March 2006, after having secured an ICC arrest warrant, the Prosecutor arranged with the DRC for Lubanga to be transferred from Kinshasa prison to The Hague. He was charged with the conscription and use of child soldiers and not with genocide or crimes against humanity. While it might be argued that Lubanga was facing more serious charges in the DRC than before the ICC, it must be pointed out that the DRC had no adequate justice system to deal with the charges and there were concerns that he might be released there (Schabas 2008, 744).

- January 2007: The Pre-Trial Chamber of the ICC confirmed the charges against Lubanga, and the trial was expected to begin in begin in March 2008.

- March 2008: The Lubanga trial was postponed to June.

- June 2008: The trial was stayed *sine die* by the Chamber when the Prosecutor refused to disclose potentially exculpatory documents to the defense because of a confidentiality agreement with his sources, the UN, and others. The Chamber ordered Lubanga's release on the basis that a fair trial was impossible, but the order was successfully overturned and he was kept in custody while the Prosecutor appealed.

- November 2008: The confidentiality claim was waived by the UN and all documents made available. That month the trial of Lubanga commenced.

- March 2012: Lubanga was convicted of enlisting and conscripting child soldiers and using them to participate actively in hostilities and sentenced to fourteen years imprisonment (the Prosecutor had asked for a thirty-year sentence). According to Human Rights Watch, this trial has raised awareness among the people of the DRC about the consequences of recruiting and using child soldiers (Feinstein and Lindberg 2009, 75).

- October 2007: Germain Katanga was transferred to The Hague from DRC and charged with murder, inhumane acts, sexual slavery, using child soldiers, intentionally attacking civilians and pillage primarily relating to an attack to a village in February 2003 (Glasius 2009, 499).

(Continued)

(Continued)

In November 2009 the trial commenced. In March 2014 he was convicted of one count of crimes against humanity (murder) and four counts of war crimes (murder, attacking a civilian population, destruction of property, and pillaging) committed on February 24, 2003, during the attack on the village of Bogoro, in the Ituri district of the DRC. In May 2014 he was sentenced to twelve years imprisonment.

- February 2008: Mathieu Ngudjolo Chui was arrested on similar charges to Katanga. In December 2009 the trial began. In December 2012 Mathieu Ngudjolo Chui was acquitted and released. The Trial Chamber found the evidence against him to be "too contradictory and too hazy." The Prosecutor has appealed the verdict.

- April 2008: An arrest warrant was unsealed for Bosco Ntaganda. A former associate of Lubanga, he was charged with conscription and use of child soldiers. He voluntarily surrendered to the ICC in March 2013. In June 2014 the charges against him confirmed. He is currently in custody awaiting trial on thirteen counts of war crimes (murder and attempted murder; attacking civilians; rape; sexual slavery of civilians; pillaging; displacement of civilians; attacking protected objects; destroying the enemy's property; and rape, sexual slavery, enlistment, and conscription of child soldiers under the age of fifteen years and using them to participate actively in hostilities) and five counts of crimes against humanity (murder and attempted murder, rape, sexual slavery, persecution, forcible transfer of population).

- October 2010: Callixte Mbarushimana was arrested by French authorities and transferred to The Hague following the issue of ICC warrant of arrest. He was charged with five counts of crimes against humanity (murder, torture, rape, inhumane acts, and persecution) and eight counts of war crimes (attacks against the civilian population, murder, mutilation, torture, rape, inhumane treatment, destruction of property, and pillaging). In December 2011, the Pre-Trial Chamber declined to confirm the charges against him and he was released from custody.

The Prosecutor and the Office of the Prosecutor

The ICC Prosecutor exercises a complex, challenging, and vital function in the scheme of international criminal justice created by the Statute of the ICC. Despite his apparent independence of action,[11] there are significant checks and balances on the Prosecutor's powers. This compares to prosecutors at Nuremberg, who chose the accused and drafted and issued indictments without any substantive judicial oversight, except that amendments to the indictment required judicial approval (Schabas 2008, 732).

In the case of the ICTY, the UN Security Council gave the Prosecutor an independent role and freedom to select the cases to be prosecuted, but later the judges of the ICTY threatened to intervene in relation to selection in a strategy designed to complete the work of the ICTY. They were able to justify this by relying on the UN Security Council Resolution that calls on the tribunal to ensure that indictments concentrate on the most senior leaders suspected of crimes (Schabas 2008, p. 733).

Discretion to Prosecute

The ICC Prosecutor has discretion in the sense that he is not obliged to initiate a prosecution once a situation has been referred to him: Article 53 permits him to decline to prosecute after a preliminary investigation. Generally, prosecutorial discretion in the case of international tribunals and courts recognizes the reality that there are potentially thousands of cases that could be prosecuted and that as a practical matter there needs to be a selection process so that the system is not overloaded. It is for this reason that prosecutors are commonly given the discretionary power to prosecute.

In a 1997 statement to the ICC Preparatory Commission, Louise Arbour (now Justice Arbour of the Supreme Court of Canada), former ICTY Prosecutor, said that in the case of prosecutions before an international tribunal as opposed to domestic prosecutions, "the discretion to prosecute is considerably larger, and the criteria upon which such prosecutorial discretion is to be exercised are ill-defined and complex." In her view, the challenge for a Prosecutor is to "choose from many meritorious complaints the appropriate ones for international intervention, rather than to weed out weak or frivolous ones"[12] (quoted in Schabas 2008, 735). It is interesting to note, for example, that the IMT that followed World War II indicted only twenty-four persons out of the thousands who were candidates for prosecution, and only twenty-eight were indicted by the Tokyo Tribunal (Brubacher 2004, 75).

Oversight of the Prosecutor

While Article 42 of the Rome Statute of the ICC declares that "the Office of the Prosecutor shall act independently as a separate organ of the Court," we have already alluded to the significant oversight exercised over the Prosecutor by both the ICC itself, and by the Security Council and the state parties. For example, the "trigger mechanisms" allow the Prosecutor to identify crimes that he proposes to investigate, but judicial authorization is first required, the Prosecutor is required to defer to national laws and jurisdictional claims, and the UN Security Council has the power under Article 16 to defer an investigation for twelve months, which can be renewed for the same period without limit.

However, the Prosecutor is tasked not simply to make decisions about complaints but to interact with states and sometimes with the UN Security Council to navigate the complex framework of safeguards and practical limitations imposed by the Statute. Consequently, it is necessary for the Prosecutor to "make decisions that are both compliant with the objective legal criteria but capable of being implemented in a manner that adapts to the prevailing political and social context" (Brubacher 2004, 74). In other words, the Prosecutor cannot function in a vacuum but must operate within a context that takes account of the need for the support of both states and the UN Security Council (Greenawalt 2007, 608).

Prosecutorial Strategy, Regulations, Policy Papers

It is quite common for prosecutors in a national criminal justice system to issue guidelines or circulars about how the prosecution function is to be exercised, that is, how the prosecutor intends to exercise her considerable discretionary powers in a common law system and, to a lesser extent, in a civil law system. (The situation of domestic prosecutors is discussed more fully in Chapter 5.) Explaining how a discretion is to be exercised, and on what principles, assists in refuting claims that a Prosecutor is political in his or her decision making, in other words, lacking in impartiality. Accordingly, the Prosecutor should, as a matter of principle, treat like cases alike and apply a coherent and consistent set of criteria to each case and, as required by the Statute, investigate both incriminating and exonerating circumstances. For example, the draft Code of Conduct for the ICC Prosecutor, issued by the International Association of Prosecutors, states that prosecutors should "be, and appear to be, consistent, objective, impartial and independent" (Danner 2003, 537).

The Office of the ICC Prosecutor (OTP) has published a number of documents, including a *Prosecutorial Strategy* (ICC 2010) and a set of *Regulations of the Office of the Prosecutor* (OTP 2009) as well as explanatory policy papers (ICC Policy Papers) that collectively explain how the OTC will conduct its functions and exercise the prosecutorial discretion. In addition, *Reports on Preliminary Examination Activities* (OTP 2013a) are published for each year of operation. These publications will be referred to in the following discussion, as appropriate, in explaining how the OTC functions within the complex framework of the Statute.

Admissibility and Jurisdiction

The Prosecutor must first consider whether "a situation meets the legal criteria established by the Statute to warrant investigation by the Court" (OTP 2013a, 3).

The first stage is for the OTP to *conduct a preliminary examination* of all situations that are submitted to the OTP. Here, the Prosecutor will make an initial assessment as to whether there exists a *prima facie* case; he must "evaluate the information" (Article 53)[13] and advise those who provided it of the outcome of his evaluation. This creates a formal channel of communication with referring states and NGOs (Brubacher 2004, 77–78). The OTP may seek additional information and even take testimony at the Court (OTP 2013a, 4). The framework of the preliminary examination is that in order to decide if there is a reasonable basis to proceed with an investigation into a situation, he must consider *jurisdiction, admissibility (issues of complementarity and gravity)*, and the *interests of justice.*

The Prosecutor must ask: Does the case come within the *jurisdiction* of the ICC? Was it committed in the territory of a state party or by a national of a state party? Is it a crime against humanity, a war crime, or the crime of genocide, and did the crime occur after July 1, 2002, when the Statute came into force? (If it occurred before that date, it is not admissible.)

On *admissibility*, the OTC must also give attention to the *complementarity principle*. As noted earlier, the OTC is required to defer to the national legal system concerned and must give notice to the state that would normally exercise jurisdiction so that state may challenge the validity of the case on the ground that it is not admissible.[14] It will therefore examine the existence of relevant national proceedings, bearing in mind the need to investigate and prosecute "those most responsible" for the most serious crime (OTP 2013b). It will also assess the "genuineness" of domestic investigations or prosecutions (OTP 2013a, 4). When the Prosecutor believes that a state is "unable or unwilling" to carry out the investigation of the case, she essentially has to prove that a state's criminal justice system lacks capacity or competence to act or that it is being controlled by the executive authority of the state. This will likely be an area of great contention (Danner 2003, 517).

It is intended that cases that lack *gravity* are dealt with by the national legal system and not the ICC (Brubacher 2004, 78). The Prosecutorial Strategy provides that "in appropriate cases the OTP will expand its general prosecutorial strategy to encompass mid- or high-level perpetrators, or even particularly notorious low-level perpetrators, with a view to building cases up to reach those most responsible for the most serious crimes" (OTP 2013a, 3, ftn. 4). According to the OTC Report for 2013, gravity "includes an assessment of the scale, nature, manner of commission of the crimes, and their impact, bearing in mind

the potential cases that would likely arise from an investigation of the situation" (OTC 2013a, 4).

In considering the *interests of justice,* the OTC says that it must assess whether there are substantial reasons to believe that an investigation would not serve those interests (OTC 2013a, 4). This is a familiar expression in legal systems and also appears in international human rights instruments. In making this assessment the OTC is required to take account of all the circumstances, including "the gravity of the crime, the interests of victims, the age or infirmity of the alleged perpetrators, and his or her role in the alleged crime" (Article 53[2]). The OTP (2007) published a substantial policy paper titled *The Interests of Justice,* which sets out the understanding of the Prosecutor of the concept. The points noted include the following:

- There is a presumption in favor of investigation or prosecution and it would be exceptional to decline to investigate or prosecute in the interests of justice. A decision not to proceed on the basis of the interests of justice "should be understood as a course of last resort," and other options, including not opening an investigation or ceasing proceedings, may be available. (p. 1)

- In assessing the interests of victims, the Prosecutor will conduct a dialogue with victims and with representatives of local communities and will seek the views of others involved in the situation, including local leaders, other states, and local and international organizations. (p. 6)

- The objects and purpose of the Statute, namely, "the prevention of serious crimes of concern to the international community through ending impunity," will guide the OTP in its decision making concerning this issue. (p. 1)

- The Prosecutor is required to inform the Pre-Trial Chamber of a decision not to investigate or prosecute, and the Chamber may review that decision and confirm or reject it. (p. 1)

In one case, the Pre-Trial Chamber in its ruling on admissibility has said that the gravity test was aimed at ensuring that the Court only pursued cases against "the most senior leaders" in any situation under investigation. They were the persons who could "most effectively prevent or stop the commission of . . . crimes" (Schabas 2008, 746). In the view of the Chamber, the gravity test was provided to maximize the deterrent effect of the Court.

Matthew Brubacher (2004, 81) has suggested that the concept of the "interests of justice" also requires that the Prosecutor take account of the interests of the international community, "including the potential political ramifications of an investigation on the political environment of the state over which he is exercising jurisdiction." Here, considerations about an ongoing armed conflict or any post-conflict reconciliation processes, including a possible amnesty, will need to be taken into account. Will a prosecution impact an ongoing negotiating or reconciliation process and operate to destabilize a situation? Fundamentally, the issue may be "indicting people [when] you may be negotiating with them," as described by one British official involved in negotiations in the former Yugoslavia (quoted in Brubacher 2004, 82). Such a situation occurred in Sierra Leone when the Special Court indictment of Charles Taylor, the former President of Liberia, threatened to disrupt power-sharing arrangements in that country (p. 82).

The Prosecutor is likely to follow the determinations of the UN Security Council in such a situation, as happened in the case of the Democratic Republic of Congo when the Prosecutor's preliminary investigation followed a determination by the UN Security Council that the situation in one province was a threat to international peace and security under Chapter VII of the UN Charter (Brubacher 2004, 83).

Time, Declining to Initiate Investigation

The OTP notes that the Statute stipulates no timelines or time limits for the conduct of preliminary examinations but that the OTP may decide to decline to initiate an investigation where the factors stated in Article 53 (1)(a)-(c) are manifestly not satisfied, or it may continue to collect information in order to make a determination, or it may initiate the investigation, subject to any judicial review.

After, or together with, the determination of jurisdiction and admissibility issues, the Prosecutor is to evaluate the *credibility and reasonableness of the evidence* received. She must decide if a sufficient evidential basis for pursuing a prosecution exists (Article 53). She must be able to satisfy the Pre-Trial Chamber of this to obtain a warrant or summons. When she decides there is no reasonable basis to proceed, she must inform those who provided the information, and if they are states, they may request a judicial review of that decision (Rule 107 ICC Rules). It appears that the first Prosecutor together with officials of the Court conducted a ranking exercise in relation to the gravest situations over which the Court could exercise jurisdiction. Major conflict zones were first identified using information from the United Nations and human rights groups. After applying the criteria of the number of violent deaths over the last several years, the Democratic Republic of Congo (DRC) emerged at the top of the rankings. Accordingly, at his first press conference in July 2003, the Prosecutor announced he would examine first the situation in eastern DRC (Bosco 2014, 90).

Pre-Trial Chamber and Arrest Warrants

When an investigation is commenced after authorization by the Pre-Trial Chamber, arrest warrants may only be issued when authorized by the Chamber. When a suspect has been arrested, the Chamber will conduct a hearing to confirm the charges that are to be tried. When the Chamber finds there is insufficient evidence, it may decline to proceed with the charges (Danner 2003, 518).

Investigations and Resources

In practical terms, the Prosecutor will need to be mindful of the costs associated with full investigations. The first ICC allocated only about 3.9 million euros to the OTP out of a total budget of about 30.8 million euros (Danner 2003, 520). The ICC is funded by contributions from state parties and by the United Nations. It may also receive voluntary contributions (p. 527).

State Cooperation, Policing, and Enforcement Powers

In conducting investigations, the Prosecutor will be dependent on states, and much of the evidence needed to prosecute will be in the hands of state authorities. Article 86 requires that states cooperate with the Court. Only in limited circumstances can the Prosecutor conduct investigations on his own in a state without the consent of that state. In other cases, the Pre-Trial Chamber may authorize the OTP to investigate in the territory of a non-cooperating state, but there are stringent conditions attached to such authorization. The state may also deny assistance where the request concerns documents or evidence that relate to national security (Danner 2003, 528–29). Justice Arbour said, about her experience with the ICTR and ICTY, that "it is more likely that the Prosecutor . . . could be chronically enfeebled by inadequate enforcement powers combined with a persistent and widespread unwillingness of States Parties to co-operate" (quoted in Danner 2003, 530). This statement has proved to be true of the ICC Prosecutor.

In contrast to national court systems, there are no policing or enforcement functions located within the ICC and it cannot seize evidence, or make arrests or searches, or compel persons to testify without the cooperation of national governments.[15] As discussed earlier, the Prosecutor will need to give some attention to the issue of likely state cooperation when deciding to initiate an investigation. It may not be possible to count on voluntary state cooperation, and while the ICC may make a finding of noncompliance and refer the issue to the UN Security Council (where it made the initial reference) or to the Assembly of State parties, this may not prove to be very effective (Brubacher 2004, 92). "Naming and shaming" may be the only recourse. Recognizing that the importance of effective cooperation with states will be essential, the Prosecutor has created a Jurisdiction, Complementarity and Cooperation Division within the OTP (ICC 2004 Regulation 7).

Both the UN and the European Union have signed cooperation agreements with the Court. Belgium, France, and the Democratic Republic of Congo have arrested and transferred accused persons to the Court. The ICC has also entered into seven agreements with state parties covering witness protection and relocation, and Austria and the United Kingdom have signed agreements indicating their willingness to accept sentenced persons (Blattmann and Bowman 2008, 723).

State Noncooperation

The issue of state noncooperation with the Court has been demonstrated in the prosecution of the President of Sudan, Omar Al-Bashir. Two arrest warrants issued by the Court in March 2009 and July 2010 remain unexecuted. In March 2013, the Pre-Trial Chamber issued a Decision on the Non-compliance of the Republic of Chad with the Cooperation Requests Issued by the Court Regarding the Arrest and Surrender of Omar Hassan Ahmad Al-Bashir (ICC 2013). On March 6, 2009, and July 21, 2010, the ICC Registry had issued a request and a supplementary request to all state parties to the Rome Statute for the arrest and surrender of Al-Bashir. The requests called for the cooperation from all state parties in the arrest and surrender of Omar Al-Bashir, according to the Statute of the ICC.[16]

In August 2010, President Al-Bashir visited Chad and this was reported to the UN Security Council by the Court. Chad, a state party since 2007, refused to comply with the cooperation request from the Court to arrest him. In February 2013 Al Bashir visited Chad again. The Court had previously sent a request for cooperation to Chad concerning his presence there, seeking to have him arrested. Chad again failed to make any arrest.

In its decision concerning the noncompliance of Chad, the Chamber said that Chad had continued to "welcome the visits of Omar Al-Bashir on its territory without any attempt to arrest him, despite several warnings on the part of the Court" (ICC 2013, 9). In acting in this way, the Court found that Chad "is engaging in a consistent pattern of deliberately disregarding not only the Court's decisions and orders related to its obligation to cooperate in the arrest and surrender of Omar Al-Bashir, but also the Security Council Resolution 1593" (p. 9). The Court noted that it had no police force and relied on states to cooperate. In accordance with the Statute, it therefore referred the noncompliance of Chad to the UN Security Council to take the necessary measures it deemed appropriate.

THE INTERNATIONAL CRIMINAL COURT AND TRANSITIONAL JUSTICE

What will the ICC, and in particular the Prosecutor, do when confronted with a claim from a perpetrator of a crime within its jurisdiction to the protection of an amnesty granted to her or him under transitional justice arrangements? (Transitional justice amnesties are extensively described in Chapter 8: Transitional Justice.) This question is fraught with political and legal complexities. So far as the Statute of the ICC is concerned, its drafters grappled with the issue of whether an amnesty might constitute a bar to prosecution, but after a brief discussion, they abandoned the topic when it became clear there was no agreement about how to deal with them (Roche 2005, 567). Consequently, there is no explicit reference to amnesties or truth commissions or the like in the Statute, nor do any of the published policy papers of the OTP discuss amnesty.

While there is a general duty to prosecute under the Statute, amnesty could be allowed under what has been called a degree of "creative ambiguity" (Mayerfeld 2003, 103). This view is supported by the Article 17 test for admissibility of a "case," which allows the Prosecutor to decline to conduct an investigation where it is determined that "taking into account the gravity of the crime and the interests of victims, there are nonetheless substantial reasons to believe that an investigation would not serve the interests of justice" (Article 53). However, such a determination may be rejected by the Pre-Trial Chamber of the ICC. Carsten Stahn (2005, 698) argues that the concept of "interests of justice" need not be confined to considerations of criminal justice but could encompass alternative methods of providing justice such as truth commissions and the like. As stated earlier, the principle of complementarity requires the ICC to complement and not supplant national proceedings. Consequently, as noted, a "case" is inadmissible before the ICC unless the state "is unwilling or unable to genuinely carry out the investigation or prosecution" (Article 17[1]).

Based on this provision, those advocating amnesty could argue that it was not intended that the ICC intervene in a case dealt with by a truth commission because such commissions do not shield persons but promote truth and justice through truth telling, reconciliation, and victim reparation (Roche 2005, 568). If this argument fails to impress, the Prosecutor could be approached with the argument that an investigation "would not serve the interests of justice" (Article 53). Here, the Prosecutor would consider the gravity of the crime and victims interests, issues commonly given a high priority in designing the powers of truth commissions (Roche 2005, 568). It is also possible that the power of the UN Security Council to temporarily halt investigations or prosecutions might be deployed to facilitate the negotiation of a post-conflict peace agreement that included an amnesty (Scharf 1999, 514; Stahn 2005, 699).

In considering its response to an amnesty, the ICC may well examine the nature of the amnesty and its place in the context of any transition to democracy in a state, usually a post-conflict state. Relevant questions could include whether the amnesty is linked to a genuine democratic transition or whether it simply allows violators of human rights a pause before resuming violations. The ICC will be concerned that an amnesty does not become a form of impunity that extends to provide protection against future crimes (Mayerfeld 2003, 101). Other relevant questions would likely include whether an end to the conflict would have occurred without an amnesty, whether the state has agreed to establish a mechanism that will enable victims to be heard and discover the truth generally, whether the state has provided reparations or compensation to victims, whether the state has taken steps to prosecute those alleged to have committed violations of international humanitarian law, and whether forms of lustration have occurred (Scharf 1999, 516).

The ICC Prosecutor could elect to cooperate with a national government negotiating transitional arrangements that include an amnesty by delaying an investigation and then selecting persons for prosecution among those who did not gain an amnesty under the transitional arrangements. Roche (2005, 566) suggests that a cooperative approach of this nature would add to the legitimacy of both institutions. However, Andrei Greenawalt (2007, 594) argues that there is broad agreement internationally that transitional states that have suffered mass atrocities may fulfill their duty to prosecute by adopting a policy of targeted selective prosecutions which leave the vast majority of offenders unprosecuted. Stahn (2005, 719) proposes that amnesties should only be permitted in exceptional cases such as when they are conditional and linked to other forms of justice but that amnesties in respect of the very serious crimes within ICC jurisdiction should not be accepted.

As noted in Chapter 8, there is now a considerable weight of international opinion, both scholarly and from within international organizations, including the UN itself, that amnesties for crimes within jurisdiction of the ICC—namely, war crimes, crimes against humanity, and genocide—may not be the subject of any amnesty and that perpetrators of such crimes must be held accountable. For example, the UN Commission on Human Rights Resolution 2002/79 on Impunity states that "amnesties should not be granted to those who commit violations of international humanitarian and human rights law that constitute serious crimes" (p. 329). As Stahn (2005, 702) has pointed out, there is also a growing trend of domestic practice that prohibits amnesties in such cases, for example, in Ecuador, Argentina, Honduras, and Macedonia, where judicial decisions and laws prohibit this. As well, several states have legislated to allow war crimes to be prosecuted within their jurisdictions on the basis of the universality principle, and courts have held that amnesty agreements have no extraterritorial effect.[17]

It is likely that, in light of its purpose and functions, the ICC will only defer prosecution in the most exceptional cases and will never endorse amnesties that include crimes within its jurisdiction (Scharf 1999, 516). However, it is interesting to reflect on the comment of the former UN Secretary-General Kofi Annan, who, in 1998, argued in relation to the amnesty and alternative justice issue,

> No one should imagine that [the ICC] would apply to a case like South Africa's, where the regime and the conflict which caused the crimes have come to an end, and the victims have inherited power. It is inconceivable that, in such a case, the Court would seek to substitute its judgment for that of a whole nation which is seeking the best way to put a traumatic past behind it and build a better future." (Quoted in Greenawalt 2007, 594)

Alternatively, as Schabas (2011, 69) has suggested, the Court "might well decide that it is precisely in cases like the South African one where a line must be drawn establishing that amnesty for such crimes is unacceptable."

VICTIMS AND THE INTERNATIONAL CRIMINAL COURT

The subject of victims' rights became prominent from the 1960s onward in the United States and before then in Europe, with measures such as victim compensation schemes and victim impact statements in addition to well-established rights in states like France and Italy for victims to participate in the criminal process as *partie civile*.[18] International law, however, tended to neglect the subject until international humanitarian law began to develop after the two world wars (Funk 2010, 30, 33). International human rights conventions then granted personal rights to victims whose rights had been violated. In 1985, victims' rights gained more specificity with the UN Declaration of Basic Principles of Justice for Victims of Crime and Abuse of Power. While it did not grant any new rights to victims, the Declaration did call upon states to adequately recognize the rights of victims by providing them with access to justice mechanisms and with prompt forms of redress for harm suffered. It also stressed the need to keep victims informed about the progress of a case and to provide assistance during the legal process. Domestic justice systems were called upon to permit victims to present their views and concerns at appropriate stages in the proceedings.

In 2006, the UN General Assembly built upon the 1985 Basic Principles when it adopted the Basic Principles and Guidelines on the Right to a Remedy and Reparations for Victims of Gross Violations of International Human Rights Law and Serious Violations of International Humanitarian Law. The Basic Principles explicitly refer to the Statute of the ICC.

The Statute of the ICC can be seen as extending this international concern for victims and their rights and breaks new ground in international criminal justice in that Article 68 requires an international court for the first time to allow the "views and concerns" of victims "to be presented and considered at stages of the proceedings."[19] Victim participation is a novel feature of trials before the ICC and has not been codified under international law. In the view of the then Senior Vice President of the ICC, René Blattmann, "The Court is, therefore, creating a unique path for victims to participate in the proceedings" (Blattmann and Bowman 2008, 728), but care must be taken to ensure that "the implementation of these rights will not jeopardise the rights of the accused . . . and result in an unfair trial" (p. 728).

As well as participation in trials and other proceedings, the ICC Statute provides two forms of redress for victims, namely, court-ordered reparations and victim support through a Trust Fund established by the Statute (McCarthy 2012, 34). Both are discussed in this section. (Unless otherwise stated, the information that follows draws on sections of the ICC website dealing with victims: http://www.icc-cpi.int/en_menus/icc/structure%20of%20the%20court/victims/Pages/victims%20and%20witnesses.aspx.)

Qualifying as a Victim

The ICC Rules define *victim* to mean "natural persons who have suffered harm as a result of the commission of any crime within the jurisdiction of the Court" (Rule 85). Persons claiming to be victims must apply for that status to the Victims Participation and Reparation Section of the Court which in turn submits the application to the Chamber to decide on the manner of victims' participation in the proceedings. Victims may request participation or reparations or both. When the Chamber considers a person is not a victim whose crime falls within the Court's jurisdiction, it may reject that application.

Victim Participation

Victim participation poses practical challenges. For example, where there are large numbers of victims in unstable situations, ensuring that all know how to participate in proceedings and are adequately supported in this role is a huge challenge (Blattmann and Bowman 2008, 728–29). In cases where there are a large number of victims, the Chamber may ask victims to choose a shared legal representative, called a "common legal representative" (Rule 90). When a victim or a group of victims lacks the means to pay for a common legal representative appointed by the Court, they may request financial aid from the Court. For example, in the Lubanga trial (see Box 9.2), there were three teams of victims' representatives, one led by the Principal Counsel of the Office of Public Counsel for Victims and the others led by non-ICC representatives (Funk 2010, 108).

In an important decision about victim participation, the Appeals Chamber decided in July 2008 that the harm alleged to have been suffered by a victim does not necessarily have to be direct in nature, but it must constitute personal harm. The Court has said that an indirect victim can suffer harm either as close family members or dependents of the direct victim or while intervening to aid victims or prevent them from becoming victims (Moffett 2014, 91). The Appeals Chamber also reversed a decision of the Trial Chamber and decided that victims who participate may bring evidence concerning the guilt or innocence of an accused, when requested, and may challenge the admissibility or relevance of evidence in a trial.

Questions about victim participation at the various stages of proceedings have been and continue to be under examination by the Pre-Trial Chamber. For example, some victims' representatives believed they possessed authority under the Statute to request that the Pre-Trial Chamber expand the charges laid against an accused to include additional charges. Consequently, in May 2009, victims' representatives formally asked the Chamber to add charges of sexual slavery and cruel and inhumane treatment to one indictment. As might be expected, the Prosecutor objected to what it considered to be "interference" with its case, and the defense argued that last-minute changes threatened the rights of the accused. The request was denied (Funk 2010, 61).

The Court has been clear that victims' legal representatives are not to function as supplementary prosecutors, as happens in some civil law systems, but rather as assistants, helping the Court to find the truth (Moffett 2014, 103). According to one Trial Chamber, this means the legal representatives' primary role is to present victim experiences of the harm those victims have suffered (p. 104). According to another Trial Chamber, however, the interests of victims include the question of which persons should be held responsible for the harm they have suffered, and this means victims "have an interest in making sure that all pertinent questions are put to witnesses" (p. 104). The Statute establishes the right of victims to present their "views and concerns" where their "personal interests . . . are affected," "at stages of the proceedings determined to be appropriate by the Court" and "in a manner which is not prejudicial to or inconsistent with the rights of the accused and a fair and impartial trial." In the practice of the Court, the following rights have been granted to victims:

- Victims may participate in court hearings about investigations but may not participate in an investigation at the "situation" stage.[20]

- Victims can participate in most pre-trial proceedings.

- Victims can participate at trial with remarks, present written submissions, and assess and present evidence.

- Victims may make oral and written submissions concerning sentencing.

- Victims can participate when the Prosecution and Defense submit appeals to the Appeals Chamber.

- Victims may appeal orders awarding reparations to victims. (AMICC 2013)

Victims must be notified of any decisions by the Prosecutor not to open an investigation or not to commence a prosecution, and may file submissions before the Pre-Trial Chamber. The same notification is required before the confirmation of charges hearing in the Pre-Trial Chamber in order to allow the victims to file submissions and present their views. All decisions taken by the Court are then sent to the victims who participate in the proceedings or to their counsel.

Office of Public Counsel for Victims

Established in September 2005, the Office of Public Counsel for Victims is tasked to ensure the effective participation of victims in the proceedings before the Court. It does this by providing legal support and assistance to the legal representatives of victims and to victims. Under Regulation 80 of the Court Regulations, members of the Office may also be appointed as legal representatives of victims, providing their services free of charge. This Office has published a manual to assist legal representatives appearing before the Court. In most cases, victims will be legally represented or represented by this Office. This ensures their concerns and views will be presented to the Court. Victims may choose their legal representative, who must be a person with extensive experience as a criminal lawyer, judge, or prosecutor and must be fluent in one of the Court's working languages (English or French).

Victim and Witness Protection

A victim may also be a witness in proceedings, and therefore witness protection is another area marked out for the attention of the Court. It is given the power to apply protection measures, including in camera proceedings and protecting a victim's identity (Article 22). The Victim and Witness Unit (VWU), under the control of the Court Registrar, is charged with recommending protective measures and providing counseling and support to victims and witnesses (Schiff 2008, 131). It must be staffed with persons possessing expertise in trauma related to crimes involving sexual violence. Child witnesses and victims are covered by specific protective measures (Blattmann and Bowman 2008, 714). When a victim is believed by their legal representative to also be a likely witness in a prosecution, notice of this must be given to the Prosecutor as soon as the legal representative becomes aware of it.

Victims and International Criminal Court Trial Practice

Like the ICTY and the ICTR, trial practice before the Court and its Chambers is an amalgam of common law and civil law systems. Accordingly, the hybrid system used by the ICC is neither fully adversarial nor fully inquisitorial. While trials are conducted with evidence being given orally, and with examination and cross-examination of witnesses and not through a written dossier as occurs in many civil law systems, there are elements of civil law systems present in the management of cases by the Pre-Trial Chamber. As in civil systems, the ICC judges are far more proactive in the pre-trial stages than is usually the case in common law systems. Similarly, there is no right to trial by jury, and Court rulings are persuasive but not binding under the *stare decisis* doctrine (Funk 2010, 64). The OTC more resembles such offices in civil law systems because it is charged with being the investigator for the prosecution and for the defense and must establish the truth by investigating both incriminating and exculpatory circumstances (p. 65).

Victims are generally permitted to make opening statements at trials, and practice so far indicates that the Court will allow victims' representatives to question a witness after the prosecution has completed its examination and before the defense begins its cross-examination. Before seeking to examine a witness, however, a victim must file a request outlining proposed questions. This reflects the notion that the victim will generally augment the function of prosecution (Funk 2010, 190).

Reparations and Trust Fund for Victims

Under Article 75 of the Statute, the Court may establish principles for granting reparations to victims which may include restitution, compensation, and rehabilitation. There is no existing body of international principles upon which the Court can draw, and therefore establishing principles will be a challenging task (McCarthy 2012, 129). The Court may also make an order against a convicted person stating the appropriate reparation for the victims or their beneficiaries. This reparation may also take the form of restitution, indemnification, or rehabilitation.

The Court may order reparations to be paid through the Trust Fund for Victims, which was set up by the Assembly of States Parties in September 2002. The Fund may receive funds from state parties and in the form of voluntary contributions and from fines and forfeitures ordered by the Court. To date, the bulk of its funds have come from state parties (McCarthy 2012, 59). The ICC does not manage the Trust Fund, which is under the control of a Board of Directors appointed by the Assembly of States Parties (p. 227).

Victims have the right to apply for reparations at any time, and where they do not do so, the Court may nevertheless order reparations but only in exceptional circumstances (McCarthy 2012, 191). Reparation proceedings take place after the person prosecuted has been declared guilty of the crimes charged. The Court may order individual or collective reparation, concerning a whole group of victims, a community, or both. If the Court decides to order collective reparation, it may order that reparation be made through the Trust Fund for Victims, and the reparation may then also be paid to an intergovernmental, international, or national organization.

In 2008 the Trust Fund expended about $2.5 million on projects in Uganda and DRC as services to victims. These projects, numbering thirty-four, provided physical rehabilitation and psychological support for men, women, and children who had experienced sexual violence and who were ex–child soldiers or abducted children. These payments did not constitute actual court ordered reparations but represented victims services (Funk 2010, 70).

How Effective Is the International Criminal Court?

Any assessment of the effectiveness of the ICC must take into account that it only commenced its task a short time ago. It began its first trial only in 2009 and its first active investigation only in 2004.

As the first permanent international criminal court, the ICC may bring an end to the practice of creating ad hoc international tribunals like the ICTY and the ICTR, both modeled on the Nuremberg trials. It may also replace the mixed international courts, such as those employed in Sierra Leone and East Timor for the crimes over which it has jurisdiction. The permanence of the ICC is a mark of its effectiveness because, unlike the ad hoc international tribunals, it is always in existence and therefore able to act in a timely manner while armed conflicts are still under way and perhaps intervene to bring about a cessation of those conflicts by investigating and punishing violations of international criminal law as they occur (Dutton 2013, 19).

In any event, it is able to investigate and prosecute war crimes as soon as there is evidence they are occurring. That in itself is said to constitute a significant measure of deterrence to would-be human rights violators (Shany 2014, 228). A contrarian view concerning the capacity of the ICC to fulfill the objective of deterring war crimes is that research based on a set of post-conflict devices used in civil armed conflicts between 1989 and 2003, including international and domestic criminal trials, has shown that international prosecutions fail to deter human rights abuses, to consolidate democracy, or to assist in peace-building. Both the ICTY and the ICTR have failed to deter subsequent international crimes, such as occurred in Sudan (Snyder and Vinjamuri 2003, 5, 20).

According to Yuval Shany (2014, 223), the ICC "has been a crucial step in the development of international criminal law." The Court has been active in issuing important decisions, issuing arrest warrants, and generally conducting its business in conjunction with an active Prosecutor. Both the Court and the Prosecutor have effectively navigated the complexities of the Statute with its procedural and substantive safeguards.

State parties have endorsed the legitimacy of the Court by referring situations to it, as has the UN Security Council, and the Prosecutor has exercised the discretion to investigate and prosecute. Accordingly, all the stakeholders with capacity to invoke the powers of the Court have done so. As well, the Prosecutor has conducted numerous investigations and the Court conducted several full trials.

In relation to UN Security Council referrals to the ICC, there is some concern among Court officials that the Security Council has not followed through with its referral to fully support the Court and ensure its effectiveness. Instead, it has used the reference power as a political and strategic instrument. An example of this was the attempt by some members of the Security Council to have the prosecution of the President of Sudan deferred under the Article 16 power despite having previously referred the situation in the Sudan to the ICC (Bosco 2014, 171). This lack of commitment by the Security Council flows through into its lack of response to the ICC on complaints of noncooperation by state parties on arrest warrants, where the Security Council has taken no enforcement action.

It has also been argued that referrals by the Security Council constitute "significant acts of control" in that the Court launches full investigations consuming limited resources and allows the major powers to shape the case load of the Court (Bosco 2014, 180). The perception that the Court is managed by the Security Council, and therefore by its permanent members, affects the overall legitimacy of the ICC, as does evidence that the major powers "have regularly communicated their preferences on investigative strategy to the court officials," such as occurred in the issue of the arrest warrant for Sudan's President (p. 181).

One outcome of the existence of the ICC has been that states have legislated on war crimes and genocide consistent with the principle of complementarity.[21] The ICC has acted as a catalyst in this regard. States have enacted new laws that punish these crimes and that will hopefully deter their nationals from committing these grave international crimes. Before the creation of the Court, war crimes were seldom prosecuted and it has been left to the international tribunals for the former Yugoslavia and Rwanda to develop international humanitarian law and punish offenders. The existence of the Court and domestic systems of laws that punish war crimes should collectively make major contributions to ending impunity—a goal of the Court as stated in the preamble of the Statute. The Court has affirmed that even Heads of State are not exempt from criminal liability.

There is, however, no mention in the Statute of the Court providing training or assistance to states in drafting their domestic war crimes legislation. Many states in the developing world lack the capacity to undertake this task. Both the Prosecutor and the Assembly of State Parties have advocated developing strategies to facilitate this work (referred to as "positive complementarity"), and it remains to be seen whether there is an appropriate role for a judicial institution in such capacity building (Dutton 2013, 163; Shany 2014, 235).

The Statute has given new prominence to victims, following the models of the ICTY and the ITCR, and the victim services and outreach activities have been seen as key to the success of the Court. Previously, the status of victims under international law was unclear, but the Statute allows victims to actively participate in proceedings and secure reparations for harms (Shany 2014, 232). At the same time, the complexity of having victim participation has affected the pace of trials and pre-trial applications.

The creation of field offices has been essential in the collection of evidence, witness protection, victim assistance, and outreach to affected communities. However, it has also revealed severe logistical challenges, the inaccessibility of some regions, and the difficulties of ensuring that all languages used in a region are accommodated (Blattmann and Bowman 2008, 724).

In relation to the conduct of trials and the necessity that they occur without undue delay, "the complexity and magnitude of international crimes are exceptional circumstances that influence the pace of conducting and concluding such trials" (Blattmann and Bowman 2008, 724).[22] Certainly the duration of trials before the ICC Trial Chamber is lengthy, but this also proved to be the case in the ICTY and the ICTR. As an example for the ICC, the trial of Lubanga (discussed in Box 9.2), commenced on January 26, 2009, and closing statements were given August 25–26, 2011. Sixty-two witnesses gave evidence: thirty-six were called by the prosecution, nineteen by the defense, three by legal representatives of witnesses, and four by the Trial Chamber (Corrie 2012, 147).

The focus of the Court on Africa has provoked adverse comment from African states and the African Union and claims that the Court can expect no state cooperation: this has proved to be true in the case of Chad's attitude to the arrest warrant issued against the President of Sudan (see "State Noncooperation," earlier). As the Chairman of the African Union, Jean Ping, stated, "We think there is a problem with ICC targeting only Africans, as if Africa has been a place to experiment with their ideas. The law should apply to everyone and not only the weak" (quoted in Bosco 2014, 151). The Court can be criticized for pursuing a double standard. While it can be said to be enforcing the rule of law in a continent ravaged by armed conflict, it can also be argued that international criminal law is being primarily enforced in weak and fragile states (Shany 2014, 245).

Issues of legitimacy and double standards were also raised when the Prosecutor declined to conduct investigations into events in Iraq and Afghanistan. In the case of Iraq, complaints were made that the U.K. Armed Forces and those of other nations committed war crimes there. In 2006, the Prosecutor advised having investigated the complaints which had been contained in some 240 referrals to the ICC. In most instances he had found no basis to conclude the ICC should exercise jurisdiction. However, the Prosecutor did find some basis for concluding that some British soldiers had committed crimes of willful killing and inhumane treatment. He declined to proceed with an investigation, relying on the fact that fewer than twenty injuries or deaths had resulted from the actions and on the need to preserve the resources of the Court for crimes of gravity. He also advised that in any event, the United Kingdom had taken action under its International Criminal Court Act 2001 to investigate the alleged crimes and prosecute its soldiers. In fact in 2006, Corporal Donald Payne became the first British soldier to be convicted of committing a war crime. Payne pleaded guilty to inhumane treatment of civilians in military activities in Iraq (Dutton 2013, 91).

The situations in Afghanistan (where the Prosecutor declined to open an investigation) and Iraq arguably reveal a tendency to avoid situations that involve major powers. Other, similar cases have occurred. For example, while the Prosecutor opened an investigation in Kenya,[23] it declined to do so in relation to the Georgia–Russia conflict and decided that the ICC lacked jurisdiction in a referral by Palestine (Bosco 2014, 186).

Has the ICC then favored the major powers and brought its legitimacy into question? The Court has been described as being "exceptionally cautious," and it is said that the Prosecutor has "operated strategically, sending conciliatory signals and orienting early court investigations so as to avoid tension with major powers" (Bosco 2014, 20–21). The first ICC Prosecutor advanced what was considered to be a novel view about how to measure the effectiveness of the Court. Speaking in April 2003, soon after his election, he said:

> The efficiency of the International Criminal Court should not be measured by the number of cases that reach the Court or by the content of its decisions. Quite on the contrary, because of the exceptional character of this institution, the absence of trials led by this court as a consequence of the regular functioning of national institutions would be its major success. (Quoted in Bosco 2014, 88)

Here, the Prosecutor is simply stating the effect of the principle of complementarity. Assuming that all or most states' domestic legislation covers war crimes, genocide, and crimes against humanity and that no offenders are improperly shielded from accountability, the Prosecutor would be correct because the Court would indeed be only a court of last resort. Where a state could not itself conduct investigations or prosecutions, the Prosecutor envisaged that the state concerned would refer its own situation to the Court "smoothing cooperation and reducing or eliminating the possibilities that the State would challenge the ICC's jurisdiction on cases admissibility"[24] (Schiff 2008, 115).

Of course, the developed states would enjoy an advantage in having justice systems that were capable of handling such cases and in adhering to the rule of law in the conduct of trials. The statement can therefore be read as reassurance to developed states and also as indicating a cautious Prosecutor and Court anxious to avoid confronting major powers.

Finally, it has to be recognized that international crimes which come to the attention of the Court are committed in the context of political events that engender high levels of violence sometimes rising to the level of atrocities and even genocide. The Court therefore operates within an environment that is political, and consequently its decisions and acts carry political implications for states and will inevitably be interpreted as political acts. While the Court seeks to act judicially, it is not always a simple matter to separate the political from the legal. Questions of legitimacy will continue to arise even while the Court acts as transparently as possible and explicitly frames the issues coming before it as matters of international criminal law (Schiff 2008, 9–10).

PART III

TRANSNATIONAL AND GLOBAL CRIMINOLOGY

PART III

TRANSNATIONAL AND GLOBAL CRIMINOLOGY

10

Transnational Crime

This chapter explains the concept of "transnational crime" (TNC) and examines how it is constituted, conducted, and combated. Essentially, TNC denotes criminality that crosses national borders. Commonly, but not always, transnational crime is also "organized crime" because the logistics of conducting criminal activities across states requires a certain degree of organization. The commonly recognized categories of TNC are drug trafficking, human trafficking, illicit sale of antiques, trafficking in endangered species, arms trafficking, and money laundering, but the categories of TNC are not closed.

TNC is often associated with weak or fragile states[1] or loss of sovereignty and is implicated in the process of globalization. It should not be regarded as committed solely by large well-organized criminal entities because some TNC is committed by individuals and TNC can be constituted by illicit actions such as dumping toxic waste by corporations whose business is otherwise quite legitimate.

Definitional issues associated with TNC remain unresolved. Essentially, the term *transnational crime* has no fixed meaning, but the international community has agreed upon a meaning for the purposes of international control. While states have adopted various definitions of TNC, it remains a criminological umbrella term under which are collected various categories of criminal activity that are conducted across national borders. The essential feature of trans-border crime is that it constitutes illicit trade that violates the laws of the importing and/or the exporting state.

TNC has been critiqued for its overemphasis on ethnicity, for example, the Italian Mafia, the so-called Russian Mafia, Chinese Triad gangs, the Japanese Yakuza. Other critiques relate to the rhetoric associated with TNC as opposed to the empirical realities disclosed by research and the reasons for this, and to the character and even the existence of TNC. These arguments are examined in this chapter.

Illicit trade is not new, but in modern times expanding cooperation between states has resulted in international campaigns against criminal activities such as drug smuggling and arms trafficking. To a great extent, this reflects the growth of American power as well as the concerns of developing state and of international nongovernmental organizations.

International Conventions, best international practice, and "soft law" in the form of recommendations that carry "name and shame" sanctions, if they are not accepted by states, are important tools for coordinating international responses to TNC and have increasingly been employed in global strategies to counter TNC. They are identified and discussed under the various categories of TNC along with some national and regional strategies designed to combat TNC.

DEFINITIONS AND EXPLANATIONS OF THE CONCEPT OF TRANSNATIONAL CRIME

During the 1980s, the war on drugs and a focus on international drug trafficking together with studies on trafficking illegal aliens, arms smuggling, currency offenses, fraud, and terrorism gave impetus to defining and explaining transnational crime. In 1990 André Bossard, in *Transnational Crime and Criminal Law,* proposed a simple definition of TNC as being an activity that is considered a criminal offense by at least two countries (Bossard 1990, 5). He further noted that TNC was located within a framework of world problems that rendered it a political and legal issue and that TNC advanced its aims by making use of global developments in transport, telecommunications, and computers (p. 141). Broader definitions include that of Nikos Passas (2002, 13): "cross border crime is conduct, which jeopardizes the legally protected interests in more than one national jurisdiction and which is criminalized in at least one of the states/jurisdictions concerned."

Internationally, TNC is explained by the UN Convention on Transnational Organized Crime, Article 3, as follows:

An offence is transnational in nature if:

(a) it is committed in more than one State;

(b) it is committed in one State but a substantial part of its preparation, planning, direction or control takes place in another State;

(c) it is committed in one State but involves an organized criminal group that engages in criminal activities in more than one State; or

(d) it is committed in one State but has substantial effects in another State.

By the final decade of the twentieth century, TNC had emerged as a major policy issue in criminal justice and attention had moved from domestic organized crime to the array of criminal activity that comprised TNC (Felsen and Kalaitzidis 2005, 5). Nevertheless, TNC still lacks a precise meaning, and its limits continue to expand as new criminal acts such as cybercrime, conducted by organizations across borders in cyberspace, add to its categories of crime. Even the categories of crime within TNC are still being debated. For example, TNC has been described as "a general-purpose, 'container'-type concept; it covers many types of crime, the main ones being organized crime, corporate crime, professional crime and political crime" (Fijnaut 2000, 120). The categories enumerated by Fijnaut are elaborated as follows:

- *organized crime,* which includes smuggling of all kinds of products, especially tobacco, alcohol, and meat;

- *corporate crime,* which includes tax evasion and social security fraud, dumping of products in foreign markets, obtaining government subsidies through fraud, the creation of cartels and monopolies, violation of intellectual property rights, industrial spying, the illegal dumping of waste and toxic substances, and the import and export of protected flora and fauna;

- *professional crime,* which includes major theft, fraud, kidnapping, piracy, illegal export of antiquities, supply of fake name products, insurance fraud, counterfeiting money, and forged papers; and

- *political crime,* which includes the activity of terrorist groups, circumventing UN sanctions, and genocide.

These categories of TNC are usually accompanied by forms of corruption such as the corruption of government officials and by money laundering (Fijnaut 2000, 122).

Some scholars highlight the organized nature of TNC so that TNC becomes TOC—*transnational organized crime.* However, this approach reflects thinking that emerged in the United States in the nineteenth century when political corruption existed in large U.S. cities and police protected gambling and prostitution. Later, the term *organized crime* was used to describe associations of gangsters involved in racketeering.[2] By the start of the Cold War, the United States had a significant history of fighting organized crime and of conceptualizing its nature. U.S. thinking about organized crime cohered with the ethnic perspective applied to opium and marijuana, and so organized crime was soon attributed to immigrant-dominated, family groups that were attempting to corrupt society. This in turn prompted a focus on mafia groups, who became regarded as the archetype of purveyors of organized crime and the lens through which such crime was viewed (Carrapico 2012, 23).

Today, the term *organized crime* usually refers to a set of organizational characteristics found in some criminal associations, such as a hierarchical structure, codes and taboos of operation, the practice of corruption, and the willingness to use violence. However, empirical evidence has shown that criminal activities are often far from organized and the use of this term assumes a homogeneous approach to crime that is not often found in practice (Felsen and Kalaitzidis 2005, 6). Instead, TNC may take the form of *networks* that are flexible and do not conform to the paradigm of an organized, managed structure.

Networks can be envisaged as a series of points that connect with each other—"a loosely knit collective with constantly shifting members" (van Dijk and Spapens 2014, 213). A network may be large or small, local or global, directed from a center or not directed at all (Williams 2001, 74). An example of a network in the case of the drug "ecstasy" is that it may involve Dutch producers who obtain the precursor chemicals to make the drug from China and Germany, manufacture the pills in the Netherlands and in Belgium, export the pills to Australia, and launder the proceeds of the illicit drug production in the Virgin Islands (van Dijk and Spapens 2014, 213).

Sometimes these networks collapse because a participant decides that more benefit is to be gained by taking over another participant's operations within the network. For example, Turkish drug traffickers allied with Albanian networks to help with the transportation of heroin through the Balkan route and then discovered that the Albanians were taking over from the Turks in some markets to the detriment of the Turks (Williams 2001, 75). Some now argue that the concept of organized crime has been emptied of meaning and distorted to such an extent that it is useful only in political terms as a bargaining tool for resources for law enforcement agencies (Beare 2003, xxv).

The Growth of Transnational Crime

TNC is not a new phenomenon because piracy, smuggling, abduction, gun-running, and counterfeiting have been crimes for centuries, but it proved impossible to bring them under control when there was a lack of international cooperation on these issues and states were only able to rely on domestic laws to counter these crimes. Accordingly, "transnational crime is new only for the manner in which law-enforcement and international agencies have recently identified it as a priority" (Findlay 1999, 51).

It was not until the 1990s that scholars began to take a close interest in TNC following the end of the Cold War, the breakup of the former Soviet Union, and the emergence of new states in Eastern Europe (Felsen and Kalaitzidis 2005, 3). In fact, some claim that the developed world's commitment to combating Communism, no longer valid in light of the disintegration of the Soviet Union, was replaced with a commitment to fight the threat of TNC "as a rationale for the reinvention of Cold War security and intelligence agencies" (Edwards and Gill 2002, 263).

In the 1990s the role and sovereignty of the nation-state came under examination by international relations scholars who began to realize that non-state actors also played an important role internationally through involvement in cross border activities, including the movement of goods, people, and finance. Theorists like Samuel Huntington (1973) and James Rosenau (1980) attempted to define and explain these non-state actors and the processes they engaged in. The role of transnational corporations as non-state actors and their actions across boundaries were called into question as a general realization grew about their economic power across the globe (Felsen and Kalaitzidis 2005, 4). At about this time in the 1970s, and more concretely later in the 1990s, a discourse of transnational crime entered criminology as organizations engaged in TNC were recognized as non-state actors who, through the process of globalization, were able to conduct an array of criminal activities across boundaries.

Factors Fostering Transnational Crime

The collapse of the Soviet Union freed Eastern European states to pursue their own economic policies and to adopt the free market system.

Citizens of these countries, realizing the employment and other opportunities now open to them, were easily able to cross European borders. Some engaged in criminal activity, including human trafficking, smuggling of various goods, and money laundering (Felsen and Kalaitzidis 2005, 12). This process was aided by the Schengen Agreement, which eliminated border controls for members of the European Union and introduced a common visa policy, thereby promoting labor mobility (McCarthy 2011, 33).

The breakup of the former Yugoslavia and the conflict in the Balkans created chaotic conditions, flows of refugees, the breakdown of institutions, and opportunities for criminal networks (Felsen and Kalaitzidis 2005, 12). In response, Western Europe began to strengthen its border controls and seek collaboration among its law enforcement agencies to counter illegal immigration, trafficking, and money laundering. The outcome included a strengthened INTERPOL and the creation of EUROPOL, the European Police Office.

Increased international trade, the internationalization of the transport of goods and persons, advances globally in information and communication, and the development of a global banking system with interlinked systems for transferring wealth across states are all said to have contributed to the growth of entrepreneurial activity, both licit and illicit. It is argued by many that the globalization process has greatly enabled the spread of TNC, as has the existence of violent conflicts in many parts of the developing world and the economic disparities that encourage the development of black economies (Fijnaut 2000, 123; Williams 2001, 67).

Globalization is said to have promoted a system of free trade worldwide that has enabled criminal associations to embed illegal products in quantities of imports and exports; expatriate ethnic communities in one state have provided an important resource to TNC by collaborating with those in the home state to create criminal networks using their trading and commercial links to facilitate illicit activity; and global financial systems are said to enable rapid and complex transactions to be performed and legitimized with ease, rendering them difficult to trace.

Why do criminal enterprises become involved in TNC? For one reason they are attracted to states where there exists a demand for the products they are able to supply. The classic case of this is the importation of cocaine into the United States starting in the 1970s. As well, a host state could be a source for products that can be stolen and trafficked to overseas markets. The widespread theft of motor vehicles in the United States and their shipment out of the country, and similar illicit activity in Europe across borders, is a case in point. Demand for a product is associated with price, and where there are significantly greater profits to be made, there is every incentive for criminal entities to take advantage of that differential.

Again, while marijuana was formerly exported from Colombia to the United States, the staggering profits obtainable from exporting cocaine caused a shift in product production in Colombia and the growth of a new industry of growing coca there.[3] Where states have lax regulations or little enforcement of the regulations that do exist, this can constitute an encouragement to TNC in that state, for example, in the case of financial regulations. Risk avoidance also constitutes an incentive to the conduct of TNC. When law enforcement is weak or can easily be suborned, TNC will be encouraged because the risk of being caught is only marginal (Williams 2001, 70–71).

The dominant role of the United States in combating TNC and the evolving status of TNC in Russia (characterized by media and scholarly references to the Russian Mafia), warrant a brief discussion of the development of organized crime and TNC in both countries. International action to counter TNC is also discussed.

Russia and Transnational Crime

During the Soviet era, both Lenin and Stalin challenged organized crime. While Lenin achieved little success in suppressing it, Stalin used harsher methods and soon filled the Soviet Gulags with criminals. After Stalin's death in 1953, about eight million prisoners were released from the Gulags, among them members of the society of the *vory-v-zakone* (thieves by law), a criminal fraternity that existed in the labor camps of the Gulag from the 1920s to the 1950s and reemerged in the 1970s. The release of the *vory* increased the criminal element within Russian society who infiltrated the Communist Party after Stalin's death, especially during the time of Leonid Brezhnev (McCarthy 2011, 58), and significantly impacted society (Cheloukhine 2012, 113; Shelley 1996, 173). For example, the *vory* were allowed to smuggle goods into the Soviet

Union in exchange for supplying members of the Communist Party with luxury items. Generally, the shadow economy that developed gave impetus to the formation of criminal associations (Cheloukhine 2012, 113). By the end of the 1980s and the collapse of the Soviet state, organized crime had become "an alternative source of economic and political power in Soviet society" (Shelley 1996, 176).

With the collapse of the Soviet Union, a series of vacuums opened up into which organized crime flowed. Thousands of former KGB officers joined organized crime gangs. In the Gorbachev period, the newly liberated media began to publish the full dimensions of crime within the Soviet Union, undermining the confidence of citizens in their own safety as the full extent of police abuse and incompetence were revealed (Shelley 1996, 176). The period from 1991 to 1999, when Vladimir Putin took power, also gave a group of powerful businessmen known as the oligarchs the opportunity to take advantage of the poorly designed privatization and restructuring of the Russian economy and to work with organized crime in forging links with the bureaucracy (Cheloukhine 2012, 116; McCarthy 2011, 59). By the end of the 1990s, a system of protection, *kryshi,* operated by criminal groups, was associated with major enterprises and reflected in security services contracts, and "the privatization of government functions was completed by a corrupt network formed by organized crime, state officials, and law enforcement agencies" (Cheloukhine 2012, 117).

United States and Transnational Crime

The United States is often viewed as the home of organized crime.[4] One of the principal means of countering organized crime in the United States has been the Racketeering Influenced and Corrupt Organizations Act 1970 (RICO). There is insufficient space here to fully explain the intricacies of this legislation or to discuss the development of organized crime in the United States,[5] but RICO was prompted by the operations of the Cosa Nostra (the Mafia) which, by the 1960s, had been identified as a dominant, nationwide, centrally organized, coherent criminal organization thought to have conducted criminal activities for generations and whose aim was to infiltrate, control, and corrupt U.S. society

(Leong 2007, 91–92; Woodiwiss 2003, 18). RICO operates as a powerful tool to combat organized crime by

- creating a series of predicate offenses that constitute racketeering[6]—to show criminal liability the accused must have committed two predicate offenses: he or she must operate or manage the criminal enterprise, and a "pattern of racketeering activity" must be proved (racketeering includes acts such as extortion, kidnapping, arson, dealing in narcotics, gambling, murder for hire, interference with commerce by threat violence, bribery, forms of white-collar crime, counterfeiting, and, under the Patriot Act amendment to RICO, terrorism);

- providing for criminal forfeiture of the proceeds of crime;

- providing for civil remedies so that victims can sue the criminal organization for damages; and

- creating substantive offenses, including using an enterprise to launder money, acquiring an interest in an enterprise through a pattern of racketeering, and broadening the definition of a conspiracy (Leong 2007, 91–97).

Numerous states (e.g., Australia and Hong Kong) have modeled their own conspiracy laws on RICO, using the predicate offenses defined to constitute organized crime (Leong 2007, 97–98).

In the United States, drug trafficking was identified early on as a key TNC and as a central national security issue. In fact, comparisons drawn by U.S. enforcement officials between TNC and the Cold War rated TNC the greater threat to U.S. national security (Felsen and Kalaitzidis 2005, 14). In the 1970s the United States declared a war on drugs and the anti-drug war was expanded during the years of the Reagan presidency in the 1980s. The United States focused its efforts on the supply of drugs into the United States, paying little or no attention to the demand side and identified Colombia, in particular, as key in stopping the supply of drugs into the United States (p. 13). U.S. legislation created a certification system for countries considered to be trafficking drugs with the power to impose sanctions on those that did not pursue what the United States considered to be adequate efforts to combat the drug trade.

International Action on Transnational Crime

The United Nations saw a role for itself in combating and coordinating the fight against TNC and created a Commission on Crime Prevention and Criminal Justice in 1991 to foster global coordination against TNC. In 1994 the Commission organized a Conference on Transnational Organized Crime attended by 142 countries which produced a *Global Action Plan against Transnational Organized Crime*. In 1994 the UN established a list of eighteen categories of TNC:

- Money laundering
- Terrorism
- Theft of art and cultural objects
- Theft of intellectual property
- Illicit arms trafficking
- Airplane hijacking
- Sea piracy
- Hijacking by land
- Insurance fraud
- Computer crime
- Environmental crime
- Trafficking in persons
- Trade in human body parts
- Illicit drug trafficking
- Fraudulent bankruptcy
- Infiltration of legal business
- Corruption and bribery of public officials/party officials/elected representatives
- Other offenses by criminal groups (e.g., auto theft)

John Mueller (2001, 14) has pointed out that the eighteen categories lack definitional precision and do not address the extent of criminality involved. As well, countries do not uniformly incorporate these categories in collecting crime data and so the crimes cannot be quantified worldwide.

By 2000 the United Nations had negotiated the Convention against Transnational Organized Crime addressing the areas of criminalization, international state cooperation, technical cooperation, and implementation (Felsen and Kalaitzidis 2005, 15). The Convention requires that state parties adopt laws prohibiting participation in organized criminal groups, money laundering, and corruption. As we shall see, other international Conventions and forms of agreement have been concluded to counter TNC. Usually they operate to control illicit trade rather than applying a complete prohibition. For example, the Single Convention on Narcotic Drugs, 1961 requires that states permit the manufacture, trade, and distribution of narcotic drugs only under license and allow export to another state only in accordance with its laws, but licit trade in drugs is limited to medical and scientific purposes.

The brief explanation of the elements, history, and development of the concept of TNC provides the foundation for the following studies of crimes that fall within the overall conceptualization of TNC:

- Drug trafficking
- Arms trafficking
- Smuggling of nuclear materials
- Money laundering
- Trading in endangered species
- Terrorism financing
- Cybercrime

DRUG TRAFFICKING

It is often said that the drug trade is "the linchpin of transnational crime" and that the U.S. war on drugs has become the lens worldwide through which TNC is perceived (Grayson 2003, 145). To a great extent this has come about because, despite the unceasing nature of the war on drugs, it is the United States that continues to demonstrate the greatest demand for trafficked narcotic drugs.

Drug traffickers illicitly supply narcotic drugs, principally heroin and cocaine. *Opium* is a naturally occurring substance found in the seeds of the opium poppy consumed as is and also used to manufacture morphine, which it contains, which is then used in the manufacture of *heroin*. The term *opiates* refers to various products derived from the opium poppy plant, including opium, morphine, and heroin. *Cocaine* is derived from coca paste or coca base, an extract of the leaves of the coca bush. Purification of coca paste yields cocaine (base and hydrochloride). *Crack cocaine* refers to cocaine base obtained from cocaine hydrochloride through conversion processes to make it suitable for smoking (*World Drug Report,* United Nations Office on Drugs and Crime 2014). Cocaine was first extracted from coca leaves in 1885, and until 1914 cocaine possession and use were legal within the United States (McCarthy 2011, 147). In 1914 the Harrison Narcotics Act prohibited the purchase of heroin or cocaine without a doctor's prescription, forcing addicts onto the streets to buy from street drug dealers (McCoy 1991, 9).

Drug traffickers and suppliers, and not the processors or farmers, benefit most from the illicit trade in narcotics. Researchers have found an 80.5 percent markup on the farm gate value of heroin grown in Pakistan and then sold in the United States compared to the 10 to 12 percent markup on traditional agricultural products. The 2011 UN World Drug Report indicates that one gram of heroin in Afghanistan at farm gate bears a value of US$2 to $3 compared to the eventual price to the consumer in the United States which varies between US$40 and $400 (Young 2013, 47).

United States and Illicit Drugs

The United States is the premier illicit narcotic drug–importing country, and it is important to understand something of how and from where narcotics came to be supplied to the United States and the history of drugs in the United States.

Beginning in the nineteenth century and for most of that century, cocaine was sold in huge quantities for popular health remedies and daily tonics. It was an ingredient of Coca-Cola until 1903 (McCoy 1991, 6). By 1896 there were about three hundred thousand addicts in the United States, and in the 1890s the medical profession first became aware of the addictive properties of opium, heroin, and cocaine (McCoy 1991, 9). In the late 1870s the Opium laws represented the first attempt to limit drug imports.[7] The legislation was aimed at Chinese immigrants and at closing down opium dens where mostly Chinese addicts went to smoke opium.

In 1914 the first laws restricting the use of cocaine were enacted following media reports about the criminal behavior of the "Cocaine Negroes" of the American South: cocaine supposedly engendered violence in southern "Negros," gave them superhuman strength, and encouraged them to rebel against white domination. In a similar ethnically focused move, early laws against marijuana reflected hostility about the settlement of Mexican migrant workers (Efrat 2012, 229; Grayson 2003, 150).

By the mid-1920s, there were some two hundred thousand addicts in the United States, and in many cities criminal groups emerged to supply the illicit demand for heroin and cocaine. Jewish gangs controlled much of the heroin traffic, smuggling the drugs in from Europe and Asia (McCoy 1991, 27). World War II imposed severe restrictions to combat possible spying and sabotage, and these affected smuggling to such an extent that most American addicts were obliged to cease drug abuse: by 1945, there were only about twenty thousand addicts remaining (p. 25).

The illegal trade in heroin and cocaine into the United States is associated with the various "families" that comprise the Italian Mafia but is not exclusive to them.[8] In the nineteenth and early twentieth centuries, immigration from Sicily brought thousands of Sicilians to the United States, some of who were prospective members of the U.S. Mafia, including Charles "Lucky" Luciano (McCarthy 2011, 87).[9] Prohibition opened up opportunities for organized criminal business, including the Italian American Mafia, to be involved in the production, selling, and transporting of liquor, and an illegal liquor market with an estimated worth of two billion dollars was created (Varese 2011, 115). Organized crime therefore gained extensive experience in the operation of complex nationwide business operations within the United States, and the New York Mafia families grew in number and consolidated their operations (p. 121).

After Prohibition, drug traffickers saw that the United States was a potentially huge market for illicit drugs and when the Mafia abandoned its previous refusal to become involved in the drug business, the end of Prohibition signaled its move into prostitution and drug trafficking. Heroin was a better option than alcohol because it was more profitable and light in weight, and controlling the sources of supply was relatively easy (McCoy 1991, 29).

After World War II, Mafia gangster Charles "Lucky" Luciano organized a narcotics syndicate that, for more than a decade, shipped morphine base from the Near and Middle East (Turkey and Lebanon) to Europe (Marseilles—the "French

Connection"), then processed it into heroin and exported it to the United States (McCarthy 2011, 47). When Turkey, China, and Iran began to eradicate their opium crop, Luciano turned to Southeast Asia, which had destabilized because of the Vietnam War. A supply and distribution center was set up in the Golden Triangle, a region that contains parts of Myanmar, Thailand, Laos, and Vietnam and which by the 1960s had become the largest source of opium, morphine, and heroin in the world (p. 49).

In 1969 President Nixon's declaration of a war on drugs made Mexico the primary target of U.S. efforts to attack drug cultivation and trafficking (Efrat 2012, 244). By the early 1970s, French police pressure on trafficking and Turkish prohibition of poppy cultivation in 1972, under U.S. diplomatic pressure with promises of financial aid, had forced a halt to the flow of heroin out of the Mediterranean through Marseilles. Traffickers into the United States developed new sources of heroin supply in Asia and Latin America (McCoy 1991, 70). When the Shah of Iran prohibited opium production in Iran, this stimulated opium production in Afghanistan, currently the world's largest opium producer (p. 125).

In the 1980s President Ronald Reagan declared that his administration was starting a war on "big time organized crime and the drug traffickers who are poisoning our young people" (quoted in Grayson 2003, 151). The new U.S. strategy was to take the fight against drugs to the Andean countries with advice and assistance being provided by the United States: the war would primarily be fought in the producing countries because U.S. law enforcement had failed to halt the supply of drugs (Ronderos 2003, 210). Also in the 1980s, cocaine became fashionable among the middle and upper middle class and crack cocaine entered the ghettos, fueling the demand for drugs. In response, harsh new laws punished drug possession and importation, causing an explosion in the rate at which offenders were incarcerated (Grayson 2003, 151).

The Sicilian Mafia (*Cosa Nostra*) was weakened in the 1990s when some of its members became government informers. The *Camorra Mafia* (located in Naples), in contrast, suffered few informers and together with the 'Ndrangheta *(the Calabrian Mafia)* moved into drug trafficking taking the place of the Cosa Nostra. The Camorra used its access to the port of Naples to attract drug shipments north from Sicily. A police crackdown on the Camorra in 2006 gave 'Ndrangheta the opportunity to gain control of the cocaine trade, reputedly controlling 80 percent of that trade between Colombia and Europe by 2008 (McCarthy 2011, 52).

U.S. anti-drug policies and practices sought to diminish the supply of drugs from South America, and the war on drugs, which had previously been a law enforcement exercise (Ronderos 2003, 210), became increasingly militarized through the Drug Enforcement Administration (DEA). In one military operation, the United States invaded Panama to seize President Manuel Noriega, who had been accused of drug smuggling and money laundering. The United States pressured states to conclude extradition treaties so traffickers could be brought to justice in the United States (Grayson 2003, 152).[10] The United States therefore internationalized its domestic drug abuse problem and made it a dominant item on the regional and international agenda.

Colombian Drug Cartels

Drug trafficking in Colombia is rooted in a tradition of smuggling contraband that dates back to the time of Spanish colonialism when smugglers developed routes and practices to evade the law. By the early 1930s the Colombian media had begun to publish reports of captured drug smugglers that suggested Colombian smugglers were involved in networks linking European drug producers with Caribbean and North American consumers and Colombian ports were involved in transshipping cocaine and opiates produced in Europe. While this trade may not have been significant in size, it reveals the early involvement of Colombians in smuggling and drug trafficking (Kenney 2012, 202–3).

Colombia currently produces about 80 percent of the world supply of cocaine, and about 60 percent of the heroin seized in the United States originates in Colombia. Cocaine was introduced to Colombia on a large scale in the 1980s by importing the base from Bolivia and Peru. In the late 1980s, opium, morphine, and heroin were added to the drug portfolio. Despite eradication efforts, the extent of the Colombia crop remains largely unaffected (Bibes 2001, 245, 247). Trafficking routes from Colombia to the United States run through Mexico (the principal route), with alternate routes through the Caribbean and Central America. Colombia also maintains organizations in Chile, Brazil, Argentina, Spain, and Italy that feed the European and Far East markets for drugs.

The Colombian drug cartels began with the *Medellín,* followed by the *Cali* and then by the *Norte del Valle.* Presently, there is no single dominant cartel but rather a number of small cartels are operating. The leader of the Medellín cartel, formed in the 1970s in response to the increase in demand for cocaine in the United States, was Pablo Escobar, killed in a shoot-out with police in 1993. Most of his associates have also been killed or imprisoned (McCarthy 2011, 150). Initially, Colombia was not set up to export white powder cocaine because it had always specialized in growing marijuana, and so Escobar imported coca leaves from Peru and Bolivia. He then began to hand out coca seedlings to Colombian farmers and so turned Colombia into a major cocaine producer (p. 151). Smuggling drugs into the United States was challenging, but Escobar used creative methods to import drugs, including

- emptying the insides of inexpensive refrigerators and televisions, filling them with about forty kilos of drugs, and shipping them as regular freight;

- mixing the drugs with dried fish from Peru, a very successful method; and

- blending cocaine into multiple products made from plastics, metal, and liquids and reconstituting the cocaine on arrival. (McCarthy 2011, 151–52)

The Medellín cartel's primary transportation method was by air, and it gradually built up a fleet of fifteen planes, six helicopters, and a Learjet. Initially, the planes landed in Jamaica and then the product was carried to Miami on fast boats. Sometimes the planes dropped the drugs packed in duffel bags on land owned by collaborators in Miami, or into the ocean close to the beaches where people would bring them ashore. As well, the cartel used small airstrips all over Florida (McCarthy 2011, 152–53).

The Cali cartel was located about two hundred miles from Medellín and was especially well connected in New York. In its early years, it specialized in marijuana but then switched to cocaine: both were profitable but cocaine extraordinarily so (McCarthy 2011, 158). The

Norte del Valle cartel began operating from around the 1990s and has probably exported the greatest amount of cocaine to the United States. The leader of this cartel pleaded guilty in U.S. federal court Miami in August 2009 to charges of conspiracy to import cocaine and was sentenced to imprisonment for forty-five years (McCarthy 2011, 166). His two brothers had both been extradited to the United States in 2005 and received long sentences for cocaine importation. Despite the collapse of these cartels, the export of cocaine from Colombia remains strong, but now many small businesses, each specializing in an element of the process of producing cocaine, make up the Colombian cocaine industry (Kenney 2012, 211; McCarthy 2011, 167).

Colombia first passed anti-drug laws in the 1990s. As the government adopted a militarized approach to counter drug trafficking, it gave the military immunity from any criminal consequences of their acts. The most recent initiative, Plan Colombia, included a national drug control strategy, a plan to introduce a comprehensive legal foundation to counter trafficking and corruption (Bibes 2001, 253) and a target of reducing the cultivation, processing, and distribution of illegal narcotics by 50 percent in six years (U.S. Government Accounting Office [GAO] 2008).[11] The strengthening of the justice sector was expected to ensure that criminals were caught, prosecuted, punished, and also extradited (Bibes 2001, 254).

In June 2000 the United States approved the spending of about $1.3 billion in counter-drug assistance to the Andean region out of which $862.3 million was allocated to Colombia alone. About 81 percent of the funds were assigned to assistance to the Colombian military (much of it for the purchase of helicopters from the United States) and to law enforcement and justice reform. Crop eradication was the principal aim of the plan (Ronderos 2003, 231). Aid to Colombia to counter trafficking has increased dramatically: from $58 million in 1998 to $309 million in 1999 and now to almost $1 billion.[12] The focus on the militarization of the counter-drug effort has been criticized by the European Union, by other Latin American states, and by scholars who see a need to address the social factors that create the conditions in which cocaine is grown and exported (Ronderos 2003, 207; Sheptycki 2003, 135).[13]

Mexican Drug Cartels

The large-scale movement of drugs from Mexico into the United States began in the late 1970s and started to gain impetus only in the 1970s. Two developments were responsible for the expansion of the Mexican drug operations: first, the popularity in the United States of cocaine, the demand for which began to grow in the 1970s, along with the use of the term *recreational drugs;* and second, efforts by the United States to close down the Caribbean transit route used to bring drugs up from Colombia into the United States. This was the central drug route into the United States in the 1970s from the south and was dominated by the Colombian cartels.

This U.S. action caused the traffickers to change routes to make Mexico the main corridor for moving drugs from South America into the U.S. market. In turn this prompted Mexican crime businesses to organize on a larger scale, responding to the increased demand for the drug product (McCarthy 2011, 119–20). Following the collapse of the Colombian cartels, many Colombian producers began selling their loads to Mexican traffickers who completed the transport and distribution process. This has led to the rise of Mexican trafficking groups (Kenney 2012, 212).

International Drug Control—Treaties

As noted, the United States has been the dominant promoter of international efforts to control the trafficking of illicit drugs. The principal international legal mechanism for this control has been the formulation of a number of anti–drug trafficking treaties that require states to create a legal control and regulatory regime in their national laws.

Three international drug agreements attempt to regulate and control drug distribution worldwide, "all established as a result of intense and long-term U.S. pressure" (Woodiwiss 2003, 24). The Single Convention on Narcotic Drugs (1961) merged all other treaties that existed at that time and created the International Narcotics Control Board (INCB). This Convention aims to secure an adequate narcotic drug supply for licit purposes such as medical and research needs while at the same time preventing illicit markets. The INCB monitors control practices and can call attention to violations (Efrat 2012, 244). The Convention applies to more than 116 narcotic drugs and divides them into four groups with varying standards of control.

The Convention on Psychotropic Substances (1971) relates to drugs that are classified as hallucinogens, stimulants, and sedatives and brings them under international control. These drugs, including amphetamines, barbiturates, and tranquilizers, became a concern after World War II. This Convention provides for fairly limited regulation with loopholes and safeguards for the manufacturing companies (Efrat 2012, 240).

The United Nations Convention against Illicit Traffic in Narcotic Drugs and Psychotropic Substances (1988) recognizes that the illicit trade in drugs has become a threat to the stability, security, and sovereignty of states and aims to strengthen the fight against organized crime. In this Convention, for the first time, international agreement was reached on the issue of international drug trafficking and on the control of precursor chemicals used in manufacturing illicit drugs. The Convention requires state parties to trace, freeze, and confiscate the proceeds of drug trafficking and for law enforcement agencies to cooperate on anti-drug strategies.

How have these treaties impacted drug trafficking? Every year the *World Drug Report* produced by the United Nations Office on Drugs and Crime (UNODC), provides an overview of developments in the various drug markets, including drug trafficking. Table 10.1 lists points made in the 2014 *World Drug Report.*

U.S. Anti–Drug Trafficking Strategy

U.S. anti–drug trafficking strategy has always focused on stopping the supply of drugs into the United States, and almost no attention has been paid to the demand side within the United States beyond imposing draconian penalties for drug possession and trafficking. This policy position dates back to 1909 when the United States believed that if other states limited drug production to medical and scientific needs, the illicit trade to the United States would simply cease. This vision, based on restricting supply, shifts the burden of drug control away from the United States and places it on other states.

Why does the United States adhere to this approach? Placing the responsibility on other states means that the United States does not need to pursue demand-side strategies which would involve considerable costs such as drug education

Table 10.1	Developments in Global Drug Markets

- Afghanistan continues to have the world's largest opium poppy cultivation: the area under cultivation increased from 154,000 hectares in 2012 to 209,000 hectares in 2013—an increase of 36 percent.

- The top three opium-producing countries are Afghanistan, Myanmar, and Laos.

- Afghan heroin is reaching new markets in Oceania and Southeast Asia that were traditionally supplied from Southeast Asia.

- The long-established Balkan route from Afghanistan to Western and Central Europe via Iran and Turkey and the Balkan states brings Afghan heroin to the markets in Western and Central Europe, but its importance has declined. The so-called southern route is expanding, with heroin being smuggled through the area south of Afghanistan reaching Europe, via the Near and Middle East and Africa, as well as directly from Pakistan.

- Cocaine use is still relatively concentrated in the Americas, Europe, and Oceania, and almost all cocaine is produced in three countries in South America: Bolivia, Colombia, and Peru.

- In North America, cocaine use has been declining since 2006, partly due to a sustained shortage. However, more recently, a slight increase in prevalence has been observed in the United States.

- In the Americas, cocaine follows cannabis as the second most prominent drug with respect to possession related to personal use and is almost equal (in first place) with respect to trafficking.

- Illicit opiates are trafficked across large distances and through multiple countries in order to meet demand. Cultivation of opium poppy occurs on a significant scale in at least three distinct areas: Southwest Asia, Southeast Asia, and Latin America.

- The Russian Federation remains a major consumer market for illicit opiates, with significant quantities of heroin flowing northward from Afghanistan via Central Asia.

- Cocaine reaching the United States is believed to originate to a large extent in Colombia and to enter the country via Mexico.

and prevention programs (Efrat 2012, 250). Even so, the cost of funding correctional systems to incarcerate huge numbers of drug offenders seems to go unnoticed because those incarcerated for drug possession are labeled as criminals in need of punishment and control rather than drug abusers in need of treatment. Also, the huge U.S. investment in the war on drugs has created, and now supports, large bureaucracies such as the Drug Enforcement Agency (DEA) which have entrenched themselves as part of the anti-drug complex in government.

In 2002 the economic cost of drug abuse (including health, crime, and the consequences of abuse) for the labor market was about $180.9 billion. It is estimated that seventeen thousand deaths in 2000 were the outcome of drug abuse (Efrat 2012, 227). For other states involved in drug production and manufacture, including Afghanistan, Colombia, and Bolivia, the drug business remains a vital source of employment and income (p. 252).

The militarization of the war on drugs has been discussed, along with U.S. demands that states conclude extradition treaties and improve their legal systems to assist in that war. How successful is the U.S. government, through its various agencies involved in the war on drugs, in halting the flow of drugs into the United States? Measuring efforts to impede the flow of drugs into the United States from Mexico, such as the number of arrests, seizures of drugs, forfeiture of assets, and confiscations, has consistently been regarded at the political level as a true account of the success of the war on drugs. However, the data collected and submitted to the U.S. Congress may have more to do with securing resources through the budget process (Andreas and Greenhill 2010, 6). These data are accepted unproblematically and go largely unchallenged despite the fact, for example, that in publishing its annual *International Narcotics Control Strategy Report,* which estimates illegal drug production outside

BOX 10.1   Viktor Bout, Pecos, and Liberia

In 2000, unhappy with a consignment of assault rifles they had ordered from a Slovak manufacturer, the Ugandan government requested that the Egyptian who had brokered the original deal return the rifles to the manufacturer. The broker agreed and dispatched an Ilyushin-IL-18 transport plane to pick up the rifles. Without the knowledge of the Uganda government, the broker had found a new buyer, a Guinean arms brokering company (Pecos) founded by a Slovak broker after criminal investigations in Europe forced him to shift his operations elsewhere. Seven tons of the rifles were loaded onto the plane and flown to Monrovia in clear violation of a UN arms embargo imposed on Liberian President Charles Taylor's regime. Three days later, the plane returned to Uganda to pick up the rest of the firearms. By this time, the Ugandan government had learned of the diversion and had impounded the guns. Subsequent investigations uncovered a vast arms trafficking network comprised of front companies operated by the infamous Viktor Bout and his associates.

SOURCE: Report of the Panel of Experts pursuant to Security Council resolution 1343 [2001], paragraph 19, concerning Liberia, UN Security Council, S/2001/1015, 26 October 2001.

The primary reason for the abundant modern-day supply of weapons, both light and heavy, can be found in the events associated with the end of the Cold War when weapons no longer needed by the states comprising the former Soviet Union, including the new Russian Federation, became available on the world market to governments and criminals (Albanese 2011, 27). For decades the arms industry was a significant sector of the former Yugoslavian economy, and the breakup of the country left massive quantities of weapons beyond government control (Arsovska and Kostakos 2008, 352).

In the case of Russia, the government actively encouraged the development of a private arms industry and this enabled the notorious Viktor Bout, the reputed Russian arms dealer, to buy Russian military equipment and sell it to both sides in conflicts in Africa and Asia.[14] When governments did not have cash to pay for arms shipments, natural resources were used to make payment, including diamonds in the case of the conflict in Sierra Leone in Africa (Albanese 2011, 28). As well, expatriate ethnic groups began to sponsor the purchase of arms, for example, the Irish in the United States for the Irish Republican Army and Kurds in Europe for Kurdish populations elsewhere (Naylor 2001, 225).

Many states began to produce arms to earn foreign exchange so that now the arms business is totally commercialized. As well, by the 1980s the end-user certificate system had become farcical, was corrupted, and had ceased to be an effective control. Rather, it constituted a means for government officials to gain personal enrichment (Naylor 2001, 217). A modern covert arms deal is therefore most likely to be effected in a series of black market deals with payments moved through coded accounts in the names of shell companies and the arms transported on a ship registered in a flag of convenience state (p. 225).

The Value of Arms Trafficking

The world production of light weapons and small arms[15] is estimated at eight million units every year, much of which is produced and purchased in the United States. However, in the Eastern European states that maintained arms industries during the Soviet time, production is now in private hands. Small Arms Survey of Geneva estimates that in 2010 the global aggregate authorized trade in small arms reached about $4.4 billion with an undocumented illicit trade of about $100 million. However, it is extremely difficult to value the global illicit trade in arms, and most analysts estimate a value of between $170 million and $320 million on the assumption that this trade represents between 10 percent and 20 percent of the legal trade (Bourne 2014, 86).

In any event putting a value on the trade does not explain much about the structure and operation of the illicit arms trade which takes place in local and regional markets where price variations can be considerable. In addition, unlike other trafficking enterprises, the arms trade is also conducted for political and not economic reasons (Bourne 2014, 87). In the former Yugoslavia from 1991 on, arms arrived in the country from South America, South Africa, the Middle East, and from stockpiles of the former Warsaw Pact states to equip forces engaged in the Balkan war (Arsovska and Kostakos 2008, 360). More than 1,200 companies in over 90 states are involved in some aspect of small arms manufacture, sale, and distribution (Efrat 2012, 62).

International Action Against Arms Trafficking

International action against illicit arms manufacturing and trafficking finally came about when states agreed to a Protocol to the UN Convention against Transnational Organized Crime called the Protocol against the Illicit Manufacturing of and Trafficking in Firearms, Their Parts and Components and Ammunition, which entered into force in 2005. The Protocol defines *illicit trade* in Article 3 to mean

> the import, export, acquisition, sale, delivery, movement or transfer of firearms, their parts and components and ammunition from or across the territory of one State Party to that of another State Party if any one of the State Parties concerned does not authorise it in accordance with the terms of this Protocol or if the firearms are not marked in accordance with Article 8 of this Protocol.

The notion of authorization remains unclear, and it is not certain what it should contain, who has authority to issue it, and exactly what it authorizes (Bourne 2014, 87). For example, some states argue that the Protocol definition applies only to transfers between non-state groups and civilians or should even be limited to transfers by TNC groups (Greene 2000, 155). Complications and lack of clarity of this nature reflect an arms market that includes a "gray market" (where the legal authority for the transfer is unclear) as well as a legal market and an illegal "black market" (Bourne 2014, 88).

The Protocol requires states to criminalize the illegal manufacture of firearms, components, and ammunition; to provide for confiscation of illegal weapons and for their destruction; for mandatory record keeping of arms sales; for documentation and licensing of arms sales; and for states to share information on organized crime groups suspected of involvement in arms trafficking (Albanese 2011, 29). The Protocol is clearly directed at arms supply, but the demand for both light and heavy weapons remains unabated.

In addition to the Protocol, the 2001 United Nations Program of Action to Prevent, Combat and Eradicate the Illicit Trade in Small Arms and Light Weapons in All Its Aspects (UN PoA), while not a document having treaty status does have political force and effect and was adopted by consensus of all UN member-states in 2001 (Efrat 2012, 66). It, too, does not define or explain "illicit trade." The UN PoA contains provisions that go beyond prohibitions on trafficking and that relate to, for example, information sharing, combating illegal manufacturing, and destroying surplus arms, but its regulatory framework is not legally binding and is quite weak because it gives governments a great deal of discretion in implementing its provisions. It does not create a monitoring authority and simply requests governments to provide information (p. 67). Nevertheless, its provisions do represent a set of internationally agreed norms and standards for the suppression of the illicit trade in small arms (p. 94).

The U.S. position on small arms control is influenced by the likely effect on domestic gun consumers of an international requirement that arms in the possession of civilians be registered. This notion has been fiercely resisted by the lobbying group the National Rifle Association (NRA), which is politically very powerful in the United States. Arms transfers also constitute an instrument of policy for the United States. At the same time, the United States generally supports humanitarian initiatives and measures that would reduce risks to U.S. military forces and that would prevent small arms getting into the hands of terrorists. Thus the United States has not ratified the Protocol and takes an "intermediate" position, preferring political rather than legally binding commitments as do other countries with major arms industries such as China and Egypt (Efrat 2012, 89, 91).

Regionally, the Organization of American States (OAS) has also concluded the Inter-American Convention against the Illicit Manufacturing of and Trafficking in Firearms, Ammunition, Explosives and Related Materials (CIFTA Convention), which mirrors the Protocol, and in Africa the

BOX 10.3 Money Laundering Through Microstructuring

At 8:50 a.m. on March 15, 2006, Luis and Carlos began visiting banks in Queens, New York, depositing cash into accounts held by others. Deposits did not exceed $2,000 each and most were from $500 to $1500. About lunchtime they crossed into Manhattan and moved along Third Avenue and then went into two banks on Madison. By 2:52 p.m., they had deposited more than $111,000 in 112 accounts. Associates of the two men in Colombia then used ATM cards there to withdraw the money in the accounts in pesos. The ATM was the washing machine.

SOURCE: McCarthy 2011, 100.

Offshore Financial Centers

Laundering the proceeds of crime is a known activity of offshore financial centers (OFCs) which have been described as places that host "financial activities that are separated from major regulating units (states) by geography and/or legislation" (cited in Leong 2007, 39). Essentially, they offer financial services to nonresidents (Young 2013, 12) with lax regulatory regimes where companies can be formed rapidly and shares held anonymously (p. 101).

Locations include the Cayman Islands, Barbados, Bermuda, and Aruba. OFCs try to attract deposits by offering low or no tax regimes and strict banking secrecy. They provide a full range of banking and financial services, including setting up trusts and managing offshore funds generally. It is estimated that over $6 trillion is held in OFCs (Leong 2007, 40). In terms of ML, OFCs have complied with the Forty Recommendations of the Financial Action Task Force (FATF) and formed a Caribbean Financial Action Task Force, mirroring the FATF, which has issued its own Nineteen Recommendations on ML (Young 2013, 82). In fact, Young concludes (p. 85), "the 19 Recommendations appear to do no more than summarise the 40 Recommendations."

In a detailed study of the Cayman Islands as an OFC, Young (2013, 4) argues that OFCs generally have only a minimal commitment to forfeit the proceeds of crime through international action because of the irreconcilable conflict that exists between their duty to counter money laundering and their duty to maintain banking confidentiality. In the Cayman Islands, while domestic laws prohibit ML and provide remedies where it is discovered to have occurred, implementation of anti-ML measures continues to be ineffective because the country remains one of the foremost destinations for ML activity.[20] Further, the Cayman Islands and other similar Caribbean small states "struggle to operate effective regulatory systems" that could counter ML (p. 5).

It is not only the OFCs that suffer internal conflicts over banking services and ML. Western nations are also conflicted because they benefit from OFCs by utilizing their financial services and the strict banking secrecy that OFCs offer. The majority of the banks located in OFCs are offshoots of the banks headquartered in the Western industrialized states,[21] and historically, states like the United Kingdom encouraged the development of small island OFCs like the Cayman Islands as an economic development option when local industries like fishing had failed.[22]

Despite pressure, especially from the U.S. Internal Revenue Service seeking to restrict tax evasion, banking secrecy in OFCs remains largely intact. In a 1998 report on ML, the U.S. General Accounting Office surveyed nine OFCs, including the Caymans, and concluded that secrecy laws in those OFCs represented "key barriers to U.S. oversight of offshore private banking activities" (Young 2013, 115). In the Caymans, the Confidentiality Law and the Proceeds Law permit banking information to be disclosed, but only to the Cayman Islands Financial Reporting Authority (p. 117).

Historically, banking secrecy has been in effect for thousands of years but is best captured by the Swiss Banking Act 1934, which created the principle of banking secrecy and made the country a safe haven for persecuted people and others in which to hide their funds (Young 2013, 135). Nevertheless, the recent agreements between the United States and the Union Bank of Switzerland "have effectively ended Swiss banking secrecy" because the Swiss Bank is now required to disclose cross border account holder information to the U.S. government. In addition, the Union Bank will no longer provide banking secrecy to U.S. clients (p. 146).[23]

Countering Money Laundering

Various methods are employed to counter ML with the majority targeting banks rather than the criminal groups attempting to launder funds. This is logical because banks dominate financial transactions and are accustomed to receiving and transferring wealth both domestically and internationally. The policy and practice of anti-ML involves laws placing due diligence requirements on those handling money to be laundered, principally the banks.

In the United States, counter-ML efforts began with the U.S. Bank Secrecy Act 1970, which requires that banks file a *Currency Transaction Report* (CTR) for every deposit, withdrawal, or exchange of funds of more than $10,000. As well, a *Currency or Monetary Instruments Report* (CMIR) must be filed with U.S. Customs for amounts of more than $10,000 in cash entering or leaving the United States. Also, citizens who hold bank accounts overseas must declare them on their annual federal tax return (Albanese 2011, 109). Common indicators that money is being laundered include the following:

- Frequent dollar cash transaction of high value

- Use of large amounts of cash when checks would have been more normal practice

- Wire transfers to known overseas offshore banking centers known for their secrecy

- Withdrawal of large amounts using check and debit cards where funds were received by wire transfer (Albanese 2011, 112)

BOX 10.4   Illegally Moving Cash

Maria Torres was stopped at Los Angeles airport by Customs officers before boarding a plane to Canada. She appeared to be weighed down with bulky clothes and was in a hurry. She said she was carrying about $3,000 in cash, but a search of her person and her purse and a plastic bag she was carrying revealed over $146,000 in U.S. currency. She was convicted and placed on probation for five years, and the cash was forfeited to the United States.

SOURCE: Albanese 2011, 114.

In 1986 the United States enacted the Money Laundering Control Act, criminalizing money laundering for the first time by making it a crime for a person to conduct a monetary transaction knowing that the funds are derived from unlawful activity. If a person is "willfully blind" to the source of the funds, or does not exercise reasonable care such as would be expected in a financial transaction, that will constitute evidence of intent.

International Action to Combat Money Laundering

International agreements on ML are constituted by the UN Convention against Illicit Trafficking in Narcotic Drugs and Psychotropic Substances 1988 and the Basle Statement of Principles on the Prevention of Criminal Use of the Banking System for the Purpose of Money Laundering 1988 (Albanese 2011, 111). Also, the UN has established a Global Programme against Money Laundering, providing technical assistance on the subject to developing countries. The United Nations also maintains the International Money Laundering Information Network on behalf of the FATF, INTERPOL, and the World Customs Organization (p. 111).

The FATF was established in 1989 by the Heads of State of the G7 group of nations and is the world's leading anti-ML enforcement agency (Leong 2007, 58). An independent, intergovernmental body, it currently comprises thirty-four nations and two regional organizations (the European Commission and the Gulf Co-operation Council)[24] and twenty-seven observer bodies

(Young 2013, 51). It develops policies and practices to counter ML and terrorist financing, monitors states' progress in implementing agreed measures, and reviews ML techniques and countermeasures. It is not a formally constituted international organization with a bureaucracy but essentially operates as a forum for making policy on ML (Efrat 2012, 258).

In 1990 the FATF published *Forty Recommendations,* revised in 1996, 2003, and 2012, to combat ML. This document set international standards and best practices covering the criminal justice system, law enforcement, the financial system, and international cooperation (Leong 2007, 59). The Recommendations are not legally binding on states, but FATF members' compliance is assessed through an evaluation process conducted by experts in the field that assesses the extent to which the Recommendations have been implemented and are properly administered. States are rated on a scale from Compliant, through Largely Compliant and Partially Compliant to Non-Complaint (Efrat 2012, 259). This process puts pressure on states through "naming and shaming."

In 2000 to 2001, FATF identified and named twenty-three states that had failed to cooperate on ML issues, Non-Co-operative Countries and Territories, a list that was reduced to zero by 2006. The FATF has therefore proved successful in "naming and shaming" countries to enact laws and to cooperate in international ML investigations (Leong 2007, 61).

BOX 10.5   Laundering Money Through Hawala

"Hawala" or "hundi" refers to an informal money transfer system operating both domestically and internationally which does not rely on banks. It is both cost effective and efficient and relies largely on trust and good relationships. It is often used by foreign workers to send remittances home. For example, an Indian working in New York wishes to transfer funds to his relative in India. He approaches a hawala dealer who agrees terms and arranges for a contact in India to pay the amount of the remittance to the relative directly. No money is sent from the United States to India (Jost and Sandhu n.d.).

Ranjha was born in Pakistan and lived in the United States where he operated a money remitting business. A witness working with the U.S. government told Ranjha he was involved in drug trafficking, smuggling of cigarettes and weapons, and providing assistance to terrorist groups. Over four years, the witness gave Ranjha $2.2 million to be transferred overseas using hawala. The money was remitted in amounts from $13,000 to $300,000. Ranjha arranged that the equivalent amounts, less deduction of commissions, were delivered to people identified by the witness and to various bank accounts in Canada, United Kingdom, Spain, Pakistan, and Australia. Ranjha was charged with money laundering and concealing terrorist financing and received a sentence of nine years imprisonment.

Despite the array of legislative and coercive measures promoted by the United States and international anti-ML agencies, there are so many methods of ML that ensuring compliance is challenging. One issue has been the very large volume of CTRs being filed by financial institutions: in one year, nine million were filed reporting on $417 billion in transactions.[25]

U.S. Measures to Counter Money Laundering

The Financial Crime Enforcement Network (FinCEN) was set up in 1990 within the U.S. Treasury to support law enforcement in anti-ML efforts with a staff of more than two hundred, and the Bank Secrecy Act was amended to prevent multiple cash transactions under the $10,000 ceiling being made to willfully avoid the Act's requirements. FinCEN is tasked with enforcing the Bank Secrecy Act and with assessing *Suspicious Activity Reports* (SARs) from banks. These reports were mandated in 1992 under the Anti-Money Laundering Act and require that SARs be filed that are "relevant to a possible violation of law or regulation." The thinking was that fixing dollar levels for reporting did not always pick up suspicious transactions (Gouvin 2003, 967).

Sometimes the U.S. Treasury proposes measures that the public considers such a significant violation of banking privacy as to be unwarranted. This happened in 1998 when rules were proposed that would have required banks to monitor customer activity. The proposal to do this, the 1998 Know Your Customer proposal, would have required financial institutions to investigate or verify a set of issues connected with an account, including the customer's identity, the source of customer funds, the "normal and expected transactions" of a customer, and a monitoring process to identify transactions by that customer that were inconsistent with that test and to determine whether such transactions were suspicious or unusual. The proposed rules were withdrawn in March 1999 following a flood of comments opposing the scheme (Gouvin 2003, 969–70).

The Patriot Act has widened the reach of the law in ML cases by forcing nonbanks also to conform to the requirements of the Bank Secrecy Act: this now applies to check cashing companies, money transmitters like Western Union, casinos, credit card companies, and issuers of traveler's checks. This Act also gives the U.S. Treasury the power to sanction overseas financial institutions that do not cooperate on ML controls, for example, by seizing assets of foreign banks operating also in the United States.

The Patriot Act also contains a set of provisions intended to improve the anti-ML process. A new version of the Know Your Customer standards requires that financial institutions verify the identity of a person opening an account, maintain records of the information used to verify that identity, and determine whether the person's name appears on any list of known or suspected terrorists or terrorist organizations according to lists supplied to the financial institution. As well, banks are required to install anti-ML programs and to establish due diligence procedures to detect ML through correspondent accounts and private banking accounts of noncitizens (Gouvin 2003, 970–71).

ML remains a key element in the conduct of TNC and, despite the host of international and national measures designed to counter it, will continue to be creatively developed for as long as there is a requirement to launder illicit funds.

TRADING IN ENDANGERED SPECIES

This form of criminal trafficking is represented by the illicit trade in natural resources, including a wide variety of plants and animals and their by-products. The trade focuses on resources of flora and fauna located in developing states which suffer from poor regulatory and enforcement practices. Consequently, there is a substantial trade from developing to developed states in these resources. Black markets for illegally trafficked flora and fauna have developed for species ranging from Siberian tigers to Thai orchids (Williams 2001, 78). While it is extremely difficult to estimate the value of illegal trade, it has been said to be in the region of $5 billion annually (p. 78).

The principal international method of protection is through the Convention on International Trade in Endangered Species of Wild Fauna and Flora 1975 (CITES), which sets out mandatory rules applying to the protection and transportation of a wide range of plants and animals and their by-products. About 5,600 species of animals and 30,000 species of plants are protected by CITES against over-exploitation through international trade.[26]

The scheme of CITES is that governments are responsible for identifying at-risk species and for prescribing sustainable harvesting under quota limits. Species are given protection according to three levels of protection:

- Appendices I and II cover species threatened by extinction, and trade is permitted only in exceptional circumstances: this comprises about 1,200 species, including the red panda, gorilla, Asian elephant, and all rhinoceros species;

- Appendix III includes species not necessarily threatened with extinction but for which trade must be controlled in order to avoid utilization incompatible with their survival: this covers about 21,000 species, including the great white shark and the American black bear.

The illicit trade in wildlife appears to be a fast growing area of criminal activity. For example, in the first months of 2012 officials in Colombia were able to take custody of more than 46,000 species destined for the illegal market; also in 2012, officials in Sri Lanka seized 1.5 tons of ivory comprising 359 tusks which came from Uganda and were en route to Dubai (Elliott 2012, 88).

Nongovernmental organizations (NGOs) such as the World Wildlife Fund (WWF) are heavily involved in monitoring and enforcing

CITES and have produced reports on subjects such as black bears, ivory poaching, polar bears, and endangered plants and species (Albanese 2011, 32). These "moral entrepreneurs" educate policymakers, disseminate information, and call public attention to issues affecting specific species. They can influence the public and governments about CITES. However, as long as there are animal and plant collectors willing and able to finance the smuggling of rare and highly valued flora for their personal purposes or for further sale, then this trade in flora and fauna will continue even when a species is put in danger of complete extinction. For example, the demand for tiger skins and traditional medicines sourced to the tiger has assisted in reducing the number of tigers so that fewer than 3,200 are now thought to exist in the wild (Elliott 2012, 89).

The rewards of illegal trafficking of species can be great. Cut pieces of illegal ivory reportedly sell for $1,863 a kilogram in Vietnam, and the endangered Lear's Macaw can sell for $60,000 on the black market. In August 2012, 16,000 dried seahorses were seized from traffickers in Peru. They were to be sent to the Asian market where their value was in the region of a quarter of a million dollars (Elliott 2012, 92).

Most recently, a report from two NGOs (C4ADS and Born Free), *Out of Africa: Mapping the Global Trade in Illicit Elephant Ivory* (Vira, Ewing, and Miller 2014), maps trends in poaching and trafficking of elephant ivory. It argues the following:

- The price of ivory has increased dramatically from US$5 per kilogram in 1989 to a wholesale price of US$2,100 per kilogram in China in 2014 with retail prices being still higher.

- At least 20,000 elephants are being illegally poached for their ivory every year out of a world population of about 450,000.

- The primary illicit ivory route runs from Africa to East Asia and uses the international container shipping trade for transportation. Most illicit shipments emanate from Kenya (Mombasa) and are routed through to China, Thailand, and Vietnam and comprise 90 percent or more of trafficked elephant ivory. Gangs lease one or multiple containers and bribe customs officials, freight operators, and others whose expertise is required to navigate the international container shipping system.

The typical shipment will contain between one and three tons of ivory, which will be concealed in cover material within a container, for example, in fish or in false backs within containers.

- China is the largest market for both licit and illicit ivory which is sent to a carving factory or other processing center or perhaps stockpiled and warehoused for gradual release into the market. In the African ivory markets, Chinese tourists, migrant workers, and businessmen are the primary customers who buy ivory because it is a status object in China. Vietnam is thought to be the second biggest ivory market as well as the center of the rhino horn trade.

- Wildlife criminals, formerly opportunistic and decentralized individuals, have been supplemented or absorbed by transnational organized networks operating out of Africa. They comprise Africans who conduct the poaching and killing and Asians who manage the supply chain to East Asia. These networks operate by ignoring the legal systems and following the models set by narcotics and weapons traffickers. The networks are made up of persons performing specific tasks along the supply chain; for example, Africans are in control from the forest to the staging area where the ivory is sold and handed over to the Asian component that handles the international transport of the ivory.

- Poaching networks have little difficulty in securing the collusion of politicians, security forces, and even wildlife rangers.

The report argues that the illicit ivory trade should be treated as an enterprise that has developed into TNC rather than as simply a wildlife protection or conservation issue, and that therefore requires an increased focus on information sharing and greater cooperation from law enforcement agencies.

TERRORISM FINANCING

Terrorism is discussed more fully in Chapter 12, and here we examine what is known about the connection between TNC groups and terrorism and how terrorism is financed. Contemporary developments in both crime and terrorism suggest that organized criminal groups and terrorist groups share common features. For example, while their long-term goals may differ, they share a common enemy, that is, the state and its agencies, and adopt similar methods to achieve their objectives. Both aim to diminish the social control of the state and promote disorder, and both use fear and violence to achieve their aims. The two forms have moved closer in recent years as criminal associations have entered the political sphere, for example, by corrupting political parties for gain. An example of the nexus between terrorism and organized crime is the combination of guerrilla-terrorist activities with organized crime in Chechnya in the conflict with Russia in 1991 (Leong 2007, 22–24).

BOX 10.6   Financing Terrorism Through Kidnapping

Kidnapping the nationals of European states for ransom is global business for Al Qaeda and finances its operations worldwide. A *New York Times* investigation found that Al Qaeda and its associates have gained at least $125 million from the proceeds of kidnapping since 2008, of which $66 million was paid in 2013.

Ransom payments are made almost exclusively by European governments (the United States and the United Kingdom refuse to pay ransoms to terrorist kidnappers) through proxies, sometimes concealing the ransom payment as development assistance. Thus kidnapping for ransom has become a major source of terrorist financing, and the rate payable per person kidnapped is increasing. While in 2003 kidnappers obtained $200,000 per person, they now expect a payment in the region of $10 million. It appears that an association between the three main Al Qaeda affiliates exists: Al Qaeda in the Islamic Maghreb (North Africa), Al Qaeda in the Arabian Peninsula (Yemen), and the Al-Shabaab (Somalia) and criminal groups. The affiliates outsource the kidnapping to criminal groups and pay them a commission for their work.

SOURCE: Callimachi 2014.

Louise Shelley (2005, 101) argues that only the more recently formed TNC groups are associated with terrorism (with the exception of Colombia), because the long-established TNC groups have developed alongside the state in which they are headquartered, maintain links with and depend upon state institutions and structures to conduct their modes of TNC, have corrupted and suborned state agencies, and therefore run little risk of being prosecuted. The newer crime groups, often originating in times of chaos in post-conflict states where the economy is informal and largely hidden from view and where the state is weak, thrive in such conditions and are said to be linking with terrorist organizations in these regions (p. 101).

Generally, when terrorists commit crimes and launder their funds in the same manner as criminal associations operating across borders, there is arguably little difference between terrorists and organized crime: wealth is the lifeblood of both (Leong 2007, 1).

Colombia and Narco-Terrorism

Drug trafficking from Colombia is associated with the term *narco-terrorism,* meaning a state of terror or insurgency created by drug traffickers, including activities such as kidnapping, extortion, and assassination. In this situation drug traffickers actively confront the state by supporting insurgency movements that oppose it: there are three such active insurgent groups in Colombia.[27] This has been the situation in Colombia since the 1980s (Bibes 2001, 244). Over the past few years both the FARC guerrillas and the right wing paramilitaries opposing them have entered the drug trade. This explains why the military strategy of the Colombian government is directed at both drug traffickers and FARC members, blurring any distinction between a war against insurgents and a narco-war.

Drug money has been used to corrupt politicians of all parties, to finance political parties and campaigns, and to lobby the legislature on issues such as money laundering and changes to the penal code. Since 1992, the Colombian military has

Cybercrime as Transnational Crime

Is there empirical evidence that cybercrime involves organized crime groups, or is it an individual criminal act performed by a lone person or a group of hackers?

Traditionally, hackers have been perceived as anti-social loners whose activities were not directed at making a profit but at causing trouble. It is now argued that hackers "work together in loosely knit units or cells" as "opportunity groups" who are "likely to collude in relation to a specific offense and thereafter disband" (McCusker 2006, 266–67). Assertions about organized cybercrime often rely on "anecdote, hearsay, extrapolation and assumption" (McCusker 2006, 258). Questions also arise as to whether "organized" cybercrime is crime committed by organized crime groups or if it is simply online crime committed in an organized fashion. The Council of Europe has stated that the data "on connections between organized crime and cybercrime are still scarce and do not permit a reliable analysis" (quoted in McCusker 2006, 259), but the Council also asserts that "organized crime groups are heavily involved in the production and distribution of child pornography" (p. 269).

Some scholars argue that organized crime is well situated to profit from the information revolution because organized crime groups are adaptable and innovative and the Internet facilitates evading detection. EUROPOL has also suggested that activities like hacking and cracking are a good fit for organized crime (McCusker 2006, 265). As to the structure of organized cybercrime groups, it has been argued that the characteristics of cyberspace—a "diffuse, evolving environment" with an absence of fixed constraints or limits—suggest that a hierarchical structure would be inappropriate (p. 266). The Council of Europe seems to adopt this perspective when it notes that cybercrime "requires less control over a geographical territory, less violence and intimidation, less personal contacts and thus less relationships based on trust and enforcement of discipline between criminals, in short, less need for formal organizations" (quoted in McCusker 2006, 267).

Rapid communication, capacity to encrypt messages, and the absence of personal contact are perceived to be assets that can be exploited by criminal groups. As a result, the use of the Internet as a tool for organized crime groups is almost taken for granted despite the absence of actual empirical evidence. For example, it has been suggested that three separate categories of perpetrators of cybercrime can be identified. In the first category are organized criminal associations who make use of information technology to profit from communication-related crime, software piracy, plastic card fraud, and malware attacks. It is said that these activities are performed by "traditional organized criminal groups," and these are identified as including the Asian Triads and the Japanese Yakuza "whose criminal activities have been known to include computer software piracy and credit card forgery and fraud" (Choo and Smith 2008, 39–40).[31]

In the second category, "organized cybercriminal groups" are constituted by small groups of like-minded persons who meet only in cyberspace and are involved in child exploitation crimes, underground malware attacks, identity crimes, and denial of service attacks. The third category comprises ideologically motivated groups, including terrorist groups and groups involved in financing terrorism, and money laundering groups (Choo and Smith 2008, 40–43). The term *cyberterrorism* has been coined to describe the use of computer technology to perform terrorist acts (Brenner 2006, 14).

Cybercrime in the United States

While there are more than forty federal laws that can be used to prosecute cybercrime, many of them predate the advent of cybercrime and are not specifically targeted at cybercrime (Brenner 2006, 19). Targeting cybercrime through federal legislation was first accomplished through the 1984 Computer Fraud and Abuse Act, which criminalized unauthorized access to computers for the first time. It has been substantially amended five times, each time extending its reach so that now its effect is to potentially regulate the use of every computer in the United States and even many located overseas (Kerr 2010, 1561). At the state level, every U.S. state prohibits hacking and cracking, and a number of states criminalize the dissemination of worms, viruses, and types of malware, denial of service attacks, and cyberstalking (Brenner 2006, 84–86). Only a few states have specifically prohibited acts of cyberterrorism (p. 91).

A key issue in the law is the concept of "unauthorized access" because the 1984 law created three new federal crimes which apply to a person who "knowingly accesses a computer without authorization, or having accessed a computer with authorization, uses the opportunity such access provides for purposes to which such authorization does not extend" (18 U.S.C. 1030 (a) (3) 1984). The three offenses created by this law relate to computer misuse to obtain national security secrets, to obtain personal financial records, and to hack into U.S. government computers (Kerr 2010, 1564). Arguably, the test of "unauthorized access" is void for vagueness because just what constitutes "access" and what makes an access "unauthorized" remain unclear (p. 1572). The question is whether the law is "so vague and standard-less that it leaves the public uncertain as to the conduct it prohibits" (p. 1573).

A 1986 amendment added unauthorized access with intent to defraud, accessing a computer without authorization and altering, damaging, or destroying information (including impairing a medical diagnosis or treatment), and trafficking in computer passwords (Kerr 2010, 1565). In 1994, the law was amended again to apply to accidental damage to computers and to give a right to victims of crimes under the law to recover damages against a convicted person (p. 1566). The amendment in 1996 effectively criminalized all interstate hacking and created a new category of "protected computers," which simply meant a computer used in interstate commerce. The USA Patriot Act of 2001 further amended the law and expanded its scope to include computers outside the United States; this was further expanded in 2008 so that the law applies to all computers within and outside the United States that are used in, or affect, interstate commerce or communication (p. 1570).

Combating Transnational Cybercrime

Generally, responses to transnational cybercrime have comprised international cooperation, legal reforms, ensuring the security of personal information, user education, and support for victims (Smith 2014, 135). In addition to the United Nations Office of Drugs and Crime (UNODC), which is working on approaches to cybercrime, there are numerous industry groups and multinational agencies working on cybercrime issues.

These include the Joint London Action Plan and the Contact Network of Spam Authorities, the European Contact Network of Spam Enforcement Authorities, and the Anti-Phishing Working Group (Smith 2014, 135).

In terms of international action, in 2010 the UN General Assembly called for a study on cybercrime, *Comprehensive Study on the Problem of and Response to Cybercrime*. In a report published in 2010, *The Globalization of Crime: A Transnational Organized Crime Threat Assessment,* UNODC claimed that more than 1.5 million people a year become victims of identity theft, at an economic loss estimated at $1 billion, and that cybercrime is endangering the security of nations, power grids, air traffic, and that even nuclear installations have been penetrated.[32] In 2012 UNODC announced that it had initiated a study of cybercrime and the responses to it by member-states, the international community, and the private sector.[33]

According to Roderic Broadhurst (2006, 409), citing the Korean Institute of Criminology, the conclusion of a UN-sponsored convention covering cybercrime is unlikely because the "digitally advanced states prefer to extend the reach of the Council of Europe Convention on Cybercrime to more countries, await assessment of the effectiveness of the convention, and are struggling to provide expertise to meet the demand for comprehensive counter measures, including the essential mutual legal assistance."

An important international initiative is the Council of Europe Convention on Cybercrime, adopted in November 2001. As of January 2014, forty-two states had ratified the Convention, including the United States and Japan but not China.[34] A Protocol to the Convention has also been concluded: Additional Protocol to the Convention on Cybercrime, Concerning the Criminalisation of Acts of a Racist and Xenophobic Nature Committed through Computer Systems, ratified by twenty states as of January 2014.[35] The Protocol seeks to control computer use for the sexual exploitation of children, aims to control acts that are racist or xenophobic in nature, and criminalizes aspects of the production and dissemination of child pornography.

The Convention aims at securing mutual legal assistance in countering cybercrime through a series of provisions that state parties would adopt in their domestic laws. For example, it states comprehensive powers to ensure the preservation of stored data and partial disclosure of traffic data, and provides for searches of computer systems, the seizure of stored data, and the interception of questionable electronic data. It provides definitions of nine criminal offenses that are intended to become common definitions applied by the state parties. This harmonization of practice and law would enable states with common systems to act rapidly to counter and prosecute cybercrime.

Importantly, the Convention contains a mechanism for an international computer crime assistance network, the 24/7 Network, comprising a network of national contact points. States are to designate a point of contact in their country who is available twenty-four hours a day, seven days a week to provide immediate assistance in investigations on issues such as technical advice, preservation of data, evidence collection, and locating suspects (Article 35). The overall objective is that international cooperation is to be provided among state parties "to the widest extent possible" (Article 23), and the Network is intended to ensure that parties can and will respond rapidly to the law enforcement challenges posed by cybercrime.

In terms of *law reform,* laws need to be revised to proscribe offenses relating to financial crime and fraud. The criminal misuse of computers and computer networks should be an offense and sanctioned, and laws ought to provide for the use of identity cards and other modes of identification. The United Kingdom has simplified the issue of what constitutes fraud by formulating a single offense of fraud. In Australia, the Cybercrime Act 2001 directly attacks the issue by largely legislating into Australian law the Convention on Cybercrime. In the United States, identity-related crime is covered by the 1998 Identity Theft and Assumption Deterrence Act, a federal law which makes identity theft a crime punishable by up to fifteen years imprisonment and a fine of up to $250,000. It also gives the victim of identity theft the right to seek restitution and gives the Federal Trade Commission the power to assist victims of identity theft (Smith 2014, 136).

BOX 10.9   Unwanted E-mail as Cyberstalking

Case One: An honor student from the University of San Diego terrorized five female students over the Internet for over a year. The victims received hundreds of violent and threatening e-mails, sometimes getting four or five e-mails a day. The student was charged and pleaded guilty and faces a sentence of up to six years imprisonment. He told police he committed the crimes because he thought the women were laughing at him and causing others to ridicule him. In fact, the victims had never even met him.

Case Two: Roger and Hannah were in a relationship that came to an end. Several months after it had ended, Roger received an e-mail from Hannah which seemed harmless. It said that she had been thinking of him and missed him. Roger did not reply to the e-mail because he did not wish to give the impression he was interested in getting back together with Hannah. Over the next months, Hannah continued to e-mail Roger, acknowledging that she should leave him alone but expressing that she was unable to do that. At first Roger was not too concerned about Hannah's e-mails, but when they continued for an entire year he felt differently and sent Hannah a strongly worded e-mail stating he wanted no further contact from her. After initially refusing to agree to this, Hannah later did cease all contact to Roger.

COMBATING TRANSNATIONAL CRIME

International action against TNC has been detailed under various categories of crime and in most cases (e.g., in relation to cybercrime where there is no global convention as yet) there exists or will exist in the future an effective international regime to which states can adhere with a range of measures to combat the particular global criminal activity, especially through mutual legal assistance and harmonized national domestic laws.

We have discussed the U.S. approach to countering drug trafficking and terrorism financing which, together with money laundering, constitute the dominant U.S. concerns on TNC. Fundamentally, the United States recognizes that the global nature of TNC requires regional and international cooperation, and its interventions and efforts have been directed to internationalizing aspects of TNC that are regarded as affecting its national interests (Kelly and Levy 2012 447).

State and regional strategies to combat TNC basically follow a model that (a) attempts to identify the nature of the threat and its operational characteristics, (b) analyzes the structure of the TNC to understand how it works, (c) develops methodologies across government agencies to better understand the distinctive features of the TNC, and (d) gains an understanding of how the TNC is vulnerable to state and international law enforcement action (Kelly and Levy 2012, 447). For the United States the 1998 International Crime Control Strategy goal of "fostering international cooperation and the rule of law" sets out a number of objectives as follows:

1. establish international standards, goals and objectives to combat international crime by using bilateral, multilateral, regional and global mechanisms, and by actively encouraging compliance;

2. improve bilateral cooperation with foreign governments and law enforcement authorities through increased collaboration, training and technical assistance; and

3. strengthen the rule of law as the foundation for democratic government and free markets in order to reduce societies' vulnerability to criminal exploitation.

Europe's approach to TNC is "fragmented and hampered by an apparent lack of institutional trust" (Goold 2012, 483). In terms of law enforcement, EU states have been reluctant to assign significant powers or provide greater resources to EUROPOL within the framework of the European Security Strategy (ESS) and the Organized Crime Threat Assessment (OCTA), and state cooperation and coordination are lacking (p. 483). The ESS states that "Europe is a prime target for organized crime" and identifies "cross-border trafficking in drugs, women, illegal migrants and weapons" as making up a large part of the criminal gang portfolio of activities. Links with terrorism and the association of criminal groups with weak states are recognized as factors associated with the growth of TNC to the extent that the ESS claims,

"In extreme cases, organized crime can come to dominate the state" (quoted in Goold 2012, 485).

In relation to the OCTA (a product of so-called intelligence-led policing), the expectation is that it will promote a more proactive approach toward TNC. In 2007, EUROPOL saw it as reflecting "a forward looking approach to fight against organized crime" (quoted in Goold 2012, 487). The OCTA for 2011 describes itself as "the product of systematic analysis of law enforcement information on criminal activities and groups affecting the EU, and is designed to assist strategic decision makers in the prioritization of organised crime threats."[36] It sees TNC in Europe as having become more "diverse" with more collaboration between criminal groups, greater mobility within the EU, a more diversified set of criminal activities, and dependence on a "dynamic infrastructure" underpinned by use of the Internet.

In Russia, highlighted by many commentators as a significant producer of TNC, it is said that efforts to counter TNC have been "largely inconsistent." Legislation has not been updated to reflect Russian ratification of the UN Convention, and legislation covering money laundering has been used by the government to discredit its opponents. It has been largely ineffective in achieving its supposed purpose. In the drug trade, law enforcement has focused on small-time dealers and users rather than TNC. A "lack of political will" has been identified as the explanation for this inactivity, along with the absence of cooperation between international law enforcement agencies and those in Russia (Orlova 2012, 503). Corruption, lack of resources, and lack of appropriate specialized training and education are also seen as contributing factors to the lack of effort in countering TNC (p. 504).

CRITIQUES OF THE CONCEPT OF TRANSNATIONAL CRIME

At different levels of analysis, scholars have questioned the concept of TNC as a category of crime as well as elements of TNC itself, for example, the supposed contribution of globalization to the origination and spread of TNC. In addition, the gap between the rhetoric about TNC and the reality of what is known about TNC through actual empirical research has caused scholarly concern.

Sometimes, the rhetoric employed in describing TNC tends to elevate TNC discourse to the level of a moral panic. For example, Michael Woodiwiss (2003, 26–27), in an account of the construction of TNC as *the* contemporary issue in crime control, reports on a conference in Washington, D.C., in September 1994 titled "Global Organized Crime: The New Empire of Evil," attended by U.S. law enforcement and intelligence officials. The then director of the FBI claimed that "the ravages of transnational crime were the greatest long-term threat to the security of the United States," and the CIA director noted that "the threats from organized crime transcend traditional law enforcement concerns. They affect critical national security interests. . . . Some governments find their authority besieged at home and their foreign policy interests imperilled abroad" (quoted in Woodiwiss 2003, 26–27).

TNC is regularly described, even in scholarly texts, in terms of a "cancer" or "disease." For example, a recent scholarly *Handbook on Transnational Organized Crime* begins its introduction as follows: "Transnational organized crime (TOC) is one of the most virulent plagues of the twenty-first century—a 'great pestilence' that we may not always notice. It is a quiet pandemic that is spreading across the world with varying degrees of potency and often unnoticed mortality" (Allum and Gilmour 2012, 1). It is questionable whether rhetoric of this nature explains anything about TNC.

Other scholars have commented on the manner of depiction or construction of this category of crime and the discourse of TNC generally. According to Ruggiero, it is presented as "a powerful and evasive menace, a looming peril whose lingering across countries adds to its destructive potential character" (Ruggiero 2000, 187). Others refer to it as possessing "a particular quality that inspires both fear and awe in the public and in governments and engenders a particular willingness to accept mythical claims about the size and magnitude of lurking dangers" (Andreas and Greenhill 2010, 5).

Peter Andreas (2010, 31) and others have examined how official estimates of the size of illicit activity worldwide construct a narrative of TNC "as a large and growing global threat." Moreover, the coupling of trafficking with terrorism has led to the securitization of trafficking activities which are now regarded as "global security threats" and not simply as organized criminality (Jackson 2005, 45).

At another level, TNC is also associated with fears by developed countries about the criminality that may be brought across their borders by nationals from developing countries. Trafficking drugs is clearly a case in point where there are fears that immigrant populations in developed states may link with criminal organizations outside of the same ethnicity, for example, in the case of Colombian drugs and immigrant Colombians in the United States. In this sense, therefore, developed countries use international law, international police resources, and their own law enforcement agencies to protect their borders and their populations from what are constructed as ethnically based criminal activities. Thus it seems that a key notion in the conception of TNC is that of outsiders attempting to infiltrate a society. At times, the rhetoric against TNC and ethnic groups can even suggest that their criminality threatens the internal security and social cohesion of a state (Edwards and Gill 2002, 252–53).

It is significant that definitions and explanations of TNC often employ ethnic designations, for example, the Japanese Yakuza, Nigerian organized crime, Chinese Triad gangs, and the so-called Russian Mafia (Ruggiero 2000, 188). Employing this crude racial stereotyping to describe TNC in terms of an alien criminal conspiracy does not explain anything about the criminality itself and treats TNC as existing within a self-contained cultural environment. In addition, limiting TNC in this manner means that criminal activity by others not part of an ethnicity is not taken into account. Nevertheless, it is fair to say that ethnicity can be a determinant in TNC when, for example, a criminal organization is operating in hostile territory, and trust, such as can be assured within kinship groups, is a key to the success of its operations. As a result, family groups are more likely to resist detection by law enforcement and already possess a degree of organizational structure (Werdmoelder 1998, 112, 117).

International pressure is considerable on states to make new anti–money laundering laws, to give law enforcement more power, and to enhance the right to seize assets, all in the interests of countering TNC and particularly TNC associated with terrorism (especially money laundering allegedly linked to terrorism). When states resist such pressures (emanating from other states, international agencies, or discrete task forces) or are slow to comply, they run a risk of being categorized as not cooperating in the fight against TNC and the war on terrorism.[37] Since the events of 9/11, "terrorism has become another major 'umbrella' concept that now subsumes a wide array of real threats, ordinary crimes, and societal annoyances" (Beare 2003, xii).

The topic of TNC has generated a host of experts, including those who are in the business of meeting, and sometimes creating, the needs of government. This professionalization of TNC topics has in turn spurred the drafting of international conventions, agreements, and the like to combat TNC. However, most importantly, there remains the issue of the absence of significant empirical research on TNC. Among the challenges faced by researchers into TNC are "the mobility and elusiveness of offenders and victims, innovation in *modus operandi,* and dangerousness of the research subject" (Barberet 2014, 48).

At best, many TNC commentaries take the form of incomplete discourse analysis and assertions about the effects of globalization together with anecdotal evidence and the perceptions of experts. Police insist on maintaining secrecy of their records and investigations, and governments hold meetings in camera with the outcome that whatever is made known to policymakers is not shared (Beare 2003, xvi). James Sheptycki contends that conflating TNC with terrorism has exacerbated the opaque nature of the policing apparatus (2003, 142). The end result may be that "unreliable conclusions reached, do not become more reliable because they are repeated over and over again" (Beare 2003, xvi).

Discussions about organized crime and TNC are inevitably political, and the rhetoric of the political leaders and policymakers is difficult to challenge when so much is kept from researchers. Nevertheless, empirical research has revealed that each of the TNC categories also has a local element that often feeds into a particular conception of TNC. Studies have revealed that a complex mix of criminals operating through networks, and not corporately organized criminals, constitute the principal criminal actors in TNC. The models of the mafia, the triads, the yakuza, and the like have for too long dominated thinking about organized crime and TNC. More research needs to be focused on the market for a particular TNC to gain understanding of methods employed, motivations, and degrees of exploitation and violence. For example, there are significant differences in trafficking persons, trafficking drugs, and trafficking arms (Beare 2003, xxv).

Globalization has operated in TNC as a means of labeling any crime "transnational" and, in the absence of real specificity about how it actually works, to promote TNC as an all-encompassing term that adds little to the knowledge base. As some researchers have shown, *globalization* as a term needs to be unpacked in the context of TNC so that different categories of crime are investigated to reveal whether, and if so exactly how and why, a criminal organization decides to conduct crime across borders and how globalization has assisted in that process.

An example of the desired empirical investigation is a study of the motivations of a mafia crime group to start operations in another country, especially when that group has been identified as local and reluctant to export itself (Varese 2011, 4).[38] Federico Varese found that the Italian Mafia did not voluntarily relocate but did so in accordance with court orders (in the case of relocation within Italy) or to escape justice or mafia infighting (p. 8). There was no interest in seeking new markets, and even where a mafia was present in a new territory, it was necessary for certain factors to exist before a new local mafia emerged to do business there. These factors were (a) that no other criminal group was present to offer illegal protection, and (b) that the state was unable to secure property rights and the like through adequate legal structures, and this in turn led to a demand for means of protection and dispute settlement outside normal conditions of governance (p. 9).

Varese found that the key to successful transplantations of the Russian Mafia in Hungary and the Calabrian Mafia to another region in Italy depended on the presence of a supply of Mafiosi and a state that, in the sudden emergence of a new free market, lacked the capacity to govern that market. In relation to China, Varese found that the triads from Hong Kong, while present in mainland China, had not offered protection services there despite the absence in many respects of government protection and booming new markets in prostitution and gambling. The reason was that corrupt officials were already providing a protective umbrella and "corrupt elements of the state apparatus, such as the military, police, and the local administration, act as the protectors of legitimate businesspeople" (Varese 2011, 178).

The boundaries of TNC appear to be ever expanding, raising the concern that persistently enriching TNC with new criminalities runs the risk that the concept itself becomes so expansive that it loses meaning and coherence (Carrapico 2012, 26–27). As well, expanding the categories of TNC can mean requests for more resources, new government agencies dedicated to fighting a category of TNC, or adding to the remit of existing agencies (Edwards and Gill 2002, 258).

Sometimes enlarging the scope of TNC reflects its politicization, for example, the insistence of the United States on establishing a nexus between terrorism and TNC. There is also the danger that, through a labeling process, TNC becomes a vehicle for declaring what is normal and what is not and which values matter and which do not. In other words, TNC becomes an ordering mechanism both domestically and internationally that governments may employ to grant enhanced law enforcement powers as part of a process of securitization. The rhetoric so often associated with TNC, both from government and scholars, underpinned as it is by a kind of moral panic, can only add to this risk.

NOTES

1. Under the Organisation for Economic Co-operation and Development's (OECD's) Fragile State Principles, a fragile state is "a state with weak capacity to carry out the basic state functions of governing a population and its territory and that lacks the ability or political will to develop mutually constructive and reinforcing relations with society."

2. The UN Convention against Transnational Organized Crime defines an organized criminal group as "a structured group of three or more persons existing for a period of time and acting in concert with the aim of committing one or more serious crimes or offences established in accordance with this Convention, in order to obtain, directly or indirectly, a financial or other material benefit."

3. According to Michael Kenney (2012, 207), the focus on exporting cocaine to the United States was the outcome of successful U.S. and Colombian efforts at eradicating and interdicting the export of marijuana to the United States in the late 1970s. This caused Colombian growers to change to cocaine where the risks were less because it was not under pressure from police operations to eradicate and interdict.

4. As Mark Findlay (1999, 150) points out, in the United States, both law enforcement and popular culture have inextricably linked the notion of organized crime with the Mafia. This in turn has led to organized crime being understood largely as "an alien conspiracy dominated by ethnic groups."

5. There is general agreement among scholars that Prohibition was a key event in the development of organized crime when criminal organizations moved into the vacuum created by liquor prohibition to ensure a sustained illegal supply through bootlegging (see, e.g., Woodiwiss 2003, 10). Others link organized crime to other prohibitions, including gambling, drugs, and prostitution (p. 10).

6. A predicate offense refers to the underlying criminal offense that gave rise to the criminal proceeds which form the subject of a money laundering charge (Leong 2007, 92).

7. Opium consumption in China in the nineteenth century, supplied by the British through India and from Turkey and Iran and later through China's own opium growers, was the impetus for international drug control. The need for international control was promoted by American missionaries who regarded drug abuse as a moral evil (Efrat 2012, 227). Thus America promoted control as a moral crusade intended to protect Oriental peoples (2012, 228). In 1900 China had 13.5 million opium addicts (McCoy 1991, 80).

8. The Mafia has existed in Italy since the 1830s (Varese 2011, 102).

9. The number of Italians in New York City increased from 12,000 in 1880 to just over 145,000 in 1900 and by 1910 immigrants and first generation Italian Americans comprised 500,000 New Yorkers or one-tenth of the population of New York. Between 1876 and 1930 about 80 percent of Italian immigrants to the United States came from southern Italy (Varese 2011, 104).

10. Military intervention began in 1986 when U.S. troops were authorized to provide logistical support on a temporary basis to the National Police Corps in Bolivia (Ronderos 2003, 210).

11. The U.S. Government Accounting Office (GAO) found that from 2000 to 2006, opium poppy cultivation and heroin production declined about 50 percent while coca cultivation and cocaine production levels increased by about 15 and 4 percent, respectively.

12. The GAO found that since fiscal year 2000, the State and Defense Departments had provided over $6.0 billion to support Plan Colombia of which nearly $4.9 billion was provided to the Colombian military and National Police.

13. In February 2001 it was reported that U.S. personnel had become directly involved in the Colombian civil war. U.S. forces on the ground, limited to five hundred at any one time, were assisted by a military consulting firm employing retired U.S. Special Forces personnel participating in search and rescue teams (Sheptycki 2003, 137).

14. A notorious arms dealer, Viktor Bout was the inspiration for the arms dealer in the film *Lord of War*. In April 2012, after being extradited from Thailand to the United States, he was sentenced to twenty-five years imprisonment in the United States after being caught in a sting operation involving a supposed arms transfer to the Colombian FARC. The supposed arms transfer would have involved between ten thousand

and twenty thousand AK47 rifles, a million rounds of ammunition, and various other light weapons that were to have been air-dropped from Bout's aircraft for FARC to collect (Bourne 2014, 89).

15. *Light weapons:* "heavy machine guns; handheld under-barrel and mounted grenade launchers; portable anti-aircraft guns; portable anti-tank guns, recoilless rifles; portable launchers of anti-tank missile and rocket systems; portable launchers of anti-aircraft missile systems; mortars of calibers of less than 100 millimetres" (Report of the United Nations Panel of Government Experts on Small Arms). *Small arms:* revolvers and self-loading pistols; rifles and carbines; submachine guns; assault rifles; light machine guns (Report of the United Nations Panel of Government Experts on Small Arms). Small arms are weapons intended for personal use and light weapons for use by several persons operating as a crew (Small Arms Survey 2005, http://www.weaponslaw.org/glossary/light-weapon).

16. See "IAEA Illicit Trafficking Database Releases Latest Aggregate Statistics," http://www.iaea.org/news center/news/2007/itdb.html.

17. The program is explained at http://www.state.gov/t/isn/offices/c55411.htm.

18. The program is explained at http://www.state.gov/t/isn/c18406.htm.

19. This Convention sets out international standards to be applied for the physical protection of nuclear material that is being transported internationally (Nillson 2001, 318).

20. The Caymans is second only to the United States in the number of *Suspicious Activity Reports* filed (Young 2013, 115).

21. In 2012, forty-five states were represented by banks in the Caymans with North America and Europe forming the largest groupings (Young 2013, 138).

22. The financial services sector was established in the Caymans in the 1960s after the collapse of the local fishing industry. Legislation governing the banking sector includes the Confidentiality Law, which is "among one of the strictest asset protection laws in the world, with criminal penalties for unauthorized disclosure of customer details" (Young 2013, 99–100). By the mid-1990s the Caymans had become a prime destination for tourism and in its financial services sector 40 percent of the workforce was expatriate. By 2001, there were over 550 banks and trust companies and more than 26,000 offshore companies had been registered. As of September 2010, US$1,725 trillion was held there in assets compared to just over US$700 billion in 2001.

23. It is estimated that US$13 trillion of untaxed wealth is located in OFCs capable of producing revenue of about US$225 billion (Young 2013, 144).

24. See http://www.fatf-gafi.org/pages/aboutus/membersandobservers/#d.en.3147 for a list of FATF members. The original membership was only sixteen states (Efrat 2012, 258).

25. The FinCEN estimated that 30 percent of the twelve million CTRs it received in 2001 were filed unnecessarily (Gouvin 2003, 968).

26. See http://www.cites.org/eng/disc/species.php.

27. The three groups are the FARC (Revolutionary Armed Forces of Colombia), ELN (National Liberation Army), and the EPL/D (People's Liberation Army; McCarthy 2011, 149).

28. The offenses defined by the Convention are illegal access, illegal interception, data interference, system interference, misuse of devices, computer-related forgery, computer-related fraud, offenses relating to child pornography, and offenses relating to copyright and neighboring rights.

29. See press release "Target Provides Update on Data Breach and Financial Performance," January 10, 2014, http://pressroom.target.com/news/target-provides-update-on-data-breach-and-financial-performance.

30. The Internet was developed in 1966 by the U.S. Defense Department with the objective of creating "a new public communications network [with] greater speed and efficiency than existing systems." By the end of 1969 it had been established that networking different types of computers was practical, and by the early 1970s a simple e-mail system had been created and the concept of linking multiple networks together into "the Internet" was conceived (Clifford 2006, 6–7).

31. The authors cite Canadian Security Intelligence Service, *Transnational Crime Activity: A Global Context* (2000) and Organisation for Economic Co-operation and Development (OECD), *The Economic Impact of Counterfeiting and Piracy* (2007) for these assertions.

32. See http://www.unodc.org/unodc/en/front page/2012/January/unodc-chief-announces-a-compre hensive-study-on-cybercrime.html.

33. See http://www.unodc.org/unodc/en/front page/2012/January/unodc-chief-announces-a-compre hensive-study-on-cybercrime.html.

34. See http://conventions.coe.int/Treaty/Commun/ C004Sig.asp?NT=185&CM=&DF=&CL=ENG.

35. See http://conventions.coe.int/Treaty/Commun/ C004Sig.asp?NT=189&CM=8&DF=&CL=ENG.

36. See https://www.europol.europa.eu/sites/ default/files/publications/octa2011.pdf.

37. In 1995 President Bill Clinton issued this warning concerning money laundering: "Nations should work together to bring their banks and financial systems into conformity with the international money laundering standards. We will work to help them do so. And, if they refuse, we will consider appropriate sanctions" (quoted in Woodiwiss 2003, 28).

38. As Varese notes (2011, 13), academic studies have found that the Sicilian Mafia, the Hong Kong Triads, and the Japanese Yakuza are local entrepreneurs, dependent on the local environment. While they may have some involvement internationally, they are essentially localized crime businesses. This research challenges the assumption and the rhetoric that see globalization as an irresistible force in the growth of TNC.

Trafficking as Business

Louise Shelley (2010, 114–131) provides a useful typology of six trafficking practices expressed in terms of business types or as criminal enterprises:

- Trade and development model

- Natural resource model

- Violent entrepreneur model

- American pimp model

- Supermarket model

- Traditional slave model with modern technology

The *trade and development model* relates to trafficking by Chinese largely for labor exploitation. Chinese smuggling operations are known to keep careful accounts and to control victims through debt bondage. Under debt bondage arrangements, victims are often only informed after arriving at their destination that they now owe a fee to the traffickers that most likely will bear no relation to that quoted before being trafficked and that this fee must be worked off by working as a prostitute. For example, Phan, a Thai woman, was told that her travel and associated fees for her trip to Japan would cost $4,000 but she was informed on arrival in Japan that she owed almost $30,000 (Farr 2012, 71). Traffickers and smugglers bribe Chinese officials and also U.S. immigration staff (Shelley 2010, 115). Victims are required to work long hours in businesses owned by the Chinese diaspora, and girls trafficked for prostitution are placed under tight controls.

The *natural resource model* relates to post-Soviet organized crime networks. Russian crime groups focus on short-term profits and sell victims as if they were a natural resource being exploited, such as timber. In this sense the business model mirrors the new Russian focus on selling gas and oil (Shelley 2010, 118). Traffickers take girls from orphanages and children's homes, take street children, and attract victims through advertisements and fake employment agencies, making extensive use of the Internet. Women taken may be sold directly to other criminal enterprises. The business is not integrated and profits are commonly used to buy other businesses, such as stores in Western Europe through which counterfeit goods can be sold. The purchase of travel agencies aids in laundering the profits of trafficking and facilitates movement of persons (p. 121).

The *violent entrepreneur model* comprises Balkan crime groups who traffic almost exclusively in women. Initially these groups (made up of family units) profited from supplying women to peacekeepers stationed in Kosovo (Shelley 2010, 121). They run an integrated enterprise acquiring women in the Balkans and relocating them in the brothels of Western Europe.

The *American pimp model* applies only to female sexual trafficking within the United States. The pimps seize persons living on the margins in U.S. society, including young runaways, street people, the homeless, and girls from malls and bars (Shelley 2010, 124). Using psychology and drugs to control the women, they appropriate all their earnings from sex work, using force when necessary. The women operate largely on the streets as opposed to apartments or through call girl arrangements. The pimps are effectively small-scale entrepreneurs working within networks, and their operations are characterized by a high consumption model using the profits to buy a range of expensive goods such as cars and jewelry. To that extent, this model mirrors contemporary American society, where the focus is on immediate consumption rather than accumulating funds for the future (pp. 124–25).

The *supermarket model* relies on moving large numbers of persons at a low cost per person. The U.S.-Mexico border is the prime location for this model, where both men and women are smuggled and trafficked. The enterprises constituting this model share profits with local border officials: on the Mexican side, it has been estimated that up to 90 percent of border staff are taking bribes (Shelley 2010, 126).

The *traditional slave model with modern technology* operates out of West Africa. Nigerian crime groups trade women and drugs and traffic them to Italy where the Nigerian diaspora is significantly represented among the immigrant community. Nigerian trafficking moves women from Edo, Nigeria, and throughout West Africa using women as recruiters and fusing old and modern methods of slavery (Shelley 2010, 129).

RECRUITMENT AND TRANSPORTATION OF TRAFFICKING VICTIMS

Techniques employed in recruiting include, in Eastern Europe and the former Soviet Union, advertisements and websites. In regions where victims are poor and uneducated, recruitment is done personally. It is common for the recruiter to be personally known to the victim: perhaps a relative or family friend and sometimes a boyfriend (Shelley 2010, 96). Persons who are trafficked are often informed that they owe a debt to the trafficker and that once it is repaid they will be free to earn as they wish. Sometimes women are told they will be working as nightclub dancers but are not told of the expectation that they will provide sexual services to customers (p. 97). Shelley argues that when impoverished families offer their children for recruitment, this should not be seen as a callous uncaring act but rather as resulting from efforts to save other children in the family from increased neglect and poverty. However, some researchers in Nigeria and Thailand attribute this practice to growing consumerism in these countries (p. 98).

Educated victims may be enticed through advertisements and through marriage and employment agencies established in the home country. Recruiters may even establish fake model agencies and film studios. Offers for study and for seemingly well-paid employment overseas may serve as inducements (Shelley 2010, 98). This approach is particularly popular in Eastern Europe where education levels are high. Matchmaking services and marriage bureaus can be used as a cover for trafficking and job offers for nannies, hotel maids, and caregivers for the elderly may be used as inducements (p. 98).

Moving persons long distances demands good planning and logistics, and some consideration needs to be given to the welfare of the persons being trafficked. However, sometimes victims travel in conditions that are inhumane, such as in the hold of cargo ships or in special compartments inside trucks (Shelley 2010, 100). If victims become ill, it is unlikely the traffickers will care for them. As Shelley notes, the conditions of travel experienced by victims mirror those experienced by slaves being transported to the new world some two centuries ago (p. 100).

It is common for traffickers to bribe or otherwise negotiate with border guards, customs officers, and embassy or consulate staff to gain entry into the receiving country (Shelley 2010, 105). Traffickers must display ingenuity and resourcefulness to gain entry. For example, in the case of entry into the United States from Mexico, one group of traffickers identified official sports and religious delegations that the victims could be attached to so as to ensure they received the requisite visas (p. 105).

OBTAINING RESIDENCE IN THE RECEIVING COUNTRY

Forged documents allowing permanent or long-term residence are used by traffickers, and sometimes the identity of the victims is changed to secure residence. In one case, trafficked sex workers were registered as students in a language school, but unfortunately for the traffickers this particular school was under close scrutiny because it had sponsored visas for two of the 9/11 hijackers (Shelley 2010, 106). Sometimes traffickers go to the extent of arranging marriages between the victims and local residents (p. 106).

Traffickers may decide to engage lawyers, at a very high cost, to obtain visas. In a well-known case involving a Harvard-educated lawyer and his wife, the couple earned $13 million from 1993 to 2000 by filing false political asylum claims for Chinese smuggled into the United States (Shelley 2010, 106). Investigations revealed that one quarter of the proceeds of this trafficking had been spent on legal fees (p. 106).

Passports and residence documents of victims are routinely taken by traffickers and retained. This means that the victim cannot prove any claim to citizenship if he or she escapes; therefore, confiscating these documents is a powerful disincentive to any escape attempts (Shelley 2010, 107). As well, escape attempts often result in severe physical punishment for the victims, and traffickers may even contract with criminal elements to sexually or physically abuse women and coerce them into compliance with traffickers' demands (p. 108). Victims often fail to seek assistance from local authorities. The reasons for this reluctance include

- they do not speak the local language and so cannot communicate with law enforcement;

- they may come from a country where police are feared and do not feel comfortable approaching police under any circumstances;

- they know that law enforcement works with the traffickers and therefore they cannot expect any assistance;

- they have been told that any attempts to escape will result in punishment being inflicted on their family back home; and

- they know that if they make any attempt to escape, they will be severely punished. (Shelley 2010, 109–10)

In parts of Africa, witchcraft has been linked to trafficking through ritual "oaths of protection," violation of which will be met with punishment from the spirit world (Willmott Harrop 2012). According to one African child advocacy organization, Nigerian traffickers use the oath as a coercive tool. A detective in the London Metropolitan Police Human Trafficking Team confirmed this practice by providing the following instance of the use of such rituals:

> One 14-year-old Nigerian victim I interviewed had taken up the offer of a family friend to become a housemaid in the United Kingdom. Before leaving she was taken to a Juju priest to undergo a ritual. She was told by the priest that if she disobeyed her trafficker, she would incur the wrath of the spirit world through nightmares, madness and death. Once in the United Kingdom, it became clear she was to be a sex slave or her trafficker would use Juju to kill her. (Quoted in Willmott Harrop 2012)

CONTROLLING VICTIMS OF TRAFFICKING

Traffickers are known to use several means to control victims, including threats of physical violence, sexual abuse, threats to inform the victim's family of the activity he or she is actually engaging in, isolation, refusal to provide food, forced alcohol or drug ingestion, restrictions on freedom to move, debt bondage arrangements, and refusal to legitimize the victim's residence status (Shelley 2010, 160). A victim's cultural obligation to support the family often means that a victim can be manipulated by traffickers who will convince the victim that he or she has a duty to pay back the family debt owed to the traffickers through unending work (p. 162).

LABOR TRAFFICKING

This form of trafficking is far less recognized as an international concern but is an acute political and social issue in developed countries. In the United States, millions migrate illegally from Mexico and Central and South America, and a significant proportion is subjected to coercion and deception when they arrive in the United States (Lee 2012). Within the United States, trafficking for labor exploitation has been found in construction, catering, clothing manufacturing, meat processing, agriculture, and labor-intensive industries generally (Lee 2012, 41). In Europe, migrants are smuggled in from North Africa or through Turkey and Eastern Europe, and the Middle East allows laborers from the Philippines, Bangladesh, Pakistan, and Thailand to enter and work (Shelley 2010, 13). The European Schengen Agreement of 1985 makes it possible to move within twenty-five European countries without a passport (p. 43).

What conduct amounts to labor exploitation? Presently, no internationally comprehensive explanation of this term exists because there are no international norms concerning employment rights. The issue of just how exploitive an employer and employee relationship must be to satisfy the Protocol definition of labor trafficking remains problematic (Lee 2012). However, some assistance on the meaning can be gained from the 1930 International Labour Organization (ILO) Convention where "forced or compulsory labour" is defined as "all work or service which is exacted from any person under the menace of any penalty and for which the said person has not offered himself voluntarily" (quoted in Lee 2012, 40).

The accident rate among trafficked laborers is especially high because they are often put to work in dangerous and hazardous conditions and are required to work long hours. In many countries they cannot seek medical assistance or treatment. Consequently, in the United Arab Emirates (UAE), boys trafficked to become camel jockeys have died or been seriously injured (Shelley 2010, 75). Box 11.1 provides two examples of labor exploitation in the United States.

BOX 11.1   Labor Exploitation in the United States

In 2004, a man was convicted of smuggling seven men into Hawaii from Tonga and enslaving them on his pig farm. They were forced to work in the man's landscaping business and were often physically assaulted with tools. They were given little food and sometimes caught and ate dogs due to extreme hunger. The owner was convicted of thirty-four charges that included forced labor, involuntary servitude, and alien smuggling. He received a sentence of twenty-six years imprisonment.

In 2006 in New Jersey, two sisters from Honduras pleaded guilty to bringing dozens of young girls into the United States, some as young as fourteen years, and forcing them to live together in substandard apartments. The girls "owed debts" to the sisters of as much as $20,000 and to repay them had to dance six days a week in bars and drink with customers. Sex work was encouraged, and the girls were beaten for rule violations. They were paid $5 an hour plus tips, most of which went toward paying off their "debt." The two sisters were part of an organization that trafficked girls out of Honduras across the Mexican border and into New Jersey. They pleaded guilty to charges that included forced labor.

SOURCE: Bales and Soodalter 2009, 195–96.

SEX TOURISM

Sex tourism is constituted by tour operators in developed countries who organize tours to other parts of the world for men to engage in sexual relations with trafficked women and children (Shelley 2010, 15).[17] Many tourists are untroubled by sex tourism. For example, when traveling on sex tours that involve sex with minors in Thailand and Cambodia, tourists rationalize that the children have made a choice to enter sex work; that the cultures are more "natural" in contrast to the moral codes of the West; that the children are, according to local cultural norms, already adults; or that the children are already sexually experienced and that having sexual relations with them is a way of providing them with financial assistance (Hartjen and Priyadarsini 2012, 158).

Whether the objective is sex with children or adults, the sex tourist "wishes to engage in a belief that the act is a voluntary one, or if not voluntary, one that is permitted by local value systems" (Ryan and Hall 2001, 56). Studies tend to show that sex tourism is associated with the "eroticization of the ethnic and cultural Other" and with power (including economic power) and dominance (O'Connell Davidson and Taylor 1999, 37). While sex tourism exists in developed states (e.g., in the Netherlands), it is experienced mostly in Asia. There are also substantial investments in sex tourism in the Caribbean and in some African states, such as Gambia and Ghana.

Sex tourism has been in evidence since the late 1960s. Beginning with prostitution associated with U.S. military bases in Southeast Asia, sex tourism has become an integral part of the economic development of some states. It is estimated that between 70 percent and 80 percent of male tourists visiting Southeast Asia from the United States, Japan, Western Europe, and Australia do so solely for sexual entertainment (Ryan and Hall 2001, 136). Tourism is a major part of the economy of many Southeast Asian states and generates employment and foreign exchange. The tourism industry has shown virtually continuous growth since the 1970s, accounting for about 10 percent of Asian gross domestic product (GDP; p. 138). Michael Hall (1992) has identified four stages in the growth of sex tourism in the Asian region:

- indigenous prostitution,
- colonialism and militarization,
- replacement of military forces with tourists, and
- rapid economic development.

Indigenous prostitution, based on concubinage and traditional prostitution, has a long history in the region and provides a ready-made foundation from which to develop sex tourism as an acceptable activity. Gendered power relations and now race and culture play a role in fostering sex tourism; for example, minorities in Myanmar and the north of Thailand are trafficked into Thailand to meet tourist demands for sex adventures in exotic Asia (Ryan and Hall 2001, 140).

During the stage of *colonization and militarization,* sex work was commodified and expanded to meet the needs of occupying military forces, leading to dependency on the business of prostitution by some sectors of the population as a means of economic survival and advancement (Ryan and Hall 2001, 141). In the Philippines, the U.S. military forces at Subic Naval Base and Clark Air Force Base supported a population of 12,000 registered and 8,000 unregistered hostesses in Olongapo City. In 1967 the U.S. and Thai governments agreed that Rest and Recreation (R and R) facilities would be provided in Thailand for U.S. forces fighting in Vietnam. As a consequence, the military presence reinforced existing structures and gender relations in the region and created new dependencies providing a firm foundation for sex tourism following the departure of the military (p. 141).

In the next stage, *international tourism replaced military forces* and governments began to promote sex tourism as an element of national development. In the developed world, tourism continued to expand, and tourism operators began to provide packaged vacations to Asia and publish media representations of countries such as Thailand that promoted stereotypes of the obedient, sexually available, and always exotic women (Ryan and Hall 2001, 143). There are now freely available published sex guides for those planning trips to Asia and a multitude of websites for potential tourists. The following is an excerpt from one guide book:

[This travel book will tell you about] places where the women will chase and fight over you, and your biggest problem will not be *who* but *when*. These are places where being an American male is a pleasure, the beaches . . . aren't polluted, the hotels are reasonable, the environment exciting, young women are appreciative, and you are a KING [emphasis original]. (Cassierer, 1992, xiv, in Davidson, 1998, 175)

The fourth stage was represented by the *rapid economic development* of the so-called Asian Tigers, with sex tourism providing an integral element in the development of various states. While the Tourism Authority of Thailand argued that creating jobs through the sex industry would enable the end of sex work, others argued that the market had already established a permanent demand for sexual services that would be fed by a continuing supply of women from the rural areas (Ryan and Hall 2001, 143). These women were migrating to the cities because of national planning policies that had downgraded agriculture and fishing within the overall country development (p. 143). As a result, Ryan and Hall argue, countries exploit women's bodies as if they were a natural resource in the interests of national economic development. In efforts to counter child prostitution in sex tourism, developed countries have legislated extraterritorially to criminalize their nationals who travel overseas to exploit children sexually and criminalize those who organize such tours (p. 144).

BOX 11.2   Sex Tourism in Nicaragua

On January 31, 2012, Edgardo Sensi, fifty-five years old, of Florida, was sentenced by the U.S. District Court in Connecticut to eighty-five years imprisonment for production of child pornography and sexual tourism offenses related to his sexual abuse of minor girls in the United States and Nicaragua.

In January 2004 in Nicaragua, Sensi seduced a nineteen-year-old woman employed as a maid, who lived in a remote and destitute area of Nicaragua. He promised to marry her and provided her with gifts and money. Through this inducement and coercion, Sensi was able to gain access to the woman's four-year-old daughter, whom he sexually abused. Sensi also videotaped sex sessions that included both the woman and her victim daughter.

SOURCE: U.S. Department of Justice 2012.

ORGAN TRAFFICKING

Body parts for transplant surgery and other medical procedures are globally trafficked, but no reliable data exist on this trade. The Palermo Protocol specifically identifies organ removal as a form of exploitation for trafficking purposes, and consent of the victim to the removal is not a relevant factor.

In China, organs are taken from imprisoned persons following their execution and are shipped to the United States for medical purposes (Shelley 2010, 15). Often, it is poor women's organs that are trafficked, but the women are left without proper care commensurate with the loss of an organ and may not be paid by the traffickers. Generally, the trafficking of organs is a product of the high world demand for organ transplants. In 2010, about 100,000 transplantations were performed worldwide and the demand for organs far outstrips supply. For example, in the United States at the end of February 2010, about 105,000 patients were on the waiting list for transplants (Francis and Francis 2010, 284). The World Health Organization (WHO) estimates that about 10 percent of the approximately 63,000 kidneys transplanted annually from living donors have been trafficked. These donors are coerced, lied to, paid very little, and frequently left with permanent disabilities for which they cannot obtain treatment (Francis and Francis 2010, 285). Organ trafficking is carried out through trafficking the organs after harvesting them from donors using coercion or by transporting the person to the receiving country and then taking his or her organs. According to the Council of Europe and the United Nations, the former method represents by far the predominant mode of operation (pp. 285–86).

Organ trafficking is condoned and facilitated in Egypt, India, Iran, Pakistan, and the Philippines, and organ brokers are most active in Israel and South Africa (Francis and Francis 2010). After recently announcing that it had broken up a ring of organ procurers, India stated that donors were paid up to $2,500 for kidneys. A broker arrested in the United States in 2009 was accused of paying $10,000 for an organ that he sold for $160,000 (p. 286).

TRAFFICKING OF MINORS

Children are trafficked primarily for commercial exploitation and because their physical size can be an asset in some industries. For example, in Nepal both boys and girls are trafficked into the local carpet-making industry because their small finger size enables them to weave complex designs (Shelley 2010). In Ghana, small boys are trafficked to mend fishing nets (p. 64). In Western Europe, children are purchased in order that the buyers may obtain welfare benefits (Hartjen and Priyadarsini 2012, 140). Minors may also be trafficked for adoption and, most recently, for their body parts. Children (most commonly girls) are also trafficked for sexual exploitation as child prostitutes, massagers, and strippers, and in the pornography industry. In terms of the scale of trafficking of minors, both the Organization for Security and Co-operation in Europe (OSCE) and the International Labour Organization (ILO) estimate that 1.2 million minors are trafficked each year with between 10 percent and 30 percent of this number destined for commercial sex work (p. 144).

Those trafficking children include the children's parents, siblings, friends, schoolteachers, the village headman, and religious groups. For example, minors trafficked from Romania for labor exploitation are usually recruited by someone known and trusted by them (Surtees 2005, 8). Often women are involved in the trafficking operation, especially in West Africa, where they may contact poverty-stricken parents to conclude an agreement they believe will lift their family out of destitution (Hartjen and Priyadarsini 2012, 156). Traffickers commonly ensure that the victim loses all and any means of communicating with his or her family (p. 160).

In some countries, the regularity of trafficking minors has now achieved a degree of normalcy. For example, in Bulgaria, recruitment involves a form of bonded labor where the minor is sold by his or her parents for an amount of about 200 to 300 euros (Surtees 2005, 11). Once the minor has repaid the bond, she is able to retain a part of what she was able to earn through street begging. In one case, a minor returned to Bulgaria with a kilogram of gold earned while begging in Austria (p. 11). Victim beggars trafficked within Eastern Europe have been forced to sit in the streets for long periods without food and in severe weather conditions in destinations like Poland, Russia, and Ukraine. Those who do not earn enough money are punished with violence (p. 11).

Surtees (2005) found that many minors trafficked in Eastern Europe were aware of the recruitment process and the sum of money paid for them to the traffickers. In many cases the minor is not the only family member who has been trafficked. A female minor trafficked to Austria in 2004 came from a family of eight children, five of whom were in Vienna, working there as beggars with different traffickers (p. 6).

REGIONAL TRAFFICKING

Asia

Trafficking in Asia is operated more by organized crime than in other regions, with some Asian crime groups specializing in human smuggling and trafficking as opposed to the drug trade (Shelley 2010, 141). The forms of human trafficking in Asia include "sexual, labor, forced marriages, trafficking of children for adoptions, child soldiers, organ trafficking, trafficking for begging and debt bondage" (p. 142). A strong tradition of trafficking for sexual purposes exists in Asia. Debt bondage has traditional connotations, especially in India and China (p. 142). Child trafficking is more prevalent in Asia than elsewhere, and children and minors figure significantly in Asian sex tourism (p. 143). The Japanese sex industry receives more than one hundred thousand women from the Philippines and Thailand each year to work in the Japanese entertainment districts (p. 153).

Trafficking in other forms has been prevalent in Asia for many years. During the nineteenth century, the colonial powers routinely exported persons to other colonies for labor, for example, from southern India to Fiji, from China to the United States, and from India to the Caribbean (Shelley 2010, 145–46). Chinese were sent to the United States where they worked on the new transcontinental railroads (Shelley 2010, 146).

Explanations for trafficking of women and girls in Asia focus on perceived gender inequality, but forced labor and organ trafficking are also prevalent as components of trafficking (Shelley 2010, 150). Trafficking is supported by the high demand for cheap labor and sexual services in the region and because of the effects of globalization, with India, China, and Japan being major elements in the spread of globalization in the region. Asian states tend to lack the protective labor laws found in the West, and there are minimal standards of health and safety at work and a practice of labor exploitation (p. 150). Family and cultural practices perpetuate trafficking in the region: there is low investment in girls' education, a general lack of access to education, and a strong preference for boys to receive education rather than girls. These factors promote trafficking (p. 158).

As noted earlier, the war in Vietnam produced a demand for sexual services at military bases and in the towns where the military congregated for rest and recreation. Thus brothels and entertainment districts were created around bases such as those adjacent to Subic Bay and Clark Air Force Base (Shelley 2010, 160). In Thailand, the sex industry is viewed as a form of development capital, and sex tourism constitutes a significant part of the local economy (p. 161). In *Guns, Girls, Gambling, Ganja,* Pasuk Phongpaichit (1998) reveals the integral role that human trafficking plays in the Thai economy because it is a major source of earnings for police who share profits with politicians and political parties (in Shelley 2010, 162).

In South Asia, Indian trafficking has its genesis in the caste system, which institutionalized bondage for lower caste people over generations, and bonded labor continues to be practiced in India (Shelley 2010, 166). Labor exploitation in India and Nepal is more widespread than sexual exploitation, and South Asian children work in bonded labor and are trafficked for a variety of purposes, including as labor and beggars (p. 168).

Why is trafficking so pervasive in Asia? Shelley (2010, 171) suggests, in relation to labor exploitation, that bonded labor is a tradition that simply continues and that the region lacks any large-scale mobilization of citizens for a cause, such as occurred with the antislavery movement in North and South America. She blames patriarchy for sex trafficking, together with the subordination of citizens to the state and the family. Thus expressions of personal rights and the right not to be a victim are uncommon in the region (p. 171).

Eurasia and Eastern Europe

Russian traditions of slavery and serfdom prior to the Revolution continued subsequently with the creation of the Gulags, where citizens were sent to do forced labor during the Stalinist period. Serfs were unable to move freely about the country, and Russian and Slavic slaves were traded in the Roman slave markets (Shelley 2010, 176). According to Shelley (2010, 177), recruits in Russia and other post-Soviet states have arrangements with directors of orphanages to regularly deliver orphans who have reached the age of eighteen to traffickers. Conditions that contribute to trafficking include the lack of a tradition of rights or respect for rights, the low status of women, corrupt practices, and ineffective and corrupt law enforcement (p. 179). A 2004 ILO report estimated that 20 percent of the five million illegal immigrants in Russia were forced labor victims (p. 179). In Russia, child exploitation can be explained by the large numbers of abandoned children coupled with Russian reluctance to adopt them (p. 180).

Organ trafficking is not prevalent in this region, and instead victims travel to other countries to have the organ removed with the assistance of crime groups (Shelley 2010, 183). According to Shelley (p. 184), "All forms of human trafficking are endemic in the region, a result of poverty, ineffective counter-measures, the frequent collusion of government officials . . . and the rise of criminal entrepreneurship." Overall, Shelley attributes the increased trafficking in this region as the outcome of the feminization of poverty, increased family violence and corresponding reduction in social protections, regional conflicts, and economic inequality (p. 184).

As socialism retreated in the region, women in particular suffered, losing their forms of social protection such as guaranteed employment and child subsidies (Shelley 2010, 185). Women had formerly held jobs with the state as teachers, doctors, nurses, and so on, but with the new policy of capital export, the state could no longer afford to pay wages for this work (pp. 186–87). Women suffered the most as a result of the transition from socialism to capitalism, including the loss of business through coercion and extortion by criminals. As the former USSR collapsed, criminal groups emerged and human trafficking became one of their core activities (p. 187). Farr (2012, 74) reports that women's income in Russia fell from 70 percent of a man's income in 1989 to just over 40 percent in 1995 and that Russia's GDP declined by 34 percent between 1991 and 1995.

Trafficking groups possess the flexibility to adjust to the changing economic and social conditions. They comprise both decommissioned military personnel and inmates formerly in Soviet labor camps as well as members of the security services (Shelley 2010, 187). Many possessed skills such as document forgery or a background in intelligence work, skills that could be readily adapted to the new criminality.

Women were trafficked into Moscow from the poorer parts of the country. There are now an estimated one hundred thousand prostitutes working in the capital alone, ten times the number in New York and London (Shelley 2010, 191). The labor migrants exploited in labor trafficking come from the poorer satellite states of the former USSR. For example, one-third of households in Tajikistan have a family member working away from home, most often in Russia or Kazakhstan (p. 191). It is estimated that up to eight hundred laborers die annually though hazardous labor conditions (p. 193).

Overall, governments in the region have shown little interest in combating trafficking of any kind. They are regularly listed as Tier 2 or 3 states[18] in the U.S. State Department's *Trafficking in Persons Report* (Shelley 2010, 196).

Europe

According to Shelley (2010, 201), most European countries have limited experience in the integration of migrants, at least compared to the United States, Canada, and Australia. Within Europe, a need for unskilled labor that is not locally available exists because of low birth rates and a well-educated labor force (p. 203). Shelley notes that there is a great demand for trafficked women in Europe because local women choose not to become prostitutes (p. 203). In Italy, low-cost labor is required for the textile industry and Chinese are smuggled in for this purpose (p. 203).

The United Nations reports that within Western Europe, five countries rate highly as destinations for human trafficking, namely, Belgium, Germany, Greece, Italy, and the Netherlands (Shelley 2010, 204). These countries have large sex markets either because of domestic demand or as an outcome of flourishing tourist industries. According to EUROPOL, the major countries from which persons are trafficked into Western Europe are Moldova, Ukraine, Bulgaria, Romania, Russia, and Nigeria (p. 206). As Shelley notes, however, EUROPOL omits other major source countries that once were colonies, such as Morocco and Algeria. Permanent residence is difficult to secure within Europe and, unlike the situation in the United States, many trafficked persons are required to return to their home countries where they are likely to be re-trafficked because of the lack of opportunities there (Shelley 2010, 215).

Slavery has a long history in Europe, back to Greek and Roman times, including an active slave market in Sicily that operated until the mid-nineteenth century (Shelley 2010, 207). With the ending of slavery, bonded labor supplied a means of meeting the labor shortage in agriculture, with the British, for example, sending Indians to Mauritius, thereby in effect, renewing the exploitation of un-free labor (p. 208). During World War II, Jews and other groups were transported to provide slave labor for the Nazis, and women were trafficked into prostitution to service the German military (p. 208).

The knowledge base of trafficking in Europe remains inadequate with limited knowledge of the sources of trafficking, the extent of the trafficking operations, the ways in which victims are exploited, and the profits that accrue to the criminal groups (Shelley 2010, 217). According to Shelley (p. 223), smuggling and trafficking have been sustained and have grown because of diminishing border controls under the Schengen Agreement and because there is a lack of cooperation in law enforcement and legal harmonization between states.

United States

The United States is distinctive among nations to which persons are trafficked because of its history of slavery, population mobility, the existence of organized criminal enterprises, its severe drug abuse issue, high birth rates, and for the role that religion still plays in the society (Shelley 2010, 239). Whereas countries in Western Europe and Japan maintain birth rates that do not even reach replacement level, the United States maintains a birth rate above the replacement level. According to Shelley, this means there are more children within the U.S. population who may not be optimally supervised or parented. Thus, in her view, it is unsurprising that a majority of trafficking victims are trafficked before they reach the age of eighteen years (p. 239).

Only a small number of sexual trafficking victims are foreigners, with an estimated 14,500 to 17,500 women and girls trafficked into the country each year for sexual exploitation (Shelley 2010, 240; U.S. Department of State 2005). In one case involving foreign women in Houston, Texas, traffickers were charged with trafficking eight women from Central American countries to work as bar girls between 2001 and 2005 (Shelley 2010, 256–57). They had been told they would be employed in restaurants but were paid only about $50 a week, incurring an even greater debt to the traffickers in addition to the smuggling fee. One nineteen-year-old girl was the subject of negotiations to sell her to another bar owner for $11,000.

Volunteerism and religiosity are characteristics of U.S. society, and both respond to trafficking with considerable victim support provided by U.S. NGOs and churches. The faith-based organizations, in particular, have played a significant role in seeking a total prohibition on prostitution worldwide (Shelley 2010, 242). Despite the passage of the Trafficking Victims Protection Act in 2000, which incorporates a strong focus on law enforcement to counter trafficking, prosecutions for trafficking in the United States remain minimal. For example, only seventy-seven convictions were obtained throughout the country in 2008 (Shelley 2010, 230).

As Shelley (p. 230) points out, those most susceptible to trafficking are the marginalized and disadvantaged within U.S. society. With a much reduced social safety net, compared to most of Western Europe for example, U.S. society generates a more than adequate supply of likely victims. In addition, the United States tolerates an undocumented migrant population of between 12.5 and 15 million persons, some of whom may have been trafficked or otherwise victimized after illegal entry into the country (p. 232).

The prevalent forms of trafficking are sex trafficking of both foreigners and native born persons, labor trafficking, and forms of debt bondage (Shelley 2010, 233). Trafficking exists in every state within the United States, and the United States is a significant destination for children who have been kidnapped and trafficked for the purposes of adoption by a family within the United States (p. 233).

In many respects, current illegal immigration mirrors the immigration patterns operating from the seventeenth to the early nineteenth centuries when persons arrived as slaves and indentured servants. Prior to 1808, it was lawful to import slaves into the United States, and indentured servitude was only prohibited in 1865. During the slave trade, it is estimated that 645,000 slaves were transported into the United States (Shelley 2010, 235). Even after it was prohibited under federal law (through the Anti-Peonage Act 1867), debt bondage and indentured servitude continued, as exemplified by the transportation of Chinese "coolies" into the United States (p. 236). Research into the facts of trafficking prosecutions has revealed some of the elements of the trafficking business in the United States (Bales and Lize 2005, 39):

- Trafficking groups ensure that victims remain vulnerable and dependent through measures like isolation and disorientation.

- Actual violence or threats of violence are used to maintain a climate of fear.

- Given the planning and organization required for successful trafficking, most instances of human trafficking and forced labor should be seen as instances of organized crime and not simply opportunism.

Significant profits are earned from trafficking. For example, a couple from Uzbekistan who trafficked two women into the United States from that country earned $400,000 from their services over eighteen months (Shelley 2010, 244). In Los Angeles, call girls from the former USSR earned $7 million annually. Generally, pimps exploiting young girls for sexual services can earn from $500 a night to several thousand dollars when demand is high, such as at conventions (p. 245).

Mexico and U.S. Border

William van Schendel (2005, 44) argues that the existence of a borderland between the United States and Mexico gives rise to a "borderland society" in the form of a social, economic, and cultural zone straddling the border. That society, he points out, possesses networks that may predate the existence of the border or that have developed because of the significance of the border. Cross border flows will be accommodated within such networks, whether clandestine or open (p. 44). The long 1,951-mile U.S. border with Mexico facilitates both trafficking and smuggling of persons into the United States. The border runs through desolate and rugged landscapes with only about six hundred miles of fencing and is policed by a Border Patrol Force of about twenty thousand agents (Schaefer and Gonzales 2012, 174).

In the early 20th century, U.S. employers informally recruited Mexicans to work in agriculture. Back then, crossing the border was relatively easy. Illegal immigration was largely overlooked, and labor shortages in the United States, the Mexican revolution, and expanded agriculture led to further immigration. The U.S. Border Patrol was formed in 1924 with its primary targets being Chinese and Europeans entering through Mexico. During the 1920s, about half a million Mexicans entered, and when the depression arrived, thousands were deported (Andreas 2001). Labor shortages in the 1940s meant encouraging Mexican workers to return.

Between 1942 and 1964 the Bracero Program established a regime for guest workers in agribusiness, thereby institutionalizing labor immigration on a mass basis (Andreas 2001, 109). Even when the Bracero Program ended, Mexican workers continued to be welcomed because hiring workers who had entered illegally had not been stipulated as a felony.

During the 1960s and 1970s, border control was minimal, and migrants either smuggled themselves across or hired a guide (Andreas 2001). However, as migrants increasingly shifted their intended destination to U.S. cities, there was a need for greater organization in crossing the border, and smugglers became more professionalized (p. 110). By the late 1970s, both governments were cooperating against organized smuggling, and in 1986 the United States rationalized its policy by enacting the Immigration Reform and Control Act. This Act created sanctions against employers who hired undocumented immigrants, expanded the Border Patrol, and legalized the status of some two million immigrants. This in turn stimulated interest in migrating to the United States, and the demand for smugglers services expanded enormously (p. 112).

By the 1990s, public opinion viewed undocumented immigration more as a threat than a source of cheap labor, and U.S. policy changed to one of regaining control of the border. The Immigration and Naturalization budget expanded from $1.5 billion in 1993 to $4 billion by 1999 (Andreas 2001, 116). As well as additional agents to police it, a massive influx of new equipment supplemented efforts to deny the border to illegal crossers, leading again to the need for professional smugglers, whose power increased given that the cost of crossing had doubled and even tripled (p. 116). Current plans by the United States to reform immigration include securing the entire border, hiring even more agents, and installing yet more monitoring equipment.

Unfortunately, the politically charged environment of the borderlands promotes a conflation of trafficking and smuggling, and trafficking tends to be subsumed under the label "smuggling." As Susan Tiano (2012, 7) puts it, "Human trafficking needs to be acknowledged as a unique phenomenon that is shaped by different socioeconomic forces and responds to different kinds of preventive strategies, than the smuggling of undocumented migrants." The two categories differ in that once delivered, the smuggled migrant is free to find his or her way in a new environment, but the trafficked victim enjoys no such liberty. In practice, Tiano (2012, 7–8) points out that the authorities tend to acknowledge trafficking cases only where there are

- living victims who can give accounts of how they were trafficked,

- women and children who are presumed to lack the agency to have voluntarily crossed the border, and

- victims working in the sex industry rather than in casual or seasonal labor.

Smuggling, on the other hand, almost always implies the migrant's consent to the crossing of the border, and smuggled migrants are not considered deserving of any special protection: in fact, once they are caught, the tendency is to punish them with the full rigor of the law. A number of specific factors shape the trafficking of persons into the United States from Mexico.

- The U.S. demand for sex workers and low-cost labor creates a constant market for trafficked victims and generates large profits for those in the trafficking business. While legal immigration into the United States remains restricted, the relational ties in the borderlands facilitate the circulation of both goods and persons though established networks. The push of depressed economic conditions in Mexico and Central and South America and the pull of the United States' need for low-cost labor combine to ensure continuous supply and demand. Undocumented migrants are now, because of recent enhancements in border controls on the U.S. side, in fear of being detected and deported, rendering them more vulnerable to abuse and exploitation. At the same time, the U.S. guest worker program comprising H-2 visa holders[19] ties the worker to a single employer, making them vulnerable to employer abuses such as substandard accommodation, poor wages, and lack of access to medical treatment[20] (Payan 2012, 150).

- The politicization of the border and the consequent obsession with preventing and apprehending migrants means that resources are devoted to preventing and chasing smuggled border crossers while little attention

is devoted to trafficking. Similarly, the war on drugs privileges drug-smuggling operations to the detriment of trafficking cases. The tension between the need for cheap labor and the desire to rigorously police the border is never really addressed at the political level.

- There is a fine line between smuggling and trafficking because, once in the control of smugglers, migrants are liable to be deceived or coerced either by the smugglers or by traffickers to whom they are linked (Tiano 2012, 11–12). The "multi-layered complexity of the borderlands muddles and confuses the issues surrounding human trafficking and human smuggling," and the two activities are often conducted by the same criminals (Payan 2012, 149–50).

The U.S. State Department lists Mexico as a Tier 2 country in its *Trafficking in Persons Reports* for 2009, 2010, and 2013. In its view, Mexico has yet to comply with the minimum standards for trafficking elimination and has not implemented effective anti-trafficking measures. According to UNODC, Mexico ranks "high" as a location from which trafficking for labor and sexual exploitation occurs (Clark 2012, 111).

Latin America and Africa

Both regions are characterized by extensive poverty, high birth rates, young populations, and, generally speaking, quite stratified societies with high rates of unemployment (Shelley 2010, 265). Governments in the region are often authoritarian, and societies have a history of slavery and colonization. The importation of slaves into South American countries like Brazil and into the Caribbean created a class of persons marginalized by their color and provided an underclass ready for exploitation by traffickers (p. 266).

Many living in the South wish to migrate to the North to find employment and generally a better life. While Europe is the preferred destination from Africa, from South America the aim is to enter the United States (Shelley 2010, 267). Barriers to migration exist in all European states, as well as in the United States, thus providing a foundation for traffickers and smugglers to prosper. The presence of diaspora communities in the wealthy states gives traffickers a foothold. Consequently, women are trafficked from the

Dominican Republic, previously a Spanish colony, into Spain. Similarly, the Nigerian diaspora in Italy facilitates the trafficking of Nigerian women into that country, which, in 2006 had 12,500 Nigerian women working as sex workers, making up about half of all sex workers in Italy (p. 268). Sex trafficking associated with international peacekeeping under United Nations auspices in particular is an issue in Africa given the increasing number of internal conflicts requiring such interventions (p. 274).

In Brazil and elsewhere in South America as well as Africa, homeless children live on the streets because of poverty, family conflicts, and drug abuse. They become easy prey for traffickers and can be coerced into begging for adults, sold as domestic servants, or trafficked into prostitution (Shelley 2010, 274). Trafficking for organs associated with ritual practices has been identified in Chad, Liberia, and Malawi (p. 275), and organ trafficking for commercial purposes exists in both South America and Africa (p. 276).

Guatemala is the center of child adoption trafficking with about 1,000 to 1,500 babies being trafficked annually. Children taken from Mexican parents for $500 can be sold in the United States for adoption for $10,000 (Shelley 2010, 278).

In sub-Saharan and North Africa, trafficking for forced labor and sexual exploitation occurs, with tourism in North Africa being a major contributing factor to the importation of women for sexual exploitation (Shelley 2010, 281).

COUNTERING HUMAN TRAFFICKING

Worldwide, intergovernmental and nongovernment organizational responses to trafficking center around three distinct strategies:

- prevention of trafficking,

- protection and support of victims, and

- prosecution of traffickers.

Most state strategies are dominated by the migration-crime-security nexus, meaning they are focused on prosecuting traffickers and are less concerned with victim protection. Prevention strategies have been concerned with preventing the entry of illegal migrants of all kinds through strengthening border security and expanding border controls beyond receiving states so that entry can be denied by taking action in states through which illegal migrants are commonly transported. In recent times, greater attention has been given to victims (Goodey 2008, 431). For example, the U.S. Department of State TIP report for 2013 states, "This Trafficking in Persons Report focuses on victim identification as a top priority in the global movement to combat trafficking in persons" (U.S. Department of State 2013, 8).

Victim Protection

Generally, only weak international obligations exist concerning trafficking victims. Accordingly, while the Palermo Protocol provides that states should assist trafficking victims, it fails to make such assistance or protection mandatory instead using "soft law" aspirational legal language that qualifies the notion of assistance with phrases such as "in appropriate cases and to the extent possible under its domestic law" and requires states to only "consider" implementing measures for victims' physical and psychological needs and to "endeavor" to ensure their physical safety (Chuang 2006, 148; Goodey 2008, 423).

In cases of sexual exploitation, immigration officials in receiving states rely heavily on stereotypes of the "trafficking victim" (Lee 2012, 63). Consequently, victims who conform to expected typifications are more likely to be assessed as "legitimate" trafficking victims, and those who do not display signs of "raw physical suffering"[21] (p. 64) or whose narrative does not exactly accord with the kind of victim judged to be acceptable for trial purposes are more likely to be rejected as unsuitable.[22] This is because the prosecution process requires that their accounts be "sanitized and simplified for state machinery to digest and act upon those experiences" (Segrave, Miliojevic, and Pickering 2011, 194).

The authorized discourse of the "legitimate" trafficking victim is exemplified by the passage of the U.S. Victims of Trafficking and Violence Protection Act (TVPA) during which legislators frequently referred to trafficking victims as meek, passive objects of sexual exploitation and largely ignored victims of trafficking for labor exploitation (Srikantiah 2007, 160). Similarly, Department of Justice publications concerning human trafficking depict victims as suffering from "paralyzing fear" and being "meek" (p. 202).[23]

Criticism of victim support measures centers on their failure to meet the realities of trafficked persons' lives and actual needs. Thus the government imperative for obtaining victim's accounts of their trafficking experience for prosecution purposes conflicts with victims' felt needs after escaping from traffickers when they are particularly fearful of reprisals and often suspicious of government authorities. In practice, women victims are often taken into custody and placed in confinement or even deported immediately. Victims' detention in welfare shelters awaiting the commencement of the prosecution against the traffickers can last for months or even years in some Asian states. The fear of "pulling" more irregular migrants into the receiving state if fuller levels of protection are offered to victims weighs heavily on receiving state protection policies. As already noted, the receiving state concerns about illegal immigration are politically much more salient than humanitarian efforts to assist victims (Lee 2012, 72).

In relation to males trafficked for labor exploitation, one study found that the vast majority of male victims from Ukraine and Belarus were recruited through employment agencies, personal contacts, and media advertisements; were subjected to forced labor in various heavy industries; and suffered substandard living conditions and a lack of basic needs such as adequate shelter and food (Lee 2012, 66). As victims of such labor conditions, male workers' needs focused on physical injury and health issues connected to the nature of their work and on the unsafe working environment, but the dominant paradigm in trafficking treatment remains focused on sexual exploitation. Consequently, male victims' needs cannot easily be met (p. 71).

Prosecution and Migration-Crime-Security

A considerable number of states regard human trafficking as a migration issue concerned with securing borders and preventing illegal immigration. This approach treats trafficked persons as violators of immigration law who enter a state illegally and work without proper documents and authorization. The problem of trafficking is therefore treated largely as one of criminality, and the state response is to expand and supplement border controls to prevent entry (Lee 2012, 29). For example, the "militarization" of policing

national borders is seen as a consequence of efforts to counter human trafficking (Lee 2012). A case in point is the U.S.–Mexico border, which has received an influx of new border agents and resources, including surveillance equipment and fencing (p. 116).

As well, in the United States and elsewhere, immigration detention facilities and their management have been expanded and privatized and reflect the growth of a "transnational security state" (Lee 2012, 119). A vast "trafficking control industry" has emerged not only comprising state personnel and assets dedicated to protecting borders but also encompassing victim programs, academic and NGO research, books, films, and commentaries describing the problem, as well as international workshops, seminars, and capacity-building programs all related to human trafficking (p. 150). This collective effort effectively marginalizes other approaches, such as identifying trafficking as a legitimate social and economic problem and seeking solutions that will reduce poverty and provide opportunities to potential victims in their states of origin.

Worldwide data contained in the 2013 U.S. State Department TIP Report on the prosecution of traffickers based on 188 country reports reveals the following for 2012:

- 7,705 *prosecutions* for trafficking, of which 1,153 related to labor trafficking;

- 4,746 *convictions,* of which 518 were for labor trafficking; and

- 46,570 victims overall.

The data reveal that there has been no significant increase in the number of prosecutions from 2005 to 2012.

U.S. Trafficking Policy

The U.S. State Department, acting under the Victims of Trafficking and Violence Protection Act (TVPA) monitors trafficking worldwide by assessing country reports provided by state parties to the Protocol. The purposes of the Act are "to combat trafficking in persons, a contemporary manifestation of slavery whose victims are predominantly women and children, to ensure just and effective punishment of traffickers, and to protect their victims" (TVPA Section 102[a]). In its annual report under the Act, the United States assigns a tier to each country indicating the extent to which the country complies with U.S. policies on anti-trafficking. (U.S. policies do not apply the international standards prescribed by the Palermo Protocol.) Thus Tier 1 indicates full compliance with U.S. policies and Tier 3 is the lowest level of compliance, denoting no significant efforts being made to comply with the TVPA standards.

A country assigned a Tier 3 rating may be subject to sanctions, including withholding non–humanitarian and non–trade-related assistance (Goodey 2008, 432). Tier 2 is divided into Tier 2 and Tier 2 Watch List. A simple Tier 2 indicates less than full compliance, but the country is making significant efforts in that direction. The Tier 2 Watch List lies somewhere between Tier 2 and Tier 3, but this classification means that a country is heading in the direction of a Tier 3 classification based on specific defaults. These are specified as a high number of victims of trafficking and no evidence having been provided of increased efforts to counter trafficking, for example, through investigations, prosecutions, or assistance to victims (U.S. Department of State 2013, pp. 44–45).

The TVPA has been criticized for emphasizing the law enforcement aspects of measures to counter trafficking at the expense of the humanitarian goal of assisting trafficking victims (Chacon 2006, 2976). The law grants protections only for victims of "severe forms of trafficking in persons" and, unlike the Palermo Protocol, makes no provision concerning victim consent. Consequently, a victim who is merely "trafficked" as the law defines that term will not be able to qualify for full relief under the law. "Severe forms of trafficking in persons" is defined to mean

(a) sex trafficking in which a commercial sex act is induced by force, fraud or coercion, or in which the person induced to perform such act has not attained 18 years of age; (b) or the recruitment, harboring, transportation, provision, or obtaining of a person for labor or services, through the use of force, fraud, or coercion for the purpose of subjection to involuntary servitude, peonage, debt bondage, or slavery. (TVPA Sections 8[a] and 8[b])

The restrictive approach to trafficking reflected in the severity test was, according to Chacon, "a deliberate effort to deny immigration benefits to individuals who, while exposed to conduct that constitutes trafficking, gave consent at some point during the process of their transportation or employment" (Chacon 2006, 3022). Victims must also demonstrate they have "complied with any reasonable request for assistance in the investigation or prosecution of acts of trafficking" (Srikantiah 2007, 159).

While the severity test concerning sex trafficking automatically includes all persons under the age of eighteen years, the same is not true of coercive labor arrangements where there is no such age stipulation. Overall, U.S. domestic trafficking legislation provides a narrower conception of trafficking then does the Palermo Protocol (Chacon 2006, 2985). The protections provided for those who satisfy the severity test are

- five thousand visas are available for those falling into this category—the "T" visa— allowing victims to stay in the United States for three years provided they cooperate in efforts to prosecute those who trafficked them and can demonstrate they would be subject to "extreme hardship involving unusual and severe harm" if returned to their country of origin; and

- a victim will be eligible for federal and state benefits and services. (Chacon 2006, 3011)

After three years on a T visa, victims may be able to remain permanently in the United States if they have displayed good moral character and either assisted in the prosecution or investigation of traffickers or would suffer extreme hardship upon removal from the United States (Chacon 2006, 3011). The principal issue with obtaining T visas is that very few are being granted: in 2003, 453 applications were received and only 172 visas granted; in 2004 out of 520 applications, only 136 were approved (p. 3018), and in 2006, out of 346 applications received, 182 were granted (Lee 2011, 73).

The reluctance to issue T visas seems connected to the regulations made under the TVPA, which show that the Department of Homeland Security is strongly encouraged to secure the endorsement of law enforcement before issuing a T visa to a victim (Chacon 2006, 3025). If a victim is unable to obtain an endorsement from law enforcement, she must provide "sufficient credible secondary evidence," which may include "trial transcripts, court documents, police reports, news articles, and copies of reimbursement forms for travel to and from court." A victim in this situation must also give a statement explaining the steps taken to report the crime to a law enforcement agency and must also show that attempts were made to obtain the endorsement (Srikantiah 2007, 176). Jayashri Srikantiah (p. 180) observes that

> the decision regarding whether or not an individual is a victim of a severe form of human trafficking . . . can [be] an arbitrary and highly subjective exercise since each Assistant U.S. Attorney, Federal Bureau of Investigation agent, or immigration officer has his or her own conception of the type of situation and events that would warrant being called severe trafficking.

Cooperating with law enforcement may not be as simple for the victim of trafficking who has been under constant threat, lost track of time, and is perhaps unable to compile a coherent narrative of events such as would satisfy the demands of evidence that can be presented in court (Chacon 2006, 3026). In addition, where a person is deemed by a prosecutor not to be a good witness in a trafficking prosecution, the prosecutor will also make the decision whether the person is a victim for the purposes of being issued a T visa. This inevitably means failing to identify as trafficking victims those who do not present themselves as good prosecution witnesses (Srikantiah 2007, 160).

Trafficking as a Human Rights Violation

States may declare trafficking to be a human rights issue but at the same time make immigration control the paramount consideration in their policy making. Within Europe, these tensions are revealed in decisions of the European Union and its organs. In 2004, the Justice and Home Affairs Council of the European Union adopted a directive concerning residence permits issued to third country nationals who are victims of trafficking and who, importantly, cooperate with the authorities. At the same time, the European Union has taken a human rights approach to trafficking in public declarations such as the 2002 Council of Europe Framework Decision on

Combating Trafficking in Human Beings and the 2005 Council of Europe Convention on Action against Trafficking in Human Beings, both of which declare human trafficking constitutes a violation of human rights. The latter Convention creates a legal framework for victim assistance and protection with a monitoring mechanism (Lee 2012, 33). Consequently, reconciling the need for successful prosecutions of traffickers with human rights and victim protection can be a challenge for states (p. 59).

Repatriation and Re-trafficking

When a rescued trafficking victim is not granted protection by the receiving state, he or she may simply be sent back to the country of origin, often to experience the same economic hardships that prompted the trafficking. As well, a victim may suffer rejection by his or her home community for bringing shame to the group. Evidence indicates that returned victims are highly susceptible to being re-trafficked. In one survey conducted in southeast Europe, between 3 percent and 34 percent of victims had been re-trafficked (Lee 2012, 79).

Re-trafficking is most likely to occur when substantial debt burdens are still owed to traffickers or others or when a victim experiences hardships in reintegrating into the community and faces sustained hostility. Strategies for trafficking and re-trafficking prevention that rely on public awareness campaigns have been found ineffective and perceived by those targeted as anti-immigration messages designed to keep the poor out of wealthy states (Chuang 2006, 155).

Assessment of Strategies

Generally, most anti-trafficking strategies and interventions have not been evaluated to assess their performance, but a 2003 report by experts to the UN Commission on the Status of Women found that, even after ten years of anti-trafficking interventions in the Balkans, there was no significant evidence of any decrease in trafficking or increase in the number of traffickers tried and convicted (Chuang 2006, 157). Likewise, a longitudinal estimate based on the 2009 TIP Report found that worldwide anti-trafficking efforts have remained stable over the past decade. This suggests that states' TIP reports' tier classifications are not improving over time despite funds being allocated to those states in need to counter trafficking (Wooditch 2011, 471).

Comment

This historical account shows that human trafficking across borders for slavery, sex work, and the like has ancient origins. From this foundation, contemporary criminal enterprises worldwide have invested in people trafficking primarily to satisfy markets for cheap labor and sexual exploitation. They trade on the human misery and desperation of the poor in the South who seek to migrate to the North to improve their own well-being and that of their family. It is striking that despite all the international effort and resources directed at countering trafficking, the scale of human trafficking for exploitation is simply not quantifiable. Moreover, the available evidence suggests that all international and domestic interventions have failed to substantially impede the trafficking business and its criminal organization. What is known is that many states, especially developed states, have conflated two modes of migration—that is, trafficking of persons for exploitation and people smuggling—and have strengthened their borders to the detriment of trafficked victims and their human rights.

A good deal is known about the actual process of trafficking: how persons are taken or recruited, the means of transportation, and what can happen to them in the receiving state at the hands of the traffickers or the government of that state. Similarly, the trafficking routes have been mapped and attempts made to monitor them. It seems obvious that strategies designed to prevent trafficking ought to focus not only on strengthening borders but also on examining how economic and social needs in states of origin can be properly addressed so that adverse economic conditions do not foster the business of trafficking.

At the country level of analysis, there are clearly attitudinal and procedural issues associated with victim identification and protection that need to be addressed if the Palermo Protocol is to be properly observed and respected. The current state and media preoccupation with trafficking for sexual exploitation is the master trafficking discourse that overshadows all other trafficking issues. States should become more cognizant of, and more concerned to combat, other modes of exploitation for which persons are trafficked, especially labor trafficking, if the international anti-trafficking regime is to be effective for all persons.

Notes

1. As Turner and Kelly (2009, 186) point out, "Most victims of human traffickers do not begin or end their journeys shackled and chained."

2. Under international law, a discrete Protocol supplementary to the Convention against Transnational Organized Crime—The Smuggling of Migrants by Land, Sea and Air—has been created and includes a definition of smuggling. The act of smuggling transitions to an act of trafficking when the smuggled person suffers exploitation at any point along the way from recruitment to arrival at destination.

3. The Protocol has been ratified by 158 states as of November 2013 (United Nations Treaty Collection, http://treaties.un.org/Pages/ViewDetails.aspx?src= TREATY&mtdsg_no=XVIII-12-a&chapter= 18&lang=en).

4. The term *prostitution* is a highly contested one. Some see prostitution as work, some as acts of immorality, while others see it as violence against women. The term *prostitution* is usually avoided by those who use the term *sex work* because of the stigma and moral judgment attached to the term *prostitution*. For some, whether exploited or coerced, no one can choose this form of work freely, while for others it is a form of labor that can be chosen by some and for others still it is an act of violence.

5. Ronald Weitzer (2007, 449) suggests that CATW is "the premier abolitionist feminist organization in the United States" and describes the abolitionist position as referring to "those who argue that the sex industry should be entirely eliminated because of its objectification and oppressive treatment of women, considered to be inherent in sex for sale" (p. 450).

6. Sheila Jeffreys (2009, 10, 18) explains that radical feminism "understands prostitution to be a harmful cultural practice originating in the subordination of women . . . and constituting a form of violence against women." She also acknowledges that those explaining prostitution as sex work have tended to "predominate in international feminist political theory."

7. Weitzer (2007, 453) points out that instead of viewing themselves as "prostituted" women offering sex services, women opt for more neutral identities such as "sex workers" and "working women" because they have made a deliberate decision to do this work and do not consider the work to be degrading or oppressive.

8. In the early part of the twentieth century, a number of international treaties were developed to address

the "traffic in women," including the 1904 International Agreement for the Suppression of White Slave Traffic, the 1910 International Convention for the Suppression of the White Slave Traffic, the 1921 International Convention for the Suppression of the Traffic of Women and Children, and the 1949 Convention for the Suppression of the Traffic in Persons and of the Exploitation of the Prostitution of Others (Lee 2012, 27).

9. Doezema (2010, 31) explains that a myth in this sense expresses a collective belief intended to make reality more comprehensible. Thus, "when it is repeated in similar form from generation to generation, a myth discloses a moral content, carrying its own meaning, secreting its own values. The power of myth lies in the totality of explanation" (Slotkin 1985, quoted in Doezema 2010, 31).

10. According to the United Nations Development Programme (UNDP), the feminization of poverty "is an increase in the difference in poverty levels between women and men, or between households headed by females on the one hand, and those headed by males or couples on the other. The term can also be used to mean an increase in poverty due to gender inequalities, though we prefer to call this the feminization of the causes of poverty" (Medeiros and Costa 2008, 1).

11. U.S. Government Accountability Office, "Human Trafficking: Better Data, Strategy and Reporting Needed to Enhance U.S. Antitrafficking Efforts Abroad," GAO-06–825, July 18, 2006, http://www.gao.gov/products/GAO-06–825.

12. U.S. Department of Justice, Office of Justice Programs, Office for Victims of Crime, http://ojp.gov/ovc/awareness/about_ncvrw.html.

13. According to one media report of September 2012, the ILO now estimates there are 20.9 million trafficking victims worldwide (Elizabeth Willmott Harrop, "Africa: A Bewitching Economy—Witchcraft and Human Trafficking [Analysis]," *Think Africa Press*, September 20, 2012, reprinted in *Africa News Update*, http://www.afrika.no/Detailed/22313.html).

14. According to Finckenauer (2001, 172), the knowledge base about human trafficking suggests that it seems "to fall more into the 'crime that is organized' category than it does into true organized crime."

15. Lee (2012, 84) criticizes the dominant framing of trafficking as "trafficking-as-organized crime" arguing that this represents a "gross simplification" of the issue because it elides the overall complexity of "doing trafficking." In this sense, therefore, the discourse of "trafficking as organized transnational crime" has become the master discourse resulting in a significant expansion and strengthening of state power over national borders and their policing, as well as transnational cooperation in law enforcement and prosecution. Lee argues that framing human trafficking in this way marginalizes victim protection, human rights protection, and trafficking prevention, including the associated socioeconomic and political causative factors (p. 108).

16. The term *diaspora* describes those in a culture or language group who have left their home country and are now scattered beyond national boundaries and sometimes throughout the world.

17. The World Tourism Organization (WTO) has explained "organized sex tourism" in the following terms: "trips organized from within the tourism sector, or from outside this sector but using its structures and networks, with the primary purpose of effecting a commercial sexual relationship by the tourist with residents at the destination," bringing about "the grave health as well as social and cultural consequences of this activity, especially when it exploits gender, age, social and economic inequality at the destination visited" (WTO, http://www.unicef.org/lac/code_of_conduct.pdf).

18. States are divided into Tier 1, Tier 2, or Tier 3. The tiers are defined as follows (U.S. Department of State 2011):

Tier 1: Countries whose governments fully comply with the TVPA's minimum standards for the elimination of trafficking.

Tier 2: Countries whose governments do not fully comply with the TVPA's minimum standards but are making significant efforts to bring themselves into compliance with those standards.

Tier 2 Watch List: Countries whose governments do not fully comply with the TVPA's minimum standards, but are making significant efforts to bring themselves into compliance with those standards AND:

(a) the absolute number of victims of severe forms of trafficking is very significant or is significantly increasing;

(b) there is a failure to provide evidence of increasing efforts to combat severe forms of trafficking in persons from the previous year, including increased investigations, prosecution, and convictions of trafficking crimes, increased assistance to victims, and decreasing evidence of complicity in severe forms of trafficking by government officials; or

(c) the determination that a country is making significant efforts to bring itself into compliance with minimum standards was based on commitments by the country to take additional steps over the next year.

Tier 3: Countries whose governments do not fully comply with the minimum standards and are not making significant efforts to do so.

19. In 2009, thirty thousand H-2A agricultural work visas were granted, and in 2009 and 2010 Congress limited the low-skill H-2B visa to seventy-eight thousand a year. Economists estimate the demand for these

low-wage and low-skill jobs in 2008–9 at four or five times the number of visas available (Schaefer and Gonzales 2012, 177).

20. According to Stephanie Hepburn (2012, 203), H-2B visa holders brought into New Orleans after Hurricane Katrina faced "squalid living conditions, denial of medical benefits for on-the-job injuries, seizure of travel and identification documents by labor brokers and/or employers, and unpaid wages."

21. Kevin Bales and Ron Soodalter (2009, 96) quote an NGO representative as follows: "The victims [of trafficking] are treated as criminals. If they're not seeing bruises, . . . overt fear, indicia of 'force, fraud and coercion plus' then it's not human trafficking."

22. The following facts help illustrate how victims who do not fit the stereotype have little chance of receiving protection. Antonio, an impoverished homeless Mexican boy, is promised by traffickers a good job in a restaurant in the United States. Upon arrival Antonio is told he must work eighteen hours a day in a *taquería* and live with other boys who work there. He is paid far less than minimum wage, and "rent" is deducted from his wages. He is threatened with severe punishment if he tries to leave, and he may not have guests or date girls. After eight years of working under these conditions, Antonio escapes and contacts the authorities, seeking protection as a victim of trafficking. Law enforcement, however, does not regard him as a true trafficking victim and consequently Antonio becomes homeless and subject to deportation (cited in Srikantiah 2007, 158).

23. As a comparison to U.S. practice, in Belgium and the Netherlands, trafficking victims receive the assistance of social service agencies immediately after gaining their freedom and are granted a reflection period within which to make an informed decision about cooperation with law enforcement. During this period (forty-five days in Belgium and three months in the Netherlands), victims are given temporary immigration status (Srikantiah 2007, 208).

12

TERRORISM

Since the events of 9/11, international terrorism has become a central concern worldwide. Terrorist attacks in Spain, the United Kingdom, and elsewhere, and the general threat of terrorism, has prompted states to introduce new laws and regulations, sometimes modeled on the USA Patriot Improvement and Reauthorization Act (2006). Immigration restrictions have been heightened, and there is now considerable international cooperation concerning the movement of known terrorists. While the measures that the United States has taken to counter terrorism have been widely discussed and documented, the same is not the case for other states. This chapter examines the incidence and history of terrorism in some other countries and their contemporary responses to combat terrorism, including new laws and practices and policy developments. The following questions are addressed: Are there policy options and ideas that other countries have advanced that are not found in the United States and what, if anything, can the United States learn from other countries? What has been the overall response of the international community to the internationalization of terrorism? In addition, the current international legal framework for combating terrorism is outlined.

Examining the various definitions of terrorism, both domestic and international, helps reveal the complexity of the concept, how we differentiate terrorism as a form of violence from other forms of violence, and what particular characteristics are associated with terrorism that are not part of other crimes. How, for example, does terrorism differ from guerrilla warfare? State terrorism stands in contrast to terrorism performed by non-state groups and persons. How is state terrorism explained, and what forms has it taken in the past? We also explore how destructive state terrorism is and if there are any plans to bring it under international control.

Terrorism can be better understood if it is situated within its particular political, social, and economic contexts. Public discourse about terrorism, shaped by the media, often ignores the sources, histories, and patterns of terrorism as if terrorism began only after 9/11. Therefore, to add context to this discussion of terrorism, we present case studies of two designated (by the United States) terrorist groups, *Boko Haram* of Nigeria and *Hamas* in the Middle East, and explore the history, politics, and social and cultural context associated with each group. What are the aims and objectives of these groups? What methods do they employ to attempt to achieve their aims, and how are their activities countered?

Many scholars differentiate terrorism before and after the events of 9/11, which is referred to as a watershed in the evolution of terrorism due to the scale and nature of the attack and its religious connotations. Given the worldwide prominence of 9/11, we review and summarize the literature in the field of terrorism and religion and discuss the articulation between terrorism and religion in terms of the causes and consequences in history.

EXPLANATIONS AND DEFINITIONS OF TERRORISM

Accounts of terrorism inevitably begin with a discussion of what is meant by the term *terrorism*. How do we classify an incident as terrorism? What distinguishes terrorism from other forms of violence? How does terrorism differ from guerrilla warfare, political assassination, and state violence? Where a spectrum of violence exists, which elements should be termed *terrorism?* (Crenshaw 1995, 12). The debate about defining terrorism "is also a debate about the classification of political violence in all its myriad forms: riot, revolt rebellion, war, conflict, uprising, revolution, subversion, intervention, guerrilla warfare and so on" (Saul 2006, 5).

What is clear is that terrorism is a method, not a movement or an ideology (Wilkinson 2001, 16). It is widely understood to be a political act performed in pursuit of a cause (Gage 2011, 74) whose meaning may change over time according to its context. Thus, for example, "a century ago, social scientists viewed terrorism as an offshoot of anticapitalist revolt; anarchists and labor radicals were the 'terrorists' of their day" to be followed by the "anticolonial guerrilla fighters and the New Left militants stirring up trouble for the world's regimes" (Gage 2011, 75; also see "The Evolution of Terrorism," later in this chapter).

In modern times, terrorism is not a neutral term; rather, it is an ideological construct "in the sense that its understanding is based on perceptions of legitimacy structured according to a bench mark of political and social 'normality'" (Hocking 1984, 103).

While terrorism is of course a real threat and danger to societies, the concept of terrorism itself is "shaped by social and political processes, by bureaucratic needs and media structures"[1] (Jenkins 2003, ix). Especially since the events of

9/11, labeling an incident or act "terrorism" or an organization "terrorist" assigns to it a great weight of moral opprobrium and scorn and attaches to it a particular stigma, namely, that those who perpetrated the act are not simply criminals but terrorists.[2] They are considered "fanatic and irrational" (Crenshaw 1995, 9).

Even where terrorism is designated as criminal action as opposed to an act of war (the "war on terrorism"), it is viewed in some way as distinct from conventional crime although it usually comprises acts such as murder or attempted murder or assault, which are considered more "usual" crimes (Hocking 1984, 104). It is therefore the political character of terrorism that differentiates it from conventional crime.

It also carries serious policy implications given that states now pursue terrorists overseas without regard to the rules of international humanitarian law,[3] and it tends to close down debate about the nature of terrorist grievances and their possible legitimacy (Kapitan 2004, 182). Since 9/11, both the media and governments have tended to describe specific acts of terrorism not by reference to the nature of the acts themselves but by reference to the religious affiliation of the group that carried them out.

The contours of terrorism need to be well understood, yet in reality, events that many view as acts of terror are regarded by others with an alternative perspective, such as guerrilla warfare, or as acts in support of freedom, or as liberation from oppression. The best known example of this is the expression that "one man's terrorist is another person's freedom fighter" (Jenkins 2003, 17). Accordingly, perceptions about what constitutes terrorism are influenced by ideology and the politics of various interest groups (Jenkins 2003, 5). For example, we might ask, "Are members of national liberation movements freedom fighters or terrorists, and were Irish Republicans fighting the British in Northern Ireland terrorists or freedom fighters?" In spite of the explicit political demands and the underlying ideology of the Irish Republican Army (IRA) and the Provisional IRA, the British government insisted on labeling their campaign "terrorism," giving it a law-and-order rather than a political context (Hocking 1984, 104). Naming an act "terrorism," therefore, involves rendering a moral and value judgment that carries considerable consequences, and "we are led to ask who calls what terrorism, why and when" (Crenshaw 1995, 9).

Terrorism is not a movement or cause: it is a tactic or method employed to achieve some particular end. We should not think of groups using terrorism as employing terrorism because it is the sole, exclusive means to achieve their purposes because it has often been associated with other tactics, for example, guerrilla warfare (Jenkins 2003, 77). It should therefore be seen as one tactic used along with others. A good example of this is the war of liberation fought in Algeria in the 1950s against the French colonists for seven years where the Algerian Arabs used both guerrilla and terrorist tactics to achieve liberation from France (p. 77).

Unfortunately there is no consensus concerning the meaning of the term internationally, and countries have adopted different definitions in their laws and administrative practices. In addition, scholars and researchers have proposed their favored definitions. In a survey conducted in the mid-1980s, fifty social scientists were asked to explain their views about this topic, and the results identified twenty-two factors that might be considered attributes of terrorism (Gage 2011, 78). In 1983, another study identified 109 different official and academic definitions (Saul 2006, 57). Thus, legal and official definitions as well as suggested explanations of the term from scholars and researchers exist. A former President of the International Court of Justice, Rosalyn Higgins, has argued that "terrorism is a term without any legal significance. It is merely a convenient way of alluding to activities, whether of States or of individuals widely disapproved of and in which either the methods used are unlawful, or the targets protected or both" (Higgins 1997, 28).

This is a helpful perspective because it confirms that the term *terrorism* is not a term of art in law but is instead descriptive only of a category of acts that states call terrorism under their domestic laws. Consequently, it is for each state to determine the constituent elements of "terrorism" from a multiplicity of acts and motivations. In fact, such is the plethora of definitions of terrorism that in the case of the United States, for example, different agencies maintain different definitions of the term. The State Department uses the definition in the U.S. Code Title 22, Chapter 38, while the Federal Bureau of Investigation (FBI) uses the definitions of both "international terrorism" and "domestic terrorism" contained in the U.S. Code Title 18 (Criminal Acts and Criminal Procedure), and the Department of Defense applies yet another definition.

What are the elements commonly found in the more than one hundred definitions or explanations of the term? It would be expected that they would reflect the generally understood concept of terrorism. Cyndi Banks (2013a, Chap. 8) discusses some of the main themes in the use of the word *terrorism*.

- Because the term used is *terrorism,* definitions commonly refer to an intention to generate fear, because terrorism is intended to inspire terror in persons.

- There is usually a reference to violence, threats of violence, or force, the use of which is intended to generate fear.

- There is usually a reference to civilians or noncombatants to reflect the fact that acts of terrorism are frequently inflicted upon innocent citizens. Since 9/11, terrorism has generally come to mean violent acts carried out against nonmilitary, civilian targets with the aim of creating public fear.

- Words such as *intimidate* and *coerce* are often used to describe the intention of the person or group conducting the terrorism.

- There is usually a reference to political objectives, political motivation, or political ideology to show that terrorism is not committed for gain or profit, as is an ordinary crime, but is a special kind of crime.

- There is usually a reference to action or a threat of action that is intended to cause death, injury, or damage to property.

- Some definitions specifically state that the act of terrorism may be performed by individuals or by groups.

- Some definitions describe terrorism in terms of the acts of persons or groups and therefore exclude terrorism by the state (see "State Terrorism," later in this chapter).

Explanations of the term by scholars and researchers include the following from Wilkinson (2001, 12–13):

the systematic use of coercive intimidation, usually to service political ends. It is used to create and exploit a climate of fear among a wider target group than the immediate victims of the violence, and to publicize a cause, as well as to coerce a target to acceding to the terrorist's claims.

In the sphere of international action against terrorism there are a number of definitions,[4] and these are discussed later, but one example of the international language of terrorism appears in UN Security Council Resolution 1566 of October 2004, which condemns terrorist acts and incorporates definitions appearing in international agreements on terrorism in its overall statement of how terrorism is constituted. The Resolution states that terrorism is

> criminal acts, including against civilians, committed with the intent to cause death or serious bodily injury, or taking of hostages, with the purpose to provoke a state of terror in the general public or in a group of persons or particular persons, intimidate a population or compel a government or an international organization to do or abstain from doing any act, which constitutes offenses within the scope of and as defined in the international conventions and protocols relating to terrorism. (UN Security Council 2004)

While not a definition as such, this statement is quite narrowly drawn but does not include any political element. This means it could equally apply to private acts that terrorize, intimidate, or coerce (Saul 2006, 247).

In 1937, the League of Nations Convention offered the following definition of terrorism: "all criminal acts directed against a state and intended or calculated to create a state of terror in the minds of particular persons or a group of persons or the general public." This leaves no room for the inclusion of state terrorism; in fact, it expressly rejects that form of terrorism. This approach is followed by the criminal definition applied by the FBI in the United States, which also refers only to methods used to intimidate or coerce a government. Similarly, the U.S. State Department definition declares that terrorism is "premeditated politically motivated violence perpetrated against non-combatant targets by sub-national groups or clandestine agents, usually intended to influence an audience" (Title 22 U.S. Code, Section 2656). This clearly excludes

state violence. Jenny Hocking (1984, 106) argues that a definition of terrorism that excludes the performance of terrorism by a state "assumes the legitimacy of the State against which it is directed" and therefore denies a perspective that terrorism is ever justifiable.

Some definitions are very broad and call into question their reasonableness because they are liable to include conduct that is not at all terroristic. For example, in the United Kingdom, the law on terrorism is principally outlined in the Terrorism Act 2006, which is reviewed annually by an expert who reports to the government (Anderson 2014). The last review report in July 2014 criticized the law on several grounds, including its definition of terrorism, which it considered too broad when compared to other countries' laws and compared to international definitions. The present definition of terrorism is in the Terrorism Act 2000 (Section 1):

> Terrorism is the use or threat of "action" designed to influence the government or an international governmental organization, or to intimidate the public or a section of the public where the use of threat is made for the purpose of advancing a political, religious, or ideological cause. The "action" referred to, amounts to terrorism if it involves serious violence against a person, involves serious damage to property, endangers a person's life, other than that of the person committing the action, creates a serious risk to the health or safety of the public or a section of the public, or is designed seriously to interfere with or seriously to disrupt an electronic system.

The independent reviewer of this law has proposed that "terrorism should be redefined so that it applies only if there is intent to coerce, compel or intimidate a Government or a section of the public" (Anderson 2014, 2). The reviewer points out that in other Commonwealth and European countries, and under the main international treaties governing terrorism, there must be an intention to coerce or intimidate (p. 2). Adopting this change would limit the scope of the law so that, for example, it would not criminalize an advocacy group that publicly expresses a religious objection to vaccination. If a group's purpose is to influence the government, and if its public statement is judged capable of creating a serious risk to public health, the members of the group could be treated as terrorists, detained for long periods of time, prosecuted, and have their assets frozen. Supporting the advocacy publicly could also be considered a terrorist crime.

This review reveals the perils to the public of an overbroad definition of terrorism and demonstrates the complexities of defining this term so that it adequately describes all the conduct deemed to be terroristic.

BOX 12.1 Why Use Terrorist Tactics?

Terrorism may facilitate a number of objectives, some revolutionary and others not. What are these objectives? Terrorists such as the *Tupamaros* of Uruguay and the *Sendero Luminoso* (Shining Path) of Peru regarded themselves as revolutionaries and sought to overthrow the ruling regime and replace it with their own. Nationalists, such as the *Algerian FLN* and the *Irish IRA,* fought to oust foreign occupiers. Minority separatists like *ETA* (the Spanish/French Basque group) fought for a homeland. Reformists against nuclear power or medical experimentation on animals may employ terror tactics in their campaigns to halt or reform a practice or development they regard as harmful to mankind, but they do not seek the overthrow of a government. Anarchists or millenarians, such as the nineteenth-century anarchists and the later *Red Brigades* and the *Japanese Red Army,* used terrorism to advance a cause. Reactionaries, such as the *Ulster Defence Association* in Northern Ireland, tried to prevent change and demanded the maintenance of the status quo (Crenshaw 1981, 385–86).

Wilkinson (2001, 7) offers the following suggested justifications for using terrorism as a tactic:

- Through a campaign of attrition, it can weaken the enemy.

- It is an effective means of inflicting harm on a hated enemy.

- It can be employed to provoke government forces into overreacting, giving more support to the terrorists and forcing the government to show that it is repressive.

- Huge publicity will result from spectacular or especially harmful attacks; terrorists want to bring media and public attention to their cause.

- It may result in the release of imprisoned fellow terrorists.

- Terrorists may gain income through kidnapping and ransoms.

- Generally, terrorism is a low-cost but potentially rewarding activity with acceptable levels of risk. It is often called the "weapon of the weak" because governments will always be more powerful than a terrorist group, but terrorism may be a simple and rapid option with an immediate, visible payoff.

In addition, as noted in Chapter 10, terrorists may ally themselves with organized crime groups for financial gain. Other inducements include the promise of compensation to relatives if they are injured or killed, and assurances of entering paradise as a martyr for a suicide bombing.[5] Terrorism may also contribute to organizational goals within a group, such as discipline, morale building, unity of purpose, and unit cohesion (Crenshaw 1981, 387), and may be a significant means of mobilizing the support of the masses over time (p. 388).

GUERRILLA WARFARE AND TERRORISM

Guerrilla warfare has been called "the war of the flea" because the classic guerrilla struggle involves highly mobile strike forces of combatants always weaker than the forces they oppose. They seek to secure a military advantage through surprise and always avoiding engagements with the enemy that might result in the complete annihilation of the guerrilla force. Theorists of this form of warfare agree that guerrilla operations do not generally result in victory unless, of course, the enemy is militarily inept. Most guerrilla operations in modern times have been associated with liberation movements, as, for example, in the case of anticolonial struggles for independence in Algeria against the French, or in Kenya against the British. Guerrilla units commonly use terrorist tactics to provoke government forces into overreacting, with the aim of gaining domestic and international support.

An example of a successful guerrilla campaign was that of the Cuban revolutionaries led by Che Guevara in 1959. He applied the theory of the *foco*, referring to a small group of fast-moving armed combatants where unit leadership combined military and political aspects of the struggle (Wilkinson 2001, 15–16). The units provided a focus for public discontent against the regime in power, giving impetus to a general uprising and arousing the solidarity and fighting spirit of the oppressed. Some guerrilla leaders refused to employ terrorist methods in their campaigns because they believed that harming the civilian population would cause them to lose the support of the people, while others like Trotsky thought that all means justified the ends sought (p. 17).[6]

STATE TERRORISM

The notion that states use terrorist methods is not contested. As philosopher Virginia Held (2004, 69) explains, "When the security forces of an unjust regime kill or brutalize detainees to deter future opposition, or shoot at random into groups of demonstrators, they engage in acts of terrorism."

States may use terrorist methods against their own citizens or may sponsor groups or use terrorism internationally as an element of foreign policy or during a conflict with another state.

Clear examples of state domestic terrorism were the methods employed by the Nazi Party in Germany and by Stalin in the Soviet Union and the regime of General Pinochet in Chile. When a state uses terrorism, it is able to deploy very significant tactical resources such as secret police units. This is in contrast to non-state terrorists, whose means and resources are usually much more limited (Primoratz 2004b, 118). Generally, it would be expected that states would implement all alternatives other than terrorism before resorting to that tactic. The one generally agreed exception would be where there exists a "supreme emergency" such as would justify extreme tactics to prevent a catastrophe (p. 120).

Many argue that the so-called terror bombing of German and Japanese cities during World War II constituted a campaign of terror. As well, the United States has been described as using terror methods, for example, in South and Central America and in Vietnam to overthrow communist governments it did not wish to see in power (Jenkins 2003, 20). In the case of the World War II bombing of German cities, it is problematic to describe this as a supreme emergency that justified the action taken because "the truth is that the supreme emergency passed long before the British bombing reached its crescendo. The greater number by far of the German civilians killed by terror bombing were killed without moral (and probably also without military) reason" (Walzer 2000, 251).

The terror bombing of Germany was clearly not a case involving collateral damage, in which innocent civilians are unintentionally killed or injured in pursuit of combatants because the British intended to attack civilians. However, just war theory requires that the harm caused through an activity that involves collateral damage must be proportionate to the importance of the military objective that cannot be satisfied in some other way (Primoratz 2004b, 124).

BOX 12.2 World War II: Terror Bombing of German Cities

In July 1943, the city of Hamburg in Germany was attacked by more than seven hundred British bomber aircraft, which dropped incendiary, phosphorous bombs and other explosives on the most densely populated section of the city, destroying about 74 percent of it. Around fifty thousand people were killed, and the attacks created more than a million refugees who fled the city for safety. The intensity of the bombing was sufficient to create a firestorm with winds of more than 150 miles per hour that literally sucked people and even entire buildings into the central area of the fires. This approach to warfare was called "area bombing." Its focus was not military or industrial targets but the cities themselves. In their targeting instructions, British aircrews were told that the city center was the prime aiming point. During the war, area bombing attacks accounted for about 70 percent of all bombing missions, and about one million tons of bombs were dropped. By 1944 about 80 percent of all German population centers of more than one hundred thousand persons had been severely damaged or devastated. It is estimated that about five hundred thousand German civilians were killed as a result of this bombing, with another one million being seriously injured and about three million homes destroyed.

In a bombing attack on the city of Dresden in February 1945, casualty estimates varied from a low of about thirty-five thousand to a high of about two hundred thousand. In relation to this attack, Winston Churchill wrote to the Chief of the Air Staff, "The destruction of Dresden remains a serious query against the conduct of Allied bombing . . . and I feel the need for more precise concentration upon military objectives . . . rather than on mere acts of terror and wanton destruction, however impressive" (in Garrett 2004, 34).

Many in Britain justified the bombing campaign by claiming there were no innocent Germans since they all bore the guilt for Hitler's aggression. The chief of British Bomber Command, Sir Arthur Harris, went so far as to claim that Germany could be defeated through airpower alone. Other arguments in support of the action centered on its capacity to divert German resources away from the war and toward protecting the cities, or that the bombing would disrupt and damage German industries that were concentrated around the cities. Arguments included the impact of the bombing on the fabric of life in Germany: it was thought they would shatter morale and dislocate war production. In retrospect, the bombing has been categorized as a form of state terrorism. However, the bombing failed to differentiate between targets that could reasonably be said to be connected to the Nazi war machine (such as arms production centers command and control centers) and the target of the broader society. As for the collective guilt of the German people, while Hitler was supported by many, he was not supported by all, so bombing all persons regardless of guilt cannot be justified.

International humanitarian law now provides that "the civilian population as such, as well as individual civilians, shall not be made the object of attack. Acts or threats of violence the primary purpose of which is to spread terror among the civilian population are prohibited" (Additional Protocol I, Geneva Conventions, Article 51).[7]

SOURCE: Garrett 2004, 141–58.

Primoratz (2004b, 115) has argued that a state ought not to be designated as a terrorist state for isolated and irregular acts of terrorism against its citizens but that the label be reserved for states that employ the tactic of terror "in a lasting and systematic way, and indeed, are defined in part, by the sustained use of terrorism against their own population." This conception of a terrorist state would therefore include totalitarian states such as Nazi Germany, Stalin's Soviet Union, and Cambodia under the rule of the Khmer Rouge (p. 115). It is arguable whether or not it would include Israel, which, since the 1950s, has "made extensive use of state terrorism in its rule over the Palestinian territories occupied in 1967 and its fight against Palestinian resistance terrorism" (p. 123).

State terrorism should be differentiated from state-sponsored terrorism when non-state actors conduct terrorism with the support of a state. State-sponsored terrorism has been explained as "a government's intentional assistance to a terrorist group to help it use violence, bolster its political activities or sustain the organization" (Byman 2005, 10). The complex methods of assistance that a state may provide to terrorists range from a state deliberately allowing use of its territory as a safe haven for terrorists to involuntary state assistance when weak or fragile states that lack capacity effectively enable terrorists to operate from their territory.

The Evolution of Terrorism

It is impossible here to provide a full account of the evolution of terrorism, but this summary will situate and contextualize the terrorism of today among acts deemed terroristic in the past.[8] When linking terrorism to its historical setting, it is necessary to consider how social, political, and economic conditions contributed to its emergence (Crenshaw 1995, 12).

David Rapoport (2001, 419; 2004, 46) has usefully identified four overlapping waves or cycles of terrorism since the 1880s, each with its own characteristics. He argues these involve similar activities occurring in different states driven by a common energy, that is, anarchism, anticolonialism, the new left, and religion. These waves and their time periods are

- First wave from the 1880s to the 1920s—the Anarchist Wave

- Second wave from the 1920s to the 1960s—the Anticolonial Wave

- Third wave from 1960s to 1979—the New Left Wave, and

- Fourth wave from the 1979 to date—the Religious Wave.

Like many others, we have adopted Rapoport's structure in the following account and first provide a brief explanation of terrorism before the 1880s.

Before 1880s

The foundation for contemporary terrorism is derived from groups and persons who used coercion to threaten society or the lives of political leaders through assassination and from militant religious groups—Islamic, Judaic, and Christian—who used murder and violence as a tactic in their causes (Miller 1995, 29). Over the centuries, from the time of the Greeks and Romans, the notion of murdering an unjust ruler is described in numerous treatises concerned with governance. For example, Cicero wrote that killing a tyrant was a virtuous act (p. 29). Whereas initially the aim was removal of the political leader or king, this later expanded to include associates of the impugned ruler or leader. Developments in terrorist weapons replaced the knife with dynamite, thereby creating the probability of collateral damage in carrying out an act of terrorism.

The term *terrorism* first appeared in political discourse as a reference to the Reign of Terror perpetrated in France by the Jacobins; therefore, this was a reference to state terror and not to terrorism perpetrated by non-state groups (Primoratz 2004a, xix).[9] The French Revolution radically changed the boundaries of terrorism when violent mobs mobilized against King Louis XVI and the ruling class, and overthrew the King to the collective horror of his fellow rulers in Europe and Russia. For the first time, citizens had turned not only against the ruler but also against the state itself, represented by those who were considered to have associated with the ruler (Miller 1995, 31). When the mobs brought terror to society, political violence had crossed all of its previous boundaries.

During the era of Napoleon, the secret organizations of the Carbonari, first formed in 1807 in Naples, called for a united independent republican Italy and in seeking national liberation set the scene for similar movements that were to come in 1848 (Miller 1995, 34). The Carbonari used terrorist tactics, arguing that governments should be overthrown through rebellion and assassination. Their terrorist attacks extended to army officials, police chiefs, and magistrates and also to loyalist members of the church. The Carbonari used the term *terrorism* to describe their tactics and approach (p. 34).

From 1880s to 1920s

Igor Primoratz (2004c, 25) argues that most who practiced terrorism have termed themselves or been termed by others as terrorists during the nineteenth century. However, most anarchists and Russian revolutionary groups did not practice terrorism in the sense we understand it today but rather engaged in political assassination (p. 25). As will be seen later, assassinating political and government leaders was the dominant terrorist tactic during this period. This was a period in which political treatises described terrorism as morally justified and explained how it would be conducted.

In 1848 Marx and Engels published the *Communist Manifesto* and in 1849 Karl Heinzen (1809–80), a German radical, wrote what has been termed the first example of "a full-fledged doctrine of modern terrorism" in an essay titled "Murder vs. Murder" (1849) that argued that murder remained an instrument to be used in achieving historical ends (Laqueur 1987, 28). He contended that violence was an acceptable tactical weapon in an amoral world and described terrorist tactics, in the form of concealed explosives, projectiles that had the capacity when thrown into a group to kill hundreds, and terrorist intimidation, and he advocated the invention of "new methods of killing" (Miller 1995, 36).

Johann Most (1846–1906) developed a reputation as an orator and agitator in Zurich and Vienna and, when he moved to London, began publishing a new journal *Freiheit* in which he declared explicitly that only through violent revolution would the social order achieve radical change. He called for the creation of anarchist cells and for organizations of armed workers to protect and defend workers' rights. Most came to the United States in 1882 where he printed even more extreme proterrorist articles. He argued for killing persons of status because of the likely greater impact of these targets, and he justified stealing from the ruling class to finance operations as morally necessary and correct. He believed that anyone who impeded "the cause" should be destroyed (Miller 1995, 44) and referred to his beliefs as "anarchist vengeance" in the belief that acts of violence would incite others to revolt. He contended that displaying posters at the sites of killings that explained the reasons for the action would be beneficial and that all weapons should be considered useful provided the skills necessary for their operation were properly acquired. He published instructions on explosive devices, poisons, and knives and advocated using dynamite to destroy homes, businesses, churches, factories, and offices used by the state (p. 45).

Anarchist activity began to increase after 1881. The major figures in the international anarchist movement believed that the people would spontaneously mount a rebellion to establish an egalitarian society (Miller 1995, 52). Anarchist cells were uncovered in Germany and anarchists in Vienna committed murders. In the 1890s, in Paris, an attack was made on the stock exchange, a bomb was set off in the Chamber of Deputies, and one anarchist accidentally blew himself up in a church. Another anarchist, who placed a bomb in a café and injured twenty people, explained at his trial that he "brought to the struggle a profound hatred, intensified every day by the revolting spectacle of society where all is base, all is cowardly" (p. 46). He called on fellow anarchists not to spare "bourgeois women and children" (p. 46) and declared that anarchism would never be defeated because of its deep roots and because it represented "egalitarian and libertarian aspirations which are battering down

existing authority. . . . It will end by killing you" (p. 47). During the 1890s anarchists succeeded in killing heads of state or their representatives at the rate of one a year, and in 1901 President William McKinley was murdered by a person thought to be an anarchist (p. 48).

In the United States, anarchists joined labor unions as the economy developed into an industrial capitalist model that employed masses of impoverished European immigrants. Johann Most used the pages of *Freiheit* to call for the use of bombs, and a "cult of dynamite" developed among the immigrant workers influenced by Most (Miller 1995, 49). In the early 1880s it was estimated that at least three thousand anarchists, mainly of German or Czech origin, were at work in Chicago (p. 49). There were anarchist newspapers in the city that called for a violent clash with the government and for a "bloody revolution." Deadly clashes with the Chicago police resulted in the police shooting into crowds of demonstrators and killing twenty persons. Following the subsequent trials of the anarchists, four were hanged for causing deaths by bombing (p. 49).

The last major theorist of political violence before the advent of the First World War was Frenchman Georges Sorel (1847–1922), who published *Reflections on Violence* in 1908. Much of his discourse was Marxist: he stressed the heroic role of the proletariat and argued for a permanent class war, for proletarian violence as the means of resistance, and for the general strike as the means of achieving liberation (Miller 1995, 55). He regarded violence as the weapon of the proletariat to be used to overthrow the bourgeois world, but he saw it as something to be directed rather than used for random killing or self-sacrifice. He was correct in some of his beliefs when political violence began to be replaced by the growth of labor unions in the United States and Europe (p. 55). The level of political violence was also diminished through the increased efforts of European governments to repress anarchism generally. Agents were infiltrated into anarchist groups, and international agreements were concluded to eradicate them (p. 55). In 1898 a conference in Rome mandated the death penalty for anyone convicted of attempting to assassinate a head of state.

The revolutionary movement in Russia extended over one hundred years, and terrorist groups evolved from their initial radical student underground movement. Reformist actions by the Russian Tsars ironically fueled terrorism because the expectations of rapid economic and social progress were not satisfied (Rapoport 2001, 420). Between 1855 and 1884, there were two cycles of revolutionary activity in Russia: the nihilist cycle and the populist cycle, with Marxism appearing in the mid-1880s (Pomper 1995, 66). The radical students of the nihilist phase were from the educated elite, but Sergey Nechaev, who emerged as their leader, came from a humble background. In 1869 he wrote the influential *Catechism of a Revolutionary,* in which he argued that in terms of political action, the end justified the means. Mikhail Bakunin (1814–76) rejected state systems of power and attacked the class system for its inequality. He believed the revolution would come from the peasants and the working class. He is considered a major figure in the anarchist movement, and his influence, over time, has been considerable. During the populist cycle, following a number of unsuccessful attempts, Tsar Alexander II was assassinated in 1881 by a radical revolutionary group called *Narodnaya Volya* (People's Will), who planned to use terrorist tactics, including assassination, against the key members of the ruling regime in the belief that this would erode the structure of the state and precipitate a revolution by the masses or at least force the rulers to offer concessions that would bring about radical societal change. They also carried out retaliatory attacks against police (Hughes 2011, 256; Pomper 1995, 83). Between 1884 and 1903, the Russian Tsarist secret police, the *Okhrana,* extensively penetrated anarchist and revolutionary organizations with the aim of identifying and forestalling terrorist acts (Jenkins 2003, 88).

Between 1905 and 1907, terrorism became so extensive as to amount to guerrilla warfare (Pomper 1995, 65). In the early 1900s, the emergence of the Socialist Revolutionary Party (SR) revived the terrorist tradition of *Narodnaya Volya* (p. 89). SR members conducted assassinations of high-ranking figures in the regime, including governors and ministers, as well as police, who were regarded as propping up the regime and guilty of taking harsh measures to suppress rebellions. Revenge was a central element in its campaigns of assassination. After 1905 the *Okhrana* was able to effectively halt the SR by infiltrating its organization, but between 1905 and 1906, strikes, action by peasants against landlords, and the appearance of soviets and peasant unions created a wave of open violence, including arson, theft, and murder, in pursuit of the goal of socialism (pp. 90–93).

The period between the World Wars was one in which fascist movements successfully took over government in Germany, Italy, and Spain and whose leaders, once in power, began programs of state terrorism. Stalinism in Russia produced its own form of terror as citizens judged to be enemies of the state were eliminated. In Britain, the Sinn Fein organization in Ireland waged a violent nationalist war from 1919 to 1921 that has only recently been brought to conclusion (Miller 1995, 57).

What can be understood about modern terrorism from these past developments? Martin Miller argues that the nineteenth-century theory that anarchism was the cause of terrorism was misconceived because, clearly, forms of terrorism were being conducted both before and after the anarchist movement had ceased to function (Miller 1995, 57). In fact "terrorism evolved.... From attacks limited to specific objects (tyrants and heads of state considered unjust) to unlimited warfare against sectors of the governing order in which the line between society and the state was completely obliterated" (p. 58).

From 1920s to 1960s

During this period, both World Wars stimulated movements for national liberation in colonized countries. The emergence of new states, which included Ireland, Israel, Cyprus, and Algeria, were associated with terrorist movements—the IRA, the *Irgun,* the *Stern Gang*[10] in Israel, *EOKA* in Cyprus, and the *FLN* in Algeria. Terrorist groups applied "hit and run" tactics against colonial troops and the appellation of "terrorist" was contested: the Stern Gang described its activities as terrorism, but the Irgun claimed the status of "freedom fighters" (Rapoport 2001, 420). In 1961 Franz Fanon[11] published *The Wretched of the Earth,* which critiqued nationalism and imperialism in the wake of the Algerian fight for liberation, analyzed violence as between colonized and colonizers, argued that a violent uprising of the masses was a justified action in the process of decolonization, and indeed that only killing was able to destroy the inferiority complex caused by colonial subjugation.

From 1960s to 1979

The war in Vietnam and the political unrest for which it was responsible in the United States and Europe, chiefly among the student population, marks the conflicts of the 1960s. It encouraged a "revolutionary ethos" that evolved into the left-wing terrorist movements of the Weathermen[12] and the *Symbionese Liberation Army* in the United States, the *Red Army Faction* and the *Baader-Meinhof* organization in Germany, the *Red Brigades* in Italy, and the *Direct Action* group in France (Rapoport 2001, 421). According to Wilkinson (2001, 23), these European groups were characterized by "Lilliputian membership and negligible popular support" (p. 24), and their unsophisticated ideologies that divided society into "oppressor-exploiters" (p. 24) and "soldiers of revolutionary justice" (p. 24) simply adopted terrorism as an end in itself.

The Cold War and its framework of direct and proxy conflict between capitalism and communism also played a role in that the leaders of these groups were generally Marxist in orientation and regarded themselves as part of an anti-imperialist movement challenging capitalist oppression and hegemony (Wilkinson 2001, 25).[13] In South America, liberation movements modeled on the Cuban Revolution emerged during the late 1960s and 1970s. For example, in Uruguay, the left-wing Tupamaros robbed banks, kidnapped political leaders, and intimidated police by assassinating its officers (Shughart 2006, 23–24).

Italy

In Italy, both fascist and leftist groups conducted terrorism, but the latter began only in the second half of the 1970s (Porta 1995, 106). Violence was executed by squads of young militants of traditional right wing organizations who carried out indiscriminate bombings and a series of attempted coups. This violence was tolerated by the government and provided a powerful incentive for a leftist response (Porta 1995, 113). A wave of protest in Italy during the second half of the 1970s, described as the 77 Movement, was fueled by grievances that included a university reform proposal, housing issues, inflation, a lack of social infrastructure around the industrial cities, youth unemployment, and working conditions (pp. 114–15). These demands were not negotiated because of the closed political system in Italy; consequently, protests became more radical. For example, protest marches that had begun with militants carrying sticks and stones changed to militants carrying firearms and Molotovs. The state lacked specialist security agencies at least until 1979, and antiterrorist laws introduced in this period that curbed civil rights proved ineffective in combating terrorism (p. 118). For example, the increased penalties had no deterrent effect (p. 118). More effective was the legislation passed in 1980 that provided for reductions in sentences and even immunity from prosecution for cooperation with the authorities.

Action by the Marxist-Leninist Italian Red Brigades (BR) included the kidnapping of U.S. General James Dozier, who was held from December 1981 to January 1982 when he was liberated by an antiterrorist unit; the killing of U.S. diplomat Leamon Hunt in February 1984; and the kidnapping and killing of Aldo Moro, former Italian Prime Minister in 1978 (Porta 1995, 120). In all, the BR was responsible for some fourteen thousand terrorist attacks in its first ten years of operation (Shughart 2006, 21). The BR justified its armed struggle by claiming there was danger of a fascist coup and insisted that this danger and the authoritarian government required violence as a response and a defense (Porta 1995, 133). From 1973 to 1983 there was a downward trend in bombings but an upward trend in attacks on persons and in conflicts with police. Donatella della Porta suggests this was necessary to gain media attention (p. 136).

Over time, the ideology of the various radical movements changed; the armed struggle intended to stimulate the working class into a process of revolution was replaced by a refusal to accept the system of governance. Thus, social reform was replaced by a private war and "outside the organization there was only evil" (Porta 1995, 137–38). Escalating violence resulted in increased police repression, and the criminality resorted to by the organizations to secure their finances further exposed them to police action and damaged their public image (p. 157). The kidnapping and murder of Aldo Moro in 1978 by the BR turned public opinion against the BR, which, combined with more effective counterterrorist policing, brought the activity of the BR to a conclusion (Shughart 2006, 21). By 1982, about 1,400 members of the BR were under arrest. Those who cooperated in exchange for lenient treatment (the *pentiti*) assisted police by identifying their leaders (Shughart 2006, 22).

Germany

In Germany, during the 1970s and 1980s, the Baader-Meinhof Group (BM) and its successor, the Red Army Faction (RAF), caused panic in the country. BM carried out bank robberies, set fire to department stores, and murdered a number of bankers, industrialists, and judges, including the Attorney-General and the head of the Berlin Supreme Court (Shughart 2006, 21). These revolutionary groups grew out of the radical student movement of the 1960s. By October 1977, Meinhof, Baader, Ensslin, and Raspe, the leaders of BM had all committed suicide in prison after having received life sentences for four murders and thirty-four attempted murders (Merkl 1995, 173, 187). The RAF was founded in May 1970 by Ulrike Meinhof and Horst Mahler. It envisioned a socialistic society for Germany and promoted the aims of Third World liberation movements. The RAF began a series of bombings in 1972 at U.S. Army headquarters in Frankfurt, and then in Heidelberg, and then the car of a federal judge. In early June, police arrested Baader and other leaders, and in June 1976, the first German antiterrorist laws were enacted.

Palestine

Links between European groups and factions of the Palestinian Liberation Organization (PLO) such as Al Fatah and the Popular Front for the Liberation of Palestine were formed after the 1967 Six Day War. One outcome was that Europeans received training in PLO camps in Jordan and Lebanon and subsequently collaborated with the PLO on a series of attacks and hijackings.[14] By the late 1970s, the PLO was the major agent in the spread of terrorism worldwide and had become synonymous with spectacular international terrorist incidents.[15] Terrorism was now described as "international" because the bonds between these groups and their chosen targets and operations—which included the Munich Olympics attack in 1972, the kidnapping of OPEC Ministers in 1973, and hijackings to Uganda in 1976—appeared to show that terrorism had gained an international dimension (Rapoport 2001, 421). Palestinian factions also assisted the Japanese Red Army, which hijacked a Japanese airliner, committed murders, and sabotaged an oil refinery in Singapore (Shughart

2006, 23). Bruce Hoffman, a prominent scholar of terrorism, has pinpointed the hijacking of an El Al flight in July 1968 as the founding moment for "modern, international terrorism" when the PLO expanded their fight against Israel to the rest of the world (p. 63).

As Miller (1995, 61) puts it, during this period the assumption was that inequality and injustice would be solved by the application of reason and by progress; however, "terrorists in the post-Holocaust era have ceased to function within the framework of this central tenet of progress." Groups like the German Baader-Meinhof and the Red Brigades were products of the evolution of terrorist organizations that developed in the nineteenth century (p. 29).

1979 to date

During this most recent period, revolutionary terrorism in Europe was defeated, the PLO lost its terrorist training facilities following the Israeli invasion of Lebanon in 1982, the Islamic Revolution occurred in Iran in 1979,[16] and the Russians withdrew from Afghanistan in 1989. Also in 1989, the Soviet Union began to disintegrate, leading to a final breakup in 1991, and this effectively undermined the ideological basis for left wing terrorism (Shughart 2006, 23). The Iranian Revolution created a theocratic Iranian state based on Sharia principles that actively supported terrorism and promoted martyrdom in the service of terrorism. For example, the militants of the Iranian Revolutionary Guard aided Shia Muslims[17] of the Hezbollah organization in a new tactic of suicide bombing in Lebanon. Hezbollah passed on the tactic to the terrorists of the *Liberation Tigers* of Tamil Eelam in Sri Lanka who used it to kill Indian Prime Minister Indira Gandhi in 1991 (Pedahzur 2005, 14). Hezbollah used suicide bombing against the U.S. Embassy and its U.S. Marine barracks, killing 241 Marines and forcing a U.S. pullback from the region (Wilkinson 2001, 31).

Due to the fact that counterterrorist agencies had developed more effective protective methods, terrorist tactics changed from aircraft hijacking, hostage taking, seizure of embassies and consulates, and the kidnapping of diplomats and business people to bombings—human-activated and suicidal and those triggered electronically from a distance. However, surprise remains an important element in terrorist tactics.

This era was marked by the rise of Al Qaeda (the Base) and its networks, the attack of 9/11, the death of Osama bin Laden, and, most recently, the rise of ISIL and its war to create a new *caliphate* in the Middle East. While terrorism motivated by religion had occurred in the past through the Thugs (Hindu), the Assassins (Muslim), and the Zealots (Jewish) (Rapoport 1984, 658), the new Muslim fundamentalist movements focused on the objective of destroying Western regimes rather than simply carrying out assassinations. The modern usage of the terms *terrorism* and *terrorist* is almost always in reference to international threats and networks (Gage 2011, 92).

The "New Terrorism"

Some see contemporary terrorism of the type pursued by Al Qaeda as "new terrorism," marking a break from the former "traditional terrorism" because new terrorism aims at disrupting not just those it specifically targets but entire populations through its transnational operations (Hoffman 2004, 549; Wilkinson 2001, 5).

In 1996, well before 9/11 and subsequent terrorist acts, Walter Laqueur (1996) wrote, "Society has also become vulnerable to a new kind of terrorism, in which the destructive power of both the individual terrorist and terrorism as a tactic are infinitely greater" (p. 26), and "current definitions of terrorism fail to capture the magnitude of the problem worldwide" (p. 35). In a detailed critique of the arguments supporting the emergence of the "new terrorism," Sandra Walklate and Gabe Mythen (2015, 47–55) note that proponents of the new terrorism point to the following as supportive of their view:

- New terrorist groups have adopted a flat organizational structure instead of the vertical structures previously favored, reducing the element of hierarchy and top-down control and allowing all groups and networks to promote various objectives and hold differing points of view.

- The magnitude of terrorist attacks, especially 9/11 with almost three thousand deaths and subsequent attacks in Europe, is significantly larger than in the past.

- The new terrorism aims at killing and wounding civilians and not at attacking and destroying infrastructure and facilities, as was the case in the past.

- The new terrorism enlists followers worldwide and seeks to launch attacks internationally. To this end, Al Qaeda has launched terrorist attacks in Algeria, Indonesia, Turkey, and Spain. Expanding territorial scope in this manner compares with the limited geographical scope of terrorism undertaken, for example, by the PLO, the IRA, or by the ETA in Spain.

- It is claimed that there has been a change in weaponry used in terrorist attacks, for example, aircraft in the events of 9/11, and the possibility of terrorists gaining access to and using nuclear, chemical, and biological weapons exists.

- Terrorists now make great use of media, networks, and the like to communicate with each other and to publicize their activities to inspire fear. Info-terrorism and cyber-warfare are now subjects of great concern.

Walklate and Mythen (2015, 52) contest this thesis concerning a new terrorism. They argue that it ignores continuities in terrorism in favor of adopting a transformative perspective. Responding to the argument about organizational change, they point out that the IRA adopted a similar structure in its operations and that this kind of change, as well as that associated with new forms of communication using the Internet, represent merely the process of social change and not a radical reconfiguration of terrorist practice. In relation to the magnitude of terrorist attacks, they note that the scale and frequency now show no significant increase and point to data showing that the United States has actually witnessed fewer attacks in recent times compared to previous decades.

As to targeting civilians and prominent structures like the Twin Towers of the World Trade Center in New York City, Walklate and Mythen (2015) point out that the IRA also attacked civilians and that the Twin Towers and the Pentagon have long been considered high-value targets. The contention concerning expanded geographical scope and the political rhetoric associated with modern terrorism suggest a view that all countries could be potential sites of attack. However, this is clearly not the case since the target states are predictable and associated with long-standing grievances. Finally, arguments about weaponry seem to relate more to the possibility that weapons of mass destruction *may* be used by terrorists rather than to the actual use. Most recently, terrorists have in fact urged the use of simple weaponry like knives in random attacks on members of the public.

Walklate and Mythen (2015, 59) also point out that the widespread acceptance by commentators, experts, and the media of the existence of a new terrorism and its embodiment in military and policing policies has had adverse consequences in that the terrorist threat has come to be seen as "not only threatening and dangerous, but potentially apocalyptic" (p. 70). Violence has come to be seen as the only acceptable form of action against terrorism and a doctrine of preemption, involving targeted killing, has evolved to prevent the apocalypse. The notion that the war on terror is a war without end has resulted in greater social control of groups thought to be hostile and the securitization of society through stringent laws and practices, including very significant restrictions on personal privacy. New practices, including extraordinary rendition, the use of drones to target suspected terrorists, detention without charge, and torture have all been justified by the security establishment as necessary to "keep us safe." As Didier Bigo (2012, 279) puts it, following 9/11, "Security was transmuted into a global common good, more important than peace or freedom."

BOX 12.3   Causes of Terrorism

Martha Crenshaw (1981, 383; 1995, 13–14) and Audrey Cronin (2004b, 20), in exploring the causes of terrorism, have suggested the following causal factors.

- *Primarily, terrorists are persons invested in a cause that has arisen from a set of social, economic, and historical circumstances.* The existence of actual grievances among a group such as an ethnic minority suffering discrimination may cause a social movement to develop as a means of redress, and terrorism may become the favored weapon of a radical element of the group. Terrorism therefore arises because of strategic decisions made by political actors. Terrorism may not be the first option for advancing a cause, but a person may become disillusioned with regular nonviolent methods that seem to be ineffective in terms of the outcome sought. Examples include separatist nationalist movements such as the ETA (the Basque separatist movement in Spain) and nationalist movements in the period of colonialism. This category does not necessarily reflect economic deprivation; for example, terrorism in the 1960s by the Red Brigades and the Baader-Meinhof Group was undertaken by the elite and the privileged.

- An *absence of opportunity for political participation where the grievance is of a political nature* such as occurred in Tsarist Russia in the 1880s. Here, the elite and privileged acted on behalf of the masses, often without their knowledge or cooperation. As Eric Hobsbawn (1977, 143) expressed this situation, "All revolutionaries regarded themselves . . . as small elites of the emancipated and progressive operating among, and for the eventual benefit of, a vast and inert mass of the ignorant and misled common people." For example, when a political system such as many of those in the Middle East provides no outlets for political dissent or seems unable to sustain antigovernment dissent, this can be a contributing cause for terrorist violence. In Egypt, for instance, during the authoritarian rules of Presidents Nasser, Sadat, and Mubarak, numerous radical organizations conducted terrorist attacks against these governments (Esposito 2003, 86).

- *When an event occurs that acts as a catalyst for terrorism* such as arbitrary government action involving the use of unexpected force in response to forms of protest. The severity of the Tsarist regime's response to the populist movement was a factor in the creation of Russian terrorist groups in the 1880s, and the British government's decision to execute the heroes of the Easter Rising laid the foundation for the creation of the IRA in Northern Ireland. When such an event occurs, the terrorist movement is regarded by the members, and perhaps by others outside the movement, as validated and moral because the regime has forfeited its legitimacy.

- *Socializing the young, especially young males, toward violent actions as a legitimate means of achieving ideals* can lead to the creation of a pool of potential terrorists imbued with ideological fervor. Evidence that this socialization can be an effective stimulant to terrorism has been found in the Islamic *madrassas*[18] in Pakistan and Afghanistan in particular.

Social science research has shown that terrorists do not greatly diverge from other people in terms of self-esteem or religiosity, socioeconomic status, or personality traits (Esposito and Mogahed 2007). While terrorists may appear as normal and not as fanatics or zealots with personality disorders (as they are commonly portrayed in the media), they may possess a generalized rage and they may join terrorist organizations for revenge or to correct a perceived injustice. For example, studies have shown that Palestinian suicide bombers have usually experienced the death or injury of a friend or relative at the hands of Israelis (Moten 2010, 46).

Why some persons channel their frustration or anger into violent action while others do not is not clearly understood but, to draw a parallel, studies of why men commit acts of domestic violence have shown the complexity associated with the intersection of factors like notions of masculinity, peer pressure, childhood experiences, and individual personality traits. While formulating profiles of potential terrorists can be a valuable tool, it can also serve to reinforce stereotypes.

Crenshaw (1981; 1995), points out that harsh responses to acts of terrorism, including military action, may be seen as an overreaction and tend to reinforce terrorists' views that their action is legitimate. For example, the Israeli policy of regularly retaliating against acts of terror by Palestinians through destroying their houses seems to perpetuate the violence and even start new outbreaks.[19]

As well as attempting to identify the proximate causes of terrorism, some have called for attention to be given to "the contributing root sources of political alienation and rage that fuel the frustrations of terrorist groups" (Cronin 2004a, 13). Economic opportunity, effective justice, and systems of governance that allow dissenting voices to be heard should all be included in strategies to combat potential and actual terrorism (p. 13).

In the Middle East, addressing the political and economic causes of terrorism—as well as understanding the origins of terrorism in the Arab street and how it grows and can become an end in itself—can contribute as much as overwhelming force applied through military and police actions to countering and defeating terrorism (Esposito 2003, 160).

RELIGION, VIOLENCE, AND TERRORISM

The association between violence, terrorism, and religion is not new. Rapoport (1984, 659) in a discussion of religious violence and terrorism, writes, "The holy terrorist believes that only a transcendent purpose which fulfils the meaning of the universe can justify terror, and that the deity reveals at some early moment in time both the end and the means and may even participate in the process as well." Here, Rapoport reminds us that religious terrorism is not the original creation of Islamic fundamentalists but was practiced by Thugs (Hindu), Assassins (Muslim), and Zealots (Jewish) over many centuries. Notably, the Assassins, founded by Hassan-i Sabbah in the late eleventh century in Persia, aimed to unify Islam and establish their own state comprising a series of mountain-fortresses and city-states and a network of cells in sympathetic urban centers (Rapoport 1984, 666). Members of this group were devoted to Sabbah and willing and eager to die for him (Green 1995, 554).

In this section, we examine the association between religion and terrorism. Given its contemporary significance and, in general, the lack of knowledge about Islam in the West,[20] we use much of this section to explore Islam, its history, and some of its beliefs with the aim of gaining a better understanding of the concept of *jihad* as it has evolved over time in the context of interactions between Islam and the West.

Since the events of 9/11, terrorism has been seen largely as a manifestation of radical Islam because of the stance adopted by Osama bin Laden, who, on April 23, 1998, issued a *fatwa*[21] announcing the establishment of a World Islamic Front for Jihad, declaring that it was "the duty of all Muslims to kill U.S. citizens—civilian or military—and their allies everywhere" (quoted in Wilkinson 2001, 5). This means that Al Qaeda is the terrorist organization *par excellence* because it has made an explicit commitment to kill civilians *en masse* (Wilkinson 2001, 43). It achieves this aim of mass killing through methods that include individual suicide bombers and car and truck bombs located in public spaces with no prior warnings before detonation. Al Qaeda is also differentiated as new terrorism by its commitment to worldwide changes rather than simply to one state or region. As a result, Al Qaeda seeks to expel all non-Muslims from the Middle East, to bring down Arab regimes that collaborate with the United States and do not follow the tenets of "true Islam," and ultimately to establish a Muslim *caliphate* across borders of Muslim states that unites all Muslims. Unlike traditional groups, Al Qaeda operates through an organizational network with cells established in a number of states. It is this dispersal that provides it with the global reach that other groups do not possess (p. 5).

Violence that is associated with religion is not limited to the religion of Islam. There are many examples of an association between religion and terrorist violence.

- In India, the movement for a separate homeland for the Sikhs and its associated terrorism (see section "Counterterrorist Responses: United States, Germany, and India") were perceived by the Sikhs as a contestation between the Sikh and Hindu religions.

- Japanese Buddhism, *Aum Shinrikyo,* was implicated in the terrorism of March 1995 when five members of this movement boarded separate trains on Tokyo's subway and, when the trains began to converge in central Tokyo, released sarin gas, causing twelve deaths (Juergensmeyer 2003, 103–4).

- In Israel, the attack by Baruch Goldstein on a mosque in Hebron on February 25, 1994, resulting in the death of 29 Muslims and the injury of 125 more, stands as an example of contemporary Jewish terrorism.

- In the United States, attacks by antiabortion advocates on medical facilities and medical personnel offering abortion services have

resulted in numerous deaths, injuries, and destruction of property. Those perpetuating such attacks are associated with Christian extremist groups such as the Christian Identity Movement,[22] who fear racial mixing and imagine Jews to be the "offspring of Satan" (Smith 2008, 94). Similarly, U.S. adherents of Reconstruction Theology advocate the creation of a theocratic Christian State where scripture will be the law and determine all social issues, and from which Christians, as the chosen people of God, will come to dominate the world (Juergensmeyer 2003, 28).

Understanding *Jihad* and Radical Islam

The terms *jihad* and *jihadist* are commonly employed in the media to describe forms of perceived Islamic militancy and generally to denote the struggles of some Muslims to prosecute a holy war against the infidel.[23] However, in Islamic thought, *jihad* is a significant religious concept referring, for most Muslims, to the internal spiritual struggle waged within oneself to become a better Muslim. It can also mean waging warfare in defense of Islam. The term has gained currency, having been used by Al Qaeda, the mujahidin in Afghanistan, the Taliban, Muslims in Chechnya and Kashmir, Hamas, Hezbollah, and most recently by the so-called Islamic State of Iraq and the Levant (ISIL). Crucial to understanding the complexities of *jihad* is knowing something of the context in which the concept was created (the early days of the foundation of Islam) and how it has been interpreted and co-opted by some Muslims in the service of their terrorist programs.

Islam emerged in the seventh century when Arabia and the city of Mecca in which the Prophet lived were subjected to tribal raids, vendettas, and cycles of vengeance. This period of unbelief and ignorance before Islam is known in Islam as *jahiliyyah*. The Prophet's message (like that of Christ in the Christian religion) challenged the status quo by calling for social justice and condemning Arabian polytheism, corruption, materialism, and avarice (Esposito 2003, 30). The radical message that Muslims were to be accountable not to tribal law but to divine law and to a single God meant that the Prophet and his followers would have to struggle to spread Islam; in other words, they would have to wage *jihad.* The ideals of *hijira* (meaning to emigrate out of a hostile anti-Islamic environment) and *jihad* were created when the Prophet moved from Mecca to Medina to establish the first Muslim city-state (p. 31).[24] The earliest Quranic verses refer to the *hijira* and to what is termed a "defensive *jihad*" as the Prophet and his followers readied themselves to fight for their beliefs and their lives. Other verses, called the "sword verses," can be quoted selectively to authorize unconditional warfare against unbelievers and were used in this way in the early period to justify expansion. In effect, it was argued that they had nullified the defensive *jihad* verses.

Under the Prophet Muhammad's leadership and that of his successors, Islam spread rapidly, creating an empire as Muslim armies overran other empires. The Qur' an states that "there is no compulsion in religion" and, aside from expansion to satisfy economic needs and religious zeal, the rationale for conquest was not to force others to convert to Islam but rather "to spread its righteous order" (Esposito 2003, 33). In the context of *jihad,* Islam reserves a special place for martyrs who die for Islam. Their acts free them from sin, and after death they avoid purgatory "and proceed to one of the highest locations in Heaven near the Throne of God" (Esposito 2003, 34).

As with most religions, over time, scholars and jurists interpreting the Qur'an and the *Hadith* (the acts and sayings of the Prophet recorded by others) became the arbiters of the various meanings of *jihad,* and when a *jihad* was planned, it was supported by *fatwas* issued to give the *jihad* legitimacy.[25] These jurists regarded *jihad* as a necessity in a world that they divided between the *dar al-Islam* (land of Islam) and the *dar al-harb* (land of war). Muslims were required to struggle for the expansion of the *dar al-Islam* so that all persons would have the benefit of living within a just social order because Islam regards disorder as a political and social evil (Esposito 2003, 35).

Religious Extremism in Islam

This can be traced back to the Assassins and the *Kharijites,* and the latter can be linked to the development of the strict Wahhabi interpretation of Islam found in Saudi Arabia today (Esposito 2003, 123). In turn, Wahhabi beliefs are associated with radical movements like Al Qaeda and can also be seen in the public statements and actions of Boko Haram (see case study "Boko Haram," later

in this chapter). The Kharijites created their own strict society, adopted a radical form of *jihad,* and waged war in the name of God, perceiving the world as divided between believers and nonbelievers. Muslims who rejected their perspective were also treated as unbelievers and either excommunicated or killed. The ends always justified the means for the Kharijites, and violence and terrorism were claimed to be morally sanctioned by Islam in the service of God. In modern times, this perspective can be seen in those who assassinated Egypt's President Sadat, in bin Laden, and in "other extremists who have called for the overthrow of "un-Islamic" Muslim rulers and for *jihad* against the West (Esposito 2003, 42).

The teachings of early Islam constitute a source of legitimacy for radical Muslims who selectively choose teachings and interpretations that support their ideology. In this way, they attempt to legitimate and give moral authority to their actions in the eyes of other Muslims. Within Islam, concepts of renewal and purification are linked to the need to follow the "straight path of Islam," meaning the "right path" (Esposito 2003, 44). Accordingly, Sunni Islam developed the notion that renewal or revival would be necessary in every age as a way to return to the unspoiled teachings of Islam.

This legacy of revivalism is exemplified in the reformer *Taqi al-Din Ahmad ibn Taymiyya* (1263–1328), whose effect on radical Islamic ideology is hugely influential (Esposito 2003, p. 45). His ideas were adopted by the eighteenth-century Wahhabi movement and by a modern activist, Sayyid Qutb. Ibn Taymiyya argued for a literal interpretation of the sacred sources of Islam with the goal of purifying Islam and thereby restoring its power and greatness. He is known for categorizing the Mongols, who were Muslims, as unbelievers because they continued to follow the laws of Genghis Khan. Modern-day extremists have used this example in their calls for a *jihad* against "un-Islamic Muslims" and against the West (p. 46).

In the eighteenth century, the Wahhabi movement led by *Muhammad ibn Abd al-Wahhab* (1703–91) called for a fresh interpretation of Islam. Al-Wahhab stressed the doctrine of the unity of God, and his forces destroyed numerous shrines, tombs, and sacred objects that they considered idolatrous, including the sacred Shia pilgrimage site of Karbala in Iraq. Many have drawn parallels between the ideology behind this destruction and the Taliban's destruction of Buddhist monuments in Afghanistan (Esposito

have begun to require that *imans* possess local language skills and have knowledge of the local cultures (Haddad and Balz 2008, 224). At a more practical level, governments are also requiring that *imans* prove they will be financially supported in a country before agreeing to issue a visa to enter. This oversight of Islamic education is not matched by similar rules or practices for other religions.

Religion can be seen as a set of beliefs that provide a structure for living one's life. The perspective of those with faith is often that without religion the world is disordered and incoherent. Religious belief therefore provides a sense of order and a moral compass to navigate society and its changes. Those with religious faith often desire to confer the benefits of faith on others, believing that they, too, need coherence and order in their lives. Most religions have been associated with violence, "from biblical wars to crusading ventures and great acts of martyrdom" (Juergensmeyer 2003, 6). Over time, Christianity, for example, rejected pacifism and conceived of "just wars" that condoned violence, and Christianity validated the Inquisition and the Crusades (pp. 25–26). Religion therefore represents and conveys moral authority and, for the individual, legitimizes individual acts done "in the name of God" or in the "name of faith," including acts of terrorism. For example, attacks on abortion clinics in the United States by religious zealots are morally justified by reference not only to the immorality of abortion but in a wider sense between what is considered good and what is thought to be evil (p. 20).

Mark Juergensmeyer argues that acts of religious terrorism are dramatic modes of public performance underpinned by images of divine warfare, often part of a religious heritage, in a "cosmic war" and not part of a political strategy (2003, xi). They are symbolic in nature and are perceived by those who perform such acts as empowering them (p. xi). The cosmic war imagines great battles of the past between the forces of good and evil and provides moral justification for acts of terrorism. Where it is known that the struggle is a hopeless one that cannot be won in real terms, it may be reimagined as a sacred struggle where the outcome is in the hands of God (p. 165). In such cases, it is believed that the struggle will ultimately succeed, but this may not be a rapid or easy process. In the cosmic war, martyrdom and sacrifice in the course of killing are seen as ennobling acts (p. 168). It might be concluded then that religion constitutes an enabling instrument that empowers religious zealots to publicly demonstrate their faith and fight a cosmic war that provides "a sense of importance and destiny to men who find the modern world to be stifling, chaotic and dangerously out of control" (Juergensmeyer 2003, 193). Therefore, in this sense, religion does not cause terrorism; rather, it is a source that can be exploited by a religiously zealous terrorist for empowerment, performance, and legitimacy in performing acts of terrorism.

INTERNATIONAL LAW AND TERRORISM

The relationship between international law and terrorism has been described as lacking a "normative fabric" and comprising "just bits and pieces of overlapping norms with significant gaps as to their coverage" (Bassiouni 2002, 86). Cherif Bassiouni points to the absence of a comprehensive convention on terrorism that is value-neutral and covers all modes of terrorism as being "consistent with the ad hoc and discretionary approach that governments have taken toward the development of effective international legal responses to terrorism" (p. 91).

Ben Saul (2006, 7) argues that the rationale for defining and criminalizing terrorism internationally is "that terrorism seriously undermines fundamental human rights, jeopardizes the State and peaceful politics, and threatens international peace and security." Since the events of 9/11, states have been encouraged by UN Security Council resolutions to act against terrorism as a discrete crime in itself and as a violation of international criminal law (p. 11). A key resolution is 1373 of September 28, 2001, which requires that states criminalize the financing of terrorism, suppress terrorist groups, deny refugee status to terrorists, prevent the movement of terrorists, bring terrorists to justice, and establish terrorist acts as serious crimes within states' domestic criminal justice systems (Saul 2006, 48). The UN Counterterrorism Committee (CTC) was established to monitor the implementation of the resolution and decided to permit states to apply their own definitions of terrorism rather than try to adopt a definition itself.

In 1972, following the killing of Israeli athletes at the Munich Olympics and the earlier attacks at an Israeli airport, as well as an attack on a Soviet diplomat, the United Nations made its first concerted effort to respond to terrorism. The UN General Assembly authorized a study on "the underlying causes of those forms of terrorism and acts of violence which lie in misery, frustration, grievance and despair and which cause some people to sacrifice human lives, including their own, to effect radical changes" (Saul 2006, 71). In an Ad Hoc Committee that was established, states offered a broad range of views on the causes of terrorism, including capitalism, neocolonialism, aggression, racism, foreign occupation, injustice, inequality, and political destabilization (UN General Assembly Ad Hoc Committee 1996, p. 71). The Ad Hoc Committee made a final report in 1979, and in the 1970s and 1980s, resolutions urged states to eliminate the causes of terrorism.

Treaties Associated With Terrorism

While there is no comprehensive convention on terrorism, terrorism has been the subject of international action under numerous sectoral conventions that cover discrete subjects that have gained international attention and are associated with terrorism. There were thirteen international treaties concluded between 1963 and 2005 that address crimes understood to be terrorist crimes (UN Treaty Collection). Many were adopted in response to acts of terrorism that took place on aircraft during the 1960s and in response to subsequent international terrorist acts. The treaties are listed here.[27]

- 1963 Tokyo Convention concerning crimes committed on board aircraft
- 1970 Hague Convention concerning the suppression of the unlawful seizure of aircraft
- 1971 Montreal Convention concerning the suppression of unlawful acts against the safety of civil aviation
- 1973 Internationally Protected Persons Convention concerned with the protection of diplomats
- 1979 International Convention against the Taking of Hostages
- 1980 Vienna Convention on the physical protection of nuclear material

- 1988 Montreal Protocol on the suppression of unlawful acts of violence at airports serving international aviation
- 1988 Rome Convention on the suppression of unlawful acts against the safety of maritime navigation
- 1988 Safety of Fixed Platforms Convention against the suppression of unlawful acts against fixed platforms located on the continental shelf
- 1991 Plastics Explosives Convention on the marking of plastic explosives for detection 1997 Terrorist Bombings Convention on the suppression of terrorist bombings
- 1999 Terrorist Financing Convention on the suppression of the financing of terrorism
- 2005 Nuclear Terrorism Convention on the suppression of acts of nuclear terrorism

Few of these treaties actually designate the prohibited conduct or acts as specifically "terrorist offenses." Instead, they require that states punish specified acts (such as hijacking, hostage taking, or financing terrorism) under their domestic laws without requiring states to provide proof of a political purpose or of an intention to cause terror. Thus, the substantive provisions do not employ the terms *terror* or *terrorism*. A few treaties do use these terms in their preambles; for example, the 1979 Hostages Convention refers to "acts of taking of hostages as manifestations of international terrorism," and the 1999 Terrorism Financing Convention states "that the "number and seriousness of acts of international terrorism depend on their financing." Saul argues that this sectoral approach to terrorist-type activities reflects a "pragmatic, empirical, problem-oriented step-by-step" approach that avoids confronting the question of securing consensus on an international definition of terrorism (2006, 133).

As well as the treaties listed earlier, a number of treaties agreed to by member-states of regional or other organizations exist that have a limited area of operation and govern relations between the member-states of the regional organization or of organizations defined by religious or cultural affiliation such as the Arab League. Some of these treaties specifically define terrorist offenses and thus contribute toward the evolution of international law on this subject (Saul 2006, 143). An example of a regional convention is the Council of Europe 1977 Convention on the Suppression of

Terrorism, which does not define terrorism as such but adopts the method of listing a variety of acts commonly committed by terrorists, while never actually using or defining the term *terrorism* (Saul 2006, 148). By contrast, the 1998 Arab Convention for the Suppression of Terrorism, concluded by the League of Arab States, opts for a very broad definition of terrorism as follows:

> Any act or threat of violence, whatever its motives or purposes, that occurs in the advancement of an individual or collective criminal agenda and seeking to sow panic among people, causing fear by harming them, or placing their lives, liberty or security in danger, or seeking to cause damage to the environment or to public or private installations or property or to occupying or seizing them, or seeking to jeopardize a national resources [sic]. (Cited in Saul 2006, 154)

Terrorism was not defined in the 1998 Statute that establishes the International Criminal Court (see Chapter 9) because

- it lacked an international definition,

- there were disagreements about how to describe violence used in movements for national liberation, and

- it was thought that it might politicize the Court.

Most states favored deferring any definition noting that it could always be included at a later date (Saul 2006, 182).

The Ad Hoc Committee established by the United Nations had been responsible for the drafting of conventions on terrorist bombings and financing and on nuclear terrorism. Between 2001 and 2002, spurred on by the events of 9/11, the Committee made substantial progress on a draft comprehensive convention on terrorism, and by 2002 agreement had been reached on most of its twenty-seven articles. However, by that time, some states had adopted final negotiating positions and it was not possible to conclude the draft (Saul 2006, 184). Mandates to continue drafting were issued in the following years. The Ad Hoc Committee did not meet in 2012, 2013, or 2014, nor will they meet in 2015 (http://www .un.org/law/terrorism/). It is working on the basis that "nothing is agreed until everything is agreed,"

and it is therefore uncertain if and when a comprehensive convention on terrorism will be concluded.

An analysis of domestic laws provided to the UN Counterterrorism Committee helps reveal that the dominant approach of most states (about half of all states) is to prosecute terrorism as ordinary crimes such as murder, assault, and so on (Saul 2006, 264). Some states that prosecute terrorism in this way also have offenses, which, while not explicitly called "terrorism," appear to function as such. Examples of this approach are the offenses of public intimidation (Argentina), creating panic (Kuwait), and intimidation (Japan, Sri Lanka, and Venezuela) (p. 265).

COUNTERTERRORIST RESPONSES: UNITED STATES, GERMANY, AND INDIA

In an unprecedented response to an international incident of terrorism, almost immediately following the events of 9/11, a number of democratic states formulated new antiterrorist laws as a means of combating and coping with any terrorist attacks that might occur in their territories. Consequently, the events of 9/11 became the referent for debates and action about security in the West (Walklate and Mythen 2015, 15). It was common to find new or expanded restrictions on freedoms like assembly, association, free speech, religion, and privacy included in these new laws. Suspicions were raised in some countries that the anxiety and insecurity raised by 9/11 were being exploited to enact unreasonably authoritarian laws and reinforce social control (p. 7). Those who protested new laws ran the risk of being accused of supporting terrorism.

Some states, like Germany, had concrete connections to the 9/11 terrorists, and new laws highlighted inadequacies in their exiting antiterrorist regimes. In addition, new counterterrorism laws had symbolic value in that they signified a commitment to protect the public (Finn 2010, 41). At the international level, UN Security Council (2001) Resolution 1373 required that all states enact necessary laws criminalizing various aspects of terrorism.

Laws reflect policies; and the overall question, therefore, is why countries pursue different counterterrorist policies when they may in fact be facing similar threats. Have restrictions on civil rights resulted in a commensurate increase in security from terrorist acts? What are the processes that interact to provide the necessary balance between civil rights and security? In a focused comparison of antiterror laws in a few countries, this section isolates the differing perspectives and politics that shaped these legislative responses.

Overall, we ask what other countries have done "in their moments of terrorist induced panic" (Scheppele 2006, 609), taking into account their legal cultures, political environments, and historical experiences. We begin with the U.S. response in order to establish a template against which other countries' responses can be contrasted. Only a summary will be provided, but this is sufficient to underscore divergences and commonalities. As well as legislative frameworks, relevant case law is presented to illustrate how laws were implemented and challenged through the court process and what considerations shaped the resultant court decisions.

United States

Antiterrorist legislation in the United States has been traced back to the 1798 Alien and Sedition Acts aimed at combating domestic unrest caused by the influx of newly arrived immigrants into the country and giving the President the power to remove aliens deemed to be "dangerous" to peace and security (Beckman 2007, 13). At that time, and this holds true for the modern period, immigration and deportation powers figured large in the management of dangerous aliens. The Sedition Act effectively prohibited criticism of the government (the Congress and the President and the country itself) by way of "false, scandalous and malicious writing or writings against the government of the United States" intended to "stir up sedition" (quoted in Beckman 2007, 14). This Act expired in 1801, as did others dealing with naturalization.

In 1917 the Espionage and Sedition Acts were again enacted following an immigrant influx, this time from Eastern Europe and Italy. The laws were aimed at those who were thought to be introducing new political philosophies considered inimical to the United States. These laws were enforced during the wartime period in a draconian manner to prevent and punish any antiwar messages. For example, on November 7, 1919, about ten thousand persons were arrested

in twenty-three different cities without warrants in an operation known as the Palmer Raids (Beckman 2007, 18). Also, during this period J. Edgar Hoover began collecting data of persons with left wing views and conducting extensive surveillance of them. The Sedition Act of this period made it an offense to speak out against the government, its armed forces, its flag, and its Constitution with the intention of bringing the government into disrepute or contempt (p. 18). During this time there was widespread public support for this kind of repressive legislation and for rigorous policing. As well, the Supreme Court largely upheld challenges to the enactment of these laws.

In 1940, the Alien Registration Act made it criminal conduct to publish, advocate, or teach with the intention of overthrowing or seeking the destruction of the United States and its government. It was used during the 1950s, when McCarthyism was ascendant, to prosecute thousands of alleged communists. This legislation was followed by the internment of thousands of U.S. citizens of Japanese origin during World War II, an executive act upheld by the Supreme Court in December 1944 (Beckman 2007, 21). The perceived threat of communism resulted in more legislation in 1950 (the Internal Security Act) and in 1956 (the Communist Control Act).

During the period of the war in Vietnam, in the 1960s and 1970s, numerous abuses of civil rights were revealed and investigated. For example, the Church Committee found that "U.S. intelligence agencies had routinely and wantonly violated the civil liberties of Americans during domestic intelligence investigations. The FBI was one of the main culprits" (quoted in Beckman 2007, 24). In 1978 the Foreign Intelligence Surveillance Act was passed ensuring judicial oversight of intelligence collection, albeit by a secret federal court which turned out to be a "virtual rubber stamp for government requests" (Beckman 2007, 24).

During the 1970s and 1980s, numerous terrorist attacks occurred outside the United States, but the feeling within the country was not alarmist because these acts were seen as happening on someone else's soil. This, in spite of the fact that some attacks involved the death or injury of many U.S. citizens. For example, 241 marines were killed in an attack in Lebanon in 1983, and 189 Americans out of 243 passengers were killed in the bombing of Pan Am Flight 103 over

Lockerbie, Scotland, in 1988. During the 1990s, the mood began to change with two domestic terrorist attacks: the attack on the World Trade Center in 1993 and the bombing of the federal building in Oklahoma in 1995.

In the belief that law enforcement required more resources to deal with such events, the passage of the Antiterrorism and Effective Death Penalty Act of 1996 was the first comprehensive antiterrorist law. While some of the more rigorous provisions of this law, such as access to personal banking records, were removed, they later appeared in the Patriot Act in 2001 (Beckman 2007, 25). Significantly, in view of events to come, the law expressed the view of Congress that the President should use "all necessary means, including covert action and military force, to destroy international infrastructure used by international terrorists" (quoted in Beckman 2007, 26).

Within one week of 9/11, the then Attorney-General had prepared a 342-page antiterrorism bill,[28] and a poll conducted within a few weeks of 9/11 found that about 60 percent of those surveyed considered certain civil liberties ought to be sacrificed in favor of security measures to combat terrorism. Congress took about forty-five days to enact the Patriot Act, but it received little debate or scrutiny. It amended numerous federal laws and became law on October 26, 2001. Generally, the Patriot Act has been viewed as tipping the balance away from civil liberties and in favor of security. The main features are listed here.

- For the first time, it empowers the FBI and the CIA to share information.

- It allows law enforcement to collect personal information and monitor persons in ways previously not permitted and with little, if any, judicial oversight.

- It defines "domestic terrorism" to include a wide range of acts.

- It broadens the previous definition of a terrorist organization and includes terrorist acts within the RICO statutes (see Chapter 10 for RICO).

- It creates new offenses of harboring and assisting others who might commit terrorist acts or providing them with material support if it is known that the resources will be used for terrorism.

- The Department of Justice is tasked with authority to investigate all suspected terrorism offenses in place of several departments with overlapping powers.

- Law enforcement was given substantially greater powers to conduct investigations, for example, by installing devices that could intercept e-mail and monitor Internet activity; to conduct "sneak and peak" secret searches without notifying the occupant of premises beforehand, thereby enabling police to enter secretly; to place eavesdropping devices without the consent or knowledge of the occupants, a major expansion of fourth amendment search powers; and to conduct warrantless monitoring of telephone conversations.

- Federal authorities were given power to collect and review records concerning a person held by a third party, such as medical records, university records, and library records, simply by issuing an administrative subpoena and with no judicial oversight under so-called national security letters, thousands of which have been issued annually[29] where the disclosure must be kept secret by the third party and where the information must be delivered before any challenge is made to the subpoena in court. (Beckman 2007, 27–31)

In addition, amendments were made to immigration laws to prohibit aliens from soliciting funds or members for a terrorist organization, or providing them with material support, to allow aliens to be refused entry for such activities and for the deportation of those legally in the United States who committed such acts. As well, the Attorney-General is given a blanket power to order taking into custody of an alien who she has reasonable grounds to believe to be engaged in activities dangerous to national security. Custody can be maintained for seven days without a hearing, but this can be extended where the person is certified to be a "suspected terrorist."

These and other regulations allowing detention of persons without charge for substantial periods of time allow the Department of Justice, when the evidence of an offense by an alien is weak, to simply take that person into custody and then deport her. Other provisions require that financial institutions document and report on the suspicious business activities of their customers, such as large cash payments, that may be intended to fund terrorist activity (Beckman 2007, 27–31).

Other elements of the counterterrorism regime include the Homeland Security Act of 2002, which established the Department of Homeland Security; executive orders on a range of issues, including military commissions for captured terrorists; and regulations concerning the detention and interrogation of suspected terrorists. There was also a Terrorist Information Awareness Program and reorganizations of the intelligence community for better coordination and information sharing (Finn 2010, 37).

The provisions of the Patriot Act noted in the previous list were renewed in November 2005 and again in 2006, and numerous provisions have been permanently enacted into law and therefore will not require annual renewal. Three of the most controversial provisions were reauthorized in 2011 for four years (ACLU, n.d.). Some provisions have been amended; notably the national security letters provision now allows challenges in court to nondisclosure, but the legal regime enacted by the Patriot Act to counter terrorism remains largely intact. Public ignorance of the contents of the Patriot Act remains considerable, but recent revelations that the National Security Agency conducted warrantless wiretapping allegedly to collect foreign intelligence and that it has been data mining under a secret order issued by the Foreign Intelligence Surveillance Court have resulted in a storm of protest about privacy violations and the need to roll back this extensive clandestine surveillance (Black 2013).

Another useful tool in the fight against terrorism has been the Material Witness Statute, which allows federal prosecutors to hold material witnesses indefinitely. It has been alleged that this law has been used to indefinitely detain persons who the government fears may commit terrorist acts in the future but where it lacks evidence to charge with a crime (Beckman 2007, 33). An example is a former cab driver in Boston who was detained under this law for about eight months in solitary confinement. In 2003 the Department of Justice admitted to holding forty to fifty persons as material witnesses. Consequently, Beckman argues that the government has exploited provisions of this nature as a form of preventive detention abusing laws that were never passed for that purpose (p. 33).

BOX 12.4   Terrorism in Court: United States

There is insufficient space to discuss all the important court decisions arising out of the war on terrorism, many of which have been concerned with the capture of alleged terrorists overseas, some of them American citizens, and how they should be dealt with under U.S. laws. In relation to the detention of persons over many years in Guantanamo Bay, Cuba, the Detainee Treatment Act prohibited judicial review and habeas corpus by the detainees, who were classed by the government as "enemy combatants" and were to be tried by military tribunals, as opposed to civilian courts (Beckman 2007, 44).

In 2004, the U.S. Supreme Court decided that even enemy combatants held by the United States but not on U.S. soil were entitled to minimum protections, including the right to challenge their detention and that the judicial power of the United States extended to Guantanamo (p. 44). In the well-known *Hamdan* case, the Supreme Court ruled that the goal of holding detainees in Guantanamo for trial by military tribunals was a violation of the Constitution and international law on the treatment of prisoners and that they must be tried under due process by the same procedures that govern courts-martial (p. 44).

In other cases, a U.S. citizen who was captured in Afghanistan in 2001, John Walker Lindh, was charged with conspiracy to kill U.S. citizens abroad but later pleaded guilty to providing support to the Taliban and received a sentence of twenty years (Beckman 2007, 49).

(Continued)

(Continued)

The British "shoe bomber," Richard Reid, who attempted to detonate explosives concealed in his shoe while on a transatlantic flight from Paris to Miami, was convicted in 2003 in the United States of attempted murder and attempted use of a weapon of mass destruction and was sentenced to life imprisonment.

The so-called twentieth hijacker of 9/11, French citizen Zacarias Moussaoui, was indicted in the United States for charges that included conspiracy to commit acts of terrorism transcending national boundaries. He ultimately pleaded guilty to six conspiracy charges in 2005, becoming the first person to be convicted in the United States for the 9/11 attacks, and received a life sentence. Despite the fact that he was not a U.S. citizen, he was not tried before a military tribunal but before a federal court.

Germany

Having experienced terrorism by non-state groups in the 1970s and 1980s, Germany came into more recent contact with terrorists when Muhammad Atta, an Egyptian and one of the leaders of the 9/11 attack, lived in Germany between 1992 and 1999 while he studied in Hamburg. An Al Qaeda cell existed in Hamburg and there were thought to be others. With a substantial Muslim population of more than three million Muslims, the German authorities had already, before 9/11, identified Germany as a possible safe haven for terrorists because of its strict constitutional protections and the special protections that existed for religious organizations (Beckman 2007, 101).

Germany is an interesting comparative study on this topic because its *Grundgesetz,* or Basic Law (BL), was greatly influenced by the United States and because of its experience in terrorism during the 1970s and 1980s (see section titled "The Evolution of Terrorism"). It was during this period of unrest that as well as targeting and arresting terrorists, Germany made changes to its laws to create a legal antiterrorist regime. Over time, it became apparent that this regime had proved to be overzealous and had limited civil rights to an unwarranted degree. Changes were made to repeal some measures and reduce the use of others (Boyne 2004, 42). After 9/11, Germany again made legal changes as part of its counterterrorist strategy. This case study of Germany explains how German postwar legal culture, its history of past terrorism, and the protection of democracy and rights embedded in its BL or Constitution have all been instrumental in shaping the German response to terrorism.

German Legal and Constitutional Framework

The legal and constitutional framework in Germany is very protective of human rights. For example, legislation approved by the two Chambers of the legislature must not conflict with the BL; to ensure this, a proposed law can be referred to the Federal Constitutional Court (FCC). The first nineteen articles of the German BL, which grant civil rights, may not be altered by parliament and explicitly promote notions of democratic governance, including a free media and freedom of speech (Haubrich 2003, 27). These rights constitute "directly enforceable law," and the FCC is set up to administer a system of judicial review to protect those rights (Beckman 2007, 90). The BL therefore guarantees individual freedom but also protects the democratic constitutional order (Lepsius 2004, 442).

The nature of German society following World War II was strongly antifascist, and democratic norms and safeguards embodied in the BL were intended to prevent any return to the horrific prewar history. In order to protect these democratic norms, attacks against the "free democratic basic order" can result in a loss of civil rights. Consequently, the balance is struck that while civil rights are granted, they may not be exercised so as to overturn the *Rechtsstaat* (Rule of Law), and the FCC has even held that individual rights may be limited by the legislature to promote the democratic order (Beckman 2007, 91).

The overall constitutional framework is therefore geared to protect a democratic society founded on the rule of law. However, laws that limit rights can be challenged by judicial review and must not in any case infringe the "essence" of the right. This means that antiterrorism measures may not be promulgated that infringe the essential content of individual rights. An example of how civil rights may trump counterterrorist measures came in 2005, when a law that allowed the government to shoot down hijacked airliners (in situations like those of 9/11) was challenged in the FCC and struck down, the Court declaring that it violated the right to life (p. 92).

Other restrictions imposed by the BL restrict Germany, unlike the United States, from engaging in offensive counterterrorist operations overseas or undertaking anticipatory self-defense when it is believed an attack may be imminent. These restrictions reflect a rejection of the aggressive practices that brought about the First and Second World Wars. Japan functions under similar constitutional restrictions concerning militarism and the use of force for the same reasons (Beckman 2007, 93). In 2005 the FCC held that Germany's indirect participation in the Iraq war violated the BL. When Germany itself is attacked and needs to defend itself, the decision has to be made with the two-thirds majority approval of both chambers of the legislature. Thus, unlike in the United States and United Kingdom, this decision does not rest with the executive government alone. This limitation seeks to avoid the abuses of the Nazi regime when the then Weimar Constitution permitted the executive, the Nazi party, to declare a state of emergency and suspend the Constitution (Beckman 2007, 93).

The dividing line between terrorism and war is therefore clearly demarcated under the German system of law so that terrorism must remain within the sphere of domestic law enforcement and cannot easily be declared a "war," as occurred in the United States.

It is argued that in the early postwar period, a democratic culture had yet to be embedded in German society, consciousness, and politics, and for this reason leaders were wary of protests and challenges to the government and adopted conservative stances for fear of being seen as weak on terrorism (Boyne 2004, 52). Accordingly, when "outspoken and extra-parliamentary political conduct" did occur in the 1970s and 1980s, it was perceived as a threat to the social order and reminiscent of the days of fascism (p. 53).

In terms of policing and intelligence collection, at the federal level, after 2001 the Federal Office for the Protection of the Constitution was empowered to monitor potential attacks by terrorists and is now the principal investigatory authority in this field of operations. The policing structure in Germany comprises state police forces in the sixteen *Lander* (states) and federal agencies that have clearly defined responsibilities. At the federal level, the Criminal Investigation Office coordinates all law enforcement agencies and activities. Unlike the United States with its plethora of police forces, the German policing system comprises only the state and federal police and there are no municipal or local law enforcement agencies as one finds in the highly decentralized U.S. policing model (Beckman 2007, 97).

A robust system of judicial and parliamentary checks scrutinizes the German intelligence apparatus. The Parliamentary Control Commission, comprising nine members of the *Bundestag,* supervises all intelligence agencies. All intelligence activities must be reported to the Commission, and it must in turn report to the *Bundestag* once every two years. Leadership of this Commission rotates between government and opposition supporters, ensuring that it does not become politically polarized in its supervisory function (Scheppele 2006, 619).

Two committees, established under the Constitution, protect the privacy of communications by reviewing the surveillance practices of the intelligence apparatus and the police. One comprises nine members of the *Bundestag* and meets every six months to review surveillance policies, and the other comprises four legal experts who meet with the intelligence agencies each month to review actual intercepts for their legality. They may order the suspension of those where legality is in doubt. They also review the content of search programs used in data mining (Scheppele 2006, 619). The previous role of the judiciary in authorizing electronic intercepts by warrant was supplanted in 1968 by replacing judicial with parliamentary oversight. Even so, a person who suspects he is under surveillance has the right to challenge this before the Parliamentary Commission and may lodge a complaint directly with the Federal Constitutional Court (FCC) (p. 620).

Unrest and Terrorism in Germany—1970s and 1980s

In 1968, during waves of terrorism and civil unrest, the government enacted emergency legislation to deal with those events. The BL at this point had few emergency-type provisions, but the new powers allowed the *Bundestag* and the *Bundesrat,* following a two-thirds majority vote, to declare a "state of defense" or a "state of tension" because of the need to respond to an armed or imminent attack, a situation approaching civil war or an international armed conflict (Boyne 2004, 47). There was also power to deploy the Federal Border Guard throughout the country, and action could be taken to restrict the right to privacy. In addition, the federal government was given power to undertake surveillance of the mail and telecommunications, and by the 1980s an extensive program of data collection and monitoring of suspected persons was being undertaken (Beckman 2007, 94).

An especially contested aspect of the new antiterrorism policy during this period was the "Termination of Radicals Policy" *(Berufsverbot),* adopted in 1972 at both federal and state levels and which barred civil service officials from taking part in what were judged to be "anticonstitutional" activities and being a member of an organization that engaged in such activities. The policy mandated that "only those persons who can show that they are prepared at all times to uphold the free democratic order and actively defend this basic order, both on and off duty, may be appointed to the civil service" (quoted in Boyne 2004, 48). This mode of loyalty screening was applied between 1972 and 1987 and affected millions of civil service applicants. When challenged in court, the policy was upheld: the court decided that civil servants must support the free democratic basic order. James Beckman (2007, 95) has suggested this policy was largely employed as a means of removing those with leftist sympathies from the civil service, much as the United States engaged in anticommunist purges in the 1950s.

In 1975 and 1976, the government revised the criminal code so that the act of forming a terrorist organization and planning illegal activities was criminalized (Boyne 2004, 49). The fear was that persons would join such groups and become a danger to society. In addition, the definition of terrorism was widened to catch almost any mass demonstration; for example, a strike that halted traffic was held by the Bavarian Supreme Court to be "violent." Given concerns that lawyers would aid terrorists who were arrested (and some did by facilitating hunger strikes and smuggling in weapons), the legal profession was regarded with some suspicion in this period (p. 49).

Legislation was passed allowing a court to exclude defense lawyers from courtrooms, and lawyers were prosecuted, for example, for attacking the sentences imposed on convicted terrorists. Broadly conceived and drafted laws like the Law for the Protection of Communal Peace criminalized anyone who supported violence through words or publications that might "disturb the public peace" (Boyne 2004, 51). The government used this legislation to penalize political dissent.

As the 1980s progressed, the judiciary began to believe that demonstrators no longer constituted a threat to the social order, and they began to dismiss some charges. Shawn Boyne suggests that the German situation during this period did not warrant legislation of this nature given the degree of the threat posed by the terrorist attacks (Boyne 2004, 51). By the 1980s, the German public had become accustomed to public forms of dissent and more tolerant of them, and this undermined appeals for stricter laws. Mass demonstrations were accepted as a normal expression of political beliefs and the traditions of "conservative-authoritarian" and "culture of subservience" were gradually eroded (p. 55). Thus, protest became part of the political culture and was not perceived as a threat to the new democratic order (p. 56).

Terrorism Laws in Germany after 9/11

Following 9/11, The German government reacted quite differently from the United States in that, while the United States saw the attack on 9/11 as an act of war, Germany located its antiterrorism strategy within its criminal justice system and within the framework of international law (Boyne 2004, 57). Accordingly, its principal strategy was to focus on the adequacy of laws required to combat whatever terrorism might be experienced after 9/11.

The legislative process in Germany (and in the United States and the United Kingdom) moved rapidly following 9/11, when, with great urgency and little debate, many changes to German law were enacted by both Chambers of the parliament. Two packages of laws were introduced, called the First and Second Security Packages *(Sicherheitspaket)*—the first in October 2001 and the second in December 2002 (Lepsius 2004, 441). Debate under the First Package was reduced from six weeks to only three weeks under an expedited procedure, and the Second Package was introduced on November 8, 2001 and had passed both chambers by December 20, 2001. Lepsius notes that the First Package focuses on "repressive measures" and the Second on "preventive protection" (p. 441).

The First Security Package extended the scope of prohibited terrorist organizations to apply to any such organization within the European Union as opposed to solely within Germany. A new offense of being a member of, or providing support to, a foreign terrorist organization where the accused was a German national or resided in Germany was created, intended to catch terrorists who planned operations in Germany and executed the terrorism in another country.

An important legal change removed the "religion privilege" under which membership in a religious organization that promoted the "common cultivation of a faith" could limit and protect persons from police investigation (Lepsius 2004, 440). Previously religious organizations had been basically off limits to government inquiries but now became subject to the same laws relating to associations of political and ideological groups (Boyne 2004, 57; Haubrich 2003, 18). Shortly after removing this religious privilege, the government banned the Union of Islamic Association and Communities (Beckman 2007, 96). Other measures were basically extensions of previously enacted laws and strengthened airport security and lessened restraints on telephone tapping and the monitoring of mail and bank records (p. 102).

The Second Security Package was overwhelmingly passed into law in the lower chamber (the *Bundestag*) and then less than a week later by the *Bundesrat,* the second chamber, comprising the sixteen German state governments. The package involved changes to seventeen laws and five regulations, but in total, security provisions had been changed in about one hundred laws (Haubrich 2003, 9–10). The following list provides information on the new laws in terms of the right to privacy.

- The new laws allowed personal data from many sources (including bank accounts, airline data and postal data, university and employment records) to be accessed by police and required Internet providers and phone companies to retain records for six months.

- Employees of security-sensitive installations such as water, electric, and telecoms could be subjected to background checks (p. 12).

- No provisions that limited freedom of speech were introduced (p. 14), and in new rules concerning freedom of movement, stricter standards were prescribed for visa applicants (p. 15).

- New counterterrorist laws permit the border police to accompany planes crossing into German airspace, and a new air marshals' unit was created while the military and civil secret services previously concerned only with targets overseas were now given power to investigate suspected persons within German territory (p. 16).

- While ID cards have been in use for many years in Germany, new provisions required that biometric data be included and stored on the card (p. 17).

- Measures included an increase in the responsibilities and resources allocated to federal agencies entrusted with protecting security.

Generally, the German legislative response was mindful of the need to protect German democracy. While this task may rest primarily with the Constitutional Court, all government agencies must implement the terms of the BL, and this includes protecting the rights of an accused person suspected of terrorism. Consequently, rights protection does not vary according to the nature of the criminal act, and judicial review gives all persons recourse to the courts (Boyne 2004, 58). Kim Lane Scheppele (2006, 622) concludes that "the German system is likely to lead to less abuse of rights than the present American system in which the system of checks is much weaker."

This recourse to judicial review was exercised in 2004 when the FCC decided that an amendment to the BL, which permitted electronic eavesdropping in the home if approved by a panel of three judges, was a violation of the BL because the legislation was required to stipulate stronger means of individual protection than it contained, especially in regard to privileged conversations between spouses, lawyer and client, doctor and patient, and so on (Scheppele 2006, 621).

BOX 12.5   Terrorism in Court: Germany

The best known prosecution mounted in Germany against an alleged terrorist was that of Mounir el-Motassadeq, the first person to be charged following the events of 9/11 (Beckman 2007, 109). He was believed to be part of the Al Qaeda cell in Hamburg that included Mohammad Atta and other hijackers who traveled to the United States to conduct the 9/11 attack. Motassadeq was thought to have stayed in Germany to manage funding for the operation and wire funds to the hijackers.

He was arrested in Germany after a long period of surveillance in November 2001. On February 19, 2003, he was convicted of being an accessory to the murder of more than three thousand persons and of being a member of a terrorist organization and was given a sentence of fifteen years imprisonment. He appealed the conviction, alleging lack of sufficient evidence for a conviction because the United States had refused to allow a key witness it held in custody to attend the trial. At the retrial in August 2005, the United States provided a statement from this key witness, but the court ruled it was not sufficient evidence to convict (Beckman 2007, 109). Accordingly, Motassadeq was acquitted of the accessory charges but convicted of the remaining charge of membership of a terrorist organization and sentenced to seven years imprisonment.

He again appealed this conviction, and on February 7, 2006, the FCC ordered his release pending appeal. On November 15, 2006, the higher court decided that the evidence brought in the original trial was sufficient to prove that Motassadeq knew about, and was involved in, the preparation of the plan to hijack the planes. He was convicted of being an accessory to 246 murders (the number of victims that died in the planes) and was sentenced to imprisonment for fifteen years (Beckman 2007, 110).

This case illustrates how the German justice system takes great care to ensure that an accused person's rights are protected and are enforced even where terrorist charges are brought. Giovanni Capoccia (2010, 287) argues that antiterrorist legislation has remained firmly within the boundaries set by the BL, largely due to the German judiciary, which has not been persuaded to reset constitutional norms even by majority public opinion that favored a national security rather than a civil rights approach to terrorism.

German antiterrorist laws have been criticized by Human Rights Watch and other international nongovernmental organizations for having introduced laws that were "panicked, ineffective, exaggerated, authoritarian and in breach of civil rights conventions" (Haubrich 2003, 7). By comparison, U.S. laws ranked first as most restrictive of civil rights, followed by the United Kingdom, Canada, France, and Germany (p. 7). Arguably, the nature of the new laws reflects the assessment made by each country of the threat level following the 9/11 attack. As a consequence, the historical "special relationship" between the United Kingdom and the United States, and British support in general for U.S. military operations in Islamic states, was a significant factor in the U.K. assessment. As for Germany, while its generally nonmilitaristic stance might have suggested a lower level of threat, the government was no doubt mindful of the large number of Turkish nationals living in Germany as well as its liberal asylum laws (p. 22).

India

The linguistic, religious, and ethnic composition of India provides the foundation for the domestic terrorism that erupted in the 1980s and has continued sporadically since then. India has experienced both international and domestic terrorism since 1947. India is vulnerable to South Asian terrorism, such as has occurred in Sri Lanka with the Liberation Tigers of Tamil Eelam (LTTE), and terrorism associated with the disputed territory of Jammu and Kashmir, where terrorist groups operating out of Pakistan have launched attacks into India (Mahmood 2000, 70). Generally, much of the ethnic and religious violence within India is characterized by the tension and rivalry between Hindus and Muslims that has been experienced since the creation of Independent India and Pakistan in 1947. The principal domestic terrorist challenges in India since 1947 have been the claims by Sikh separatists for their own homeland in the Punjab and, in

Kashmir, claims by Muslims for Kashmir to be incorporated into Pakistan or to be established as an independent Kashmiri State (p. 70).

Overall, the Indian government's response to terrorism in its states and territories has been to adopt a robust military or paramilitary strategy with the aim of crushing militant movements and disregarding civil rights[30] (Bhoumik 2004, 335). The Indian perspective on both movements was that "a successful secessionist effort . . . could have a dangerous domino effect . . . perhaps pulling India's fragile union apart" (Mahmood 2000, 71). While this strategy has been successful in the Punjab, it has not proved adequate to forestall attacks by various Islamic militant groups operating out of Kashmir and in other parts of the country. In the case of both conflicts, India has been criticized by human rights groups for the abuses committed by armed force and police, including extrajudicial executions, enforced disappearances, rapes of women in custody, and torture (p. 70).

Sikh Terrorism—Khalistan

A significant internal terrorist threat that now appears to have subsided was the struggle waged by Indian Sikhs of the Punjab from 1984 for a separate homeland, which they termed "Khalistan." The monotheistic Sikh religion was founded in the fifteenth century in the Punjab region. During the time of the Muslim Mughals in India, Sikhs had become militant in defense of their religion. At the end of the sixteenth century they were joined by a tribal group, the Jats, who were renowned warriors. In 1699 Sikhs came together to fight for a new *Khalsa,* a community possessing a religious foundation and a military discipline (Wallace 1995, 362). In this brotherhood all men took the name Singh (lion). They could be distinguished from non-Sikhs by the command never to cut their hair, to carry a sword and wear a steel bracelet, a comb, and knee-length shorts then worn by soldiers. Today, Sikhs are recognized by their uncut hair tucked in a turban (p. 362). *Khalsa* Sikhism became the mainstream element of the Sikh community.

Sikhs had established a powerful kingdom before they were defeated by the British in 1849, but they became an important element in the British Army (Wallace 1995, 366). By 1873, Sikhs had begun a religious revival united by displays of Hindu artefacts in the Golden Shrine and other Sikh temples and shrines. By 1920, groups

of Sikhs had begun to agitate for the removal of Hindus and their artefacts from Sikh shrines, and in 1925, the British acceded to these demands and established a board of control that became a meeting place for Sikh politics (Juergensmeyer 2003, 97–98).

Following the partition of India in 1947, Punjab became a state within India. The state was split between India and Pakistan, but Sikhs remained a minority in the Indian Punjab. They called for Punjab to be restricted to only Punjabi speakers, a demand essentially for a Sikh state, and in 1966, the Indian government agreed to a new Punjab drawn on linguistic lines with a small Sikh majority (Juergensmeyer 2003, 98). In 1978, Sant Jarnail Singh Bhindranwale, a rural preacher, attempted to reshape Sikhism, and violence became a key element of the movement he led from the Golden Temple complex in the city of Amritsar (Wallace 1995, 363). Bhindranwale sought a pure form of Sikhism and the unification of his followers to protect them from outside forces, especially from what was regarded as Hindu domination. He justified the use of violence in extraordinary circumstances, including as a defensive act (Juergensmeyer 2003, 100).

From his base in the Golden Temple, Bhindranwale began to establish a government and to surround himself with armed militants challenging the central government in Delhi and the state authorities (Biswas 2014, 24). Terrorism began in 1981 based on the Sikh claim to establish a homeland they called Khalistan, a claim resisted by successive Indian governments who treated it as a claim for secession (Wallace 1995, 385). Thousands of young men and some women joined the movement and were initiated into groups such as the Babbar Khalsa and the Khalistan Commando Force (Juergensmeyer 2003, 90). Prime Minister Gandhi refused to allow Bhindranwale to continue his activities, fearing that she would be perceived as losing control of a prosperous state (Biswas 2014, 25).

The government opted for a military response in the form of Operation Bluestar and, in June 1984, began a massive military assault on the Golden Temple complex as well as a military occupation of the Punjab, involving approximately seventy thousand troops. Before the assault, the Punjab was sealed off and a shoot-on-sight curfew was imposed in the state (Biswas 2014, 26). In three days and nights of fighting around the Temple (the army expected the operation would last only a few hours), about one thousand were killed, including Bhindranwale and two other leaders of the movement, and the Indian Army desecrated the Sikh's most sacred shrine. The Sikh Reference Library was burned to the ground (Mahmood 2000, 77; Wallace 1995, 385). After the operation, about two thousand Sikh soldiers mutinied, and prominent Sikhs resigned positions or handed back honors they had been awarded. As well, the operation mobilized diaspora Sikhs into supporting the separatist movement (Biswas 2014, 27). In spite of the loss of their leaders, Sikh militancy continued, and in October 1984 then Prime Minister Gandhi was killed by two of her Sikh bodyguards. This was widely believed to be in revenge for Operation Bluestar (Juergensmeyer 2003, 99). Pakistan began to provide training camps for young Sikh militants, bringing an international dimension to the conflict (Biswas 2014, 28).

Retaliatory violence by mobs in Delhi the day after Gandhi's death resulted in the killing of more than two thousand Sikhs and the burning of their property (Wallace 1995, 387). New Prime Minister Rajiv Gandhi opted for a political approach, set up a commission of inquiry to investigate the violence against Sikhs after the death of Indira Gandhi, released jailed Sikhs, and reached an agreement with Sikh leaders in 1985 in the Punjab Accord, which promised greater autonomy for Punjab (Biswas 2014, 29; Wallace 1995, 389). In spite of this initiative, terrorism continued with new tactics involving the placing of bombs in bus and train stations. Nineteen bomb blasts were recorded in Delhi on May 10 and 11, 1985. Also in 1985, an Air India 747 flight was blown up with the loss of 329 passengers and crew. The bombing was believed to have been carried out by the Sikh militant group Babbar Khalsa (Biswas 2014, 37).

The Punjab Accord was not implemented by the Indian government, and on January 26, 1986, Sikh militants retook control of the Golden Temple complex, but this was short-lived when military action caused them to flee. Police adopted harsh methods to combat the insurgency, including torture, extended detention, and causing young Sikh men to become "disappeared" (Gossman 2002, 263). The government practice of paying rewards to police who eliminated known militants promoted extrajudicial executions, and police maintained secret "hit lists" of those who were to be shot on sight (p. 268). In 1987, the central government took

back control over the state, declaring President's Rule (Biswas 2014, 29).

During early 1988, more than one hundred people each month were being killed. In February 1988, the Punjab was designated a "notified area" under the Terrorists and Disruptive Activities (Prevention) Act 1987 and the Indian Constitution was amended to enable a state of emergency to be declared in Punjab (Juergensmeyer 2003, 91; Wallace 1995, 393). Also in 1988, Operation Black Thunder successfully targeted militants in the Golden Temple complex (Biswas 2014, 29). By this time, the militants had only a low level of support from within Punjab, but the central government did not capitalize on this by stepping in and making a final settlement because of internal political struggles (p. 30). From 1989 to 1993, factions developed within the militants (by some counts there were more than 160 groups operating in the Punjab), and the central government entered a state of "policy inertia," partly because of the difficulty of identifying the correct groups with whom to negotiate (p. 31). In the end, the decision was made to follow an aggressive approach and take advantage of the fragmentation of the movement by conducting a police-led counterinsurgency campaign (p. 31). Sikh militants regarded the rise of the Hindu nationalist party (BJP) as a threat and in January 1992 attacked supporters of the BJP being transported through Punjab, killing five and wounding sixteen others (Juergensmeyer 2003, 89). However, militant groups had lost the support of the people of the Punjab, and by 1993 most militant groups had disbanded or at least ceased operations (Biswas 2014, 32).

In 1995, the Chief Minister of Punjab State, Beant Singh, and fifteen of his aides and security guards were killed in a bombing of the government buildings in the state capital of Chandigarh. The attack was carried out by members of the Babbar Khalsa, one of the Sikh terrorist cells (Juergensmeyer 2003, 86). This event did not signal an escalation but rather the end of the conflict, and by 1998, peace had been restored to the state (Biswas 2014, 32).

The Indian government has largely been able to suppress the Khalistan movement, but diaspora Sikhs, for example, in Canada, the United Kingdom, and the United States, continue to provide resources for the movement (Juergensmeyer 2003, 196). In 2010, it was reported that Sikh terrorism in Canada was "on the rise" (Delaney

2010), and in April 2014, it was reported that Canada would deport a British Sikh with ties to a Sikh terrorist group ("Canada to Deport British Sikh" 2014).

The response of the central Indian government to the violence in Punjab has been criticized for police abuse. Patricia Gossman argues that police pursued a strategy that included the covert extra-judicial execution of suspected militants taken into custody with the overt justification for their death being a police claim that they had been killed in armed "encounters" between police and militants (2002, 262). As well, police formed units to infiltrate militant groups and targeted their leaders. In terms of the framework of India's national security laws, Anil Kalhan and colleagues have argued that "India's antiterrorism laws have functioned more as preventive detention laws than as laws intended to obtain convictions for criminal violations" (Kalhan et al. 2006, 97–98).

The military was able to fence off that part of the Punjab border with Pakistan, and this closed off much support to the militants. Coercive policing and the factionalism that developed among the Sikh militants aided the central government's approach, which, although at times appearing conciliatory, was essentially to treat the situation as an insurgency and apply robust counterinsurgency techniques. Nevertheless, a series of elections assisted in normalizing the situation as well as the central government's willingness to assist the state with building infrastructure in the rural areas (Biswas 2014, 34–35).

Islamic Terrorism—Kashmir

Kashmir has long been a source of contention between India and Pakistan. The root of the conflict is the undecided fate of Jammu and Kashmir at the time of the 1947 partition of India into Pakistan (Muslim) and India (predominantly Hindu). While Hindu- and Muslim-occupied parts of India were divided between the two religious groups, the status of 562 princely states was left unresolved at partition. These included the State of Jammu and Kashmir, which had a predominantly Muslim population but was ruled by a Hindu prince. Kashmir's position was anomalous because it shared borders with both India and Pakistan. When militants from Pakistan made an incursion into Kashmir in October 1947, Pakistan argued they were responding to atrocities committed against Muslims in Kashmir.

The Kashmir ruler sought assistance from India and in return agreed to an Indian annexation of the territory (Bhoumik 2004, 331).

Despite Muslims being the majority community in Kashmir,[31] the rise of Hindu nationalism prompted protests in 1986–87 led by the Muslim United Front. In 1988, elements formed the Kashmir Liberation Front, allegedly supported by Pakistan, which called for Kashmir's secession from India. By May 1989, after incidents of violence with police and demonstrations, the militants began terming themselves *mujahedeen* (holy warriors), characterizing their struggle against the government as a holy war (Juergensmeyer 2003, 92).

In December 1989, the Jammu and Kashmir Liberation Front (JKLF) abducted the daughter of the Indian Home Minister and freed her in exchange for the release of five militants. This event, together with popular protests, caused the central government to impose direct rule on the state in January 1990. From the outset, police and army violated human rights when they shot unarmed demonstrators and summarily executed detainees. The once flourishing tourist industry in the Kashmir Valley virtually collapsed (Biswas 2014, 45). By 1989–90, Pakistan was actively supporting the Kashmiri militants by providing funds and training (p. 46).

By 1992, there was a push for the government to apply similar methods to those used in Punjab, and by 1995, the use of former militants who were in police custody to infiltrate militant groups and assassinate group leaders was a well-established tactic. Militants were promised rewards and protection for their services (Gossman 2002, 272, 275). Several attempts at holding elections in 1994–95 were unsuccessful (p. 275). In its report on human rights for 1996, the U.S. State Department noted that "killings and abductions of suspected militants . . . by pro-government countermilitants emerged as a significant pattern" (p. 278). A state government was finally elected in 1996 (the first since 1990), and by 1996, it was clear that the militants had become weakened and could not secure a military victory against the Indian Army (Biswas 2014, 49).

By early 1999, militants had been driven out of the urban areas in Kashmir, but groups supported by Pakistan were continuing to conduct killings of civilians in other parts of the state (Gossman 2002, 280). In 1999, members of one militant group hijacked an Indian Airlines airliner to Kandahar in Afghanistan (Subramaniam 2012, 398).

In December 2001, a five-man suicide squad, armed with automatic weapons and grenades, drove onto the grounds of India's Parliament in New Delhi. Carrying grenades, they entered the building and gunned down all who came into contact with them. The final death toll was fourteen, including the five terrorists. The terrorists were members of two groups, *Lashkar-e-Tayyiba* (Army of the Righteous) and *Jaish-e-Mohammed* (Army of Muhammad). The latter group was linked to a previous suicide and bombing attack in October 2001 on the legislature of the State of Jammu and Kashmir, which killed thirty-eight people (Bajpai 2003, 113).

The incident at Parliament inflamed tensions between India and Pakistan. By December 19, Indian and Pakistan forces were massing on their borders and exchanging fire, and by December 28, the two sides were firing shells along the border that separates them in Kashmir. Under continuing pressure from India, Pakistan finally reported that it had rounded up more than two dozen militants. While tensions continued for some time, the possibility of a major war was averted after diplomatic efforts by the United States and the United Kingdom brought calm. At one point then President Musharraf of Pakistan denounced "all forms of terrorism—including groups that operate under the pretext of Kashmir" (Smith 2008, 42).

The state conducted elections in 2002, 2005, and 2006. Violence reached a peak in 2001, but from a fatality level of about 4,500 in 2001, the casualty rate dropped to 117 in 2012 (Biswas 2014, 51). In 2010, the state was again subjected to demonstrations and protests when a young Kashmiri was fatally injured by being struck on the head by a tear gas canister while passing by a street protest. This sparked protests against police brutality. The central government intervened with special police units and curfews, and the Indian Army marched through Srinagar for the first time in twenty years (p. 52). In contrast to previous actions, the central government acted quickly to bring the situation under control by releasing prisoners, announcing compensation for those killed or injured, and offering assistance with infrastructure development and education.

The state has been relatively calm since 2010, but the special legislation for the state, that is, the Armed Forces (Jammu and Kashmir) Special Powers Act first introduced in 1990, remains a point of contention because of the extensive powers it grants the military, including an almost total immunity for its actions (Biswas 2014, 52). In terms of the dispute between India and Pakistan over Kashmir, a Composite Dialogue Process that began in 1997 has continued at intervals since then, but the general lack of trust between the two countries is the major problem in finally resolving the dispute (p. 56). It appears that India is intent on keeping the dispute a bilateral matter and has resisted all suggestions that it be internationalized and resolved using different processes (p. 62).

Indian Antiterrorist Laws

The Indian Constitution guarantees fundamental rights of "equality before the law" and "equal protection of the laws" as well as rights to freedom of speech and expression, peaceable assembly, free association, freedom of movement, and residence although Parliament may legislate "reasonable restrictions" on some of these rights in the interests of the "sovereignty and integrity of India," "security of the state," or "public order" (Constitution of India). The Constitution also allows judicial enforcement of these rights to be suspended during periods of declared emergency. The Constitution is actively enforced by the Supreme Court, which has, however, shown great deference to the executive in matters of national security (Kalhan et al. 2006, 116). Following India's colonial legal framework, the Constitution explicitly authorizes preventive detention during ordinary, nonemergency periods that generally may not extend beyond three months without the approval of an advisory board of current or former High Court judges (Kalhan et al. 2006, 134–35).

India was no stranger to emergency and security laws before 9/11. India experienced a period of Emergency Rule from 1975 to 1977 under Prime Minister Indira Gandhi, who suspended the Constitution, ruled by decree, and imprisoned thousands of her political opponents claiming that India faced national security threats from the forces of the opposition (Krishnan 2004, 268). The National Security Act of 1980 applied where a state of emergency had been declared within the country and allowed detention without charge or trial for one year. The period was extended to two years in 1984 for the declared emergency in the Punjab (Finn 2010, 51). The National Security Act represented "the first serious attempt to tackle terrorism" (Vijayakumar 2005, 352).

In 1987, the Terrorist and Disruptive Activities (Prevention) Act (TADA) was enacted in part as a response to the assassination of Prime Minister Indira Gandhi in 1984 by Sikh militants (Krishnan 2004, 266). TADA provided for trials of accused terrorists to be held in camera and created a presumption in law that suspected terrorists were guilty as charged unless they could prove their innocence. It also permitted arrest on suspicion of engaging in terrorism and authorized custody without bail for up to one year, enabling police to detain persons for long periods without bringing any charges (p. 268). In India, confessions to police are generally excluded from evidence because of the need to protect an accused from coercion or torture, but TADA allowed confessions made to senior police officers to be admitted into evidence (R. Singh 2012, 425).

By 1994, more than 76,000 persons had been arrested under TADA, but only about 1 percent had ever been convicted of a crime. In Punjab the conviction rate was 0.37 percent out of about 14,500 persons detained (R. Singh 2012, 428). TADA had a sunset provision that provided for its automatic expiry after two years. It was extended three times but ceased operation in 1995 when public pressure, forthcoming elections, and opposition from the National Human Rights Commission[32] brought it to an end (Krishnan 2004, 268; Vijayakumar 2005, 354).

In 2001, TADA was replaced with a Prevention of Terrorism Ordinance (POTO) made by the President while parliament was not in session.[33] It was justified as a response to a Muslim terrorist bombing in Bombay in 1993 and subsequent attacks attributed by the government to Muslim terrorists. This Ordinance was blocked by opponents who argued that it would be used for the mass arrest of Muslims (TADA had been used for this purpose; Krishnan 2004, 271).

The Prevention of Terrorism Act, 2002 (POTA) was passed in March 2002 after a "bitter debate" between the Hindu nationalist ruling party (BJP) and the opposition (Whitaker 2007, 1026). It contained a provision for its expiry after three years, but it was repealed in October 2004, before its expiry, following the Congress Party victory in elections whose campaign had promised to repeal it (Finn 2010, 77). It drew on the USA Patriot Act in its provisions, allowing the deportation of aliens from India who were suspected of having links to terrorist organizations (Krishnan 2004, 273). Prosecutions under POTA were brought in Special

Courts[34] where evidence rules were relaxed, especially in relation to drawing inferences where an accused exercised his or her right to silence during a criminal trial or was found in possession of weapons or whose fingerprints were found at the place of a terrorist attack (Finn 2010, 46; Krishnan 2004, 283). POTA expanded police powers, provided a broad definition of terrorism, and allowed detention without charge for 180 days. Bail could only be granted with the consent of the prosecutor (U. K. Singh 2012, 429). It also conferred immunity from prosecution on government authorities for actions done in good faith to combat terrorism and allowed the identity of prosecution witnesses to be kept secret (Krishnan 2004, 275, 286).

Beth Elise Whitaker proposes that POTA was used not against terrorists but against political opponents and minorities when state governments used POTA against opposition politicians who spoke in favor of Tamil separatists and against Muslims who attacked Hindus in sectarian violence (2007, 1026). As well, POTA is said to have placed few checks on the exercise of executive and police powers (Krishnan 2004, 266) and to have "established a permissive set of legal rules to prosecute acts of terrorism largely outside the ordinary rules of the regular criminal justice system" (Kalhan et al. 2006, 96). A contrary view is that POTA "was a balanced piece of legislation that has taken national security seriously without diluting too much the rights and liberties of individuals" (Vijayakumar 2005, 362).

The repeal of POTA in 2004 was characterized as merely "cosmetic" because many of its key provisions were reenacted in 2004 and 2008 amendments to the Unlawful Activities (Prevention) Act of 1967 (Kalhan et al. 2006, 100; U. K. Singh 2012, 420). In addition, despite its repeal, prosecutions brought under POTA that were pending on repeal were saved, and a review committee was established to determine which charges should proceed (Whitaker 2007, 1026). Concurrently with the repeal of POTA, states began to enact their own terrorism laws (U. K. Singh 2012, 421). In 2008 the National Investigating Agency Act was passed, providing for the creation of a National Investigating Agency to investigate terror-related offenses for trials in special courts. It could take up any case in the country if so directed by the central government (p. 437).

Ujjwal Kumar Singh (2012, 446) argues that India's regime of antiterrorist laws represents a trajectory that reveals "a deepening reliance on extraordinary laws through a process of normalization and expansion." Laws created for specific and extraordinary situations have been abused in that they have enabled the government, state and federal, to exercise preventive detention powers for non-terrorist purposes and have facilitated and fostered a militaristic strategy in some states rather than an approach that seeks to resolve issues through dialogue (p. 446).

The activist Indian Supreme Court has validated a number of antiterrorist laws, beginning in the 1950s with a decision upholding the Preventive Detention Act. In 1994 the Court upheld the Terrorist and Disruptive Activities (Prevention) Act 1987. The Prevention of Terrorism Act 2002 was challenged in the Court several times, usually without success, although in a few cases the Court narrowed the effect of some provisions. This approach by the Court reflects its continued inclination to allow the government to legislate without much judicial interference in the field of national security (Finn 2010, 69).

Comment

This section's case studies of responses to domestic and international terrorism in three countries (the United States, Germany, and India) reveal differing approaches in responding to terrorism. While each country has enacted laws over time against acts that can broadly be described as terrorism, each reacted to the events of 9/11 by rapidly enacting more such laws, with only Indian leaders engaging in significant debate about the balance between civil rights and security. Each country had a history of terrorism before 9/11, with India and Germany having far greater experience in the field. While the German and U.S. approaches have relied on changes to the law and intrusive policing and, in the case of the United States, military action, India has adopted a predominantly policing and military strategy that has been criticized for abuse of power, especially in the form of extrajudicial killings. While there have been abuses in the exercise of U.S. military power, they have occurred overseas and not domestically as in India. In Germany, thanks to a strong legal framework that protects democratic ideals and the rule of law, the judiciary has not been persuaded to favor security over the protection of civil rights. However, in both India and the United States (the United States to a lesser extent), the courts

have been generally reluctant to challenge executive acts said to be necessary to protect citizens against terrorism, and in the United States the special intelligence court has authorized very intrusive forms of policing. It is remarkable how, despite the abundance of legislation, so few prosecutions for terrorism have been brought in any of these countries.

This brief comparison of countries' antiterrorist strategies provides an added dimension to the issue of responses to terrorism and highlights commonalities and divergences in state policy making, counterterrorist action, and antiterrorist laws.

TERRORIST GROUPS

Our aim in this chapter has been to add context to debates about terrorism, to promote a greater level of awareness of the roots and causes of terrorism and its development over time, and to critically assess assumptions about how terrorism should be countered. This section presents case studies of two designated (by the United States) terrorist groups: Hamas in the Middle East and Boko Haram of Nigeria. The studies explore the history, politics, and social and cultural context associated with each group. What are the aims and objectives of these groups? What methods do they employ to attempt to achieve their aims, and how are their activities countered? What are their beliefs, and why do they conduct acts of terrorism to further them?

Hamas

Hamas is the acronym for *Harakat al-Muqawama al-Islamiya* (Islamic Resistance Movement), but the word also means "zeal" or "fervor" in Arabic (Jenkins 2003, 1). It is an offshoot of the Palestinian Muslim Brotherhood and was founded in 1987 by Shaykh Ahmad Yassin[35] during the Palestinian uprising *(intifada)*,[36] in which it played a leading role against Israeli rule in Gaza and the West Bank (Esposito 2003, 95). Before 1987 the PLO had controlled Palestinian politics and the advent of Hamas was to be a source of concern for the PLO. Hamas gained support from Iran and the Lebanese Shia group Hezbollah (Løvlie 2014, 101) and from Saudi Arabia, Syria, Libya, Sudan, Yemen, and Qatar, either through direct state funding as Iran provides or through the provision of training facilities or safe havens (Levitt 2006, 171).

Becoming the principal alternative to the PLO, Hamas initially operated only against military targets in the occupied territories but later began a campaign of suicide bombings. While justifying its actions on religious grounds, Hamas also relies on an argument that it is acting in self-defense against those employing violence to dispossess Palestinians of the remainder of their land (Kapitan 2004, 185). From the outset, Hamas has struggled to end the Israeli occupation using political action, social welfare, and acts of violence and terrorism (Esposito 2003, 95).

The evolution and actions of Hamas must first be situated within the context of the conflict between Arabs and Jews arising from the situation of Palestine and its designation as a national home for the Jews. Hamas and its actions must also be located in the context of its difficult and complex relationship with the PLO (Fatah).[37] The following discussion adds important dimensions to our understanding of the entity known as Hamas, which is commonly perceived only as a contemporary anti-Israeli terrorist organization.

The Palestinian cause has been a key element in the evolution of contemporary forms of terrorism. The political context to the Palestinian cause is that in the early twentieth century, Palestine was mainly occupied by Arabs. In 1897, Palestine comprised about six hundred thousand persons, 95 percent Arab and 5 percent Jewish (Kapitan 2004, 176). When, following the end of World War II, Jews wished to establish a national home in the land from which they had been expelled long ago, they began to immigrate to Palestine. The policy followed by the Zionist leaders was first, to promote migration into Palestine and second, to encourage Arabs in Palestine to move out to the neighboring Arab countries. The desire for a national home dates back to the foundation of the Zionist movement in the late nineteenth century (p. 176). In 1917, the British, who occupied Palestine, pledged to facilitate it as a national home for the Jews and to allow Jewish immigration. The outcome was that the Jewish proportion of the population went from 8 percent in 1918 to 20 percent by 1931 and by 1948, Jews comprised one-third of the two million occupants of Palestine (p. 176).

By 1918 it had become clear to the British that the Palestinian Arabs would resist, through violent means, the establishment of a Jewish State in Palestine (Kapitan 2004, 177). By 1935, Jewish immigration was running at sixty thousand persons a year, and Arab farmers were being moved off their lands and into the cities (p. 178). In 1937, responding to attacks on Jewish settlements and the British, Jews formed an underground group, the *Irgun Zvai Leumi,* which planted bombs in Arab marketplaces killing hundreds of Arabs (p. 179). By 1939, Britain had abandoned its policy of establishing a Jewish state and was at odds with the Jewish population as it attempted to restrict Jewish immigration. In response, the Irgun bombed the British headquarters at the King David Hotel in Jerusalem, killing ninety persons (p. 179). The British announced in September 1947 that it would no longer govern Palestine (Shughart 2006, 20).

In 1948, the land was partitioned between the Jewish State of Israel and other territories controlled by Arabs following a recommendation of the UN General Assembly. The State of Israel was proclaimed on May 15, 1948. Fighting broke out, and by 1949 Israel controlled over 77 percent of Palestine and about 750,000 Arabs had fled to the West Bank, Gaza, or the surrounding Arab states, especially Jordan, from what was now the State of Israel (Kapitan 2004, 179). The exodus of Palestinians and the creation of a State of Israel "remain crucial markers of Palestinian identity and nationalism," and therefore the conflict with Israel constitutes a force for unity among Palestinians (Løvlie 2014, 102).

Following a series of wars in 1956, 1967, and 1973, millions of Palestine Arabs were expelled from their homes and forced to live in refugee camps on the West Bank of the Jordan River, in the Gaza Strip, and in neighboring Arab states, especially Jordan. Following the 1967 War, radical and revolutionary elements emerged from the Arab population dedicated to expelling the Israelis and regaining Arab lands (Jenkins 2003, 70). Having been unable to defeat Israel through conventional warfare, the radicals turned to guerrilla and terrorist tactics to bring pressure on Israel to meet their demands. During the 1970s and 1980s, waves of attacks took place: hijackings and bombing of aircraft and attacks on airports and embassies worldwide. From the late 1980s, groups like Hamas and Palestinian Islamic Jihad had begun to practice and advocate Islamic fundamentalist doctrines. In 2000, with the outbreak of a fresh wave of violence, the fundamentalists began a campaign of suicide bombing. The aim was to inflict the maximum possible damage (p. 70). This would demonstrate that Israel was unable to protect its citizens because it no longer had a monopoly on the use of violence. Business as usual became impossible when buses and markets might be bombed at any time. Thus, the aim was to create a societal breakdown (p. 71). One of the founders of Hamas, Mahmoud al-Zahar, has justified suicide bombing arguing the following:

> If Israelis are killing Palestine civilians then why are we not using the same means? An eye for an eye. . . . None of them are civilians . . . they say they are a military society and in civil uniform. . . . So don't waste your time in Europe discussing is it civilian or not. . . . This is a dirty war. (Quoted in Onapajo, Uzodike, and Whetho 2012, 341)

Hamas attributes the Palestinian predicament to a loss of faith and to Muslims straying from the true path of Islam. It calls upon all Muslims to exchange their secular culture and ways for a return to religious observance that includes "prayer, fasting, Islamic dress, moral and social values to re-create a proper Islamic society" able to wage a successful *jihad* that will liberate Palestine (Esposito 2003, 96). In contrast to Hamas, the PLO regards the enemy as Zionism, the movement from Europe that created the State of Israel, and seeks a secular state with rights for all citizens. Hamas sees no distinction between Judaism and Zionism and views the Palestinian conflict with Israel as a confrontation between Islam and Judaism. Al-Zahar has asserted that the Israelis "have declared war on Islam" and "we are obliged by our religion to defend ourselves" (quoted in Esposito 2003, 97).

Most of the members of Hamas are professionals and technocrats recruited from a variety of sources, including mosques, schools, and charities. Public support for Hamas has been linked to its social activism as well as its political objectives, and its extensive network of community and charitable projects distinguishes it from other terrorist groups. Through these social welfare programs, Hamas provides emergency cash, food, medical care, and educational services. Rashmi Singh (2012, 532) has suggested that because of these activities, Hamas "is much more than just a terrorist organization and should be seen, first and foremost, as a social movement that is deeply rooted in Palestinian society."

Hamas also engages in political education and protest, competing with the PLO in asserting that it offers a more authentic Islam. A contrary view argues that the social welfare organizations of Hamas report to the same political leaders who conduct terrorist attacks and should not therefore be regarded as distinct from its political and terrorist operations (Levitt 2006, 3).

Hamas maintains a specialized military wing called the Qassam Brigade, operational since 1992, which, operating in small clandestine cells, conducts guerrilla warfare against the Israeli State (Esposito 2003, 98). Hamas is designated by the United States as a foreign terrorist organization (since October 1997). After initially attacking only military and political targets in the occupied territories,[38] Hamas dramatically shifted tactics following the 1993 Oslo Accords[39] and in response to two specific events that took place in Israel and the West Bank and Gaza. The first event, in February 1994, involved a Jewish settler, Baruch Goldstein, who entered a mosque in Hebron and killed twenty-nine worshippers. In response, Hamas began to use suicide bombers, and the Qassam Brigade began attacks on civilian targets within Israel, the most deadly of which occurred in October 1994 in Tel Aviv when a bus was bombed killing twenty-three and wounding nearly fifty persons. The subsequent Israeli assassination of a Hamas bomb-maker led to further Hamas retaliation (Esposito 2003, 99). A second *intifada* began in September 2000. Since 2001 Hamas has included rocket attacks in its tactics. In 2002 Israel reoccupied most of the West Bank in Operation Defensive Shield, dismantled the infrastructure for suicide missions, and imprisoned or killed many militants (Araj and Brym 2010, 850).

Currently, Hamas continues its struggle with Israel, but the agreement reached between Israel and the PLO that resulted in the creation of a Palestinian Authority puts it at odds with both Israel and the PLO. Both Hamas and the PLO claim to constitute the legitimate leadership of the Palestinian national movement. Questions about how to liberate Palestine, how much to liberate, and who is to liberate have occupied the two Palestinian movements (Løvlie 2014, 103). While the PLO has accepted the legitimacy of the State of Israel within its pre-1967 borders, Hamas has never acceded to this position. It therefore boycotted the Palestinian Authority elections but later chose to recognize the election of the late

Yasser Arafat as President of the Palestinian Authority and disassociated itself from militant action (Esposito 2003, 102).

Over the years, the PLO has modified its original secularism and adopted an Islamist stance. For example, the 2003 Constitution of the Palestinian Authority proclaims that Sharia shall be the principal source of laws (Løvlie 2014, 108). Frode Løvlie (2014, 109) proposes that this pragmatic exchange of revolutionary ideals for religiosity can be seen as political maneuvering and as a self-serving alignment with the increasingly religious Palestinian population in the occupied territories. Hamas, on the other hand, proclaimed early its ultimate goal as raising "the banner of Islam on every inch of Palestine" (its Charter declares there is no solution to the Palestinian issue except through *jihad*) and establishing a Palestinian state on what now constitutes the State of Israel and the occupied territories.

Hamas defines Palestine as a *waqf* (an Islamic trust), thereby communicating the imperative that all Muslims are required to liberate Palestine (Løvlie 2014, 110–11).[40] Nevertheless, Løvlie contends that there is evidence of reduced religiosity by Hamas because Hamas official publications from 2005 and 2006 dwell more on practical politics and dilute the religious rhetoric (p. 112). One reason for this is its need to appeal to the median Palestinian voter (p. 114). From 2007 onward, Hamas has governed Gaza but has not taken the opportunity to establish an Islamic, Sharia-based state. Instead, it has "prioritized security over politics" and been preoccupied with contesting control of Gaza with the powerful extremist opposition groups there (Løvlie 2014, 113; R. Singh 2012, 544).

In 2006 in the Palestinian parliamentary elections, Hamas defeated the PLO, but future foreign assistance to the Palestinian Authority was made conditional on Hamas committing to a policy of nonviolence and to recognizing the State of Israel. Hamas's refusal to agree to recognize the State of Israel resulted in a cessation of foreign assistance and to Israel imposing sanctions on the Hamas-led Palestinian Authority. In the 2007 Battle of Gaza, Hamas took control of Gaza, but its officials lost control of the West Bank. In 2011, Hamas and the PLO announced an agreement for a joint caretaker Palestinian government. Using tunnels from Gaza and rocket attacks, Hamas continues to attack Israel. In 2014 the Israel military entered Gaza primarily to destroy rockets and demolish the tunnels.

Boko Haram

Islam is deeply rooted in the northern part of Nigeria, having been established there in the tenth and eleventh centuries by which time major northern cities such as Kano (the North's largest city) were already Muslim or had a significant Muslim presence. At that time, the ethnic group[41] known as the *Hausa* practiced Islam but with significant nonorthodox variations derived from indigenous religious beliefs and practices (Falola and Heaton 2008, 32). These variations were called "innovations" and were challenged as departures from orthodoxy by reformer cleric Shehu Uthman Dan Fodio (1754–1817), an ethnic Fulani living in the then Hausa states (Cook 2011, 4).[42] Dan Fodio, a charismatic orator, believed in a strict interpretation of Islam and led a *jihad* against the Hausa in 1804 to force them to adopt conventional Islamic practice. He achieved this objective and created a theocratic state in the North, the Sokoto Caliphate, that extended into present-day Niger and Chad and which subsisted until 1903 when it fell to British forces (Falola and Heaton 2008, 73). These early religious struggles have a close connection to the present-day situation in the North and to the ideology of Boko Haram and are crucial to understanding the desire of Boko Haram to "purify" Islam in the North and extend it throughout the country (Cook 2011, 4).

The boundaries of the present-day Nigeria were determined arbitrarily by the British colonizers in the late nineteenth and early twentieth centuries and had no association or relationship with the indigenous people who inhabited the regions that now form part of Nigeria (Falola and Heaton 2008, 17). Northern Nigeria received much less attention during the British colonization of Nigeria than did the mainly Christian South. As a consequence, in terms of economic development, infrastructure, and facilities, the North lags behind the rest of the country and the South has "higher levels of westernization" than the North (Onapajo et al. 2012, 345). Outbreaks of violence by radical groups have a long history in northern Nigeria (Waldek and Jayasekara 2011, 168).

The British declared a protectorate over the North in 1897 and ruled in a noninterventionist manner through local chiefs in the process known as indirect rule (Falola and Heaton 2008, 7). In 1914, the British colonial government amalgamated the northern and southern protectorates of Nigeria to form one unified country (p. 6). The

North is divided into thirteen states, with Kano being the largest. In the South, the British established missionary schools staffed by Christian missionaries. The missions were the primary means of bringing education to the people, but only a handful of missions operated in the North where missionary activity was restricted on the grounds of "Islamic cultural preservation" (p. 128). In the North, Western education is nowadays associated with attempts by proselytizing Christians to convert northern Muslims as well as with a general fear of political and economic domination. Within the North, there are ethnic tensions between the various tribal groups (Waldek and Jayasekara 2011, 170).

During the 1980s and 1990s, Christian proselytizing in the middle belt of the country resulted in numerous converts to Christianity. Riots erupted in the North as a response to evangelical crusades and also in relation to the publication of the Danish cartoons of the Prophet Muhammad in 2006 (Cook 2011, 6). As a result, considerable religious tension existed in the area, which, so far as the Muslim population was concerned, could only be eased by the introduction of Sharia law (p. 6). In the early 1980s, the Maitatsine uprisings led by a radical Islamic preacher, Muhammad Mawa, paralleled the ideology of Boko Haram. In both cases, Islamic fomenting of public opinion has tended to subsume other causal factors such as economic deprivation, income inequality, and high levels of poverty exacerbated by drought, cattle diseases, and, in terms of religion, the 1979 Iranian Revolution (Adesoji 2010, 98). Generally, it has proved difficult for civilian administrations to provide good governance for the country, and the lack of stability has resulted in Nigeria being governed by military regimes for twenty-eight of its first forty-seven years of political independence (Falola and Heaton 2008, 9).

During the 1970s and 1980s, disputes between Muslims in the North centered on the different schools of thought among the Muslim community. In addition to the traditional Sufi Muslims, there were conservative and modernist groups and a radical group supported by wealthy Gulf states' Arabs whose mission was to suppress innovations that had occurred under Dan Fodio (Cook 2011, 5). The traditional Sufi Muslims were regarded by the radical group as innovators despite the fact that Dan Fodio himself was a devout Sufi and that most of the history of Islam in northern Nigeria was associated with Sufism (p. 5).

When Nigeria returned to democratic rule in 1999, most of the northern states proclaimed a new, stricter form of Sharia. Decisions taken under that system of law provoked international controversy when, in 2002, a woman was sentenced to death for adultery, even though she said she had been raped (Falola and Heaton 2008, 238). While her sentence (and those sentences imposed on others) was eventually commuted, the international publicity associated with the operation of Sharia created tensions between Christians and Muslims. One example of these tensions occurred in 2002 when the Miss World beauty contest (something not permitted by orthodox Islam) was relocated from Abuja to London after violent protests in the North in which more than two hundred people were killed (p. 239).

The group known as Boko Haram emerged in 1995 under various names but was little known until 2003 when it claimed responsibility for several attacks against officials in two provinces. Calling itself the Nigerian Taliban, the group conducted further attacks against security forces, including the ambush of a police patrol in October 2004 that resulted in the death of fifteen police (Waldek and Jayasekara 2011, 169). The name Boko Haram was not chosen by the group itself which, since 2002, has called itself *Jama'atu Ahlus-Sunnah Lidda'Awati Wal Jihad* (People Committed to the Prophet's Teachings for Propagation and Jihad) but is a name given them by the local communities (Solomon 2012, 6). The origin of the name Boko Haram is contested but is generally accepted as being a statement of the group's opposition to Western education, with the rejection of education symbolizing a rejection of all things Western. The word *Boko* is from the Hausa language (the Hausa being one of the principal ethnic groups of the North); some say it means "book" and others that it is a corruption of the Hausa word *bako* meaning "sorcery" or "witchcraft." It is combined with the Arabic word *haram* meaning "forbidden" so that, taken together, the two words may signify "Western education is sacrilege" (Waldek and Jayasekara 2011, 168).

Boko Haram as a group does not limit its thinking only to Western education but generally espouses an ideology that "rejects all forms of secular authority and seeks to establish a Nigerian state governed entirely by Sharia law" (Waldek and Jayasekara 2011, 170). As well, the group regards the Nigerian State as a stooge of the West and Nigerian Christians as aligned with the West (Onapajo et al. 2012, 342).

Boko Haram rejects the modern economy based on Western ways and culture, forbidden profits, and modern forms of communication that divert attention from the worship of God (Onapajo et al. 2012, 342). The group supports a system of education based on the Qur'an, a political system modeled on that created by the Taliban in Afghanistan, and an economy based largely on trading and farming. It regards the secular Nigerian State as illegitimate and its laws as without validity. State officials are therefore seen as agents for the transmission of Western culture and consequently have been targeted throughout Boko Haram's campaigns of violence. In an interview with the BBC in 2009, Muhammad Yusuf, the founding leader, explained Boko Haram's ideology as follows:

> There are prominent Islamic preachers who have seen and understood that the present Western-style education is mixed with issues that run contrary to our beliefs in Islam. Like rain. We believe it is a creation of God rather than an evaporation caused by the sun that condenses and becomes rain. Like saying the world is a sphere. If it runs contrary to the teachings of Allah, we reject it. We also reject the theory of Darwinism. (Quoted in Cook 2011, 8)

Boko Haram accuses the elites of the North of having failed to properly implement Sharia in the northern states (Onapajo et al. 2012, n344). In 2011, a leader of the group stated in an interview,

> What we are demanding is that those states that have independently declared their states Sharia states should implement it to the letter. Have you seen Sharia cut the hand of someone who steals a cow head, while someone who corruptly enriches himself is left to go free? They [northern elites] have chased away local prostitutes and brought in international red light prostitutes to replace them. They have also banned local alcoholic drinks, yet they drink imported spirits in their respective government houses. Is that Sharia? They are insincere, so they must be effective in the implementation of Sharia. Sharia is being abused. (Quoted in Onapajo et al. 2012, 344–45)

The fact that Sharia law has been enacted in twelve of the northern states has not satisfied Boko Haram, which accuses government leaders in those states of corruption and of adopting Western ways. In fact, when Sharia was applied in 2002 and 2003 in a number of cases of adultery where a punishment of death by stoning was imposed, the resulting international outcry no doubt influenced the overturning of these decisions and has weakened the effectiveness and applicability of Sharia and therefore of an ideal Muslim society (Cook 2011, 8).

Boko Haram's membership was originally from the middle class, especially students from religious schools, and it appears that it is supported by persons of wealth and status within Nigeria (Waldek and Jayasekara 2011, 171). Its current membership comprises unemployed, uneducated urban youth[43] and some civil servants and elites primarily from the North. Some members are citizens of neighboring states such as Mali, Cameroon, Chad, and Niger because of cultural links between the North and ethnic groups in those states (Onapajo et al. 2012, 345).

The founding leader of Boko Haram, Muhammad Yusuf, had a background of participating in activist Muslim movements in Nigeria and debated Muslim issues in the media. In 2006 and 2008 he was arrested on terrorism and violence-related charges but released without charge in both cases. When arrested again on July 25, 2009, he died in police custody. His death is said to be the outcome of a shooting incident when he attempted to escape, and his arrest provoked four days of violence (Cook 2011, 11).[44] It is claimed that he was the victim of an extrajudicial killing. Following his death, reports indicated that the new leader was Mallam Sanni Umaru, who pledged to continue fulfilling Boko Haram's objectives. However, in a video of July 2010, a new leader was announced, Abu Muhammed Abubakar bin Muhammed Shekau, a local Maiduguri businessman (p. 13). According to Cook (p. 13), "Available material does not seem to indicate a central authoritative leadership, but rather one that is local and made up of cells." About a week following Yusuf's death, Umaru issued a statement that included the following passages:

> First of all that Boko Haram does not in any way mean "Western education is a sin" as the infidel media continue to portray us. Boko Haram actually means "Western Civilisation" is

forbidden. The difference is that while the first gives the impression that we are opposed to formal education coming from the West, that is Europe, which is not true, the second affirms our believe in the supremacy of Islamic culture (not Education), for culture is broader, it includes education but not determined by Western Education.

In this case we are talking of Western ways of life which include: constitutional provision as it relates to, for instance the rights and privileges of women, the idea of homosexualism, lesbianism, sanctions in cases of terrible crimes like drug trafficking, rape of infants, multi-party democracy in an overwhelmingly Islamic country like Nigeria, blue films, prostitution, drinking beer and alcohol and many others that are opposed to Islamic civilization. (Quoted in Cook 2011, 14)

The statement asserts that Boko Haram is "a version of the Al Qaeda" and that the group lost more than one thousand members "killed by the wicked Nigerian army and police mostly of Southern Nigeria extraction." The Southern states are said to be the group's "immediate target." The group's aim is to "Islamize Nigeria" and bombings will continue with the aim of making the country "ungovernable." This will include to kill "irresponsible political leaders" and "hunt and gun down those who oppose the rule of Sharia in Nigeria" (quoted in Cook 2011, 14–15).

The Nigerian government has claimed that Boko Haram receives funding from Al Qaeda, but this has not been verified. Private persons who have funded the organization have died at the hands of the police, perhaps through extrajudicial killing, or have been arrested and disappeared (Waldek and Jayasekara 2011, 173). There has also been speculation that prominent religious leaders and northern businessmen have contributed funds (Adesoji 2010, 101).

The terrorist tactics adopted by Boko Haram have generally been small-scale attacks against security forces and infrastructure. It has raided police stations and convoys and seized weapons. It has also conducted targeted assassinations of security force members and local leaders. The first signs of its strategy were revealed in December 2003 when it attacked local government installations and a police station in a village about a mile from its camp and killed thirty people (Cook 2011, 10). At that point it was estimated

that the group comprised about sixty members, all but seven of which were captured. The raid seems to have been aimed at securing weapons. In January 2004, the group attempted an attack on a police station south of the city of Maiduguri, and in June 2004 it attempted a prison break in the capital city of Yobe State which failed. At the conclusion of this initial period of violence, the group attacked a convoy of sixty police in October 2004, taking twelve of them hostage and either executing them or forcing them to join the group. These operations indicated a group of around eight hundred to one thousand members, and the primary aim appears to have been to secure weapons (p. 10).

A period of truce ended in July 2009, and between July 2009 and January 2012, more than 935 persons were killed and many more wounded in 164 attacks. Boko Haram also suffered losses with about 800 members killed by police (Cook 2011, 11). Moreover, Boko Haram has intensified attacks with more than 253 people killed in twenty-one attacks in the first three weeks of 2012. Initially attacks were concentrated in the four northern states of Bauchi, Kano, Yobe, and Borno but have now extended throughout the country, even including the capital, Abuja. A suicide attack on the National Police Headquarters in Abuja was carried out in June 2011; this was the first time such a tactic had been deployed by the group (Waldek and Jayasekara 2011, 174). Other attacks have been against banks, suggesting that the group has to generate funds from robberies (Cook 2011, 21).

In response to the terrorist tactics of Boko Haram, the Nigerian federal government under President Goodluck Jonathan has employed counterterrorist measures intended to halt the group's activities. The government's tactical approach has been to meet violence with violence (Solomon 2012, 6). In July 2009 a security team raided the group's hideout in Bauchi State and nine members were arrested, resulting in violent retaliatory riots in the four states of Bauchi, Kano, Yobe, and Borno. Fighting over the next four days resulted in the destruction of infrastructure, including police stations, prisons, government offices, schools, and churches and seven hundred deaths. It was during this raid that Muhammad Yusuf was arrested and met his death in police custody.

In June 2011, the federal government established a task force in Maiduguri (the capital of, and largest city in, Borno State) that included all units of the armed forces, state security, and the police to adopt a coordinated approach to combating and eliminating Boko Haram (Amnesty International 2011). Checkpoints were also set up around Abuja and a state of emergency declared in areas of the northern states. In all, around thirty thousand army, police, and state security personnel were deployed. As well, the northern border was closed to prevent escapes and halt any flow of reinforcements to Boko Haram from outside the country. Nevertheless, the border remained porous given its length and the terrain. As well as organizing a violent military response in February 2011, the government enacted an antiterrorism law. According to Amnesty International (2011), security forces engaged in "unlawful killings, dragnet arrests, arbitrary and unlawful detentions, extortion, and intimidation" (p. 2). In August 2011 the group targeted the UN headquarters in Abuja, signifying a variation in tactics that had previously seen attacks on only domestic targets. At least eighteen UN staff died in the car bomb attack that destroyed the lower floors of the building ("Abuja Attack" 2011). In a Christmas Day bombing in the same year in Madalla in Niger State, forty-two Christian worshippers were killed. In January 2012 multiple bombings and shootings by group members occurred in Kano State with almost two hundred casualties, and on April 8, 2002, an Easter Day bombing killed thirty-eight people in Kaduna State (Onapajo et al. 2012, 337).

Generally, counterterrorist efforts against Boko Haram are constrained by police lack of intelligence about the group, few trained forensic staff, and an overall lack of general policing capacity. Police rely largely on confession evidence to secure convictions, which are often coerced. In addition, the brutality of the security forces, including practices such as extrajudicial killings, blanket arrests, and extorting and intimidating residents, has proved counterproductive serving only to alienate the civilian population (Solomon 2012, 9). As well, the sheer geographical extent of the North renders much of it inaccessible with poor roads and inadequate communication. It is said the northern border areas, in particular, have always been "bandit country" (Okeowo 2014).

Recently, government strategies have reportedly been supplemented by a populist vigilante-type movement against Boko Haram—a Civilian Joint Task Force made up of volunteers who are professionals, traders, students, and civil servants using machetes and homemade weapons and operating out of Maiduguri, capital of Borno State, a city of more than one million (Okeowo 2014). According to this report, the Force numbers about eight thousand and dispenses a form of summary justice after it has tracked down suspected Boko Haram members. In August 2014, Amnesty International released a video showing what appear to be Nigerian soldiers and Civilian Joint Task Force members cutting the throats of suspected Boko Haram members and pushing them into an open grave. Amnesty accused the Civilian Joint Task Force of making arbitrary arrests and carrying out extrajudicial killings (Okeowo 2014).

Local criticism of the Nigerian Army became more vocal in April 2014 following the kidnapping of about three hundred schoolgirls from Chibok, a town about eighty miles from Maiduguri. Residents claim that the army was told of the possible abduction four hours before its occurrence, but military reinforcements did not arrive. There have been complaints that soldiers have deserted to avoid engagements with Boko Haram and have not been paid, affecting their morale.[45] As the Civilian Joint Task Force gains confidence and strength, residents fear that members may use their power to intimidate enemies of Force members. The Force reportedly works closely with the government Joint Task Force known as Operation Restore Order or JTORO. A 2014 report (Nossiter 2014) indicates that the group is continuing attacks in the North. On December 1, 2014, two attacks—one a suicide bombing of a market by two women and the other an attack on military police and security facilities—were carried out in state capitals. It appeared Boko Haram was trying to seize weapons in the latter attack, which failed after militants were driven off by a Nigerian Air Force jet. Another attack occurred on July 2 and 3, 2015, in Borno, killing two hundred people (Akubakar 2015). A regional fighting force comprised of Nigeria, Niger, Chad, Cameroon, and Benin planned to deploy 8,700 troops at the end of July 2015 (Akubakar 2015).

Questions about the terror campaign of Boko Haram have focused on the cause of the terrorism, which has been associated with the motivations of individual members, the founder's ideology, revenge, the benefits to be gained from membership, and the inadequacies of governance in Nigeria (Adesoji 2010, 95). Religious tensions and sensitivities both historically and in the present clearly are a key element. One scholar has suggested that the accomplishments of the group can be attributed to

> the prevailing economic dislocation in Nigerian society, the advent of party politics (and the associated desperation of politicians for political power), and the ambivalence of some vocal Islamic leaders, who, though they did not actively embark on insurrection, either did nothing to stop it from fomenting, or only feebly condemned it. These internal factors coupled with growing Islamic fundamentalism around the world make a highly volatile Nigerian society prone to violence, as evidenced by the Boko Haram uprising. (Adesoji 2010, 95)

Whether Boko Haram has transnational linkages with other terrorist groups remains an open question, but the United States and others believe there is evidence of Boko Haram having gained knowledge from these groups[46] and having received training from them in Somalia and Mali (Onapajo et al. 2012, 338, 347). There is no clear evidence suggesting any link between Boko Haram and Al Qaeda or its affiliates such as Al Qaeda in the Maghreb, which, in any event, is largely focused on the North of Africa (Cook 2011, 32; Waldek and Jayasekara 2011, 170).[47]

The United States designated Boko Haram as a foreign terrorist organization on November 14, 2013.[48] Scholars associated with Nigeria within the United States argued against this action, claiming that it would "internationalise Boko Haram's standing and enhance its status among radical organizations elsewhere" (Onapajo et al. 2012, 349). Nigeria has received U.S. assistance in its antiterrorist campaign in the form of military training and collaboration with the FBI as well as funding of at least eight million dollars (p. 349). The African Union has also designated the group as a terrorist group along with Somalia's Al-Shabaab and Uganda's Lord's Resistance Army (p. 351). It is believed that were Boko Haram able to establish some kind of Islamic state in northern Nigeria, it would seek to incorporate other states in the region where there are ethnic and traditional ties, such as Cameroon, Niger, and Chad (Cook 2011, 24).

Nonmilitary, nonviolent strategies to counter Boko Haram have been proposed, including an economic development package for the North, where poverty is acute and is widely regarded as an outcome of government neglect, corruption, and abuse (Onapajo et al. 2012, 350). Scholars have urged that attention be given to the "root causes" of the movement (Adesoji 2010, 104).

The ideology of Boko Haram is fundamentally the same as that proclaimed by the Egyptian Muslim Brotherhood (established in 1928) and the Pakistan Jamaat-i-Islami (established in 1941), which "became the primary models for new activist organizations across the Muslim world" and which place "primary blame for the ills of their society and the decline of the Muslim world upon European imperialism and Islamized Muslim elites" (Esposito 2003, 50–51). The statements of Boko Haram concerning the West and Western influences can be traced back to the words of Ayatollah Khomeini after the Iranian Revolution when he said,

> The foul claws of imperialism have clutched at the heart of the lands of the people of the Qur' an with our national wealth and resources being devoured by imperialism. . . . With the poisonous culture of imperialism penetrating to the depths of our towns and villages throughout the Muslim world, displacing the culture of the Qur' an. (Quoted in Esposito 2003, 76)

Consequently, for the members of Boko Haram, only through *jihad* and following a "straight path of Islam" will Muslim pride, success, and power be restored and the Islamization of society be achieved (Esposito 2003, 53).

Notes

1. Bassiouni (2002, 85) points out that terrorists' selection of targets is based on expectations of media attention, and that extensive media attention often causes an overreaction by the government which in turn "tends to undermine the legitimacy of the state's response and to give such groups more legitimacy in the eyes of their constituencies."

2. The U.S. Department of State publishes a list of "Designated Foreign Terrorist Organizations" under the Immigration and Nationality Act.

3. Held (2004, 65) points out that "news reports frequently equate terrorism with evildoing" and that

"politicians often use the term as an automatic term of abuse."

4. Saul (2006, 5) points out that the absence of an internationally agreed definition of terrorism renders problematic the UN Security Council's requirement that states implement measures against terrorist acts and terrorists.

5. According to the Qur' an, "To die for one's faith is the highest form of witness to God." "When *jihad* is invoked to urge Muslims to take part in wars against nonbelievers, its main motivator is the belief that someone who is killed on the battlefield, called a *shahid,* will go directly to Paradise" (Esposito 2003, 69).

6. Leon Trotsky wrote that "the revolution does require of the revolutionary class that it should attain its end by all methods at its disposal—if necessary by an armed rising; if required, by terrorism" (Trotsky 2007, 55). For Trotsky, "The question of the form of repression, or its degree, of course, is not one of 'principle.' It is a question of expediency" (p. 55).

7. In raids on Tokyo from March 9–10, 1945, American incendiary bombing caused a firestorm that killed at least 80,000 persons and destroyed 250,000 buildings (Lackey 2004, 132).

8. The seminal work on the history of terrorism is Walter Laqueur's *Terrorism,* published in 1977 and subsequently updated and retitled *The Age of Terrorism* in 1987.

9. The period of violence that followed the French Revolution between September 1793 and July 1794 was known as the "Reign of Terror." It was distinguished by mass executions of those considered to be enemies of the Revolution and symbolized by the guillotine.

10. The British gave the name Stern Gang to a radical offshoot of the Irgun, *Lohameni Herut Yisrael* (Freedom Fighters for Israel) known as *Lehi,* who adopted a strategy of political assassination (Shughart 2006, 19).

11. Franz Fanon was a black psychiatrist born in Martinique in the Caribbean who was posted as a staff physician in a hospital in the French colony of Algeria during the 1950s.

12. The Weathermen, later named the Weather Underground and the Weather People, were responsible for nineteen bombing incidents within the United States over a four-year campaign in the late 1960s and early 1970s. They emerged out of the organization known as Students for a Democratic Society (Shughart 2006, 23).

13. Gage (2011, 89) points out that the narrative of left-wing terrorist organizations in the United States in this period usually ignores the coexistence of abundant right-wing terrorism, for example, the Ku Klux Klan.

14. More than one hundred aircraft hijackings occurred every year during the 1970s (Rapoport 2001, 421).

15. Paul Smith (2008, 70) correctly points out that the rise of cable television and satellite broadcasting has enabled spectacular terrorist events to reach a worldwide audience; for example, the Black September attack at the 1972 Munich Olympics was seen by more than eight hundred million people.

16. Esposito (2003, 36) points out that although Islam is the second largest world religion "many in the West knew nothing about it until Iran's Islamic revolution catapulted Islam into the consciousness of the world."

17. The Islamic community comprises Sunni and Shia Muslims. Shia means the party or followers of Ali and Shia comprise only about 15 percent of the Muslim community (2003, 36). Following the death of the Prophet Muhammad in 632 CE, a crisis occurred over his successor—should it be the most pious Muslim, or should it be a direct descendant of the Prophet? The companions of the Prophet acted quickly to select Abu Bakr, the father-in-law of the Prophet as his successor or *caliph.* The majority who accepted this decision became known as Sunni, meaning followers of the *Sunnah,* the example of the Prophet. The minority, the Shia, rejected this choice of Abu Bakr, arguing that before his death the Prophet had designated the senior male of his family, Ali, who was the Prophet's cousin and son-in-law, to be leader or *Iman* of the community. While Ali did become the fourth *caliph,* he was assassinated after five years of rule and later his son suffered death during the battle of Karbala. This death symbolized for the Shia, the profound injustice of the world (Esposito 2003, 37). Iran is the only totally Shia Islamic nation (Shughart 2006, 28).

18. *Madrassas* are Islamic religious schools.

19. For example, on November 19, 2014, Reuters reported that Israel had blown up the home of a twenty-one-year-old man who had in the previous month run over and killed two persons at a Jerusalem tram stop and had been subsequently shot dead by the police (Lewis 2014). Israel had ceased this method of retaliation in 2005 after it was introduced in the late 1960s, but it has been revived. The assumption behind the practice of demolishing houses is that it will deter suicide bombers because of the pain that would be suffered by their families; however, no correlation has ever been shown between suicide bombers and housing demolition, and in any event, families are usually compensated when this occurs. Ami Pedahzur and Arie Perliger (2010, 342) argue that the policy "increased the animosity of Palestinians toward Israel" and "undermined some of the basic foundations of a democratic regime, such as the dictates to avoid collective punishment and to adhere to the laws that enforce domestic and international civil liberties" (p. 343).

20. A good example of ignorance of Islam is the fact that the majority of the world's Muslims live in Asia and Africa and not in the Arab world, and only about one in five Muslims worldwide is Arab. The largest Muslim communities are in Indonesia, Bangladesh, Pakistan, India, and Nigeria, and not, as so commonly presented in the media, in Saudi Arabia,

Egypt, or Iran. In the United States, Islam is the third largest religion (Esposito and Mogahed 2007, 2).

21. A *fatwa* is, according to the Islamic Supreme Council of America, "an Islamic legal pronouncement, issued by an expert in religious law *(mufti)*, pertaining to a specific issue, usually at the request of an individual or judge to resolve an issue where Islamic jurisprudence *(fiqh)*, is unclear. Typically, such uncertainty arises as Muslim society works to address new issues—issues that develop as technology and society advance" (http://www.islamicsupremecouncil.org/understanding-islam/legal-rulings/44-what-is-a-fatwa.html).

22. Juergensmeyer (2003, 31, 32) suggests that Timothy McVeigh, the convicted bomber of the Oklahoma federal building, had been exposed to Christian Identity ideas through publications that included the notorious *Turner Diaries,* said to be his favorite book or "bible." Published in 1978, *The Turner Diaries,* which became an underground classic, describes an apocalyptic battle between the U.S. federal government and freedom fighters.

23. *Infidel* is a term used to refer to someone with no religious beliefs or to someone outside of one's religion. Under Islam it refers to "unbelievers" of Allah or of the Prophet Muhammad and who can also be considered ritually impure and unclean.

24. The concept of *hijira* was co-opted by Osama bin Laden to describe his departure from his home in Saudi Arabia to Afghanistan. This practice of reaching back into the past to situate one's own actions in an Islamist framework has been used by both mainstream and extremist movements (Esposito 2003, 32).

25. This practice of issuing *fatwas* is followed today, so for example, during the Gulf War against Saddam Hussein's *jihad,* Muslim leaders secured *fatwas* to legitimate their participation in the coalition of forces and Saudi Arabia obtained a *fatwa* to authorize the presence of U.S. troops in that Kingdom (Esposito 2003, 34).

26. An *iman* is a religious leader or cleric of a mosque who provides religious guidance. *Iman* can also be used to refer to a Muslim scholar.

27. United Nations Treaty Collection, https://treaties.un.org/Pages/DB.aspx?path=DB/studies/page2_en.xml

28. Many of the provisions of the USA Patriot Act had been formulated and rejected during the Clinton administration (Finn 2010, 42).

29. In March 2013 a federal judge found these letters to be unconstitutional, but this decision was appealed in October 2014 ("Appeals Court to Determine" 2014).

30. Although policing and public order are under state control in India's federal system, there are several federal paramilitary forces, with a total force strength of over 685,000, that can be deployed to assist state police. Commonly, these forces may be deployed only following a request from a state, but the scope of the central government's authority to deploy these forces

has been controversial (Kalhan et al. 2006, 113). Senior police are under the control of the center, not the states, and the Indian Army may be deployed in aid of the civil power and has regularly been granted special powers of arrest and detention whenever this power has been exercised (p. 114).

31. Kashmir was, and is, the only Muslim-majority state in India (Biswas 2014, 42). It is given special treatment under the Indian Constitution in that Article 370 restricts the power of the Indian parliament to make laws relating only to defense, communications, and foreign relations. In all other areas of law making, the center requires the agreement of the state. This appears to give Kashmir a greater level of autonomy than all other Indian states (p. 42).

32. Among its comments, the National Human Rights Commission stated that TADA was "draconian in effect and character," made "considerable deviations from the normal law," and was "incompatible with India's cultural traditions, legal history and treaty obligations" (U. K. Singh 2012, 427).

33. Under Indian law, an Ordinance is essentially a temporary Presidential executive order that has to be put to parliament to be a duly enacted law or it will cease to have effect. The Ordinance was therefore a stopgap measure until parliament reconvened to enact POTA (U. K. Singh 2012, 429).

34. The regular Indian criminal courts face huge backlogs of cases, and there is a practice in India of creating special courts to deal with specific criminal issues that gain public attention, thereby bypassing the regular justice system (Krishnan 2004, 280).

35. Yassin was assassinated by Israeli security forces on March 22, 2004 (Levitt 2006, 203).

36. The first Palestinian intifada began in December 1987 and lasted until 1993 when the Oslo Accords were concluded (Løvlie 2014, 116).

37. *Fatah* was founded in the late 1950s by Palestinian university students led by Yasser Arafat and Khalil Wazir. In 1969 Fatah gained control of the PLO, which had been created in an Arab summit meeting in 1964 (Araj and Brym 2010, 843). Fatah emerged as a "leftist liberation movement dependent on Soviet sponsorship" and modeled on movements of the time in Algeria, Cuba, and Vietnam; as a result, it adopted a secular ideology combined with nationalist rhetoric. After the 1979 Iranian Revolution, Fatah began to supplement its secular ideology with references to Islam (Løvlie 2014, 101, 107).

38. The occupied Palestinian territories are the West Bank (including East Jerusalem) and the Gaza Strip, which Israel occupied in the 1967 War and has continued to occupy since then. In 1980, Israel annexed East Jerusalem and declared its capital to comprise all of the city of Jerusalem. The annexation is not recognized internationally.

39. The Palestinian Authority was formed in 1994 under the Oslo Accords between the PLO and

Israel as a five-year interim body. Further negotiations were to take place regarding its final status, but this has not occurred. The Accords involved five main principles: (1) recognition of the PLO as the legitimate representative of the Palestinians, (2) recognition of Israel's right to exist, (3) the renunciation by the PLO of terrorism and violence, (4) agreement by Israel to withdraw by stages from the West Bank and Gaza, (5) the creation of the Palestinian Authority to govern Gaza and the West Bank (Araj and Brym 2010, 844).

40. In a poll taken in 2010, 82 percent of Palestinians said they preferred a theocratic rather than a secular state (Løvlie 2014, 118).

41. Nigeria has a very diverse population with more than two hundred ethnolinguistic groups, but three groups predominate. The Hausa in the North make up about 21 percent of the population, the Yoruba in the Southwest another 20 percent, and the Igbo of the Southeast with 17 percent. Most Nigerians are either Christian or Muslim with about 50 percent Sunni Muslim who are concentrated in the northern savannas where Islam first appeared (Falola and Heaton 2008, 4).

42. Before the *jihad* of Dan Fodio, Islam was a religion of the elite. Kings and merchants adopted the faith to facilitate commercial and diplomatic ties with North Africa and the Middle East (Falola and Heaton 2008, 4).

43. Nigeria's population is overwhelmingly young. In 2005, it was estimated that 64.7 million citizens were under the age of 24 and only 2.9 percent over the age of 65 (Falola and Heaton 2008, 5).

44. Yusuf's death was videotaped by soldiers and later broadcast on television (U.S. House of Representatives 2011, 6). Cook (2011, 11) reports that Yusuf was beaten by police, forced to beg for his life (all videotaped), and then summarily shot.

45. It is said that senior commanders did not take the threat of Boko Haram seriously (U.S. House of Representatives 2011, 24).

46. It is argued that Boko Haram has acquired knowledge and supplies of high explosives and bomb-making techniques that would not have been possible without links to other terrorist groups (Onapajo et al. 2012, 347).

47. The view of the commander of U.S. Africa Command, however, is that Boko Haram intends to coordinate its campaign with Al Qaeda in the Maghreb and internationalize its efforts, perhaps also in association with the Somali militant group Al-Shabaab (Solomon 2012, 8). Boko Haram has publicly claimed that it has sent fighters to Somalia and Yemen for training.

48. U.S. law requires that to be designated a foreign terrorist organization (FTO), the organization must be foreign; it must engage in terrorist activity or terrorism as defined under laws administered by the Department of State, or retain the capacity and intent to engage in terrorist activity or terrorism; and the organization's terrorist activity or terrorism must threaten the security of U.S. nationals or the national security of the United States (U.S. House of Representatives 2011, 26–27). According to Michael Sheehan (2004, 105), designation as an FTO serves as an instrument in gathering international antiterrorist support and as "an important signaling effect for other countries."

13

VIOLENCE AGAINST WOMEN

Globally, research has revealed that violence against women is a universal, systemic phenomenon that takes many forms, including

- violence against women within the family (including domestic violence, harmful traditional practices such as female circumcision, marital rape, and honor crimes);

- violence against women in the community (including femicide, sexual violence by non-partners, sexual harassment and trafficking, and honor crimes);

- violence against women authorized and condoned by the state (including women in custody suffering violence, allowing domestic violence to be perpetrated on women through inadequate laws or poor implementation of laws, and forms of forced sterilization); and

- violence against women in armed conflict (including unlawful killings, torture and other cruel, inhuman, or degrading treatment or punishment, abductions, maiming and mutilation, forced recruitment of women combatants, rape, sexual slavery, sexual exploitation, arbitrary detention, forced prostitution). (United Nations 2006, 40–44)

These categories of violence are considered to be violence against women because these kinds of violence are experienced by women at least partly because they are women. In this chapter we focus on domestic violence, honor crimes, and violence against women in armed conflict, specifically examining rape.

Over the past twenty-five years, the approach of the international community to violence against women, as expressed through the United Nations, has changed from a focus on crime control and criminal justice to one based on human rights (Connors 2005, 22). For this reason, the UN Secretary-General's report *In-Depth Study of All Forms of Violence Against Women* (United Nations 2006) states that violence against women has been recognized internationally as a form of discrimination and therefore as a violation of human rights.

Within the human rights framework, the specific causes of such violence are to be found in systemic gender-based discrimination against women and other forms of subordination. Violence against women "is a manifestation of

Research in the United States and elsewhere indicates that the majority of DV survivors leave the perpetrator of the abuse, often after having attempted to overcome the violence through actions such as temporary separation, seeking outside interventions, and using self-defense. A woman's options in responding to DV are often constrained by circumstances such as community attitudes, availability of local resources to assist, and access to financial help. Thus, the specific circumstances of the woman must always be taken into account in trying to understand her response to acts of DV (Ellsberg et al. 2001, 547–48).

Why do women remain in abusive relationships? Women worldwide give similar reasons for remaining in abusive relationships. These reasons include "fear of reprisals, shame and self-blame, economic and emotional dependence on the abuser, concern for the children, lack of support from family and friends, and the hope that 'he will change'" (Ellsberg et al. 2001, 548). Even when women do seek assistance, they often face institutional and personal barriers based on attitudes and perceptions about DV generally, and in some countries, on customs and traditions that condone a level of DV as a cultural norm. Feminist scholars regard the home as an unsafe place for women because it is structured and controlled by men, but women are aware of the dangers of the home and devise coping strategies to survive violence. Accordingly, remaining in an abusive relationship speaks to women's knowledge of the men in their lives (Walklate 1995, 91).

What have studies revealed about attitudes toward DV? Multiple factors affect attitudes toward DV against women, but gender and culture are powerful influences. Gender and culture intersect as cultural contexts weave together norms and gender relations that shape attitudes to violence. Other influences not discussed here include individual factors (the experience of witnessing violence, age, and development), organizational factors (sports, universities, religions), community factors (peer groups and informal social relations, religion), and societal factors (media, social movements, laws, criminal justice policies; Flood and Pease 2009, 137).

Attitudes toward DV are important because they influence and shape the perpetration of the violence, institutional and individual responses to it, and responses to it by the victim and others (Flood and Pease 2009, 125). Attitudes are formed by a wide range of social processes and translate into a causal relationship to the perpetration of DV. Thus, men with traditional, misogynistic gender-role attitudes are more likely to engage in DV and to accept its use. Conversely, those who hold egalitarian gender attitudes will have less tolerance of DV. Men who sustain sexist, patriarchal, and/or sexually hostile attitudes are more likely to be associated with DV (p. 126). In other words, norms about gender and sexuality shape judgments on violence against women. Traditional and long-standing social and gender norms and beliefs, embedded in legal systems, legitimize the following norms and beliefs through, if necessary, using DV:

- In order to maintain the dominant role in households, men may have to physically discipline women.

- Men have uncontrollable sexual urges that must be satisfied when they so choose.

- Women are deceiving and malicious.

- Marriage gives a man the right to assume consent to sexual relations.

- Female victims of DV who are verbally aggressive or act in ways that are perceived to inspire their husband's jealousy should be judged more harshly.

A gender gap has been found to exist in violence against women: men are more likely than women to agree with beliefs supporting violence against women, perceive a smaller number of behaviors as violent, blame and fail to empathize with the victim, minimize the harm resulting from a violent assault, and regard violence against women as less serious (Flood and Pease 2009, 127). This gap, however, has been closing, and this is best shown in the United States where, since the 1970s, there has been "a dramatic and widespread liberalization of gender role attitudes" (p. 129).

The cultural context within which violence against women occurs is an important factor in attitudes toward DV. Attitudes vary across cultural groups and from one nation to another. For example, one U.S. study found that Southeast Asian respondents were more supportive of the use of violence and of male privilege than East Asian respondents (Flood and Pease 2009, 130). As the discussion of honor crimes (see "Violence Against Women: Honor Crimes," later in this chapter) indicates, key elements in so-called honor cultures include traditional attitudes to gender, a firm belief in male dominance, norms of female chastity, and the centrality of the role of the family. Accordingly, in such cultures, both men and women are more tolerant of men's violence toward women (p. 130).

However, attitudes shaped within one culture toward DV are dynamic and may change as people move from a more violence-prone cultural context to a less violent, more supportive one. Conversely, some immigrant groups may import their cultural norms into a new cultural context as occurs with honor crimes. Of course, within a culture, changes can also occur because cultures are not frozen in time or immutable

(Flood and Pease 2009, 130). In a number of traditional cultures such as the !Kung of Botswana, physical aggression and "any form of harsh treatment more severe than an occasional scolding" were strongly discouraged. Previously a hunter-gatherer society, the !Kung have now settled, but elements of their former way of life (e.g., living in close proximity to one's kin and living mostly out of doors in full view of others) continue to offer women protection from possible abuse by their husbands (Draper 1999, 58, 61–63).

Box 13.1 presents case studies of two contrasting cultures from the developing country of Papua New Guinea that reveal opposite attitudes to DV.

BOX 13.1   Wife Beating in Kaliai, Papua New Guinea

The Lusi-Kaliai people of the West New Britain Province, Papua New Guinea, say that wife-beating is common and village women (there are five villages) expect to be beaten by their husbands sometime during their marriage. Women strike their children and fight with their co-wives, and adults laugh with approval when older children hit those who are younger. In the past, marriages were between people of the same or neighboring villages, and wives lived only two or three hours from their natal families. Nowadays, wives may live days away from their families as young educated partners choose their partner from friends in high school or from another town they have visited. Domestic violence does not usually result in serious injury because onlookers intervene to prevent this from happening. Both men and women believe a husband is entitled to hit his wife for cause, for example, if she flirts with men, commits adultery, draws blood in punishing the children, fails to perform her domestic obligations, publicly shames or insults her husband, or fights with co-wives.

While both men and women agree that domestic violence is customary, there are clear limits that situationally define the level of abuse that is considered acceptable. The parameters surrounding abuse levels include the wife's perceived offense and the willingness of her kin to give her support. A woman's kin will usually intervene where the beating is prolonged, if the husband publicly exposes her genitals, kicks her like a dog, draws blood, or hits her with a weapon larger than a small stick. Women do not often fight back for fear of more violence or public shaming, but they may return to their relatives who may or may not accept them because leaving the marriage means returning the bride wealth they received on marriage. An abused woman may also make sorcery against her husband by collecting his hair or cigarette butts and using them in the sorcery to cause illness.

SOURCE: Counts 1999, 73.

Wape Men Don't Beat Their Wives

The Wape people live in the Sandaun Province of Papua New Guinea in a mountainous tropical forest environment where they live by slash and burn horticulture. The Wape number about ten thousand and live in villages. There are several factors that render Wape society less prone to domestic violence. In their society, emotions are to be kept under control, especially those that might result in violence. Accordingly, children who become aggressive toward others are left

(Continued)

(Continued)

alone, and being aggressive in public brings only embarrassment. The Wape have been socialized toward nonviolence through fear of supernatural retribution by their ancestors if they do not control their anger. They believe that on death, the spirit returns to clan lands in the forest and is a frequent visitor to the village, where the spirit takes care of its descendants by sending illness and bad luck to enemies of the family.

As well as the power of the ancestors, the Wape tend to minimize gender differences. While they recognize the gender division of labor, they do not follow many of the gender rules found in many Papua New Guinea societies. For example, their boys and girls play together, menstruating mothers and daughters are not secluded in menstrual huts to avoid polluting the male but stay at home with their husbands and continue to eat food prepared by the wife, and boys are not secluded from their mothers and sisters for initiation into manhood. A critical factor in the absence of domestic violence is that the women produce most of the food. Typically the Wape consume sago and boiled greens, a diet sometimes supplemented with a little meat, but due to the prevalence of shotguns, the local game has all but been totally depleted. Consequently, a husband has become dependent on his wife for food. A diet of sago is deficient in protein and calories, and the Wape region suffers from poor soils. Thus, the nature of the diet may be a contributing factor in the domestic peace found among the Wape.

When a woman believes she is being abused, she will immediately move in with her relatives, stay for a week or more, and then return with them to her house. The husband may not seek to have her return. Women develop strong bonds. When a husband and wife begin to shout at each other, women in the village, a few carrying sticks, will go to the house until the wife comes outside to join them. Shaming is an important element in domestic violence. When domestic violence does occur, it may cause a wife to attempt suicide to shame her husband for humiliating or shaming her through anger or violence.

SOURCE: Mitchell 1999, 100.

Measuring Domestic Violence

The Conflict Tactics Scale (CTS) and Revised CTS are commonly used internationally to measure both lifetime and twelve months' prevalence of violence. The CTS lists behaviors used in resolving conflicts ranging from "discussed the issue calmly" to "used a knife or gun," and respondents are asked which of the specified behaviors they used (Ferraro 2006, 18). There are eighteen items that are intended to assess how interpersonal conflict was handled. One item is "verbal aggression" (from insults and swearing to throwing, smashing, hitting, or kicking something). It therefore measures both physical and psychological acts of violence but not attitudes toward violence (Straus, Hamby, Boney-McCoy, and Sugarman 1996, 283).

The CTS has been criticized on a number of grounds, some of which were addressed by the Revised version, but the introduction to the CTS is said to be problematic. Respondents are introduced to the CTS as a survey document and informed that the items on the scales constitute a list of ways of "settling differences." This seems, to many, to be an inappropriate formulation because while some will consider violent experiences to be ways of settling differences, others will not. Thus, acts of aggression by men to women are often not preceded by any argument or disagreement that amounts to a precipitating factor (Dobash and Dobash 1998, 28).

Another issue with surveys generally on DV is the tendency in cross-cultural research to assume that concepts and meanings are universal. Consequently, a survey that has been developed in the United States and applied there is unproblematically translated into another language, administered in other countries, and then used to make "cross-cultural comparisons." A better approach is to first ask intended respondents for their definitions of what in the West is termed *domestic violence* because many countries do not have a term in local languages that describes abuse as applied by English speakers to this form of aggression. Accurate and adequate translation and discovering the correct local terms for the subject of the survey are therefore critical issues in research among different cultures (Malley-Morrison 2004, 11). More generally, as noted by Madeline Fernández (2006, 258), specific cultural beliefs should be considered key elements in designing and implementing strategies to combat DV.

Theories Concerning Domestic Violence

In attempting to explain DV, numerous theories have been advanced, many of which see the roots of this violence in *patriarchy*, "a system of social structures and practices in which men dominate, oppress and exploit women" (quoted in Ferraro 2006, 78). In the traditional ideology of patriarchy, men are the providers and heads of households while women provide emotional support and domestic services, but the exact nature of patriarchy differs depending on culture and context (p, 79). Patriarchy as a system of domination and oppression has been embedded in social and cultural norms and in global and local economies and institutionalized in the law and in political structures. It is rooted in public discourse and thinking and while it limits women's choices, it does not render women helpless or without power as the history and development of the women's movement clearly shows (United Nations 2006).

Patriarchy is shaped by its history in a particular place and functions in different ways. It is a product of colonialism, armed conflict, and migration and is influenced by race, culture, ethnicity, class, and other factors. It is crucial, therefore, in any analysis of violence against women to contextualize women's experience of such violence to not only reveal the absence of women's power but also to make explicit how women exercise agency and control over their lives even in an environment of subordination. The relationship between violence against women and patriarchy was expressed in a decision of the South African Constitutional Court in 1999. The Court said that the Constitution of South Africa required the state to provide protection from DV and that "to the extent that it is systemic, pervasive and overwhelmingly gender-specific, domestic violence both reflects and reinforces patriarchal domination, and does so in a particularly brutal form" (quoted in United Nations 2006, 30).

There is no single unified feminist perspective on DV, but the approach of all feminist research is to address the question "Why do men beat their wives?" (Bograd 1988, 13). Feminist approaches to DV may apply various principles.

- *Radical feminist principles* argue that gender-based violence can only be completely eliminated following a fundamental reorganization of international and state structures of power. Only by restructuring legal systems to include women's concerns and interests will gender equality be achieved and violence against women eliminated (MacKinnon 1987, 40). Radical feminism is criticized for presuming that all men exercise the same power and control over their own lives as they have over women. Of all the feminist positions, radical feminism has been the most vocal on gender and violence (Walklate 1995, 40, 95).

- *Liberal feminist principles* work for political and civil equality within the existing social order and advocate for changes in the law that will bring about equality of rights and equal opportunity (Walklate 1995, 38). Liberal feminists are criticized for simply seeking to move toward the male standard (Dobash and Dobash 1992, 24).

- *Cultural feminist principles* apply a psychological approach and argue that women have their own moral perceptions and their own ways of thinking and believing. Much cultural feminism has developed out of the work of Carol Gilligan. Cultural feminists, also known as psychoanalytic feminists, have been criticized for concentrating exclusively on the workings of the psyche and ignoring societal factors such as race and class (Tong 1989, 157 172).

- *Postmodern feminist principles* criticize attempts to produce a "grand narrative" or to find universal truths and instead focus on identity and multiple viewpoints. They argue that knowledge is always partial and that the subject does not exist but rather is produced through discourse. They examine the multiple and shifting dimensions of women's oppression and reject the notion that it can be reduced to a single or universal set of factors (Kapur 2005, 103–4; Tong 1989, 222).

- *Third-world feminist principles* criticize what they regard as an overemphasis on gender to the detriment of other salient factors, such as race, diversity among women, colonialism, and the effects of globalism on women's economic status, lack of wealth, and the feminization of poverty (Mohanty 1988, 61).

Social learning theory, also known as *the cycle of violence*, argues, for example, that boys who witness the use of violence by one parent against another may come to believe that violence is an effective instrumental strategy (Flood and Pease 2009, 131). Studies of the effect on girls of witnessing such violence are inconclusive, however. In a wider sense, the association between witnessing violence by adults may also reflect the generational learning of such norms within a local community (p. 131). The individualistic focus of the cycle of violence model has been criticized for pathologizing behaviors within families and ignoring social, cultural, and economic factors. It suggests that behavior can be controlled and predicted so that DV can be eliminated without altering the basic social structures that support DV. Thus, "it does not draw public or scholarly attention to the multiple, intersecting factors that shape experiences within families and the behavior of youth" (Ferraro 2006, 112, 116). Attributing acts of DV solely to individual psychological factors overlooks the broader impact of systemic inequality and the social context of power relations (United Nations 2006, 29).

Studies of risk factors for DV have found that of forty-two markers of risk in female victims, only one, having witnessed violence between parents in childhood, was consistently correlated with being a victim of a male partner's violence[3] (Heise 1998, 266). Other risk factors, including alcohol use, income, and education, were not found to be consistently related. Thus, for males, only two experiences have been identified as especially predictive of future spousal abuse: witnessing DV as a child and experiencing physical or sexual abuse as a child (but the effect is less strong in this case; p. 267). While it is not clear how being a witness to violence in childhood translates into abuse behavior in adulthood, social learning theory indicates that understanding the

instrumentality of violence as a means of achieving one's desires is a relevant factor (p. 268).

Sociological approaches to DV are not concerned with individual psychological factors but contend that social structural factors result in DV. Thus researchers might focus on class, education, race, or religion and through empirical studies examine how the family responds to the dynamics of society and how violence becomes a response to structural and social impacts. Studies may be quantitative, based largely on survey data,[4] or qualitative where researchers will try to fully contextualize women's experience of DV (Bograd 1988, 18–19).

Heise (1998, 262) has put forward an *ecological approach* that proposes an "integrated, ecological framework for understanding the origins of gender-based violence." This conceives violence as "a multifaceted phenomenon grounded in an interplay among personal, situational, and sociocultural factors." It is argued that theories relying on a single factor that depend on individual or social/political explanations ignore the multiple levels involved in gender abuse. Feminists have been reluctant to take into account factors other than patriarchy in theorizing the causes of DV, but their disregard of social and individual factors has not explained why some men beat women and others do not, even when all men are impacted by cultures that assert male superiority and affirm their right to control women. While male dominance must be the cornerstone to any theory of DV, life experience suggests it cannot stand as the single explanatory factor.

The ecological approach builds on research on child abuse and neglect that have been applied to battering by a number of theorists (Heise 1998, 264). The ecological framework comprises four levels of analysis: (1) personal history factors, (2) the microsystem (the immediate context of the violence, often the family or intimate relationship), (3) the exosystem (comprising institutions and social structures such as the working environment, the neighborhood, social networks), (4) the macrosystem (the cultural perspective). Other theorists have identified a further level of analysis, the mesosystem, meaning the interplay between the aspects of a person's social environment, such as between family and extended family or group of peers, as well as linkages with institutions such as police, courts, and social services (p. 264).

Theoretical frameworks that attempt to explain domestic violence continue to be developed and refined, and almost all argue that DV cannot be explained by a single cause. Rather, multiple intersecting factors are implicated in DV. This means that single interventions and responses to DV, such as treating it only as an issue of criminal conduct, are unlikely to be successful.

Violence Against Women: International Advocacy

In this section we look at how international advocacy placed violence against women on the international agenda and how ultimately, sustained efforts by academics and NGOs caused violence against women to be defined as a violation of women's human rights.

In the 1970s the issue of DV was little discussed in academia, there were no shelters for abused women, and police policies mandated they did not arrest men who assaulted their wives. Between 1939 and 1969 the *Journal of Marriage and the Family* contained not a single article on DV (Ferraro 2006, 19). Marital violence was considered a private matter. In the United Kingdom and the United States, advocacy on behalf of "battered women" resulted in the creation of shelters and refuges. In the United States, class action lawsuits played a major part in raising public awareness of the issue of DV and in securing police cooperation to mandatory arrests of perpetrators of abuse (Dobash and Dobash 1992, 76, 165–66). In 1976 a group of Western women organized the International Tribunal on Crimes Against Women in Belgium, gathering more than two thousand women from more than forty states. The meeting was planned to be a counterreaction to the 1975 UN Women's Conference in Mexico City. The Tribunal wanted to hear testimonies from women victims of violence. The Tribunal's outcomes included the formation of international networks of activists and the beginning of national initiatives on gender violence. Testimonies from women revealed that while violence against women differed across regions and states, it was nevertheless universal. Women blamed patriarchal structures[5] and traditions for the violence against them. Following this event, women continued to organize their own events separate from established structures because they had little confidence in the efficacy of the UN Conference, which they considered politicized (Joachim 2003, 254–56).

In 1985 at the third UN Women's Conference in Nairobi, Kenya, governments were ready to identify violence against women as an obstacle to gender equality and as a priority issue in the coming decade. By 1985 women had learned how to exert political force and pressure and were able also to move beyond their geographical and political divergences in common cause. Violence against women "brought women to their strongest point of common experience" (Charlotte Bunch[6] interview 1995, quoted in Joachim 2003, 256).

In December 1986 UN agencies organized a meeting of experts in Vienna on "Violence in the Family with Special Emphasis on Women." Experts in sociology, criminology, and law agreed to provide, for the first time, data on the causes and consequences of violence against women and strategies to counteract it. Statistical and other data and case studies, including from developing countries, revealed that violence had significant long-term effects on women, children, and societies. At this time the issue was clouded by the notion that the family unit was a private and sacred domain and victims remained silent because of guilt, shame, loyalty, or fear of repercussions. At this time there was a perception that DV was a "societal ill" and both the victim and the perpetrator were abnormal. The outcome of this thinking was to offer therapeutic or welfare solutions stressing mediation as a way to restore the harmony of the family unit. The expert group called instead for the intervention of the criminal justice system and for DV to be treated as any other crime. The experts believed that, apart from its practical effect, the prosecution of the perpetrator would send a message to all that violence was unacceptable and that the perpetrator would be held accountable. This view was a radical departure from previous therapy and welfare approaches and strategies (Joachim 2003, 257). The technical knowledge of the experts gave legitimacy to the strategy of criminalization, and following this meeting the UN commissioned the first comprehensive survey on *Violence Against Women in the Family* (Joachim 2003, 258).

In 1992 the Convention on the Elimination of All Forms of Discrimination Against Women (CEDAW) Committee (see discussion of CEDAW, later in this chapter) adopted Recommendation 19 on Violence Against Women stating that violence against women constitutes a form of discrimination against women and that it reflects and perpetuates their subordination to men and calling upon states to eliminate violence in all spheres.

The 1993 World Conference on Human Rights in Vienna was the next major opportunity for the issue to be discussed. Prominent women's groups organized meetings prior to the Conference and formulated a broad definition of violence against women that included acts of violence (physical, emotional, or psychological) in the public and private spheres that are used against women because of their gender or sexual orientation. At this time a division between women's rights and human rights was maintained within the United Nations. It was argued this was justified because, unlike human rights violations, women's rights violations occurred exclusively in the domestic domain where the state had no right to intervene.

The claim that women's rights were also human rights was advanced in technical terms by Charlotte Bunch's article titled "Women's Rights as Human Rights," published in *Human Rights Quarterly* in 1990. Other activities by activist groups tried to show a linkage because it constituted a powerful frame for further international action and resonated with cultural groups worldwide. Attempts were made to present the issue to the media; for example, women staged an eighteen-hour Tribunal at the Conference and provided kits to the media. By this time the two leading human rights international NGOs, Human Rights Watch and Amnesty International, had established Women's Human Rights Programs and begun to investigate violations of women's rights perpetrated or condoned by states and their agencies. Women's groups lobbied states hard at the Conference, camping on corridors, offering improved drafts of texts, and generally planning their lobbying to ensure it would be effective (Joachim 2003, 259).

The 1993 World Conference on Human Rights in Vienna recognized that violence against women constitutes a severe violation of rights, whether it is perpetrated publicly or privately. The Conference called for the development of international, regional, and national programs to eliminate violence and discrimination against women. Shortly after the Conference ended, the UN General Assembly adopted the Declaration on the Elimination of All Forms of Violence Against Women, which condemns "any act of gender-based violence that results in, or is likely to result in, physical, sexual or psychological harm or suffering to women, including threats of such acts, coercion or arbitrary deprivations of liberty, whether occurring

in public or private life." A special rapporteur on violence against women was also appointed to investigate the causes and consequences of the issue (Joachim 2003, 260).

The Fourth World Conference on Women in Beijing, 1995, declared that violence against women interferes with the enjoyment of women's human rights and fundamental freedoms. The platform for action required that states condemn violence against women and adopt policies to eliminate it. At the Conference the issue of violence against women emerged as a key item on the policy agenda for the international women movement and for international development (Hemment 2004, 819).

This section has described the development trajectory of the notion of violence against women (VAW), beginning with its recognition as an international issue starting in the 1970s and concluding with its acceptance as a violation of women's human rights in 1993. The success of the campaign for the internationalization of violence against women was largely attributable to the linkage of women's rights and human rights that brought together two groups of social activists in a dynamic social movement: feminists and human rights activists from the academy and feminist advocates from NGOs. The following section explains and assesses progress made on the implementation of international action to combat violence against women.

Violence Against Women: International Action

The international advocacy against violence against women described in this section led to concrete international steps intended to combat such violence worldwide. In the next section, we examine in more detail particular international instruments that have established international norms concerning violence against women, including DV.

WOMEN'S RIGHTS AS HUMAN RIGHTS

Perhaps the most fundamental of strategies to end violence against women was arguing that women's rights were human rights (Ulrich 2000, 629). Historically, states and not persons were the subject of international law, and consequently international human rights mandates were directed at the conduct of states. However, it is clear that states commit violence against women. For example, in Peru, military personnel systematically assaulted females, and in El Salvador, judges regularly dismissed prosecutions for rape on the basis that the rape victim provoked the crime (p. 636). If the traditional scope of international law is set aside, women can be protected against violence through international instruments. What are these international instruments, and what norms do they set?

The Universal Declaration of Human Rights 1948

This provides the norm or standard by which states are to judge the civil, political, cultural, economic, and social rights of their citizens, that is, their human rights. The Declaration does not expressly confer rights on women and uses the term *man* generically. It contains no actual protections for women and depicts them as wives and mothers through constant references to the family. Accordingly it reflects a masculinist conception of human rights protection, and women's rights were not addressed substantively until 1979 with the finalization of CEDAW.

Convention on the Elimination of All Forms of Discrimination Against Women (CEDAW)

CEDAW specifies that women's rights are human rights and aims at ending discrimination against women. The capacity of the CEDAW, as an international instrument, to eliminate violence against women through enforcement action against states is limited. While Article 17 sets up a monitoring and enforcement mechanism in the form of a Committee on the Elimination of Discrimination Against Women, it has limited effectiveness. Member-states are required to submit reports to the Committee within one year of ratification, and every four years afterward, on the progress and performance of their efforts to end discrimination. However, because CEDAW meets infrequently, there is always a large backlog of reports (Ulrich 2000, 644).

It was not until 1992 that CEDAW issued Recommendation No. 19 on Violence Against Women, stating that violence against women constitutes a form of discrimination against women, that it reflects and perpetuates their subordination to men, and calling upon states to eliminate violence in all spheres. It also articulates a standard of due diligence that states should apply in protecting women effectively from such violence: "Under general international law and specific human rights covenants, states may also be responsible for private acts if they fail to act with due diligence to prevent violation of rights, or to investigate and punish acts of violence, and for providing compensation." This duty has been enunciated also by the Inter-American Commission on Human Rights in *Maria da Penha Maia Fernandes v. Brazil*, in which the Commission found that the failure of the state to prosecute and punish a DV perpetrator more than fifteen years after the start of an investigation was a violation of the state's international commitments and an indication that the state condoned such violence (United Nations 2006, 76).

Optional Protocol to the Convention on the Elimination of Discrimination Against Women

In 1999, an Optional Protocol to the Convention on the Elimination of Discrimination Against Women was adopted. It entered into force in December 2000. Following the model of other human rights instruments, the Protocol grants the right to individuals and groups to communicate directly to the Committee on the Elimination of Discrimination Against Women, where they claim to be victims of violations of any of the rights contained in the CEDAW. Domestic remedies must first be exhausted by the claimants except in cases where domestic remedies will be unreasonably prolonged or unlikely to bring effective relief (Article 4).

The state concerned in the claim has six months to submit written explanations, after which the Committee is to examine communications in closed session and then transmit its views to the parties. Within six months of receiving its view, the state party is to submit a response to the Committee with information on any action taken. Where there is evidence of "grave and systematic" violations of the CEDAW by a state, the Committee has the power to designate its members to conduct an inquiry, which can include a visit to the state, with the state's consent (Article

8). States have the right to opt out of Article 8 when ratifying the Protocol: as of August 2014, only six states had done so. A total of 105 states had ratified the Optional Protocol as of August 2014 (the United States and Nicaragua have not ratified, but Ghana and Russia have ratified).

Declaration on the Elimination of Violence Against Women 1993 (DEVAW)

DEVAW makes significant advances in the international campaign against violence against women. It recognizes that gender-based violence is the outcome of "historically unequal power relations between men and women, which has led to domination over and discrimination against women by men." DEVAW rejects the notion that culture and tradition should permit violence against women and provides that states may be accountable for failing to protect their female citizens from violence. Nevertheless, it also qualifies the universality of human rights by insisting that "the significance of national and regional particularities and various historical, cultural and religious backgrounds must be borne in mind."

The Fourth World Conference on Women's Platform for Action, Beijing 1995[7]

This Conference formulated a comprehensive set of measures to combat violence against women. There are three strategic objectives:

- Adopt integrated measures to prevent and eliminate violence against women.

- Study the causes and consequences of that violence and the effectiveness of preventive measures.

- Eliminate trafficking in women and assist victims of violence resulting from prostitution and trafficking.

Each strategic objective is accompanied by a list of "Actions to Be Taken" comprising an effective agenda for change. The Actions in relation to violence against women are summarized as follows:

- Governments are to be responsible for policy and operational measures, including the development of a national policy on domestic violence. These measures would include strengthening and expanding domestic laws, preferably by enacting a separate law on domestic violence; creating and funding training programs on violence against women for judges, prosecutors, police, and medical and immigration officials; and designing a set of measures to sanction police and other state agents who engage in violence against women. Also, governments are to ensure that due diligence is exercised to investigate and prosecute cases of violence against women.

- Governments are expected to provide for victims of violence, to design training programs aimed at preventing violence, and to set up counseling and allied services for victims. All levels of government are required to provide shelters and support for victims and to conduct awareness campaigns so that victims know where assistance is available to them. Also, governments must adopt measures to modify the social and cultural patterns of conduct of men and women and to eliminate prejudices, customary practices, and all other practices based on the idea of the inferiority or superiority of either of the sexes and on stereotyped roles for men and women. Adequate resources must be provided for all these measures.

- Governments must conduct research, collect data, and compile statistics on the causes and consequences of violence; disseminate research studies; and provide support for women's NGOs who are recognized as important actors in policy implementation.

- Governments must establish a state office responsible for combating violence against women that should collaborate with other government agencies and NGOs.

The first step in implementing the Platform of Action was that states were to submit National Plans of Action. Some states did not include violence against women in the National Plans because governments were free to decide the critical areas of concern to them within the overall Platform (Avdeyeva 2007, 885). The Commission on the Status of Women (CSW) is the UN agency responsible for monitoring the implementation of national plans; it analyzes national reports, issues question-naires to governments, and collects data. It is clear that implementation of the Platform is voluntary in the sense that there are no official sanctions that can be imposed for lack of action (p. 886). Nevertheless, in policy and operational terms, the Platform and the detailed Actions constitute a comprehensive strategy and set of measures to prevent, counter, and eliminate violence against women.

UNiTE to End Violence Against Women

In 2008 the UN Secretary-General initiated a campaign called UNiTE to End Violence Against Women, which designated violence a "global pan-demic" and called violence against women "never acceptable, never excusable, never tolerable." The campaign, now operated by UN Women, "aims to raise public awareness and increase political will and resources for preventing and ending all forms of violence against women and girls in all parts of the world." Its goals include changes in domestic laws, action plans, data collection and analysis, and local campaigns through civil society groups.[8]

In the following section, we examine strategies and national responses to the international agenda to end violence against women. What form have these strategies taken, and have they proved to be successful? Have the global norms about violence against women been successfully disseminated worldwide, and what has been the outcome of publicizing them in countries? Strategic studies that take a global approach covering many coun-tries can be contrasted with local country profiles of DV in Russia, Nicaragua, and Ghana that appear in the following section. Comparing the global and the local gives greater insight into prog-ress on translating global norms about violence against women into a local context: has the global linked to the local, or have local practices and beliefs mediated or resisted global norms?

NATIONAL STRATEGIES TO COMBAT VIOLENCE AGAINST WOMEN

In the late 1980s, major U.S. foundations and funding agencies concerned with international development decided that violence against women should become a major funding priority

and began channeling funds to NGOs for that purpose (Hemment 2004, 819). International NGOs commonly work with local NGOs to develop and implement advocacy, awareness, and training programs about DV and many other topics, with the local NGOs being responsible for translating concepts of human rights into local terms, in other words, remaking them in the ver-nacular (Merry 2006a, 1).

These programs, based on The Fourth World Conference on Women's Platform for Action, Beijing 1995, are conducted in developing coun-tries where local customs and traditions regulate and bring social order to daily life. Western transnational discourses about human rights and DV are often unknown, especially in rural areas, and as indicated in the country profile of Ghana (discussed later), often come into tension with local practices, values, and beliefs. For Ghana and other developing countries, DV is deeply embedded in systems of kinship, and implement-ing measures to combat DV is challenging, requires patience, demands attention to local practices, and represents a major social change in communities and families. It requires nothing less than a reshaping of "the rules people carry in their heads" (Merry 2006a, 2–3).

Transnational discourses about human rights for women usually meet local resistance in both developed and developing countries (e.g., see "Russian Federation" under "Country Profiles: Domestic Violence," later in this chapter). While local values and beliefs must be examined for consistency with messages about human rights and adjustments made to framing and methodol-ogy, as Sally Engle Merry (2006a, 5) points out, it is nevertheless necessary that these discourses be framed in transnational rights terms because only then will funding be secured from interna-tional donor agencies.

For many Asian leaders and citizens, the West-ern discourse of women's rights is subordinated to an Asian discourse that values and promotes cul-ture, community, and the nation (Ong 1996, 111). This Asian focus on economic development of the nation, as well as community support for that focus, means that within Asia, gender issues may be situated within the context of a set of compet-ing problems that affect developing countries generally, taking into account global inequalities. Thus, Asian leaders are likely to privilege eco-nomic and social responsibilities and place limits on the rights of individuals (p. 116). At the same time, however, these discourses about community, family, and the nation commonly contain "the unspoken assumption of sexual inequality" (p. 121) and fix women within "webs of power relations." In addition, it has been claimed that the Asian perspective on human rights that stresses "economic development over political rights and collective duties over individual freedoms, is largely a self-serving construct of Asian governments that has been widely rejected by Asian human rights activists" (Human Rights Watch/ Asia, quoted in Ong 1996, 121).

Drawing on data from China, Indonesia, and Malaysia, Aihwa Ong gives examples of alternative strategies to the Western formulated approaches to violence against women. In these countries, struggles for human rights are usually framed in terms of community, class, religion, or nation and not in terms of gender (Ong 1996, 107). In Malaysia, Muslim feminists have formed Sisters in Islam,[9] a civil society group that does not form alliances with Western feminists in pursuing women's rights but instead engages local males in examining gender within the framework of Islamic morality. Thus, Ong calls for "a feminist sisterhood with men in interpreting and formulating public morality." Sisters in Islam articulate issues within Islam by arguing with male Islamic scholars for an interpretation of Islam that rejects a narrow and anachronistic reading of the Qur'an rooted in yesterday in favor of a reading that creates a space for the renegotiation of gender roles and rights (pp. 131–32).

Some scholars assert that strategies perceived to be effective in the North, for example, in the United States, where resources are extensive and there is a significant history of campaigning against DV, are not appropriate for Africa, where resources are always lacking. This view cites the existence of a significant traditional sphere of life "much of which reinforces the subordinate position of women within the family" even though it is acknowledged to have been eroded by development (so that customary sanctions against DV are no longer effective) and severe economic constraints, like effective law enforcement and inadequate medical facilities (Bowman 2003, 474).

As Cynthia Bowman (2003) acknowledges, questions about this assertion might include why, in spite of virtually unlimited resources, the United States has failed to eliminate DV in the United States and why attitudes toward gender in the United States ("traditional" attitudes) have not

changed radically despite the focus on women and DV since the 1970s. In other words, the issue is not simply one of choice of strategy but *effective* strategies.[10] The following discussion examines implementation of some of the strategies that have been employed and notes where questions have been raised about government responses to them.

Policy Strategies: Government Responses to Violence Against Women

The issue of government responsiveness to DV action has been examined cross-culturally by S. Laurel Weldon (2002) in an empirical study that asks how responsive governments have been in implementing a series of actions designed to prevent or combat violence against women. For her study, Weldon selected thirty-six countries that had been continuously democratic from 1974 to 1994. She examined the extent to which these thirty-six governments had implemented the following actions:

- Legal reform for domestic violence

- Legal reform for sexual assaults

- Establishment of, and government funding for, shelters, emergency housing, and crisis centers

- Training of judges, police, social workers, and other service providers and professionals dealing with violence against women through government-sponsored programs

- Public education/awareness programs about violence against women

- Establishment of a central coordinating government authority to coordinate national policies on violence against women

The objective of the study was to identify the measures to which governments had been most responsive.[11] This should not be confused with effectiveness; responsiveness does not necessarily imply effectiveness, which is an assessment of the impact of government actions in a particular field (Weldon 2002, 7).

The data showed that none of the thirty-six states, except Canada, had addressed any of these policy areas in 1974, but by 1984 France had addressed four areas, other industrialized countries (Sweden, United Kingdom) three areas, eight countries (seven developed countries, including the United States and India) two areas, four countries (Costa Rica, Iceland, Luxembourg, Spain) one area, and the remaining twenty-one countries still had not addressed any areas of policy action.

By 1994 however, only four countries had failed to take any action (Botswana, Italy, Nauru, and Venezuela); two had addressed all seven areas (Australia and Canada); the United States had addressed six areas; five countries (including Costa Rica) had addressed five areas; four countries had addressed four areas (including the United Kingdom and India); seven had addressed three areas (including Bahamas, Barbados and Colombia); seven had addressed two areas (including Germany and Trinidad and Tobago); and five had addressed one area (including Japan, Jamaica, and Papua New Guinea; Weldon 2002, 31).

In seeking an explanation for these differing responses, Weldon examined a number of factors but found that no single factor or set of factors could satisfactorily explain the bulk of the variation in government response. Thus, while there was some correlation between the level of development of a country to government responsiveness, it was not determinative (Weldon 2002, 60).

Taking the same set of seven actions, Weldon examined whether the existence of social movements, such as women's movements, affected government responsiveness. She found that "strong, independently organized women's movements" improved government responsiveness to violence against women. Commonly, women's movements were the first to articulate the violence issue and urge for its recognition as a public problem that required government action. Women's movements work through "everyday politics"; that is, they challenge assumptions and discourse as a daily event and through constant dialogue; through cultural productions such as books, movies, magazines, street theater, and events like "speak outs" and Take Back the Night marches; and through making moral and political arguments to gain public support for their views and bring pressure to bear on policymakers (Weldon 2002, 69–70).

The importance of women's movements is highlighted by the finding that in all the countries included in the study, during the period 1974 to 1994 no government initiative on violence against women was adopted in the absence of a women's movement (Weldon 2002, 78). A key factor in this success was that the women's movement was autonomous; that is, it was not attached to a political party, union, or other political institution (p. 80).

Weldon also found that, generally, women in government, elected or appointed (members of the legislature or government Ministers at Cabinet level), are unlikely to be able to increase responsiveness in governments on their own. However, if allied with an autonomous women's movement, their influence increases significantly as they have an external support base to counter resistance to the implementation of women-centered policies and actions (Weldon 2002, 97).

Does creating a woman-centered policy organization within government render a government more responsive to issues like violence against women? Almost all the countries included in Weldon's study had set up some kind of institution concerned with women's policy by 1994. They ranged from women's desks in low-ranking Ministries to complex collections of advisory bodies (Weldon 2002, 125). It is vital, however, that whatever its structure, the woman's policy body has the bureaucratic power to coordinate policy across sectors of government—it must be an effective agency. Important attributes of an effective women's policy body include

- adequate resources must be provided to it;

- it must have at least equal status with other government agencies or ministries;

- it must possess a degree of autonomy; and

- it must possess the institutional power to review and comment on government policy across sectors; it must be perceived as having "cross-cutting powers."

An example of the optimum model comes from Australia where, in 1976, women's offices were created in every department within government to analyze the gender impact of policies. Moreover, these offices were connected to a central office within the Office of the Prime Minister (Weldon 2002, 129).

When an active and autonomous women's movement is linked to effective, powerful women's policy machinery within government, the most comprehensive policy responses to women's concerns can be achieved. This was the case in both Canada and Australia (Weldon 2002, 156).

In a similar study (Htun and Weldon 2012, 548), the researchers extended the time frame for the comparative policy analysis to 2005 from 1975 and to seventy countries. Again, their analysis shows that a strong autonomous feminist movement is a predictor of government responsiveness to addressing violence against women across all policy actions, that "autonomous organizing ensures that words become deeds," and that organizing of this kind institutionalizes international norms about violence against women (p. 564).

Nongovernmental Watch Groups

These groups are able to address DV on a global level through identifying problems, publicizing issues, and pressuring governments. They may monitor and report abuses to the UN agencies. A good example of such a group is the International Women's Rights Action Watch (IWRAW),[12] established in 1985 at the Third World Conference on Women in Nairobi, Kenya, to promote recognition of women's human rights under the CEDAW. IWRAW undertakes advocacy for women's human rights under all the international human rights treaties and is an international resource and communications center that serves activists, scholars, and organizations throughout the world. IWRAW pioneered shadow reporting (NGO participation in the review of a country that has ratified a treaty) to the CEDAW Committee and shadow reporting on women's human rights to the Committee on Economic, Social and Cultural Rights.

Crime-Centered Approach: Britain and the United States

Recourse to the law as a strategy for responding to violence against women has followed different pathways in England and in the United States. In England, Home Office Circulars in 1986, 1990, and 2000 promoted the policing of DV to a more central position within the policing function, required that clear strategies for DV be developed, urged a presumption of arrest where an offense had been committed, and encouraged the setting up of specialist units to deal with incidents of DV (Silvestri and Crowther-Dowey 2008, 93). This meant that the legal authority of the police could be applied in the private home and in public spaces. Thus, for the first time, there was a "presumption to arrest" for acts of DV (Walklate 2008, 41). Previously, the police had been very

reluctant to intervene in what they considered to be a civil matter and had described shelters for abused women as likely to precipitate the breakup of families and DV cases as "very time consuming and a distraction to the overall police effort" (quoted in Dobash and Dobash 1992, 151).

Nevertheless, there remains within U.K. police culture an underlying belief that DV is a domestic family matter, more appropriately dealt with under civil law procedures (Silvestri and Crowther-Dowey 2008, 94), despite evidence that DV constitutes nearly one-quarter of all recorded crime in England and Wales and the police receive a call for domestic assistance every minute (Silvestri and Crowther-Dowey 2008, 89). Also in the United Kingdom, DV attrition within the criminal justice process results in DV cases being excluded. Exclusion is justified by a number of reasons, including

- when police decide not to proceed,

- when police refuse to refer a case to the Crown Prosecution Service (CPS),

- when the CPS itself decides not to proceed or reduces the charge to a less serious one, and

- when the court dismisses the case or finds the accused not guilty.

The dropping out of cases for these reasons has been a cause of growing concern, especially when cases are not proceeded with because police have decided not to prosecute in the exercise of their wide discretion.

In the United States the strength of the movement against DV was such that arrest for DV became mandatory despite studies that revealed this approach to be problematic.[13] For example, the short-term gain of having an offender arrested could result in long-term losses in that the violence worsened. This was especially so in the case of minority women who also had to depend on the criminal justice system, but this continued to be the policy notwithstanding studies showing that arrest worked more effectively when combined with other community-based resources like shelters and crisis centers (Walklate 2008, 41). In addition, there is evidence that women who fight back in DV situations are also being arrested. This has resulted in calls for action to be taken to stem the increase in the level of female violence (p. 43).

Other perspectives on a crime-centered approach see it as ineffective when the intervention is against the wishes of the woman and where counter-charging (i.e., bringing charges against the victim if there is any evidence of retaliatory violence or self-defense) has become common and operates as a deterrent to reporting offenses at all. In addition, it is asserted that there is an absence of evidence to show that reliance on the criminal justice system has resulted in better outcomes for the woman in terms of personal safety or in diminished violence by men (Snider 1998, 2). The legacy of a DV policy dominated by criminalization and by constituencies of professionals within the justice system with an interest in perpetuating criminalization is that DV is perceived to be only about punishment (Snider 1998, 3, 9). Arguing against criminalizing DV as the dominant anti-DV strategy, scholars have pointed out that dependence on the criminal justice system alone runs the risk of ignoring the existence of legal, social, and political structures that are the foundation of male privilege. It is contended that DV should be located in these wider and deeper social structures and not in the individual pathologies of perpetrators and victims and in the details and complexity of procedures and practices (Walklate 2008, 51).

Feminists working in criminology and law "have long acknowledged that deep-seated social problems such as domestic assault can only be ameliorated by ideological and structural change" (Snider 1998, 2). Laureen Snider suggests that this lengthy process has been marginalized by the policy of criminalization (p. 2). Valorizing criminalization also has the effect of diverting funding away from shelters and programs designed to assist victims of DV (p. 2).

Australian researchers have found that the impact of legal protection is variable according to factors such as the severity of the violence experienced and whether or not the woman has asked for police help or for police and court assistance. Researchers have demonstrated that an approach that established an automatic link between protection orders and police intervention is most effective at securing protection against violence (Walklate 2008, 42). The development of specialist units to handle DV and provide victim support has raised questions in England about the degree of understanding of ethnic women's needs and whether or not this approach militates against victim empowerment.

In England, establishing fast-track DV courts has been evaluated and found to be an effective strategy because it has improved victim confidence in the justice system and facilitated advocacy and information sharing. However, half of the victims appearing in these courts retract their statements and withdraw their support from the prosecution (Walklate 2008, 43).

DISSEMINATION AND DIFFUSION OF GLOBAL NORMS ON VIOLENCE AGAINST WOMEN

How successfully have international and national NGOs, UN and international agencies, and development agencies of developed countries disseminated and diffused these global norms about ceasing DV and violence against women in all its forms, and what have been their impact?

Scholars have documented the impact of global norms, usually determined under international agreements in a number of policy areas, for example, human rights, democracy, women's political participation and women's voting rights, female circumcision, and gender mainstreaming (Pierotti 2013, 241). Essentially, diffusing norms about violence against women means linking the global and the local, and in this task the growth in the number of international NGOs focused on women and violence has been very influential. Through a multitude of methods, "pathways of influence" have affected both national policies and individual attitudes. These methods include

- donor-funded programs, NGO campaigns (awareness, education, and outreach), and publications;

- media coverage;

- public discussions (conferences, seminars, and the like);

- inclusion in school curricula; and

- dialogue in various forms. (Pierotti 2013, 242)

The outcome of these activities in terms of national policy addressing DV is that since 1975, 119 countries have enacted about 260 legal changes in the form of new laws, changes to laws, decrees, and constitutional changes concerning DV. Almost 95 percent of these changes have come about since the 1995 Beijing Conference. This suggests the development of a trend as national governments responded to the pressures generated on this subject and gradually institutionalized violence against women as a violation of human rights (Pierotti 2013, 244). While this outcome represents changes in government policies, the question arises whether individual attitudes, especially of non-elite women who are not activists, have also been influenced.

Using data from fifty-two Demographic and Health Survey (DHS) data sets—two from each of twenty-six countries, including Ghana, collected in two surveys, the first in early to mid-2000 and the second in mid- to late 2000 (usually five years apart, for Ghana 2003 and 2008)—Pierotti (2013, 248) analyzed responses to the same five questions used in the Ghana DHS, namely, whether a husband is justified in hitting or beating his wife in the following circumstances:

- If she goes out without telling him

- If she neglects the children

- If she argues with him

- If she refuses to have sex with him

- If she burns the food

Across the fifty-two sets of data, an average of 51 percent of respondents rejected all the circumstances indicated in the five questions/scenarios. There were some exceptions (i.e., Indonesia, Jordan, and Madagascar) where, for reasons yet to be explained, there was a significant decrease in the percentage of men and women rejecting DV. In twenty-three countries, there was a significant increase in the proportion of women rejecting violence: twelve countries revealed a more than 10 percentage point increase in the rejection rate, with Nigeria showing the largest of 19 percent and Zambia, Kenya, Rwanda, and Armenia showing a 15 percent increase. The results did not vary significantly for married and never-married women where both were surveyed in a country. The analysis shows a similar trend for men, with twelve countries showing a significant increase in the percentage of men rejecting DV. In the Dominican Republic, there was no significant change for men and, as in the case of women, Indonesia and Jordan showed a significant decrease in the percentage of men rejecting DV (Pierotti 2013, 252–53).

Living in an urban area also impacted the results because in twenty-two countries, women living in urban areas had higher odds of rejecting DV. In all but four countries, women who had attended high school had much higher odds of rejecting DV with an even larger effect for further education beyond high school. Media access was associated with higher odds of rejection in fourteen countries. Older women were more likely to reject DV in seventeen countries. In fourteen of the twenty countries that did not restrict the sample based on marital status, never-married women were more likely than married women to reject DV.

Women in marriages with husbands who had more education were more likely to reject DV, and married women who had more education than their spouses were less likely to reject DV. In almost all countries, a husband's level of education had a positive association with his wife's attitudes about DV, independent of her own educational level (Pierotti 2013, 254).

In summary, after only five years, a significantly larger percentage of women in twenty-three countries, including Ghana, rejected DV. As noted earlier, some changes were very rapid, for example, in Nigeria, where the percentage of women who rejected DV rose from 33 percent in 2003 to 52 percent in 2008. The rapidity of change in only five years cannot be explained by socioeconomic or demographic shifts, both of which customarily occur over generations (Pierotti 2013, 260). Consequently, the results appear to provide evidence of rapid cultural diffusion in terms of attitudes to DV. Since the study was concerned with the diffusion of norms on DV, it is arguable that the new knowledge gained by the respondents about DV is evidence that diffusion has been effective.

COUNTRY PROFILES: DOMESTIC VIOLENCE

Having considered the nature and scope of violence against women, including DV, and the international advocacy and action that has occurred to recognize this violence as a worldwide problem and to find solutions, we now present detailed country profiles of DV. The countries selected are Russia, Nicaragua, and Ghana: one developed and two developing states all with very different cultures. The country profiles situate

DV within a local framework that contextualizes DV by reference to social, cultural, and economic factors. In this way, a fuller understanding is gained concerning how and why DV continues to be an issue in these countries and the factors that continue to sustain DV. These studies can be contrasted with those noted earlier which have examined global strategies.

Russian Federation

In Russia, violence against women was first emphasized by North American feminist activists employing the language of women's human rights. Prior to this, family violence generally was not discussed publicly; this was in line with the communist ideology of ignoring the negative aspects of the lives of Soviet citizens. State organizations, however, gave some attention to problems that might contribute to DV, such as alcoholism (Fastenko and Timofeeva 2004, 111). In Russia, feminist theories trace DV in Russia to a set of gendered beliefs from the past known as *Domostroi*[14] that prescribe a way of life in which women are to devote themselves to domestic functions and duties while men have authority to apply discipline if these duties are perceived to be performed inadequately.

After the 1917 Communist revolution, women benefited to some extent from the socialist principle that the cultural and economic progress of a country was linked to the status of women. The Soviet Constitution proclaimed the equality of men and women and provided for maternity care, legal abortion, child care, and the right to a divorce, but in practical terms, while this gave women the capacity to work full-time, they were expected to continue to perform their domestic duties in addition to engaging in paid employment (Fastenko and Timofeeva 2004, 113).

Prior to 1991, DV had been somewhat regulated criminally under the rubric of the crime of "hooliganism," a crime constituted by acts that violated public order and revealed a clear disrespect for society. It has been estimated that up to 40 percent of crimes charged as hooliganism in fact comprised instances of DV. Soviet police commonly ignored DV, but extreme cases could be treated as a "family scandal" and police might then intervene with the aim of reconciliation.

The Soviet housing system was also problematic for abused women because occupation was regulated by the state through a permit system and there was no property ownership. This meant that abused women were often forced to live with their husbands who held the residential permit, or they could be forced to share living space with violent men with whom they had no relationship (J. E. Johnson 2009, 24).

In the Soviet era, women's organizations in government comprised a Women's Department within the Communist Party, chiefly concerned with recruiting women into the party, and women's councils, established during the Khrushchev regime, intended to assist women in reconciling their work and home lives. In both cases, the state decided upon the goals and mission of the organizations (J. E. Johnson 2009, 26). Even after the end of the Soviet era, women's organizations emerged only slowly until 1991, when the First Independent Women's Forum met. By 1992, two hundred organizations were registered, and by 1998, there were six hundred registered. Nevertheless, these organizations remain small and unable to exercise significant influence (p. 40).

During the Soviet time, DV was not thought of as a distinct structural problem: the prevailing traditional gender ideology perceived women's role to be mothers with responsibility to promote motherhood and marriage. Gender, as social construct, remained undiscovered and unexamined. Teachers and parents promoted traditional physiological norms of weakness in women and strength in men, of women as caretakers and men as providers (J. E. Johnson 2009, 25). Olga Voronina (2009, 253) agrees that biological determinism, and not gender, has been the dominant national ideology expressed in literature, textbooks, the media, and official ideology, "all of which assign the role of soldier and defender of the fatherland to men and the role of mother, naturally, to women." After the fall of the Soviet Union, funding from the United States, the European Union, and groups of European countries generated numerous DV programs such as those that funded shelters and crisis centers for abused women. Awareness campaigns and training of law enforcement promoted policy change to recognize the existence of DV and to design measures to counter it. By 2004, some two hundred women's organizations throughout Russia provided hotline counseling, some provided shelter for DV survivors, and others conducted awareness campaigns (J. E. Johnson 2009, 2). The promotion of anti-DV measures in Russia was spurred by a new global feminism that overcame divisions between feminists from the North and the South and was based on "norms of inclusivity" that recognized feminists could sustain consensus even with dissent (p. 11). From the outset, DV activism in Russia drew on transnational norms and was linked to transnational feminist activism but was defined by existing Russian values and was referred to as "violence in the family" (p. 100).

From 1990 on, democracy assistance programs poured funds into the post-Soviet countries to support the new democracy. Between 1990 and 2002, Russia received some $860 million in this form of assistance from the United States and a further 800 million euros from the European Union. It is believed that about 10 percent of this funding went to civil society NGOs (J. E. Johnson 2009, 46). In order to access this funding, many women's organizations became formal NGOs despite warnings that Soviet history showed that the state had always co-opted social organizations.

The first women's organizations to address DV were formed between 1993 and 1995 in Moscow and St. Petersburg. Moscow-based ANNA (No to Violence Association)[15] began as a one person hotline and was registered with the authorities in 1995. The St. Petersburg Crisis Center began work in 1991, opened officially in 1994, and began to operate a regular hotline in 1995. Interest expanded to the regions, and activists established a scheme to facilitate the provision of lawyers to victims of sexual violence (J. E. Johnson 2009, 49). Crisis centers were established relatively easily and cheaply but could not expand to include shelters for abused women because of lack of resources and oppressive post-Soviet regulations (p. 52). Most centers received public funding and were heavily regulated while also claiming to be NGOs to funding donors (p. 55). By 2001, crisis centers could claim to be a success (p. 57).

The events of 9/11 caused international donors to cease funding post-communist civil society. As a result, by 2002, USAID, which had been funding crisis centers, ceased to do so, and by 2003, there was much less interest worldwide in funding women's issues, other than trafficking, which became the new donor focus in Russia (J. E. Johnson 2009, 60). Organizations funded by the government, such as twenty-two crisis centers in 2005, continued to survive, but the autonomous organizations that relied on overseas funding support began to close down (p. 64) or seek state funding or associate themselves with universities.

DV is prevalent in Russia, which still has no discrete legislation dealing with DV.[16] One survey found that one-half of married women respondents reported at least one incident involving physical violence (e.g., striking, pushing, shaking, arm-twisting) from their present husbands (J. E. Johnson 2009, 14). According to a 1998 report by the Ministry of Internal Affairs, violence against women occurs in one out of every four families (Fastenko and Timofeeva 2004, 116). Russia does not publish any official statistics on DV. Another survey conducted in 1998 in a small Russian town found that 99 percent of respondents believed that male aggression was a natural attribute of masculinity. Women excused men's aggression by reference to various factors such as the negative influences of the school and the street, "tough times while serving in the army," and "unbearable stress of economic burden" (p. 114).

After 1991, Russian police continued to ignore DV incidents and because more people had begun to live more privately, this gave police even less justification to intervene. As well, police argued that intervening in DV would violate the Russian Constitution's right to privacy or that DV should be dealt with by way of a private prosecution. The decline in state services after the Soviet era meant that women suffered more because it was estimated that the social service system could meet only 7 percent of demand, including that resulting from DV (J. E. Johnson 2009, 31). According to Janet Johnson, post-Soviet society is characterized by "gender neotraditionalism," an ideology that "draws upon pre- and anti-Soviet beliefs and practices advocating women's roles as mothers and homemakers" (p. 38). This was seen in action in the 1990s when women were called upon to give up their jobs and return to the home and in the widespread rejection of feminism and the concept of gender. Under communism, feminism had been regarded as anti-male, and even the notion that gender was a social construct was resisted by most women, who believed that men and women had essential roles (p. 39). Voronina (2009, 252) agrees that Russian popular culture sees feminism as posing "a threat to Russian national values" and believes the media "creates the image of feminists as masculinized, sexually unsatisfied, and/or morally degraded women whose core values are rights, power over men, and money—not family and children, which a "normal woman is expected to prefer."

Tensions Between the Local and the Global

As noted earlier, with financial assistance from overseas, women's crisis centers began to be established beginning in 1991. How was the Western conception and model of a crisis center received in Russia? In the United States and Western Europe, campaigns against DV had led to the development of women's crisis centers, the first of which were established by grassroots survivors of that violence. Providing shelters for women—secret safe places where women victims of domestic violence could take temporary shelter—was a key element of campaigning. By the late 1980s and early 1990s, the international women's movement had globalized the issue of DV so that it constituted a "common advocacy position" of both the women's and the human rights movements (Hemment 2004, 818). By the late 1990s, the United Nations and its organizations and international foundations and NGOs were working with women's groups in what were "determinedly transnational" campaigns (p. 818). It was assumed, therefore, that elements of strategies evolved to counter DV (such as crisis centers and shelters) would migrate worldwide.

Activist Russian women, after meeting with Western feminists in the early 1990s, set up the first Russian women's shelters in Moscow and St. Petersburg and then in provincial cities. Only a minority of Russian women's groups described themselves as feminist, and they were located in institutes and universities and composed of elite, highly educated women who were familiar with Western feminist literature. Their education, language skills, and familiarity with Western thinking made them a good fit for the representatives of the donor agencies (Hemment 2004, 822), and the crisis centers they established were enthusiastically received by the donor agencies. However, these elite groups did not enjoy broad support within Russia, and both men and women regarded them with "suspicion and hostility especially if they identified as feminist" (p. 822).

Tensions became apparent between local concerns, perceptions, and values and the beliefs held by international advocacy and activist groups promoting women's needs. In Russia, while elite women supported such interventions, the work of crisis centers was generally not well understood and Western models of such centers failed to understand and respond to local knowledge and local activist priorities (Hemment 2004, 816). The work of Russian women activists at the local level was shaped by "a distinct history and a distinct set of gender alignments." These included a local context of extreme economic dislocation as the free market took over from the planned economy (p. 817). Deep cuts in social security, changes in employment, and cuts in health care disproportionately affected women and so informed their perception of needs.

Julie Hemment found that Russian women with violent spouses were unlikely to regard their experience as gendered violence and therefore seek assistance from crisis centers. The Western conception of a crisis center assumes that women are economically dependent on men and trapped in the private sphere, but this is not true for Russian women, who were welcomed into the workforce and enjoyed only notional formal equality guaranteed by the paternalistic state. Women's concerns usually centered on chronic shortages of housing that required extended families to live communally. Thus, domestic conflict was dominated by tension caused by overcrowding, alcoholism, and personal conflicts (Hemment 2004, 823). However, one study conducted in St. Petersburg found that living communally significantly reduced the risk of the woman experiencing DV (Stickley, Timofeeva, and Sparen 2008, 483). Hence, the notion of a crisis center was inconsistent with Soviet and later Russian lifestyles. For one thing, the Western conception is that a stay in a crisis center is temporary until a woman moves on elsewhere. In Russia, there is often nowhere else to move on to. Also, in practical terms, it was often difficult to secure accommodation for a crisis center from the local authority (Hemment 2004, 824).

Following the promotion of women's programs by NGOs and Russian activists, Russian crisis centers have been created based on what Russian women call the "international model" using telephone hotlines and individual consultations (Hemment 2004, 825). In her research from 1995 to 1997, Hemment found that the crisis that occupied women's minds was not DV but that of existing in the larger Russian society. She argues that women did not feel any connection to DV as an issue as one they could coalesce around because it was considered to be too private a matter (p. 826). Russian women argued that violence was much less of a problem in Russia than economic violence and discrimination, which touched every woman daily (p. 827).

one woman, the DV was justified. As she put it, "On two occasions he slapped me because I was too loud when arguing with him. . . . Anyway he made it up to me later. . . . It was just a little problem." Another woman said: "Fighting in marriage is nothing serious. It happens all the time. I tell you, very few women have not received a slap or two from their husbands since they married. . . . If they won't tell you about it, it does not mean that it does not happen" (Amoakohene 2004, 2377). As Kathleen Ferraro (2006, 42) notes, when women blame themselves, this helps them to restore a sense of control in their lives; thus, "if I don't do X, that caused me to be hurt, then I won't get hurt again." When this respondent rationalizes the abuse, it operates as a means of making what occurred more explicable and less of a random event (p. 43).

Nonphysical forms of abuse included excessive control, verbal insults, and threatening behavior, and all thirty-five respondents who had suffered abuse reported experiencing these forms of violence. (Coker-Appiah and Cusack [1999, 21] reported threats, bullying, and destruction of property as the most frequently cited instances of psychological violence.) The cases of psychological abuse included the husband screaming at the woman in front of the children and a form of control termed "close marking," described as follows: "My husband is always suspicious of me. Any time I leave the house, he gives me close-marking even when I have told him where I'm going and for how long I'll be away. I really feel like a prisoner" (Amoakohene 2004, 2377).

Economic forms of control in terms of obtaining money from a husband for household expenses were experienced by only 10 percent of the women. None of the women in this study reported any physical injuries received from DV, but the nonphysical forms of abuse engendered stress and tension with 84 percent reporting being hypertensive. As one woman described it, "I panic and feel jittery in his presence. . . . It seems I can never get over this" (Amoakohene 2004, 2379). For these women, traditional gender roles, especially the gender division of labor in Ghana, had not evolved despite their employment and education. Women's roles were explained as: "The woman is required to keep the house. She cleans, cooks, washes, bathes the children and takes care of them. In former times when the woman was a housewife, this was not a problem but today it is a big problem" (p. 2378).

Another woman expressed the persistence of tradition: "Tradition has been overtaken by events. . . . It is about time our men folk realized that things have changed" (p. 2378).

In a group of fifty women clients of the Legal Aid Clinic of FIDA,[22] Ghana, respondents gave the following reasons for the DV they experienced:

- He would beat me whenever he was drunk.

- I confronted him with evidence of his sleeping with another woman.

- There was no particular reason.

- He accused me of sleeping with another man.

- My cooking was not to his taste.

- He said I was rude in public.

- I had insulted his mother.

- I spent too much money.

None of the women who had suffered DV had reported it to police or other authorities or even to family members despite the fact that all the women were aware of governmental and non-governmental agencies that existed to assist with DV. Their reasons for not reporting included that DV was condoned among their ethnic group and they did not want to be ridiculed for complaining about it; they did not want to "wash dirty linen in public"; they did not want to "unduly expose" their husbands and families; and they wanted to avoid social stigma, family disgrace, and bad repute. They believed that "family matters should be kept within the family" (Amoakohene 2004, 2378).[23]

Nancy Cantalupo and colleagues (2006, 544) also found in numerous interviews with a range of leaders, justice officials, and others that DV is widely considered to be a family matter and that women are under pressure from the family to keep such matters out of the justice system. As Rosemary Ofeibea Ofei-Aboagye (1994, 3) puts it, "Ghanaians wish it out of existence and deliberately downplay its visibility."

Women used a number of strategies to confront and cope with abuse. These included keeping silent, using distractions ("pretending to be busy with the kids. . . . so I leave him to fight alone"), and leaving the home temporarily to stay with friends or neighbors until "tempers would have cooled down" (Amoakohene 2004, 2378–79). In

Ghana, abused women commonly do not permanently leave their husbands. Women have given the following reasons for staying and continuing to suffer abuse: "I felt shy at my 'failure' to keep my husband happy.... I would not be able to keep the children in the comfort to which they were accustomed.... So long as the danger to my health was not bad I felt that I could manage.... My family would not support me if I left.... I did not want my children to have different fathers.... I had no money to sue him in court.... We have to be obedient to our husbands ... I know of no organization that could advise and support me if I left" (Ofei-Aboagye 1994, 7).

In their study, Dorcas Coker-Appiah and Cusack (1999, 126–27) found that where the husband and wife had children this was the predominant reason for the wife electing not to leave the marriage, and that pressure from family and friends was also a significant factor in 20 percent of women who elected not to leave. When the husband apologized, 61 percent of women returned to violent relationships. The study reveals that the group of educated, economically independent, married women considered DV to be "normal" (Amoakohene 2004, 2383). Only when a physical assault resulted in injury or death would it be considered an offense against the woman. These accounts of violence from affluent educated women suggest that women with lower socioeconomic status are likely to experience higher levels of violence. If that is correct, it may suggest that the husbands of this group of women have, to some extent, restructured customary norms about the treatment of women in marriage by using physical violence less often.

The educated Ghanaian women in the Coker-Appiah and Cusack study were all earning incomes, and only 10 percent expressed any problems in obtaining household expense money from their husbands. While multiple factors are associated with DV, the role of resources has been found to be of significance. Hence it is argued that when men are unable to provide the resources concomitant with the role as breadwinner, they are more likely to express anger within an intimate relationship. When women have little access to resources or when they have access to more resources than their partner, they are likely to be at a higher risk of suffering DV (Mann and Takyi 2009, 323). Financial autonomy and independence may operate to protect

women from DV, or at least restructure the kind of violence they may be subjected to, as indicated in the Ghanaian study. There are some studies that suggest this may only be true so long as women do not possess resources in excess of their partner's (p. 324).

Data from the 2003 Ghana Demographic Health Survey, which contains detailed information on attitudes to DV but not on actual behavior, have been used to test a number of hypotheses concerning resources and DV. Based on a sample of 2,099 men and 2,106 women (the women tended to be younger, had fewer children, and had lower levels of education than their partners), researchers found that a higher percentage of women than men (26.6 percent compared to 12.5 percent) believed that physical abuse was justified in the following situations:

- If the wife went out without telling the husband

- If the wife neglected the children

- If the wife argued with the husband

- If the wife refused to have sex with the husband

- If the wife burned the food

Two-thirds of the men (64.2 percent) believed abuse was never justified, compared to 44.6 percent of women. On the basis of these data, the researchers suggest that in Ghana, married women "tend to believe that abuse is justifiable far more often than their husbands" (Mann and Takyi 2009, 329).

In relation to resources within the family unit, the relative quantity of resources was found to be significant in shaping attitudes to DV. As a result, women who contributed one half or less to the household expenses believed abuse to be justified less often than those who contributed the total amount of expenses. Education was also found to be an important factor. Both men and women who had completed higher education were less likely to believe abuse was justifiable in any situation (Mann and Takyi 2009, 335).

Strategies to Counter Domestic Violence

Governmental and nongovernmental strategies against DV in Ghana have included legislation, forms of public education, awareness campaigns, counseling, and prosecuting offenders. Institutional responses include the creation of the WAJU and establishment of a Ministry of Women and Children's Affairs (Amoakohene 2004, 2379). However, WAJU has limited resources and is overwhelmed by the number of cases reported to it (Cantalupo et al. 2006, 531),[24] and there are fears that the Ministry will be politicized and not be an active driver of change in combating violence against women. There are numerous civil society organizations operating shelters and providing counseling and legal aid. For example, the Federation of Women's Lawyers has been active since the mid-1970s, and its lobbying has resulted in a Domestic Violence Bill (Amoakohene 2004, 2381).

DV victims may seek help from community leaders who have traditionally served as peacemakers and mediators in the settlement of disputes, including marital disputes. However, leaders often endorse and sustain traditional gender roles and advise women not to complain and to endure the DV, thus keeping it private (Cantalupo et al. 2006, 551). Similarly, religious leaders often counsel DV victims to be more submissive and are reluctant to refer abused women to police. One Christian leader quoted by Cantalupo and coworkers (p. 555) said of one such case:

> The woman was not the type who had patience. She talks. The man believed she did not respect him. Once, he broke the window in the house and handled a gun. He tried to beat her when she was pregnant. The violence continued every day. We counsel that being the woman, she must submit. We never advised her to go to the police [because] that's the end of the marriage.

In a study of fifty abused women, each had reported the DV to relatives at some point, ten had reported it to their priests, nine had reported their husbands to the chief of their husband's village, but all admitted that "it did not help much." Of the fifty women, only four had considered the option of reporting the incident to the police, and two had reported it to their husband's workplace superiors. Two had made reports to the Department of Social Welfare, but neither received a "meaningful response." All fifty women decided to seek advice from the Legal Aid Clinic of FIDA because they believed their health to be in danger, that the abuse created a

detrimental atmosphere for their children, and, as one woman put it, because "she was going insane" (Ofei-Aboagye 1994, 8). However, where the DV involves "serious injuries," chiefs may sanction a husband. In one such case, the husband struck his wife on the jaw with a hammer and the chief fined the husband three bottles of gin, which he reported was "a harsher punishment than normally given because he used a weapon" (Cantalupo et al. 2006, 557).

Traditional healers may also be consulted for advice on DV. They treat broken bones and other injuries, they charge less than hospitals, and women believe they maintain a higher level of confidentiality. Nevertheless, healers also consider themselves to be the guardians of tradition. In one case, even though the woman had suffered being kicked, had injuries to her elbow, leg, and ribs, and was regularly beaten for not cooking food on time and not coming home on time after a visit to her parents, the healer's advice to her was to modify her behavior so as to avoid any further violence (Cantalupo et al. 2006, 558).

What constitutes a serious injury such that it violates traditional norms and calls for a response? The following were suggested in one study: "he beats her to leave a scar or deformity. . . . He leaves her with a fracture. . . . He beats her publicly. . . . The beating is more than three slaps or he beats her three or four times." Women considered an excessive beating to be deplorable because "a man should not use his strength to 'cheat' a woman. . . . She is not a slave. . . . She is his partner and not his child. . . . It does not show respect for the woman . . . it has an adverse effect on the children. . . . It is not fair" (Ofei-Aboagye 1994, 6–7).

In 2007, Ghana enacted the Domestic Violence Act. The Act makes it an offense to engage in DV. On conviction, a penalty of up to two years imprisonment or a fine, or both, can be imposed, and the court can also order the payment of compensation. Courts may issue protection orders and interim protection orders that prohibit a respondent from committing or threatening to commit an act of domestic violence personally or otherwise against an applicant or a relation or a friend of the applicant. The Court may also order a respondent to vacate the family home.[25]

The numerous studies on DV in Ghana provide a rich source of information about DV and its social, economic, and cultural context. Qualitative studies are especially important in providing explanations for abuse because they describe the forms of abuse and the coping strategies used and report on community responses to abuse. Government has responded to the issue in Ghana in appropriate ways, especially by enacting specific legislation.

Summary

Commonalities in perceptions about gender and gender roles are apparent in all three country profiles. Recourse to the criminal justice system seems to be problematic in all three countries. Other strategies, such as education, awareness raising, and adequate legislation, appear to have some degree of effectiveness in Ghana and, to a limited extent, in Nicaragua. The NGO sector is an important change agent in Ghana and Nicaragua but not in Russia where the government imposes restrictions to hamper the sector's activities. The country profiles suggest that the progress achieved in disseminating global norms about violence against women has been limited because the local studies summarized and analyzed here reveal entrenched beliefs about gender and culture that have not as yet been appreciably eroded by the internationalization of violence against women. Governments in Ghana and Nicaragua are supportive of change, but this is not the case in Russia. This partial analysis of these country profiles indicates that all three countries have been impacted by global norms about violence against women but that overcoming the local social and cultural beliefs and adverse economic conditions will be a long-term challenge for governments and for civil society.

VIOLENCE AGAINST WOMEN: HONOR CRIMES

The introduction to this chapter identified honor crimes as an instance of violence against women in the family and as a harmful traditional practice. In some cases such crimes may also involve the community. What are these crimes, who commits them, for what reasons and how? What is the cultural context within which such crimes are committed? What measures are being taken to end honor killings, and how successful are they? These and other questions will be addressed here with the aim of adding to Western knowledge this form of violence against women.

Honor crimes have been variously described as "extreme acts of domestic violence culminating in the murder of a woman by her family or community" (Meeto and Mirza 2007, 187) or "the killing of women for suspected deviation from sexual norms imposed by society" (Faqir 2001, 66). The concept of "honor" is associated with such crimes (which do not always involve killings) in religious and ethnic communities as justification for these acts because murdering the woman (and sometimes the man where they are involved in a perceived illicit relationship[26]) is thought to salvage the good name of the family and the family's status and reputation.

In research into honor crimes in Iraqi Kurdistan, Cyndi Banks (2010, 28) found that a variety of sanctions were applied to women and girls for breaches of honor. These included home imprisonment, denial of education, withholding food, poisoning, beating, forced marriage, *Zhin be Zhin* marriage (woman for woman—a woman is traded for another in an arranged marriage), suicide through self-immolation (women may douse themselves with kerosene and set themselves alight), and murder (by shooting, suffocation, stabbing, burning, and drowning), payment of compensation, and divorce.

"Honor," therefore, relates to the violation of a code of conduct that is perceived to have brought shame upon the family. The UN Special Rapporteur on violence against women explains honor crimes by reference to such crimes in Lebanon as follows: "Honour is defined in terms of women's assigned sexual and familial roles as dictated by traditional family ideology. Thus, adultery, premarital relationships (which may or may not include sexual relations), rape and falling in love with an 'inappropriate' person may constitute violations of family honour" (quoted in Welchman and Hossain 2005, 5).

Women's sexuality is at the core of concerns about women's behavior, and the need to preserve a woman's virginity for her husband places limits not only on how she is to act sexually but also on the nature of her contacts with men outside the circle of the extended family, contacts that may hold sexual potential (Sen 2005, 48).

Violations of honor can extend beyond these parameters of sexual conduct to include other behaviors that are perceived to challenge male control such as staying out late and smoking (Welchman and Hossain 2005, 5). Codes of honor construct not only what constitutes a woman but also what it means to be a man, and therefore the codes are linked to both genders (Sen 2005, 48). The traditional family ideology can often be sourced to tribal rules. In Iraqi Kurdistan, gendered clan-based values serve as a powerful force for nationalism among the Kurds so that challenging patriarchal ideology becomes a challenge to the nationalist cause, rendering the dismantling of that ideology highly problematic (Begikhani 2005, 220).

These frameworks of shame and honor "control, direct and regulate women's sexuality and freedom of movement by male members of the family" (Coomaraswamy 2005, xi). Mothers often support these controls; for example, mothers

interviewed following the death of daughters often state that their daughters deserved the death (Coomaraswamy 2002, 496). In Egypt, older women gain status by supervising younger women to ensure that the honor (*sharaf*) of the tribe is maintained. They may use gossip as an instrument of control, for example, "Because you are a girl, and people will talk if you do this" (Abu-Odeh 2010, 919).

Honor crimes are characterized by the notion that the family and community of the woman and not simply her husband or partner are empowered to perform the killing (Meeto and Mirza 2007, 187). Forms of killing can include stoning, ritual stabbing, or killing in public spaces (Devers and Bacon 2010, 360).

BOX 13.2   Prosecutor Modernity Versus Tradition

An incident chronicled by Banks (2010, 16) shows how modern communication techniques highlight the tensions between modernity and tradition. An incident occurring in 2004 (the year that mobile phones were introduced into Iraq) involved a teenage boy and girl in Erbil and became a notorious instance of this tension. The boy encouraged the girl to drink alcohol, and she became drunk and insensible. He drove her to an isolated place and had sexual relations with her. During his assault the boy took pictures of their relations on his mobile phone. He later showed the pictures to his friends, who in turn showed them around the community. The pictures were also uploaded to the Internet. In response, the girl's family killed her to redeem their honor. The boy's family attempted to settle the affair with the girl's family, but the latter insisted that the boy must also be killed. The girl's family argued that the incident could only be resolved by an honor killing, given the enormity of widespread public knowledge of the incident on the Internet and the powerlessness to erase that record. Finally, the boy's family agreed that their son must be killed, and the boy's father took his son to an isolated place and killed him. No criminal charges were brought against the parents.

Migration away from one's own country can be associated with DV and honor crimes because migrant women may be perceived by the family and community to be the guardian of patriarchal practices and traditions sustained in the home country and this cultural responsibility can be amplified in the new country. Diaspora women from India, for example, are often expected to protect the cultural specificity of their communities by not dating men, not arranging their own marriages, and abstaining from same-sex relationships (Narayan 1997, 177). As Coomaraswamy (2005, xi) puts it, "Honour is generally seen as residing in the bodies of women," but at the same time "a woman's honor is the property of her male relatives, not her own property" (Hoyek, Sidawi, and

Mrad 2005, 112). Thus, immigrant women who live in the West and refuse to marry men chosen for them by their parents run the risk of honor killing.

Clare Beckett and Marie Macey (2001) argue that women in the United Kingdom who are at risk of honor crimes because of religion or ethnicity are placed in more danger because discourses of multiculturalism and respect for other cultures and traditions operate to engender nonintervention in cases where honor killings may occur. The emphasis in multiculturalism on "non-interference in minority lifestyles and its insistence on community consultation (with male self defined community leaders)," while not directly causing DV, does facilitate it (p. 311).

According to data from the UN Population Fund (UNFPA), about five thousand women are killed annually in the name of honor in states as widespread as Bangladesh, Brazil, Ecuador, Egypt, India, Israel, Italy, Jordan, Morocco, Pakistan, Sweden, Turkey, Uganda, Afghanistan, Saudi Arabia, Iran, Iraq, and the United Kingdom. Data on the number of honor crimes committed in countries is unreliable because many such crimes go unreported, but Pakistan reports a far higher number of such crimes than other countries where they are known to occur. This may be an indication of underreporting in other countries (Devers and Bacon 2010, 361).

Honor Crimes in Court

Legal scholars in the Middle East state that legal regimes in that region favor men who kill in the name of honor (Devers and Bacon 2010, 362) even though "honor" as such is not expressly stated to be a mitigating or even an exculpatory factor in such killings. Rather, laws explain the nature of conduct that will allow a penalty to be reduced. For example, the 1961 Penal Code of Jordan, Article 340[27] provides: "The perpetrator of a killing, wounding or injury benefits from a mitigating excuse if he surprises his wife or one of his female ascendants or siblings with another in an unlawful bed" (quoted in Devers and Bacon 2010, 364).

The Article was later amended to give a wife the same right to claim mitigation if she surprises her husband committing adultery due to concerns that it violated the Jordanian Constitutional right to equality (Devers and Bacon 2010, 364). While Article 340 is very specific about the conduct that can mitigate a penalty (similar provisions apply in Iraqi Kurdistan and in Lebanon), it is rare for an accused person in an honor killing to rely on this defense. Instead, defendants in honor crime cases plead that the crime was committed in a "fit of fury" or "a sudden spurt of anger," and if this plea is accepted it will reduce premeditated murder to manslaughter. This then is the favored defense of those accused of honor killings (Abu-Odeh 2010, 918; Welchman and Hossain 2005, 11).[28]

In the case of Jordan, Article 98 of the Penal Code provides that "whosoever commits a crime in a state of extreme rage resulting from an unrightful and dangerous act on the part of the victim shall benefit from the mitigating/extenuating excuse"

(quoted in Hassan and Welchman 2005, 204). Recent decisions in Jordan (1999–2003), however, have required that in order to take advantage of this defense, the rage, or "fit of fury" as it is commonly referred to, must be immediate in relation to gaining knowledge of the act. This would negate any period of reasoning prior to the act, and the Jordanian courts have indicated that the time involved can be no more than fifteen minutes (Hassan and Welchman 2005, 205). As to the concept of "dangerous" in this Article, the courts have interpreted this to cover a broad range of conduct, including talking with a strange man and leaving home for a week with no prior explanation for the absence (Madek 2005, 55).

In Egypt the law contains no general excuse of provocation, nor is there any excuse where a murder is committed in circumstances of *in flagrante delicto* (Abu-Odeh 2010, 921). However, those who commit crimes of honor are likely to ask the court for compassion under Article 17 of the Egyptian Penal Code, an issue solely within the discretion of the judge and that cannot be appealed because it is not an issue of law (p. 921). When this discretion is exercised in favor of a defendant, this can result in a significant reduction in punishment; for example, the death penalty can be replaced with life imprisonment or imprisonment for a fixed term (CEWLA 2005, 143). Here is an example of such a case from Egypt:

> The brother of the victim was suspicious of his sister's behaviour and thought that she had fallen pregnant through extramarital sexual relations; her husband had been out of the country for a period. He asked her to abort her pregnancy and she refused so he hit her on the head and then set her on fire. She managed to put out the fire and then shut herself in the water closet. He then poured petrol under the door jamb, set it alight and she burned to death. The forensic report showed that the victim was pregnant and with that the court issued a ruling of prison for three years for the man who murdered his sister. (Quoted in CEWLA 2005, 144)

Here, the court accepted that the murderer was under severe emotional pressure and required to defend his honor because the victim deviated from accepted standards of behavior. The murderer's act of killing his sister was justified as an attempt to "wash away" or bury the shame that

Rape as a Crime Against Humanity: The Former Yugoslavia

As well as grave breaches of the Convention, IHL also prescribes offenses that constitute *crimes against humanity*. The notion of a crime against humanity came out of the proceedings of the Nuremberg Tribunal as a means of criminalizing the actions of the Nazis against distinct communities, such as the Jews (Buss 2002, 94). The charters of the Nuremberg and Tokyo tribunals after World War II did not specifically enumerate rape as a crime against humanity, although it could be subsumed within the phrase "inhumane act" used in both charters (Niarchos 1995, 660). Crimes against humanity are described also in numerous international instruments of more recent origin, including the statute of the recently established International Criminal Court (see Chapter 9), and explicitly include rape.

While there is no agreed international consensus on the elements required to constitute a crime against humanity because the concept is defined differently in different international instruments (Askin 1999b, 70), a report of the United Nations[32] contains a commonly adopted interpretation stating that crimes against humanity "refer to inhumane acts of a very serious nature . . . committed as part of a widespread or systematic attack against any civilian population on national, political, ethnic, racial or religious grounds." Thus, where rape is committed on a wide scale against a civilian population for the specified grounds, it could be prosecuted as a crime against humanity. Up to the time of the formation of the ICTY, no prosecution had been taken. The statute of the ICTY gives it jurisdiction over crimes against humanity, and these are enumerated to explicitly include rape (O'Brien 1993, 645). In the context of the former Yugoslavia, charges of crimes against humanity are aimed at acts amounting to "ethnic cleansing," the forced removal of populations from specific locations that led to widespread violations of IHL (Buss 2002, 94).

Can rape amount to a crime against humanity? In 2001, in the landmark case of *Prosecutor v. Kunarac,* the Trial Chamber of the ICTY found that the mass rape, torture, and enslavement of Muslim women in the municipality of Foca during the conflict in Bosnia amounted to a crime against humanity. This was the first case to successfully prosecute rape as a crime against humanity (Buss 2002, 91). The Trial Chamber also found that the rapes were an element of a broader policy agenda that comprised terrorizing Muslims, evicting them, and making the area a Serbian stronghold. The accused Kunarac stated that the rapes "were one of the many ways in which the Serbs could assert their superiority and victory over the Muslims" (Buss 2002, 94). The decision makes it clear that wartime violence against women will be taken seriously and those who rape women will be held accountable.

BOX 13.4   Prosecutor v. Kunarac—*Rape as a Crime Against Humanity*

In April 1992, the city and area of Foca in Bosnia were invaded by Serb forces. Muslims residing in the city and its environs were attacked, deported out of the region, and/or detained. Women, children, and some older men were transported to detention centers located at the local high school and sports hall. Before the war in Bosnia, 52 percent of the approximately forty thousand residents of the municipality of Foca were Muslim. After the war, only ten remained. Conditions for those placed in detention were horrendous, with unhygienic facilities, little food, beatings, and repeated rapes. Serb soldiers habitually raped the women kept in the high school and sports hall. The accused Kunarac, along with two others, was involved in the rapes and in the removal of a group of women and girls, aged from twelve to twenty years, to houses and apartments where they were raped repeatedly by the accused and other soldiers. Some of this group were detained for months and subjected to constant rapes, taken as the "property" of the accused and made to perform housework, cooking, and cleaning. After some time, some women were sold to other soldiers. The twelve-year-old girl was never seen again. Kunarac and others were charged with rape as a crime against humanity.

SOURCE: Buss 2002, 92–93.

Rape as Genocide: The Former Yugoslavia

Genocide is defined by Article 2 of the Convention on the Prevention and Punishment of the Crime of Genocide 1948 and requires an intention to destroy, wholly or partly, a national, ethnic, racial, or religious group by committing acts such as killing; causing serious bodily or mental harm to group members; inflicting conditions on the group calculated to bring about its physical destruction, wholly or partly; imposing measures to prevent births in the group; or forcibly transferring children of the group to another group. Rape is not specifically mentioned, but it is argued that, where it has been conducted on a massive and systematic basis to produce babies of the ethnicity of the rapists or to destroy family life and to cleanse the area of all other groups, rape becomes genocidal (Chinkin 1994, 334). It is also argued that rape that amounts to serious bodily or mental harm to members of a group must be seen as an act of genocide (Eboe-Osuji 2007, 252).

Where rape is prosecuted as an act of genocide, it must be shown that the intention was to destroy a group, in whole or in part, and thus coercion or use of violence must be a key feature of the narrative given in genocide trials. Questions of consent, often the focus of domestic laws on rape, are irrelevant (Eboe-Osuji 2007, 258). In charging rape as genocide, it can be challenging to fulfill the requirements of the elements of genocide. For example, a UN report found no genocidal intent in Darfur, Sudan, because counterinsurgency and an intent to drive the victims from the land were additional motivations in what occurred there (Faucette 2012, 56).

Can rape amount to genocide? In the Akayesu case before the ICTR, rape was tried as genocide for the first time, with the ICTR noting that sexual violence was "an integral part of the process of destruction" and that the evidence of victims showed that sexual violence was a "fundamental and integral part of the genocide" with the use of HIV-positive soldiers providing evidence of intent to destroy. The ICTY focused on the systematic nature of rape, the targeting of Tutsi women, and the degree of harm and concluded that rape was used as an instrument of genocide. Akayesu was found guilty of rape as genocide, an unprecedented finding in international law. The decision has been described as of "monumental legal significance" (Faucette 2012, 59).

BOX 13.5 Prosecutor v. Akayesu—*Rape as Genocide*

Jean-Paul Akayesu was the *bourgmestre* (akin to a mayor) of Taba commune, Rwanda. The Tribunal found that a widespread and systematic attack against the civilian ethnic population of Tutsi took place in Taba between April 7 and the end of June 1994. Many Tutsi women endured sexual violence, mutilations, and repeated rapes, often in public and often by multiple men. One witness said, "Each time that you met assailants, they raped you." It was proved that some armed communal policemen and Akayesu himself were present during the commission of some of the rapes. While there were no allegations that Akayesu committed rape, it was held that he could be held accountable for the rapes and sexual violence that occurred in the area of Taba, perpetrated by Hutu on Tutsi women because he was involved in ordering, instigating, or aiding and abetting the rapes, forced public nudity, and sexual mutilation. He did this by being present and by verbally encouraging during or before instances of sexual violence. His presence and words sent "a clear signal of official tolerance" for the acts that took place.

SOURCE: Askin 2003, 320–21.

The incorporation of the crime of rape into international crimes is a significant step in the protection of women during times of armed conflict. Those involved in such conflicts who commit acts of rape can now be held accountable, depending on the evidence and circumstances, for the most serious international crimes. One outcome of the decisions discussed in this chapter is that rape as torture, rape as a crime against humanity, and rape as genocide can all be prosecuted in any state. Finally, it can be said that this is "compelling evidence that crimes of sexual violence are now considered amongst the most serious international crimes" (Askin 2003, 349).

NOTES

1. The public sphere focuses on the political public life of rational thinking and is where political and legal activity traditionally occurs. This contrasts with the private sphere where the focus is on the family, privacy, and the domestic and emotional life, where political and legal regulation is, in theory, believed to be inappropriate. In fact, there is a good deal of regulation of the private sphere, for example, in the case of abortion. Feminists have pointed out that the division between public and private is gendered and hierarchical and works to the disadvantage of women. The public world is male oriented and assumes greater power than the private world to which women are assigned. Thus, the domestic sphere entrenches inequality and renders women's concerns invisible.

2. The WHO (2013, 8) reported that psychological trauma and stress resulting from intimate partner violence can result in mental health problems, including post-traumatic stress disorder, anxiety, depression, eating disorders, suicidality, as well as substance abuse through alcohol, drugs, and tobacco.

3. Ninety-four percent of empirical studies found a significant relationship for men between witnessing violence against their mother and later abusing a partner themselves. This suggests that violence in adulthood is learned as boys grow up in a violent home (Heise 1998, 267).

4. As Rebecca Dobash and Russell Dobash (1992, 276) point out, "The survey is particularly poor at investigating complex behaviours, emotions and social processes such as those associated with violence, and its necessary brevity means it can rarely be used to explore the contexts associated with social behavior."

5. In the traditional ideology of patriarchy, men are the providers and heads of households while women provide emotional support and domestic services, but the exact nature of patriarchy differs depending on culture and context (Ferraro 2006, 79).

6. Charlotte Bunch is an activist for women's and human rights. She was a major lobbyist for the United Nations to consider women's rights as human rights.

7. See http://www1.umn.edu/humanrts/instree/e5dplw.htm.

8. See http://www.un.org/en/women/endviolence/about.shtml.

9. See http://www.sistersinislam.org.my/.

10. For example, in the United States, the strategy of providing treatment to abusers has been found to be ineffective. Studies have found that men arrested and treated for violence against women resume their violent conduct at the same rate as men arrested but not treated, and other studies have found no significant difference in recidivism rates between those who complete treatment programs and those who do not (Hanna 1998, 1505, 1533).

11. Weldon (2002, 7) explains that in her study, "responsiveness" in relation to governments means asking "whether governments are taking action to address violence against women or whether they are avoiding such action."

12. See http://www1.umn.edu/humanrts/iwraw/.

13. In the United States, police concerns about arresting perpetrators of DV centered on the dangers that conflict in the home presented to police. The police view was that they should become counselors and mediators and be trained in crisis intervention rather than make an arrest (Dobash and Dobash 1992, 161).

14. Historical Russian literature casts women as possessing evil and magical powers and as calling for rules and punishments to control them. Women were considered to be sinful and depraved. This set of beliefs about women found further expression in the *Domostroi*, a household manual that, as well as proscribing appropriate gendered roles for women and men, contained the appropriate dimensions for whips and instructed that a wife should be whipped without her blouse on and in private (Horne 1999, 56).

15. By 1998 ANNA had twelve staff and numerous volunteers, and by 2001 its leaders had become national advocates for DV by participating in conferences all over the country funded by programs operated by the American Bar Association (J. E. Johnson 2009, 54).

16. Reuters news agency reported in August 2013 that a new draft law on DV was being considered by committees of the Lower House of the Russian Parliament. This draft is the third such draft, the others having been "watered down" and dropped (Gabriela Baczynska, "Victims of Domestic Violence Face Uphill Battle for Protection in Russia," Reuters, August 20, 2013, http://www.reuters.com/assets/print?aid—USBR E97JOCX20130820).

17. The Human Development Index measures three basic dimensions of human development: long and healthy life, knowledge, and decent standard of living. Four indicators are used to calculate the index: life expectancy at birth, mean years of schooling, expected years of schooling, and gross national income per capita.

18. In an article published in 1994, Ofei-Aboagye (1994, 1) indicated there were no published studies on domestic violence in Ghana at that time.

19. Ghana's Country Reports to CEDAW submitted under Article 18 of CEDAW are referenced in Cantalupo et al. 2006, 531, footnote 22.

20. Where a woman asks for money, this is associated with perceptions that women are "greedy and have insatiable material desires" (Coker-Appiah and Cusack 1999, 16).

21. The WAJU was subsequently renamed the Domestic Violence and Victim Support Unit (Immigration and Refugee Board of Canada, *Ghana: Domestic Violence, Including Protection, Services and*

Recourse Available to Victims, GHA103468.E, June 10, 2010, available at Refworld, http://www.refworld.org/docid/4dd22ae92.html).

22. FIDA (Federación Internacional de Abogadas) is an international organization of women lawyers.

23. In the United States, survey data from the National Crime Victimization Study show that the reason most often given for failing to report DV (25 percent) is that it was a "private matter" (Ferraro 2006, 51).

24. While WAJU asserts that it refers all DV cases to court, WAJU officers reportedly refer cases for counseling. In addition, some WAJU officers do not sympathize with victims of DV (Cantalupo et al. 2006, 531).

25. See http://www.refworld.org/docid/4dd22ae92.html.

26. Men are rarely victims of honor crimes, but this can occur when both the man and the woman are murdered as a consequence of an act of adultery (Devers and Bacon 2010, 361).

27. The origins of Article 340 are the Ottoman Penal Code of 1858 and the French Penal Code of 1810, repealed only in 1975. Provisions similar to Article 340 are found in almost every Arab Penal Code and were in the Italian Penal Code, which was repealed in 1979 (Abu-Odeh 2010, 913–14).

28. The defense of provocation is available under almost all legal regimes. For example, in England and Wales, provocation is a partial defense to homicide where the killing is claimed to have taken place as a result of a sudden and temporary loss of control (Homicide Act 1957).

29. Resolution A/c.3/59/L.25 of 15 October 2004.

30. The 1995 Beijing Declaration and Platform for Action recognized the pervasiveness of sexual violence against women in times of armed conflict and noted, "Parties to a conflict often rape women with impunity, sometimes using systematic rape as a tactic of war and terrorism" (quoted in Askin 1999b, 61).

31. The Trial Chamber reviewed a case from the Inter-American Commission on Human Rights of 1996 in which the Commission found that rape constituted torture. The case, *Raquel Mejía v. Peru,* concerned events in 1989 when, during the evening, Peruvian military units with their faces covered entered the Mejía home and abducted Fernando Mejía on suspicion of being a subversive. Subsequently, Raquel Mejía was raped twice by a single soldier. The Commission found that she had been raped with the aim of intimidating her and inflicting punishment upon her. As to the level of suffering involved in torture, the Commission found that the rapes constituted an act of violence that caused physical and psychological pain and suffering, shock, fear of public ostracism, feelings of humiliation, fear of her husband's reaction, damage to the integrity of the family, and an apprehension that her children would feel humiliated if they came to know about the rapes. The European Court of Human Rights in the case of *Aydin v. Turkey,* in 1997, involving the rape of a woman in a police station after being blindfolded, beaten, stripped and sprayed with high pressure water, also found that the acts constituted torture. Also, in the case of *Akayesu,* 1998, the International Criminal Tribunal for Rwanda found that rape constituted torture because it degraded and humiliated, violated personal dignity, and was inflicted by a public official. All three cases involved rape by public officials.

32. Report of the Secretary-General Pursuant to Para. 2 of the Security Council Resolution 808 1993.

14

HUMAN RIGHTS AND CULTURAL RELATIVISM

Female Circumcision and Child Soldiers

ultural relativism is the notion that every society possesses its own moral code that explains what acts are permitted or prohibited. Thus, where the moral code of a society determines that an act occurring within that society is right, then it is right within that society and persons not of that society cannot judge the conduct of others in that society. Believers in cultural relativism argue that it is not possible to judge one moral code as being superior to another because there is no objective standard from which to make such a judgment. Cultural relativism is rejected by the discourse and practice of human rights, which applies a universalist approach to rights and practices in all societies. Thus international treaties and conventions establishing and protecting human rights fix universalist norms without regard to societies' moral codes. When societies continue practices that conflict with these norms, they are criticized and their practices are marginalized or even demonized. These universalist norms tend to be Eurocentric in nature because human rights treaties and conventions are largely the product of developed Western societies.

In the context of culture and cultural relativism, this chapter looks at female circumcision and child soldiers as instances of practices condemned in the West. We seek to contextualize these practices and events and explain why and how they occur. For example, the childhood of many in third world countries contrasts starkly with that enjoyed by many middle- and upper-class children in the West. Similarly, the notion of childhood itself is socially constructed and, as in the case of child soldiers, notions of what constitutes childhood differ between societies. We explore female circumcision and child soldiers in the context of the Western critique of such practices. The complex issue of female circumcision is fully addressed within context as a prime instance of Western universalist discourses about women, and an account is given of how and why this issue became a site of contestation between Western feminists and third world women.

Child soldiering, like female circumcision, became an international moral panic conducted and managed by nongovernmental organizations (NGOs) and international agencies who promoted specific discourses and forms of international legal regulation based on a Western conception of what constituted a child soldier. As female circumcision created the "mutilated woman," so the campaign against child soldiers created an idealized child soldier, vulnerable and innocent, always a victim and never a perpetrator. Our discussion draws a contrast between Western perspectives and the empirical and lived realities of both of these subjects, traces the international discourse and its outcome, describes the international legal frameworks that have been created around these subjects, and assesses the implications for subjects of female circumcision and child soldiering.

FEMALE CIRCUMCISION

Over the past fifty years, the issue of female circumcision has moved from a local to a global concern. Female circumcision (FC) has been referred to as "female genital mutilation" (FGM), and a practice designated as "traditional" or as "custom" has been redefined internationally as "a human rights violation" and as "violence against women." Female circumcision has engendered debates about cultural relativism, feminism, the image of Africa, arrogant imperialism, medicalization, sexuality, and the patriarchal oppression of women. The literature on female circumcision, whether in women's studies, law, politics, anthropology, medicine, or public health, has reached huge proportions (Shell-Duncan and Hernlund 2000, 1). Despite numerous international and national interventions to eliminate or eradicate the practice, it persists in those countries in which it is concentrated. While Western feminist activism has been responsible for most of the attention given to FC, it seems that much of the outrage and passion generated by the subject has subsided over the past ten years or so as the different constituencies involved have engaged in substantive dialogue (Obiora 2007, 69).

Terminology

A number of terms are used by academics, commentators, the media, and ordinary people to describe this practice, including *female genital cutting* (FGC), *female genital mutilation* (FGM), *genital surgery,* and *female circumcision.* Ellen Gruenbaum (2001, 3) notes that the term *female genital mutilation* has been widely used since the 1990s, but the word *mutilation* connotes an intention to cause harm, and many who favor female circumcision find the term offensive since that is never the intention of the operation. The term *female circumcision* suggests equivalence with male circumcision, which, to many persons, trivializes the act and the scale of its practice. *Female circumcision* is the term used most often in the communities in which the practice occurs, whereas the term *female genital mutilation* is generally employed for international audiences. We have therefore opted to use the term *female circumcision* in this account, which focuses on the cultural, social, and economic dimensions of the practice in the various communities in which it is concentrated. This account does not conceptualize FC only as a practice that violates the rights of women and girls. The word most commonly used in Arabic to describe the practice is *tahur,* which means "purification," denoting the cleanliness that follows a ritual process, although it is questionable whether FC constitutes a ritual because it is administered in a matter-of-fact manner without any spiritual association.

What Is Female Circumcision?

Whatever term is used, generally speaking, *female circumcision* is a term used "for the cutting and removal of genitalia of young girls to conform to social expectations" (Gruenbaum 2001, 2). From the viewpoint of health, the World Health Organization reports that female genital mutilation comprises all procedures involving partial or total removal of the external female genitalia or other injury to the female genital organs for nonmedical reasons (WHO and UNICEF, 1997).[1] FC is classified by the WHO into four types.[2]

- *Type I.* Partial or total removal of the clitoris and/or the prepuce (clitoridectomy).

- *Type II.* Partial or total removal of the clitoris and the labia minora, with or without excision of the labia majora (excision). In Sudan, this describes a *sunna* circumcision.

- *Type III.* Narrowing of the vaginal orifice with creation of a covering seal by cutting and appositioning the labia minora and/or the labia majora, with or without excision of the clitoris (infibulation). This is also known as a pharaonic circumcision and is the most extreme form, which leaves a perfectly smooth vulva of skin and scar tissue with a single tiny opening for urination and menstruation, rendering sexual intercourse very difficult.

- *Type IV.* All other harmful procedures to the female genitalia for nonmedical purposes, for example, pricking, piercing, incising, scraping, and cauterizing. Also known as a "*sunna* circumcision," where *sunna* means "tradition," usually referring to the traditions that the Prophet Muhammad did or advocated during his lifetime. However, in some countries, for example, Sudan, a *sunna* circumcision is more severe than a type I circumcision (Gruenbaum 2001, 2).

Given the type of FC practiced varies according to the country concerned, when discussing FC in various countries we refer to its manner of practice by reference to this typology. For example, in Somalia, the most common type of FC practiced is type III, infibulation. The WHO reports that type II is the most commonly performed mode of FC, accounting for 80 percent of all cases, and that type III is used in 15 percent of cases (Skaine 2005, 50).

In Somalia and Sudan, infibulation commonly involves removal of the clitoris, in whole or in part, and all of the labia minora. The labia majora are incised and stitched together, leaving a sheath of skin covering the urethra and obstructing the vaginal opening to a greater or lesser extent. A reed or similar narrow artefact is usually inserted to allow for urine and menstrual blood to pass. As the wound heals, it forms a layer of tissue, and a midwife may be required to enlarge the vaginal opening when the woman marries. During labor, a midwife must be present to cut through the scar tissue and release the child. After birth, the vagina is re-stitched or reinfibulated because many women say they "feel naked" or ashamed because the body is no longer "closed" (Boddy 2007, 49, 51).

FC can be compared to Western practices of performing female genital cosmetic surgery, commonly referred to as "designer vaginas," which include reduction of the labia, remodeling of the labia majora, pubis reduction, and clitoral reduction, some of which practices quite closely resemble FC as performed "traditionally" in Africa in their outcomes (Hernlund and Shell-Duncan 2007, 19).

Origins of Female Circumcision

The origins of FC are unclear. Some say that it was practiced by nomadic Arabs long before the coming of Islam "to protect the shepherd girls against likely male attacks while they were out unescorted with their grazing sheep" (Al-Safi 1970, quoted in Gruenbaum 2001, 42). Another origin narrative is that an Egyptian pharaoh with a small penis demanded that women undergo FC to facilitate his pleasure. References to FC being practiced in the Nile Valley during the time of the civilizations of Egypt and Sudan have been discovered, and among the people of that area there is a widespread belief that it began in the time of the pharaohs although no evidence of FC has been found in Egyptian mummies (Gruenbaum 2001, 43). Nevertheless, Herodotus stated that Egyptians, Hittites, Ethiopians, and Phoenicians performed FC five hundred years before the birth of Christ. As well, a Greek papyrus kept in the British Museum and dated to 163 BCE refers to the circumcision of girls in Egypt at the city of Memphis. There are other scattered references to FC in other Roman texts (p. 43).

Some have speculated that FC was performed because the pharaohs believed in the bisexuality of the gods. It was thought that the woman's soul was located in the clitoris, and therefore removal of the clitoris would result in a complete man (Gruenbaum 2001, 43). None of these ancient references explains why FC remains a tradition today. Over the centuries, however, FC became deeply embedded in local cultures and acquired meanings associated with the "complex sociocultural arrangements of women's subordination in a patriarchal society" (p. 45).

While FC is always described as an "ancient" practice, research has revealed that in some countries it is a recently acquired practice. For example, research in Chad has shown that it dates back only a single generation in some groups, and it is said that FC has spread in Sudan outward from the Arabized north to other parts of the country (Shell-Duncan and Hernlund 2000, 35).

Age of Female Circumcision

There are significant variations in age, and sometimes it is performed on infants and toddlers. For example, it has been performed on Egyptian girls aged one or two and among the Maasai of Kenya at fourteen or fifteen years or even older, but most commonly it is effected between the ages of four and eight (Gruenbaum 2001, 2) or four and twelve (Skaine 2005, 14).

Health Risks of Female Circumcision

Given the conditions under which it is normally carried out, there are significant health risks with all types of FC. In the short term, during and following completion of the procedure, the conditions are commonly unhygienic, and those performing the FC are usually minimally trained. Infection of the wound can occur, and uncontrolled hemorrhages can be difficult to control. Shock and blood poisoning can occur, and in the days following the surgery, girls may experience retention of urine (Gruenbaum 2001, 5).

According to the WHO, types I, II, and III cause severe pain because anesthesia is not commonly used and the healing period remains painful. The pain is most severe in type III where the surgery takes longer (fifteen to twenty minutes). The possible long-term effects are many and various and explained at http://www.who.int/reproductivehealth/topics/fgm/health_consequences_fgm/en/. To summarize, from the health and medical viewpoint, the WHO reports the procedure is never performed for any medical reasons and is clearly painful in three modes and liable to produce a host of ill effects in both the short term and long term.

Some scholars have taken issue with the claim that FC produces harmful effects or have concluded that the research shows little evidence of health complications. For example, Carla Obermeyer (1999, 92) completed the first systematic review of the biomedical research and found that only eight studies met her criteria for inclusion into a summary of major findings. She concluded that "severe complications are relatively infrequent" and that medical complications are "the exception rather than the rule." Other issues relate to the lack of information for all types of FC, that cases of infibulation are "often used to generalize about health risks associated with all types of FC," and that research does not always establish causality because many reported conditions may be the outcome of factors other than FC. It is argued there is a need for better data (Hernlund and Shell-Duncan 2007, 15–16).

Performing Female Circumcision

Commonly, FC is performed by traditional midwives, but health care professionals provide the service in some countries, including Egypt, Sudan, and Kenya. In Kenya, reportedly, while women have been sensitized to the health risks associated with FC, they have not abandoned the practice but pay medical professionals to perform it (Skaine 2005, 111). In Egypt, health professionals regularly perform FC, and mothers have reported that in three out of four cases (77 percent), FC was performed on their daughters by a trained medical professional who was usually a medical practitioner. In other countries, the procedure is carried out by nurses, midwives, and trained health professionals rather than by medical practitioners. Since 1996, the WHO has taken the position that willfully damaging healthy organs for nontherapeutic reasons "violates the injunction to 'do no harm' and is unethical by any standards" (quoted in Skaine 2005, 33).

Methods of Performing Female Circumcision

The WHO has described the instruments used in FC done in the home as "special knives, scissors, razors or pieces of glass." Sharp stones have been used, but rarely, and in Gambia fingernails have been used to pluck out babies' clitorises (Skaine 2005, 11). Depending on the skill of the traditional circumciser, usually a woman, the procedure may take up to twenty minutes (Skaine 2005, 13).

BOX 14.1   Female Circumcision in Egypt

The ceremony took place in the courtyard of the house in which a family was staying while visiting their home village. The girl was the daughter of that visiting family. Several women and girls from the neighborhood gathered in the courtyard. The girl's mother remained in a room away from the courtyard because she could not bear to watch the operation. The girl was seated by some women on an overturned basin that was large enough for the midwife to reach her. The women held the girl firmly, and the midwife sat in front of the girl with a pot of charcoal by her side. The girl began squirming and showed some fear. One woman pulled the girl's dress over her face, obscuring her sight of what was to happen, and exposed her genitals. The midwife, holding a knife, spread the girl's legs apart and dipped her hand in the charcoal so her hand would not slip during the procedure. She took hold of the girl's genitals and made a series of small cuts. The girl was screaming and bleeding—no anesthetic was used. On completion of the cutting, the midwife washed off the blood with water. She smeared egg yolk over the wound and applied henna leaves, then pressed the girl's legs together and bound them with strips of cloth at the thighs and ankles.

At this point, the women in the courtyard gave cries of joy calling out, "You are a woman now," "you are now a bride." The girl's mother came and put two necklaces, one silver and one gold, around her neck. This represented a gift of mother-daughter bonding and celebrated the girl's transition into sexuality, which made her ready for marriage. The mother then picked up her daughter, who had previously been wrapped in a white cloak, and carried her out of the courtyard and then reentered the courtyard. This represented a public announcement that the circumcision had been completed and the daughter had transitioned from one life phase to another. After she had placed the girl in the shade on a mat, the mother circled the courtyard giving the guests gifts of perfume and candy and later served everyone lentil soup. Other women came to offer congratulations. Before departing, each guest gave the mother a money gift, and the midwife was paid her fee and given cigarettes, dates, and soap.

This description of a circumcision and its attendant rituals is based on anthropological fieldwork conducted in Nubia, Egypt.

SOURCE: El Guindi 2006, 43.

The Geography of Female Circumcision

It is estimated that there are more than 125 million women and girls who have had some form of FC and about 2 million are believed at risk of having the procedure carried out each year (Skaine 2005, 35). FC in some form is practiced in twenty-nine African and Middle Eastern countries (UNICEF 2013, 5). As well, small populations practice FC in Colombia, Jordan, Oman, Saudi Arabia, and parts of Indonesia and Malaysia, and there is evidence that FC is being performed in parts of Europe and North America, which, for the past several decades, have been destinations for migrants from countries where FC is a long-standing tradition (pp. 22–23).[3]

Scholars have begun to try to understand how diaspora communities have responded to living in Western societies where the reaction to FC is outrage and horror. For example, Somali women living in *London* are acutely aware their bodies are different from those in mainstream society and the fact of circumcision, a sign of excellence and perfection in Somali culture, has taken on the character of "a mark of deficiency and difference,"

rendering Somali women in London "marked and marginalized as incomplete and inferior women" (Talle 2007, 103).

Among Somali women in *Sweden,* while no cases of FC have been prosecuted or even authenticated, there is a widespread belief that FC is practiced in the country on a large scale. In research in Malmö, Sweden, in the late 1990s (Johnsdotter cited in Talle 2007, 107) found that in Somalia, FC was understood as both a Somali tradition and a religious duty, but in Sweden, circumcised girls are "the ones to be different and feel ashamed" (p. 112). The overwhelmingly majority of Somalis in Sweden were opposed to FC, but native Swedes, applying stereotypes of circumcised African women, firmly believe that circumcisers are imported to undertake FC within Sweden despite the fact that there are about twenty thousand Somalis in the country, many of whom have lived there for more than ten years, and no cases of FC have ever been found and prosecuted (p. 116).

For Mandinga women of Guinea-Bissau living in *Lisbon, Portugal,* notions about the meaning and practice of FC vary as they move between Africa and Portugal (M. C. Johnson 2007, 203).

In their own country, FC is regarded as a cleansing rite that makes women "true Muslims" by enabling them to pray in the correct manner. It is thought that the genitals of uncircumcised women produce an odor that "spoils" prayers, a common belief among West African FC countries. They believe FC to be mandated by Islam, claiming that the passage where this is stated is secret and may only be seen by certain qualified persons (p. 210). For the Mandinga, ethnicity and religious identity are fused in one and inscribed on their bodies.

In Guinea-Bissau, men consider FC a woman's issue, but Mandinga men in Portugal who have traveled to Arab countries and been on the Haj strongly argue that African customs are not Muslim ones and that identity and religion are separate, not fused. In contrast to the men, women are uncertain, but many are losing confidence in the connection between religion and ethnicity (Johnson 2007, 212). For some Mandinga women now living in Portugal, the decision about circumcising their daughters rests on their residence; staying in Europe means not circumcising because there it is "big trouble," but if they return to Guinea-Bissau the link there between FC and initiation rituals is seen as important because there is a "traditional" context there that is absent in Europe (2007, 218).

In Africa and the Middle East, based on information published by UNICEF (2013), the following is a list of countries with the highest estimated prevalence of FC.

- Somalia 98%
- Guinea 96%
- Djibouti 93%
- Egypt 91%
- Eritrea, Mali 89%
- Sierra Leone, Sudan 88%
- Gambia, Burkina Faso 76%
- Mauritania 69%
- Liberia 66%
- Guinea-Bissau 50%
- Chad 44%
- Côte d'Ivoire 38%
- Kenya, Nigeria 27%
- Central African Republic 24%
- Tanzania 15%
- Benin 13%
- Iraq 8%
- Ghana, Togo 4%
- Niger 2%
- Cameroon, Uganda 1%

In terms of the typology of FC, in Djibouti, type III (infibulation) is used almost exclusively, and in Somalia, FC is almost universal with at least 80 percent being type III. In Sudan, 83 percent of FC are type III. While FC is most prevalent among predominantly Muslim countries, it is also found among other religions, for example, among the Coptic Christians of Sudan, Ethiopia, and Egypt (Abu-Sahlieh 2006, 54; Gruenbaum 2001, 60). FC is not however practiced in all countries where the Muslim faith predominates; for example, it is not found in Iran, Jordan, Lebanon, Syria, Turkey, or any North African countries and is found only in a few parts of Indonesia, India, and Malaysia.

Female Circumcision and Islam

There is a tendency in the West to believe that FC is associated with the practice of Islam and is therefore required of Muslims. Many Muslims also believe that this is the case; for example, one culture in Guinea-Bissau believes that FC is a purification rite that establishes a woman's Muslim identity (Gruenbaum 2001, 62). In rural Sudan, many believe that FC is expected of them as Muslims. Thus Muslims who practice FC think it constitutes part of their religion (Abu-Sahlieh 2006, 59). In Sudan, pharaonic circumcision (type III circumcision—infibulation), as a tradition that predates the coming of Islam, was, over time, syncretized into Sudanese Islamic belief, so that it seems to people to be an element of Islam (Gruenbaum 2001, 44).

In fact, nearly all Islamic scholars agree that Islam does not require FC to be performed on women and girls. The Qur'an contains no reference to FC in any form (Abu-Sahlieh 2006, 54), but Muslims who wish to associate FC with Islam do so by justifying it on the basis of *hadith* (see Chapter 3 on Islamic Law Systems), reports on the actions and sayings attributed to the Prophet. These reports include attributing to the

Chapter 14 Human Rights and Cultural Relativism 457

Prophet the saying, "Reduce, but do not destroy," supposedly said to a midwife conducting a circumcision in the early Muslim period. Versions of *hadith* concerning FC have been interpreted in different ways as the following alternative interpretations show:

Do not go deep. That is enjoyable to the woman and is preferable to the husband.

Do not go deep. It is more illuminating to the face and more enjoyable to the husband.

Circumcise but do not go deep, this is more illuminating to the face and more enjoyable to the husband. (Quoted in Gruenbaum 2001, 64)

While each of these statements condemns infibulation (type III), it is uncertain whether it can be said that the Prophet was actively encouraging some lesser form of FC. One interpretation maintains that the Prophet was expressing disapproval of severe FC practices that existed before Islam and recommending mitigation and therefore not requiring rejection of FC altogether; another is that the Prophet was endorsing FC and in fact recommending it, but only in the less severe forms. Consequently, it is believed that the majority of Muslim authors agree that FC is *makrumah,* meaning a meritorious act as opposed to *haram,* meaning a forbidden act, and that "it is better to do it, although it is not obligatory from a religious point of view" (Abu-Sahlieh 2006, 56; Skaine 2005, 119). Since there is no single authoritative interpretative voice in the practice of Islam, the debate about meaning will presumably continue (Gruenbaum 2001, 65).

Colonial Activity to Combat Female Circumcision

During the British colonial period in Sudan, FC was a topic of interest to colonial policymakers (Gruenbaum 2001, 20). In 1945, a pamphlet was published in Arabic and English titled *Female Circumcision in the Anglo-Egyptian Sudan* (Pridie et al. 1945). The publication was intended to promote the elimination of FC, and the key arguments against FC included statements from three prominent Sudanese religious and political leaders, including the then Mufti of Sudan. The religious arguments concluded that male circumcision was a *sunna* (tradition) and that female circumcision

was merely "preferable," meaning while it was permitted, it was not a requirement of Islam. The pamphlet also included arguments about the health risks of FC and provided anatomical information and descriptions of the operation (Gruenbaum 2001, 62). This publication was issued shortly before the date of legislation that criminalized FC (p. 63).

Around 1940 the Mufti of Sudan issued a *fatwa* against FC in the infibulation form, and in Egypt, a *fatwa* was issued in 1950 that recited, "Female circumcision is an Islamic practice mentioned in the tradition of the Prophet, and sanctioned by Imans and Jurists, in spite of the difference on whether it is a duty or a sunna (tradition). We support the practice as sunna and sanction it in view of its effect on attenuating the sexual desire in women and directing it to the desirable moderation" (quoted in Gruenbaum 2001, 63). Members of the Gikuyu culture in Kenya believed during the 1930s and 1940s that FC was central to their way of life and viewed it as a "symbol of ethnic pride pitted against colonial domination" (Gruenbaum 2001, 103). Thus ethnic identity and nationalism coalesced through the medium of the practice of FC.

Cultural and Social Context of Female Circumcision

Numerous studies reveal that when women in FC countries were asked why they supported FC, the inevitable reply involved some variation of "because it's our tradition/custom." It is necessary then to ask, What social practices and norms of behavior are implicated in that tradition or custom that are so enduring and of such weight that they function to resist any changes to the practice, let alone its elimination?

Marriage

When women's social standing and economic security are an outcome of their roles as wives and mothers, it is to be expected that local norms concerning marriage will be rigorously followed (Gruenbaum 2001, 45). This is true even where, as in many African societies and cultures, women engage in productive work such as subsistence agriculture, wage employment, and commodity production. A husband and children are commonly essential in guaranteeing a woman's economic security. Many roles may be gender specific; for example, men may build fences and provide forms of physical protection. Children often contribute their labor at a young age, especially in rural areas. The aggregate work and effort of the wife, husband, and children form an economic as well as a social unit. Especially in rural areas, unmarried women are uncommon, and while if unmarried they may live with family members, they will often receive the bare minimum in subsistence and have no one committed to their interests. As a result, the social practice of marriage is vital to a woman's identity and to her economic security (Gruenbaum 2001, 46). For many societies, therefore, an uncircumcised female is not a woman (Abusharaf 2006, 9).

In many such societies and cultures, it is imperative that a woman come to a marriage as a virgin. In Sudan, even rumors that question a woman's virginity can be destructive of any marriage prospects and can damage and shame her family honor (Gruenbaum 2001, 46). It is, therefore, in the context of a woman's marriage and virginity that FC plays such a vital role: it "guarantees virginity, morality, marriageability, and the hope of old age security, all in one decisive action taken when she is too young to object" (p. 46). Thus "virginity is both socially constructed and physically constructed through infibulation," and the family that does not inflict infibulation on a daughter is regarded as abdicating its responsibility to provide a guarantee of her virginity (p. 79).

Islam especially views prohibitions on sexual relationships outside marriage as issues of family honor (see Chapter 13 for a discussion of Honor Crimes). For example, Boddy (1989, 53) reports that a community in Sudan perceived FC as a means "to curb and socialize their sexual desires lest a woman should, even unwittingly, bring irreparable shame to her family through misbehaviour." FC will establish that the woman has not had premarital sex because her sexuality has been diminished by the removal of the clitoris, and when she has undergone infibulation (type III), she has presented a physical barrier to sexual intercourse. When the woman has not undergone an infibulation but a type I or type II surgery, doubts may still be raised about her morality and virginity and therefore to her marriageability (Gruenbaum 2001, 46).

Gender Identity

Gender plays a significant role in FC. For example, in numerous cultures, removal of perceived male-like or masculine parts of the body (such as the clitoris, which is regarded as such in Egypt and Somalia) is seen as feminizing the body and clearly establishing gender. It is reported that for the Gikuyu of Kenya and in Mali, removing the clitoris displaces gender ambiguity and crystallizes status and gender (Gruenbaum 2001, 67). Consequently, removal of the foreskin in boys through circumcision eliminates any femininity, and removal of the clitoris in females eliminates any masculinity. Some believe that if the clitoris is not removed, it will grow into a phallus (Gruenbaum 2001, 68). In Mali, the Dogon and Bambara cultures believe that a newly born child possesses two souls, male and female, and is inhabited by an evil power that prevents fertility. They consider the boy's "female soul" is located in the prepuce, the "female" element of the genitals, and that the girl's "male soul" is located in the clitoris. Removal of the clitoris and the prepuce destroys the evil power that inhibits fertility (Skaine 2005, 21).

Some cultures see removal of both the clitoris and the labia as essential to fixing gender. For the Sudanese who support and practice FC, the clitoris and labia are not only considered male body parts but are also regarded as ugly. Those who advocate infibulation (type III) also view the smooth, infibulated vulva as highly feminine and aesthetically pleasing (Gruenbaum 2001, 68). Women in Sudan stressed the clean, smooth, and pure body that is the outcome of FC (p. 79).

Maintaining ethnic identity can also be a barrier to change in FC practices. Among culture groups in Sudan, the nature of the FC can operate as a marker of the status of the woman who undergoes it. Thus, among the Beni Halba of Sudan, women of higher status families underwent infibulation while women of lesser status had a *sunna* circumcision. The same concern for status is shown by the Beri people of Chad and western Sudan, where FC is only performed on the daughters of royal clans (Gruenbaum 2001, 105). Status and ethnicity differentiate circumcising and non-circumcising groups within Sudan: the Muslims of West African descent and the groups of Ethiopian immigrants and refugees hold a lower social status and are also ethnically different (p. 105). FC can therefore operate as "an important marker of privileged ethnic group status" (p. 107).

Tradition and Culture

An adequate response to the question concerning why women undergo and support FC would necessitate an interrogation of multiple cultures, many of which would give different reasons and explanations for FC. For example, one survey conducted in Sudan of 1,804 females and 1,787 males found that the response to the question of why FC was practiced varied considerably. While 59 percent of males said it was for "religious demand," only 14 percent of women gave that response. Women most often responded that FC was a "good tradition" (42 percent), but only 28 percent of men gave that reason. The promotion of cleanliness was also advanced as a reason by 28 percent of men and 19 percent of women. Only about one tenth mentioned protecting virginity and preventing immoral behavior (10 percent of women and 11 percent of men). As to increasing the chance of marriage, even fewer chose this reason (9 percent of women and 4 percent of men). Increasing the pleasure of the husband in having sex was mentioned by 13 percent of women and 21 percent of men (Rushwan, Slot, El Dareer, and Bushra 1983, 92–93). The researchers in this survey noted that respondents found it difficult to give a reason for a practice they thought so obviously "right" that they resorted to "some vague reference to religion." The outcome of this survey is illustrative of the difficulty in ascribing a reason for FC, even in a single society (Gruenbaum 2001, 49).

Similar results were shown for a survey conducted in Somalia in 1991 when respondents were permitted only one choice of reason to justify FC. Researchers found that of the two hundred female respondents, 70 percent named "religion," 20 percent named "to remain virgin in order to get married," and 10 percent responded with "tradition" (Dirie and Lindmark 1991, 583). It is suggested that the reasons given do not substantially differ because Muslims consider preserving virginity is the will of God and this is achieved through infibulation (Gruenbaum 2001, 50). In Egypt, similar results were reported from a survey in a village in Upper Egypt in 1992 which found the most prevalent reason given for FC (77 percent) was "because it followed customs and traditions" (Sayed, El-Aty, and Fadel 1996, 285).

Ritual

Among the Maasai of Kenya, FC marks the transition from girlhood to womanhood and marriageable age. In this culture, FC is not performed until a marriage has been arranged for a girl, usually in her teenage years; thus FC merges marriage and womanhood. Also in Kenya, among the Gikuyu, a similar process is followed where FC forms an element in a complex initiation ritual that includes instruction about how to behave appropriately. It is through this ritual that girls obtain respect and are considered ready to marry. In Tanzania, it is said that the ritual of FC "represents a celebration of courage, self-giving and self-denial, and suffering. The girl's identity is established and she experiences the unity of the clan and its members. She is now ready to move into adult womanhood" (Skaine 2005, 113). In a study of FC in Guinea-Bissau, FC was found to be a cleansing rite that defined women as Muslim and enabled them to pray appropriately. Thus, in this country, FC establishes a religious identity and fuses ethnicity and religion (p. 122).

In many societies, however, FC is performed at a young age and cannot be considered as a transition ritual from girlhood to womanhood. It follows that it is incorrect to designate all FC as ritual or rites of passage (Gruenbaum 2001, 70). For women in some societies, FC plays a crucial role in marriage, identity, culture and tradition, as well as in rituals that mark the transition from girlhood to womanhood. These are key events and phenomena in women's lives and understanding the links between marriage, identity, tradition, ritual, and the practice of FC adds greatly to our knowledge of all the dimensions of FC. The overall context within which FC is practiced demonstrates a complex association between FC and social practices and shows that FC is not to be understood solely as a practice that violates the rights of women and girls.

CULTURAL RELATIVISM AND FEMALE CIRCUMCISION

The central questions about FC and traditional cultures and practices have been posed as follows:

> Is female circumcision a vicious act of mutilation and injury, or a virtuous act of purity and rectitude? Two opposing views dominate

current debates, one authorizing cultural accommodation and the other advocating the observance of universal standards of human rights. The former view has been widely vilified for sanctioning violence under the guise of culture, and the latter has been reproved for its ethnocentric stance toward cultural rights. (Abusharaf 2006, 6)

In this section we examine the notion of cultural relativism, explore varying cultural perspectives on FC, gain an understanding of how Western feminists created and then continued to influence the international discourse on FC, and map out international action taken on FC, including its international designation as a "harmful traditional practice." Finally, we consider how the issue of FC and its effect on sexuality are viewed from different cultural perspectives.

Cultural Relativism and Female Circumcision as Violence Against Women

Notions of human rights and women's rights granted and protected by international treaties and conventions constitute universalist discourses about human rights and women's rights. It is argued that while such discourses use criteria that are ostensibly international, they actually reflect the values of Western culture. Cultural relativist arguments have been raised in response to these universalist discourses with such arguments sometimes attempting to justify restrictions on women's human rights by asserting that restrictions are required to defend local cultural traditions against universalist domination. Claims are made by leaders that universalist rights discourses are a form of Western hegemony and ought to be challenged and resisted.

Cultural relativism argues that knowledge of other cultures is limited when an observer has not been brought up in that culture (and therefore lacks a full understanding of the significance of the practices of that culture) and that all cultures have equal legitimacy regardless of content. Accordingly, it is argued that cultural practices should not be presented in a simplistic manner or misrepresented altogether. For example, the veil carries multiple meanings[4] because of differing cultural and historical contexts, but in the

West the veil is almost always presented as an oppressive practice that typifies Islam's degrading treatment of women (Kapur 2005, 107).

There are degrees of cultural relativism. "Hard" or "strong" relativists assert that the validity of a moral right may only be judged by the culture that is its source, whereas "soft" or "weak" relativists claim only that culture may constitute an important source of the validity of a moral right. Relativists assert that each culture maintains its own moral code about what is normative or nonnormative and that one culture's moral code cannot be judged as the superior of another in the absence of any objective standard that would allow such a judgment to be made. Thus the moral code that citizens of the United States subscribe to is not special: it is simply one among many. Relativists claim that the Western conception of individual rights as embodied in numerous international instruments is inappropriate for many developing countries, where the needs of the community are dominant and paramount. Consequently, in those countries, the rights of the individual are subsumed to community rights, and many cultures reject the notion that individuals are autonomous beings (Kim 1993, 57–58). This critique of individual autonomy is expressed by anthropologist Aihwa Ong, who argues that transnational feminist campaigns incorporating a North-South alliance of sisterhood are driven by Northern (Western) women who ignore geopolitical inequalities and are insensitive to non–first world cultural values. She asserts such campaigns are based on a distinctly individualistic formulation of rights that is Western specific (Ong 1996). Thus cultural relativists argue that certain practices are integral to cultural identity and cannot be radically changed without an adverse impact on the community.

The response of the human rights community to relativist arguments is to argue that international human rights law represents "the collective response of the international community to the uniqueness of the human condition and the unity of the human race" (Kim 1993, 63). This collective response is evidenced by many non-Western countries having ratified human rights conventions and therefore adopting the international norms created by those instruments. This positivist approach to the issue of cultural relativism is rejected by relativists who say that in international treaty making processes, non-Western nations were dominated by Western nations and that their consent to international norms is simply a legacy of colonialism (p. 65). Human rights activists argue that discrimination against women cannot be justified by local circumstances and differences. While cultural differences will be respected, this happens only within limits (Merry 2006a, 91). As Sally Engle Merry (2006a, 91) reports in her observation of the process of the CEDAW Committee,[5] when culture is invoked by states presenting their reports on women's status, it is more often regarded "as an obstacle to change, than as a resource or a mode of transformation." Thus, according to this standpoint, FC, as a form of violence against women, is grouped with murder, rape, trafficking, forced prostitution, and sexual harassment (Abusharaf 2006, 10).

Cultural relativism becomes especially salient when many countries maintain customs and traditions that are not only seen to oppress women but also violate international instruments that protect women's human rights. Thus rights granted to women by international instruments relating to human rights are often in tension with cultural practices that impact the everyday lives of women worldwide. This tension is revealed when, for example, women publicly celebrate practices that in fact disguise experiences, such as FC, which are said to be coercive and subjugating. Accordingly, it is argued that "respect for culture does not require embracing traditions that marginalize and victimize women" (Hernandez-Truyol 1999, 37).

Radhika Coomaraswamy (2002, 498) argues that a number of traditional or customary forms of violence against women closely resemble torture because of the degree of pain and suffering involved. FC and honor crimes fall into this category and should, she asserts, receive the highest degree of international scrutiny and groups working against these practices in their own countries should receive the utmost assistance. She suggests that all areas of customary and religious law and practice must give way to international standards, and the optimum strategy may be progressive realization over time, propelled by women's groups. This approach is more likely to result in durable solutions (p. 509). As Coomaraswamy puts it, "Being sensitive to cultural relativism cannot imply putting hard-won battles on human rights up for grabs" (p. 513).

FC practices represent deeply held cultural beliefs, and hard cultural relativists would argue that there is no basis for challenging and radically altering the beliefs and values of others. Often, the reaction of outsiders to cultural practices they find "backward" or "barbaric" provokes a response from insiders that brings a defense of culture. For example, Jomo Kenyatta, the President of Kenya, in *Facing Mount Kenya* (published in 1938), mounted a defense of FC in the face of British colonial criticism, which he regarded as cultural imperialism (Gruenbaum 2001, 25). Thus critical comment or writing is liable to be perceived as ethnocentrism and, as Gruenbaum (2001, 25) notes, is often exacerbated when delivered in a tone of "scolding, distaste, condescension, and condemnation." About this ethnocentric and condescending approach by Westerners toward FC, El Guindi (2006, 42) writes, "Most interventionist debate . . . assumes that women in non-Western societies are childlike and helpless, passive victims of their men, who must be saved by Western missionaries and feminists. This stance is arrogant and ethnocentric." Alternative stances are always more productive in terms of social change.

Tolerance for the beliefs of others, also known as ethical pluralism, argues that there are many truths in most situations rather than one single "truth" (see, e.g., Hinman 1998, 67–68; Hinman 2012, 45). Tolerance or ethical pluralism includes the principle of accepting difference (as opposed to denying any diversity in ethical perspectives) and the principle of understanding. The latter principle requires that we fully understand the ethical standards of another culture from the perspective of that culture: we should recognize that our perspective on FC is shaped by our own cultural values and not those of the relevant culture (Banks 2012, 6–7).

There are few hard cultural relativists concerning the practice of FC (James and Robertson 2002, 1) and, as Janice Boddy (1991, 16) has observed, no scholar who studies FC in its cultural context is "so theoretically myopic or inhumane as to advocate its continuance. . . . Understanding the practice is not the same as condoning it." Thus, as Richard Shweder (2002, 227) states in his discussion of FC, "Seeing the cultural point and getting the scientific facts straight is where tolerance begins." Fully understanding the cultural context of FC informs how best to change it because it takes "far more than overheated rhetoric and offended sensibilities to justify a cultural 'eradication campaign'" (p. 227).

**BOX 14.2   Harborview Hospital,
Seattle (United States), and Female Circumcision**

In September 1996, Harborview Hospital, serving a largely immigrant population, many of whom were Somali, initially refused requests from women to circumcise their daughters. However, following lengthy discussion, the hospital concluded that refusal would do more harm than good. If the hospital did not do the surgery, it was clear that daughters would be sent back to Somalia or visit one of the three local midwives to be circumcised. These options increased the likelihood the girls would be infibulated (type III).

Therefore, in September 1996, the hospital offered a plan concerning FC: it would nick the head of the clitoris in a procedure that would draw blood but would not remove tissue or leave any scarring and would use a local anesthetic. The girls would have to give consent, and informed parental consent would also have to be given.

The proposal was never implemented because the hospital was "besieged by outraged opponents" and inundated with letters and phone calls protesting the plan. It was said that even suggesting the plan would legitimize a "barbaric practice," and a physician who was sympathetic to the plan because he believed in the need to understand other cultural practices received death threats and hate mail. One physician suggested the abandonment of the plan would simply result in the hospital dealing with the medical consequences of the work of local midwives.

SOURCE: Boyle 2002, 112–13.

Western Feminist Perspectives on Female Circumcision and Responses

In 1980, the publication of *The Hosken Report: Genital and Sexual Mutilation of Females,* by Fran Hosken, generated popular Western interest in FC, its prevalence, and the nature of the practice. Hosken delivered a plea for activists and governments to take a strong stand against the practice, even including withholding overseas aid to require countries to cease the procedure (Gruenbaum 2001, 22). Her demand to eliminate the practice forthwith contrasted with the gradualist approach that had been followed, for example, in Sudan since the 1970s of providing improved hygiene, having the procedure performed by doctors in their surgeries, providing midwives with medical supplies, and encouraging the use of milder forms of FC (p. 22).

During the 1970s and early 1980s, few Middle Eastern feminists wrote about FC, but Egyptian doctor Nawal El Saadawi was an exception. "The Circumcision of Girls," a chapter in her book *The Hidden Face of Eve* (1980), was reprinted in *Ms.* magazine in the early 1980s and was influential, especially the section describing her own circumcision. This publication attracted the attention of North American feminists (Gruenbaum 2001, 22).

As concern in the West about FC began to grow, Hanny Lightfoot-Klein's 1989 publication *Prisoners of Ritual* was prominent among other titles that used dramatic and emotive descriptors such as "crimes," "pain," "brutal ritual," and "torture" to characterize FC. Examples of such publications included "Battling the Butchers" (Brownsworth 1994), *Possessing the Secret of Joy* (Walker 1992), and the book and film by Alice Walker and Pratibha Parmar, *Warrior Marks,* which in 1993 promoted the notion that an oppressive ritual designed to perpetuate male domination over women was being imposed on women (Gruenbaum 2001, 23). Texts by anthropologists and social scientists[6] offered contextual analysis rather than outrage and demands for immediately eliminating the practice and pointed out that FC practices were already undergoing change and that those affected were already debating the issue among themselves. Generally, this group argued for a greater understanding of the cultural, social, and economic context in which the practice was occurring (p. 23). It was also observed that in the practice and performance of FC, albeit a practice embedded in patriarchal societies, women are the direct agents of FC and often share its ideologies. Thus, in the Arab cultures that practice FC, the decision to circumcise is made by women for their daughters

(El Guindi 2006, 35). Feminists have responded by claiming that women are demonstrating "false consciousness" in affirming FC, suggesting they have no agency, and that therefore international action is required to save them from this practice (Hernlund and Shell-Duncan 2007, 30).

FC has not always and only been confined to largely African countries. Removal of the clitoris was regularly applied in the West in the nineteenth century as a cure for "excessive masturbation and nymphomania" and as a procedure for other medical reasons, including hypertrophy, tumors, and "infantile, adolescent, or adult masturbation regarded as excessive" (Gruenbaum 2001, 9). During the 1860s, Isaac Baker Brown, an eminent obstetrical surgeon, founded the London Surgical Home for Women and observed that many of the female epileptics masturbated. He developed a theory that masturbation led to a progression of stages from "hysteria" to epilepsy and finally to "idiocy or death" (p. 11). Symptoms that might result in eventual removal of the clitoris included becoming "restless and excited or melancholy and retiring, listless, and indifferent to the social influences of domestic life" as well as, in married women, "distaste for marital intercourse" (Sheehan 1997, 327). The practices of Baker Brown were adopted in the United States in the late 1860s and continued in some form until at least the 1940s, when the last known clitoridectomy to correct emotional disorder was performed on a five-year-old girl (p. 333).

As discussed, Western feminist perspectives on FC have generally regarded it as a deeply patriarchal practice that sanctions the mutilation of the bodies of helpless female victims with the objective of controlling a woman's sexuality (Abusharaf 2006, 12). An international discourse of the practice of female genital mutilation has unreservedly condemned it and called for its immediate elimination. According to Shweder (2002, 247), this global discourse "portrays African mothers as mutilators, murderers and torturers of their children." In response to that account of FC, an alternative discourse has emerged, constructed by women in FC countries and by anthropologists who have researched FC. It has rejected what it regards as the simplistic and ethnocentric representation of FC offered by Western feminists and called for a far greater understanding of FC as a complex social practice. As Shweder (2002, 247) puts it, "We should be dubious of representations that suggest African

mothers are bad mothers, or that First World mothers have a better idea of what it means to be a good mother." Thus it is contended that feminist reductionist arguments that perceive FC to concern "men's domination and oppression of women" or "controlling a woman's sexuality" have little or no explanatory power given the sociocultural context within which FC occurs, although they may of course be important elements of such explanation. Poverty and economic restrictions also play a role, and may be assigned a higher priority for those affected by FC. In other words, FC should not be seen in isolation from other, equally pressing problems affecting persons and communities in countries where FC is concentrated (Abusharaf 2006, 5).

As Angela Gilliam (1991, 217) characterizes the division between the Western and non-Western viewpoints on FC, there are those who believe "the major struggle for women is increasing their access to, and control over, the world's *resources* and those who believe that the main issue is access to, and control over, *orgasms.*"

It has been argued that an adequate analysis of FC ought to include "listening to what women who do it have said about it, and trying to understand the reasons for resistance to change" (Gruenbaum 2001, 26). Gaining an understanding of the complexity of local knowledge about FC is critical (Abusharaf 2006, 9), as is respecting and giving equal treatment to various and different cultures (Gunning 1991, 191). An ethnocentric approach inhibits useful dialogue and disregards context. Adopting a more relativistic approach facilitates an interrogation of the process of change, for example, giving intimations about which changes are most likely to meet obstacles and which will more readily facilitate change and eventual elimination of the practice (Gruenbaum 2001, 28). As well, it is contended that reducing FC to a crime means ignoring the web of complex social practices associated with it (Abusharaf 2006, 6).

It is clear that despite efforts to reduce or even eliminate FC, it continues to have a strong hold in many countries. For its adherents, the act of FC invokes excitement, exaltation, and joy because of its role in defining and reinforcing ethnicity; in constituting an element of a rite of passage into sexuality and womanhood; in maintaining gender conditioning and thus social cohesion considered appropriate in specific communities. According to its adherents, FC has been honored by the passage of time and because of what it symbolizes in terms of religious practice. Suffering and pain are associated with FC but tend to subside as age mates who undergo the practice together form bonds between themselves and their families so that the pain and suffering are appropriated to create social cohesion (Abusharaf 2006, 8).

An international movement against FC has been under way since the 1950s, and it is instructive to examine how that campaign against FC has developed, both as a discrete effort and as an element in the international movement to stop forms of violence against women (see Chapter 13 for a fuller discussion of the development of the concept of violence against women). Before it entered international discourse, FC was considered a private matter that did not fall within the scope of government policy making. As explained in the following discussion, in international discourse and practice, FC was first designated an issue of custom or tradition, then reconfigured as a health issue (a frame that was deemed less political), and then reframed as a violation of human rights and a "harmful traditional practice."

International Action to Eliminate Female Circumcision

International action concerning FC first occurred in 1958 when the Economic and Social Council (ECOSOC) of the United Nations asked the WHO to undertake a study of the persistence of customs subjecting girls to ritual operations. In 1960, the issue of FC was debated at the Seminar on the Participation of Women in Public Life, held in Ethiopia. The Seminar included a call to the WHO to make a statement condemning all forms of medicalization of FC. In 1961, ECOSOC again asked the WHO to study the medical aspects of operations based on customs. The WHO, up to that point, had resisted involvement in the issue, considering it a matter of culture and not a health issue. A seminar convened in 1979 by the WHO in Khartoum set the pace and direction for international and national plans of action. It recommended the formation of the Inter-African Committee on Traditional Practices Affecting the Health of Women and Children. In addition, the seminar urged governments to collaborate with international bodies in a concerted effort to eliminate harmful traditional practices, including FC (Gunning 1991, 242).

As will be seen, the notion of *harmful traditional practices* and the international transformation of FC as an issue of health to an issue of *women's rights* are the principal elements in the pathway taken by FC from a domestic customary practice to an international concern.

Female Circumcision as a Harmful Traditional Practice

FC is the central issue in the internationally conceived notion of harmful cultural practices; yet, as Merry (2006a, 28) points out, "in the United States, domestic violence, rape in wartime and stalking are not labelled as harmful cultural practices nor are forms of violence against women's bodies such as cosmetic surgery, dieting, and the wearing of high heels."

Cultural norms associated with harmful traditional practices such as FC, child marriage, preferences for sons over daughters, honor crimes, and restrictions that women face on marriage have now been identified as causal factors in violence against women (UN 2006, 30). Culture is not immutable, however, and is constantly influenced by local and global processes. Culture is part of the constantly contested and negotiated social practices whose meanings are affected by the power and status of their interpreters and participants. As anthropologist Sally Engle Merry (2006a, 11) describes it,

> Cultures consist of repertoires of ideas and practices that are not homogeneous but continually changing because of contradictions among them or because new ideas and institutions are adopted by members. . . . Cultures are not contained within stable borders but are open to new ideas and permeable to influences from other cultural systems.

Women, too, influence cultural values and beliefs, and their identities are shaped and supported by their participation in traditional ceremonies and customs and through daily interaction with their local communities. Thus, while women may suffer from the harmful aspects of a culture, they also value and benefit from the positive cultural values they experience within their communities. In light of the fluidity of culture, women's agency in challenging oppressive cultural practices represents the most effective method of addressing the articulation between culture and violence against women (UN 2006, 31).

Eliminating Female Circumcision

Article 5 of the 1979 Convention on the Elimination of All Forms of Discrimination Against Women (CEDAW) requires state parties to eliminate all forms of discrimination against women and to take all appropriate measures

> to modify the social and cultural patterns of conduct of men and women, with a view to achieving the elimination of prejudices and customary and all other practices which are based on the idea of the inferiority or the superiority of either of the sexes or on stereotyped roles for men and women.

In 1990, General Recommendation 14 of the CEDAW Committee recommended that state parties take appropriate and effective measures to eradicate female circumcision, to collect and disseminate basic data on traditional practices, and to support women's organization at the national and local levels that work for the elimination of harmful practices.

In 1999, General Recommendation 24 of the CEDAW Committee emphasized that certain cultural or traditional practices such as FC carry a high risk of death and disability and recommended that state parties should ensure the enactment and effective enforcement of laws that prohibit FC.

Other regional international instruments that are concerned with sociocultural patterns of behavior include the Inter-American Convention on the Prevention, Punishment and Eradication of Violence Against Women ("Convention of Belém do Pará"), 1994, which requires states to "modify legal or customary practices that sustain the persistence and tolerance of violence against women" and provisions of the Protocol to the African Charter on Human and Peoples' Rights on the Rights of Women in Africa, 2003, which address the elimination of discrimination and harmful practices and require states to "modify the social and cultural patterns of conduct of women and men. . . . with a view to achieving the elimination of harmful cultural and traditional practices" (Article 2.2). "Harmful practices" are those which "negatively affect the human rights of women and which are contrary to recognised international standards."

Child Rights and Female Circumcision

The 1990 Convention on the Rights of the Child (CRC), to which all states except the United States and Somalia are parties, specifies that a dominant guiding principle in all actions concerning children is "the best interests of the child." While parents who decide to submit a child to FC perceive FC to be in the child's best interests because they are satisfying social and cultural expectations that mandate FC, this does not, according to UNICEF, justify the violation of the rights of the girl or woman.

The CRC requires state parties to "take all effective and appropriate measures with a view to abolishing traditional practices affecting women and children" (Article 24). As against this, the CRC also states that children have a right to practice their culture (Article 30). Some scholars have cast doubt on the applicability of FC to human rights doctrines, and a United Nations report of 1986 found that no international treaty addressed the practice and determined that the issue raised "challenging questions" (Hernlund and Shell-Duncan 2007, 12).

According to UNICEF (2005, 15), the practice of FC on girls violates the right to life, the right to physical integrity, the right to the highest attainable standard of health (including, with maturity, reproductive and sexual health), as well as the right to freedom from physical or mental violence, injury, or abuse. The practice is also a violation of the rights of the child to development, protection, and participation. The CRC establishes a Committee on the Rights of the Child, which receives reports from state parties on the implementation of the Convention. UNICEF reports that FC has often been raised as a matter of concern by the Committee, which has called upon state parties to take all "effective and appropriate measures" with a view to abolishing the practice.

Female Circumcision as a Violation of Women's Rights[7]

The campaign against FC as a violation of women's rights has resulted in a number of international actions seeking to eliminate the practice. In 1993, at the World Conference on Human Rights in Vienna, female circumcision was effectively redefined and reconceptualized as violence against women and a human rights violation (UNICEF 2013, 8). Previously, it had been presented internationally as a health issue. In 1994, the UN Conference on Population and Development held in Cairo, Egypt, issued a Program of Action that included within the part dealing with the girl child, the following statement on FC: "Governments are urged to prohibit female genital mutilation wherever it exists and to give vigorous support to efforts among nongovernmental and community organizations and religious institutions to eliminate such practices."[8] In 1995, a joint statement by the WHO, UNICEF, the UN Family Planning Association (UNFPA), and the UN Development Programme (UNDP) declared the medical basis for anti-FC policies to have been a "mistake in policy strategy." They agreed that the medicalization of FC had undermined the urgency for the elimination of the practice and had effectively medicalized the practice rather than eliminating it, in some areas. Also, health professionals had generally failed to distinguish between the different types of FC, rendering the health discourse, which assumed infibulation only, false and misleading. While FC did indeed have health consequences, these agencies affirmed that, more importantly, it was a violation of women's rights (Boyle 2002, 55, 140). The agencies declared that their aim was "to convince people, including women, that they can give up a specific practice without giving up meaningful aspects of their own cultures" (quoted in Boyle 2002, 68).

In 2001, the Parliamentary Assembly of the Council of Europe passed a resolution declaring "genital mutilation should be regarded as inhuman and degrading treatment within the meaning of Article 3 of the European Convention on Human Rights, even if carried out under hygienic conditions by competent personnel." The resolution called on member states to legislate against FC, declare FC a violation of human rights, create awareness of the law banning FC, and adopt flexible measures concerning the right of asylum (Skaine 2005, 148). In 2011, the Council of Europe Convention on Preventing and Combating Violence Against Women and Domestic Violence required that state parties ensure that the following intentional conduct be criminalized:

"excising, infibulating, or performing any other mutilation to the whole or any part of a woman's labia majora, labia minora or clitoris; coercing or procuring a woman to undergo any of the acts listed; inciting, coercing or procuring a girl to undergo any of the acts listed" (Article 38).

Most recently, in 2012, the UN General Assembly adopted a resolution intensifying global efforts for the elimination of female genital mutilation. It noted that a number of countries were using a coordinated approach to elimination that promoted social change at community, national, regional, and international levels and that there are signs of progress. The resolution calls upon states to develop standardized methods of data collection and develop indicators to measure progress. States are urged to pursue "a comprehensive, culturally sensitive, systematic approach that incorporates a social perspective and is based on human rights and gender-equality principles" (quoted in UNICEF 2013, 3). Actual progress on eliminating FC is discussed later in this chapter.

Female Circumcision and Sexuality

Central to the Western feminist discourse about FC is the issue of sexuality. For example, Alice Walker and Pratibha Parmar used the expression "sexual blinding of women" in the subtitle of their text *Warrior Marks* to denote the supposed destruction of sexuality as a result of FC (Gruenbaum 2001, 133). As Gruenbaum notes, Western feminist concerns about a diminution in, or even the destruction of, sexuality in FC countries reflects their concern about the centrality of female sexuality in their cultures and is therefore a projection that is wholly ethnocentric (p. 134). It is also reductionist in that it ignores the cultural context of sexuality in other cultures. For many Western feminists, the clitoris in particular has become a symbol of female emancipation, and therefore removing the clitoris in FC becomes a symbol of extreme patriarchal oppression (Shell-Duncan and Hernlund 2000, 21). As well, in the West, the experience of orgasm has come be regarded as both a woman's right and a goal, creating the expectation that women should regularly experience orgasm (Dopico 2007, 231).

What evidence is there of the actual sexual sensations experienced by circumcised women? A key issue here is whether women are able to experience orgasm without a clitoris. Masters and Johnson's research found that stimulation of the clitoris, directly or indirectly, is almost always an element in a woman achieving orgasm (Gruenbaum 2001, 137). The clitoris came to be central to female sexuality in Western feminist thinking because it displaced the notion that lovemaking was a passive exercise for women. The clitoris enabled women to control their wants and needs, and the male penis and penetration of the woman could even be entirely dispensed with altogether (p. 138). Thus terms such as *mutilation, sexual castration,* and *sexual blinding* are consistent with the practice of removing the clitoris and depriving women of the power to control their own sexuality. However, against the Western feminist view of sexuality is the notion that culture influences and structures sexuality and that there are multiple ways to experience pleasure in sex and even to achieve orgasm (p. 139). Gruenbaum concludes, after examining the research in Egypt and Sudan, that FC is "not uniformly destructive to female sexuality, even in countries where infibulation is the norm" and the effects of FC on sexuality are not well understood (pp. 142, 156).

Culture impacts sexuality in that women supporting FC have concerns about "the sexual energy expended as a girl is growing and her body maturing into womanhood." Thus slimness is seen as a sign that sexual energy is "wasting the body" and FC operates to control sexuality until marriage. "[FC] is not considered a mechanism for the permanent reduction of the woman's sexuality" but the intention is to "promote sexual pleasure within marriage" (El Guindi 2006, 37).

In FC-concentrated countries, men generally desire tight openings, and the cultural expectation that men have this preference likely influences parents in continuing to have their daughters circumcised. As well, both men and women in these cultures favor the smoothness of the vulva attained by infibulation (Gruenbaum 2001, 154). Research among Egyptian Nubians affirmed men's preference for vaginal tightness. In this culture, "the cultural assumption is that a man's arousal and pleasure give much pleasure to the woman," and the sexual experience is said to be "integrative and mutual, rather than a matter of individualized pleasure-seeking" (El Guindi 2006, 32).

Studies of the effects of FC on women's sexuality show wide variations in findings. In some cases, up to 90 percent of women with type III

(infibulated) circumcisions reported pleasurable sex and frequent orgasms, but other studies show 50 percent of women claimed to experience diminished sexual pleasure. While FC has the potential to affect sexual response, it does not necessarily affect receptivity to sexual stimulation because the clitoris is deeply embedded and is not necessarily removed in its entirety in FC. As well, other studies suggest that the labia minora or other erogenous zones increase their sensitivity in cases of FC, thus allowing for increased pleasure (Shell-Duncan and Hernlund 2000, 17).

Researchers have found that in some cultures, sex is primarily about having children. Thus, when one woman in southern Chad was asked how she found sex after having been circumcised, she responded, "Both circumcised and uncircumcised women give birth so I don't see the difference" (Boyle 2002, xi). This instance points to the need to critically assess the social construction of sexuality and the family in cultures and societies (p. xi) and at the same time to recognize the subjective nature of what constitutes enjoyment or satisfaction in one's sexual life. As Henrietta Moore (2007, 320) reminds us,

Sexual pleasure is . . . an intimate experience that lends itself only marginally to verbal articulation. . . . So the "uncircumcised" woman talking to the "circumcised" woman can have no certainty as to the nature and comparability of their forms of sexual pleasure, just as the "circumcised woman" cannot know definitively whether the "uncircumcised woman" experiences her forms of sexual pleasure.

CLAIMS FOR ASYLUM BASED ON THE PRACTICE OF FEMALE CIRCUMCISION

A consequence of the internationalization of FC has been women and girls applying for political asylum in states other than their own under the 1951 Refugee Convention, claiming that FC will be performed on them, against their will, if they return to their country of birth. Thus claims for political asylum have been founded on the international condemnation of FC as violence against women and a violation of women's human rights. Women claiming asylum argue that the risk of FC satisfies the Convention requirement that a person seeking asylum have a well-founded fear of being persecuted on the specified grounds, including "membership of a particular social group."

A significant asylum case of this nature is that of Fauziya Kassindja of Togo who succeeded in gaining asylum in the United States in 1996. She had left her home and family to resist FC that she claimed was being forced upon her before her arranged marriage took place. She was able to satisfy an Immigration Appeal Board (after her initial appeal for asylum had been rejected by an immigration judge on the grounds that it was "inconsistent" and "irrational"; Piot 2006, 226) that she had a well-founded fear of persecution as a member of a particular social group. According to Charles Piot (2006, 226), who was involved in the case, the claim for asylum was facilitated by the willingness of the Immigration and Naturalization Service lawyer not to oppose the claim, provided it was based on narrow grounds so that the United States would not be flooded with similar asylum claims. It was for this reason that the claim was held to be justified based on the facts that (1) she was an uncircumcised woman of a distinct social group, (2) who resist FC, and (3) justifiably fear they will suffer persecution country-wide (p. 228).

In another case in 1994 involving a Nigerian woman, Lydia Oluloro, who was illegally in the United States, an immigration judge suspended her deportation based on evidence that her two daughters, who were U.S. citizens, would suffer FC if she were deported to Nigeria (Skaine 2005, 81). However, in a similar case in 2003, also involving a Nigerian mother, Doris Oforji, who also had U.S. citizen children, the court refused to suspend her deportation because of her fear for her children based on the fact that as U.S. citizens, the children could remain in the United States without her (pp. 81–82).

In 1996, the U.S. Board of Immigration Appeals explicitly recognized FC as "persecution" according to the terms of the Refugee Convention. Australia, Canada, and Sweden have also recognized FC as persecution. In 1993 Canada granted refugee status to a mother from Somalia who had fled her country with her ten-year-old daughter, fearing she would be forced to undergo FC. The Canadian Immigration and Refugee Board determined that her "right to personal security would be grossly infringed" if she were returned to Somalia (Skaine 2005, 78). In Australia, the Guidelines on Gender Issues for Decision Makers 1996 recognize that FC may be classed as persecution and satisfy a claim for asylum. The French Refugee Appeal Commission takes a similar position (p. 79).

CHANGING THE PRACTICE OF FEMALE CIRCUMCISION: WHAT WORKS?

As noted earlier, simply demanding that a long established and deeply embedded practice like FC be eliminated forthwith is problematic, to say the least. After all, slavery was recognized as an immoral practice long before it ceased to be an accepted system in the West. In advocating change to an entrenched cultural practice, it has been suggested that it is best not to "start by proclaiming that you possess the truth" (Geertz 1993, quoted in Gruenbaum 2001, 203) because social change is almost always a long-term process that is contingent on formulating strategies that take full account of local beliefs, values, and expectations. This is especially so in the case of traditional practices believed to be sanctioned or even required by religion.

As a practice that is so vital to issues of marriageability and therefore to a woman's economic security and social status, FC is unlikely to be rejected for the medical risks it poses, especially when, in many FC countries, medical professionals can be persuaded to perform the procedure (Gruenbaum 2001, 87). Interventions aimed at modifying and ultimately eliminating the tradition of FC may therefore have to be able to respond to questions such as "Will my daughter be marriageable if she does not undergo FC?"

The key change agent in relation to most if not all harmful traditional practices, including deeply rooted gender practices generally, is the agency of the local population in a society or culture. In the case of FC, it is argued that programs and interventions designed to eliminate FC ought to recognize the role of FC in determining the marriageability and reputation of daughters under patriarchy in the countries in which it is practiced. Above all, only through an understanding of the historical, social, and cultural context is it possible to analyze how best to develop the means to change the practice and eventually to even eliminate it (Gruenbaum 2001, 46–47). However, it is clear that the means chosen ought to be designed and implemented by local actors (El Guindi 2006, 42). One strategy in regard to FC is to follow a staged process that begins with replacing infibulation (the most severe form of FC) with *sunna* (a less severe form of FC). In other words, one approach is first to modify rather than attempt an immediate elimination of FC because, as one anthropologist put it, "To us it looks barbaric. . . . Westerners are quick to be pejorative. But by and large, women in nations where this is done are not in revolt against this" (Gruenbaum 2001, 195, 202). El Guindi (2006, 42) reports on how FC practice can change, describing how Nubian women in Egypt chose to abandon the most severe forms of FC and change to a form they considered "more humane," thus ending the older practice.

Prohibiting Female Circumcision by Law

The effectiveness of laws alone in eliminating a deeply rooted traditional practice like FC is questionable. While enacting a law against FC demonstrates a state's commitment to its treaty obligations, effective implementation cannot be assumed. Moreover, as UNICEF (2013, 8) has recognized, where there is support for FC among communities, legislation should be part of change strategies "that complement efforts in the social sphere and contribute to collective abandonment of the practice." Legislation is, however, important in providing legitimacy for new behaviors that are the outcome of the process of social change (UNICEF 2013, 9), but there is always the risk that legislation will drive the practice underground. Some argue that laws against FC are unenforceable on the basis that "it is not possible to criminalize the entirety of a population or the entirety of a discrete and insular minority of the population without methods of mass terror" (Mackie 2000, 278).

According to UNICEF (2013, 8), twenty-six states in Africa and the Middle East have prohibited FC by law or decree. As well, legislation has been adopted in thirty-three states elsewhere to protect children with origins in FC states. In the twenty-nine states where FC is concentrated, legislative activity on FC has been actively pursued since 2000. For example, laws were enacted in Egypt in 2008, Iraq in 2011, Sudan (some states) in 2008–9 (in addition to colonial legislation), Kenya in 2001 and 2011 and Somalia in 2012.

However, the legislation is not uniform. For example, in Mauritania, the law is limited to a ban on practicing FC in government health facilities and by medical practitioners. In Kenya, the ban on FC of minors in 2001 was extended to include a ban on adults in 2011. Kenya also extended the law to apply to its citizens who commit the crime outside Kenya. In some countries (e.g., Burkina Faso), prosecutions have been brought against the circumcisers, while in other countries (e.g., Senegal and Tanzania), parents are targeted (Hernlund and Shell-Duncan 2007, 37).

Sudan has had legislation prohibiting FC that uses the infibulation method (but allowing the *sunna* method) since 1946 and has punished convicted midwives with imprisonment for up to seven years. Enforcement was attempted by the British colonial administration and resisted by the local populations. Gruenbaum (2001, 206) provides an example of what occurred in the town of Rufa'a on the Blue Nile:

> The police took a midwife into custody for circumcising a girl and put her in the local jail. Outraged at this affront to their customs and abuse of their midwife, an angry crowd of Rufa'a citizens attacked the jail and "tore it to the ground" to free the midwife. Government troops fired on the crowd, and there were injuries.

In Kenya, in 1982, FC was condemned by then President Moi, who called for prosecution of those involved in FC, thereby reversing support for FC declared by the first President, Jomo Kenyatta. During the colonial period, missionaries worked with the Gikuyu tribal councils to try to ban at least the most severe forms of FC, to improve hygiene where FC was performed, and to regulate midwives. However, they met with resistance from the councils where the opposing forces argued that this was another measure directed at the indigenous people while colonial policies favored settlers and introduced land and population controls (Gruenbaum 2001, 207).

Recent reports[9] indicate that Kenya established a national unit in April 2014 to ensure that laws prohibiting FC are enforced. The unit has found that the enforcement action has caused women to take their daughters to remote regions of Kenya to have FC performed. In addition, the unit has found that FC is being conducted covertly by doctors and nurses on girls admitted to hospital on the pretext of illness. Resistance to the laws is often led by older women. In a prosecution in June 2014, a Maasai couple pleaded guilty to the murder of a thirteen-year-old girl who bled to death after a FC. Since 2011, seventy-one cases of FC have been prosecuted and sixteen have resulted in convictions; the remaining cases are still pending.

In Uganda, a report[10] indicates that five persons were arrested in eastern Uganda in November 2014. All pleaded guilty to aiding or procuring FGM and were convicted and imprisoned for four years. There have been few such prosecutions since the anti-FC law was enacted in 2010.

A number of countries have no specific legislation on FC because they consider their existing penal laws and codes to be adequate to prosecute cases of FC, using offenses such as assault, child abuse, and the like (Gruenbaum 2001, 208). In the United Kingdom, the Female Genital Mutilation Act 2003 makes FC an offense punishable on indictment with imprisonment for up to five years. In March 2014 it was reported[11] that the first prosecutions for FC were being brought by the U.K. Crown Prosecution Service against a female doctor who allegedly committed FC at a hospital and a man who allegedly aided and abetted the procedure. The same report indicates that in France there have been more than one hundred such prosecutions. From 1983 to 1999, France prosecuted twenty-six FC cases of which twenty-five resulted in convictions with the accused usually being the parents, but in three trials medical practitioners were charged. In 1999, a prosecution in France convicted a woman of performing the procedure on forty-eight girls between the ages of one month and ten years. In 2004, a French court sentenced a mother from Mali who resided in Paris for complicity in the FC of her daughter (Skaine 2005, 67).

In the United States, the Female Genital Mutilation Act criminalized FC in 1996 and explicitly excluded a defense based on beliefs. American consulates are required to inform would-be immigrants of the law banning FC. It is a crime to knowingly perform FGM on girls under the age of eighteen or to take a girl abroad for FGM. The maximum sentence is up to five years imprisonment. Twenty-two U.S. states have passed their own laws on FC: in Florida, FGM is punishable by up to thirty years imprisonment, and in Illinois from six to thirty years, while in Oklahoma, the penalty is three years to life (AHA Foundation).

In February 2004, a couple was arrested in an area outside Los Angeles in a "sting" operation: both persons had agreed with an undercover FBI agent to circumcise two girls who they believed were the FBI agent's daughters. No FC occurred, but a fee of $8,000 had been agreed for the procedures on the two daughters.

In Canada, the extent to which FC occurs is not known, but it is probably performed by health professionals (Macklin 2006, 210). Initially, the Canadian Justice Department did not favor creating a separate crime of FC, believing it was adequately covered by existing offenses. However, in 1993 the criminal code was amended to criminalize taking a girl out of Canada with the intention of subjecting her to FC elsewhere. Then, in 1997, the criminal code was amended to explicitly define and include FC as a form of aggravated assault to which no person could consent (p. 211).

In two countries, Canada and Australia, specific legislation prohibiting FC and rendering a category of women the subjects of management or criminalization has been questioned for its stigmatization of these women by the dominant culture. Criminalizing the practices of some members of a particular community by special laws raises significant moral and policy issues. In investigating this question in Canada, Macklin (2006, 212) discovered that the political pressure to criminalize came from women in immigrant communities who had lobbied for the change in the law. Macklin (p. 218) argues that in considering explicit criminalization of FC, what must be considered is whether "the law will in fact be interpreted as a matter of white, Judeo-Christian Canadians inscribing their moral superiority on African Muslim bodies through the text of the criminal law."

In her study of the introduction of anti FC legislation in the State of Victoria, Australia, Juliet Rogers (2007, 136) like Macklin, sees the legislation as exemplifying and reifying the right of white Australians "to manage Australia's social and political spaces, simultaneously defining 'others' as people requiring management." Pointing out that the Crimes (Female Genital Mutilation) Act 1996 was produced by the Family Law Council of Australia, whose report recommending the law described the women as "mutilated women," Rogers argues that the Council defined the problem and wrote the solution to it, ignoring in the process representations from organized groups of circumcised women who sought the right themselves to define and manage strategies for the elimination of FC that would not include legislation.

Effective Strategies and Programs

Among the many strategies and programs intended to change or even eliminate FC, a number have been shown to be effective. Many programs suffer from poor program design, meaning they cannot easily be evaluated or evaluated at all to determine success or failure (Diop and Askew 2006, 127). We briefly describe a few programs and strategies that are generally considered to have reduced the incidence of FC or changed its form within a culture in some way. As will be seen, integrated interventions that convey knowledge, raise awareness, and empower women have shown the most success.

Alternative Rites of Passage Program (ARP)

In Kenya, the Maendeleo Ya Wanawake Organization (MYWO), a local NGO with a focus on the health and well-being of Kenyan women, began to give priority to FC in 1991. They conducted a survey in four rural districts and found that nine out of ten women had undergone some form of FC. With overseas funding and technical assistance from an international NGO, MYWO began working in these four districts to raise awareness of human rights and the health consequences of FC and involve secular and religious leaders, teachers, and others in mobilizing for social change. The development of an Alternative Rites of Passage Program (ARP) was an element within the overall change strategy.

In many Kenyan cultures, FC is part of a ritualized communal process that marks a girl's transition to sexuality and womanhood. The rite of passage was less common in urban areas but still widely practiced in rural areas. As well as FC itself, the rite involves keeping the girls in seclusion for a week during which they receive guidance about appropriate forms of behavior, including the avoidance of inappropriate sexual relationships. They also learn how their behavior is monitored by others (Diop et al. 2006, 88). The traditional rites of passage ceremony was being criticized by some for becoming too expensive

and for constituting a competition for social status between families. Some families had taken to having the FC performed in a hospital or in their homes by a visiting health professional.

The change strategy conceived by MYWO involved preserving the ritual and its social meaning and building on it but eliminating the act of FC.[12] While passing on traditional aspects of the rite of passage, the strategy would also provide information and awareness about HIV/AIDS, sexuality, and family life. Thus ARP was designed to avoid the stigmatism that girls who did not undergo FC commonly suffered. The first ARP was conducted in 1996, and within six years, seven thousand girls had taken part in this alternative rite of passage (Mohamud, Radeny, and Ringheim 2006, 76–77). At the beginning of the MYWO campaign, 78 percent of women younger than age twenty in the four districts had been circumcised; by 1999, after four years of the program, this proportion had fallen to 56 percent. Only 47 percent of women now favor continuation of FC as opposed to almost 63 percent at the commencement of the program. The proportion of all girls aged fourteen who had already been circumcised declined from more than half at the time of the baseline survey to less than one-third six years later (p. 94).

Educational and awareness activities conducted by MYWO included encouraging women and girls to relate their experiences of FC; having women who had already decided FC was a harmful practice explain the different kinds of FC and build a strong non-circumcising community; and, subsequently, bringing men into the discussion. The key messages used to convince women to cease the practice included circumcision is, in fact, genital mutilation; when a tradition outlives its usefulness, it has to be discarded; and circumcision violates the rights of Kenyan girls to health, gender equity, and freedom from torture and degrading practices (Mohamud, Radeny, and Ringheim 2006, 87). In their baseline survey of the four districts, researchers found that

- circumcised girls were believed to make better, more obedient wives, and to behave more respectfully to parents and elders, and to show more maturity;

- men said that women who had not been circumcised were oversexed, unclean, rude, bossy, and disrespectful;

and killing unarmed civilians, adults, and children, often to acquire natural resources or political power. In this mode of violent conflict, torture, killing, rape, and the slaughter of ethnic groups have been frequent outcomes.

Especially in Africa, armed conflicts are often struggles to gain control of valuable natural resources like the diamond fields of Sierra Leone and the coltan mines of the Democratic Republic of Congo (DRC). In Asia and South America, the profits of the drug trade have fueled armed conflicts. Like organized crime, violent conflicts are led by leaders, often referred to as "warlords" (local leaders who are able to mobilize forces using terror tactics and tribal loyalty), who seek the plunder and spoils of war (Honwana 2006, 34).

Civil wars are the most prevalent form of armed conflict today. These conflicts are characterized by forms of guerrilla warfare involving generally small groups of fighters who undertake raids and ambushes, terrorize civilian populations, loot, and kill. There are seldom exchanges in which combatants face each other (Gates 2011, 32). The aim is often to control the population by expelling or killing all those with a different identity, which may be tribal or religious. Typically, in armed conflicts of this kind, children may perform as well as adults. Children have not only suffered as the victims of this violence but have also perpetrated it. Significant numbers of children have participated in local wars as armed combatants, some as young as six years old (Singer 2006, 6). In Liberia and Sierra Leone, militias created "small-boy units" in which the boys typically were younger than twelve years and were renowned for their fearlessness. Worldwide, most child soldiers are aged between thirteen and eighteen years (Wessells 2006, 7). Alcinda Honwana (2006, 27) notes, "The participation of children and youth in armed conflicts is a defining feature of our times." Child soldiers have participated in conflicts in

- Colombia (eleven thousand child soldiers), Ecuador, El Salvador, Guatemala, Mexico, Nicaragua, Paraguay, and Peru; Northern Ireland and Bosnia; and Turkey (in the Kurdish Workers' Party [PKK]);

- Sierra Leone (where they constituted as much as 80 percent of the Revolutionary United Front [RUF]);

- Liberia (where the United Nations estimates some twenty thousand served in combat);

- Angola (where as many as one million children were exposed to the conflict as civilians and combatants; Honwana 2006, 14);

- Mozambique (where between eight thousand and ten thousand children participated in the conflict; Honwana 2006, 11);

- Uganda (where the Lord's Resistance Army [LRA] is thought to have abducted more than fourteen thousand children with the youngest being only five years of age);

- the Democratic Republic of the Congo (where one warlord commanded a group of some ten thousand child solders between the ages of seven and sixteen);

- Palestine;

- the war between Iran and Iraq (some one hundred thousand child soldiers from Iran are thought to have died in this conflict);

- Sudan (estimates are one hundred thousand on both sides of the civil war);

- Ethiopia;

- Afghanistan (with the Taliban and the Northern Alliance); and

- many conflicts in Asia, especially in Myanmar and Sri Lanka (UNICEF has estimated more than six thousand child soldiers were recruited between 2003 and 2008 by the rebel Tamil Tigers; Drumbl 2012, 30; Singer 2006, 15–28).

Why Use Child Soldiers?

Despite prohibitions under international law, children continue to be recruited to fight and participate in other ways in armed conflicts. Singer (2006, 38) offers two concrete reasons for this: first, having children use lethal weapons is now possible because small arms are light and portable so that children can easily deploy and use them;[20] and second, mobilizing children to fight is a cost-effective way to participate in armed conflicts. Force commanders have therefore concluded that children are sufficiently cheap to employ to compensate for their lower military efficiency (Gates 2011, 34). The strategy of using children provides a ready source of "manpower" at very little cost to almost any protagonist because children are rarely paid (Singer 2006, 52). Wessells (2006, 34) draws attention to a more sinister basis for recruiting children, that is, their tactical value as shock troops. Adult soldiers opposing children are asked to confront the prospect of killing them, sowing confusion and doubt in their minds and adversely affecting their cohesion as a unit and force.

The dramatic impact of HIV/AIDS in African states means that children now constitute an overall majority of persons, with 51 percent of the continent's population of 340 million under the age of eighteen. It is argued that the death of so many mature adults because of HIV/AIDS has destabilized the large youth population so that the young males, lacking any social controls or family structure and "angry" and "listless," are drawn into violence. The large group of orphans created by HIV/AIDS has proved to be susceptible to the attractions of child soldiering (Singer 2006, 41–42). As the case study of Sierra Leone (later in this chapter) shows, other factors at play in some states include a history of youth involvement in political violence and crime that has made for an easy transition from one form of violence to another. The demand for cheap fighters has been accelerated as the number and extent of violent internal conflicts have grown.

The general level of poverty within a country, a lack of employment, and an inability to gain an education have all contributed to situations where children are drawn into conflicts as a means of surviving. In a war zone, therefore, the poorest, least educated children are vulnerable to recruitment. In some states, children have only ever been exposed to an environment of violence and conflict. As one child in Northern Uganda noted, "If you are under 20 and living here, you have known virtually nothing else your whole life but what it is like to live in a community enduring armed conflict—conflict in which you are a prime target" (quoted in Singer 2006, 44).

It is also contended that economic and structural issues in postcolonial Africa have impacted households and communities and weakened their capacity to maintain established norms that once protected and nurtured children. Children have been commodified as their labor has become vital to the survival of the family group. In such conditions, child soldiering can function and flourish as a survival strategy, and children are drawn into internal conflicts as they move to towns searching for employment following the collapse of social and economic structures in the rural areas (Honwana 2006, 46–47).

Child Soldiers in Combat

A rebel commander in the DRC is quoted as saying, "Children make good fighters because they are young. . . . They think it's a game, so they're fearless" (Singer 2006, 80). Another rebel Congolese officer reported, "They obey orders; they are not concerned with getting back to their wife and family; and they don't know fear" (quoted in Gates 2011, 34). Drugs or alcohol are sometimes supplied to counter any fears. A report chillingly summarizes the value of the child soldier to a commander in the field.

> Children make very effective combatants. They don't ask a lot of questions. They follow instructions, and they often don't understand and aren't able to evaluate the risks of going to war. Victims and witnesses often said they feared the children more than the adults because the child combatants had not developed an understanding of the value of life. They would do anything. They knew no fear. Especially when they were pumped up on drugs. They saw it as fun to go into battle. (Singer 2006, 83)

While child fighters may be used in concert with adult forces, or to attack easy targets like villages, it is also common for them to be used in human wave attacks and in a mass charge, firing automatic weapons, screaming, and yelling (Singer 2006, 85). Newly recruited child fighters experience the same fears of combat as adults but often rapidly adapt partly because commanders punish those who show fear (Wessells 2006, 75).

Over time, children can become extremely proficient soldiers, like the child fighters of the LTTE Leopard Brigade, whose members grew up in Liberation Tigers of Tamil Eelam (LTTE) orphanages and who took on elite Sri Lanka commando forces, surrounding and killing nearly two hundred, or the Sierra Leone West Side Boys who fought the highly trained British special forces (the SAS) for six hours, killing one and wounding twenty-five others (Singer 2006, 87–88). Child soldiers develop coping skills to survive in the uncertain, unpredictable environment of an armed group. These skills may include knowing which orders can be refused without running the risk of being put to death. A sixteen-year-old male from Sierra Leone, abducted by the RUF, provides this example: "The leader told us to beat women and saw it [watched us] with his within a group through sex and relationships and actively manage their survival. In Colombia, a similar system operated, with girls competing for access to important fighters for protection.

> When girls join the FARC, the commanders choose among them. There's pressure. The women have the final say, but they want to be with a commander to be protected. The commanders buy them. They give a girl money and presents. When you're with a commander, you don't have to do the hard work. So most of the prettiest girls are with the commanders. (Honwana 2006, 85–86)

In Liberia, during the period 2000–2002, girls were often raped or threatened with rape by armed groups and then taken into the group as followers to perform duties such as cooking, cleaning, and providing sex to the soldiers. Some of the girls would transition to becoming fighters or become the wife of a commander to escape sexual abuse from many others in the group (Podder 2011a, 69).

In Colombia and Sierra Leone, girls were recruited and trained for combat (Honwana 2006, 93). In Angola, girls were used for domestic tasks in the camps and for sexual purposes. Reportedly, if a girl refused to have sex with a soldier, she would be taken away and killed (Honwana 2006, 86). The sexual violence directed against girls forms part of the wide-ranging pattern of violence used against girls and women in zones of war, but it is important to note the diversity of experiences suffered by girls and that some groups did expressly prohibit sexual violence (Wessells 2006, 86–87). Stereotypes of the passive victim are inappropriate in view of the survival strategies girls employed to actively manage their predicament. As well, some girls joined groups willingly, for ideological reasons.

In Guatemala, a civil war lasted for more than thirty years until a peace agreement between the government and the rebels was signed in 1996. A survey of the members of the insurgent force showed that many were still quite young and must therefore have joined as children or teenagers. Qualitative interviews conducted with girl soldiers after the end of the conflict revealed that political violence by government forces was a major factor in prompting many to join the guerrillas. Other factors included a desire to change society and improve the condition of the poor,

witnessing and escaping massacres and torture, or having relatives already in the guerrilla movement. None of those interviewed had been abducted (Hauge 2011, 97). Some girls had very long experience with the guerrillas; one girl had joined at twelve years of age and stayed for thirty years (p. 98).

Sometimes girls resisted commands. In one case, a girl abducted by the RUF at fourteen years of age told her captors that she was too young for sex. She tried to shame her captors, telling them they should be ashamed of themselves for wanting sex with her at her age. In response, the RUF took her to the capital and cut off her left arm above the elbow (Wessells 2006, 95). Attempts to resist sexual violence in the RUF also took the form of pretending to be menstruating or even using violence to repel an attempted rape ("I stabbed one guy to death—he was always harassing me for sex"), and girls developed a solidarity among themselves to support their mental and physical well-being (Denov 2010, 135–36).

Honwana (2006, 79) notes the secrecy that still surrounds the participation of girls in internal conflicts, largely because few girls are willing to share their experiences because of the social implications within the family and community. Explicit discussion of sexual matters is ordinarily proscribed and rape and forms of sexual slavery more so. The discourse concerning girl soldiers has therefore tended to portray them as "silent victims particularly as 'wives,' in tangential supporting roles, and as victims of sexual slavery" (Denov 2010, 13).

COERCION, AGENCY, AND VICTIMS

Research studies have shown that children become soldiers for a diversity of reasons and that there is no single narrative such as that of forced recruitment that adequately describes how they came to be soldiers. In every case, therefore, the actual process of the recruitment should be examined because children may be recruited through coercion, they may be volunteers, or they may be abducted. However, in all cases, whatever the mode of recruitment, the process should always be perceived as embedded within wider structures of violence and oppression (Wessells 2006, 32, 55).

Constructing Child Soldiers— Recruitment and Training

A common means of recruiting children is through abduction, sometimes directly, for example, from a school[24] or a marketplace, or simply by sweeps in the streets, or through imposing conscription targets in an area (Singer 2006, 58–59). Camps for refugees and internally displaced persons are also favored by recruiters because they are not well policed and contain large numbers of children (Wessells 2006, 38). Another mode of forced recruitment is to require all households under the control of an armed group to provide one soldier (Gates 2011, 36).[25] In Uganda, the LRA is notorious for having abducted thousands of children with an average age of fourteen years. A large proportion of these abductees developed a loyalty to the LRA such that they remained with the LRA into adulthood (p. 30). In Sierra Leone, it is estimated that the RUF abducted 87 percent of its recruits (p. 37).

Sometimes children chose to join a group through their own initiative, and in fact their agency accounts for about two out of every three children who are recruited (Singer 2004, 61). In Liberia, for example, while most child soldiers reported on a first meeting to being forced, as they became more familiar with the researcher, they tended "to shift their story to one of opportunism and volition" (Podder 2011a, 60). However, in Liberia the high level of insecurity within the country meant that if there was no chance to leave the country or escape the fighting in some way, there were few options other than to join an armed group as a means of securing food and personal security (p. 62).

Joining a group may most often be prompted by the need for food and shelter, but the desire to exact revenge for the loss of a family member may also be a precipitating factor, as may a desire to experience the excitement of having weapons and fighting. Recent research has shown that some children join groups to escape negative family pressures and situations such as parental abuse, perhaps seeing the group as a better "family" than the one they have escaped from (Wessells 2006, 48). Some join simply to better themselves by acquiring skills and training, as explained by one sixteen-year-old girl who had been a commander with the RUF in Sierra Leone: "I'm proud of what I learned—how to speak to groups, organize people, command, use weapons.

I never got this from [the] government. How else am I supposed to have a future? If I had to do it again, I'd join again" (Wessells 2006, 50).

Children may also respond to ideological messages and propaganda and acquire a genuine desire to serve a particular cause (Wessells 2006, 53). Sometimes, the promise of future benefits will evoke a favorable response, as in Liberia where poor children were offered free access to education after the end of the war if they joined Charles Taylor's armed group. Similarly, in the Democratic Republic of Congo (DRC), children were promised payment or a job after the war (Gates 2011, 34).

Agency and Victims

A key question in considering child soldiering is should child soldiers be regarded as victimized, innocent children, or should their agency, where exercised, exclude them from the category "child"? Honwana (2006, 4) contends that children affected by conflict "do not constitute a homogeneous group of helpless victims but exercise an agency of their own, which is shaped by their particular experiences and circumstances." When child soldiers disrupt so many cultural and social categories and dualities, such as protector and protected, victim and perpetrator, and civilian and soldier, they lack a fixed identity and "occupy a world of their own." Thus it is argued that children should not be regarded as victims devoid of agency even though their capacity to make rational decisions is questioned.

In Mozambique and Angola, child soldiers were not without agency but displayed what Honwana (2006, 51), calls "tactical agency," a limited mode of agency, "an agency of the weak," necessary as a coping mechanism in the environment in which they had to survive. In this sense they lacked power to exercise a full "strategic" agency, where they would have been aware of the purposes of their actions and any long-term gains or benefits. Nevertheless, they were conscious of the immediate outcomes of their actions. Former boy soldiers reported that "insecurity, vulnerability, and lack of food" were among the causes that led them to volunteer, but in some cases the main inducement was "wearing military gear and carrying an AK-47" (p. 58). Honwana warns against applying Western conceptions of responsibility to the actions of child

child who was initially charged with crimes against humanity. However, the case was resolved through a plea bargain in 2002 on the first trial day when the prosecutor amended the indictment to bring only an ordinary charge of murder, not an international crime. Thus the prosecution was brought outside the framework of international criminal law (Drumbl 2012, 125).

National legal systems have prosecuted child soldiers, for example, in Rwanda before the gacaca courts,[30] and imprisonment was consistently imposed as the punishment for crimes committed during the genocide there. In the DRC, child soldiers were prosecuted and received harsh sentences until 2002, when a law prohibited children younger than age eighteen from being prosecuted before military courts. Civil society mobilized to prevent national prosecutions of child soldiers in Uganda when, for example, in 2002 two youths aged fourteen and sixteen were charged with treason and the charges were withdrawn following an appeal from the international NGO Human Rights Watch (Drumbl 2012, 177).

While child soldiers enjoy virtual impunity under international criminal law, countries have taken a contrary approach to claims for asylum by former child soldiers implicated in crimes against humanity. In Canada, for example, a child aged between eleven and thirteen years, a member of a terrorist organization in Turkey could be denied asylum if it were shown that he had knowledge of acts of violence; in another case, a minor from El Salvador was denied asylum because he had voluntarily enlisted in government armed forces to avenge atrocities committed against his family by rebel forces; and in 2005 the Canadian courts affirmed the deportation of a minor who had distributed terrorist propaganda for a terrorist organization in Iran while aged between sixteen and eighteen (Drumbl 2012, 131). Thus, while countries are reluctant to prosecute child soldiers or to support their prosecution before international criminal tribunals, they are willing to refuse to admit child soldiers seeking refugee status.

In transitional justice processes in Sierra Leone, the Truth and Reconciliation Commission (TRC) determined that children younger than eighteen years were not responsible for their actions; in South Africa the TRC adopted a policy of not taking evidence from children younger than eighteen in accordance with "advice given by child specialists" (Drumbl 2012,

181). In Liberia, the TRC collected statements from children and children also testified. It was found that children made up about 10 percent to 20 percent of members of armed groups, but the TRC concluded that children were not culpable or responsible for violations of human rights or for war crimes (Drumbl 2012, 186).

As this discussion reveals, international tribunals and domestic systems of justice are very reluctant to prosecute child soldiers, however horrendous may be the crimes they perpetrated. There seems little doubt that, with the exception of nonjudicial processes like the grant of asylum and transitional justice where the status of victim is less readily accepted, the case for the establishment of an international norm prohibiting such prosecutions for those below the age of eighteen years is now generally accepted by states.

REINTEGRATING AND RESTORING THE CHILD SOLDIER

In light of the experiences described in the previous section, how best can child soldiers be restored to their community and regain their childhood? Wessells (2006, 23) observes that while former child soldiers may have suffered greatly, they are "neither uniquely vulnerable nor definable in terms of vulnerability" and that most display "remarkable resilience." Looking to the community that will receive the child soldier, Wessells (2006, 141) suggests "the reintegration of former child soldiers is less a matter of helping individual children than of strengthening family and community supports, enabling children to adapt and function well despite difficult past experiences and current living situations."

After disarming and demobilizing them through the DDR process, child soldiers become ex-combatants, many of them now adults but still in need of support services.[31] Many suffer from post-traumatic stress, which may continue for months or even years. Reintegrating former child fighters into their communities has proved to be a difficult process (Singer 2006, 193). For example, one survey in Africa found that 82 percent of parents considered former child soldiers to represent a potential danger to the population (p. 200). Some communities in Northern Uganda refused to accept the absence of any accountability for the acts of child soldiers and would not welcome them back (Akello, Richters, and Reis 2006, 235). In Northern Uganda, three months after the rescue of three hundred abducted children in 2004–5, none were located in the community in which they were supposed to have been reintegrated. Data showed that more than 70 percent of detainees in the juvenile crime unit of Gulu District were former child soldiers detained on charges of rape, assault, and theft (Akello, Richters, and Reis 2006, 229). In Sierra Leone, DDR began in mid-1998 and 6,774 children (513 were female) were processed through DDR with children younger than fifteen commonly sent to care centers and older children placed in group homes or permitted to live independently. Reintegration followed. In Liberia, 11,870 children were demobilized, and about 9,000 were boys (Drumbl 2012, 170).

DDR design and programming has focused on treating trauma, providing education, tracing and reuniting with family, providing short stays in interim care centers or with foster parents, giving vocational training, and offering some cash payment.[32] Generally, community support is the preferred course of action (Podder 2011b, 147). DDR programs have been criticized for their lack of attention to the special needs of girl soldiers (Drumbl 2012, 171). In Sierra Leone, addressing a group of similarly abducted girls, one girl explicitly acknowledged their marginalization in society as a result of their experiences.

> We are not like other girls, because we were taken in the bush. Our minds are not steady, and we cannot eat off the same plates as our families. People call us bad names and do not accept us. They call us bad names. How can they do that? We worry about where we will get money to live and feed our babies. Our hearts are heavy even after the war. (Wessells 2006, 195)

A typical reintegration program was that in the Côte d'Ivoire, where the reintegration process comprised two stages. In the first, which lasted for three months, the elements included counseling, individual profiling, medical care, sports, a career orientation session, and literacy courses. This was conducted at a transition center where facilities included shared accommodation, a canteen, and basic entertainment. In the second stage, a short-term vocational education program placed youth with local businesses such as tailors, welders, and auto mechanics for six

months to learn basic skills. During this stage, they had to leave the center; some were reunited with family and others placed with foster families (Chelpi-den Hamer 2010, 20–21).

Honwana (2006, 4) calls for a culturally specific approach to reintegration that takes account of local practices and values that often prescribe rituals for those returning from war. For child soldiers in Angola and Mozambique where internal wars lasted more than twenty years and fifteen years, respectively, a process of ritual purification is required to reincorporate a child into the community, and the community itself is understood as disturbed and in need of rituals to cleanse and reconcile (p. 106). Similar rituals are employed in Mozambique in a holistic approach to health and healing. In these countries, former child soldiers opt to undergo these culturally specific forms of treatment rather than the Western therapeutic models that look back into events and involve individual verbal externalization of the traumatic experience of being a child soldier.[33] A cleansing and welcoming ceremony for community members who have been absent for long periods has been used to welcome back and reestablish relationships with former child soldiers in the Acholi community of Northern Uganda (Drumbl 2012, 190).[34] Wessells (p. 137) agrees that Western models used in diagnosing post-traumatic stress might not generalize to other cultures, which have their own understandings about trauma, and notes that former child soldiers often express their desire to see a traditional healer who can cleanse them (Wessells 2006, 194). As he points out, the trauma approach is ethnocentric, and imposing outsider categories runs the risk of marginalizing, or even entirely displacing, local knowledge.

Comment

These detailed accounts of FC and child soldiering have revealed the cultural, social, economic, and historical context within which these practices are located as well as the local nature and content of FC and child soldiering. Opposed to the local context are international rights discourses, whose origin, growth, and effect have been mapped in these accounts. As international issues, child soldiering and FC share numerous commonalities that reveal the tensions between universalism and cultural relativism. The commonalities include the following:

- Both concerns have been rendered issues of international attention, primarily through the efforts of the international NGO complex with support from UN agencies who collectively apply a rights-based approach to both issues. In the case of child soldiers, as David Rosen (2007, 304) points out, "Little attention was paid to the presence of child soldiers in the era of national liberation movements, but it has become a significant issue now that postcolonial states face their own insurgencies." FC as an international cause became noticed in the West only from the 1980s but is an ancient social practice.

- Both issues are constituted by Western concerns about rights violations: in the case of child soldiering, the rights are those protected by the CRC and child soldiering is declared to be an abuse of those rights; in the case of FC, women's human rights, specifically violence against women, and the continuation of a "harmful traditional practice" are opposed to the practice.

- In each case, claims of violations are based on universalist discourses about rights that are based on Eurocentric or ethnocentric standards; assumptions are made that all cultures adhere to the notion that "childhood constitutes a coherent group or a state defined by identical needs and desires, regardless of class, ethnic or racial differences [and is] based on an assumed identity of the biological and physiological attributes of children across the world" (Fernando 2001, 18); and to notions about women and sexuality and what constitutes a violation of women's rights.

- Both issues involve the denial of agency: to women, who are presumed in the West to be demonstrating "false consciousness" if they support or refuse to opt out of FC, and to child soldiers who are regarded as never responsible or legally accountable for their acts, even when they amount to war crimes and who are always perceived as "a deviant product of adult abuse" (Rosen 2007, 297).

- Both issues have been pursued by the West through globalized master narratives of rights in which most commentators have been indifferent to local contexts, history, culture, and social practices, creating tensions between these narratives and local expectations, values, and needs.

- It was assumed or asserted that both FC and child soldiering could be rapidly eliminated through the application of transformative Western techniques, but this has proved to be untrue. Both practices endure because of their grounding in local cultures and social practices and through the persistent exercise of agency by women and youth.

These accounts strongly suggest that between the "twin traps of relativism and universalism" there is clearly a need for a "constructive dialogue" that does not ignore heterogeneity (Fernando 2001, 20) and that does not offer simplified perspectives that deride or ignore local cultural issues. Moreover, adopting a more relativistic approach facilitates an interrogation of the process of change and the likely constraints and obstacles in the way of the eventual elimination of these practices.

NOTES

1. A number of scholars have pointed to the similarities between FC and male circumcision: both practices remove healthy tissue, often without anesthesia; both are considered to be medically unnecessary; and both often take place without the consent of the person being circumcised (Boyle 2002, 37). Nevertheless, the debate over FC far overshadows that concerning male circumcision. It has been noted that "the reasons cited by families for altering the genitalia of their children is nearly identical whether it is a girl in Africa or a boy in the United States," namely, "cleanliness, preventing illness, religion, looking like other children or like their parents, fear of promiscuity, and acceptance of the altered genitalia as more attractive by the opposite sex" (Hernlund and Shell-Duncan 2007, 19).

2. See http://www.who.int/reproductivehealth/topics/fgm/overview/en/.

3. For example, in the United Kingdom, the British Medical Association has estimated that three thousand procedures are performed annually (Skaine 2005, 47).

4. In Iran the veil was a sign of the rejection of the Shah and of Western imperialism, and in immigrant communities it can stand as a rejection of assimilation policies. In other contexts it grants the wearer privacy (Kapur 2005, 107).

5. The Committee is established to receive state reports on the status of women under the Convention on the Elimination of All Forms of Discrimination against Women (CEDAW); see Chapter 13: Violence Against Women.

6. Examples include Scheper-Hughes 1991, "Virgin Territory: The Male Discovery of the Clitoris

(Commentary to Gordon)," *Medical Anthropology Quarterly* 5 (1): 25–28; Gruenbaum 1996, "The Cultural Debate over Female Circumcision: The Sudanese Are Arguing This One Out for Themselves," *Medical Anthropology Quarterly* 10 (4): 455–75; Obermeyer 1999, "Female Genital Surgeries: The Known, the Unknown and the Unknowable," *Medical Anthropology Quarterly* 13 (1): 79–106; Hicks 1993, *Infibulation: Female Mutilation in Islamic Northeastern Africa*, New Brunswick, NJ: Transaction; and Walley 1996, "Searching for 'Voices': Feminism, Anthropology, and the Global Debate over Female Genital Operations," *Cultural Anthropology* 12 (3): 405–38.

7. See Chapter 13 for a discussion of the international conception and development of "violence against women" as a violation of human rights.

8. See http://www.un.org/popin/icpd/conference/offeng/poa.html.

9. A. Topping, "Kenyan Girls Taken to Remote Regions to Undergo FGM in Secret," *Guardian*, July 24, 2014, http://www.theguardian.com/global-develop ment/2014/jul/24/kenya-girls-female-genital-mutilation-fgm-secret.

10. "Uganda Jails Five over FGM," *Guardian*, November 21, 2014, http://www.theguardian.com/world/2014/nov/21/uganda-jails-five-female-genital-mutilation.

11. BBC News UK, "FGM: UK's First Female Genital Mutilation Prosecutions Announced," March 21, 2014, http://www.bbc.com/news/uk-26681364.

12. In Gambia, where a similar project was tried, Ylva Hernlund (2000, 249) reports that not everyone supported the idea of having a ritual without any actual cutting. Some respondents thought that "ritual without cutting" was nonsensical: "What is there to celebrate if they haven't been cut?" Others considered the rituals to be un-Islamic and therefore inappropriate, and some complained that the rituals were too costly and should be discouraged. Gerry Mackie (2000, 276) suggests that rituals are falling out of favor in Gambia, Mali, and Kenya and that girls are being circumcised at younger ages and without the associated rituals. This suggests that FC is a stronger element than the ritual.

13. Research studies by NGOs involving interviews with child soldiers normally generate "responses in victim modes" and conceal aspects of the lived reality. As well, children may believe "they must present themselves as helpless and dependent in order to be seen as deserving of assistance" (Drumbl 2012, 51).

14. Drumbl (2012, 12) points out that most child soldiers are not young children but adolescents in the age range of fifteen to seventeen years. He contends that "the marketing and advertising work of charity organizations however, still inclines toward underscoring the tender age of child soldiers."

15. It has been suggested that the simplistic framing of child soldiers is designed to create sympathy and funding and that representing all child soldiers as having "100% victim status" is vital to eliciting sympathy from the West (Drumbl 2012, 37).

16. Drumbl (2012, 15) points out that contrary to media representations, many children "neither fight nor carry weapons."

17. In a 2002 report titled *Adult Wars, Child Soldiers: Voices of Children Involved in Armed Conflict in the East Asia and Pacific Region*, UNICEF stated that 57 percent of children interviewed had volunteered while 24 percent reported being coerced. Despite these data, the report concluded that most children were forcibly recruited because volunteering does not demonstrate free choice but is a response to economic, cultural, social, and political pressures (Drumbl 2012, 75).

18. See Chapter 7: Juvenile Justice for more on this Convention.

19. Rosen (2005, 5) suggests that as many as 250,000 to 420,000 boy soldiers, including many in their early teens or even younger, served in both the Union and Confederate Armies.

20. Rosen (2005, 14–16) disagrees with the argument that small arms and child soldiers are connected, pointing out that the weapon of choice in armed groups is the Kalashnikov AK47, which weighs about 9 lbs approximately 4 kilos) as compared, for example, to the U.S. M16 rifle, which is rarely found in such armed groups and weighs only about 6 lbs (2.72 kilos). In addition, children in Lebanon often used rocket-propelled grenade launchers that weigh more than 17 lbs (7.7 kilos). Moreover, most of those murdered in Sierra Leone and Rwanda were killed with knives and machetes and not with guns.

21. Some researchers have suggested that the experience of being abducted by the RUF resonated with a traditional practice among Sierra Leone rural youth in which, as a rite of passage to adulthood, youth are taken away, sometimes violently, from their village by the "Bush Devil" to the bush where they undergo weeks or even months of initiation rituals. This practice of kidnapping and isolating youth in the bush promotes a strong bonding between youth which often endures their whole lives (Peters 2011, 81).

22. All countries except the United States and Somalia are parties to this Convention.

23. Demography is also important because in developing country conflict societies, the proportion of the populations constituted by youth is often 50 percent or more. This compares to a figure of 24 percent for the United States. For example, data in 2005 calculated that 47.1 percent of the population of the DRC and 50.4 percent of the population of Uganda were under the age of fifteen years (Drumbl 2012, 47).

24. Steven Zyck (2011, 162) says that the Taliban in Afghanistan focused their recruitment efforts on madrassas in Western Pakistan and that child soldiering among the Taliban was "widely noted" despite statements from Taliban leaders to the contrary.

Beare, M. E. 2003. "Introduction." In *Critical Reflections on Transnational Organized Crime, Money Laundering, and Corruption*, edited by M. E. Beare, xi–xxix. Toronto: University of Toronto Press.

Beck, A., and A. Robertson. 2009. "Policing in the 'New' Russia." In *Policing Developing Democracies*, edited by M. S. Hinton and T. Newburn, 50–72. New York: Routledge.

Beckett, C., and M. Macey. 2001. "Race, Gender and Sexuality: The Oppression of Multiculturalism." *Women's Studies International Forum* 24 (3/4): 309–19.

Beckman, J. 2007. *Comparative Legal Approaches to Homeland Security and Anti-Terrorism*. Aldershot, UK: Ashgate.

Begikhani, N. 2005. "Honour-Based Violence among the Kurds: The Case of Iraqi Kurdistan." In *'Honour': Crimes, Paradigms and Violence Against Women*, edited by L. Welchman and S. Hossain, 209–29. London: Zed Books.

Beirne, P. 2008. "Foreword." In *Global Criminology and Criminal Justice: Current Issues and Perspectives* edited by N. Larsen and R. Smandych, vii–ix. Peterborough, ON: Broadview Press.

Belkin, I. 2000. "China's Criminal Justice System: A Work in Progress." *Washington Journal of Modern China* 6 (2): 61–84.

Bennett, R. 2004. "Comparative Criminology and Criminal Justice Research: The State of Our Knowledge." *Justice Quarterly* 21 (1): 1–21.

Bennett, T. W. 2008. "Comparative Law and African Customary Law." In *The Oxford Handbook of Comparative Law*, edited by M. Reimann and R. Zimmerman, 642–73. Oxford: Oxford University Press.

Bernard, T., and M. Kurlychek. 2010. *The Cycle of Juvenile Justice*, ed. 2. Oxford: Oxford University Press.

Bernault, F. 2003. "The Politics of Enclosure in Colonial and Post-Colonial Africa." In *A History of Prison and Confinement in Africa*, edited by F. Bernault, 1–54. Portsmouth, NH: Heinemann.

Bernault, F. 2007. "The Shadow of Rule: Colonial Power and Modern Punishment in Africa." In *Cultures of Confinement: A History of the Prison in Africa, Asia and Latin America*, edited by F. Dikötter and I. Brown, 55–94. Ithaca, NY: Cornell University Press.

Bhoumik, A. 2004. "Democratic Responses to Terrorism: A Comparative Study of the United States, Israel and India." *Denver Journal of International Law and Policy* 33 (2): 285–345.

Bibes, P. 2001. "Transnational Organized Crime and Terrorism: Colombia, a Case Study." *Journal of Contemporary Criminal Justice* 17 (3): 243–58.

Biddulph, S. 2005. "Mapping Legal Change in the Context of Reforms to Chinese Police Powers." In *Asian Socialism and Legal Change: The Dynamics of Vietnamese and Chinese Reform*, edited by J. Gillespie and P. Nicholson, 212–38. Canberra: ANU E Press & Asia Pacific Press.

Bigo, D. 2012. "Security, Surveillance and Democracy." In *Handbook of Surveillance Studies*, edited by K. Ball, K. D. Haggerty, and D. Lyon, 277–84. Abingdon, UK: Routledge.

Birkbeck, C. 1993. "Against Ethnocentrism: A Cross-Cultural Perspective on Criminal Justice Theories and Policies." *Journal of Criminal Justice Education* 4: 307–23.

Bischoff, J. L. 2003. "Reforming the Criminal Procedure System in Latin America." *Texas Hispanic Journal of Law and Policy* 9: 27–52.

Biswas, B. 2014. *Managing Conflicts in India: Policies of Coercion and Accommodation*. Lanham, MD: Lexington Books.

Black, I. 2013. "NSA Spying Scandal: What We Have Learned." *Guardian*, June 10. http://www.theguardian.com/world/2013/jun/10/nsa-spying-scandal-what-we-have-learned

Blatier, C. 1999. "Juvenile Justice in France: The Evolution of Sentencing for Children and Minor Delinquents." *British Journal of Criminology* 39 (2): 240–52.

Blattmann, R., and K. Bowman. 2008. "Achievements and Problems of the International Criminal Court." *Journal of International Criminal Justice* 6: 711–30.

Blomberg, T., and K. Lucken. 2000. *American Penology: A History of Control*. Hawthorne, NY: Aldine de Gruyter.

Bloom, R. M. 2006. "Jury Trials in Japan." *Loyola of Los Angeles International and Comparative Law Review* 28: 35–68.

Bloss, W. 2007. "Escalating U.S. Police Surveillance after 9/11: An Examination of Causes and Effects." *Surveillance and Society* 4 (3): 208–28.

Bodde, D., and C. Morris. 1967. *Law in Imperial China: Exemplified by 190 Ching Dynasty Cases*. Cambridge, MA: Harvard University Press.

Boddy, J. 1991. "Body Politics: Continuing the Anti-circumcision Crusade." *Medical Anthropology Quarterly* 5 (1): 15–17.

Body-Gendrot, S. 2012. *Globalization, Fear and Insecurity: The Challenges for Cities North and South*. London: Palgrave Macmillan.

Bograd, M. 1988. "Feminist Perspectives on Wife Abuse: An Introduction." In *Feminist Perspectives on Wife Abuse*, edited by Yllo, K. and Bograd, 11–27. Newbury Park, CA: Sage.

Bonelli, L. 2007. "Policing the Youth: Toward a Redefinition of Discipline and Social Control in French Working-Class Neighborhoods." In *Youth, Globalization, and the Law*, edited by S. A. Venkatesh and R. Kassimir, 90–123. Stanford, CA: Stanford University Press.

Bordenkircher v. Hayes, 434 U.S. 357 (1978).

Borlini, L. 2014. "The Economics of Money Laundering." In *Handbook of Transnational Crime and Justice,* edited by P. Reichel and J. Albanese, 227–42. Thousand Oaks, CA: Sage.

Bosco, D. 2014. *Rough Justice: The International Criminal Court in a World of Power Politics.* Oxford: Oxford University Press.

Bossard, A. 1990. *Transnational Crime and Criminal Law.* Chicago: University of Chicago.

Botsman, D. V. 2005. *Punishment and Power in the Making of Modern Japan.* Princeton, NJ: Princeton University Press.

Bottoms, A. 1995. "The Philosophy and Politics of Punishment and Sentencing." In *The Politics of Sentencing Reform,* edited by C. M. V. Clarkson and R. Morgan, 17–49. Oxford: Oxford University Press.

Bourne, M. 2014. "Transnational Trafficking in Weapons." In *Handbook of Transnational Crime and Justice,* edited by P. Reichel and J. Albanese, 85–10. Thousand Oaks, CA: Sage.

Bowling, B. 2011. "Transnational Criminology and the Globalization of Harm Production." In *What Is Criminology?* edited by M. Bosworth and C. Hoyle, 361–79. Oxford: Oxford University Press.

Bowling, B., and J. Foster. 2002. "Policing and the Police." In *The Oxford Handbook of Criminology,* edited by M. Maguire, R. Morgan, and R. Reiner, 980–1019. Oxford: Oxford University Press.

Bowling, B., and J. Sheptycki. 2012. *Global Policing.* Thousand Oaks, CA: Sage.

Bowman, C. G. 2003. "Domestic Violence: Does the African Context Demand a Different Approach?" *International Journal of Law and Psychiatry* 26: 473–91.

Boylan, S. P. 1998. "The Status of Judicial Reform in Russia." *American University International Law Review* 13 (5): 1327–44.

Boyle, E. H. 2002. *Female Genital Cutting: Cultural Conflict in the Global Community.* Baltimore: Johns Hopkins University Press.

Boyne, S. 2004. "Law, Terrorism and Social Movements: The Tension between Politics and Security in Germany's Anti-Terrorism Legislation." *Cardozo Journal of International and Comparative Law* 12: 41–79.

Boyne, S. 2012. "Is the Journey from the In-box to the Out-box a Straight Line? The Drive for Efficiency and the Prosecution of Low-Level Criminality in Germany." In *The Prosecutor in Transnational Perspective,* edited by E. Luna and M. L. Wade, 37–53. Oxford: Oxford University Press.

Bradley, C. 2012. "The Prosecutor's Role: Plea Bargaining and Evidentiary Exclusion." In *The Prosecutor in Transnational Perspective,* edited by E. Luna and M. L. Wade, 91–101. Oxford: Oxford University Press.

Brand, L. A. 1998. "Women and the State in Jordan: Inclusion or Exclusion?" In *Islam, Gender and Social Change,* edited by Y. Y. Haddad and J. L. Esposito, 100–23. New York: Oxford University Press.

Brants, C. 2011. "Comparing Criminal Process as Part of Legal Culture." In *Comparative Criminal Justice and Globalization,* edited by D. Nelken, 49–68. Farnham, UK: Ashgate.

Brenner, S. W. 2006. "Defining Cybercrime: A Review of State and Federal Law." In *Cybercrime: The Investigation, Prosecution and Defense of a Computer-Related Crime,* edited by R. D. Clifford, 13–186. Durham, NC: Carolina Academic Press.

Broadhurst, R. 2006. "Developments in the Global Law Enforcement of Cyber-crime." *Policing: An International Journal of Police Strategies and Management* 29 (3): 408–33.

Brodeur, J. P. 2010. *The Policing Web.* Oxford: Oxford University Press.

Brown, D. 2005. "Continuity, Rupture, or Just More of the 'Volatile and Contradictory'? Glimpses of New South Wales' Penal Practice behind and through the Discursive." In *The New Punitiveness: Trends, Theories, Perspectives,* edited by J. Pratt, D. Brown, S. Hallsworth, and W. Morrison, 27–46. Cullompton, UK: Willan.

Brown, R. C. 1997. *Understanding Chinese Courts and Legal Process: Law with Chinese Characteristics.* The Hague: Kluwer Law International.

Brown, S. 2005. *Understanding Youth and Crime: Listening to Youth?* Maidenhead, UK: Open University Press.

Brownsworth, V. 1994. "Battling the Butchers: The Fight against Female Sex Mutilations." *Lesbian News* 19 (7): 46–47, 59–61.

Brubacher, M. R. 2004. "Prosecutorial Discretion within the International Criminal Court." *Journal of International Criminal Justice* 2: 71–85.

Buckley-Zistel, S., T. K. Beck, C. Braun, and F. Mieth. 2014. "Transitional Justice Theories: An Introduction." In *Transitional Justice Theories,* edited by S. Buckley-Zistel, T. K. Beck, C. Braun, and F. Mieth, 1–16. Abingdon, UK: Routledge.

Bunch, C. 1990. "Women's Rights as Human Rights: Toward a Re-Vision of Human Rights." *Human Rights Quarterly* 12 (4): 486–98.

Burke-White, W. W. 2008. "Proactive Complementarity: The International Criminal Court and National Courts in the Rome System of International Justice." *Harvard International Law Journal* 49 (1): 53–108.

Burnet, J. E. 2010. "(In)justice: Truth, Reconciliation, and Revenge in Rwanda's Gacaca." In *Transitional Justice: Global Mechanisms and Local Realities after Genocide and Mass Violence,* edited by A. L. Hinton, 95–117. Piscataway, NJ: Rutgers University Press.

Burt, M. 2012. "Accountability After Atrocity in Peru: The Trial of Former President Alberto Fujimori in Comparative Perspective." In *Critical Perspectives in Transitional Justice,* edited by N. Palmer, P. Clark, and D. Granville, 119–46. Oxford Transitional Justice Research. Cambridge: Intersentia.

Buss, D. 2002. "Prosecuting Mass Rape: *Prosecutor v. Dragoljub Kunarac, Radomir Kovac and Zoran Vukovic.*" *Feminist Legal Studies* 10: 91–99.

Mediation in France: A Very UnFrench Legal Response?" *Social and Legal Studies* 9 (1): 29–53.

Crenshaw, M. 1981. "The Causes of Terrorism." *Comparative Politics* 13 (4): 379–99.

Crenshaw, M. 1995. "Thoughts on Relating Terrorism to Historical Contexts." In *Terrorism in Context,* edited by M. Crenshaw, 3–26. University Park: Pennsylvania State University.

Criminal Procedure Law of the People's Republic of China. July 1, 1979. Amended March 17, 1996, and March 14, 2012.

Crombag, H. F. M. 2003. "Adversarial or Inquisitorial: Do We Have a Choice?" In *Adversarial versus Inquisitorial Justice: Psychological Perspectives on Criminal Justice Systems,* edited by P. J. Van Koppen and S. D. Penrod, 21–26. New York: Kluwer Academic.

Cronin, A. K. 2004a. "Introduction: Meeting and Managing the Threat." In *Attacking Terrorism: Elements of a Grand Strategy,* edited by A. K. Cronin and J. M. Ludes, 1–18. Washington, DC: Georgetown University Press.

Cronin, A. K. 2004b. "The Sources of Contemporary Terrorism." In *Attacking Terrorism: Elements of a Grand Strategy,* edited by A. K. Cronin and J. M. Ludes, 19–45. Washington, DC: Georgetown University Press.

Cumes, G. 2009. "Impunity, Truth and the Rule of Law: The Political Compromise of Accountability and Justice for Human Rights Atrocities in East Timor." In *Timor-Leste: Challenges for Justice and Human Rights in the Shadow of the Past,* edited by W. Binchy, 475–504. Dublin: Clarus Press.

Czarnota, A. 2012. "Transitional Justice in Post-Communist Central-Eastern Europe: Decommunisation and the Rule of Law." In *Critical Perspectives in Transitional Justice,* edited by N. Palmer, P. Clark, and D. Granville, 425–42. Cambridge: Intersentia.

Dai, Y. 2001. "New Directions of Chinese Policing in the Reform Era." In *Crime and Social Control in a Changing China,* edited by J. Liu, L. Zhang, and S. E. Messner, 151–57. Westport, CT: Greenwood Press.

Dai, Y. and Y. Pi. 2006. "Introduction to the Juvenile Justice System in China: Traditional Crime Control Meets the Challenges of Modernization." In *Delinquency and Juvenile Justice Systems in the Non-Western World,* edited by P. C. Friday and X. Ren, 191–210. Monsey, NY: Criminal Justice Press.

Damaska, M. 1975. "Presentation of Evidence and Factfinding Precision." *University of Pennsylvania Law Review* 123: 1083–1105.

Damaska, M. R. 1986. *The Faces of Justice and State Authority.* New Haven, CT: Yale University Press.

Dammer, H., & E. Fairchild. 2006. *Comparative Criminal Justice Systems,* ed. 3. Belmont, CA: Wadsworth/Thomson Learning.

Danner, A. M. 2003. "Enhancing the Legitimacy and Accountability of Prosecutorial Discretion at the International Criminal Court." *American Journal of International Law* 97 (3): 510–52.

Death Penalty Worldwide (database). 2012. "Methods of Execution." Ithaca, NY: Cornell University Law School. www.deathpenaltyworldwide.org/methods-of-execution.cfm

de Cruz, P. 2007. *Comparative Law in a Changing World.* London: Routledge.

Deflem, M., and S. McDonough. 2010. "International Law Enforcement Organizations." In *Comparative and International Policing, Justice, and Transnational Crime,* edited by S. Kethineni, 127–46. Durham, NC: Carolina Academic Press.

De Grieff, P. 2006. "Justice and Reparations." In *The Handbook of Reparations,* edited by P. De Grieff, 451–77. Oxford: Oxford University Press.

Delaney, J. 2010. "Sikh Extremism on the Rise in Canada, Says Terrorism Expert." *Epoch Times,* April 29. http://www.theepochtimes.com/n2/canada/sikh-extremism-on-the-rise-in-canada-says-terrorism-expert-34375.html

Demleitner, N. V. 2001. "The Law at a Crossroads: The Construction of Migrant Women Trafficked into Prostitution." In *Global Human Smuggling: Comparative Perspectives,* edited by D. Kyle and R. Koslowski, 257–93. Baltimore: Johns Hopkins University Press.

De Muniz, P. J. 2004. "Judicial Reform in Russia: Russia Looks to the Past to Create a New Adversarial System of Criminal Justice." *Willamette Journal of International Law and Dispute Resolution* 11: 81–121.

Denov, M. 2010. *Child Soldiers: Sierra Leone's Revolutionary United Front.* Cambridge: Cambridge University Press.

Devers, L. N., and S. Bacon. 2010. "Interpreting Honor Crimes: The Institutional Disregard Towards Female Victims of Family Violence in the Middle East." *International Journal of Criminology and Sociological Theory* 3 (1): 359–71.

Deville, D. 1999. "Combating Russian Organized Crime: Russia's Fledging Jury System on Trial." *George Washington Journal of International Law and Economics* 32: 73–105.

Diehm, J. W. 2001. "The Introduction of Jury Trials and Adversarial Elements into the Former Soviet Union and Other Inquisitorial Countries." *Florida State Journal of Transnational Law and Policy* 11 (1): 1–38.

Di Frederico, G. 1998. "Prosecutorial Independence and the Democratic Requirement of Accountability in Italy." *British Journal of Criminology* 38 (3): 371–87.

Dikötter, F. 2002. *Crime, Punishment and the Prison in Modern China.* New York: Columbia University Press.

Dikötter, F. 2007. "Introduction." In *Cultures of Confinement: A History of the Prison in Africa, Asia and Latin America,* edited by F. Dikötter and I. Brown, 1–13. Ithaca, NY: Cornell University Press.

Diop, N. J., and I. Askew. 2006. "Strategies for Encouraging the Abandonment of Female Genital Cutting: Experiences from Senegal, Burkina Faso and Mali." In *Female Circumcision: Multicultural Perspectives,* edited by R. M. Abusharaf, 125–43. Philadelphia: University of Pennsylvania Press.

Dirie, M. A., and G. Lindmark. 1991. Female Circumcision in Somalia and Women's Motives. *Acta Obstetricia et Gynecologica Scandinavica* 70 (7/8): 581–85.

Dobash, R. E., and R. P. Dobash. 1992. *Women, Violence and Social Change.* New York: Routledge.

Dobash, R. E., and R. P. Dobash. 1998. *Rethinking Violence Against Women.* Thousand Oaks, CA: Sage.

Dodson, M. 2002. "Assessing Judicial Reform in Latin America." *Latin American Research Review* 37 (2): 200–220.

Doezema, J. 2010. *Sex Slaves and Discourse Masters: The Construction of Trafficking.* London: Zed Books.

Doob, A., and M. Tonry. 2004. "Varieties of Youth Justice." In *Youth Crime, and Youth Justice: Comparative and Cross-National Perspectives,* edited by M. Tonry and A. Doob, 1–20. Chicago: University of Chicago Press.

Dopico, M. 2007. "Infibulation and the Orgasm Puzzle: Sexual Experiences of Infibulated Eritrean Women in Rural Eritrea and Melbourne, Australia." In *Transcultural Bodies: Female Genital Cutting in Global Context,* edited by Y. Hernlund and B. Shell-Duncan, 224–47. New Brunswick, NJ: Rutgers University Press.

Dorange, A., and S. Field. 2012. "Reforming Defence Rights in French Police Custody: A Coming Together in Europe?" *International Journal of Evidence and Proof* 16 (2): 153–74.

Downes, D., and P. Rock. 1988. *Understanding Deviance,* ed. 2. Oxford: Clarendon Press.

Drake, D. 2010. "Punitiveness and Cultures of Control." In *Criminal Justice: Local and Global,* edited by D. Drake, J. Muncie, and L. Westmarland, 37–70. Cullompton, UK: Willan.

Drake, D., and J. Muncie. 2010. "Risk Prediction, Assessment and Management." In *Criminal Justice: Local and Global,* edited by D. Drake, J. Muncie, and L. Westmarland, 105–40. Cullompton, UK: Willan.

Drake, D., J. Muncie, and L. Westmarland. 2010. "Interrogating Criminal Justice." In *Criminal Justice: Local and Global,* edited by D. Drake, J. Muncie, and L. Westmarland, 1–36. Cullompton, UK: Willan.

Draper, P. 1999. "Room to Maneuver: !Kung Women Cope With Men." In To Have and to Hit: Cultural Perspectives on Wife Beating, edited by D. A. Counts, J. K. Brown, and J. C. Campbell, 53–72. Chicago: University of Illinois Press.

Drexler, E. F. 2010. "The Failure of International Justice in East Timor and Indonesia." In *Transitional Justice: Global Mechanisms and Local Realities after Genocide and Mass Violence,* edited

by A. L. Hinton, 49–66. Piscataway, NJ: Rutgers University Press.

Driver, F. 1990. "Discipline without Frontiers? Representations of the Mettray Reformatory Colony in Britain, 1840–1880." *Journal of Historical Sociology* 3: 272–93.

Drumbl, M. A. 2012. *Reimagining Child Soldiers in International Law and Policy.* New York: Oxford University Press.

du Bois-Pedain, A. 2012. "Post-Conflict Accountability and the Demands of Justice: Can Conditional Amnesties Take the Place of Criminal Prosecutions?" In *Critical Perspectives in Transitional Justice,* edited by N. Palmer, P. Clark, and D. Granville, 459–84. Cambridge: Intersentia.

Duff, A. 2001. *Punishment, Communication and Community.* Oxford: Oxford University Press.

Duguid, S. 2000. *Can Prison Work? The Prisoner as Object and Subject in Modern Corrections.* Toronto: University of Toronto Press.

Duncan, M. C. 1998. "Playing by Their Rules: The Death Penalty and Foreigners in Saudi Arabia." *Georgia Journal of International and Comparative Law* 27: 231–48.

Dupont, B. 2008. "The French Police System: Caught between a Rock and a Hard Place—The Tension of Serving Both the State and the Public." *Comparative Policing: The Struggle for Democratization,* edited by M. R. Haberfield and I. Cerrah, 247–72. Thousand Oaks, CA: Sage.

Dutton, M. 1992. *Policing and Punishment in China: From Patriarchy to "the People."* Cambridge: Cambridge University Press.

Dutton, M. 2000. "The End of the (Mass) Line? Chinese Policing in the Era of the Contract." *Social Justice* 27 (2): 61–105.

Dutton, M. R., and Z. Xu. 2005. "A Question of Difference: The Theory and Practice of the Chinese Prison." In *Crime, Punishment, and Policing in China,* edited by B. Bakken, 103–40. Lanham, MD: Rowman and Littlefield.

Dutton, Y. 2013. *Rules, Politics, and the International Criminal Court: Committing to the Court.* London: Routledge.

Dwyer, D. H. 1990. "Law and Islam in the Middle East: An Introduction." In *Law and Islam in the Middle East,* edited by D. H. Dwyer, 1–14. New York: Bergin and Garvey.

Eboe-Osuji, C. 2007. "Rape as Genocide: Some Questions Arising." *Journal of Genocide Research* 9 (2): 251–73.

Eckert, S. E., and T. J. Biersteker. 2010. "(Mis) Measuring Success in Countering the Financing of Terrorism." In *Sex, Drugs, and Body Counts: The Politics of Numbers in Global Crime and Conflict,* edited by P. Andreas and K. M. Greenhill, 247–63. Ithaca, NY: Cornell University Press.

Edwards, A., and P. Gill, P. 2002. "The Politics of 'Transnational Organized Crime': Discourse,

Reflexivity and the Narration of 'Threat.'" *British Journal of Politics and International Relations* 4 (2): 245–70.

Efrat, A. 2012. *Governing Guns, Preventing Plunder: International Cooperation against Illicit Trade.* New York: Oxford University Press.

El Guindi, F. 2006. "'Had This Been Your Face, Would You Leave It As Is?' Female Circumcision among Nubians of Egypt." *In Female Circumcision: Multicultural Perspectives,* edited by R. M. Abusharaf, 27–46. Philadelphia: University of Pennsylvania Press.

Elias, N. 1994. *The Civilizing Process.* Oxford: Blackwell.

Elliott, L. 2012. "Fighting Transnational Environmental Crime." *Journal of International Affairs* 66 (1): 87–104.

Ellison, G. 2007. "Fostering a Dependency Culture: The Commodification of Community Policing in a Global Marketplace." In *Crafting Transnational Policing: Police Capacity Building and Global Police Reform,* edited by A. Goldsmith and J. Sheptycki, 203–42. Portland, OR: Hart.

Ellsberg, M. C., A. Winkvist, R. Pena, and H. Stenlund, H. 2001. "Women's Strategic Responses to Violence in Nicaragua." *Journal of Epidemiological Community Health* 55: 547–55.

Elrod, P., and M. Yokoyama. 2006. "Juvenile Justice in Japan." In *Delinquency and Juvenile Justice Systems in the Non-Western World,* edited by P. C. Friday and X. Ren, 211–28. New York: Criminal Justice Press.

Elster, J. 2006. "Introduction." In *Retribution and Reparation in the Transition to Democracy,* edited by J. Elster, 1–14. Cambridge: Cambridge University Press.

Ericson, R., and K. Carriere. 1996. "The Fragmentation of Criminology." In *Criminological Perspectives: A Reader,* edited by J. Muncie, E. McLaughlin, and M. Langan, 508–16. London: Sage.

Ericson, R. V., and K. D. Haggerty. 1997. *Policing the Risk Society.* Toronto: University of Toronto Press.

Esposito, J. L. 1998. "Introduction: Women in Islam and Muslim Societies." In *Islam, Gender and Social Change,* edited by Y. Y. Haddad and J. L. Esposito, ix–xxviii. New York: Oxford University Press.

Esposito, J. L. 2003. *Unholy War: Terror in the Name of Islam.* Oxford: Oxford University Press.

Esposito, J. L., and Mogahed, D. 2007. *Who Speaks for Islam? What a Billion Muslims Really Think.* New York: Gallup Press.

Esquirol, J. L. 2008. "The Failed Law of Latin America." *American Journal of Comparative Law* 56 (1): 75–124.

Ezeonu, I. 2008. "Crimes of Globalization: Health Care, HIV and the Poverty of Neoliberalism in Sub-Saharan Africa." *International Journal of Social Inquiry* 1 (2): 113–34.

Falola, T., and M. H. Heaton. 2008. *A History of Nigeria.* New York: Cambridge University Press.

Fanon, F. 1961. *The Wretched of the Earth.* New York: Grove Press.

Faqir, F. 2001. "Intrafamily Femicide on Defence of Honour: The Case of Jordan." *Third World Quarterly* 22 (1): 65–82.

Farr, K. 2012. "Trafficking in Women and Girls: Commodification for Profit." In *Borderline Slavery: Mexico, the United States and the Human Trade,* edited by S. Tiano and M. Murphy-Aguilar, 67–88. Burlington, VT: Ashgate.

Farrington, D., P. Langan, and M. Tonry. 2004. *Cross-National Studies in Crime and Justice.* Washington, DC: Bureau of Justice Statistics.

Fastenko, A., and I. Timofeeva. 2004. "Russia." In *International Perspectives on Family Violence and Abuse: A Cognitive Ecological Approach,* edited by K. Malley-Morrison, 111–30. Mahwah, NJ: Lawrence Erlbaum Associates.

Faucette, A. 2012. "Improvements in the Legal Treatment of Systematic Mass Rape in Wartime: Where Do We Go from Here?" In *Conflict-Related Sexual Violence: International Law, Local Responses,* edited by T. St. Germain and S. Dewey, 53–70. Bloomfield, CT: Kumarian Press.

Feest, J., and M. Murayama. 2000. "Protecting the Innocent through Criminal Justice: A Case Study from Spain, Virtually Compared to Germany and Japan." In *Contrasting Criminal Justice: Getting from Here to There,* edited by D. Nelken, 49–76. Aldershot, UK: Ashgate.

Feinstein, L., and T. Lindberg. 2009. *Means to an End: U.S. Interest in the International Criminal Court.* Washington, DC: Brookings Institution Press.

Feld, B. C. 2006. "The Inherent Tension of Social Welfare and Criminal Social Control: Policy Lessons from the American Juvenile Court Experience." In *Juvenile Law Violators, Human Rights, and the Development of New Juvenile Justice Systems,* edited by E. L. Jensen and J. Jepsen, 407–42. Portland, OR: Hart.

Feldman, O. 1998. "Materialism and Individualism: Social Attitudes of Youth in Japan." In *Cross-Cultural Perspectives on Youth and Violence,* edited by M. W. Watts, 9–26. Stamford, CT: JAI Press.

Felsen, D., and A. Kalaitzidis. 2005. "A Historical Overview of Transnational Crime." In *Handbook of Transnational Crime and Justice,* edited by P. Reichel and J. Albanese, 3–19. Thousand Oaks, CA: Sage.

Fenrich J., P. Galizzi, and T. E. Higgens. 2011. "Introduction." In *The Future of African Customary Law,* edited by J. Fenrich, P. Galizzi, and T. E. Higgins, 1–8. New York: Cambridge University Press.

Fenwick, C. R. 1996. "Law and Order in Contemporary Japan: Commitment, Sanctions and the Quality of Life." In *Comparative Criminal Justice:*

Traditional and Nontraditional Systems of Law and Control Fields, edited by C. B. Field and R. H. Moore, 97–114. Prospect Heights, IL: Waveland Press.

Fenwick, M. 2006. "Japan: From Child Protection to Penal Populism." In *Comparative Youth Justice: Critical Issues,* edited by J. Muncie and B. Goldson, 146–58. London: Sage.

Fenwick, M. 2007. "Youth Crime and Crime Control in Contemporary Japan." In *The Blackwell Companion to Criminology,* edited by C. Sumner, 125–42. London: Blackwell.

Fernández, M. 2006. "Cultural Beliefs and Domestic Violence." *Annals of the New York Academy of Sciences* 1087: 250–60.

Fernando, J. L. 2001. "Children's Rights: Beyond the Impasse." *Annals of the American Academy of Political and Social Science* 575: 8–24.

Ferraro, K. J. 2006. *Neither Angels nor Demons: Women, Crime, and Victimization.* Boston: Northeastern University Press.

Fijnaut, C. 2000. "Transnational Crime and the Role of the United Nations in Its Containment through International Cooperation: A Challenge for the 21st Century." *European Journal of Crime, Criminal Law and Criminal Justice* 8 (2): 119–27.

Finckenauer, J. O. 2001. "Russian Transnational Organized Crime and Human Trafficking." In *Global Human Smuggling: Comparative Perspectives,* edited by D. Kyle and R. Koslowski, 166–86. Baltimore: Johns Hopkins University Press.

Findlay, M. 1999. *The Globalisation of Crime: Understanding Transitional Relationships in Context.* Cambridge: Cambridge University Press.

Findlay, M., L. Boon Kuo, and L. Si Wei. 2013. *International and Comparative Criminal Justice: A Critical Introduction.* Abingdon, UK: Routledge.

Finn, J. E. 2010. "Counterterrorism Regimes and the Rule of Law: The Effects of Emergency Legislation on Separation of Powers, Civil Liberties, and Other Fundamental Constitutional Norms." In *The Consequences of Counterterrorism,* edited by M. Crenshaw, 33–93. New York: Russell Sage Foundation.

Fischer, M. M. J. 1990. "Legal Postulates in Flux: Justice, Wit and Hierarchy in Iran." In *Law and Islam in the Middle East,* edited by D. H. Dwyer, 115–42. New York: Bergin and Garvey.

Fishman, S. 2002. *The Battle for Children: World War II, Youth Crime, and Juvenile Justice in Twentieth-Century France.* Cambridge, MA: Harvard University Press.

Fitzpatrick, J. 1994. "The Use of International Human Rights Norms to Combat Violence Against Women." In *Human Rights of Women: National and International Perspectives,* edited by R. J. Cook, 532–72. Philadelphia: University of Pennsylvania Press.

Fletcher, L. E., and H. M. Weinstein. 2002. "Violence and Social Repair: Rethinking the Contribution of Justice to Reconciliation." *Human Rights Quarterly* 24 (3): 573–639.

Flood, M., and B. Pease. 2009. "Factors Influencing Attitudes to Violence Against Women." *Trauma, Violence and Abuse* 10 (2): 125–42.

Fon, V., and F. Parisi. 2006. "Judicial Precedents in Civil Law Systems: A Dynamic Analysis." *International Review of Law and Economics* 26: 519–35.

Foucault, M. 1977. *Discipline and Punish: The Birth of the Prison.* New York: Vintage Books.

Francis, L. P., and J. G. Francis. 2010. "Stateless Crimes, Legitimacy, and International Criminal Law: The Case of Organ Trafficking." *Criminal Law and Philosophy* 4: 283–95.

Fraser, A. 2013. "Ethnography at the Periphery: Redrawing the Borders of Criminology's World-Map." *Theoretical Criminology* 17 (2): 251–60.

Freeman, J. C. 1987. "England." In *Major Criminal Justice Systems: A Comparative Survey,* edited by G. F. Cole, S. J. Frankowski, and M. C. Gertz, 48–70. Newberry Park, CA: Sage.

Freeman, M. 2009. *Necessary Evils: Amnesties and the Search for Justice.* Cambridge: Cambridge University Press.

Frase, R. S. 2001. "Comparative Perspectives on Sentencing Policy and Research." In *Sentencing and Sanctions in Western Countries,* edited by M. Tonry and R. S. Frase, 259–92. Oxford: Oxford University Press.

French Code of Criminal Procedure. http://legislationline.org/download/action/download/id/1674/file/848f4569851e2ea7eabfb2ffcd70.htm/preview

Fretland, K. 2014. "Oklahoma Execution: Clayton Lockett Writhes on Gurney in Botched Procedure." *Guardian,* April 30. http://www.theguardian.com/world/2014/apr/30/oklahoma-execution-botched-clayton-lockett

Friday, P. C. 1996. "The Need to Integrate Comparative and International Criminal Justice into a Traditional Curriculum." *Journal of Criminal Justice Education* 7 (2): 227–39.

Friedman, L. M. 1993. *Crime and Punishment in American History.* New York: Basic Books.

Friedrichs, D. O. 2011. "Comparative Criminology and Global Criminology as Complementary Projects." In *Comparative Criminal Justice and Globalization,* edited by D. Nelken, 163–82. Farnham, UK: Ashgate.

Friman, H. R. 2010. "Numbers and Certification: Assessing Foreign Compliance in Combating Narcotics and Human Trafficking." In *Sex, Drugs, and Body Counts: The Politics of Numbers in Global Crime and Conflict,* edited by P. Andreas and K. M. Greenhill, 75–109. Ithaca, NY: Cornell University Press.

Fu, H. 2000. "Procuracy." *Doing Business in China,* edited by M. J. Moser. Huntington, NY: Juris.

Fu, H. 2001. "After Dictatorship: The Nature and Function of the Police in Post-Mao China." In *Policing, Security and Democracy: Theory and Practice,* edited by S. Einstein and M. Amir, 259–85. Huntsville, TX: OICJ Press.

Fu, H. 2003. "Putting China's Judiciary into Perspective: Is It Independent, Competent and Fair?" In *Beyond Common Knowledge: Empirical Approaches to the Rule of Law,* edited by E. G. Jensen and T. C. Heller, 193–219. Stanford, CA: Stanford University Press.

Fu, H. 2005. "Zhou Yongkang and the Recent Police Reforms in China." *Australia and New Zealand Journal of Criminology* 38: 241–53.

Funk, T. M. 2010. *Victims' Rights and Advocacy at the International Criminal Court.* New York: Oxford University Press.

Furlong, A. 2008. "The Japanese Hikikomori Phenomenon: Acute Social Withdrawal among Young People." *Sociological Review* 56 (2): 309–25.

Gage, B. 2011. "Terrorism and the American Experience: A State of the Field." *Journal of American History* 98 (1): 73–94.

Gahima, G. 2013. *Transitional Justice in Rwanda: Accountability for Atrocity.* Abingdon, UK: Routledge.

Gannon, M. 2001. *Crime Comparisons between Canada and the United States.* Statistics Canada Catalogue no. 85–002-XIE, Vol. 21, no. 11. Ottawa: Canadian Centre for Justice Statistics.

Gargarella, R. 2012. "Human Rights, International Courts and Deliberative Democracy." In *Critical Perspectives in Transitional Justice,* edited by N. Palmer, P. Clark, and D. Granville, 101–18. Cambridge: Intersentia.

Garland, D. 1985. *Punishment and Welfare: A History of Penal Strategies.* Aldershot, UK: Gower.

Garland, D. 1990. *Punishment and Modern Society.* Oxford: Oxford University Press.

Garland, D. 2001. *The Culture of Control: Crime and Social Order in Contemporary Society.* Chicago: University of Chicago Press.

Garland, D. 2010. *Peculiar Institution: America's Death Penalty in an Age of Abolition.* Cambridge, MA: Belknap Press.

Garland, D., and R. Sparks. 2000. "Criminology, Social Theory, and the Challenge of Our Times." In *Criminology and Social Theory,* edited by D. Garland and R. Sparks, 1–22. Oxford: Oxford University Press.

Garrett, S. A. 2004. "Terror Bombing of German Cities in World War II." In *Terrorism: The Philosophical Issues,* edited by I. Primoratz, 141–60. Basingstoke, UK: Palgrave Macmillan.

Gaspard, T. 2004. *A Political Economy of Lebanon 1948–2002: The Limits of Laissez-faire.* Boston: Brill.

Gates, K. 2012. "The Globalization of Homeland Security." In *Routledge Handbook of Surveillance Studies,* edited by in K. Ball, K. D. Haggerty, and D. Lyon, 292–99. Abingdon, UK: Routledge.

Gates, S. 2011. "Why Do Children Fight? Motivations and the Mode of Recruitment." In *Child Soldiers: From Recruitment to Reintegration,* edited by A. Ozerdem and S. Podder, 29–49. Basingstoke, UK: Palgrave Macmillan.

Gendrot, S. 2006. "The Politicization of Youth Justice." In *Comparative Youth Justice,* edited by J. Muncie and B. Goldson, 48–64. London: Sage.

Gerber, T. P., and S. E. Mendelson. 2008. "Public Experiences of Police Violence and Corruption in Contemporary Russia: A Case of Predatory Policing?" *Law and Society Review* 42 (1): 1–40.

Gibbs, C., M. L. Gore, E. F. McGarrell, and L. Rivers. 2010. "Introducing Conservation Criminology: Towards Interdisciplinary Scholarship on Environmental Crimes and Risk." *British Journal of Criminology* 50 (1): 124–44.

Giddens, A. 1990. *The Consequences of Modernity.* Cambridge: Polity Press.

Giddens, A. 1999. "Globalisation: London. Episode 1: Runaway World." *The BBC Reith Lectures 1999,* BBC Online Network.

Gilliam, A. 1991. "Women's Equality and National Liberation." In *Third World Women and the Politics of Feminism,* edited by C. T. Mohanty, A. Russo, and L. Torres, 215–36. Bloomington: Indiana University Press.

Ginsburg, T. 2008. "The Clash of Commitments at the International Criminal Court." *Chicago Journal of International Law* 9: 499–512.

Glasius, M. 2009. "What Is Global Justice and Who Decides? Civil Society and Victim Responses to the International Criminal Court's First Investigations." *Human Rights Quarterly* 31: 496–520.

Glaze, L. E., and E. J. Herberman. 2013. *Correctional Populations in the United States, 2012.* Washington, DC: Bureau of Justice Statistics.

Glaze, L. E., and D. Kaeble. 2014. *Correctional Populations in the United States, 2013.* NCJ 248479. Washington, DC: Bureau of Justice Statistics.

Glendon, M. A., P. G. Carozza, and C. B. Picker. 1982. *Comparative Legal Traditions.* St. Paul, MN: West.

Glendon, M. A., P. G. Carozza, and C. B. Picker. 2008. *Comparative Legal Traditions,* ed. 3. St. Paul, MN: Thomson/West.

Glenn, H. P. 2010. *Legal Traditions of the World: Sustainable Diversity in Law.* Oxford: Oxford University Press.

Goldsmith, A. 2009. "Turkey: Progress towards Democratic Policing?" In *Policing Developing Democracies,* edited by M. S. Hinton and T. Newburn, 31–49. Abingdon, UK: Routledge.

Goldsmith, A., and J. Sheptycki. 2007. "Introduction." In *Crafting Transnational Policing: Police*

Capacity-Building and Global Policing Reform, edited by A. Goldsmith and J. Sheptycki, 1–28. Portland, OR: Hart.

Goldsmith, J. 2003. "The Self-Defeating International Criminal Court." *University of Chicago Law Review* 70 (1): 89–104.

Goldson, B., and J. Muncie. 2012. "Towards a Global 'Child Friendly' Juvenile Justice?" *International Journal of Law, Crime and Justice* 40: 47–64.

Goodey, J. 2008. "Human Trafficking: Sketchy Data and Policy Responses." *Criminology and Criminal Justice* 8 (4): 421–42.

Goodman, R. 2012. "Shifting Landscapes: The Social Context of Youth Problems in an Ageing Nation." In *A Sociology of Japanese Youth: From Returnees to NEETs,* edited by R. Goodman, Y. Imoto, and T. Toivonen, 159–73. London: Routledge.

Goold, B. 2012. "'Mind the (Information) Gap': Making Sense of the European Union's Strategic Approach to Transnational Organized Crime." In *Routledge Handbook of Transnational Organized Crime,* edited by F. Allum and S. Gilmour, 483–93. New York: Routledge.

Gordon, S., and R. Ford. 2006. "On the Definition and Classification of Cybercrime." *Journal of Computer Virology and Hacking Techniques* 2: 13–20.

Gorman, T. "Back on the Chain Gang: Why the Eighth Amendment and the History of Slavery Proscribe the Resurgence of Chain Gangs." *California Law Review* 85: 441, 448–52.

Gossman, P. 2002. "India's Secret Armies." In *Death Squads in Global Perspective: Murder with Deniability,* edited by B. B. Campbell and A. D. Brenner, 261–86. London: Palgrave Macmillan.

Gottfredson, M. R., and D. M. Gottfredson. 1988. *Decision Making in Criminal Justice: Toward the Rational Exercise of Discretion.* New York: Plenum Press.

Gouvin, E. J. 2003. "Bringing Out the Big Guns: The USA Patriot Act, Money Laundering and the War on Terrorism." *Baylor Law Review* 55 (3): 955–90.

Grayson, K. 2003. "Discourse, Identity, and the U.S. 'War on Drugs.'" In *Critical Reflections on Transnational Organized Crime, Money Laundering, and Corruption,* edited by M. E. Beare, 145–70. Toronto: University of Toronto Press.

Green, J. D. 1995. "Terrorism and Politics in Iran." In *Terrorism in Context,* edited by M. Crenshaw, 553–96. University Park: Pennsylvania State University.

Greenawalt, A. K. A. 2007. "Justice without Politics? Prosecutorial Discretion and the International Criminal Court." *New York University Journal of International Law and Politics* 39: 583–640.

Greenberg, J. D. 2009. "The Kremlin's Eye: The 21st Century Prokuratura in the Russian Authoritarian Tradition." *Stanford Journal of International Law* 45 (1): 1–50.

Greene, O. 2000. "Examining International Responses to Illicit Arms Trafficking." *Crime, Law and Social Change* 33: 151–90.

Grisso, T., L. Steinberg, J. Woolard, E. Cauffman, E. Scott, S. Graham, N. D. Reppucci, and R. Schwartz. 2003. "Juveniles' Competence to Stand Trial: A Comparison of Adolescents' and Adults' Capacities as Trial Defendants." *Law and Human Behavior* 27 (4): 333–62.

Grose, R. G., and S. Grabe. 2014. "The Explanatory Role of Relationship Power and Control in Domestic Violence Against Women in Nicaragua: A Feminist Psychology Analysis." *Violence Against Women* 20 (7): 1–22.

Grundlingh, A. 1991. "'Protectors and Friends of the People?' The South African Constabulary in the Transvaal and the Orange River Colony, 1900–08." In *Policing the Empire: Government, Authority and Control, 1830–1940,* edited by D. M. Anderson and D. Killingray, 168–82. Manchester, UK: Manchester University Press.

Gruenbaum, E. 2001. *The Female Circumcision Controversy: An Anthropological Perspective.* Philadelphia: University of Pennsylvania Press.

Gunning, I. R. 1991. "Arrogant Perception, World Travelling and Multicultural Feminism: The Case of Female Genital Surgeries." *Colombia Human Rights Law Review* 23: 189–248.

Hackler, J. 1988. "Practising in France What Americans Have Preached: The Response of French Judges to Juveniles." *Crime and Delinquency* 34 (4): 467–85.

Hackler, J., A. Garapon, C. Frigon, and K. Knight. 1987. "Locking Up Juveniles in Canada: Some Comparisons with France." *Canadian Public Policy* 13 (4): 477–89.

Haddad, Y. Y., and M. J. Balz. 2008. "Taming the Imans: European Governments and Islamic Preachers since 9/11." *Islam and Christian-Moslem Relations* 19 (2): 215–35.

Hadi, A. A. 2006. "A Community of Women Empowered: The Story of Deir El Barsha." In *Female Circumcision: Multicultural Perspectives,* edited by R. M. Abusharaf, 104–24. Philadelphia: University of Pennsylvania Press.

Hafetz, J. L. 2002. "Pretrial Detention, Human Rights and Judicial Reform in Latin America." *Fordham International Law Journal* 26 (6): 1754–77.

Haggerty, K. D., and R. V. Ericson. 2000. "The Surveillant Assemblage." *British Journal of Sociology* 51 (4): 605–22.

Hakeem, F. 2008. "Emergence of Modern Indian Policing: From Mansabdari to Constabulary." In *Comparative Policing: The Struggle for Democratization,* edited by M. R. Haberfield and I. Cerrah, 169–79. Thousand Oaks, CA: Sage.

Hall, M. 2011. "Environmental Victims: Challenges for Criminology and Victimology in the 21st Century." *Journal of Criminal Justice and Security* 13 (4): 371–91.

Hall, M. C. 1992. "Sex Tourism in South-east Asia." In *Tourism and the Less Developed Nations,* edited by D. Harrison, 64–74. London: Belhaven Press.

Hamai, K., and T. Ellis. 2006. "Crime and Criminal Justice in Modern Japan: From Re-integrative Shaming to Popular Punitivism." *International Journal of the Sociology of Law* 34: 157–78.

Hanna, C. 1997. "Paradox of Hope: The Crime and Punishment of Domestic Violence." *William & Mary Law Review* 39 (1998): 1505.

Hanson, T. O. 2014. "The Vertical and Horizontal Expansion of Transitional Justice: Explanations and Implications for a Contested Field." In *Transitional Justice Theories,* edited by S. Buckley-Zistel, T. K. Beck, C. Braun, and F. Mieth, 105–24. Abingdon, UK: Routledge.

Hardie-Bick, J., J. Sheptycki, and A. Wardak. 2005. "Introduction: Transnational and Comparative Criminology in a Global Perspective." In *Transnational and Comparative Criminology,* edited by J. Sheptycki and A. Wardak, 1–18. London: GlassHouse Press.

Harriott, A. 2000. *Control in Jamaica: Problems of Reforming Ex-Colonial Constabularies.* Kingston, Jamaica: University of West Indies Press.

Harris, D. A. 2012. "The Interaction and Relationship between Prosecutors and Police Officers in the United States, and How This Affects Police Reform Efforts." In *The Prosecutor in Transnational Perspective,* edited by E. Luna and M. L. Wade, 54–66. Oxford: Oxford University Press.

Hart, J. 2006. "Saving Children: What Role for Anthropology?" *Anthropology Today* 22 (1): 5–8.

Hartjen, C. A. 2008. *Youth, Crime and Justice: A Global Inquiry.* New Brunswick, NJ: Rutgers University Press.

Hartjen, C. A., and S. Priyadarsini. 2012. *The Global Victimization of Children: Problems and Solutions.* New York: Springer.

Hassan, R. A., and L. Welchman. 2005. "Changing the Rules? Developments on 'Crimes of Honour' in Jordan." In *'Honour': Crimes, Paradigms and Violence Against Women,* edited by L. Welchman and S. Hossain, 199–208. London: Zed Books.

Haubrich, D. 2003. "September 11, Anti-Terror Laws and Civil Liberties: Britain, France and Germany Compared." *Government and Opposition* 38 (1): 3–28.

Hauge, W. 2011. "Girl Soldiers in Guatemala." In *Child Soldiers: From Recruitment to Reintegration,* edited by A. Ozerdem and S. Podder, 91–103. Basingstoke, UK: Palgrave Macmillan.

Hawkins, R. 1991. "The 'Irish Model' and the Empire: A Case for Reassessment." In *Policing the Empire: Government, Authority and Control, 1830–1940,* edited by D. M. Anderson and D. Killingray, 18–32. Manchester, UK: Manchester University Press.

Hayner, P. B. 2002. *Unspeakable Truths: Facing the Challenge of Truth Commissions.* New York: Routledge.

Head, J. W. 2011. *Great Legal Traditions: Civil Law, Common Law and Chinese Law in Historical and Operational Perspective.* Durham, NC: Carolina Academic Press.

Heinzen, K. 1901. "Murder vs. Murder." *Freiheit.* First published 1849.

Heise, L. L. 1998. "Violence Against Women: An Integrated, Ecological Framework." *Violence Against Women* 4 (3): 262–90.

Held, D., and A. McGrew. 2007. *Globalization/Anti-Globalization: Beyond the Great Divide.* Cambridge: Polity Press.

Held, V. 2004. "Terrorism, Rights and Political Goals." In *Terrorism: The Philosophical Issues,* edited by I. Primoratz, 5–79. Basingstoke, UK: Palgrave Macmillan.

Hemment, J. 2004. "Global Civil Society and the Local Costs of Belonging: Defining Violence Against Women in Russia." *Signs: Journal of Women in Culture and Society* 29 (3): 815–40.

Henrichson, C., and R. Delaney. 2012. *The Price of Prisons: What Incarceration Costs Taxpayers.* New York: Center on Sentencing and Corrections, Vera Institute of Justice.

Hepburn, S. 2012. "Aftermath of Hurricanes Katrina and Rita: Labor Exploitation and Human Trafficking of Mexican Nationals to the Gulf Coast." In *Borderline Slavery: Mexico, the United States and the Human Trade,* edited by S. Tiano and M. Murphy-Aguilar, 197–217. Burlington, VT: Ashgate.

Hernandez-Truyol, B. E. 1999. "Human Rights through a Gendered Lens: Emergence, Evolution, Revolution." In *Women and International Human Rights Law,* vol. 1, edited by K. D. Askin and D. M. Keonig. New York: Transnational.

Hernlund, Y. 2000. "Cutting without Ritual and Ritual without Cutting: Female 'Circumcision' and the Re-ritualization of Initiation in the Gambia." In *Female "Circumcision" in Africa: Culture, Controversy, and Change,* edited by B. Shell-Duncan and Y. Hernlund, 235–52. Boulder, CO: Lynne Rienner.

Hernlund, Y., and B. Shell-Duncan. 2007. "Transcultural Positions: Negotiating Rights and Culture." In *Transcultural Bodies: Female Genital Cutting in Global Context,* edited by Y. Hernlund and B. Shell-Duncan, 1–45. New Brunswick, NJ: Rutgers University Press.

Higgins, R. 1997. "The General International Law of Terrorism." In *Terrorism and International Law,* edited by R. Higgins and M. Flory. London: Routledge.

Hill, R. S. 1991. "The Policing of Colonial New Zealand: From Informal to Formal Control, 1840–1907." In *Policing the Empire: Government, Authority and Control, 1830–1940,* edited by

D. M. Anderson and D. Killingray, 52–70. Manchester, UK: Manchester University Press.

Hills, A. 1996. "Towards a Critique of Policing and National Development in Africa." *Journal of Modern African Studies* 34 (2): 271–91.

Hills, A. 2008. *Policing Post-Conflict Cities.* London: Zed Books.

Hills, A. 2009. "The Possibility of Transnational Policing." *Policing and Society: An International Journal of Research and Policy* 19 (3): 300–317.

Himonga, C. 2011. "The Future of Living Customary Law in African Legal Systems in the Twenty First Century and Beyond, with Special Reference to South Africa." In *The Future of African Customary Law,* edited by J. Fenrich, P. Galizzi., and T. E. Higgins, 31–57. New York: Cambridge University Press.

Hinman, L. 1998. *Ethics: A Pluralistic Approach to Moral Theory.* Fort Worth, TX: Harcourt Brace.

Hinman, L. 2012. *Ethics: A Pluralistic Approach to Moral Theory,* ed. 5. Boston: Wadsworth.

Hinton, A. L. 2010. "Introduction: Towards an Anthropology of Transitional Justice." In *Transitional Justice: Global Mechanisms and Local Realities after Genocide and Mass Violence,* edited by A. L. Hinton, 1–24. Piscataway, NJ: Rutgers University Press.

Hinton, M. 2006. *The State on the Streets: Police and Politics in Argentina and Brazil.* Boulder, CO: Lynne Rienner.

Hinton, M. S., and T. Newburn. 2009. "Introduction." In *Policing Developing Democracies,* edited by M. S. Hinton and T. Newburn, 1–27. Abingdon, UK: Routledge.

Hirsch, A. J. 1992. *The Rise of the Penitentiary Prisons and Punishment in Early America.* New Haven, CT: Yale University Press.

Hobsbawn, E. 1977. *Revolutionaries: Contemporary Essays.* London: Quartet Books.

Hocking, J. 1984. "Orthodox Theories of 'Terrorism': The Power of Politicised Terminology." *Politics* 19 (2): 103–10.

Hodgson, J. 2001. "The Police, the Prosecutor and the Juge D'Instruction: Judicial Supervision in France, Theory and Practice." *British Journal of Criminology* 41: 342–61.

Hodgson, J. 2002. "Defendants and Victims in the French Criminal Process: The Context of Recent Reform." *International and Comparative Law Quarterly* 51 (4): 781–815.

Hodgson, J. 2004. "The Detention and Interrogation of Suspects in Police Custody in France: A Comparative Account." *European Journal of Criminology* 1: 163–99.

Hodgson, J. 2005. *French Criminal Justice.* Oxford: Hart.

Hodgson, J. 2010. "The French Prosecutor in Question." *Washington and Lee Law Review* 67: 1361–1411.

Hodgson, J. 2012. "Guilty Pleas and the Changing Role of the Prosecutor in French Criminal Justice." In *The Prosecutor in Transnational Perspective,* edited by E. Luna and M. L. Wade, 116–34. Oxford: Oxford University Press.

Hoffman, B. 2006. *Inside Terrorism.* New York: Colombia University Press.

Hogg, R. 2002. "Criminology beyond the Nation State: Global Conflicts, Human Rights and the 'New World Disorder.'" In *Critical Criminology: Issues, Debates, Challenges,* edited by R. Hogg and K. Carrington, 185–217. Cullompton, UK: Willan.

Holscher L. M., and R. Mahmood. 2000. "Borrowing from the Shariah: The Potential Uses of Procedural Islamic Law in the West." In *International Criminal Justice: Issues in a Global Perspective,* edited by D. Rounds, 82–96. Boston: Allyn & Bacon.

Home Office, U.K. 2014. *Strengthening the Law on Domestic Abuse—A Consultation.* London: Home Office.

Honwana, A. 2006. *Child Soldiers in Africa.* Philadelphia: University of Pennsylvania Press.

Hood, R. 2001. "Capital Punishment: A Global Perspective." *Punishment and Society* 3 (3): 331–54.

Hood, R., and C. Hoyle. 2008. *The Death Penalty: A Worldwide Perspective,* ed. 4. Oxford: Oxford University Press.

Hood, R., and C. Hoyle. 2015. *The Death Penalty: A Worldwide Perspective,* ed. 5. Oxford: Oxford University Press.

Horelt, M. A. 2010. "Performing Reconciliation: A Performance Approach to the Analysis of Political Apologies." In *Critical Perspectives in Transitional Justice,* edited by N. Palmer, P. Clark, and D. Granville, 347–68. Cambridge: Intersentia.

Horiguchi, S. 2012. "Hikikomori: How Private Isolation Caught the Public Eye." In *A Sociology of Japanese Youth: From Returnees to NEETs,* edited by R. Goodman, Y. Imoto, and T. Toivonen, 122–38. London: Routledge.

Horne, S. 1999. "Domestic Violence in Russia." *American Psychologist* 34 (1): 55–61.

Hoyek, D., R. R. Sidawi, and A. A. Mrad. 2005. "Murders of Women in Lebanon: 'Crimes of Honour' between Reality and the Law." In *'Honour': Crimes, Paradigms and Violence Against Women,* edited by L. Welchman and S. Hossain, 111–36. London: Zed Books.

Hoyle, C. 2012. "Can International Justice Be Restorative Justice? The Role of Reparations." In *Critical Perspectives in Transitional Justice,* edited by N. Palmer, P. Clark, and D. Granville, 189–210. Cambridge: Intersentia.

Htun, M., and S. L. Weldon. 2012. "The Civic Origins of Progressive Policy Change: Combating Violence Against Women in Global Perspective, 1975–2005." *American Political Science Review* 106 (3): 548–69.

Hudson, B. 1996. *Understanding Justice: An Introduction to Ideas, Perspectives and Controversies in Modern Penal Theory.* Buckingham, UK: Open University Press.

Hudson, J. 1996. *The Formation of the English Common Law: Law and Society in England from the Norman Conquest to Magna Carta*. London: Longman.

Huggins, M. K. 1998. *Political Policing: The United States and Latin America*. Durham, NC: Duke University Press.

Hughes, M. J. 2011. "British Opinion and Russian Terrorism in the 1880s." *European History Quarterly* 41 (2): 255–77.

Human Rights Watch. 2003, June 20. *Bilateral Immunity Agreements*. http://www.iccnow.org/documents/HRWBIATableJune03.pdf

Huntington, S. P. 1973. "Transnational Organizations in World Politics." *World Politics* 25 (3): 333–68.

Huntington, S. P. 1993. "The Clash of Civilizations." *Foreign Affairs* 72 (3): 22–49.

Huntington, S. P. 1996. *The Clash of Civilizations and the Remaking of World Order*. New York: Simon & Schuster.

Ignatieff, M. 1978. *A Just Measure of Pain: The Penitentiary in the Industrial Revolution, 1750–1850*. New York: Pantheon Books.

Immigration and Nationality Act. http://www.state.gov/j/ct/rls/other/des/123058.htm

Inda, J. X., and R. Rosaldo. 2008. "Tracking Global Flows." In *The Anthropology of Globalization: A Reader*, edited by J. X. Inda and R. Rosaldo, 3–46. Malden, MA: Blackwell.

International Convention against the Taking of Hostages, G.A. Res. 146 (XXXIV). U.N. GAOR, 34th Sess., Supp. No. 46, at 245, U.N. Doc. A/34/46 (1979), entered into force June 3, 1983.

International Convention for the Suppression of the Financing of Terrorism. Adopted by the General Assembly of the United Nations in resolution 54/109 of 9 December 1999.

International Covenant on Civil and Political Rights (ICCPR). 1966.

International Criminal Court (ICC). 2004. *Regulations of the Court*. Adopted by the Judges of the Court on May 26, 2004. Fifth Plenary Session. The Hague, 17–28 May 2004. ICC-BD/01–01–04.

International Criminal Court (ICC). 2009, April 23. *Regulations of the Office of the Prosecutor*. ICC-BD/05–01–09. http://www.icc-cpi.int/NR/rdonlyres/FFF97111-ECD6–40B5–9CDA-792BCBE1E695/280253/ICCBD050109ENG.pdf

International Criminal Court (ICC). 2010, February 1. *Prosecutorial Strategy, 2009–2012*. The Hague: Office of the Prosecutor. http://www.icc-cpi.int/NR/rdonlyres/66A8DCDC-3650–4514-AA62-D229D1128F65/281506/OTPProsecutorialStrategy20092013.pdf

International Criminal Court (ICC). 2013, March 26. *Pre-Trial Chamber II. Situation in Darfur, Sudan*. ICC-02/05–01/09. http://www.icc-cpi.int/iccdocs/doc/doc1573530.pdf

International Criminal Court (ICC). *Policy Papers*. http://www.icc-cpi.int/FR_Menus/Search/Pages/results.aspx?k=Policy%20Papers

International Criminal Court (ICC). *Situations and Cases*. http://www.icc-cpi.int/en_menus/icc/situations%20and%20cases/Pages/situations%20and%20cases.aspx

International Labour Organization (ILO). 2005. *A Global Alliance against Forced Labour, Global Report under the Follow-up to the ILO Declaration on Fundamental Principles and Rights at Work*. International Labour Conference, 93rd Session 2005. Geneva: International Labour Office.

Istanbul Statement on the Use and Effects of Solitary Confinement. Adopted on December 9, 2007, at the International Psychological Trauma Symposium, Istanbul.

Jackson, J. 2006. "The Ethical Implications of the Enhanced Role of the Public Prosecutor." *Legal Ethics* 9 (1): 35–55.

Jackson, N. 2005. "The Trafficking of Narcotics, Arms and Humans in Post-Soviet Central Asia: (Mis)perceptions, Policies and Realities." *Central Asian Survey* 24 (1): 39–52.

"Jamaica to Abolish Flogging Punishment." *Guardian*, Associated Press in Kingston Jamaica, November 16, 2012. http://www.theguardian.com/world/2012/nov/16/jamaica-abolish-flogging-punishment

James, S. M., and C. C. Robertson. 2002. "Prologue: Position Paper on Clitoridectomy and Infibulation, Women's Caucus of the African Studies Association." In *Genital Cutting and Transnational Sisterhood: Disputing U.S. Polemics*, edited by S. M. James and C. C. Robertson, 1–4. Urbana: University of Illinois Press.

Jamieson, R., and K. McEvoy. 2005. "State Crimes by Proxy and Judicial Othering." *British Journal of Criminology* 45 (4): 504–27.

Janson, C. G. 2004. "Youth Justice in Sweden." In *Youth Crime and Youth Justice: Comparative and Cross-National Perspectives*, edited by M. Tonry and A. N. Doob, 391–442. Chicago: University of Chicago Press.

"Japan's Death Row." Editorial. *New York Times*, April 6, 2014. http://www.nytimes.com/2014/04/07/opinion/japans-death-row.html?_r=0

Jeffreys, S. 2009. *The Industrial Vagina: The Political Economy of the Global Sex Trade*. New York: Routledge.

Jenkins, P. 1988. "Whose Terrorists? Libya and State Criminality." *Contemporary Crises* 12: 5–24.

Jenkins, P. 2003. *Images of Terror: What We Know and Can't Know about Terrorism*. New York: Aldine de Gruyter.

Jiang, N. 2014. *China and International Human Rights: Harsh Punishments in the Context of the International Covenant on Civil and Political Rights*. New York: Springer.

Jiang, S., E. G. Lambert, J. Liu, and T. Saito. 2014. "Formal and Informal Control Views in China, Japan, and the U.S." *Journal of Criminal Justice* 42: 36–44.

Jiao, A. Y. 2001a. "Police and Culture: A Comparison between China and the United States." *Police Quarterly* 4 (2): 156–85.

Jiao, A. Y. 2001b. "Traditions and Changes of Police Culture: Organization, Operation, and Behavior of the Chinese Police." In *Crime and Social Control in a Changing China,* edited by J. Liu, L. Zhang, and S. E. Messner, 159–76. Westport, CT: Greenwood Press.

Joachim, J. 2003. "Framing Issues and Seizing Opportunities: The UN, NGOs, and Women's Rights." *International Studies Quarterly* 47 (2): 247–74.

Johnsdotter, S. 2007. "Persistence of Tradition or Reassessment of Cultural Practices in Exile: Discourses on Female Circumcision among and about Swedish Somalis." In *Transcultural Bodies: Female Genital Cutting in Global Context,* edited by Y. Hernlund and B. Shell-Duncan, 107–34. New Brunswick, NJ: Rutgers University Press.

Johnson, D. T. 2002. *The Japanese Way of Justice: Prosecuting Crime in Japan.* New York: Oxford University Press.

Johnson, D. T. 2006. Where the State Kills in Secret: Capital Punishment in Japan. *Punishment and Society* 8 (3): 251–285.

Johnson, D. T. 2009. "Early Returns from Japan's New Criminal Trials." *Asia-Pacific Journal* 36: 3–9.

Johnson, E. H. 1998. "The Japanese Experience: Effects of Decreasing Resort to Imprisonment." In *Comparing Prison Systems: Toward a Comparative and International Penology,* edited by R. P. Weiss and N. South, 337–366. Amsterdam: Gordon and Breach.

Johnson, H. 1991. "Patterns of Policing in the Post-Emancipation British Caribbean, 1835–95." In *Policing the Empire: Government, Authority and Control, 1830–1940,* edited by D. M. Anderson and D. Killingray, 71–91. Manchester, UK: Manchester University Press.

Johnson, J. E. 2009. *Gender Violence in Russia: The Politics of Feminist Intervention.* Bloomington: Indiana University Press.

Johnson, M. C. 2007. "Making Mandinga or Making Muslims? Debating Female Circumcision, Ethnicity, and Islam in Guinea-Bissau and Portugal." In *Transcultural Bodies: Female Genital Cutting in Global Context,* edited by Y. Hernlund and B. Shell-Duncan, 202–23. New Brunswick, NJ: Rutgers University Press.

Johnstone, G. 2002. *Restorative Justice: Ideas, Values, Debates.* Cullompton, UK: Willan.

Jones, T., and Newburn, T. 2007. *Policy Transfer and Criminal Justice: Exploring U.S. Influence over British Crime Control Policy.* Maidenhead, UK: Open University Press.

Jost, P. M., and H. S. Sandhu. n.d. *The Hawala Alternative Remittance System and Its Role in Money Laundering.* U.S. Department of Treasury and INTERPOL. http://www.treasury.gov/resource-center/ terrorist-illicit-finance/Documents/FinCEN-Hawala-rpt.pdf

Juergensmeyer, M. 2003. *Terror in the Mind of God: The Global Rise of Religious Violence.* Berkeley: University of California Press.

Juma, L. 2011. "Putting Old Wine in New Wine Skins: The Customary Code of Lerotholi and Justice Administration in Lesotho." In *The Future of African Customary Law,* edited by J. Fenrich, P. Galizzi., and T. E. Higgins, 129–52. New York: Cambridge University Press.

Junger-Tas, J. 2008. "Trends in International Juvenile Justice: What Conclusions Can Be Drawn?" In *International Handbook of Juvenile Justice,* edited by J. Junger-Tas and S. Decker, 505–32. New York: Springer-Verlag.

Justice Management Institute and Vera Institute of Justice. 1996. *How to Use Structured Fines (Day Fines) as an Intermediate Sanction.* Report no. NCJ156242. Washington, DC: U.S. Bureau of Justice Assistance.

Kagan, R. A. 2001. *Adversarial Legalism: The American Way of Law.* Cambridge, MA: Harvard University Press.

Kaldor, M. 2012. *New and Old Wars: Organized Violence in a Global Era.* Stanford, CA: Stanford University Press.

Kalhan, A., G. P. Conroy, M. Kaushal, S. S. Miller, and J. S. Rakoff. 2006. "Colonial Continuities: Human Rights, Terrorism, and Security Laws in India." *Colombia Journal of Asian Law* 20 (1): 93–234.

Kapitan, T. 2004. "Terrorism in the Arab-Israeli Conflict." In *Terrorism: The Philosophical Issues,* edited by I. Primoratz, 175–91. Basingstoke, UK: Palgrave Macmillan.

Kapur, R. 2005. "Revisioning the Role of Law in Women's Human Rights Struggles." In *The Legalization of Human Rights: Multidisciplinary Perspectives,* edited by S. Meckled-García and B. Çali, 101–16. London: Routledge.

Karstedt, S. 2001. "Comparing Cultures, Comparing Crime: Challenges, Prospects and Problems for a Global Criminology." *Crime, Law and Social Change* 36: 285–308.

Kawasaki, K. 1994. "Youth Culture in Japan." *Social Justice* 21 (2): 185–203.

Kearney, M. 1995. "The Local and the Global: The Anthropology of Globalization and Transnationalism." *Annual Review of Anthropology* 24: 547–65.

Kelley, J. 2007. "International Commitments and Why? The International Criminal Court and Bilateral Nonsurrender Agreements." *American Political Science Review* 101 (3): 573–89.

Kelly, R. J., and S. A. Levy. 2012. "The Endangered Empire: American Responses to Transnational Organized Crime." In *Routledge Handbook of Transnational Organized Crime,* edited by F. Allum and S. Gilmour, 443–54. New York: Routledge.

Kenney, M. 2012. "The Evolution of the International Drugs Trade: The Case of Colombia, 1930–2000." In *Routledge Handbook of Transnational Organized Crime,* edited by F. Allum and S. Gilmour, 201–16. New York: Routledge.

Kent, L. 2012. *The Dynamics of Transitional Justice: International Models and Local Realities in East Timor.* Abingdon, UK: Routledge.

Kerr, O. S. 2010. "Vagueness Challenges to the Computer Fraud and Abuse Act." *Minnesota Law Review* 94: 1561–87.

Khadduri, M. 1984. *The Islamic Conception of Justice.* Baltimore: Johns Hopkins University Press.

Kilkelly, U. 2008. "Youth Justice and Children's Rights: Measuring Compliance with International Standards." *Youth Justice: An International Journal* 8 (3): 187–92.

Killingray, D. 1991. "Guarding the Extending Frontier: Policing the Gold Coast, 1865–1913." In *Policing the Empire: Government, Authority and Control, 1830-1940,* edited by D. M. Anderson and D. Killingray, 106–25. Manchester, UK: Manchester University Press.

Killingray, D. 2003. "Punishment to Fit the Crime? Penal Policy and Practice in British Colonial Africa." In *A History of Prison and Confinement in Africa,* edited by F. Bernault, 97–118. Portsmouth, NH: Heinemann.

Kim, N. 1993. "Toward a Feminist Theory of Human Rights: Straddling the Fence between Western Imperialism and Uncritical Absolutism." *Columbia Human Rights Law Review* 25: 49–105.

Komiya, N. 1999. "A Cultural Study of the Low Crime Rate in Japan." *British Journal of Criminology* 39 (3): 369–90.

Koszeg, F. 2001. "Introduction." In *Police in Transition: Essays on the Police Forces in Transition Countries,* edited by A. Kadar, 1–14. Budapest: Central European University Press.

Krishnan, J. K. 2004. *India's "Patriot Act": POTA and the Impact on Civil Liberties in the World's Largest Democracy.* Faculty Publications Paper 379. Bloomington: Indiana University, Maurer School of Law.

Krug, E. G., K. E. Powell, and L. L. Dahlberg. 1998. "Firearm-Related Deaths in the United States and 35 Other High- and Upper-Middle-Income Countries." *International Journal of Epidemiology* 27: 214–21.

Krug, P. 2002. "Prosecutorial Discretion and Its Limits." *American Journal of Comparative Law* 50: 643–64.

Kumari, V. 2004. *The Juvenile Justice System in India: From Welfare to Rights.* New Delhi: Oxford University Press.

Kurki, L. 2001. "International Standards for Sentencing and Punishment." In *Sentencing and Sanctions in Western Countries,* edited by M. Tonry and R. S. Frase, 331–78. Oxford: Oxford University Press.

Lackey, D. 2004. "The Evolution of the Modern Terrorist State: Area Bombing and Nuclear Deterrence." In *Terrorism: The Philosophical Issues,* edited by I. Primoratz, 128–40. Basingstoke, UK: Palgrave Macmillan.

Lambourne, W. 2012. "Outreach, Inreach and Civil Society Participation in Transitional Justice." In *Critical Perspectives in Transitional Justice,* edited by N. Palmer, P. Clark, and D. Granville, 235–62. Cambridge: Intersentia.

Langer, M. 2007. "Revolution in Latin American Criminal Procedure: Diffusion of Ideas from the Periphery." *American Journal of Comparative Law* 55: 617–76.

Laqueur, W. 1987. *The Age of Terrorism.* Boston: Little, Brown.

Laqueur, W. 1996. "Postmodern Terrorism." *Foreign Affairs* 75 (5): 24–36.

Larsen, N. 2010. "Nuclear Facilities in the Russian Far East: A Weak Link in the War on Terrorism: 21 Steps to Better Nuclear Security in the Russian Far East." *Issues and Insights Pacific Forum CSIS* 10 (13): iv–31.

Larsen, N., and R. Smandych. 2008. "Preface." In *Global Criminology and Criminal Justice: Current Issues and Perspectives,* edited by N. Larsen and R. Smandych, xi–xii. Peterborough, Ontario: Broadview Press.

Lawoko, S. 2008. "Predictors of Attitudes toward Intimate Partner Violence: A Comparative Study of Men in Zambia and Kenya." *Journal of Interpersonal Violence* 23 (8): 1056–74.

Lawyers Committee for Human Rights. 1998. *Wrongs and Rights: A Human Rights Analysis of China's Revised Criminal Law.* New York: Lawyers Committee for Human Rights.

League of Nations Convention. 1937.

Lee, M. 2012. *Trafficking and Global Crime Control.* Thousand Oaks, CA: Sage.

Lemarchand, R. 2009. "The 1994 Rwanda Genocide." In *Century of Genocide: Critical Essays and Eyewitness Accounts,* edited by S. Totten and W. S. Parsons, 483–506. New York: Routledge.

Lenz, N. 2002. "'Luxuries' in Prison: The Relationship between Amenity Funding and Public Support." *Crime and Delinquency* 48 (4): 499–525.

Leong, A. V. M. 2007. *The Disruption of International Organized Crime: An Analysis of Legal and Non-Legal Strategies.* Aldershot, UK: Ashgate.

Lepsius, O. 2004. "Liberty, Security, and Terrorism: The Legal Position in Germany." *German Law Journal* 5 (5): 435–60.

Levi, M. 2002. "Money Laundering and Its Regulation." *Annals of the American Academy of Political and Social Sciences* 582 (1): 181–94.

Levitt, M. 2006. *Hamas: Politics, Charity, and Terrorism in the Service of Jihad.* New Haven, CT: Yale University Press.

Lewis, C. 2012. "The Evolving Role of the English Crown Prosecution Service." In *The Prosecutor in Transnational Perspective,* edited by E. Luna and M. L. Wade, 214–34. Oxford: Oxford University Press.

Lewis, N. 2005. "Expanding Surveillance: Connecting Biometric Information Systems to International Police Cooperation." In *Global Surveillance and Policing: Borders, Security, Identity,* edited by E. Zureik and M. B. Salter, 97–112. Cullompton, UK: Willan.

Lewis, O. 2014. "Israel Destroys Home of Palestinian Who Crashed Car into People at Jerusalem Tram Stop." *Huffington Post,* November 19. http://www.huffingtonpost.com/2014/11/19/israel-retaliation-tram-stop-attack_n_6183142.html

Li, Y. 2014. *The Judicial System and Reform in Post-Mao China: Stumbling towards Justice.* Farnham, UK: Ashgate.

Liang, B., and H. Lu. 2006. "Conducting Fieldwork in China: Observations on Collecting Primary Data Regarding Crime, Law and the Criminal Justice System." *Journal of Contemporary Criminal Justice* 22: 157–72.

Liu, J. 2007. "Developing Comparative Criminology and the Case of China." *International Journal of Offender Therapy and Comparative Criminology* 51 (1): 3–8.

Liu, J., L. Zhang, and S. Messner, eds. 2001. *Crime and Social Control in a Changing China.* Westport, CT: Greenwood Press.

Longman, T. "Justice at the Grassroots? Gacaca Trials in Rwanda." In *Transitional Justice in the Twenty-First Century,* edited by in N. Roht-Arriaza and J. Mariezcurrena, 206–28. Cambridge: Cambridge University Press.

Løvlie, F. 2014. "Questioning the Secular-Religious Cleavage in Palestinian Politics: Comparing Fatah and Hamas." *Politics and Religion* 7: 100–121.

Lu, H., and Zhang. L. 2005. Death Penalty in China: The Law and Practice. *Journal of Criminal Justice* 33: 367–76.

Lucas, E. 2009. *The New Cold War: Putin's Russia and the Threat to the West.* New York: Palgrave Macmillan.

Luna, E., and M. L. Wade, eds. 2012. *The Prosecutor in Transnational Perspective.* Oxford: Oxford University Press.

Lundy, P., and M. McGovern. 2008. "Whose Justice? Rethinking Transitional Justice from the Bottom Up." *Journal of Law and Society* 35 (2): 265–92.

Lynch, M. 1990. "The Greening of Criminology." *Critical Criminologist* 2: 1–5.

Lyon, D. 2001. *Surveillance Society: Monitoring Everyday Life.* Buckingham, UK: Open University Press.

Lyon, D. 2003. *Surveillance after September 11.* Cambridge: Polity Press.

Lyon, D. 2004. "Globalizing Surveillance: Comparative and Sociological Perspectives." *International Sociology* 19 (2): 135–49.

Ma, Y. 1997. "The Police Law 1995: Organization, Functions, Powers and Accountability of the Chinese Police." *Policing: An International Journal of Police Strategy and Management* 20 (1): 113–35.

Ma, Y. 2008. "The Chinese Police." In *Comparative Policing: The Struggle for Democratization,* edited by M. R. Haberfield and I. Cerrah, 13–59. Thousand Oaks, CA: Sage.

MacCormack, G. 1990. *Traditional Chinese Penal Law.* Edinburgh: Edinburgh University Press.

Mackie, G. 2000. "Female Genital Cutting: The Beginning of the End." In *Female "Circumcision" in Africa: Culture, Controversy, and Change,* edited by B. Shell-Duncan and Y. Hernlund, 253–84. Boulder, CO: Lynne Rienner.

MacKinnon, C. 1987. *Feminism Unmodified: Discourses on Life and Law.* Harvard, MA: Harvard University Press.

Macklin, A. 2006. "The Double-Edged Sword: Using the Criminal Law against Female Genital Mutilation." In *Female Circumcision: Multicultural Perspectives,* edited by R. M. Abusharaf, 207–23. Philadelphia: University of Pennsylvania Press.

Madek, C. A. 2005. "Killing Dishonor: Effective Eradication of Honor Killing." *Suffolk Transnational Law Review* 29: 53–75.

Maguire, R. 1997. "Crime, Crime Control and the Yakuza in Contemporary Japan." *Criminologist* 21 (3): 131–41.

Mahmood, C. K. 2000. "Trials by Fire: Dynamics of Terror in Punjab and Kashmir." In *Death Squad: The Anthropology of State Terror,* edited by J. A. Sluka, 70–90. Philadelphia: University of Pennsylvania Press.

Mallat, C. 2006. "Comparative Law and the Islamic (Middle Eastern) Legal Culture." In *The Oxford Handbook of Comparative Law,* edited by M. Reimann and R. Zimmermann, 609–40. Oxford: Oxford University Press.

Malley-Morrison, K. 2004. "Introduction." In *International Perspectives on Family Violence and Abuse: A Cognitive Ecological Approach,* edited by K. Malley-Morrison, 3–16. Mahwah, NJ: Lawrence Erlbaum Associates.

Malley-Morrison, K., and D. A. Hines. 2004. *Family Violence in a Cultural Perspective: Defining, Understanding, and Combating Abuse.* Thousand Oaks, CA: Sage.

Mallinder, L. 2008. *Amnesty, Human Rights and Political Transitions: Bridging the Peace and Justice Divide.* Portland, OR: Hart.

Mani, R. 2002. *Beyond Retribution: Seeking Justice in the Shadows of War.* Cambridge: Polity Press.

Mann, J. R., and B. K. Takyi. 2009. "Autonomy, Dependence or Culture: Examining the Impact of Resources and Socio-Cultural Processes on Attitudes towards Intimate Partner Violence in Ghana, Africa." *Journal of Family Violence* 24: 323–35.

Manning, Peter K. 1986. "Police: Community." In Louis A. Radelet, *The Police and the Community*. (4th Ed.). New York: Macmillan.

Manning, P. 2001. "Police: Community." In *The Police and the Community*, edited by L. A. Radelet, 486–92. New York: Macmillan.

Manning, P. 2005. "The Study of Policing." *Police Quarterly* 8 (1): 23–43.

Mareinin, O. 2007. "Implementing Police Reforms: The Role of the Transnational Policy Community." In *Crafting Transnational Policing*, edited by A. Goldsmith and J. Sheptyck, 177–202. Oxford: Hart.

Marshall, J. 2005. *Humanity, Freedom and Feminism*. Aldershot, UK: Ashgate.

Martinson, R. 1974. "What Works? Questions and Answers about Prison Reform." *Public Interest* 35: 22–54.

Marx, K., and F. Engels. 1969. *The Communist Manifesto*. Moscow: Progress. First published 1848.

Mastrofski, S. D., and J. J. Willis. 2010. "Police Organization Continuity and Change: Into the Twenty-First Century." *Crime and Justice* 39 (1): 55–144.

Masur, L. 1989. *Rites of Execution: Capital Punishment and the Transformation of American Culture, 1776-1865*. New York: Oxford University Press.

Mattelart, A. 2010. *The Globalization of Surveillance: The Origin of the Securitarian Order*. Cambridge: Polity Press.

Mawby, R. I. 2001. "The Impact of Transition: A Comparison of Post-Communist Societies with Earlier 'Societies in Transition.'" In *Police in Transition: Essays on the Police Forces in Transition Countries*, edited by A. Kadar, 19–38. Budapest: Central European University Press.

Mawby, R. I. 2008. "Models of Policing." In *Handbook of Policing*, edited by T. Newburn, 17–46. Cullompton, UK: Willan.

Mayer, A. E. 1990. "Reinstating Islamic Criminal Law in Libya." In *Law and Islam in the Middle East*, edited by D. H. Dwyer, 99–114. New York: Bergin and Garvey.

Mayerfeld, J. 2003. "Who Shall Be Judge? The United States, the International Criminal Court, and the Global Enforcement of Human Rights." *Human Rights Quarterly* 25 (1): 93–129.

McCarthy, C. 2012. *Reparations and Victim Support in the International Criminal Court*. Cambridge: Cambridge University Press.

McCarthy, D. M. P. 2011. *An Economic History of Organized Crime: A National and Transnational Approach*. New York: Routledge.

McConville, S. 1995. "The Victorian Prison: England, 1865-1965." In *The Oxford History of the Prison: The Practice of Punishment in Western Society*, edited by N. Morris and D. J. Rothman, 117–50. Oxford: Oxford University Press.

McCoy, A. W. 1991. *The Politics of Heroin: CIA Complicity in the Global Drug Trade*. New York: Lawrence Hill Books.

McCracken, J. 1986. "Coercion and Control in Nyasaland: Aspects of the History of a Colonial Police Force." *Journal of African History* 27 (1): 127–47.

McCusker, R. 2006. "Transnational Organized Cyber Crime: Distinguing Threat from Reality." *Crime, Law and Social Change* 46: 257–73.

McEvoy, K. 2007. "Beyond Legalism: Towards a Thicker Understanding of Transitional Justice." *Journal of Law and Society* 34 (4): 411–40.

McGowen, R. 1995. "The Well-Ordered Prison: England 1780-1865." In *The Oxford History of the Prison: The Practice of Punishment in Western Society*, edited by N. Morris and D. J. Rothman, 71–99. Oxford: Oxford University Press.

McKillop, B. 1997. "Anatomy of a French Murder Case." *American Journal of Comparative Law* 45 (3): 527–83.

Medeiros, M., and J. Costa. 2008. "What Do We Mean by 'Feminization of Poverty'?" *One Pager*, no. 58. Brasília, Brazil: International Poverty Centre. http://www.ipc-undp.org/pub/IPCOnePager58.pdf

Meetoo, V., and H. S. Mirza. 2007. "There Is Nothing 'Honourable' about Honour Killings: Gender, Violence and the Limits of Multiculturalism." *Women's Studies International Forum* 30: 187–200.

Mehigan, J., R. Walters, and L. Westmarland. 2010. "Justice, Globalization and Human Rights." In *Criminal Justice: Local and Global*, edited by D. Drake, J. Muncie, and L. Westmarland, 213–51. Cullompton, UK: Willan.

Mendez, J. E. 2012. "Foreword." In *Amnesty in the Age of Human Rights Accountability: Comparative and International Perspectives*, edited by F. Lessa and L. A. Payne, xxii–xxix. New York: Cambridge University Press.

Merkl, P. 1995. "West German Left-Wing Terrorism." In *Terrorism in Context*, edited by M. Crenshaw, 160–210. University Park: Pennsylvania State University Press.

Meron, T. 1993. "Comment: Rape as a Crime under International Humanitarian Law." *American Journal of International Law* 87: 424–31.

Merry, S. E. 2006a. *Human Rights and Gender Violence: Translating International Law into Local Justice*. Chicago: University of Chicago Press.

Merry, S. E. 2006b. "Transnational Human Rights and Local Activism: Mapping the Middle." *American Anthropology* 108 (1): 38–51.

Merryman, J. H., and R. Perez-Perdomo. 2007. *The Civil Law Tradition: An Introduction to the Legal Systems of Europe and Latin America*. Stanford, CA: Stanford University Press.

Merton, R. K. 1957. *Social Theory and Social Structure.* New York: Free Press.

Metzler, A. 2003. "The Juvenile Training Schools of Japan: Teaching Young Serious Offenders How to Live and 'How to Be.'" In *Juvenile Delinquency in Japan: Reconsidering the "Crisis,"* edited by G. Foljanty-Jost, 221–52. Leiden: Brill.

Miller, M. A. 1995. "The Intellectual Origins of Modern Terrorism in Europe." In *Terrorism in Context,* edited by M. Crenshaw, 27–62. University Park: Pennsylvania State University Press.

Miller, M. L., and R. F. Wright. 2012. "Reporting for Duty: The Universal Prosecutorial Accountability Puzzle and an Experimental Transparency Alternative." In *The Prosecutor in Transnational Perspective,* edited by E. Luna and M. L. Wade, 392–407. Oxford: Oxford University Press.

Ministère de la Justice. 2005. *Head of Court's Youth Protection Services—The Juvenile Justice System in France.* http://www.afmjf.fr/IMG/pdf/youth_justice_system_in_France.pdf

Mitchell, W. E. 1999. "Why Wape Men Don't Beat Their Wives: Constraints toward Domestic Tranquility in a New Guinea Society." In *To Have and to Hit: Cultural Perspectives on Wife Beating,* edited by D. A. Counts, J. K. Brown, and J. C. Campbell, 100–109. Chicago: University of Illinois Press.

Miyazawa, S. 2008. "The Politics of Increasing Punitiveness and the Rising Populism in Japanese Criminal Justice Policy." *Punishment and Society* 10 (1): 47–77.

Moffett, L. 2014. "Realising Justice for Victims before the International Criminal Court." ICD Brief 6. http://www.internationalcrimesdatabase.org/upload/documents/20140916T170017-ICD%20Brief%20-%20Moffett.pdf

Mohamud, A., S. Radeny, and K. Ringheim. 2006. "Community-Based Efforts to End Female Genital Mutilation in Kenya: Raising Awareness and Organizing Alternative Rites." In *Female Circumcision: Multicultural Perspectives,* edited by R. M. Abusharaf, 75–103. Philadelphia: University of Pennsylvania Press.

Mohanty, C. T. 1988. "Under Western Eyes: Feminist Scholarship and Colonial Discourses." *Feminist Review* 61–88.

Mohsen, D. K. 1990. "Women and Criminal Justice in Egypt." In *Law and Islam in the Middle East,* edited by D. H. Dwyer, 15–34. New York: Bergin and Garvey.

Montgomery, H. 2009. *An Introduction to Childhood: Anthropological Perspectives on Children's Lives.* Chichester, UK: Wiley-Blackwell.

Moohr, G. S. 2004. "Prosecutorial Power in an Adversarial System: Lessons from Current White Collar Crime Cases and the Inquisitorial Model." *Buffalo Criminal Law Review* 8 (1): 165–220.

Moon, C. 2007. "Reconciliation as Therapy and Compensation: A Critical Analysis." In *Law and the Politics of Reconciliation,* edited by S. Veitch, 163–84. Aldershot, UK: Ashgate.

Moore, H. L. 2007. "The Failure of Pluralism?" In *Transcultural Bodies: Female Genital Cutting in Global Context,* edited by Y. Hernlund and B. Shell-Duncan, 311–30. New Brunswick, NJ: Rutgers University Press.

Morita, A. 2002. "Juvenile Justice in Japan: A Historical and Cross-Cultural Perspective." In *A Century of Juvenile Justice,* edited by M. K. Rosenheim, F. E. Zimring, D. S. Tanenhaus, and B. Dohrn, 360–80. Chicago: University of Chicago Press.

Moten, A. R. 2010. "Understanding Terrorism: Contested Concept, Conflicting Perspectives and Shattering Consequences." *Intellectual Discourse* 18 (1): 35–63.

Mueller, G. O. W. 2001. "Transnational Crime: Definitions and Concepts." *Combating Transnational Crime: Concepts, Activities and Responses,* edited by P. Williams and D. Vlassis, 13–21. London: Frank Cass.

Muhlhahn, K. 2009. *Criminal Justice in China: A History.* Cambridge, MA: Harvard University Press.

Muncie, J. 2000. "Decriminalising Criminology." In *Rethinking Social Policy,* edited by G. Lewis, S. Gewirtz, and J. Clarke, 217–28. London: Sage.

Muncie, J. 2007. "Youth Justice and the Governance of Young People: Global, International, National and Local Contexts." In *Youth, Globalization, and the Law,* edited by S. A. Venkatesh and R. Kassimir, 17–60. Stanford, CA: Stanford University Press.

Muncie, J. 2009. *Youth and Crime.* London: Sage.

Muncie, J. 2011. "On Globalisation and Exceptionalism." In *Comparative Criminal Justice and Globalization,* edited by D. Nelken, 87–106. Farnham, UK: Ashgate.

Murphy, C. 2007. "The Cart before the Horse: Community Oriented versus Professional Methods of International Police Reform." In *Crafting Transnational Policing: Police Capacity-Building and Global Police Reform,* edited by A. Goldsmith & J. Sheptycki 243–62. Portland, OR: Hart.

Mutlu, K. 2000. "Problems of Nepotism and Favouritism in the Police Organization in Turkey." *Policing: An International Journal of Police Strategies and Management* 23 (3): 381–89.

Nagorcka, F., M. Stanton, and M. Wilson. 2005. "Stranded between Partisanship and the Truth? A Comparative Analysis of Legal Ethics in the Adversarial and Inquisitorial Systems of Justice." *Melbourne University Law Review* 29: 448–77.

Nagy, R. 2008. "Transitional Justice as Global Project: Critical Reflections." *Third World Quarterly* 29 (2): 275–89.

Narayan, U. 1997. *Dislocating Cultures: Identities, Traditions, and Third World Feminism.* New York: Routledge.

National Registry of Exonerations. http://www.law.umich.edu/special/exoneration/Pages/Exoneration-by-Year.aspx

Naylor, R. T. 2001. "The Rise of the Modern Arms Black Market and the Fall of Supply-Side Control." In *Combating Transnational Crime: Concepts, Activities and Responses,* edited by P. Williams and D. Vlassis, 209–36. London: Frank Cass.

Neild, R. 2001. "Democratic Police Reforms in War-Torn Societies." *Conflict, Security & Development* 1 (1): 21–43.

Nelken, D. 2000. "Virtually There, Researching There, Living There." In *Contrasting Criminal Justice: Getting from Here to There,* edited by D. Nelken, 23–48. Aldershot, UK: Ashgate.

Nelken, D. 2002. "Comparing Criminal Justice." In *The Oxford Handbook of Criminology,* edited by M. Maguire, R. Morgan, and R. Reiner, 175–202. Oxford: Oxford University Press.

Nelken, D. 2010. *Comparative Criminal Justice: Making Sense of Difference.* Thousand Oaks, CA: Sage.

Nelken, D. 2011a. "Introduction." In *Comparative Criminal Justice and Globalization,* edited by D. Nelken, 1–8. Farnham, UK: Ashgate.

Nelken, D. 2011b. "Making Sense of Punitiveness." In *Comparative Criminal Justice and Globalization,* edited by D. Nelken, 11–26. Farnham, UK: Ashgate.

Nelken, D. 2011c. "Studying Criminal Justice in Globalised Times." In *Comparative Criminal Justice and Globalization,* edited by D. Nelken, 183–210. Farnham, UK: Ashgate.

Nelken, D. 2013. "The Challenge of Globalization for Comparative Criminal Justice." In *Globalization and the Challenge to Criminology,* edited by F. Pakes, 9–26. Abingdon, UK: Routledge.

Neyroud, P. 2003. "Policing and Ethics." In *Handbook of Policing,* edited by T. Newburn, 578–602. London: Willan.

Niarchos, C. N. 1995. "Women, War, and Rape: Challenges Facing the International Tribunal for the Former Yugoslavia." *Human Rights Quarterly* 17 (4): 649–90.

Nillson, A. 2001. "International Atomic Agency Programme against Illicit Trafficking of Nuclear Materials and Radioactive Sources." In *Combating Transnational Crime: Concepts, Activities and Responses,* edited by P. Williams and D. Vlassis, 315–20. London: Frank Cass.

Nossiter, A. 2014. "Boko Haram Attacks with Ease, Causing Death and Mayhem in Nigeria's Provinces." *New York Times,* December 1. http://www.nytimes.com/2014/12/02/world/boko-haram-attacks-with-ease-causing-death-and-mayhem-in-nigerias-capitals.html

Oba, A. A. 2011. "The Future of Customary Law in Africa." In *The Future of African Customary Law,* edited by J. Fenrich, P. Galizzi, and T. E. Higgins, 58–82. New York: Cambridge University Press.

Obermeyer, C. M. 1999. "Female Genital Surgeries: The Known, the Unknown and the Unknowable." *Medical Anthropology Quarterly* 13 (1): 79–106.

Obiora, L. A. 2007. "A Refuge from Tradition and the Refuge of Tradition: On Anticircumcision Paradigms." In *Transcultural Bodies: Female Genital Cutting in Global Context,* edited by Y. Hernlund and B. Shell-Duncan, 67–90. New Brunswick, NJ: Rutgers University Press.

O'Brien, J. C. 1993. "Current Development: The International Tribunal for Violations of International Humanitarian Law in the Former Yugoslavia." *American Journal of International Law* 87: 639–62.

O'Connell Davidson, J. 1998. *Prostitution, Power and Freedom.* Ann Arbor: University of Michigan Press.

O'Connell Davidson, J., and J. S. Taylor, 1999. "Fantasy Islands: Exploring the Demand for Sex Tourism." In *Sun, Sex, and Gold: Tourism and Sex Work in the Caribbean,* edited by K. Kempadoo, 37–54. Lanham, MD: Rowman and Littlefield.

Ofei-Aboagye, R. O. 1994. "Domestic Violence in Ghana: An Initial Step." *Colombia Journal of Gender and Law* 4: 1–25.

Office of Juvenile Justice and Delinquency Prevention. 2013. "Juvenile Justice System Structure and Process: Jurisdictional Boundaries." http://www.ojjdp.gov/ojstatbb/structure_process/qa04101.asp

Office of the Prosecutor (OTP). 2007. *The Interests of Justice.* Policy paper, ICC-OTP-2007. http://www.icc-cpi.int/iccdocs/asp_docs/library/organs/otp/ICC-OTP-InterestsOfJustice.pdf

Office of the Prosecutor (OTP). 2009. *Regulations of the Office of the Prosecutor.* The Hague: International Criminal Court.

Office of the Prosecutor (OTP). 2013a. *Report on Preliminary Examination of Activities 2013.* . The Hague: International Criminal Court. http://www.icc-cpi.int/en_menus/icc/press%20and%20media/press%20releases/Documents/OTP%20Preliminary%20Examinations/OTP%20-%20Report%20%20Preliminary%20Examination%20Activities%202013.PDF

Office of the Prosecutor (OTP). 2013b. *Strategic Plan June 2012–2015.* . The Hague: International Criminal Court. http://www.icc-cpi.int/en_menus/icc/structure%20of%20the%20court/office%20of%20the%20prosecutor/reports%20and%20statements/statement/Documents/OTP%20Strategic%20Plan.pdf

Okeowo, A. 2014. "Inside the Vigilante Fight against Boko Haram." *New York Times Magazine,* November 5. http://www.nytimes.com/2014/11/09/magazine/inside-the-vigilante-fight-against-boko-haram.html?_r=0

Olayanju, L., R. N. G. Naguib, Q. T. Nguyen, R. K. Bali, and N. D. Vung. 2013. "Combating Intimate Partner Violence in Africa: Opportunities and Challenges in Five African Countries." *Aggression and Violent Behavior* 18: 101–12.

O'Malley, P. 2011. "Monetary Sanctions as Misguided Policy: Politicizing the Case for Fines." *Criminology and Public Policy* 10 (3): 547–53.

Onapajo, H., U. O. Uzodike, and A. Whetho. 2012. "Boko Haram Terrorism in Nigeria: The International Dimension." *South African Journal of International Affairs* 19 (3): 337–57.

Ong, A. 1996. "Strategic Sisterhood or Sisters in Solidarity? Questions of Communitarianism and Citizenship in Asia." *Indiana Journal of Global Legal Studies* 4 (1): 107–35.

Orentlicher, D. 2004. "Unilateral Multilateralism: United States Policy toward the International Criminal Court." *Cornell International Law Journal* 36: 415–38.

Orland, L. 2002. "A Russian Legal Revolution: The 2002 Criminal Procedure Code." *Connecticut Journal of International Law* 13: 133–319.

Orlova, A. V. 2012. "The Fight against Transnational Organized Crime in Russia." In *Routledge Handbook of Transnational Organized Crime,* edited by F. Allum and S. Gilmour, 494–508. New York: Routledge.

Ossman, S., and S. Terrio. 2006. "The French Riots: Questioning Spaces of Surveillance and Sovereignty." *International Migration* 44 (2): 5–22.

Ozerdem, A., and S. Podder. 2011. "The Long Road Home: Conceptual Debates on Recruitment Experiences and Reintegration Outcomes." In *Child Soldiers: From Recruitment to Reintegration,* edited by in A. Ozerdem and S. Podder, 3–28. Basingstoke, UK: Palgrave Macmillan.

Pahl, M. R. 1992. "Wanted: Criminal Justice—Colombia's Adoption of a Prosecutorial System of Criminal Procedure." *Fordham International Law Journal* 16 (3): 608–34.

Pakes, F. 2004. *Comparative Criminal Justice.* Cullompton, UK: Willan.

Pakes, F. 2010. "The Comparative Method in Globalized Criminology." *Australian and New Zealand Journal of Criminology* 43 (1): 17–30.

Papua New Guinea Constitution, Schedule 2, Part 1. http://www.wipo.int/wipolex/en/text.jsp?file_id=199188

Parker, L. C. 2013. *Crime and Justice in Japan and China: A Comparative View.* Durham, NC: Carolina Academic Press.

Passas, N. 2002. "Cross-Border Crime and the Interface between Legal and Illegal Actors." In *Upperworld and Underworld in Cross-Border Crime,* edited by P. C. van Duyne, K. von Lampe, and N. Passas, 11–42. Nijmegen, Netherlands: Wolf Legal Publishers.

Paton, D. 2001. "The Penalties of Freedom: Punishment in Post-Emancipation Jamaica." In *Crime and Punishment in Latin America: Law and Society since Late Colonial Times,* edited by R. D. Salvatore, C. Aguirre, and G. M. Joseph, 275–307. Durham, NC: Duke University Press.

Payan, T. 2012. "Human Trafficking and the U.S.-Mexico Border: Reflections on a Complex Issue in a Binational Context." In *Borderline Slavery: Mexico, the United States and the Human Trade,* edited by S. Tiano and M. Murphy-Aguilar, 141–61. Burlington, VT: Ashgate.

Pedahzur, A. 2005. *Suicide Terrorism.* Cambridge: Polity.

Pedahzur, A., and A. Perliger. 2010. "The Consequences of Counterterrorist Policies in Israel." In *The Consequences of Counterterrorism,* edited by M. Crenshaw, 335–66. New York: Russell Sage Foundation.

Peerenboom, R. 2006. "What Have We Learned about Law and Development? Describing, Predicting, and Assessing Legal Reforms in China." *Michigan Journal of International Law* 27 (3): 823–46.

Peters, K. 2011. "Group Cohesion and Coercive Recruitment: Young Combatants and the Revolutionary United Front of Sierra Leone." In *Child Soldiers: From Recruitment to Reintegration,* edited by A. Ozerdem and S. Podder, 76–90. Basingstoke, UK: Palgrave Macmillan.

Pfeiffer, C. 1998. "Juvenile Crime and Violence in Europe." In *Crime and Justice: A Review of Research,* vol. 23, edited by M. Tonry, 255–328. Chicago: University of Chicago Press.

Phongpaichit, P. 1998. *Guns, Girls, Gambling, Ganja: Thailand's Illegal Economy and Public Policy.* Seattle: University of Washington Press.

Pierce, W. L. (Andrew MacDonald, nom de plume). 1978. *The Turner Diaries.* https://archive.org/stream/TheTurnerDiariesByAndrewMacdonald/turner-diaries-william-luther-pierce#page/n1/mode/2up

Pierotti, R. S. 2013. "Increasing Rejection of Intimate Partner Violence: Evidence of Global Cultural Diffusion." *American Sociological Review* 78 (2): 240–65.

Pino, N., and M. D. Wiatrowski. 2006. "The Principles of Democratic Policing." In *Democratic Policing in Transitional and Developing Countries,* edited by N. Pino and M. Wiatrowski, 69–98. Aldershot, UK: Ashgate.

Piot, C. 2006. "Representing Africa in the Kasinga Asylum Case." In *Female Circumcision: Multicultural Perspectives,* edited by R. M. Abusharaf, 224–33. Philadelphia: University of Pennsylvania Press.

Pisciotta, A. 1994. *Benevolent Repression: Social Control and the American Reformatory Movement.* New York: New York University Press.

Pizzi, W. T. 2012. "A Perfect Storm: Prosecutorial Discretion in the United States." In *The Prosecutor in Transnational Perspective,* edited by E. Luna and M. L. Wade, 189–99. Oxford: Oxford University Press.

Pizzi, W. T., and L. Marafioti. 1992. "The New Italian Code of Criminal Procedure: The Difficulties of Building an Adversarial Trial System on a Civil Law Foundation." *Yale Journal of International Law* 17 (1): 1–40.

Platt, A. M. 1977. *The Child Savers: The Invention of Delinquency,* ed. 2. Chicago: University of Chicago Press.

Podder, S. 2011a. "Child Soldier Recruitment in the Liberian Civil Wars: Individual Motivations and Rebel Group Tactics." In *Child Soldiers: From Recruitment to Reintegration,* edited by A. Ozerdem and S. Podder, 50–75. Basingstoke, UK: Palgrave Macmillan.

Podder, S. 2011b. "Neither Child nor Soldier: Contrasted Terrains in Identity, Victimcy and Survival." In *Child Soldiers: From Recruitment to Reintegration,* edited by A. Ozerdem and S. Podder, 141–58. Basingstoke, UK: Palgrave Macmillan.

Podgor, E. S. 2012. "Prosecution Guidelines in the United States." In *The Prosecutor in Transnational Perspective,* edited by E. Luna and M. L. Wade, 9–19. Oxford: Oxford University Press.

Pomorski, S. 2006. "Modern Russian Criminal Procedure: The Adversarial Principle and Guilty Plea." *Criminal Law Forum* 17: 129–48.

Pomper, P. 1995. "Russian Revolutionary Terrorism." In *Terrorism in Context,* edited by M. in Crenshaw, 63–104. University Park: Pennsylvania State University.

Popkin, M., and N. Bhuta. 1999. "Latin American Amnesties in Comparative Perspective: Can the Past Be Buried?" *Ethics and International Affairs* 13 (1): 99–122.

Porta, D. D. 1995. "Left-Wing Terrorism in Italy." In *Terrorism in Context,* edited by M. Crenshaw, 105–59. University Park: Pennsylvania State University.

Potter, P. B. 2001. *The Chinese Legal System: Globalization and Local Legal Culture.* New York: Routledge.

Powell, K. 2004. "Nicaragua." In *International Perspectives on Family Violence and Abuse: A Cognitive Ecological Approach,* edited by K. Malley-Morrison, 381–96. Mahwah, NJ: Lawrence Erlbaum Associates.

Power, S. 2007. *"A Problem from Hell": America and the Age of Genocide.* New York: Harper Perennial.

Pratt, J. 2007. *Penal Populism.* London: Routledge.

Pratt, J., D. Brown, S. Hallsworth, and W. Morrison. 2005. *The New Punitiveness: Trends, Theories, Perspectives.* Cullompton, UK: Willan.

Preyer, Kathryn. 1982. "Penal Measures in the American Colonies: An Overview." *American Journal of Legal History* 26: 326–53.

Pridie, E. D., A. E. Lorenzen, A. Cruickshank, J. O. Hovel, and D. R. MacDonald. 1945. *Female Circumcision in the Anglo-Egyptian Sudan.* Khartoum: Sudan Medical Service.

Prillaman, W. C. 2000. *The Judiciary and Democratic Decay in Latin America.* Westport, CT: Praeger.

Primoratz, I. 2004a. "Introduction." In *Terrorism: The Philosophical Issues,* edited by I. Primoratz, x–2. Basingstoke, UK: Palgrave Macmillan.

Primoratz, I. 2004b. "State Terrorism and Counter-Terrorism." In *Terrorism: The Philosophical Issues,* edited by I. Primoratz, 113–27. Basingstoke, UK: Palgrave Macmillan.

Primoratz, I. 2004c. "What Is Terrorism?" In *Terrorism: The Philosophical Issues,* edited by I. Primoratz, 15–30. Basingstoke, UK: Palgrave Macmillan.

Quigley, J. 1989. "Socialist Law and the Civil Law Tradition." *American Journal of Comparative Law* 37 (4): 781–808.

Qutb, S. 2007. *Milestones.* New Delhi: Maktabah Publishers. First published 1964.

Ralph, J. 2011. "The International Criminal Court and the State of the American Exception." In *International and Comparative Criminal Justice and Urban Governance: Convergence and Divergence in Global, National and Local Settings,* edited by A. Crawford, 67–85. Cambridge: Cambridge University Press.

Ranger, T. 1983. "The Invention of Tradition in Colonial Africa." In *The Invention of Tradition,* edited by E. Hobsbawn and T. Ranger, 211–62. London: Cambridge University Press.

Rap, S., and I. Weijers. 2014. *The Effective Youth Court: Juvenile Justice Procedures in Europe.* The Hague: Eleven International Publishing.

Rapoport, D. C. 1984. "Fear and Trembling: Terrorism in Three Religious Traditions." *American Political Science Review* 78 (3): 658–77.

Rapoport, D. C. 2001. "The Fourth Wave: September 11 in the History of Terrorism." *Current History* 100 (650): 419–24.

Rapoport, D. 2004. "The Four Waves of Modern Terrorism." In *Attacking Terrorism: Elements of a Grand Strategy,* edited by A. K. Cronin and J. M. Ludes, 46–73. Washington, DC: Georgetown University Press.

Rautenbach, C., and W. Plessis. 2011. "Reform of the South African Customary Law of Succession: Final Nails in the Customary Law Coffin?" In *The Future of African Customary Law,* edited by J. Fenrich, P. Galizzi, and T. E. Higgins, 336–62. New York: Cambridge University Press.

Reames, B. N. 2008a. "Neofeudal Aspects of Brazil's Public Security." In *Comparative Policing: The Struggle for Democratization,* edited by M. R. Haberfield and I. Cerrah, 61–87. Thousand Oaks, CA: Sage.

Reames, B. N. 2008b. "Paths to Fairness, Effectiveness, and Democratic Policing in Mexico." In *Comparative Policing: The Struggle for Democratization,* edited by M. R. Haberfield and I. Cerrah, 97–115. Thousand Oaks, CA: Sage.

Reichel, P. 2013. *Comparative Criminal Justice Systems: A Topical Approach,* ed. 6. Upper Saddle River, NJ: Prentice Hall.

Reiss, A. J. 1992. "Police Organization in the Twentieth Century." *Crime and Justice* 15: 51–97.

Reitz, K. R. 2001. "The Disassembly and Reassembly of U.S. Sentencing Practice." In *Sentencing and Sanctions in Western Countries,* edited by M. Tonry and R. S. Frase, 222–58. Oxford: Oxford University Press.

Ren, X. 1996. "People's Republic of China." In *International Handbook on Juvenile Justice,* edited by D. J. Shoemaker, 57–59. Westport, CT: Greenwood Press.

Ren, X. 1997. *Tradition of the Law and Law of the Tradition: Law, State, and Social Control in China.* Westport, CT: Greenwood Press.

Renner, J. 2012. "A Discourse Theoretic Approach to Transitional Justice Ideals: Conceptualizing 'Reconciliation' as an Empty Universal in Times of Political Transition." In *Critical Perspectives in Transitional Justice,* edited by N. Palmer, P. Clark, and D. Granville, 51–72. Cambridge: Intersentia.

Riego, C. 1998. "The Chilean Criminal Procedure Reform." *International Journal of the Sociology of Law* 26: 437–52.

Roach, K. 2010. "Wrongful Convictions: Adversarial and Inquisitorial Themes." *North Carolina Journal of International Law and Commercial Regulation* 35 (2): 387–446.

Robben, A. C. G. M. 2010. "Testimonies, Truths, and Transitions of Justice in Argentina and Chile." In *Transitional Justice: Global Mechanisms and Local Realities after Genocide and Mass Violence,* edited by A. L. Hinton, 179–205. Piscataway, NJ: Rutgers University Press.

Roberts, A., and G. Lafree. 2004. "Explaining Japan's Postwar Violent Crime Trends." *Criminology* 42 (1): 179–209.

Robertson, A. 2012. "Police Reform and Building Justice in Russia: Problems and Prospects." In *Building Justice in Post-Transition Europe? Processes of Criminalization within Central and Eastern European Societies,* edited by K. Goodall, M. Malloch, and B. Munro, 158–76. London: Routledge.

Robinson, D. 2003. "Serving the Interests of Justice: Amnesties, Truth Commissions and the International Criminal Court." *European Journal of International Law* 14 (3): 481–505.

Roche, D. 2005. "Truth Commission Amnesties and the International Criminal Court." *British Journal of Criminology* 45: 565–81.

Roff, W. R. 2010. "Customary Law, Islamic Law, and Colonial Authority: Three Contrasting Case Studies and Their Aftermath." *Islamic Studies* 49 (4): 455–62.

Rogers, J. 2007. "Managing Cultural Diversity in Australia: Legislating Female Circumcision, Legislating Communities." In *Transcultural Bodies: Female Genital Cutting in Global Context,* edited by Y. Hernlund and B. Shell-Duncan, 135–56. New Brunswick, NJ: Rutgers University Press.

Roht-Arriaza, N. 2006. "The New Landscape of Transitional Justice." In *Transitional Justice in the Twenty-First Century,* edited by N. Roht-Arriaza and J. Mariezcurrena, 1–16. Cambridge: Cambridge University Press.

Rome Statute of the International Criminal Court. As Corrected by the process-verbaux of 10 November 1998 and 12 July 1999. http://legal.un.org/icc/statute/99_corr/cstatute.htm

Ronderos, J. G. 2003. "The War on Drugs and the Military: The Case of Colombia." In *Critical Reflections on Transnational Organized Crime, Money Laundering, and Corruption,* edited by M. E. Beare, 207–36. Toronto: University of Toronto Press.

Rosen, D. M. 2005. *Armies of the Young: Child Soldiers in War and Terrorism.* New Brunswick, NJ: Rutgers University Press.

Rosen, D. M. 2007. "Child Soldiers, International Humanitarian Law, and the Globalization of Childhood." *American Anthropologist* 109 (2): 296–306.

Rosenau, J. 1980. *The Study of Global Interdependence: Essays on the Transnationalization of World Affairs.* London: Pinter.

Rosenzweig, J. 2013. "Disappearing Justice: Public Opinion, Secret Arrest and Criminal Procedure Reform in China." *China Journal* 70: 73–97.

Ross, J. I., ed. 2013. *The Globalization of Supermax Prisons.* New Brunswick, NJ: Rutgers University Press.

Rotberg, R. 2000. "Truth Commissions and the Provision of Truth, Justice, and Reconciliation." In *Truth v. Justice: The Morality of Truth Commissions,* edited by R. Rotberg and D. Thompson, 3–21. Princeton, NJ: Princeton University Press.

Rothe, D., and D. O. Friedrichs. 2015. *Crimes of Globalization.* New York: Routledge.

Rothman, D. 1990. *The Discovery of the Asylum: Social Order and Disorder in the New Republic.* Boston: Little, Brown.

Roudik, P. 2008. "Policing the Russian Federation." In *Comparative Policing: The Struggle for Democratization,* edited by M. R. Haberfield and I. Cerrah, 139–64. Thousand Oaks, CA: Sage.

Ruggiero, V. 2000. "Transnational Crime: Official and Alternative Fears." *International Journal of the Sociology of Law* 28 (3): 187–99.

Rusche, G., and O. Kirchheimer. 1939. *Punishment and Social Structure.* New York: Russell and Russell.

Rushin, S. 2011. "The Judicial Response to Mass Police Surveillance." *University of Illinois Journal of Law, Technology and Policy* 281–328.

Rushwan, H., C. Slot, A. El Dareer, and N. Bushra. 1983. *Female Circumcision in the Sudan: Prevalence, Complications, Attitudes and Changes.*

Khartoum, Sudan: University of Khartoum, Faculty of Medicine.

Ryan, C., and C. M. Hall. 2001. *Sex Tourism: Marginal People and Liminalities*. Abingdon, UK: Routledge.

Sachs, J. 1998. "Globalization and the Rule of Law." *Yale Law School Occasional Papers* series 2, no. 4.

Safeguards Guaranteeing Protection of the Rights of Those Facing the Death Penalty. 1984.

Santiso, C. 2003. "The Elusive Quest for the Rule of Law: Promoting Judicial Reform in Latin America." *Brazilian Journal of Political Economy* 23 (3): 112–34.

"Saudi Criticises World Reaction to Maid's Beheading." 2013. *World Politics Review,* January 14. http://www.breitbart.com/news/cng-a501c43080aa337116c8686dbf98acf7–601

Saul, B. 2006. *Defining Terrorism in International Law.* Oxford: Oxford University Press.

Savelsberg, J. 2010. *Crime and Human Rights: Criminology of Genocide and Atrocities.* Thousand Oaks, CA: Sage.

Savelsberg, J. J. 2011. "Globalization and States of Punishment." In *Comparative Criminal Justice and Globalization,* edited by D. Nelken, 69–86. Farnham, UK: Ashgate.

Savino, M. 2010. "Global Administrative Law Meets 'Soft' Powers: The Uncomfortable Case of Interpol Red Notices." *New York University Journal of International Law and Politics* 42 (2): 263–36.

Sayed, G. H., M. A. A. El-Aty, and K. A. Fadel. 1996. "The Practice of Female Genital Mutilation in Upper Egypt." *International Journal of Gynecology and Obstetrics* 55 (3): 285–91.

Schabas, W. 2004. "United States Hostility to the International Criminal Court: It's All about the Security Council." *European Journal of International Law* 15 (4): 701–20.

Schabas, W. 2008. "Prosecutorial Discretion v. Judicial Activism at the International Criminal Court." *Journal of International Criminal Justice.* 6: 731–61.

Schabas, W. A. 2011. "An Introduction to the International Criminal Court." Cambridge: Cambridge University Press.

Schaefer, R. J., and C. Gonzales. 2012. "Human Trafficking through Mexico and the Southwest Border: Accounts from Hidalgo and Cochise Counties." In *Borderline Slavery: Mexico, the United States and the Human Trade,* edited by S. Tiano and M. Murphy-Aguilar, 173–96. Burlington, VT: Ashgate.

Scharf, M. P. 1999. "The Amnesty Exception to the Jurisdiction of the International Criminal Court." *Cornell International Law Journal* 32: 507–29.

Scheper-Hughes, N. 2004. "Introduction: Making Sense of Violence." In *Violence in War and Peace: An Anthology,* edited by N. Scheper-Hughes and P. Bourgois, 1–31. Oxford: Blackwell.

Scheppele, K. L. 2006. "We Are All Post-9/11 Now." *Fordham Law Review* 75 (2): 607–29.

Schiff, B. N. 2008. *Building the International Criminal Court.* New York: Cambridge University Press.

Schneider, C. L. 2008. "Police Power and the Race Riots in Paris." *Politics and Society* 36 (1): 133–59.

Scott, K. 2010. "Why Did China Reform Its Death Penalty?" *Pacific Rim Law and Policy Journal* 63: 63–80.

Second Optional Protocol to the International Covenant on Civil and Political Rights of 1989.

Segrave, M., S. Milivojevic, and S. Pickering. 2011. *Sex Trafficking: International Context and Response.* Abingdon, UK: Taylor & Francis.

Sen, P. 2005. "'Crimes of Honour,' Value and Meaning." In *'Honour': Crimes, Paradigms and Violence Against Women,* edited by L. Welchman and S. Hossain, 42–63. London: Zed Books.

Serajzadeh, S. H. 2001. "Islam and Crime: The Moral Community of Muslims." *Journal of Arabic and Islamic Studies* 4: 111–31.

Seymour, J. D., and R. Anderson. 1998. *New Ghosts, Old Ghosts: Prisons and Labor Reform Camps in China.* Armonk, NY: M. E. Sharpe.

Shadle, B. L. 1999. "Changing Traditions to Meet Current Altering Conditions: Customary Law, African Courts and the Rejection of Codification in Kenya, 1930–1960." *Journal of African History* 40 (3): 411–31.

Shalhoub-Kevorkian, N. 2005. "Researching Women's Victimization in Palestine: A Socio-Legal Analysis." In *'Honour': Crimes, Paradigms and Violence Against Women,* edited by L. Welchman and S. Hossain, 160–80. London: Zed Books.

Shany, Y. 2014. *Assessing the Effectiveness of International Courts.* Oxford: Oxford University Press.

Shaw, M., J. van Dijk, and W. Rhomberg. 2003. "Determining Trends in Global Crime and Justice: An Overview of Results from the United Nations Surveys of Crime Trends and Operations of Criminal Justice Systems." *Forum on Crime and Society* 3 (1–2): 35–63.

Shaw, V. N. 1998. "Productive Labor and Thought Reform in Chinese Corrections: A Historical and Comparative Analysis." *Prison Journal* 78 (2): 186–211.

Sheehan, E. A. 1997. "Victorian Clitoridectomy: Isaac Baker Brown and His Harmless Operative Procedure." In *The Gender/Sexuality Reader: Culture, History, Political Economy,* edited by R. N. Lancaster and M. Leonardo, 325–34. New York: Routledge.

Sheehan, M. D. 2004. "Diplomacy." In *Attacking Terrorism: Elements of a Grand Strategy,* edited by A. K. Cronin and J. M. Ludes, 97–114. Washington, DC: Georgetown University Press.

Sheleff, L. 1999. *The Future of Tradition: Customary Law, Common Law and Legal Pluralism.* London: Frank Cass.

Shell-Duncan, B., and Y. Hernlund. 2000. "Female Circumcision in Africa: Dimensions of the Practice and Debates." In *Female "Circumcision" in Africa: Culture, Controversy, and Change,* edited by B. Shell-Duncan and Y. Hernlund, 1–39. Boulder, CO: Lynne Rienner.

Shelley, L. I. 1996. *Policing Soviet Society: The Evolution of State Control.* New York: Routledge.

Shelley, L. I. 2005. "The Unholy Trinity: Transnational Crime, Corruption and Terrorism." *Brown Journal of World Affairs* 11 (2): 101–11.

Shelley, L. I. 2010. *Human Trafficking: A Global Perspective.* Cambridge: Cambridge University Press.

Sheptycki, J. 2003. "Against Transnational Organized Crime." In *Critical Reflections on Transnational Organized Crime, Money Laundering, and Corruption,* edited by M. E. Beare, 120–44. Toronto: University of Toronto Press.

Sheptycki, J. 2004. "Accountability of Transnational Policing Institutions: The Strange Case of Interpol." *Canadian Journal of Law and Society* 19 (1): 107–34.

Sheptycki, J. 2007. "The Constabulary Ethic and the Transnational Condition." In *Crafting Transnational Policing: Police Capacity-Building and Global Policing Reform,* edited by A. Goldsmith and J. Sheptycki, 31–72. Portland, OR: Hart.

Sheptycki, J. 2011. "Transnational and Comparative Criminology Reconsidered." In *Comparative Criminal Justice and Globalization,* edited by D. Nelken, 145–62. Farnham, UK: Ashgate.

Sherman, T. C. 2010. *State Violence and Punishment in India.* Abingdon, UK: Routledge.

Shughart, W. F. 2006. "An Analytical History of Terrorism, 1945–2000." *Public Choice* 128: 7–39.

Shweder, R. 2002. "'What about Female Genital Mutilation?' and Why Understanding Culture Matters in the First Place." In *Engaging Cultural Differences: The Multicultural Challenge in Liberal Democracies,* edited by R. Shweder and M. Minow, 216–51. New York: Russell Sage Foundation.

Silvestri, M., and C. Crowther-Dowey. 2008. *Gender and Crime.* London: Sage.

Simmons, B. 2009. *Mobilizing for Human Rights: International Law in Domestic Politics.* Cambridge: Cambridge University Press.

Simon, J. 2007. *Governing through Crime: How the War on Crime Transformed American Democracy and Created a Culture of Fear.* Oxford: Oxford University Press.

Sinclair, G. 2006. *At the End of the Line: Colonial Policing and the Imperial Endgame 1945–80.* Manchester, UK: Manchester University Press.

Singer, P. W. 2006. *Children at War.* Berkeley: University of California Press.

Singh, R. 2012. "The Discourse and Practice of 'Heroic Resistance' in the Israeli-Palestinian Conflict: The Case of Hamas." *Politics, Religion and Ideology* 13 (4): 529–45.

Singh, U.K. 2012. "Mapping Anti-Terror Regimes in India." In *Global Anti-Terrorism Law and Policy,* edited by V. V. Ramraj, M. Hor, K. Roach, and G. Williams, 420–46. Cambridge: Cambridge University Press.

Skaine, R. 2005. *Female Genital Mutilation: Legal, Cultural and Medical Issues.* Jefferson, NC: McFarland.

Smith, P. J. 2008. *The Terrorism Ahead: Confronting Transnational Violence in the Twenty-First Century.* Armonk, NY: M. E. Sharpe.

Smith, R. G. 2014. "Transnational Cybercrime and Fraud." In *Handbook of Transnational Crime and Justice,* edited by P. Reichel and J. Albanese, 119–42. Thousand Oaks, CA: Sage.

Snacken, S. 2010. "Resisting Punitiveness in Europe?" *Theoretical Criminology* 14 (3): 273–92.

Snider, L. 1998. "Towards Safer Societies: Punishment, Masculinities and Violence Against Women." *British Journal of Criminology* 38 (1): 1–39.

Snyder, J., and L. Vinjamuri. 2003. "Trials and Errors: Principle and Pragmatism in Strategies of International Justice." *International Security* 28 (3): 5–44.

Sobanet, A., and S. Terrio. 2005. "Silence in the Court and Testimony behind Bars: Juvenile Defendants and the French Judicial System." *French Cultural Studies* 16 (1): 21–39.

Solomon, H. 2012. "Counter-Terrorism in Nigeria." *RUSI Journal* 157 (4): 6–11.

Solomon, P. H. 2005a. "The Criminal Procedure Code of 2001: Will It Make Russian Justice More Fair?" In *Ruling Russia: Law, Crime and Justice in a Changing Society,* edited by W. A. Pridemore, 77–100. Lanham, MD: Rowman and Littlefield.

Solomon, P. H. 2005b. "The Reform of Policing in the Russian Federation." *Australian and New Zealand Journal of Criminology* 38: 230–40.

Solomon, P. H., and T. Foglesong. 2000. *Courts and Transition in Russia.* Boulder, CO: Westview Press.

Sorel, G. 1914. *Reflections on Violence.* Translated by T. E. Hulme. New York: Red and Black. First published 1908.

Souryal, S. 1988. "The Role of Shariah Law in Deterring Criminality in Saudi Arabia." *International Journal of Comparative and Applied Criminal Justice* 12 (1): 1–25.

Souryal, S., A. I. Alobied, and D. W. Potts. 1996. "The Penalty of Hand Amputation for Theft in Islamic Justice." In *Comparative Criminal Justice: Traditional and Nontraditional Systems of Law and Control,* edited by C. B. Fields and R. H. Moore, 429–52. Prospect Heights, IL: Waveland Press.

Sowa, H., A. A. M. Crijnen, L. Bengi-Arslan, and F. C. Verhulst. 2000. "Factors Associated with Problem Behaviors in Turkish Immigrant

Children in the Netherlands." *Social Psychiatry and Psychiatric Epidemiology* 35 (4): 177–84.

Srikantiah, J. 2007. "Perfect Victims and Real Survivors: The Iconic Victim in Domestic Human Trafficking Law." *Boston University Law Review* 87: 157–211.

Stahn, C. 2005. "Complementarity, Amnesties and Alternative Forms of Justice: Some Interpretative Guidelines for the International Criminal Court." *Journal of International Criminal Justice* 3: 695–720.

Stanley, E. 2009. *Torture, Truth and Justice: The Case of Timor-Leste*. Abingdon, UK: Routledge.

Starr, J. 2015. *Continuing the Revolution: The Political Thought of Mao*. Princeton, NJ: Princeton University Press.

Steger, M. B. 2009. *Globalization: A Very Short Introduction*. Oxford: Oxford University Press.

Steinberg, M. 1982. "The Twelve Tables and Their Origins: An Eighteenth Century Debate." *Journal of the History of Ideas* 43 (3): 379–96.

Stephan, J. J. 2004. *State Prison Expenditures, 2001*. Washington, DC: U.S. Department of Justice, Office of Justice Programs, Bureau of Statistics.

Stern, V. 2001. "An Alternative Vision: Criminal Justice Developments in Non-Western Countries." *Social Justice* 28 (3): 88–104.

Stickley, A., I. Timofeeva, and P. Sparen, P. 2008. "Risk Factors for Intimate Partner Violence Against Women in St. Petersburg, Russia." *Violence Against Women* 14 (4): 483–95.

Stoebuck, W. B. 1968. "Reception of English Common Law in the American Colonies." *William and Mary Law Review* 10 (2): 393–426.

Stohl, R. 2005. "Fighting the Illicit Trafficking of Small Arms." *SAIS Review of International Affairs* 25 (1): 59–68.

Stojanovic, S., and M. Downes. 2009. "Policing in Serbia: Negotiating the Transition between Rhetoric and Reform." In *Policing Developing Democracies*, edited by M. S. Hinton and T. Newburn, 73–98. Abingdon, UK: Routledge.

Stone, C., & Ward, H. 2000. "Democratic Policing: A Framework for Action." *Policing and Society: An International Journal of Research and Policy*. 10 (1): 11–45.

Straus, M. A., S. L. Hamby, S. Boney-McCoy, and D. B. Sugarman. 1996. "The Revised Conflict Tactics Scales (CTS): Development and Preliminary Psychometric Data." *Journal of Family Issues* 17 (3): 283–316.

Stromseth, J., D. Wippman, and R. Brooks. 2006. *Can Might Make Right? Building the Rule of Law after Military Interventions*. New York: Cambridge University Press.

Subramaniam, A. 2012. "Challenges of Protecting India from Terrorism." *Terrorism and Political Violence* 24 (3): 396–414.

Sugimori, S. 1998. "Bullying in Japanese Schools: Cultural and Social Psychological Perspectives." In *Cross-Cultural Perspectives on Youth and Violence*, edited by M. W. Watts, 175–86. Stamford, CT: JAI Press.

"Sultan of Brunei Unveils Strict Sharia Penal Code." *Guardian*, April 30, 2014. http://www.theguardian.com/world/2014/apr/30/sultan-brunei-sharia-penal-code-flogging

Sun, I. Y., and Y. Wu. 2010. "Chinese Policing in a Time of Transition, 1978–2008." *Journal of Contemporary Criminal Justice* 26 (1): 20–35.

Surtees, R. 2005. *Other Forms of Trafficking in Minors: Articulating Victim Profiles and Conceptualizing Interventions*. Vienna: Nexus Institute to Combat Human Trafficking and International Organization of Migration.

Szabo, D. 1975. "Comparative Criminology." *Journal of Criminal Law and Criminology* 66 (3): 366–79.

Tak, P. J. P. 2012. "The Dutch Prosecutor: A Prosecuting and Sentencing Officer." In *The Prosecutor in Transnational Perspective*, edited by E. Luna and M. L. Wade, 135–55. Oxford: Oxford University Press.

Talle, A. 2007. "Female Circumcision in Africa and Beyond: The Anthropology of a Difficult Issue." In *Transcultural Bodies: Female Genital Cutting in Global Context*, edited by Y. Hernlund and B. Shell-Duncan, 91–106. New Brunswick, NJ: Rutgers University Press.

Tanioka, I., and H. Goto. 1996. "Japan." In *International Handbook on Juvenile Justice*, edited by D. J. Shoemaker, 191–206. Westport, CT: Greenwood Press.

Tanner, M. S. 2005. "Campaign-Style Policing in China and Its Critics." In *Crime, Punishment, and Policing in China*, edited by B. Bakken, 171–88. Lanham, MD: Rowman & Littlefield.

Taylor, B. D. 2014. "Police Reform in Russia: The Policy Process in a Hybrid Regime." *Post-Soviet Affairs* 30 (1): 226–55.

Teitel, R. 2000. *Transitional Justice*. Oxford: Oxford University Press.

Teitel, R. 2003. "Transitional Justice Genealogy." *Harvard Human Rights Journal* 16: 69–94.

Ten, C. L. 1987. *Crime, Guilt and Punishment: A Philosophical Introduction*. Oxford: Clarendon Press.

Terrio, S. 2007. "Youth, (Im)migration, and Juvenile Law at the Paris Palace of Justice." In *Youth, Globalization, and the Law*, edited by S. A. Venkatesh and R. Kassimir, 163–91. Stanford, CA: Stanford University Press.

Terrio, S. 2009. *Judging Mohammed: Juvenile Delinquency, Immigration, and Exclusion at the Paris Palace of Justice*. Stanford, CA: Stanford University Press.

Terry, G. 2007. "Conclusion." In *Gender-Based Violence*, edited by G. Terry and J. Hoare, 154–62. Oxfam GB.

Thaman, S. C. 1999. "Europe's New Jury Systems: The Cases of Spain and Russia." *Law and Contemporary Problems* 62 (2): 233–59.

Thaman, S. C. 2012. "The Penal Order: Prosecutorial Sentencing as a Model for Criminal Justice Reform?" In *The Prosecutor in Transnational Perspective*, edited by E. Luna and M. L. Wade, 156–76. Oxford: Oxford University Press.

Thibault, J. W., and L. J. Walker. 1975. *Procedural Justice: A Psychological Analysis*. New York: Wiley.

Tiano, S. 2012. "Introduction." In *Borderline Slavery: Mexico, the United States and the Human Trade*, edited by S. Tiano and M. Murphy-Aguilar, 3–13. Burlington, VT: Ashgate.

Toivonen, T., and Y. Imoto. 2012. "Making Sense of Youth Problems." In *A Sociology of Japanese Youth: From Returnees to NEETs*, edited by R. Goodman, Y. Imoto, and T. Toivonen, 1–29. London: Routledge.

Tollefson, H. 1999. *Policing Islam: The British Occupation of Egypt and the Anglo-Egyptian Struggle over Control of the Police 1882–1914*. Westport, CT: Greenwood Press.

Tomlinson, J. 1999. *Globalization and Culture*. Chicago: University of Chicago Press.

Tong, R. 1989. *Feminist Thought: A Comprehensive Introduction*. Boulder, CO: Westview Press.

Tonry, M. 1999. "Parochialism in U.S. Sentencing Policy." *Crime and Delinquency* 45 (1): 48–65.

Tonry, M. 2001. Punishment Policies and Patterns in Western Countries." In *Sentencing and Sanctions in Western Countries*, edited by M. Tonry and R. S. Frase, 3–28. Oxford: Oxford University Press.

Tonry, M. 2012. "Prosecutors and Politics in Comparative Perspective." *Crime and Justice* 41 (1): 1–33.

Tonry, M., and A. Doob, eds. 2004. *Youth Crime and Youth Justice: Comparative and Cross-National Perspectives*. Chicago: University of Chicago Press.

Touma-Sliman, A. 2005. "Culture, National Minority and the State: Working against the 'Crime of Family Honour' within the Palestine Community in Israel." In *'Honour': Crimes, Paradigms and Violence Against Women*, edited by L. Welchman and S. Hossain, 181–98. London: Zed Books.

Trebilcock, M. J., and R. J. Daniels. 2008. *Rule of Law Reform and Development: Charting the Fragile Path of Progress*. Cheltenham, UK: Elgar Press.

Trevaskes, S. 2002. "Courts on the Campaign Path in China: Criminal Court Work in the 'Yanda 2001' Anti-crime Campaign." *Asian Survey* 42 (5): 673–93.

Trevaskes, S. 2008. "The Death Penalty in China Today: Kill Fewer, Kill Cautiously." *Asian Survey* 48 (3): 393–413.

Trevaskes, S. 2010. *Policing Serious Crime in China: From "Strike Hard" to "Kill Fewer."* London: Routledge.

Trotsky, L. 2007. *Terrorism and Communism: A Reply to Karl Kautsky*. London: Verso.

Turner, J. 2012. "Prosecutors and Bargaining in Weak Cases: A Comparative View." In *The Prosecutor in Transnational Perspective*, edited by E. Luna and M. L. Wade, 102–15. Oxford: Oxford University Press.

Turner, J., and L. Kelly. 2009. "Trade Secrets: Intersections between Diasporas and Crime Groups in the Constitution of the Human Trafficking Chain." *British Journal of Criminology* 49: 184–201.

Tyldum, G., and A. Brunovskis. 2005. "Describing the Unobserved: Methodological Challenges in Empirical Studies on Human Trafficking." *International Migration* 43 (1/2): 17–34.

Ubink, J. 2011. "The Quest for Customary Law in African State Courts." In *The Future of African Customary Law*, edited by J. Fenrich, P. Galizzi, and T. E. Higgins, 83–102. New York: Cambridge University Press.

Ulrich, J. L. 2000. "Confronting Gender-Based Violence with International Instruments: Is a Solution to the Pandemic within Reach?" *Indiana Journal of Global Legal Studies* 7 (2): 629–54.

"UN Releases Report on Sex Abuse by Peacekeepers." 2015. *Aljazeera*, June 16. http://www.aljazeera.com/news/2015/06/peacekeepers-sex-abuse-150616012115509.html

United Nations. 2006. *In-Depth Study of All Forms of Violence Against Women: Report of Secretary-General*. New York: United Nations.

United Nations Children's Fund (UNICEF). 2005. *Changing a Harmful Social Convention: Female Genital Mutilation/Cutting*. Florence, Italy: UNICEF.

United Nations Children's Fund (UNICEF). 2013. *Female Genital Mutilation/Cutting: A Statistical Overview and Exploration of the Dynamics of Change*. New York: UNICEF.

United Nations Commission on Human Rights Resolution 2002/79. "Impunity." 56th meeting. 25 April 2002. Commission on Human Rights. Report on the Fifty-Eighth Session. Economic and Social Council. Official Records 2002. Supplement No. 3. http://www.un.org/en/terrorism/pdfs/2/G0215272.pdf

United Nations Declaration of Basic Principles of Justice for Victims of Crime and Abuse of Power. New York, 29 November 1985.

United Nations General Assembly Ad Hoc Committee. 1996. Measures to Eliminate International Terrorism. Ad Hoc Committee established by General Assembly resolution 51/210 of 17 December 1996. http://legal.un.org/terrorism/index.html

United Nations Minimum Standard Rules for the Treatment of Prisoners 1955.

United Nations Office of the High Commissioner for Human Rights. 1984. Convention against Torture and Other Cruel, Inhuman or Degrading Treatment or Punishment. http://www.ohchr.org/EN/ProfessionalInterest/Pages/CAT.aspx

United Nations Office of the High Commissioner for Human Rights. 2005. Basic Principles and Guidelines on the Right to a Remedy and Reparations for Victims of Gross Violations of International Human Rights Law and Serious Violations of International Humanitarian Law.

Adopted and proclaimed by General Assembly Resolution 60/147 of 16 December 2005.

United Nations Office on Drugs and Crime. 2014. *World Drug Report 2014.* New York: United Nations. https://www.unodc.org/documents/wdr2014/World_Drug_Report_2014_web.pdf

United Nations Office on Drugs and Crime. 2015. "Human Trafficking FAQs: What Is the Most Commonly Identified Form of Human Trafficking?" http://www.unodc.org/unodc/en/human-trafficking/faqs.html

United Nations Security Council. 2001. Resolution 1373 (2001). Adopted by the Security Council on 28 September 2001. S/RES/1373 (2001). http://www.un.org/en/sc/ctc/specialmeetings/2012/docs/United%20Nations%20Security%20Council%20Resolution%201373%20%282001%29.pdf

United Nations Security Council. 2004. Resolution 1566 of October 2004. http://www.state.gov/j/ct/rls/other/un/66959.htm

United Nations Security Council. 2004, August. *The Rule of Law and Transitional Justice in Conflict and Post-Conflict Societies.* Report of the Secretary-General, UN document S/2004/616, New York.

U.S. Agency for International Development. 2007. "Anticorruption and Police Integrity: Security Sector Reform Program." http://pdf.usaid.gov/pdf_docs/PNADN948.pdf

USA Patriot Improvement and Reauthorization Act of 2005. 120 STAT.192. Public Law 109–177, March 9, 2006.

U.S. Code Title 18 (Criminal Acts and Criminal Procedure).

U.S. Code Title 22, Chapter 38.

U.S. Department of Justice. *United States Attorneys' Manual.* Revised 1997. http://www.justice.gov/usam/united-states-attorneys-manual.

U.S. Department of Justice. *Criminal Resource Manual,* 1–99. http://www.justice.gov/usam/criminal-resource-manual.

U.S. Department of Justice. 2012. "Edgardo Sensi Sentenced to 85 Years in Federal Prison for Production of Child Pornography and Sexual Tourism Offenses." Press release, United States Attorney's Office, District of Connecticut. http://www.justice.gov/archive/usao/ct/Press2012/20120131-1.html

U.S. Department of State. 2005. *Trafficking in Persons Report 2005,* NCJ 211300. Washington, DC: U.S. Department of State.

U.S. Department of State. 2011. "Tiers: Placement, Guide, and Penalties for Tier 3 Countries." *Trafficking in Persons Report 2011.* http://www.state.gov/j/tip/rls/tiprpt/2011/164221.htm

U.S. Department of State. 2013. *Trafficking in Persons Report 2013.* http://www.state.gov/documents/organization/210737.pdf

U.S. Government Accounting Office (GAO). 2008. *Plan Colombia.* GAO-09-71. Washington, DC: GAO.

U.S. House of Representatives, Committee on Homeland Security, Subcommittee on Counterterrorism and Intelligence. 2011, November 30. *Boko Haram: Emerging Threat to the U.S. Homeland.* Washington, DC: U.S. House of Representatives.

Utas, M. 2004. "Fluid Research Fields: Studying Ex-Combatant Youth in the Aftermath of the Liberian Civil War." In *Children and Youth on the Front Line: Ethnography, Armed Conflict and Displacement,* edited by J. Boyden and J. de Berry, 209–36. London: Berghahn.

Utas, M. 2011. "Victimcy as Social Navigation: From the Toolbox of Liberian Child Soldiers." In *Child Soldiers: From Recruitment to Reintegration,* edited by A. Ozerdem and S. Podder, 213–30. Basingstoke, UK: Palgrave Macmillan.

Uvin, P., and C. Mironko. 2009. "The International Criminal Tribunal for Rwanda." In *The Genocide Studies Reader,* edited by S. Tottens and P. R. Bartrop, 465–67. New York: Routledge.

Van Caenegem, R. C. 1973. *The Birth of the English Common Law.* Cambridge: Cambridge University Press.

Vanderwiele, T. 2006. "A Commentary on the United Nations Convention on the Rights of the Child. Optional Protocol." *The Involvement of Children in Armed Conflicts.* Leiden: Martinus Nijhoff.

Van Dijk, J. 2008. *The World of Crime: Breaking the Silence on Problems of Security, Justice, and Development across the World.* Thousand Oaks, CA: Sage.

Van Dijk, J., and T. Spapens. 2014. "Transnational Organized Crime Networks." In *Handbook of Transnational Crime and Justice,* edited by P. Reichel and J. Albanese, 213–26. Thousand Oaks, CA: Sage.

Van Koppen, P. J., and S. D. Penrod. 2003. "Adversarial or Inquisitorial? Comparing Systems." In *Adversarial versus Inquisitorial Justice: Psychological Perspectives on Criminal Justice Systems,* edited by P. J. Van Koppen and S. D. Penrod, 2–17. New York: Kluwer Academic.

van Schendel, W. 2005. "Spaces of Engagement: How Borderlands, Illegal Flows and Territorial States Interlock." In *Illicit Flows and Criminal Things: States, Borders and the Other Side of Civilization,* edited by W. van Schendel and I. Abraham, 38–68. Bloomington: Indiana University Press.

Vansina, J. 2003. "Confinement in Angola's Past." In *A History of Prison and Confinement in Africa,* edited by F. Bernault, 55–68. Portsmouth, NH: Heinemann.

Van Swaaningen, R. 2011. "Critical Cosmopolitanism and Global Criminology." In *Comparative Criminal Justice and Globalization,* edited by D. Nelken, 125–44. Farnham, UK: Ashgate.

Van Wilsem, J. 2004. "Criminal Victimization in Cross-National Perspective: An Analysis of Rates of

Theft, Violence and Vandalism across 27 Countries." *European Journal of Criminology* 1 (1): 89–109.

Varese, F. 2011. *Mafias on the Move: How Organized Crime Conquers New Territories.* Princeton, NJ: Princeton University Press.

Venema, D. 2012. "Transitions as States of Exception: Towards a More General Theory of Transitional Justice." In *Critical Perspectives in Transitional Justice,* edited by N. Palmer, P. Clark, and D. Granville, 73–89. Cambridge: Intersentia.

Victims of Trafficking and Violence Protection Act (TVPA). Public Law 106–386, October 28, 2000. 114 STAT. 1464. 106th Congress.

Vijayakumar, V. 2005. "Legal and Institutional Responses to Terrorism in India." In *Global Anti-Terrorism Law and Policy,* edited by V. V. Ramraj, M. Hor, and K. Roach, 351–67. Cambridge: Cambridge University Press.

Vira, V., T. Ewing, and J. Miller. 2014. *Out of Africa: Mapping the Global Trade in Illicit Elephant Ivory.* Washington, DC: Born Free USA and C4ADS.

Vogel, F. E. 2000. *Islamic Law and Legal System: Studies of Saudi Arabia.* Leiden: Brill.

Vogler, R. 2005. *A World View of Criminal Justice.* Aldershot, UK: Ashgate.

Voronina, O. 2009. "Has Feminist Philosophy a Future in Russia?" *Signs: Journal of Women in Culture and Society* 34 (2): 252–57.

Waldek, L., and S. Jayasekara. 2011. "Boko Haram: The Evolution of Islamist Extremism in Nigeria." *Journal of Policing, Intelligence and Counter Terrorism* 6 (2): 168–78.

Waldorf, L. 2006. "Mass Justice for Mass Atrocity: Rethinking Local Justice as Transitional Justice." *Temple Law Review* 79 (1): 1–87.

Walker, A. 1992. *Possessing the Secret of Joy.* Orlando, FL: Harcourt Brace Jovanovich.

Walker, N. 1991. *Why Punish?* Oxford: Oxford University Press.

Walker, N. 2008. "The Pattern of Transnational Policing." In *Handbook of Policing,* edited by T. Newburn, 119–46. Cullompton, UK: Willan.

Walklate, S. 1995. *Gender and Crime: An Introduction.* London: Prentice Hall.

Walklate, S. 2008. "What Is to Be Done about Violence Against Women? Gender, Violence, Cosmopolitanism and the Law." *British Journal of Criminology* 48: 39–54.

Walklate, S., and G. Mythen. 2015. *Contradictions of Terrorism: Security, Risk and Resilience.* Abingdon, UK: Routledge.

Wallace, P. 1995. "Political Violence and Terrorism in India: The Crisis of Identity." In *Terrorism in Context,* edited by M. Crenshaw, 352–409. University Park: Pennsylvania State University.

Walmsley, R. 2013. *World Prison Population List,* ed. 10. London: International Centre for Prison Studies.

Walters, R. 2006. "Crime, Bio-Agriculture and the Exploitation of Hunger." *British Journal of Criminology* 46 (1): 26–45.

Walzer, M. 2000. *Just and Unjust Wars: A Moral Argument with Historical Illustrations.* New York: Basic Books.

War Child. 2014. *Child Soldiers.* http://www.warchild.org.uk/issues/child-soldiers

Wardak, A. 2005. "Crime and Social Control in Saudi Arabia." In *Transnational and Comparative Criminology,* edited by J. Sheptycki and A. Wardak, 91–116. New York: Routledge.

Watts, J. 2002. "Japan's Teen Hermits Spread Fear." *Guardian,* November 16. http://www.theguardian.com/world/2002/nov/17/film.japan

Weber, L., and B. Bowling. 2004. "Policing Migration: A Framework for Investigating the Regulation of Global Mobility." *Policing and Society: An International Journal of Research and Policy* 14 (3): 195–212.

Weber, R. 2001. "Police Organization and Accountability: A Comparative Study." In *Police in Transition: Essays on the Police Forces in Transition Countries,* edited by A. Kadar, 39–70. Budapest: Central European University Press.

Weigend, T. 2001. "Sentencing and Punishment in Germany." In *Sentencing and Sanctions in Western Countries,* edited by M. Tonry and R. S. Frase, 188–221. Oxford: Oxford University Press.

Weigend, T. 2012. "A Judge by Another Name? Comparative Perspectives on the Role of the Public Prosecutor." In *The Prosecutor in Transnational Perspective,* edited by E. Luna and M. L. Wade, 377–91. Oxford: Oxford University Press.

Weitzer, R. 2007. "The Social Construction of Sex Trafficking: Ideology and Institutionalization of a Moral Crusade." *Politics and Society* 35 (3): 447–75.

Welch, M. 1999. *Punishment in America: Social Control and the Ironies of Imprisonment.* Thousand Oaks, CA: Sage.

Welchman, L., and S. Hossain. 2005. "Introduction: 'Honour': Rights and Wrongs." In *'Honour': Crimes, Paradigms and Violence Against Women,* edited by L. Welchman and S. Hossain, 1–21. London: Zed Books.

Weldon, S. L. 2002. *Protest, Policy, and the Problem of Violence Against Women: A Cross-National Comparison.* Pittsburgh: University of Pittsburgh Press.

Werdmoelder, H. 1998. "Moroccan Organized Crime in the Netherlands." *International Journal of Risk, Security and Crime Prevention* 3: 111–20.

Wessells, M. 2006. *Child Soldiers: From Violence to Protection.* Cambridge, MA: Harvard University Press.

Westmarland, L. 2010. "Transnational Policing and Security." In *Criminal Justice: Local and Global,* edited by D. Drake, J. Muncie, and L. Westmarland, 177–212. Cullompton, UK: Willan.

Whitaker, B. E. 2007. "Exporting the Patriot Act? Democracy and the 'War on Terror' in the Third World." *Third World Quarterly* 28 (5): 1017–32.

White, M. 2007. *Current Issues and Controversies in Policing.* Boston: Allyn & Bacon.

Whittlesey, D. 1937. "British and French Colonial Technique in West Africa." *Foreign Affairs* 15 (2): 362–72.

Wilkinson, P. 2001. *Terrorism versus Democracy: The Liberal State Response.* Abingdon, UK: Routledge.

Williams, G. 2002. *The Other Side of the Popular: Neoliberalism and Subalternity in Latin America.* Durham, NC: Duke University Press.

Williams, P. 2001. "Organizing Transnational Crime: Networks, Markets and Hierarchies." In *Combating Transnational Crime: Concepts, Activities and Responses,* edited by P. Williams and D. Vlassis, 57–87. London: Frank Cass.

Willis, J. 1991. "Thieves, Drunkards and Vagrants: Defining Crime in Colonial Mombasa, 1902–32." In *Policing the Empire: Government, Authority and Control, 1830–1940,* edited by D. M. Anderson and D. Killingray, 219–35. Manchester, UK: Manchester University Press.

Willmott Harrop, E. 2012. "Africa: A Bewitching Economy—Witchcraft and Human Trafficking (Analysis)." *Think Africa Press,* September 17. http://allafrica.com/stories/201209181007.html

Wilson, D. 2014. *Pain and Retribution: A Short History of British Prisons, 1066 to the Present.* London: Reaktion Books.

Winslow, R. n.d. "Saudi Arabia." In *Crime and Society: A Comparative Criminology Tour of the World,* http://www-rohan.sdsu.edu/faculty/rwinslow/asia_pacific/saudi_arabia.html

Wong, D. S. W. 2001. "Changes in Juvenile Justice in China." *Youth and Society* 32 (4): 492–509.

Wong, D. S. W. 2004. "Juvenile Protection and Delinquency Prevention Policies in China." *Australian and New Zealand Journal of Criminology* 37: 52–66.

Wong, K. C. 2001. "The Philosophy of Community Policing in China." *Police Quarterly* 4 (2): 186–214.

Wong, K. C. 2004. "The Police Legitimacy Crisis and Police Law Reform in China: Part 1." *International Journal of Police Science and Management* 6 (4): 199–218.

Wood, D. M., and C. W. R. Webster. 2009. "Living in Surveillance Societies: The Normalisation of Surveillance in Europe and the Threat of Britain's Bad Example." *Journal of Contemporary European Research* 5 (2): 259–73.

Wooditch, A. 2011. "The Efficacy of the *Trafficking in Persons Report*: A Review of the Evidence." *Criminal Justice Policy Review* 22: 471–93.

Woodiwiss, M. 2003. "Transnational Organized Crime: The Strange Career of an American Concept." In *Critical Reflections on Transnational Organized Crime, Money Laundering, and Corruption,* edited by M. E. Beare, 3–34. Toronto: University of Toronto.

Woodman, G. 2011. "A Survey of Customary Laws in Africa in Search of Lessons for the Future." In *The Future of African Customary Law,* edited by J. Fenrich, P. Galizzi, and T. E. Higgins, 9–30. New York: Cambridge University Press.

World Health Organization (WHO). 2013. *Global and Regional Estimates of Violence Against Women: Prevalence and Health Effects of Intimate Partner Violence and Non-partner Sexual Violence.* Geneva: WHO.

World Health Organization (WHO) and UNICEF. 1997. *Female Genital Mutilation/Cutting.* New York: United Nations.

World Tourism Organization. *Protect Children from Exploitation in Tourism: Code of Conduct for the Protection of Children from Sexual Exploitation in Travel and Tourism.* http://www.unicef.org/lac/code_of_conduct.pdf

Wyness, M. *Childhood and Society,* ed. 2. Basingstoke, UK: Palgrave Macmillan.

Wyvekens, A. 1997. "Mediation and Proximity: Community Justice Centres in Lyons." *European Journal on Criminal Policy and Research* 5 (4): 27–42.

Wyvekens, A. 2008. "The French Juvenile Justice System." In *International Handbook of Juvenile Justice,* edited by J. Junger-Tas and S. H. Decker, 173–86. New York: Springer.

Yamamiya, Y. 2003. "Juvenile Delinquency in Japan." *Journal of Prevention and Intervention in the Community* 25 (2): 27–46.

Yoder, R. S. 2011. *Deviance and Inequality in Japan: Japanese Youth and Foreign Migrants.* Bristol, UK: Policy Press.

Yokoyama, M. 2015. "Juvenile Justice and Juvenile Crime: An Overview of Japan." In *Juvenile Justice: International Perspectives, Models, and Trends,* edited by J. A. Winterdyk, 179–208. Boca Raton, FL: CRC Press.

Yokoyama, M. 2002. "Juvenile Justice and Juvenile Crime: An Overview of Japan." In *Juvenile Justice Systems: International Perspectives,* edited by J. Winterdyk, 321–52. Toronto: Canadian Scholars Press.

Young, M. A. 2013. *Banking Secrecy and Offshore Financial Centers: Money Laundering and Offshore Banking.* Abingdon, UK: Routledge.

Zedner, L. 1995. "In Pursuit of the Vernacular: Comparing Law and Order Discourse in Britain and Germany." *Social and Legal Studies* 4: 517–34.

Zernova, M. 2012. "Coping with the Failure of the Police in Post-Soviet Russia: Findings from One Empirical Study." *Police Practice and Research: An International Journal* 13 (6): 474–86.

Zhang, L. 2008. "Juvenile Delinquency and Justice in Contemporary China: A Critical Review of the Literature over 15 Years." *Crime, Law, and Social Change* 50: 149–60.

Zhang, L., and J. Liu. 2007. "China's Juvenile Delinquency Prevention Law: The Law and the Philosophy." *International Journal of Offender Therapy and Comparative Criminology* 51 (5): 541–54.

Zhao, R., H. Zhang, and J. Liu. 2015. "China's Juvenile Justice: A System in Transition." In *Juvenile Justice: International Perspectives, Models, and Trends*, edited by J. Winterdyk, 137–62. Baton Rouge, LA: CRC Press.

Zhong, L. Y. 2009. "Community Policing in China: Old Wine in New Bottles." *Police Practice and Research* 10 (2): 157–69.

Zila, J. 2012. "Prosecutorial Powers and Policy Making in Sweden and the Other Nordic Countries." In *The Prosecutor in Transnational Perspective*, edited by E. Luna and M. L. Wade, 235–49. Oxford: Oxford University Press.

Zimring, F. E. 2003. *The Contradictions of American Capital Punishment.* Oxford: Oxford University Press.

Zimring, F. E., and G. Hawkins. 1997. *Crime Is Not the Problem: Lethal Violence in America.* New York: Oxford University Press.

Zimring, F. E., and D. T. Johnson. 2006. "Public Opinion and the Governance of Punishment in Democratic Political Systems." In "Democracy, Crime and Justice," Special issue, *Annals of the American Academy of Political and Social Sciences* 605: 266–80.

Zimring, F. E., and D. T. Johnson. 2008. "Law, Society, and Capital Punishment in Asia." *Punishment and Society* 10 (2): 103–15.

Zorbas, E. 2007. "Reconciliation in Post-Genocide Rwanda: Discourse and Practice." PhD diss., London School of Economics and Political Science, University of London.

Zureik, E., and M. B. Salter. 2005. "Introduction." In *Global Surveillance and Policing: Borders, Security, Identity*, edited by E. Zureik and M. B. Salter, 1–10. Cullompton, UK: Willan.

Zyck, S. A. 2011. "'But I'm a Man': The Imposition of Childhood on and Denial of Identity and Economic Opportunity to Afghanistan's Child Soldiers." In *Child Soldiers: From Recruitment to Reintegration*, edited by A. Ozerdem and S. Podder, 159–72. Basingstoke, UK: Palgrave Macmillan.

INDEX

Kaushal, M.
  see Kalhan, A.
Kawasaki, K., 208, 230
Kazakhstan, 313
Kearney, M., 6
Kelley, J., 275, 292
Kelling, G., 229
Kelly, L., 340, 341, 357
Kelly, R. J., 329
Kenney, M., 304, 305, 306, 332
Kent, L., 239, 248 (box), 252, 253, 254, 261, 263
Kenya
  colonial policing, 66, 67, 93
  colonial punishment regimes, 168, 169, 187
  customary law, 53
  decolonization period, 67
  domestic violence, 425
  endangered species trading, 320
  female circumcision, 453, 454, 456, 457, 458, 459, 461,
    469–470, 471–472, 474, 493
  International Criminal Court (ICC), 276, 292, 293
Kenyatta, Jomo, 461, 469
Kenyatta, Uhuru, 293
Kerr, O. S., 326, 327
Kessai system, 141 (box)
Khadduri, M., 46, 48, 50
Khadr, Omar, 488 (box)
Khalistan, 391–393
Khalistan Commando Force, 391
Khalsa Sikhism, 391
Kharijites, 377
Khomeini, Ayatollah, 404
Khrushchev, Nikita, 73
Kidnapping operations, 95, 321 (box), 403, 493
Kidney transplants, 347
Kilkelly, U., 227
Killias, M., 22
  see also Aebi, M. F.
Killingray, D., 64, 65, 167, 168, 169, 187
Kim, N., 460–461
Kirchheimer, O., 148
Knight, K.
  see Hackler, J.
Koban, 24
Komiya, N., 24–25
Koran
  see Islamic law
Korea
  colonial punishment regimes, 178
  crime rates, 219
  International Criminal Court (ICC), 276
  nuclear weapons programs, 313
  penal policy, 181, 188
  rape, 441, 442
Kosovo, 237, 238
Kostakos, P. A., 310, 311
Koszeg, F., 72
Krishnan, J. K., 394, 395, 406
Kritz, N., 237
Krug, E. G., 29
Krug, P., 102 (table)

Kryshi, 301
Ku Klux Klan, 405
Kumari, V., 191
Kurds, 310, 437, 438, 439
Kurki, L., 152
Kurlychek, M.
  see Bernard, T.
Kuwait
  capital punishment, 154
  crime rates, 26
  Islamic law, 45
  rape, 441
  terrorism policies, 382

Labor camps, 184, 188, 300, 349
Labor commissions, 55
Labor trafficking, 342, 344, 344–345 (box), 348,
    350, 353, 354
Lackey, D., 405
Lafree, G., 24
Laissez-faire system, 99, 143
Lal Sena group, 481
Lambert, E. G.
  see Jiang, S.
Lambourne, W., 252, 259 (box)
Langan, P., 186
Langer, M., 109–110, 111, 143
Laogai system, 81–82 (box), 184, 221
Laojiao system, 81–82 (box)
Laos, 304, 307 (table)
Lapeyronnie, D., 197
Laqueur, W., 368, 373, 405
Larceny rates, 26 (table)
Larsen, N., 4, 313
Lashings, 50
Latin America
  arms trafficking, 311
  child soldiers, 476, 481, 482
  colonial punishment regimes, 171
  contemporary armed conflicts, 476
  criminal justice system reforms, 109–113, 143
  democratization, 109–110
  domestic violence, 425, 430–432
  drug trafficking, 304–305, 307, 307 (table), 321–322, 332
  endangered species trading, 319
  firearm-related deaths, 29
  honor crimes, 439
  human trafficking, 352–353
  inquisitorial criminal justice systems, 109–110
  labor trafficking, 344
  legal system, 31
  lustration, 248
  minimum age of criminal responsibility (MACR), 489
  narco-terrorism, 321–322
  nuclear weapons programs, 313
  organ trafficking, 353
  policing models, 68, 92
  post-independence criminal procedures, 110–111
  reparations and compensation, 246
  revolutionary movements, 39, 371
  terror bombings, 366